T0180045

Communications in Computer and Information Science   1252

Commenced Publication in 2007
Founding and Former Series Editors:
Simone Diniz Junqueira Barbosa, Phoebe Chen, Alfredo Cuzzocrea,
Xiaoyong Du, Orhun Kara, Ting Liu, Krishna M. Sivalingam,
Dominik Ślęzak, Takashi Washio, Xiaokang Yang, and Junsong Yuan

More information about this series at http://www.springer.com/series/7899

Xingming Sun · Jinwei Wang ·
Elisa Bertino (Eds.)

Artificial Intelligence
and Security

6th International Conference, ICAIS 2020
Hohhot, China, July 17–20, 2020
Proceedings, Part I

 Springer

Editors
Xingming Sun 🆔
Nanjing University of Information Science
and Technology
Nanjing, China

Jinwei Wang 🆔
Nanjing University of Information Science
and Technology
Nanjing, China

Elisa Bertino 🆔
Purdue University
West Lafayette, IN, USA

ISSN 1865-0929   ISSN 1865-0937 (electronic)
Communications in Computer and Information Science
ISBN 978-981-15-8082-6   ISBN 978-981-15-8083-3 (eBook)
https://doi.org/10.1007/978-981-15-8083-3

This Springer imprint is published by the registered company Springer Nature Singapore Pte Ltd.
The registered company address is: 152 Beach Road, #21-01/04 Gateway East, Singapore 189721, Singapore

Preface

The 6th International Conference on Artificial Intelligence and Security (ICAIS 2020), formerly called the International Conference on Cloud Computing and Security (ICCCS), was held during July 17–20, 2020, in Hohhot, China. Over the past five years, ICAIS has become a leading conference for researchers and engineers to share their latest results of research, development, and applications in the fields of artificial intelligence and information security.

We used the Microsoft Conference Management Toolkits (CMT) system to manage the submission and review processes of ICAIS 2020. We received 1,064 submissions from 20 countries and regions, including Canada, Italy, Ireland, Japan, Russia, France, Australia, South Korea, South Africa, Iraq, Kazakhstan, Indonesia, Vietnam, Ghana, China, Taiwan, Macao, the USA, and the UK. The submissions cover the areas of artificial intelligence, big data, cloud computing and security, information hiding, IoT security, multimedia forensics, encryption, cybersecurity, and so on. We thank our Technical Program Committee (PC) members and external reviewers for their efforts in reviewing papers and providing valuable comments to the authors. From the total of 1,064 submissions, and based on at least three reviews per submission, the program chairs decided to accept 186 papers, yielding an acceptance rate of 17%. The volume of the conference proceedings contains all the regular, poster, and workshop papers.

The conference program was enriched by a series of keynote presentations, and the keynote speakers included: Xiang-Yang Li, University of Science and Technology of China, China; Hai Jin, Huazhong University of Science and Technology (HUST), China; and Jie Tang, Tsinghua University, China. We look forward to their wonderful speeches.

There were 56 workshops organized in ICAIS 2020 which covered all hot topics in artificial intelligence and security. We would like to take this moment to express our sincere appreciation for the contribution of all the workshop chairs and their participants. We would like to extend our sincere thanks to all authors who submitted papers to ICAIS 2020 and to all PC members. It was a truly great experience to work with such talented and hard-working researchers. We also appreciate the external reviewers for assisting the PC members in their particular areas of expertise. Moreover, we want to thank our sponsors: Nanjing University of Information Science and Technology, New York University, ACM China, Michigan State University, University of Central Arkansas, Université Bretagne Sud, National Natural Science Foundation of China, Tech Science Press, Nanjing Normal University, Inner Mongolia University, and Northeastern State University.

May 2020

Xingming Sun
Jinwei Wang
Elisa Bertino

Organization

General Chairs

Yun Q. Shi	New Jersey Institute of Technology, USA
Mauro Barni	University of Siena, Italy
Elisa Bertino	Purdue University, USA
Guanglai Gao	Inner Mongolia University, China
Xingming Sun	Nanjing University of Information Science and Technology, China

Technical Program Chairs

Aniello Castiglione	University of Salerno, Italy
Yunbiao Guo	China Information Technology Security Evaluation Center, China
Suzanne K. McIntosh	New York University, USA
Jinwei Wang	Nanjing University of Information Science and Technology, China
Q. M. Jonathan Wu	University of Windsor, Canada

Publication Chair

Zhaoqing Pan	Nanjing University of Information Science and Technology, China

Workshop Chair

Baowei Wang	Nanjing University of Information Science and Technology, China

Organization Chairs

Zhangjie Fu	Nanjing University of Information Science and Technology, China
Xiaorui Zhang	Nanjing University of Information Science and Technology, China
Wuyungerile Li	Inner Mongolia University, China

Technical Program Committee Members

Saeed Arif	University of Algeria, Algeria
Anthony Ayodele	University of Maryland, USA

Zhifeng Bao   Royal Melbourne Institute of Technology University,
                                  Australia
Zhiping Cai   National University of Defense Technology, China
Ning Cao   Qingdao Binhai University, China
Paolina Centonze   Iona College, USA
Chin-chen Chang   Feng Chia University, Taiwan, China
Han-Chieh Chao   Taiwan Dong Hwa University, Taiwan, China
Bing Chen   Nanjing University of Aeronautics and Astronautics,
                                  China
Hanhua Chen   Huazhong University of Science and Technology,
                                  China
Xiaofeng Chen   Xidian University, China
Jieren Cheng   Hainan University, China
Lianhua Chi   IBM Research Center, Australia
Kim-Kwang Raymond   The University of Texas at San Antonio, USA
  Choo
Ilyong Chung   Chosun University, South Korea
Robert H. Deng   Singapore Management University, Singapore
Jintai Ding   University of Cincinnati, USA
Xinwen Fu   University of Central Florida, USA
Zhangjie Fu   Nanjing University of Information Science
                                  and Technology, China
Moncef Gabbouj   Tampere University of Technology, Finland
Ruili Geng   Spectral MD, USA
Song Guo   Hong Kong Polytechnic University, Hong Kong, China
Mohammad Mehedi Hassan   King Saud University, Saudi Arabia
Russell Higgs   University College Dublin, Ireland
Dinh Thai Hoang   University Technology Sydney, Australia
Wien Hong   Sun Yat-sen University, China
Chih-Hsien Hsia   National Ilan University, Taiwan, China
Robert Hsu   Chung Hua University, Taiwan, China
Xinyi Huang   Fujian Normal University, China
Yongfeng Huang   Tsinghua University, China
Zhiqiu Huang   Nanjing University of Aeronautics
                                  and Astronautics, China
Patrick C. K. Hung   Ontario Tech University, Canada
Farookh Hussain   University of Technology Sydney, Australia
Genlin Ji   Nanjing Normal University, China
Hai Jin   Huazhong University of Science and Technology,
                                  China
Sam Tak Wu Kwong   City University of Hong Kong, Hong Kong, China
Chin-Feng Lai   National Cheng Kung University, Taiwan, China
Loukas Lazos   University of Arizona, USA
Sungyoung Lee   Kyung Hee University, South Korea
Chengcheng Li   University of Cincinnati, USA
Feifei Li   Utah State University, USA

Arun Kumar Sangaiah	VIT University, India
Di Shang	Long Island University, USA
Victor S. Sheng	University of Central Arkansas, USA
Zheng-guo Sheng	University of Sussex, UK
Robert Simon Sherratt	University of Reading, UK
Yun Q. Shi	New Jersey Institute of Technology, USA
Frank Y. Shih	New Jersey Institute of Technology, USA
Biao Song	King Saud University, Saudi Arabia
Guang Sun	Hunan University of Finance and Economics, China
Jianguo Sun	Harbin University of Engineering, China
Krzysztof Szczypiorski	Warsaw University of Technology, Poland
Tsuyoshi Takagi	Kyushu University, Japan
Shanyu Tang	University of West London, UK
Jing Tian	National University of Singapore, Singapore
Yoshito Tobe	Aoyang University, Japan
Cezhong Tong	Washington University in St. Louis, USA
Pengjun Wan	Illinois Institute of Technology, USA
Cai-Zhuang Wang	Ames Laboratory, USA
Ding Wang	Peking University, China
Guiling Wang	New Jersey Institute of Technology, USA
Honggang Wang	University of Massachusetts-Dartmouth, USA
Jian Wang	Nanjing University of Aeronautics and Astronautics, China
Jie Wang	University of Massachusetts Lowell, USA
Jin Wang	Changsha University of Science and Technology, China
Liangmin Wang	Jiangsu University, China
Ruili Wang	Massey University, New Zealand
Xiaojun Wang	Dublin City University, Ireland
Xiaokang Wang	St. Francis Xavier University, Canada
Zhaoxia Wang	A*STAR, Singapore
Sheng Wen	Swinburne University of Technology, Australia
Jian Weng	Jinan University, China
Edward Wong	New York University, USA
Eric Wong	The University of Texas at Dallas, USA
Shaoen Wu	Ball State University, USA
Shuangkui Xia	Beijing Institute of Electronics Technology and Application, China
Lingyun Xiang	Changsha University of Science and Technology, China
Yang Xiang	Deakin University, Australia
Yang Xiao	The University of Alabama, USA
Haoran Xie	The Education University of Hong Kong, Hong Kong, China
Naixue Xiong	Northeastern State University, USA
Wei Qi Yan	Auckland University of Technology, New Zealand

Aimin Yang	Guangdong University of Foreign Studies, China
Ching-Nung Yang	Taiwan Dong Hwa University, Taiwan, China
Chunfang Yang	Zhengzhou Science and Technology Institute, China
Fan Yang	University of Maryland, USA
Guomin Yang	University of Wollongong, Australia
Qing Yang	University of North Texas, USA
Yimin Yang	Lakehead University, Canada
Ming Yin	Purdue University, USA
Shaodi You	The Australian National University, Australia
Kun-Ming Yu	Chung Hua University, Taiwan, China
Weiming Zhang	University of Science and Technology of China, China
Xinpeng Zhang	Fudan University, China
Yan Zhang	Simula Research Laboratory, Norway
Yanchun Zhang	Victoria University, Australia
Yao Zhao	Beijing Jiaotong University, China

Organization Committee Members

Xianyi Chen	Nanjing University of Information Science and Technology, China
Yadang Chen	Nanjing University of Information Science and Technology, China
Beijing Chen	Nanjing University of Information Science and Technology, China
Baoqi Huang	Inner Mongolia University, China
Bing Jia	Inner Mongolia University, China
Jielin Jiang	Nanjing University of Information Science and Technology, China
Zilong Jin	Nanjing University of Information Science and Technology, China
Yan Kong	Nanjing University of Information Science and Technology, China
Yiwei Li	Columbia University, USA
Yuling Liu	Hunan University, China
Zhiguo Qu	Nanjing University of Information Science and Technology, China
Huiyu Sun	New York University, USA
Le Sun	Nanjing University of Information Science and Technology, China
Jian Su	Nanjing University of Information Science and Technology, China
Qing Tian	Nanjing University of Information Science and Technology, China
Yuan Tian	King Saud University, Saudi Arabia
Qi Wang	Nanjing University of Information Science and Technology, China

Lingyun Xiang   Changsha University of Science and Technology,
                             China
Zhihua Xia   Nanjing University of Information Science
                             and Technology, China
Lizhi Xiong   Nanjing University of Information Science
                             and Technology, China
Leiming Yan   Nanjing University of Information Science
                             and Technology, China
Li Yu   Nanjing University of Information Science
                             and Technology, China
Zhili Zhou   Nanjing University of Information Science
                             and Technology, China

Contents – Part I

Contents – Part II

Information Security

Contents – Part III

Big Data and Cloud Computing

Information Processing

Artificial Intelligence

Fast Texture Image Retrieval Using Learning Copula Model of Multiple DTCWT

Chaorong Li[1,2,3]($\boxtimes$), Tianxing Liao[4], and Xingchun Yang[5]

[1] Computer College of Chongqing University of Science and Technology,
Chongqing 400054, China
lichaorong88@163.com

[2] Department of Computer Science and Information Engineering, Yibin University,
Yibin 644000, China

[3] University of Electronic Science and Technology of China, Chengdu 611731, China

[4] Department of Computer Science and Information Engineering, Yibin University,
Yibin 644000, China

[5] The Department of Computer Science and Technology, Sichuan Police College,
646000 Luzhou, China

Abstract. In this work, we proposed a fast texture image retrieval method by using the learning Copula model of multiple Dual-tree complex wavelet transforms (DTCWTs). Compared with the discrete wavelet transform, DTCWT provides multiple-directions and multiple-scales decomposition to image and also has the fast calculation capability. In the proposed method Multiple DTCWTs is incorporated to get more texture features; compare to Gabor wavelet, DTCWT has less computational cost of decomposition. In DTCWT domains, we developed a Learning Copula Model (called LCMoMD) to describe the dependence between the subbands of multiple DTCWTs. For improving the retrieval performance, LCMoMD is first embedded in the linear space by utilizing matrix logarithm and Kernel Principal Component Analysis (KPCA) is used to calculate the features from the embedding Copula model in the linear space. Experiments demonstrate that our method has fast and robust performance of texture extraction compared to the state-of-the-art methods.

Keywords: Image retrieval · Dual-Tree Complex Wavelet Transforms (DTCWTs) · Copula model · Kernel Principal Component Analysis (KPCA) · Log-euclidean embedding

1 Introduction

Texture analysis is a fundamental and important image processing task. It has been widely used in the content-based information retrieval system [1,2]. To texture image retrieval method, the two stages are necessary: feature extraction and feature matching. Feature extraction will affect the retrieval accuracy and

X. Sun et al. (Eds.): ICAIS 2020, CCIS 1252, pp. 3–15, 2020.
https://doi.org/10.1007/978-981-15-8083-3_1

feature matching will affect the retrieval run-time. From the point of feature extraction, existing retrieval methods can be categorized into following classes: local pattern descriptor [3–5], wavelet transform [6–10], dictionary learning [11, 12], and deep learning [13].

The idea of local pattern is that the image is composed of a number of local patterns. By counting the number of local patterns in the image, the features of image are obtained. Local binary pattern (LBP) [3] is a simplest and effective local pattern descriptor. The main advantage of LBP is they have low computing cost because it just need simple comparing operation between pixels. However, the drawback of LBP is that it is sensitive to image noise because the local pattern codes may be totally different if the intensity of one pixel in the local neighborhood is changed by noise. In order to improve the performance of LBP, a few variants of LBP have been developed like local ternary patterns (LTP) [4] and the local tetra patterns (LTrP) [5].

The goal of dictionary learning is to obtain a sparse representation of the image by using the atoms which compose the dictionary, and the linear combination of the atoms [14]. In order to obtain the dictionary and the optimal linear combination, learning process (called dictionary learning) is required. The algorithmic theory consists of two phases: Dictionary Generate and Sparse coding with a precomputed dictionary. k-SVD [15] and SGK [16] are two state-of-the-arts dictionary-learning algorithms.

Deep learning technique has attracted much attention in recent years. The theoretical basis of this approach is based on the standpoint of David Hubel, Torsten Wiesel et al. [17]: The visual information processing mechanism of primates is a hierarchical processing from simple to complex. Deep learning technique is mainly based on artificial neural network (ANN), especially based on Back Propagation (BP) neural network. Various deep-learning-based methods have been designed in succession for image representation [18]: sparse auto-encoder, Convolutional Neural Network, Deep Belief Nets, Restricted Boltzmann Machine and so on. Deep-learning-based method requires numerous samples to train the network model, so its computational overhead is very large, and it is necessary to design a different network structure for a type of image database. Therefore, this critical drawback limits its applications in many fields.

Wavelet is a commonly used technique in image analysis and processing. Its most prominent advantage is its multi-resolution analysis. As we all know, there are two types of features extracted according to the wavelets coefficients produced by using wavelet decomposition to image: one is wavelet signature features including the norm-1 energies, norm-2 energies and standard deviations calculated from the coefficients of each wavelet subband [19,20]; the other one is the statistical models such as probability distribution (Generalized Gaussian Model (GGD) [6], Gaussian Mixture Model (GMD) [21,22]). Statistical models can capture the distribution of wavelet coefficients by using maximum likelihood estimation to estimate the model parameter. Studies have shown that the feature extraction method based on a statistical model in wavelet domains is a useful feature extraction technique, and it has a wide range of applications in the fields of image analysis and pattern recognition. Early methods mainly focus on establishing a univariate statistical model for each wavelet subband independently. Recent researches [23, 24] have demonstrated that the dependencies exist in the wavelet transform domain and in wavelet transform domain we can effectively increase discriminative capacity of the wavelet features by using multidimensional joint distribution. For example, Multivariate Generalized Gaussian Distribution (MGGD) and Multivariate Laplace Distribution (MLD) [25] and Copula model [26] are employed to join the subbands of orthogonal wavelet transform such as discrete wavelet transform [27] and stationary wavelet transform [28].

Multivariate models are effective to model the subbands of wavelet; however, there are two drawbacks of multivariate model: (1) expensive computational cost of calculating the similarity between models; (2) it is difficult to incorporate learning approach to improve its performance. To address these issues, we proposed the learning based Copula model in DTCWT domain for image representation. This work has three contributions:

* In the previous works, just one DTCWT are used to extract the texture. In this work, a novel multiple Dual-tree complex wavelet transforms (DTCWTs) is proposed to produce more robust texture feature.
* We construct Copula model on both the lowpass and highpass subbands of DTCWT. Lowpass subbands of DTCWT is often ignored by researchers. By combination lowpass and highpass, the performance of the proposed model can be further improved for texture representation.
* We proposed a learning technique of Copula model for texture image retrieval. Copula model has complex formula and the expensive computational cost of similarity between two Copula models hinders the development of image feature extraction with Copula model. The introduction of learning technology not only reduces the computational cost of the copula model, but also improves the recognition accuracy of the texture representation method.

The rest of this paper is organized as follows: Sect. 2 introduces copula model including the Gaussian copula model, and Sect. 3 introduces DTCWT for image decomposition. The proposed method image feature extraction scheme based on multiple DTCWTs is presented in Sect. 4. Experimental results are presented in Sect. 5 and conclusions are drawn in Sect. 6.

2   Copula Model

Copula is a useful statistic model in finance, and it has been widely used for analyzing and forecasting financial data by constructing joint distribution. Copulas have been studied in wavelet domain for image analysis and achieved success [29, 30]. Copula C is a d-dimensional function and it has following properties:

– $C = [0, 1]^d$;
– C is d-increasing, i.e., for every a and b in $[0, 1]^d$ such that $a \leq b$, the C-volume $V_C([a, b])$ of the box $[a, b]$ is positive.

– C has margins C_n, and $C_n(u) = C(1, \cdots, u_n, 1 \cdots 1) = u_n$ for $u \in [0,1]^d$

Sklar's theorem: Let $H(\mathbf{x}|\Theta)$, $(x = [x_1, \cdots, x_d])$ be a d-dimensional distribution function with continuous margins $F_1(x_1|\alpha_1), \cdots, F_d(x_d|\alpha_d)$, then there exists an unique copula function C such that for x :

$$H(\mathbf{x}|\Theta) = C(F_1(x_1|\alpha_1), \cdots, F_d(x_d|\alpha_d)|\phi) \tag{1}$$

where α_i are the parameters of $F_i(x_i)$, Θ is the parameter of $H(x)$, and ϕ is the parameter of $C(u)$.

Sklar's theorem provides a useful solution for constructing a multivariate distribution relying on the marginal distributions. That is, a copula function C can be used to join a set of margins $F_1(x_1), \cdots, F_d(x_d)$, for constructing a multivariate distribution. Copula function C has the following form according to (3):

$$C(\mathbf{u}|\phi) = H(F_1(x_1|\alpha_1), \cdots, F_d(x_d|\alpha_d)|\Theta) \tag{2}$$

where $\mathbf{u} = [u_1, \cdots, u_d] = [F_1(x_1|\alpha_1), \cdots, F_d(x_d|\alpha_d)]$.

The PDF of the d-dimensional distribution $H(\mathbf{x}|\Theta)$ is useful for representing the texture image. Based on (1), the PDF of $H(\mathbf{x}|\Theta)$ is represented by

$$h(x|\Theta) = \frac{\partial C}{\partial F_1 \cdots \partial F_d} \frac{\partial F_1}{\partial x_1} \cdots \frac{\partial F_d}{\partial x_d} = c(\mathbf{u}|\phi) \prod_{i=1}^{d} f_i(x_i|\alpha_i) \tag{3}$$

where $c(\mathbf{u}) = c(F_1(x_1|\alpha_1), \cdots, F_d(x_d|\alpha_d))$ indicates the pdf of copula C $f_i(x_i|\alpha_i)$ are the PDFs of $F_i(x_i|\alpha_i)$; $\Theta = \{\phi, \alpha_1, \cdots, \alpha_d\}$ is the parameter set of $h(\mathbf{x}|\Theta)$. One can observe from (3) that density $h(\mathbf{x}|\Theta)$ is composed of a copula function and the margins, then $h(\mathbf{x}|\Theta)$ is called copula model. For instance, if Gaussian copula function is used as the joint part in $h(\mathbf{x}|\Theta)$, then $h(\mathbf{x}|\Theta)$ is called Gaussian copula model.

Given the observations of the random vector $x_1, \cdots, x_d$, the copula function $c(\mathbf{u}|\phi)$ and the copula model $h(\mathbf{x}|\Theta)$ can be constructed by the two-step maximum likelihood (TSML) approach [31], described as follows:

1. First step, the parameters of margins $f_i(x_i|\alpha_i)$ are calculated by maximum likelihood estimation (MLE) based on observation of x_i. With the estimated parameters $\tilde{\alpha}_i$, the points of CDF are calculated by $F_i(x_i) = \int f_i(x_i|\tilde{\alpha})dx_i$;
2. Second step, the parameters of copula function are calculated by maximum likelihood estimation with the calculated CDFs $F_i(x_i)$, denoted by $\tilde{\phi}$. Then the PDF of copula can be established from $F_i(x_i)$, denoted by $c(\mathbf{u}|\tilde{\phi})$.

Once the PDFs of margins $f_i(x_i|\tilde{\alpha}_i)$ and the copula $c(\mathbf{u}|\tilde{\phi})$ are determined, the copula model $h(\mathbf{x}|\tilde{\Theta})$ is constructed by using (3), where $\tilde{\Theta} = \{\tilde{\phi}, \tilde{\alpha}_1, \cdots, \tilde{\alpha}_d\}$.

The commonly used copula functions are Gaussian copula, t-copula as well as Archimedean copulas, [31]. In this work, Gaussian copula is used since it has better performance compared with other copulas. The CDF (Cumulative

Distribution Function) and the PDF (Probability Density Function) of Gaussian copula are respectively defined as [31]:

$$G(\mathbf{u}|\boldsymbol{R}) = \Phi(\Phi^{-1}(u_1), \cdots, \Phi^{-1}(u_d)) \tag{4}$$

$$g(\mathbf{u}|\boldsymbol{R}) = |R|^{-1/2} \exp\left(-\frac{1}{2}\xi^T(R^{-1} - I)\xi\right) \tag{5}$$

where $\boldsymbol{R}$ denotes the correlation matrix which is the unique parameter of Gaussian copula. Φ denotes the standard univariate Gaussian distribution function with correlation matrix $\boldsymbol{R}$, and Φ^{-1} denotes the quantile function corresponding to Φ. $\boldsymbol{\xi} = [\xi_1, \cdots, \xi_d]$, $\xi_i = \Phi^{-1}(u_i), i = 1, \cdots, d$. The parameter $\boldsymbol{R}$ can be calculated using MLE with following expression

$$\boldsymbol{R} = \frac{1}{N}\xi\xi^T \tag{6}$$

where N is the length of ξ.

3 Dual-Tree Complex Wavelet Transform (DTCWT)

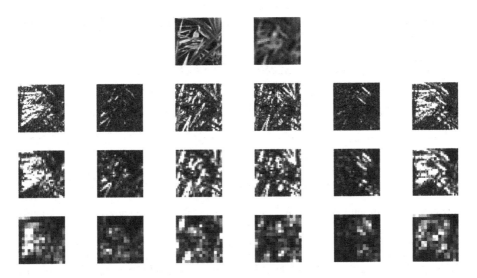

Fig. 1. Image 3-scale decomposition with DTCWT. The left at the first row is the original image and right is the lowpass subband. From second row to fourth row are respectively the subbands at scale 1 to scale 3.

Dual-tree Complex Wavelet Transform (DTCWT) [32] is implemented by filtering an image with several filters, respectively: 2 filter trees are used for the rows of the image and 2 filter trees for the columns in a quad-tree structure with 4:1

redundancy. This scheme produces 6 directional subbands for each scale of the 2-dimensional DTCWT at approximately $\pm 15°, \pm 45°, \pm 75°$. Figure 1 show an example of DTCWT three-scale decomposition. It can be seen that an image is decomposed into six highpass subbands and a lowpass subband by DTCWT. To RGB image, DTCWT is applied on each of the channel (R, G, and B), and there will produce 16 highpass subbands at each scale and 3 lowpass subbands.

The strong correlation (dependence) exists between the subbands of DTCWT. If we can use this correlation to build a multidimensional statistical model, the performance of the model can be improved. We use chiplots to demonstrate the dependence between the subbands of DTCWT. In chi-plot, the values of λ_i indicate the distance of points (x_i, y_i) from the center of the points, while the values of λ_i indicate the dependence of (x_i, y_i). If X and Y are independent, then most of the points (χ_i, λ_i) should be close to the line of $\chi = 0$. We can observe that the dependencies exist between the subbands including color channels, directional subbands and Filter Banks (FB) (Fig. 2).

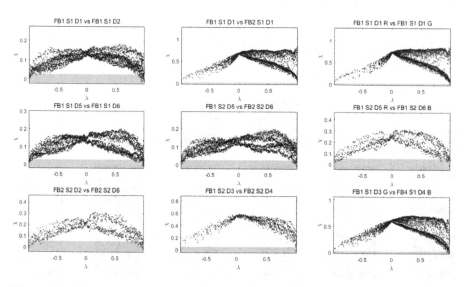

Fig. 2. Chiplots in multiple DTCWT domains. The first column shows the dependence between directional subbands. The second column shows the dependence between Filter banks. The third column shows the dependence between color channels. Tuple in title describe the dependence between two subbands which are denoted by two tuples T_1 *vs* T_2. For example in (FB1 S1 D1 R): FB1 indicate the filter bank 1; S1 indicates scale 1; D1 indicate direction 1; R indicates the R channel of RGB image.

4   Learning Copula Model of Multiple DTCWTs

4.1   Constructing CM-DTCWT

In order to improve the performance, we design novel multiple DTCWT scheme by employing multiple Kinkgsbury's filter banks [33]. In the proposed method, two DTCWTs which constructed with two Filter banks are used:

- Filter bank 1 (DTCWT 1): Antonini (9, 7) tap filters, Q-Shift (10, 10) tap filters;
- Filter bank 2 (DTCWT 2): Near-Symmetric (5, 7) tap filters, Q-Shift (18, 18) tap filters;

One can use more DTCWT filter banks (or different filter banks) to design inter-filter dependence structure. However, taking into account the computational efficiency, we only used two sets of filter banks for constructing inter-filter dependence. Figure 3 illustrates the scheme of constructing Copula models in multiple DTCWT domains. Furthermore, lowpass subband of DTCWT is often ignored in previous researches. In fact, lowpass subband of wavelet contains rich texture information. In this work, we incorporate the lowpass subbands of DTCWT into Copula model for image representation. Three-scale decomposition of DTCWT is performed in our scheme. The 6 highpass subbands at each scale and the lowpass are used. The subband of DTCWT can be regarded as observation data generated by a random variable. Each subband of DTCWT is vectorized into the column of the observation matrix. Hence the size of the observation matrix is $n \times 21$ $(2 \times (6+1))$ at each scale, where n is the number of coefficients in the subband (see Eq. 7).

$$M_s = \left[L_1, H_1, \ldots, H_6, \tilde{L}_1, \tilde{H}_1, \ldots, \tilde{H}_6\right] = \begin{bmatrix} l_1 & h_{1,1} & \cdots & h_{1,6} & \tilde{l}_1 & \tilde{h}_{1,1} & \cdots & \tilde{h}_{1,6} \\ l_2 & h_{2,1} & \cdots & h_{2,6} & \tilde{l}_2 & \tilde{h}_{2,1} & \cdots & \tilde{h}_{2,6} \\ & & \ddots & & & & \\ l_n & h_{6,1} & \cdots & h_{n,6} & \tilde{l}_n & \tilde{h}_{n,1} & \cdots & \tilde{h}_{n,6} \end{bmatrix}$$

$$(7)$$

where s indicates the scale; n is the number of the coefficients in a subband. To RGB image, the observation matrix is

$$M_s = [L_{R,1}, H_{R,1}, \ldots, H_{R,6},$$

$$\tilde{L}_{R,1}, \tilde{H}_{R,1}, \ldots, \tilde{H}_{R,6}, \cdots, \tilde{H}_{B,6}]$$

$$(8)$$

To color image, the size of observation matrix is $n \times 42$ $(3 \times 2 \times (6+1))$.

In the proposed method Gaussian copula is used as the joint part of Copula model, and Weibull distribution is used as the margins of Copula model in DTCWT domain. The Probability Distribution Function (PDF) of Weibull has following expression

$$f_{WBL}(x|\alpha, \beta) = \left(\frac{\alpha}{\beta}\right)\left(\frac{x}{\beta}\right)^{\alpha-1} e^{-(x/\beta)^\alpha}$$

$$(9)$$

where α is shape parameter, and β is scale parameter. The Cumulative Distribution Function (CDF) of Weibull is

$$F_{WBL}(x|\alpha,\beta) = 1 - e^{-(x/\beta)^\alpha}. \tag{10}$$

Algorithm 1. Constructing CM of DTCWT

Require: Image I.

Ensure: Copula model $\{\boldsymbol{R}_s, \alpha_{s,i}, \beta_{s,i}\}_{s=1,i=1}^{L,D}$, where L is the number of scales and D is the dimensions of Copula model;

1: Multiple DTCWTs are used to decompose I into 3-scale and 6-direction subbands.
2: Calculating observation matrix $\boldsymbol{M}_s$ according EQ.7 or EQ.8
3: **for** each scale **do**
4:     **for** each column c_i of $\boldsymbol{M}_s$ **do**
5:         Calculate the parameter $\alpha_{s,i}, \beta_{s,i}$ of Weibull from c_i using MLE according EQ.9
6:         Calculate the CDF F_i of Weibull by EQ.10
7:     **end for**
8:     Calculate the parameter $\boldsymbol{R}_s$ of Gaussian copula function based on F_i using EQ.6
9: **end for**

If L-scale decomposition of DTCWT is performed, we will obtain L Copula models. The specific step of constructing copula models on the input image is presented in Algorithm 1.

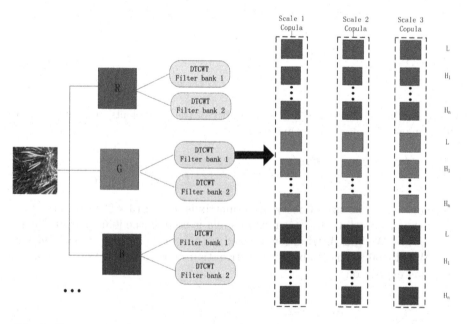

Fig. 3. Constructing Copula models base on multiple DTCWTs (CM of DTCWT).

4.2   Learning CM of DTCWT

Given an image, it will be produced a Gaussian Copula model denoted by $\{\boldsymbol{R}_s, \alpha_{s,i}, \beta_{s,i}\}_{s=1,i=1}^{L,D}$. However, the high computational cost is needed to calculate the similarity of Gaussian Copula models. Previous work [26,30,34] use Kullback-Leibler Divergence (KLD) to calculate the similarity between two Gaussian Copula models. In this work, we propose an efficient approach to calculate the similarity of two Gaussian Copula models based on logarithm which has been used for embedding the Symmetric Positive Definite (SPD) matrix into Euclidean space (Log-Euclidean) [35]. First, we use logarithm to embed $\boldsymbol{R}_s$ into Euclidean space and vectorize it into a vector. Then we concatenate f_s and $\{\alpha_s, \beta_s\}$ to form the final feature of image, denoted by

$$\boldsymbol{f}_s = [Vect(Log(\boldsymbol{R}_s)), \alpha_s, \beta_s] \tag{11}$$

The image features can be expressed as the combination of all the $\boldsymbol{f}_s$, denoted by

$$\boldsymbol{f} = [\boldsymbol{f}_1, \boldsymbol{f}_2, \boldsymbol{f}_3] \tag{12}$$

To color image, the size of $Log(\boldsymbol{R})$ is 1812 ($42 \times 42 + 2 \times 42$) and the dimensions of $\boldsymbol{f}$ is 5436 ($3 \times (1812)$). In order to obtain the discriminative feature and reduced feature dimension, we use Kernel Principal Component Analysis(KPCA) [36] to learn low-dimensional and robust features from CM-DTCWT (see Fig. 4).

5   Experiment

To evaluate the retrieval performance of the proposed MDCM on wavelet features, we use Average Retrieval Rate (ARR) as the measure of retrieval performance. ARR is defined as the average percentage of the retrieved subimages

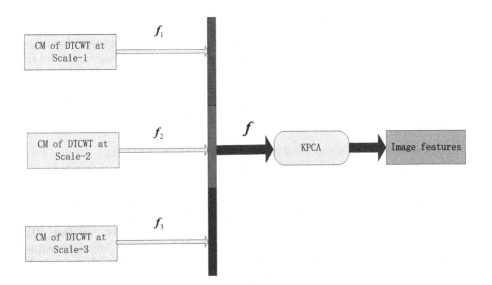

Fig. 4. Learnig Copula model of multiple DTCWTs (LCMoMD).

Table 1. Retrieval performance comparison on the three color texture datasets.

Method	VisTex (40)	ALOT (250)	STex (476)
LBP [3]	85.84	39.57	54.89
CLBP [37]	89.4	49.6	58.4
DDBTC [38]	92.09	48.64	44.79
Power Exp. [27]	91.2	49.3	71.3
LECoP [39]	92.99	–	74.15
Gabor-Copula [26]	92.40	60.8	76.4
CIF-LBP-PSO [40]	95.28	–	45.61
LED+RD [41]	94.70	–	80.08
MS-SLED [42]	94.95	–	79.87
AlexNet [43]	91.76	59.01	68.32
VGG16 [44]	92.48	**60.34**	72.16
VGG19 [44]	92.02	59.15	71.68
LCMoMD	91.38	58.32	78.61
LCMoMD-PCA	92.49	58.58	78.70
LCMoMD-KPCA	**95.53**	59.83	**80.17**

Table 2. Computation time (in second) of LCMoMD and the-state-of-the-art methods on VisTex(40)

Method	Dimension	FE	FM	Total
Gabor-Copula	$3 \times 42 \times 42$	0.517	0.199	0.716
LCMoMD-KPCA	40		0.158	0.099	0.257

from the same original texture class in the top N_R retrieved subimages (including the query image). Let I_k is the query subimage and $t(I_k)$ is a query function which returns the number of the relative subimages (these subimages and the I_k belong to a same original texture image), then ARR is defined as [6]

$$ARR = \frac{1}{N} \sum_{k=1}^{N} \frac{t(I_k)}{N_R}. \tag{13}$$

where N indicates the total number of subimages in the dataset.

Three commonly used texture databases were included in the retrieval experiments: MIT Vision Texture (VisTex) Database [45], Amsterdam Library of Textures (ALOT) database [46], and Salzburg Textures (STex) database [29]. In the databases, each texture class is divided into 16 nonoverlapping subimages, $N_R = 16$ is adopted in the experiments on the three datasets. **VisTex(40)** dataset. The goal of VisTex is to provide texture images that are representative of real-world conditions. We used the 40 grayscale texture classes which are widely used for texture image retrieval [29,30]. There are 640 subimages

(40×16) in this dataset. **ALOT (250)** dataset [46]. ALOT is a color image collection of 250 rough textures which are recorded under different illumination conditions and viewing directions. We used the textures captured under the c1l1 condition for the experiments. There are 4000 subimages (250×16) in this dataset. **STex (476)** dataset. STex (Salzburg Textures) is a novel texture image dataset captured under real-world conditions; it consists of 476 different texture classes, and these textures are captured under real-world conditions; there are 7616 subimages in this dataset (476×16).

Our method called LCMoMD-KPCA is performed with 3-scale DTCWT decomposition and Gaussian kernel (the parameter of Gaussian kernel gamma is set to 0.001) is used in KPCA. We make a comparison of our method with other state-of-the-art methods and the retrieval results are listed in Table 1. It can be seen that LCMoMD-KPCA has the best ARRs on VisTex (40) and STex(476); and its ARR is slightly less than the ARR of VGG16 ranking second on ALOT (250).

MDCM has the lower computational cost compared with copula based methods both in Feature Extraction (FE) step and Feature Matching (FM) step. We took a test on VisTex(40) for evaluating the computational performance of the proposed methods. All the tests have been carried out using matlab 2016a on a computer (Core i7 6700 4 GHz, 32 GB RAM). It can be observed from Table 2 that the run time of LCMoMD-KPCA is always less than the Gabor-Copula.

6   Conclusions

We have proposed a simple and fast texture image retrieval method by using Copula model in multiple DTCWT domains combining KPCA, called LCMoMD-KPCA. LCMoMD-KPCA is easy to implement and has low computational cost compared to other multivariate statistical models and deep learning based methods. Experiments on the public texture databases show our method achieved the promising retrieval accuracy. In future work, we will combine the features of LCMoMD-KPCA with deep network features to improve the performance of the texture image representation method.

Acknowledgements. This work is supported by the Foundation of Central Universities in China (No. ZYGX2016J123), Project of Sichuan Science and Technology Program (Nos. 2018JY0117 and 2019YFS0068).

References

1. Mellor, M., Hong, B.W., Brady, M.: IEEE Trans. Pattern Anal. Mach. Intell. **30**(1), 52 (2008)
2. Chen, Q., Song, Z., Dong, J., Huang, Z.: IEEE Trans. Pattern Anal. Mach. Intell. **37**(1), 13 (2015)
3. Ojala, T., Pietikainen, M., Maenpaa, T.: IEEE Trans. Pattern Anal. Mach. Intell. **24**(7), 971 (2002)

4. Tan, X., Triggs, B.: IEEE Trans. Image Process. **19**(6), 1635 (2010)
5. Murala, S., Maheshwari, R., Balasubramanian, R.: IEEE Trans. Image Process. **21**(5), 2874 (2012)
6. Do, M.N., Vetterli, M.: IEEE Trans. Image Process. **11**(2), 146 (2002)
7. Kokare, M., Biswas, P., Chatterji, B.: IEEE Trans. Syst. Man Cybern. Part B (Cybern.) **36**(6), 1273 (2006)
8. Qian, Y., Ye, M., Zhou, J.: IEEE Trans. Geosci. Remote Sens. **51**(4), 2276 (2013)
9. Li, C., Huang, Y., Yang, X., Chen, H.: Pattern Recogn. **92**, 246 (2019)
10. Li, C., Guan, X., Yang, P., Huang, Y., Huang, W., Chen, H.: IEEE Access **7**, 30693 (2019)
11. Mairal, J., Bach, F., Ponce, J., Sapiro, G., Zisserman, A.: IEEE Conference on Computer Vision and Pattern Recognition, CVPR 2008, pp. 1–8. IEEE (2008)
12. Liu, L., Fieguth, P.: IEEE Trans. Pattern Anal. Mach. Intell. **34**(3), 574 (2012)
13. Zhao, W., Du, S.: IEEE Trans. Geosci. Remote Sens. **54**(8), 4544 (2016)
14. Mairal, J., Bach, F., Ponce, J., Sapiro, G.: International Conference on Machine Learning, ICML 2009, Montreal, Quebec, Canada, pp. 689–696, June 2009
15. Aharon, M., Elad, M., Bruckstein, A.: IEEE Trans. Signal Process. **54**(11), 4311 (2006)
16. Sahoo, S.K., Makur, A.: IEEE Signal Process. Lett. **20**(6), 587 (2013)
17. Hubel, D.H., Wiesel, T.N.: J. Physiol. **195**(1), 215 (1968)
18. Schmidhuber, J.: Neural Netw. Official J. Int. Neural Netw. Soc. **61**, 85 (2014)
19. Pun, C.M., Lee, M.C.: IEEE Trans. Pattern Anal. Mach. Intell. **25**(5), 590 (2003)
20. Ekici, S., Yildirim, S., Poyraz, M.: Expert Syst. Appl. **34**(4), 2937 (2008)
21. Kim, S.C., Kang, T.J.: Pattern Recogn. **40**(4), 1207 (2007)
22. Allili, M.S., Baaziz, N., Mejri, M.: IEEE Trans. Multimedia **16**(3), 772 (2014)
23. Portilla, J., Simoncelli, E.P.: IEEE Workshop on Statistical and Computational Theories of Vision (1999)
24. Po, D.Y., Do, M.N.: IEEE Trans. Image Process. **15**(6), 1610 (2006)
25. Bombrun, L., Berthoumieu, Y., Lasmar, N.E., Verdoolaege, G.: IEEE International Conference on Image Processing, pp. 3637–3640 (2011)
26. Li, C., Huang, Y., Zhu, L.: Pattern Recogn. **64**, 118 (2017)
27. Verdoolaege, G., De Backer, S., Scheunders, P.: 15th IEEE International Conference on Image Processing, ICIP 2008, pp. 169–172. IEEE (2008)
28. Pascal, F., Bombrun, L., Tourneret, J.Y., Berthoumieu, Y.: IEEE Trans. Signal Process. **61**(23), 5960 (2013)
29. Kwitt, R., Meerwald, P., Uhl, A.: IEEE Trans. Image Process. **20**(7), 2063 (2011)
30. Lasmar, N.E., Berthoumieu, Y.: IEEE Trans. Image Process. **23**(5), 2246 (2014)
31. Cherubini, U., Luciano, E., Vecchiato, W.: Copula Methods in Finance. Wiley, Hoboken (2004)
32. Kingsbury, N.: The Dual-tree complex wavelet transform: a new technique for shift invariance and directional filters. In: Proceedings of IEEE Dsp Workshop (1998)
33. Kingsbury, N.: Appl. Comput. Harmonic Anal. **10**(3), 234 (2001)
34. L. C, X. Y, H. Y., Computational Intelligence (SSCI) pp. 1–5 (2017)
35. A. V, F. P, P. X, A. N, Magnetic Resonance in Medicine 56(2), 411 (2010)
36. Yang, J., Frangi, A.F., Yang, J., Zhang, D., Jin, Z.: IEEE Trans. Pattern Anal. Mach. Intell. **27**(2), 230 (2005)
37. Guo, Z., Zhang, L., Zhang, D.: IEEE Trans. Image Process. **19**(6), 1657 (2010)
38. Guo, J.M., Prasetyo, H., Wang, N.J.: IEEE Trans. Multimedia **17**(9), 1576 (2015)
39. Verma, M., Raman, B., Murala, S.: Neurocomputing **165**(C), 255 (2015)
40. Liu, P., Guo, J.M., Chamnongthai, K., Prasetyo, H.: Inf. Sci. **390**, 95 (2017)

41. .
42. Pham, M.T. (2018). arXiv.org
43. Krizhevsky, A., Sutskever, I., Hinton, G.E.: International Conference on Neural Information Processing Systems, pp. 1097–1105 (2012)
44. Simonyan, K., Zisserman, A.: Computer Science (2014)
45. Vistex texture database. http://vismod.media.mit.edu/vismod/imagery/Vision/Texture/Images/Reference/
46. Alot texture database. http://aloi.science.uva.nl/public_alot/

Joint Generic Learning and Multi-source Domain Adaptation on Unsupervised Face Recognition

Zhi Xu, Han Han, Jianqiu Ji$^{(\boxtimes)}$, and Baohua Qiang

Guangxi Key Laboratory of Image and Graphic Intelligent Processing,
Guilin University of Electronic Technology, Guilin 541004, China
{xuzhi,qiangbh}@guet.edu.cn, lengyu_hanhan@163.com, stocton@163.com

Abstract. For most machine learning algorithms, the performance of model trained on the source domain degenerates obviously when it is applied to the target domain because the distributions of both domains are different. Besides, in many cases, there is a lack of adequate supervised target domain training samples. In order to solve the mismatch between the domains and the lack of training samples, this paper proposes jointing domain adaptation and generic learning on solving unsupervised face recognition. Firstly, samples are selected randomly from multiple source and target domains which do not contain interest subjects and construct multiple sub-datasets. Secondly, learning a common subspace for each sub-dataset. In the common subspace, source and target domains can mutual interlace and their structures are well preserved, and we can get more discrimination information from multiple feature subspaces. Finally, the recognition is obtained by using combine strategies. The experimental results show that the recognition performance of the framework is better than that of the competitive ones.

Keywords: Face recognition · Generic learning · Domain adaptation · Multi-source domain

1 Introduction

Traditional machine learning algorithms such as Linear Discriminative Analysis (LDA), Support Vector Machine (SVM) [6,15] have successfully solved the classification prediction problem. But the precondition is assumed that the training and test data are sampled from identical distribution. Generally speaking, when traditional machine learning algorithms are used to solve classification problems, it relie on the consistency of data distribution between training and test data, and need lots of labeled data. However, in many cases, there is a lack of adequate supervised training samples with the same distribution, and it is a costly task to collect and annotate information. Lots of experiments show that the performance will seriously degenerate when the training and test data come from the different domains.

© Springer Nature Singapore Pte Ltd. 2020
X. Sun et al. (Eds.): ICAIS 2020, CCIS 1252, pp. 16–27, 2020.
https://doi.org/10.1007/978-981-15-8083-3_2

For solving the inadequate of supervised training target samples, generic learning [5,10,21,22,25] attempted to boost the performance of traditional recognition solutions by using a training database which has not interested classes, but it cannot solve the problem of different distribution. The emergence of transfer learning [14] solved the problem of inconsistent data distribution, it can transfer knowledge from source domain to target domain by reducing the distribution difference between domains and then do classification task. Common subspace is frequently discussed in domain adaptation methods which belonging to the field of transfer learning. Geng proposed a new metric learning method for domain adaptation [2], it minimized the empirical maximum mean discrepancy between domains in the reproducing kernel Hilbert space by introducing a data-dependent regularizer. In the work [17], a latent common space was obtained by minimizing the discrepancy between the marginal distributions of source and target domains to learn a transform pattern. The work [4] learned a common intermediate feature representation by projecting the source and target data to the subspace on Grassman manifold. Domain adaptation dictionary learning [16] was proposed and S Shekhar et al. developed generalized domain adaptation based on Fisher Discrimination Dictionary Learning (FDDL) [12,23], which utilized data from each domain together and generated subspace for each domain.

The methods presented above utilize only the common features of the source and target domains, but ignore the specific knowledge of the target which may be beneficial for the task. Kan et al. proposed a conversion method called TSD [7], in which the source domain data with labels are represented by target domain data in the common subspace. The common subspace of TSD satisfied the samples from both domains should be well interlaced and the structures of source and target domains should be well preserved. It not only used the common features, but also the specific knowledge of the target. The work (TMSD)[24] proposed the multi-source domain adaptation [1,11,18] in face recognition based on TSD. It transferred the rich supervision knowledge from more than one source domain. But the subspace methods proposed above only use a single subspace, when the cost function is minimum, the optimal result of source domain which is represented by target domain is fixed. However, a single subspace cannot provide a various discriminative information due to the neglect of sample diversity.

For learning a better face recognition model [9,19], we propose a multi-source domain generic learning framework on domain adaptation(MDGL). Different from other methods, this work combines domain adptation and generic learning. We adopt multiple systems to obtain multiple optimal results, then combine all identity results. In this paper, the contributions are as follows: (1) We propose a multi-source domain adaptation method on FR and do the theoretical derivation. (2) MDGL is proposed and the advantages of the framework are analyzed. (3) Extensive experimental results suggest that MDGL significantly improves the recognition performance on face recognition task.

The rest of this paper is organized as follows: In Sect. 2, we propose MDGL and describe a multi-source domain adaptation method. In Sect. 3, we evaluate the proposed framework and compare with other methods. Finally, a conclusion is given in the Sect. 4.

2   A Multi-source Domain Generic Learning Framework on Domain Adaptation

2.1   Notations and Definition

The data matric of the training samples from i-th source domain is denoted as $\mathbf{X}_i = [\mathbf{x}_1^i, \mathbf{x}_2^i, \cdots, \mathbf{x}_{n_i}^i] \in \mathbf{R}^{d_i \times n_i}, \mathbf{x}_j^i \in \mathbf{R}^{d_i \times 1}, i = 1, 2, \cdots, s$ with the labels defined as $\mathbf{Y}_i = [y_1^i, y_2^i, \cdots, y_{n_i}^i], y_j^i \in \{1, 2, \cdots c_s\}$, where s is the number of source domains. x_j^i is the feature representation of the j-th sample in i-th source domain and it's feature dimension is d_i, y_j^i is the class label of the j-th sample in source domain and c_s is the total number of classes in the i source domain. Similarly, the target domain is defined as $\mathbf{X}_t = [\mathbf{x}_1^t, \mathbf{x}_2^t, \cdots, \mathbf{x}_{n_t}^t] \in \mathbf{R}^{d_t \times n_t}$ and it's label is $Y_t = [y_1^t, y_2^t, \cdots, y_{n_t}^t], y_i^t \in \{1, 2, \cdots c_t\}$.

Denote $\mathbf{X}^g = \left[\mathbf{x}_1^g, \mathbf{x}_2^g, \cdots, \mathbf{x}_{n_g}^g\right]$ as gallery and the labels set is $\mathbf{L} = \{\mathbf{L}_i\}_{i=1}^c$, let $\mathbf{x}^p$ denoted as probe set which will be identity and $label(\mathbf{x}^p) \in \mathbf{L}$. The gallery and the probe sets satisfy their distributions are the same as target domain. Calculating the label of $\mathbf{x}^p$ by comparing with gallery.

2.2   The Design of Framework

For clarity, the overall algorithm of MDGL is summarized in Fig. 1. Preprocessing of this framework, multiple sub-datasets can be obtained by randomly selecting samples from source and target domains. We use *subset 1, subset 2, ..., subset M* to donate the sub-datasets. Then learning a common subspace by domain adaptation method for each sub-dataset and jointing the idea of generic learning. The training samples do not contain the categories which will eventually be identified.

In this paper, we choose the multi-source domain adaptation method to learn the common subspace and using Fisher's Liner Discrimination analysis extract features. Similarity of images is calculate via cosine function for classification. In addition, the part of combination we adopt two strategies to estimate the classification performance. These are briefly introduction in the following content.

MDGL is divided into two parts: training part and testing part. In training part, we adopt domain adaption method to make the distribution of source domain closer to target domain, then a feature subspace is extracted by training a feature extraction algorithm on the new source domain set. Speaking specifically, there are 3 steps as follows:

1. Constructing multiple subsets by randomly selecting samples in the source and target domains.

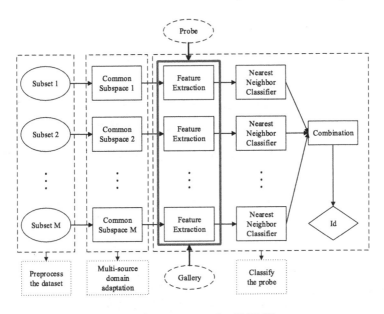

Fig. 1. The framework of MDGL.

2. Learning a feature subspace for every sub-dataset and a new source domain dataset will be represented by target samples.
3. Choosing an approach for discriminative feature extraction, in this paper, we employ FLD:

$$\mathbf{W}_{fld}^{*} = \arg\max_{\mathbf{W}} \frac{\left|\mathbf{W}^{T}\mathbf{S}_{b}\mathbf{W}\right|}{\left|\mathbf{W}^{T}\mathbf{S}_{t}\mathbf{W}\right|}, \tag{1}$$

where $\mathbf{S}_b$ is the between-class scatter matrix that is calculated from the targetize source domain and the total scatter matrix $\mathbf{S}_t$ is calculated from the target domain.

In testing part, both gallery and probe samples are projected into each subspace to obtain the corresponding feature representation $\mathbf{W}_{fld}^{*T}\mathbf{x}_i^g$ and $\mathbf{W}_{fld}^{*T}\mathbf{x}^p$. The identity of probe is calculated by each subsystem using nearest neighbor classifier, i.e.,

$$Label(\mathbf{x}^p) = Label(\mathbf{x}_i^{g*}), i = \arg\min_{i} \|\varphi(\mathbf{x}^p) - \varphi(\mathbf{x}_i^g)\|, \tag{2}$$

where $\|\cdot\|$ denotes the distance metric and $\varphi(\cdot)$ is the feature extraction function. The final identity is determined by combining the decision from all systems.

2.3 Multi-source Domain Adaptation Learning

In order to transfer the richer supervised knowledge from multi-source domains, we propose multi-source domain adaptation based on the TSD method.

We project multiple domains into a common subspace which need to satisfy two conditions: samples should be well interlaced and the structure should be well preserved. We use sparse reconstruction [13] and Max-Variance to meet the conditions.

Learning projection for each source and target domains, which are defined as $\mathbf{W}_1, \mathbf{W}_2, \cdots \mathbf{W}_s$ and $\mathbf{W}_t$, to project the source and target domain into a common subspace respectively due to domains may have large discrepancy or even in different space. What the samples in the common subspace are denoted as $\mathbf{Z}_i = [\mathbf{z}_1^i, \mathbf{z}_2^i, \cdots, \mathbf{z}_{n_i}^i], \mathbf{Z}_i = \mathbf{W}_i^T \mathbf{X}_i$ and $\mathbf{Z}_t = [\mathbf{z}_1^t, \mathbf{z}_2^t, \cdots, \mathbf{z}_{n_t}^t], \mathbf{Z}_t = \mathbf{W}_t^T \mathbf{X}_t$ respectively.

Sparse Reconstruction: Reconstructing the source domains samples by using a limited number of samples from target domain. We define $\|v\|_0 < \tau$, τ is the parameter to control the sparsity in terms of the number of samples used for the reconstruction. Specifically, the source and target domains samples are reconstructed by each other as bellow:

$$[\mathbf{V}_{s_i}^*, \mathbf{W}_i^*, \mathbf{W}_t^*] = \arg \min_{\mathbf{V}_{s_i}, \mathbf{W}_i, \mathbf{W}_t} \|\mathbf{Z}_i - \mathbf{Z}_t \mathbf{V}_{s_i}\|_F^2 \tag{3}$$

$$[\mathbf{V}_{t_i}^*, \mathbf{W}_t^*, \mathbf{W}_i^*] = \arg \min_{\mathbf{V}_{t_i}, \mathbf{W}_i, \mathbf{W}_t} \|\mathbf{Z}_t - \mathbf{Z}_i \mathbf{V}_{t_i}\|_F^2 \tag{4}$$

with $\mathbf{V}_{s_i} = [\mathbf{v}_1^{s_i}, \mathbf{v}_2^{s_i}, \cdots, \mathbf{v}_{n_{s_i}}^{s_i}]$, $\mathbf{V}_{t_i} = [\mathbf{v}_1^{t_i}, \mathbf{v}_2^{t_i}, \cdots, \mathbf{v}_{n_t}^{t_i}]$.

Max-Variance: The structure of each domain is preserved by simply maximizing the variance of source and target domains as follows:

$$\mathbf{W}_i^* = \arg \max_{\mathbf{W}_i} Tr(\mathbf{W}_i^T \mathbf{X}_i \mathbf{X}_i^T \mathbf{W}_i), i = 1, 2, \cdots, s, t. \tag{5}$$

where $\mathbf{X}_1, \mathbf{X}_2, \cdots, \mathbf{X}_s$ and $\mathbf{X}_t$ are assumed to have zero mean. Combining Eqs. (3)–(5) together by formulating it as a Fisher criterion-like objective function:

$$[\mathbf{W}_i^*, \mathbf{W}_t^*, \mathbf{V}_{s_i}^*, \mathbf{V}_{t_i}^*] = \arg \max_{\mathbf{W}_i, \mathbf{W}_t, \mathbf{V}_{s_i}, \mathbf{V}_{t_i}}$$

$$\frac{Tr(\sum_{i=1}^{s} \frac{1}{n_i} \mathbf{W}_i^T \mathbf{X}_i \mathbf{X}_i^T \mathbf{W}_i + \frac{1}{n_t} \mathbf{W}_t^T \mathbf{X}_t \mathbf{X}_t^T \mathbf{W}_t)}{\sum_{i=1}^{s} (\frac{1}{n_i} \|\mathbf{W}_i^T \mathbf{X}_i - \mathbf{W}_t^T \mathbf{X}_t \mathbf{V}_{s_i}\|_F^2 + \frac{1}{n_t} \|\mathbf{W}_t^T \mathbf{X}_t - \mathbf{W}_i^T \mathbf{X}_i \mathbf{V}_{t_i}\|_F^2)} \tag{6}$$

$$s.t. \|\mathbf{v}_j^{s_i}\|_0 \leq \tau, j = 1, 2, \cdots, n_{s_i}; \|\mathbf{v}_l^{t_i}\|_0 \leq \tau, l = 1, 2, \cdots, n_t.$$

Because the Eq. (6) isn't convex for all variables, we choice iterative updating method for solving the projection matrices $(\mathbf{W}_i, \mathbf{W}_t)$ and the sparse reconstructing coefficients $(\mathbf{V}_{s_i}, \mathbf{V}_{t_i})$. In optimization $\mathbf{V}_{s_i}$, by assuming a weight $\mathbf{h}_{t_i} \in \mathbf{R}^{n_t \times 1}$ indicates the times of the target sample which has been used, adding an additional penalty $\lambda \|1 - \mathbf{h}_{t_i}^T \mathbf{v}_j^{s_i}\|_F^2$ to avoid losing sample's intrapersonal variations. In optimization projection matrices, by rewriting W_s and W_t as one matrix $\mathbf{W} = \left[\mathbf{W}_i^T \mathbf{W}_t^T\right]^T$, it can be re-formulated with a norm-1 constraint and relax into a more tractable ratio trace form:

$$\mathbf{W}^* = \arg \max_{\mathbf{W}} Tr\left(\frac{\mathbf{W}^T \Sigma_b \mathbf{W}}{\mathbf{W}^T \Sigma_w \mathbf{W}}\right), s.t. \|w_j\|^2 = 1, \tag{7}$$

For clarity, the algorithm of multi-source domain adaptation is summarized in Algorithm 1.

Algorithm 1. mulit-source domain adaptaion

Input: the domain samples $\mathbf{X}_i, \cdots, \mathbf{X}_s$ and the target domain samples $\mathbf{X}_t$.

1. Initialize $\mathbf{W}_s, \mathbf{W}_t$ as random matrices with the norm of each column as 1;

2. Update $\mathbf{W}$ and $\mathbf{V}$

while less than a maximum number of iterations and the changes of variables is larger than ε **do**

  2.1 Optimize the sparse reconstruction coefficients

  for i=1:s **do**

    for j=1:n_{s_i} **do**

$$[\mathbf{v}_j^{s_i*}] = \arg\min_{\mathbf{v}_j^{s_i}} \left\| \mathbf{W}_i^T x_j^i - \mathbf{W}_t^T \mathbf{X}_t \mathbf{v}_j^{s_i} \right\|_F^2 + \lambda \left\| 1 - \mathbf{h}_{t_i}^T \mathbf{v}_j^{s_i} \right\|, h_{t_i} \Leftarrow \mathbf{h}_{t_i} -$$

$$\frac{0.5}{\max(|\mathbf{v}_j^{s_i*}|)} |\mathbf{v}_j^{s_i*}|.$$

    end for

    for j=1:n_t **do**

$$[\mathbf{v}_j^{t_i*}] = \arg\min_{\mathbf{v}_j^{t_i}} \left\| \mathbf{W}_t^T x_j^t - \mathbf{W}_i^T \mathbf{X}_i \mathbf{v}_j^{t_i} \right\|_F^2 + \lambda \left\| 1 - \mathbf{h}_{s_i}^T \mathbf{v}_j^{t_i} \right\|, \mathbf{h}_{s_i} \Leftarrow \mathbf{h}_{s_i} -$$

$$\frac{0.5}{\max(|\mathbf{v}_j^{t_i*}|)} |\mathbf{v}_j^{t_i*}|.$$

    end for

  end for

  2.2 Optimize the projection matrices

$$\mathbf{W}^* = \arg\max_{\mathbf{W}} Tr\left(\frac{\mathbf{W}^T \Sigma_b \mathbf{W}}{\mathbf{W}^T \Sigma_w \mathbf{W}}\right), \mathbf{W} = [\mathbf{W}_i^T \mathbf{W}_t^T], i = 1, 2, \cdots, s.$$

end while

3. Calculate the targetized source domain: $\mathbf{X}_{s \to t} = \mathbf{X}_t \mathbf{V}_{s_i}^*$

Output: the targetized source domain $\mathbf{X}_{s \to t}$.

2.4 Combination Strategy

The final identity of the probe sample is determined by combining the decisions from all subsystems. The paper selects majority vote and sum rule as the combination strategies because of their robustness and simplicity [3,8].

We define the $\mathbf{D}_g$ as the distance between the probe sample and the gallery dataset in each subsystem. d_{ki} is the distance between the probe and the gallery sample $\mathbf{x}_i^g$ in the k-th feature subspace where $i = 1, 2, \cdots, n_g$, $k = 1, 2, \cdots, M$, M is the number of subsystems. The formula is as follows:

$$\mathbf{D}_g = \begin{pmatrix} d_{11} & \cdots & d_{1n_g} \\ \vdots & \ddots & \vdots \\ d_{M1} & \cdots & d_{Mn_g} \end{pmatrix}, d_{ki} = \frac{d_{ki} - \mu}{\sigma}, \tag{8}$$

where μ and σ are the mean and variance of all distance d_{ki} respectively. The similarity to each gallery sample is calculated via cosine function as $sim(\mathbf{x}_i^g, \mathbf{x}^p) = \cos ine(\mathbf{W}_{fld}^{*T}\mathbf{x}_i^g, \mathbf{W}_{fld}^{*T}\mathbf{x}^p)$, The confidence degree is measured by a sigmoid function:

$$r_{ki} = \frac{1}{1 + \exp(d_{ki})}, r_{ki} = \frac{1}{\Sigma_{i=1}^{n_g} r_{ki}}, \tag{9}$$

where r_{ki} is class score, representing the posterior probability output by the k-th subsystem. The identify of $\mathbf{x}^p$ is obtained by combining the decisions from all subsystems.

Majority vote: Each subsystem provides a class decision of the probe, the final identity of the probe is the one which receives the majority votes.

Sum rule: Summing up the class score provide by every system for the final score and determining the label corresponding to the largest score.

Almost classification methods expect the inter-class variations are large while the intra-class is small, meaning the eigenvectors of between-class scatter matrix with a large value and the within-class scatter matrix with small are important. As the magnitude of eigenvalue increases, the estimation variance of the corresponding eigenvectors increases too, it can negatively impact recognition performance which is proved in the work [21]. Thus, inter-class variation determination and recognition performance can be improved by combining a set of weak learners.

3   Experiments and Results

In this section, we test the insensitivity of the method, comparing the validity with domain adaptation and generic learning methods respectively on the MultiPIE face dataset which is widely used to evaluate the performance of various face recognition algorithms.

3.1   Experimental Settings

In all experiments, we align the face images according to the manually labeled eye locations and normalized the images as 40×32 pixels on MultiPIE settings. Each image is resized to a column vector by stacking its raw pixels. Then, reducing the dimension of source domains and target domain separately through principal component analysis (PCA) [20] with 98% energy kept. To keep consistent with the parameters of the comparison algorithm, the parameters of τ and λ are empirically set to 3 and 0.05. For convince and fairness, the training samples our method used are all a subset of the training samples used in the comparative experiments and all the results are the mean accuracy of 10 trials.

The MultiPIE dataset contains 337 subjects, more than 750,000 images under various poses, illuminations and expressions. A dataset including 5 poses $(-45°, -30°, 0°, 30°, 45°)$ from four collecting session and is further divided into five sub-datasets according to view angle. For each subset, the images of

200 subjects are used for training. The remaining of 137 subjects with about 1 and 4 images randomly selected per subject as the gallery and probe respectively. The class labels are given in all source domain data for training but are not given for target training data.

We divide the experiment settings into two schemes: "samples randomly" and "subjects randomly". The detailed description is as follows:

(1) n images are selected randomly per subject when the number of subjects is 200.
(2) m subjects are selected randomly when there are 7 images per subject.

Through relevant experiments, the parameters of n and m are set to 2 and 100. The best dimension of feature space is 50 and the number of systems M are 5, 10, 15 and 20 respectively.

3.2   Comparison with the Existing Works

In this section, we compare with the common face recognition methods and the combination strategies. In order to prove MDGL universality and advantage, we compare the single-source domain adaptive method and the multi-source domain adaptive method respectively, and then compare with the method which only uses generic learning framework. In the experiments, acc_maj5 represents 5 subsystems with the strategy of majority vote, and acc_sum5 represents 5 systems with the strategy of sum rule. 0_ 30_ 45 represent the source domains are $0°$ and $30°$, $45°$ is target domain. TSD1 express that TSD use the first source domain. The experiment is divided into two schemes: (1) 2 samples randomly selected per subject (number of subjects is 200). (2) Selecting 100 subjects from 200 subjects respectively(7 samples per subject).

The Framework on the Scheme of "Samples Randomly". MDGL compares with other method including FLD which is a widely-used supervised method for feature extraction, TSD and TMSD. TSD is domain adaptation method by targeting source domain, it uses the target domain information. TMSD uses more than one source domains to get more discriminate information, and then training model by adaptation method.

As seen in Table 1, MDGL achieves much better performance than other methods in all cases. FLD has the worst performance because the data distribution of source domain is different from target domain and it cannot achieve a better recognition performance by training model on source domain without domain adaptation. TSD is better than FLD, it adopts domain adaptation method and learns discriminate information from both domains. On the basis of TSD, TMSD adds multiple source domains and learns more information by adaptation. But these methods what we compared with are worse than MDGL. The improvement of our method benefits from two aspects. On the one hand, MDGL makes the data distribution of source domain and target domain close by sparse reconstruction of multiple source domains in common subspace, and

Table 1. The recognition accuracy (%) of "subjects randomly"

View angles		0_30_45	0_30_−45	30_0_−30	−30_0_30	45_30_−30	−45_−30_30	45_30_−45
FLD		65.29	51.66	64.34	64.09	66.73	64.49	54.71
TSD1		71.68	69.18	76.93	78.21	77.04	78.65	70.18
TSD2		71.84	69.43	76.64	78.38	76.88	78.28	70.20
TMSD		73.12	70.38	78.08	79.80	77.68	79.67	71.33
MDGL	maj_5	**75.60**	**72.86**	79.43	80.18	78.87	80.22	73.25
	maj_10	**76.42**	**73.05**	79.93	80.69	79.31	80.35	73.14
	maj_15	**76.42**	**73.38**	**80.11**	81.08	79.47	80.55	**73.49**
	maj_20	**76.50**	**73.54**	80.05	81.11	79.45	80.66	**73.59**
	sum_5	**75.49**	72.10	79.32	80.05	78.91	79.76	72.81
	sum_10	**75.47**	**72.52**	79.78	80.24	78.92	79.98	72.59
	sum_15	**75.42**	**72.63**	79.73	80.42	79.20	80.44	72.57
	sum_20	**75.55**	**72.88**	**80.15**	80.47	79.25	80.13	72.74

on the other hand, MDGL constructs multiple subsystems by selecting different samples, so as to extract more discriminant information of samples.

According to the result in Table 1, the majority vote is better than sum rule. Especially, the best performance can be improved 3.38% than TMSD and 33.93% recognition rate which are bolded are improved more than 2%. As the number of subsystems increases, the advantages gradually emerge. Overall, the improvement of MDGL benefits that more discriminant information is retained and the reliability of the recognition result is improved by the selection of relevant combination strategies.

The Framework on the Scheme of "Subjects Randomly". Comparing with other methods on the scheme of "subjects randomly", we select 100 subjects randomly. The results are shown in Table 2. It can be observed that almost all of recognition results have improved. Especially, the best performance can be improved 3.14% than TMSD and 39.2% recognition rate are improved more than 2%. Increasing domains can provide more knowledge, so the performance improvement is more significant. Similarly, the results suggest that MDGL improves the recognition performance when the more subsystems participate.

The two combination strategies adopted in this experiment are also a positive in performance improvement. Majority vote helps to reduce the variance in the estimation of S_w and S_b, then, the reliability of confidence is enhanced. And the sum rule is the addition of confidence degree for the same class in each subsystem, therefore, it can avoid the errors of individual systems and the learning capacity of the algorithm increases resulting (Table 2).

The Framework Compare with Generic Learning Method. In this part, The framework compares with the generic learning method. We randomly select 4 groups of angles, they are $0°_−45°$, $30°_−−30°$, $45°_−−30°$ and $−45°_−45°$ respectively. In the scheme of "samples randomly", choosing 5 samples can show the

Table 2. The recognition accuracy (%) of "subjects randomly"

View angles		0_30_45	0_30_.−45	30_0_.−30	−30_0_30	45_30_.−30	−45_.−30_30	45_30_.−45
FLD		65.29	51.66	64.34	64.09	66.73	64.49	54.71
TSD1		71.68	69.18	76.93	78.21	77.04	78.65	70.18
TSD2		71.84	69.43	76.64	78.38	76.88	78.28	70.20
TMSD		73.12	70.38	78.08	79.80	77.68	79.67	71.33
MDGL	maj_5	**75.31**	**72.48**	79.58	80.24	79.03	79.95	72.88
	maj_10	**76.08**	**72.65**	**80.09**	80.77	79.16	80.35	**73.43**
	maj_15	**76.17**	**72.99**	**80.31**	80.80	79.38	80.55	**73.50**
	maj_20	**76.26**	**72.96**	**80.31**	81.09	79.64	80.73	**73.67**
	sum_5	**75.29**	72.06	79.14	80.16	78.61	79.53	72.41
	sum_10	**75.69**	72.28	79.49	80.31	79.09	80.15	73.08
	sum_15	**75.93**	**72.83**	79.42	80.58	78.98	80.35	**73.39**
	sum_20	**75.89**	**72.59**	79.40	80.80	79.34	80.40	**73.36**

best performance with 200 subjects. Choosing 150 subjects with 7 samples per subject in the scheme of "subjects randomly". The combination strategy is sum rule. 0_45 represent the source domain and target domain are 0° and 45° respectively. In Table 3, it shows the different number of samples per subject and the different number of subjects.

Table 3. The performance with different schemes and combine strategies

Scheme	View angles	0_45	30_.−30	45_.−30	−45_45
5 samples	acc_sum5	67.34	63.69	68.43	63.14
	acc_sum10	66.97	63.50	68.98	63.14
	acc_sum15	66.97	62.77	68.43	63.14
	acc_sum20	66.97	62.96	68.80	63.32
150 subjects	acc_sum5	68.07	61.31	69.53	62.23
	acc_sum10	67.88	62.96	69.71	61.50
	acc_sum15	68.25	63.32	70.44	61.86
	acc_sum20	68.25	63.87	69.71	61.13

It is obvious that the performance of generic learning method is worse than MDGL. That is because it does not joint the idea of domain adaptive, it only can learn feature information from source domain rather than both source and target domains. Meanwhile, it also proves that the generic learning method does not have the ability to solve the problem of different distribution.

4   Conclusion and Future Works

In this work, we propose MDGL on unsupervised learning to address face recognition problem. The method selects samples randomly and converts the source domains data into target domain data in the common feature subspace. It can obtain more discriminating information from different feature subspaces. The evaluations demonstrate the superiority of our framework to the other domain adaptation and generic learning methods. Although the combination strategies method adopted in this paper are simple, performance improvement is still obvious. In the following work, we will improve the integration strategy to get better recognition performance. Besides, we will discuss the impact of different domains on the recognition results and try to study the domain selection strategies.

Acknowledgments. This work is partially supported by The National Natural Science Foundation of China (61662014, 61702130, 61762025), Image intelligent processing project of Key Laboratory Fund (GIIP1804) and Innovation Project of GUET Graduate Education (2018YJCX44).

References

1. Ding, Z., Zhao, H., Fu, Y.: Multi-source transfer learning. Learning Representation for Multi-View Data Analysis. AIKP, pp. 175–202. Springer, Cham (2019). https://doi.org/10.1007/978-3-030-00734-8_8
2. Geng, B., Tao, D., Xu, C.: DAML: domain adaptation metric learning. IEEE Trans. Image Proces. **20**(10), 2980–2989 (2011). https://doi.org/10.1109/TIP.2011.2134107
3. Ghosh, J.: Multiclassifier systems: back to the future. In: Roli, F., Kittler, J. (eds.) MCS 2002. LNCS, vol. 2364, pp. 1–15. Springer, Heidelberg (2002). https://doi.org/10.1007/3-540-45428-4_1
4. Gopalan, R., Li, R., Chellappa, R.: Domain adaptation for object recognition: an unsupervised approach. In: IEEE International Conference on Computer Vision, pp. 999–1006 (2011). https://doi.org/10.1109/ICCV.2011.6126344
5. Ho, T.K., Hull, J.J., Srihari, S.N.: Decision combination in multiple classifier systems. IEEE Trans. Pattern Anal. Mach. Intell. **16**(1), 66–75 (1994). https://doi.org/10.1109/34.273716
6. Joachims, T.: Text categorization with support vector machines: learning with many relevant features. In: Nédellec, C., Rouveirol, C. (eds.) ECML 1998. LNCS, vol. 1398, pp. 137–142. Springer, Heidelberg (1998). https://doi.org/10.1007/BFb0026683
7. Kan, M., Wu, J., Shan, S., Chen, X.: Domain adaptation for face recognition: targetize source domain bridged by common subspace. Int. J. Comput. Vis., 94–109 (2013). https://doi.org/10.1007/s11263-013-0693-1
8. Kittler, J., Hatef, M., Duin, R.P.W., Matas, J.: On combining classifiers. IEEE Trans. Pattern Anal. Mach. Intell. **20**(3), 226–239 (1998). https://doi.org/10.1109/34.667881
9. Li, S., Liu, F., Liang, J., Cai, Z., Liang, Z.: Optimization of face recognition system based on azure IoT edge. Comput. Mater. Continua **61**(3), 1377–1389 (2019)

10. Liu, C.L.: Classifier combination based on confidence transformation. Pattern Recogn. **38**(1), 11–28 (2005). https://doi.org/10.1016/j.patcog.2004.05.013

11. Mansour, Y., Mohri, M., Rostamizadeh, A.: Domain adaptation with multiple sources. In: Advances in Neural Information Processing Systems, pp. 1041–1048 (2008)

12. Meng, Y., Lei, Z., Feng, X., Zhang, D.: Fisher discrimination dictionary learning for sparse representation. Proceedings **24**(4), 543–550 (2011). https://doi.org/10.1109/ICCV.2011.6126286

13. Nguyen, H.V., Patel, V.M., Nasrabadi, N.M., Chellappa, R.: Sparse embedding: a framework for sparsity promoting dimensionality reduction. In: Fitzgibbon, A., Lazebnik, S., Perona, P., Sato, Y., Schmid, C. (eds.) ECCV 2012. LNCS, vol. 7577, pp. 414–427. Springer, Heidelberg (2012). https://doi.org/10.1007/978-3-642-33783-3_30

14. Pan, S.J., Yang, Q.: A survey on transfer learning. IEEE Trans. Knowl. Data Eng. **22**(10), 1345–1359 (2010). https://doi.org/10.1109/TKDE.2009.191

15. Shawe-Taylor, J., Sun, S.: A review of optimization methodologies in support vector machines. Neurocomputing **74**(17), 3609–3618 (2011). https://doi.org/10.1016/j.neucom.2011.06.026

16. Shekhar, S., Patel, V.M., Nguyen, H.V., Chellappa, R.: Generalized domain-adaptive dictionaries. In: 2013 IEEE Conference on Computer Vision and Pattern Recognition, pp. 361–368 (2013). https://doi.org/10.1109/CVPR.2013.53

17. Sinno Jialin, P., Tsang, I.W., Kwok, J.T., Qiang, Y.: Domain adaptation via transfer component analysis. IEEE Trans. Neural Netw. **22**(2), 199–210 (2011). https://doi.org/10.1109/TNN.2010.2091281

18. Sun, S., Shi, H., Wu, Y.: A survey of multi-source domain adaptation. Inf. Fusion **24**(C), 84–92 (2015). https://doi.org/10.1016/j.inffus.2014.12.003

19. Tang, Z., et al.: Robust image hashing via random Gabor filtering and DWT. Comput. Mater. Continua **55**(2), 331–344 (2018)

20. Turk, M.A., Pentland, A.P.: Face recognition using eigenfaces. In: International Conference on Computer Research & Development (2011)

21. Wang, J., Plataniotis, K.N., Lu, J., Venetsanopoulos, A.N.: On solving the face recognition problem with one training sample per subject. Pattern Recogn. **39**(9), 1746–1762 (2006). https://doi.org/10.1016/j.patcog.2006.03.010

22. Wang, X., Xiong, C., Pei, Q., Qu, Y.: Expression preserved face privacy protection based on multi-mode discriminant analysis. Comput. Mater. Continua **57**(1), 107–121 (2018)

23. Xu, Y., Li, Z., Yang, J., Zhang, D.: A survey of dictionary learning algorithms for face recognition. IEEE Access **5**, 8502–8514 (2017). https://doi.org/10.1109/ACCESS.2017.2695239

24. Yi, H., Xu, Z., Wen, Y., Fan, Z.: Multi-source domain adaptation for face recognition. In: 24th International Conference on Pattern Recognition (ICPR), pp. 1349–1354 (2018). https://doi.org/10.1109/ICPR.2018.8546299

25. You, K., Long, M., Cao, Z., Wang, J., Jordan, M.I.: Universal domain adaptation. In: IEEE Conference on Computer Vision and Pattern Recognition, CVPR 2019, Long Beach, CA, USA, 16–20 June 2019, pp. 2720–2729 (2019)

Reset Attack: An Attack Against Homomorphic Encryption-Based Privacy-Preserving Deep Learning System

Xiaofeng Wu, Yuanzhi Yao, Weihai Li$^{(\boxtimes)}$, and Nenghai Yu

CAS Key Laboratory of Electromagnetic Space Information, University of Science and Technology of China, Hefei 230027, China
wxf12345@mail.ustc.edu.cn, {yaoyz,whli,ynh}@ustc.edu.cn

Abstract. In some existing privacy-preserving deep learning systems, additively homomorphic encryption enables ciphertext computation across the gradients. Therefore, many learning participants can perform neural network-based deep learning over a combined dataset without revealing the participants' local data to a central server. However, this privacy-preserving deep learning system is not secure against participant-level attack. We present an effective participant-level attack method against collaboration deep learning by uploading specific gradients to control the training process. With our method, even a single attacker can attack a learning task which is conducted by several participants. We implement our method and test it over the privacy-preserving learning framework. Considerable results show that this attack can greatly decrease the model accuracy.

Keywords: Privacy-preserving deep learning · Attack · Neural network

1 Introduction

Recently large-scale deep learning via crowdsourcing data becomes a hot topic in cloud computing [13] field. Thanks to the breakthrough of the distributed training technique [4] and edge-computing [16,19], the model train over a large number of devices like smartphones becomes available.

However, massive data collection raises privacy problems. Users usually need to train model over some sensitive data such as financial data and medical data, they do not want anyone else can get information about their data. Shokri et al. [17] presented a system for privacy-preserving deep learning that enabled multiple parties to jointly learn a model without sharing their private datasets. Le Trieu Phong et al. [10] enhanced Shokri's system to defense the server's attack by using additively homomorphic encryption. The system in [10] protects privacy from the server but misses an attack surface that attackers can control user's devices in the task. Especially, if the number of participants grows to thousands level, it is impossible to detect or exclude the attacker in users.

© Springer Nature Singapore Pte Ltd. 2020
X. Sun et al. (Eds.): ICAIS 2020, CCIS 1252, pp. 28–38, 2020.
https://doi.org/10.1007/978-981-15-8083-3_3

The system in [10] uses encryption to protect the gradients, which also protect the abnormal gradients from the attacker, i.e. server cannot get any information about the attacker. By exploiting this vulnerability, we can construct an attack more effective because we can directly operate the gradients. And we proved this by constructing a new participants-level attack.

In this paper, we constructed an attack against the system in [10] named Reset Attack by uploading specific fake gradients to intervene in the training process. We got considerable results that by using our method, the attacker can force the global model's accuracy into a neighborhood of the value the attacker gives.

The remainder of this paper is organized as follows. Section 2 reviews the progress in privacy-preserving deep learning. Section 3 introduces the target framework we use. Section 4 demonstrates the proposed approach, and Sect. 5 shows the experimental results. Finally, Sect. 6 gives conclusions and future work.

2 Related Works

Distributed Deep Learning. Xu Zhang et al. [21] presented a distributed multi-node synchronous SGD algorithm with Data Parallelism. Jeffrey Dean et al. [5] presented downpour sgd to train a large-scale with tens of thousands of CPU cores which has higher performance against traditional sgd. Feng Niu et al. [15] presented a Lock-Free parallelizing SGD named HOGWILD!. It can run parallelizing SGD using shared memory, which improves memory access efficiency. These technologies are the foundation of collaborative learning.

Secure Machine Learning. Nathan Dowlin et al. presented a method to convert a learned neural network to CryptoNets [20]. CryptoNets use homomorphic encryption to protect test-time security. Morten Dahl et al. [3] presented a framework using secure multi-party computation [6] to construct private machine learning in TensorFlow. Mohassel et al. [14] presented SecureML using secure two-party computation(2PC). In SecureML, users distribute their private data among two non-colluding servers who train various models on the joint data using 2PC. These protection methods focus on the attack outside of the users but cannot defense participants-level attack.

Adversarial Examples. Adversarial examples [8] are constructed to be misclassified by applying small but intentionally worst-case perturbations. In many cases, a human cannot notice the modification but the classifier gives error output in high confidence. Our method is train-time attack and the Adversarial examples are a test-time attack.

Backdoor Attack. Data poisoning attack [2] try to inject fake data into the dataset, to insert backdoors into the model. But the backdoor only works when input is specifically selected, and traditional poisoning attack is proved not work against federated learning [1]. Bagdasaryan et al. [1] presented a new backdoor attack by model replacement in federated learning. It is like two-task learning, where the global model learns the main task during normal training and learns the backdoor task during attackers are selected. By contrast, our method attacks the performance over the whole input-space.

GAN Attack. Briland Hitaj et al. [9] used the real-time nature of the learning process to train a GAN [7,12,18] that can generate other users' private data. They proposed that any privacy-preserving collaborative deep learning is unsecured with this attack. GAN-attack focuses on the information leak while training.

3   Privacy-Preserving Deep Learning

Privacy-Preserving Deep Learning [10,17] allows users running large-scale deep learning without sharing private data.

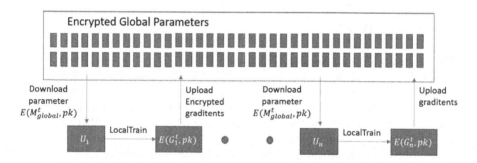

Fig. 1. Overview of the learning framework.

Figure 1 gives the structure of privacy-preserving deep learning with n participants. pk, sk_i are the key pair between the server and user i, sk_i is the private key belongs to i. $E(\cdot), D(\cdot)$ are the pair of encrypt function and decrypt function. For each user i and server state t, user i downloads the encrypted global parameters $E(M_{global}^t, pk)$ from the server, decrypts it using sk_i and calculates the gradients G_i^t using their private data $data_i$. Finally encrypts the gradients using pk and uploads the encrypted gradients to the server.

$$
\begin{aligned}
G_i^t &= LocalTrain(E(M_{global}^t, pk), data_i, sk_i) \\
&= SGD(D(E(M_{global}^t, pk), sk_i), data_i) \\
&= SGD(M_{global}^t, data_i)
\end{aligned}
\tag{1}
$$

Server updates the global parameters using the gradients from users. Since the encryption scheme is additively homomorphic, the update step with user i is:

$$
E(M_{global}^{t+1}, pk) = E(M_{global}^t, pk) + E(G_i^t, pk)
\tag{2}
$$

It is optional that users can upload a part of gradients to avoid information leakage [17]. As Fig. 1 and these equations show, the training data never leave participants' machine. There exist a lot of flavors of distributed deep learning, like system using synchronous SGD [21], but they are trivial to our attack method in Sect. 4. So we no longer consider them.

4   Reset Attack: An Attack Against Privacy-Preserving Deep Learning

Structure in [10] gives a secure channel for crowd-sourced Deep Learning. By using additively homomorphic encryption, it solves the problem of privacy disclosure to the server. However, it also disables the server's ability to audit, which allows attackers to easily participate in the training task with no abnormality to the server.

4.1   Threat Model

The attackers have the full control permission of their devices, and we assume that attackers have the following capabilities.

(1) The attacker can run any program on its own devices;
(2) it can participate in the training task as one or several legal users;
(3) it can modify the gradients uploaded to the server;
(4) it has some local data which is i.i.d. to the train data;
(5) it does not try to interfere legal users, i.e., it only attacks the server by uploading fake gradients.

Objectives of Attack. The attacker wants to reset the model state to the old state, which finally causes the performance to decrease. Furthermore, our attacker wants to control the model's performance accurately, and force it close to the value that the attacker gives.

4.2   Attack Model Structure

Naive Approach: Opposite Gradients Attack. The attacker runs the local training step as same as legal users, but uploads the opposite gradients. The overview of the attack is Fig. 2. It is intuitive that, when the attacker uploads the opposite gradients, the global optimization will be dragged in the opposite direction. It will be effective when the attacker controls a large part of the users' devices. But it does not work or archive a low effect when the attacker controls only one or a small part of the participants. (See Sect. 5.1) It reflects the fake gradients will be easily averaged by the legal gradients. We use this naive approach as the baseline in the experiment.

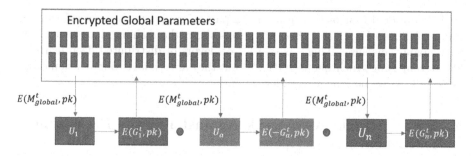

Fig. 2. Opposite gradients attack model

Our Method: Reset Attack. In this method, the attacker tries to save the global parameters for each step, e.g. the global model of state t is M^t_{global}. The attacker upload the scaled difference with the latest model and M^t_{global}.

It can be expressed by the following formulas.

The attacker upload the fake gradients when server's state is $t + l$:

$$G_a = (M^t_{global} - M^{t+l}_{global}) \tag{3}$$

$$
\begin{aligned}
E(M^{t+l+1}_{global}, pk) &= E(M^{t+l}_{global}, pk) + E(G_a, pk) \\
&= E(M^{t+l}_{global}, pk) + E(M^t_{global} - M^{t+l}_{global}, pk) \\
&= E(M^t_{global}, pk)
\end{aligned}
\tag{4}
$$

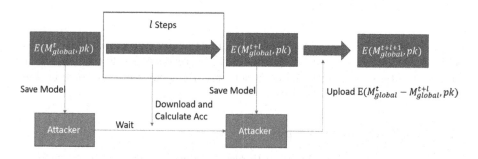

Fig. 3. Reset attack model

These equations show that once attacker upload fake gradients, the Model of $t + l$ state will be reseted to the Model of t state, and the M_{t+l+1} is usually near to M_{t+l}. The performance of global model will stay in a low level after attacker started attacking if attacker uploads fake gradients frequently (Fig. 3).

We do not give any limitation to variable l and t, so it is flexible that attacker can hack in the task at any time. For example, attacker can set a stop_acc as a flag, and evaluate the global model using his local data for each round.

When the global model performance exceeds the stop_accuracy, attacker start attacking. Then the global model will be reset to the point near the model whose performance close to the stop_accuracy.

5   Experiments

In this section, we implement privacy-preserving deep learning with 30 participants. We use MNIST [11] as the dataset with the training images are split into 30 parts, and use structure as Fig. 6 in [17] as the DeepLearning model. Each participant uses 0.001 as the learning rate and SGD optimizer. We train the model 100 epochs on 1 NVIDIA Tesla K80 GPU, and each epoch traversing the smallest dataset.

We test the Opposite Gradients Attack in Sect. 5.1, and test Reset Attack in Sect. 5.2. The backend of these experiments is Pytorch 1.1.0.

5.1   Opposite Gradients Attack

In this section, we implement the Opposite Gradients Attack. In each round, the attacker's devices calculate the normal gradient using their local dataset and return the opposite item.

The number of devices attacker controls takes values in $\{0, 1, 3, 5, 7, 9, 12, 15, 18\}$. When the number is 0, it expresses that the attacker controls no device. In Fig. 4 we can see that decrease of accuracy is not significant, only 4.03% decrease even when 12 attackers in 30 participants. Table 1 lists the detailed information. It shows the privacy-preserving deep learning has high robustness against opposite gradients attack. The reason is the effects of fake gradients are easily overwritten by the normal gradients.

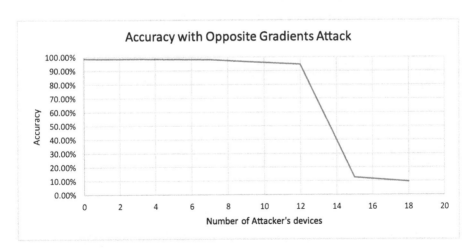

Fig. 4. The Accuracy decrease via the number of the attacker's devices grows. But the decrease is small until the number reaches 15, the half of the users.

Table 1. Accuracy with opposite gradients attack.

Num of the attackers	Max accuracy	Decrease
0	0.9871	0
1	0.9854	0.0017
3	0.9849	0.0022
5	0.9836	0.0035
7	0.9811	0.0060
9	0.9667	0.0204
12	0.9468	0.0403
15	0.1263	0.8608
18	0.0974	0.8897

5.2 Reset Attack

In this section, we implement Reset Attack with 30 participants, the attacker controls only 1 device of them. We use the hyperparameter stop_acc to control the time attack happen and use c to control the percentage gradients upload. For each round, the attacker downloads the global model from sever and uses local data to evaluate the model's accuracy. The attacker upload zero tensors until the global model's performance exceed stop_acc, and attack continually after the attack begins. We use round-robin as the schedule method.

We test stop_acc in $\{0, 0.2, 0.3, 0.5, 0.8, 0.9\}$ and use result in [10] as the baseline accuracy without attack.

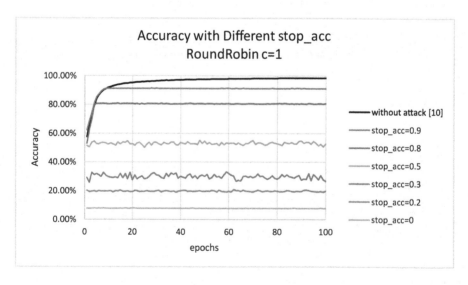

Fig. 5. Accuracy on test dataset with different stop_acc

Figure 5 shows the result under different stop_acc with all the participants uploading the whole gradients. We can see the accuracy is limited in the neighborhood of stop_acc, the bound is below 6% (see Table 2). The performance stays under 10% if attack starts from the beginning, almost random guess. Reset Attack is effective, with 90.78% decrease when attack start from beginning.

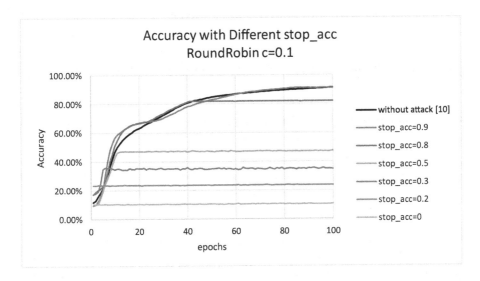

Fig. 6. Accuracy on test dataset with different stop_acc

For every stop_acc, accuracy stops growing after the attack started, but when the stop_acc falls on the middle part, the accuracy becomes oscillation. We think the limitation of the attacker's dataset is the main cause of the error between final accuracy and the stop_acc, because the attacker cannot start attacking at the precise moment.

Figure 6 shows the result with 10% of the gradients will be accepted. The update speed slows down, but the final result is similar to Fig. 5. It expresses that our method is also effective in privacy-preserving deep learning using selective SGD. It seems training is not convergence when stop_acc = 0.9 and without attack. So we rerun these tests with more epochs and fix the result in Table 2.

Comparing to the result in Sect. 5.1, Reset Attack is more effective with less cost. In Sect. 5.1, we need 12 controlled devices to get only 4.03% performance degradation, but when we use Reset Attack, we only need 1 controlled device and can get 90.78% performance degradation.

Table 2. Accuracy with reset attack.

stop_acc	Accuracy, c = 1	Accuracy, c = 0.1
0	0.0808	0.1062
0.2	0.2083	0.2374
0.3	0.3319	0.3580
0.5	0.5511	0.4746
0.8	0.8089	0.8186
0.9	0.9131	0.9140 **fixed**
Without attack	0.9857 [10]	0.9882 [10] **fixed**

5.3 Estimating the Computational Costs

To estimating the running time of our method, we use the formulas in [10], the cost each participant has to bear can be expressed as bellow:

$$T_{user,one\ run} = T_{CNN,one\ run} + T_{enc} + T_{dec} + T_{upload} + T_{download} + T_{add}$$
$$\approx T_{CNN,one\ run} + 401\,(\text{ms}) \tag{5}$$

where, $T_{user,one\ run}$ is the running time of the participant i when doing the following: waiting for the addition of ciphertexts at the server (T_{add}), downloading the encrypted parameters from the server ($T_{download}$), decrypting the encryped parameters (T_{dec}), computing the gradients ($T_{CNN,one\ run}$), encrypting the gradients (T_{enc}) and uploading the results to the server (T_{upload}).

Since the number of parameters and gradients are not change, we use $T_{attack,one\ run}$ to express the time of offline computing and $T_{attacker,one\ run}$ is the running time of the attacker:

$$T_{attacker,one\ run} = T_{attack,one\ run} + T_{enc} + T_{dec} + T_{upload} + T_{download} + T_{add}$$
$$\approx T_{attack,one\ run} + 401\,(\text{ms}) \tag{6}$$

We counted the time needed for the offline calculation, and fixed (5) and (6).

$$T_{ours,one\ run} \approx 4.052\,(\text{ms}) + 401\,(\text{ms}) \approx 405\,(\text{ms})$$
$$T_{attack,one\ run} \approx 2.388\,(\text{ms}) + 401\,(\text{ms}) \approx 403\,(\text{ms}) \tag{7}$$

Results in (7) prove that our attacker has almost the same cost as the legal participants.

6 Conclusions and Future Work

In this paper, we present a new attack on privacy-preserving deep learning. Our method is a participant-level attack that directly destroys the integrity of the training task. Since the server cannot learn any information from the data we uploaded because of the encryption, the participant-level attack cannot be avoided. But, if there is no protection on uploaded data, the attack will be detected because the fake gradients are abnormal. It seems that protecting the privacy of data is inconsistent with the participant-level security, so we should find the balance between two types of security.

Acknowledgments. This work was supported by the National Key Research and Development Program of China under Grant 2018YFB0804101 and the National Natural Science Foundation of China under Grant 61802357.

References

1. Bagdasaryan, E., Veit, A., Hua, Y., Estrin, D., Shmatikov, V.: How to backdoor federated learning (2018). http://arxiv.org/abs/1807.00459
2. Biggio, B., Nelson, B., Laskov, P.: Poisoning attacks against support vector machines. In: Proceedings of the 29th International Conference on International Conference on Machine Learning, ICML 2012, Omnipress, USA, pp. 1467–1474 (2012). http://dl.acm.org/citation.cfm?id=3042573.3042761
3. Dahl, M., et al.: Private machine learning in TensorFlow using secure computation (2018). http://arxiv.org/abs/1810.08130
4. Dean, J., et al.: Large scale distributed deep networks. In: Pereira, F., Burges, C.J.C., Bottou, L., Weinberger, K.Q. (eds.) Advances in Neural Information Processing Systems, vol. 25, pp. 1223–1231. Curran Associates, Inc. (2012). http://papers.nips.cc/paper/4687-large-scale-distributed-deep-networks.pdf
5. Dean, J., et al.: Large scale distributed deep networks. In: Proceedings of the 25th International Conference on Neural Information Processing Systems - Volume 1, NIPS 2012, pp. 1223–1231. Curran Associates Inc. (2012). http://dl.acm.org/citation.cfm?id=2999134.2999271
6. Du, W., Atallah, M.J.: Secure multi-party computation problems and their applications: a review and open problems. In: Proceedings of the 2001 Workshop on New Security Paradigms, NSPW 2001, pp. 13–22. ACM, New York (2001). http://doi.acm.org/10.1145/508171.508174
7. Goodfellow, I., et al.: Generative adversarial nets, pp. 2672–2680 (2014). http://papers.nips.cc/paper/5423-generative-adversarial-nets.pdf
8. Goodfellow, I., Shlens, J., Szegedy, C.: Explaining and harnessing adversarial examples. In: International Conference on Learning Representations (2015). http://arxiv.org/abs/1412.6572
9. Hitaj, B., Ateniese, G., Perez-Cruz, F.: Deep models under the GAN: information leakage from collaborative deep learning, pp. 603–618 (2017). https://doi.org/10.1145/3133956.3134012
10. Le, T.P., Aono, Y., Hayashi, T., Wang, L., Moriai, S.: Privacy-preserving deep learning via additively homomorphic encryption. IEEE Trans. Inf. Forensics Secur. **13**(5), 1333–1345 (2018)
11. Lecun, Y., Bottou, L., Bengio, Y., Haffner, P.: Gradient-based learning applied to document recognition. Proc. IEEE **86**, 2278–2324 (1998). https://doi.org/10.1109/5.726791
12. Li, X., Liang, Y., Zhao, M., Wang, C., Jiang, Y.: Few-shot learning with generative adversarial networks based on WOA13 data. Comput. Mater. Continua **58**, 1073–1085 (2019). https://doi.org/10.32604/cmc.2019.05929

13. Marston, S., Li, Z., Bandyopadhyay, S., Ghalsasi, A.: Cloud computing - the business perspective. In: Proceedings of the 2011 44th Hawaii International Conference on System Sciences, HICSS 2011, pp. 1–11. IEEE Computer Society, Washington, DC (2011). https://doi.org/10.1109/HICSS.2011.102

14. Mohassel, P., Zhang, Y.: SecureML: a system for scalable privacy-preserving machine learning. In: 2017 IEEE Symposium on Security and Privacy (SP), pp. 19–38, May 2017. https://doi.org/10.1109/SP.2017.12

15. Niu, F., Recht, B., Ré, C., Wright, S.: Hogwild!: A lock-free approach to parallelizing stochastic gradient descent. In: NIPS, vol. 24 (2011)

16. Shi, W., Jie, C., Quan, Z., Li, Y., Xu, L.: Edge computing: vision and challenges. IEEE Internet Things J. 3(5), 637–646 (2016)

17. Shokri, R., Shmatikov, V.: Privacy-preserving deep learning. In: Proceedings of the 22Nd ACM SIGSAC Conference on Computer and Communications Security, CCS 2015, pp. 1310–1321. ACM, New York (2015). https://doi.org/10.1145/2810103.2813687

18. Tu, Y., Lin, Y., Wang, J., Kim, J.U.: Semi-supervised learning with generative adversarial networks on digital signal modulation classification. Comput. Mater. Continua 55(2), 243–254 (2018)

19. Wei, Y., Wang, Z., Guo, D., Yu, F.: Deep Q-learning based computation offloading strategy for mobile edge computing. Comput. Mater. Continua 59, 89–104 (2019). https://doi.org/10.32604/cmc.2019.04836

20. Xie, P., Bilenko, M., Finley, T., Gilad-Bachrach, R., Lauter, K., Naehrig, M.: Crypto-nets: Neural networks over encrypted data. Comput. Sci. (2014)

21. Zhang, X., Yu, F.X., Kumar, S., Chang, S.F.: Learning spread-out local feature descriptors. In: Proceedings of the IEEE International Conference on Computer Vision, pp. 4595–4603 (2017)

Intelligent Contract for Power Market Transaction Based on the BlockChain

Yutong Zhang[1]([✉]), Yuan Meng[1], Shanshan Tu[1][ID], Muhammad Waqas[1,4][ID], Sadaqat Ur Rehman[1,2][ID], Wei Zhao[3], Ghulam Abbas[4], and Ziaul Haq Abbas[4]

[1] Beijing Key Laboratory of Trusted Computing, School of Computing, Beijing University of Technology, Beijing 100124, China
zyj990@163.com, sstu@bjut.edu.cn, 690146986@qq.com
[2] College of Science and Engineering, Hammad Bin Khalifa University, Al Rayyan, Qatar
engr.sidkhan@gmail.com
[3] Beijing Electro-Mechanical Engineering Institute, Beijing 100074, China
[4] Telecommunications and Networking (TeleCoN) Research Lab, Ghulam Ishaq Khan Institute of Engineering Sciences and Technology, Topi 23460, Pakistan
{abbasg,ziaul.h.abbas}@giki.edu.pk

Abstract. The power market is changing with the development of distributed energy. The development of the micro-grid introduces a small power generation system for distributed energy. It has become a trend for the micro-grid to participate in the power market. Blockchain is a database technology with transparent distribution through a decentralization mechanism. In the blockchain, the transaction data are maintained by entire nodes in the power market. It solves the trust problem between the transaction agents. Intelligent contract technology can make transaction contracts computerized and executed automatically, which has dramatically improved transaction efficiency. In this paper, an intelligent contract for the power transaction is analyzed based on the concepts of the blockchain. The roles of the micro-grid and the related intelligent contract technologies in the power market are also investigated in the electricity reform. Finally, a blockchain scheme for point-to-point trading is designed for future purposes.

Keywords: Power market · Micro-grid · BlockChain · Intelligent contract · Distributed database

1 Introduction

Nowadays, power generation and distribution system, and micro-grid have gained tremendous attention due to the development of distributed energy. Micro-grid is an effective way to achieve an active power distribution network. As a result, the traditional energy trading system cannot adapt to the complex transaction system in the future anymore. Electricity trading is facing significant challenges. Under the background of national reform on the electric power system, there is a

© Springer Nature Singapore Pte Ltd. 2020
X. Sun et al. (Eds.): ICAIS 2020, CCIS 1252, pp. 39–49, 2020.
https://doi.org/10.1007/978-981-15-8083-3_4

long way for the operation system of the electric power market to make changes and achieve the goal of the reform. During the construction of the energy internet, the bilateral transactions are essential in the power market trans-action system due to the enrolment of many different producers and consumers. The main body of the power market has developed with more diversity, which has made the management of the power transactions and the storage of the transaction information more difficult. At present, power transaction management mainly uses a centralized system in which the operations are stored and maintained by the central organization. The centralized system results in the information asymmetry. If hackers threaten the information security of the central organization, large amounts of private information will be leaked [1–3]. Consequently, it damages the interest of the traders. Therefore, a trust mechanism is needed to ensure mutual trust, preserve the transaction information, enhance the transaction efficiency, and reduce the transaction costs in bilateral transactions.

Blockchain technology is a trust mechanism that has the characteristics of transparency and decentralization. Blockchain is also used in Bitcoin. It develops the proof of technical workload, the timestamp and the public key system. Due to its traceability and unalterable transaction mode, blockchain has a significantly lowered security risk. Meanwhile, the development of Ethereum Virtual Machine (EVM) intelligent contract has enabled the users to observe the process and results of machine language operation in the blockchain. Currently, many companies and research institutes are focusing on the application of blockchain technology in the energy area. Different theoretical frameworks have been proposed and conduct a significant amount of experiments on the trading frameworks. In [4,5] the authors used an electronic currency as a token, and the electricity is considered as the commodity correspondingly. The electronic currency is used to exchange electricity, as proposed in [6]. The authors investigated a three-tier energy architecture. In [7], a system with intelligent devices is considered as nodes. The power transaction between devices is achieved through intelligent contracts. A framework of blockchain technology combined with the virtual power plant is analyzed in [8]. Moreover, many companies in countries other than China have established power trading projects based on the small-scale micro-grid blockchain, including the micro-grid blockchain project in Brooklyn in the United States, and the micro-grid blockchain sale project in New York. However, there is still a long way for these projects to be applied commercially. Most of the studies in the literature and the research projects focused on the transactions between the internet devices or the trading architecture of the energy market based on the energy internet. However, very few studies have considered the national reform on electric power while investigating the trading modes of the micro-grid electric power market in China.

Therefore, we have analyzed the relationship between the micro-grid and the trading entities involved in the electric power reform. We also investigate the micro-grid to participate in the trading entities used in the blockchain. Thus, we construct an intelligent contract system for the micro-grid electricity trading based on the intelligent contract. In this regard, we propose our scheme to improve the blockchain platform. Finally, a case study on the intelligent contract is discussed and is offered future development direction for the power trading blockchain.

2   Intelligent Contract System for Power Transaction in Micro-grid

2.1   Micro-grid

Micro-grid is a small distribution system consisting of distributed power supply, energy storage devices, loading and monitoring, protection devices and energy conversion devices. Micro-grid can be operated either independently or in parallel with the large grid (in-parallel micro-grid). In micro-grid, energy conversion is achieved by controlling the electronic power devices. According to Electric Power Reform (EPR), the micro-grid is encouraged to participate in the power market. There are two strategies for the in-parallel micro-grid to join in the power market. First, we consider the single user micro-grid, such as photovoltaic micro-grid. It is considered as the primary user in the power market, similar to the factory user. Second, the power supply network identical to the local area network is considered, in which a single grid connection point should be used to provide the power supply to multiple types of users. In the power market, micro-grid should participate as a company to offer either the integration of transmission and distribution services or the distribution service only. The difference between the above two participation modes is the distributed power supply in the micro-grid.

2.2   Intelligent Contract System for Power Transaction in Micro-Grid

This system adopts the token incentive, utilizes the agreement mechanism of proof of work (PoW) + Proof of stake (PoS) similar to (exchange traded funds) ETF, uses the account as the basic unit, and applies the private key to sign the transaction. Every user utilizes the system client terminal and the intelligent meter. The intelligent meter stores the power quantity in the blockchains, and eventually generates the intelligent terminal containing the public blockchains. The electricity is a special commodity and the intellectualization of the power system. Thus, power transactions cannot be completely decentralized. Therefore, a central node is necessary to provide transaction supervision, congestion management, and account management [9]. The transaction flow is shown in Fig. 1.

The games trading entities are carried out to determine the content of the transaction. The game process contains three stages. In the first stage, the bilateral free negotiation transactions are conducted among the power generation side, the micro-grid side, the grid side, and the user side. After the negotiation,

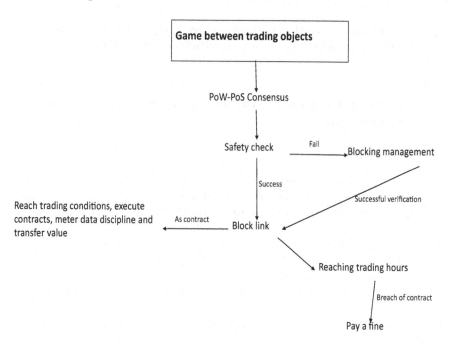

Fig. 1. The transaction process among multiple entities with a weak central node.

the electricity quantity and the price in the transaction are determined and confirmed in the contract using the website as the medium. In the second stage, the power generation side initiates the trading with the listing price.

Meanwhile, the micro-grid users, the market users, the regulated users, the micro-grid, and power grid provide offering price for the trading. In the third stage, the centralized bidding of the transactions between the users, the micro-grid, the power generation side, and the large power grid is conducted. The match of the transaction is based on the price difference. Both the power generation side and the purchaser provide their bidding prices. The price difference is calculated by subtracting the cost from the purchaser from the power generation side. The system attempts to match each of the transactions using the maximum price difference. When the price difference is less than 0, the matching attempts will end. If the same price difference occurs in multiple transactions, the transaction with larger electricity quantity has a higher priority. For all the successfully matched transactions, the final price equals to the arithmetic average of the costs from both the purchaser and the power generation side. Also, to follow "the strategies of significantly developing the low-carbon, environment-friendly, and clean energy" described in [10], the carbon factor was introduced into the equation to calculate and revise the price provided by the power generation side. By adding the carbon factor, it is easier for the clean-unit group to match the cost from the purchaser. The revised equation on the price of the power generation company side is in Eq. (1):

$$P_k = \frac{u_k \sum_{i=1}^{n} Q_i}{\sum_{i=1}^{n} u_i Q_i} P_k \tag{1}$$

Where Q_i is the electricity quantity from the power generation side i, P_k is the initial listing price, u is the intensity of carbon emissions, n is the number of power generation companies, and K is the label of the power generation side. From Eq. (1), the listing price from the power generation side for the low-carbon electricity decreases and the average price difference is increased. Thus, it is easier for low-carbon electricity to achieve a price match.

When the game is completed, the transaction information and scheduling information are broadcasted to other users through the converted contract by a background application in the system. The users pack the transaction sets and determine the accounting rights and blocks using the incentive mechanism. As discussed above, the PoW agreement mechanism requires a lot of computation power and wastes resources, which has been proved by the application of Bitcoin. Thus, the PoS agreement mechanism is added to determine the accounting right. The PoS agreement is based on the concept of currency age, which is calculated by multiplying the number of tokens held by users with the number of days owned by the user. The larger the currency age, the higher the probability of the user to get the accounting right. After a user obtains the opportunity to keep the account, his/her currency age will be cleared. Meanwhile, the user will get some income from the blocks by following the account. The income can be calculated by Eq. (2):

$$S = \frac{B \times 5\%}{365} \tag{2}$$

Where S is the number of the interest coins, 5% is the annual interest rate, and B is the cleared currency age. Therefore, this mechanism to determine the accounting right is called incentive mechanism. The PoS agreement encourages the users who hold large amounts of tokens to participate actively; however, the users with small amounts of tokens only get little interest; thus, their participation ratio is meagre. Therefore, the hybrid agreement of PoW+PoS is adopted to increase the participation ratio of small users. With the hybrid agreement of PoW+PoS, both criteria of the mining participation, and the holding number of tokens are used to vote for the accounting the block. The implementation of the hybrid agreement of PoW+PoS is described as follows. PoW miners determine the accounting rights and the blocks based on the calculation using the random number Nonce. Then, the PoS holders verify the legitimacy of blocks by voting. The PoW miners pack $K(k \geq 5)$ votes from the PoS holders into the new blocks to indicate that the new blocks have been certified by the PoS holders. Finally, the incentive tokens are distributed proportionally to the PoW miners and the POS holders. The PoW miners get the dominate share of the incentive tokens. In this way, the miners, the token holders, and the developers can participate in the system more actively.

After the accounting right and the block are determined, the security check will be run on the electricity transaction. If the transaction is insecure, the weak central node will adjust the price using the minimum trading amount as the objective function or changes the transaction matrix to adjust the transaction in the block. The accounting node will verify whether the public key and private key of the transaction are paired and whether the transaction is legitimate. After the verification, the block will be broadcasted, and each node can get a copy of the block. Then the block is connected to the blockchain. When the conditions for contract execution are met, the intelligent contract will be automatically executed, and the value will be transferred according to the data in the electricity meter. When the micro-grid is working as a company with the integrated transmission and distribution services, it first sells the electricity power to the micro-grid users and then purchases from the power generation side when the electricity power is insufficient. In contrast, when the micro-grid is working as a company with only distribution service, it first purchases a full amount of energy from (distributed energy resource) DER and then buys more from the power generation side when the electricity power is insufficient. Micro-grid is more competitive comparing to other power distribution companies (Fig. 2).

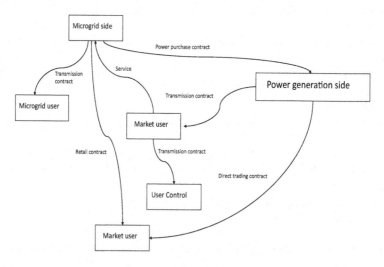

Fig. 2. Four types of intelligent contracts when the in-parallel micro-grid participates in the power market as the electricity seller.

3   A Case on the Intelligent Contract

In this study, based on the analysis of the working principle of the intelligent contract system, we have created a study case on the transaction contract between the micro-grid and the power generation side, and then deployed and tested the transaction contract on the blockchain. Assume that a micro-grid finds that the power generated by a distributed energy system is insufficient for the participating users; the micro-grid then plays the first-stage game with the power generation plant and obtains a purchasing and selling contract. Based on the agreement, the micro-grid sends the purchasing request message to the power generation side, and then both sides make plans on the purchasing quantity and the unit price based on negotiation. After the actual transaction is completed, if the exact purchasing quantity by the micro-grid is higher than 110% of the amount planned, the first 110% of the scheduled purchasing quantity will be at the original price, while the excessive part will be priced at 150% of the original price. Otherwise, if the actual purchasing amount of electricity by the micro-grid is lower than 90% of the planned purchasing quantity, the actual purchasing will be at the original price. However, the micro-grid needs to pay the penalty to the power plant for the losses arising from the transaction. The amount of the penalty is three times the difference between the planned and actual purchasing quantities. The unit of the penalty is based on the relationship between tokens and RMB. Based on the test result, the catalogue price was 3. The test results of the intelligent contract are shown in Fig. 3.

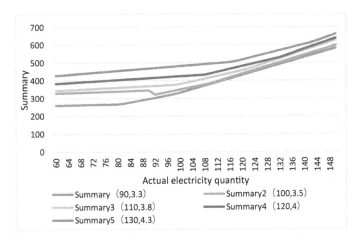

Fig. 3. Relationship between actual electricity quantity and summary based on four different planned electricity quantity and planned unit price factor conditions.

It can be seen that the summary values are quite different, but the overall trend is similar. There are two more obvious turning points at 90% and 110% of the planned electricity quantity. Based on the data of electricity quantity and unit price in previous years, we roughly simulate the actual summary in the specific electricity quantity range. Compare the real summary and the summary calculated from the intelligent contract shown in Fig. 4.

Calculation of the ratio of 45% sets of real data to analog data is shown in the result of Fig. 5. It can be seen that the gap between the actual summary and the theoretical summary is large but the same trend, and the gap is due to the fact that the proposed unit price is not in line with the actual situation. The generation of this gap cannot prove that this algorithm has errors.

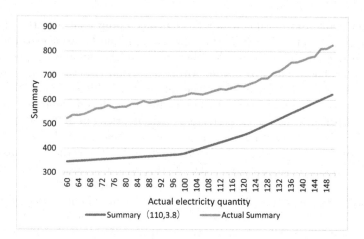

Fig. 4. Comparison of he actual summary and the summary calculated from intelligent contract. Based on the test results, the data of the transaction in five cases were all correct.

Fig. 5. Relationship between real data and analog data. The 45 sets of data are not stable but the overall trend is closer to 1.

The result of executing this smart contract in a P2P network consisting of 4,000 nodes shown in Fig. 6.

The contract was compiled by the Ethereum Virtual Machine (EVM) [11]. In addition, the transaction cost which was determined by the transaction quantity and the unit price. If gas exceeded the budget or the price of gas was too low, the transaction would fail. The reason for the expiration of the contract is mainly due to the lack of security of the power buyer or the depletion of the contract issuer's gas. At the same time, the average transaction confirmation time per payment at the time of contract performance was approximately 16 s.

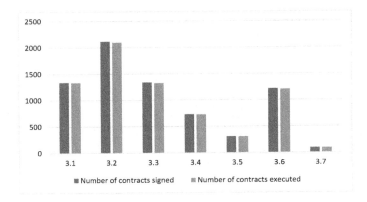

Fig. 6. Smart contract in a P2P network consisting of 4,000 nodes. Within a week, a total of 7,129 smart contracts were signed, of which 7,085 were successfully performed, 44 were expired, and the success rate was approximately 99.38%.

4 Potential Point-to-Point Trading Alliance Chains in the Future

Nowadays, the development of an intelligent grid is in the initial stages. For instance, the authors in [12] proposed a private chain for the finance department in the power grid. By preserving the settlement basis of the trading center into the purchasing blockchain, a bidirectional anchor between the private chain and the side blockchain, which kept the transaction information of the distribution company, was achieved. Based on the above test results on the intelligent contract case, we find that the public chain of tokens had significant shortcomings in the transaction speed. Although the open-chain is the embodiment of decentralization, it will be challenging to use the public chain in future point-to-point power transactions because of four factors. First, the speed and quantity of the power transactions in the future are very high, which is difficult to be supported by the public chains. Second, the transaction cost of the encrypted currency has a significant impact on the transactions. Third, the maintenance of the public chains is complicated, and the dividing pathways in the power network will have serious consequences. Finally, as a national service, the information security of power trading is critical. However, intelligent contracts in public chains are more vulnerable. The previous attack, "The DAO," is an example.

In the future, we can investigate the double-chain architecture, which includes the public chain and the alliance chain. The public chain can use a platform similar to ETF, is to provide services to users. For instance, the users pay the service fees with tokens. The platform helps users' choice to more environment-friendly power sources. The alliance chain is the leading chain for power transactions. Thus, the Byzantine fault-tolerant algorithm (BFTA) is used to ensure user privacy. The essence of the BFTA is to exchange the number of communications for credit. Moreover, the alliance chain has higher partial decentralization, strong controllability, non-open data, and high transaction speed. The double-chain architecture is shown in Fig. 7.

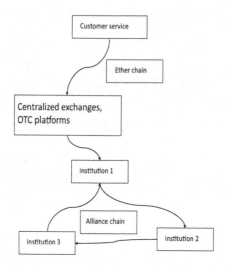

Fig. 7. Double-chain trading architecture, including public chain and alliance chain.

5   Conclusions

In this paper, we study the application of the blockchain technology in the power market, including the agreement mechanism, the incentive mechanism, and the encryption technology with the private key. We also analyze the gradual reform of the power market due to the development of distributed energy. Then the intelligent contract among different participating entities was established based on the intelligent contract system in the micro-grid power market using these technologies. We present a case on the power purchasing and selling contract between the micro-grid and the power generation side. Based on the case study, we find out that there are some issues with the transaction speed and cost in the current system. Therefore, we recommend some future direction of point-to-point blockchain power trading. The blockchain technology in the power market is only in its infancy. Therefore, more studies will be conducted to solve the specific technical problems of point-to-point blockchain. In order to have these technologies applied in practice, the introduction of related policies and rules, as well as the establishment of the intelligent contract system, are needed.

Acknowledgement. This work was partially supported by the National Natural Science Foundation (NNSF) of China (No. 61801008), National Key R&D Program of China (No. 2018YFB0803600), Beijing Natural Science Foundation National (No. L172049), Scientific Research Common Program of Beijing Municipal Commission of Education (No. KM201910005025).

References

1. Haus, M., Waqas, M., Ding, A.Y., Li, Y., Tarkoma, S., Ott, J.: Security and privacy in Device-to-Device (D2D) communication: a review. IEEE Commun. Surv. Tutorials **19**(2), 1054–1079 (2017)
2. Ahmed, M., Shi, H., Chen, X., Li, Y., Waqas, M., Jin, D.: Socially aware secrecy-ensured resource allocation in D2d underlay communication: an overlapping coalitional game scheme. IEEE Trans. Wireless Commun. **17**(6), 4118–4133 (2018)
3. Waqas, M., Ahmed, M., Li, Y., Jin, D., Chen, S.: Social-aware secret key generation for secure device-to-device communication via trusted and non-trusted relays. IEEE Trans. Wireless Commun. **17**(6), 3918–3930 (2018)
4. Alam, M.T., Li, H., Patidar, A.: Bitcoin for smart trading in smart grid. In: 2015 IEEE International Workshop on Local and Metropolitan Area Networks (LANMAN) (2015)
5. Hua, Z., Zhengyu, L., Chunyi, C., Yupeng, H., Bo, Z.: Research of demand-side response of clients based on power market. Comput. Digit. Eng. (2019)
6. Cai, J., Shuxian, L.I., Fan, B., Tang, L.: Blockchain based energy trading in energy internet. Electric Power Constr. (2017)
7. Wei, W., Dawei, H., Weihua, L.: The power trading mechanism of distributed micro grid. Inf. Technol. (2019)
8. She, W., Hu, Y., Yang, X., Gao, S., Liu, W.: Virtual power plant operation and scheduling model based on energy blockchain network. Zhongguo Dianji Gongcheng Xuebao/Proc. Chinese Soc. Electr. Eng. **37**(13), 3729–3736 (2017)
9. Tai, X., Sun, H., Guo, Q.: Electricity transactions and congestion management based on blockchain in energy internet. Power Syst. Technol. **40**, 3630–3638 (2016)
10. Hui, W., Kun, L., Bobo, C., Binbin, J.: Low carbon situation based on the technique of blockchain containing micro-grid power market clearing model. Modern Power **36**(1), 18–25
11. Suliman, A., Husain, Z., Abououf, M., Alblooshi, M., Salah, K.: Monetization of IoT data using smart contracts. IET Netw. **8**(1), 32–37 (2018)
12. Jing, L.U., Song, B., Xiang, W.H., Zhou, Inc, Y., Education, U.O.: Smart contract for electricity transaction and charge settlement based on blockchain. Comput. Syst. Appl. (2017)

Survey on Zero-Trust Network Security

Xiangshuai Yan[1] and Huijuan Wang[2(✉)]

[1] The Network Security Bureau of the Ministry of Public Security of P.R.C, Beijing, China
[2] The Information Security Department of the First Research Institute of the Ministry of Public Security of P.R.C, Beijing, China
whj409@163.com

Abstract. As a promising tool to cope with the current phishing attacks, zero-trust is gradually being taken seriously while the situation of network security becoming more and more severe. In zero trust, no unit is fully trusted even if it passes the certification. They only have the least privilege, access to data requires authentication, these processes need to be logged. This paper performs a typical survey of the composition and key technologies of zero trust, and combines the application of this technology in some scenarios to introduce the advantages of zero trust, such as big data function, cloud network and IoT. Moreover, this paper also discusses some of the challenging research issues in the field that can provide ideas for future researchers.

Keywords: Zero-Trust · Network security · Big data · IoT

1 Introduction

Nowadays, more and more terminal devices are adding to the network, and data interaction and resource access are frequently performed. Information sharing in the era of big data has brought us great convenience, at the same time an issue can not be ignored that the massive amount of devices and data accessing the network has also brought a series of security risks, resulting in frequent network security incidents. [1] predicted that by 2020, the number of Internet users will reach up to 6 billion, and by 2030 this number will exceed 7.5 billion. The damage caused by cybercrime will also increase from 3 trillion in 2015 to 6 trillion in 2021. Cybercrime is becoming the most serious threat in the next two centuries. This series of figures also motivates people to increase their research on network security and improve their network defense capabilities.

The traditional concept of network security is based on the framework of border security. It needs to find out the security boundary of the network and divide the network into different areas such as external network and intranet [2]. This concept holds that the inside of the network is secure and credible, but once the attacker breaks through the defense and enters the intranet, the entire network security is lost, and the boundaries of the security boundary with the emergence and development of the Internet of Things become blurred. It is difficult to confirm a network boundary. Traditional security concepts are difficult to cope with. In May 2016, the global information finance network was attacked. Banks in Bangladesh and other places suffered huge losses. Attackers tried

© Springer Nature Singapore Pte Ltd. 2020
X. Sun et al. (Eds.): ICAIS 2020, CCIS 1252, pp. 50–60, 2020.
https://doi.org/10.1007/978-981-15-8083-3_5

to cover up their evidence of theft by controlling the system equipment in the bank [3]. This incident fully demonstrates that it is not enough to treat external users and devices as untrustworthy objects. It is necessary to further strengthen the security of the intranet.

Zero-trust security was first proposed by the National Institute of Standards and Technology (NIST) [4]. It subverts the traditional concept of network security, and believes that the entire network is untrustworthy, does not trust any users, device terminals and data, and needs to perform certain identity authentication and authorization mechanisms before entering the network to access resources. The mechanism follows the method of least privilege. When a user want to access other resource after obtaining the trusted access to one of the resource, it still needs to perform related authentication, and different trust rights are required for accessing different resources in the network.

Since the introduction of the zero-trust model in 2010, Google has been working to build and improve a network architecture based on a zero-trust security model. In [6], a new enterprise security method is proposed, which abandons the traditional internal privileged network. It pointed out that Beyondcrop aims to create a new access mode, which is only related to the user and device credentials and regardless of its location. [7] mentioned that Google has gradually migrated from the traditional border security mode to Beyondcrop to implement access control based on inventory and trust level. [8] pointed out that Google migrates to Beyondcrop mode step by step by dividing the migration work into independent tasks to achieve the user's fundamental access to network mode changes and minimize the impact on users. [9, 10] further enhances the security of the Beyondcrop zero-trust model by defining the concept of fleet from a common control perspective and ensuring strong enforcement of various control measures.

The structure of this paper is as follows. Firstly, the origin, concept and development of the zero-trust network architecture are introduced. The second part introduces the architecture, implementation methods and key technologies of the zero-trust network security model in detail, including identity authentication and access control. The third part briefly introduces the application of the current zero-trust model in the fields of Internet of Things, cloud network and big data, etc. The fourth part presents the challenges of the zero-trust architecture and the future development direction. Lastly, summarizes the paper as a whole.

2 Key Technology

2.1 Three Basic Principles of Zero Trust

Zero-trust security is proposed in the face of today's network security problems. It was first proposed by John Kindwig, an analyst at Forresterde, a well-known research institute in the United States. Subsequently, with the increasing security vulnerabilities of Internet resources, how to effectively solve the security protection of enterprises has also been put on the agenda. Zero-trust technology has increasingly become the mainstream technology of enterprise data security protection [11]. Evan Gilman once thought that zero-trust model was mainly based on five considerations. He believed that:

1. Internet security is exposed everywhere.
2. There are both internal and external security threats.

3. The trust relationship established by the network is unreliable and unreliable.
4. All participants, including enterprise equipment, users and network traffic, need to be certified and authorized professionally.
5. The core of data source access control strategy is dynamic anti-access control, which aims at data source evaluation model.

He transformed the concept of zero trust from conditional trust to unconditional trust. Then in 2010 [4], the National Institute of Standards and Technology (NIST) put forward the zero trust model, which is based on Evan Gilman's research content and transforms the "trust but verification" method into "never trust, always verify"; this is confirmed again in the report submitted by the House of Representatives Supervision and the Government Reform Committee in 2016 [12]. Nowadays, the zero-trust model has been applied in theory. It is used in practice and in various enterprises and government organizations. According to the IDG survey in 2018, about 71% of IT decision makers focused on the zero-trust model, and 8% of them successfully applied the zero-trust model to their own enterprises. Ten percent are trying it out. The establishment of zero trust model does not require enterprises to completely reset their own network architecture. Its implementation process can gradually upgrade their own equipment. From a technical point of view, the main purpose of zero trust model is security. It can automatically arrange and repair data, load personnel, network equipment and network protection, visualize security threats, and with A. PI is associated, all of which are based on three basic:

1. There are no trusted domains in the resource access area of the architecture; all domains are secure access.
2. By default, all access users are not credited. They strictly implement access control policies in the gateway and anti-firewall areas, and follow the minimum privilege policy.
3. Check and record all visiting network traffic, whether from its own LAN or WAN.

2.2 Zero Trust Network Architecture Diagram

The construction of zero-trust architecture model effectively responds to foreign invasion threats and penetration attacks, builds a good barrier for equipment, improves the security situation of enterprises, guarantees the accuracy of authentication mechanism, and provides infrastructure without technical constraints.

The traditional construction model of zero trust architecture is to connect user equipment, gateway or business agent with authentication platform. Its main functions are: user equipment is authenticated and authorized to ensure user information security; business access agent mainly realizes access control to business platform, and can build relevant business data only after user equipment is authenticated. Channels and conditions require business access subject to have relevant privileges and resource sharing mechanism; authentication of identity platform is mainly the evaluation process of experimental trust, sharing data between user access subject and proxy device, completing dynamic authorization of information and data analysis of authentication process [2]; the practice of zero trust architecture requires that all access is based on identity. In order to achieve the validity and accuracy of authentication, the dynamic access control of the center needs a continuous process of authentication. In the process of identity analysis, it needs to evaluate and diagnose the acquired data intelligently, reduce the interference to other potential threats as much as possible, and adjust it adaptively [2].

The experimental model proposed by Dayna Eidle is as follows: gateway, user equipment, firewall, etc. The red pointer represents the data plane in the system architecture diagram, and the blue pointer represents the control plane. The innovation of the experimental platform lies in the dynamic arrangement (ACL) of the firewall access control list. The dynamic arrangement includes the authentication of the gateway. Configuration of dynamic trust level [13]. These authentication devices meet the requirements of packet authentication and transmission access control. The traditional network security architecture places firewalls between untrusted networks and protected resources on internal networks. The architecture diagram established in this chapter mainly uses FPA and TAC [14] technology in authentication and control devices. For example, in Fig. 1, different gateways are deployed in the network architecture. The first gateway is to insert identity tokens, and the second gateway is to insert identity tokens. They are distributed on the edge of the untrusted network, and their information transmission process is to first issue authentication requests by inserting identity tokens into the gateway. Then, Gateway 2 validates request 1 [14], extracts authentication information of Gateway 1 identity token, and sends connection requests. All authentication processes in the device are independent, and access to the device requires authorization from the server.

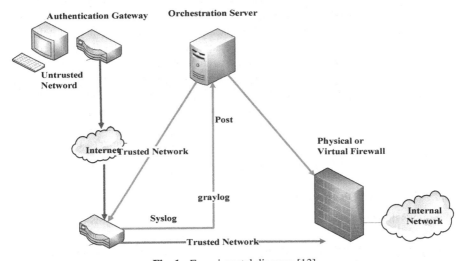

Fig. 1. Experimental diagram [13]

2.3 How to Achieve Zero Trust

Zero trust is designed to provide a scalable security infrastructure. Zero trust is guaranteed mainly through four methods: identity authentication, access control, continuous diagnosis and mitigation [13].

2.3.1 Identity Authentication and Access Control

The essence of zero trust is dynamic access control centered on identity, and full identity is the premise of zero trust [2]. Based on comprehensive identity, establish a unified digital identity and governance process for physical entities such as users, devices, applications, and business systems, and further construct a dynamic access control system to extend security boundaries to identity entities. Identity authentication and access control are implemented by First Packet Authentication and Transport Access Control technologies, both of which rely on an authentication gateway [14].

The authentication gateway has its own dynamic trust level configuration. It uses eight defined system trust levels. They are exposed by the gateway API [13]. If the user's trust level is low, then its operation will be more restricted. For instance, level zero disables all operations and level seven allows all operations. Levels 3 through 6 have security policies that define application or client-specific. These policies can enforce one of three options, identity, group and global. The identity level can only perform operations related to personal identity. The group level allows the operation of the set of identities configured on the gateway. The global level allows operations through the gateway. Only system administrators can change user operation rights for each trust level.

The basic principle of zero trust involves ensuring secure access to all resources. It assumes that all network operations are threat before being authorized, checked, and protected. Establishing a network identity token during session can establish an explicit trust. The network token is a 32-bit encrypted object [14]. It contains the session ID, user IP, and other information. The token contacts the existing Identity Access Management system. Trusted users have such network identity token, and untrusted users do not. Validating these tokens on the first packet of TCP can establish trust before a traditional three-way handshake is completed and the session for the cloud or network resource is established. Each network session needs to be independently verified before giving any access to the network or server. This approach makes the resource behind the second gateway unaffected by access requests. Only authorized access can connect to the protected resource. The external server will log all access attempts. The server has enough memory to not overwrite log entries. A record of all access attempts ensures that any access attempts are monitored. This is consistent with the zero-trust network approach.

2.3.2 Continuous Diagnosis and Mitigation

Continuous diagnosis and mitigation come from near real-time analysis of all network operations [15].

One method involves a feedback loop of the control plane. It performs a quick analysis at the location where the attack was detected. Then perform a more accurate response to prevent long-term threats [16]. This loop responds faster than the attacker's response. It obtains intelligence by parsing large amounts of data, preventing specific attacks in a relatively short period of time. In this way, the defense system does not need to store all log data. It simply parses the log, then uses a small amount of data to provide current valid information.

Another approach comes from autonomic calculations. Human security administrators are unable to keep up with the number and speed of security alerts, so they cannot respond to security alerts in a timely manner. Or the processing of security alerts can take several minutes to a few hours, so that the attack cannot be effectively mitigated [17]. Autonomic calculation is a self-management feature of distributed resources to accommodate near-real-time unpredictable changes while hiding its inherent complexity [18]. Autonomic computing can improve the automation of network defenses and protect cloud and enterprise data center networks.

3 Application

In recent years, network security incidents have occurred frequently. For these network attacks, a zero-trust platform can be built based on the OODA model [13]. Dynamic management of security threats for their own responses and authentication. These security issues are addressed by combining log resolution, orchestration software, and open source log management tools for security threats from firewalls, authentication gateways, and other devices on the network. The zero-trust model can be applied to big data, cloud networks, and the Internet of Things.

3.1 The Application of Zero Trust Method in Big Data

With the rapid development of information technology, we are ushered in the era of big data. Under this new situation, the security of big data has received much attention.

Due to the huge amount of data, monitoring of network traffic becomes more difficult. Therefore, a secure data traffic monitoring architecture can be built by correlating multiple data sources to solve this problem [19]. The architecture can realize the storage management of data, and can also be used for subsequent development and utilization. Under the Spark and Shark framework, the performance is better. N. Sirisha et al. proposed using Apache Sentry to improve the security performance of Hadoop in HDFS [20]. The article starts with sensitive data, uses Apache whistle to provide authorization and strengthen the protection of private data, and strengthens the security of data authorization.

Traditional big data security technology has a lot of disadvantages in processing power, efficiency and security. Therefore, based on the zero trust model, a new method is proposed to ensure the security of big data [21]. Firstly, a zero-trust model is built for user identification, and then the accessed network traffic information is audited. In this way, access to potentially risky access is intercepted. This method effectively identifies security risks in big data access control.

3.2 Application of Zero Trust Method in Cloud Network

The advantages of cloud computing virtualization technology, powerful computing storage capacity and scalability make it more and more familiar, but the security and privacy of cloud computing is also a hot issue.

Traditional security mechanisms have been vulnerable, so a new solution is proposed to introduce trusted third parties [22]. In order to assess the security of cloud networks and eliminate potential threats, trusted third parties are introduced to ensure the security of information and to achieve a trust network between users. Xiangjian He et al. proposed a new tree rule firewall technology [23]. In this paper, the security problems of traditional firewall technology (listing rule firewalls) are introduced and proved. To solve the above problems, a tree rule firewall is proposed. This rule is based on tree structure and shows better performance. It is more suitable for cloud networks..

Because the security mode of network segmentation can not adapt to the rapid changes of the environment, a new network architecture is proposed. The network token is embedded in the TCP packet request to resolve the identity of the requester. If it does not meet the requirements, Reject the connection request for unauthorized network traffic [14]. This method implements a zero-trust application and effectively enhances security in large server and cloud environments.

3.3 Application of Zero Trust Method in Public Cloud Infrastructure as a Service (IaaS) Platform

With the explosive growth of network data, cloud computing technology has been favored by major companies around the world. But as major companies providing more and more scalable services to cloud computing providers, the security of data becomes more and more complex [24]. In this complex network environment, in order to ensure the security of user's data, scholars have done a lot of research against malicious attacks. Because of the concept of zero trust, scholars began to study how to use the zero trust method on the IaaS platform. The so-called IaaS is a cloud computing service model that provides core computing, network, and storage infrastructure. Based on this, users can build their own platform-as-a-service (PaaS) or software-as-a-service (SaaS) environment. In essence, IaaS provides an easy way to deploy virtualized servers in the cloud by leveraging servers and automation [31]. It is precisely because of the importance of IaaS that its security issues are widely studied.

Scott et al. mentioned the use of zero-trust methods in Amazon Web Services (AWS)'s IaaS platform to secure the environment. They proposed six ways to extend existing security methods for data centers to the IaaS platform. This includes creating a common security and compliance model across cross-premises and cloud resources, accountability, auditing, requiring users to log in with their personal accounts and escalating permissions as needed, integrating identity and multi-factor authentication (MFA) [24]. And Saleh A S A et al. proposed a hybrid model of construction, evaluation and open trust applied to the cloud computing environment [27, 28]. In the article [27], the author also established a new evaluation standard to ensure the credibility of the entity before the transaction. In the new model, the author also added a new registration module to identify the communicating entity to prevent malicious attacks.

The point raised by Scott et al. is that an identity-centric zero-trust approach is needed in the cloud. To build a fair shared responsibility model in the cloud, every organization that enjoys cloud services needs to recognize its responsibilities and cannot extract excessively. Customer data [24]. While Saleh A S A and others did not explicitly put forward the idea of zero trust, they pointed out that it is necessary to track the behavior of cloud consumers and cloud service providers and conduct trust management, which coincides with the method of zero trust [27].

3.4 Application of Zero Trust Method in Internet of Things (IOT) Environment

The Internet of Things is an Internet system that connects things with things without anyone's participation and interference [29]. The Internet of Things emphasizes the connection between things and things, enabling things to form an organic network as a whole through the Internet platform. And the Internet of Things uses objects as the main body to emphasize the subjective role of things in the Internet of Things system. In addition, the purpose of interconnection of IoT objects is not only to realize information transmission and information processing, but to realize intelligent utilization of information through information transmission and provide information services for the society. With the rise of artificial intelligence and machine learning technology, Internet of Things technology has become an inevitable trend of social development [26]. However, since the entities in the Internet of Things are all exposed to the network, the sharp increase in access devices makes the entire system difficult to manage, and the security issues become more and more complicated. Scholars have done a lot of research on the trust of access devices [30]. With the deepening of research, scholars believe that all devices inside the network and outside the network must be treated with zero trust, so as to ensure the entire Internet of Things.

Ben Saied Y et al. proposed a context-aware trust management system based on the state of the upper and lower nodes in the network and the services of the auxiliary nodes. From the global perspective, a trust management system was created for the Internet of Things environment to solve Some common malicious attacks in the network environment [25]. Samaniego, M et al. recently applied a layered IoT trust architecture by applying the Amatista management middleware in the blockchain to the Internet of Things. It is a new zero-trust layer mining process. The focus of the Internet of Things has shifted from a centralized architecture to a hierarchical structure, enabling the processing of infrastructure and access transactions at different levels of trust [26].

The difference between Ben Saied Y and Samaniego, M is that they construct a zero-trust method in the Internet of Things environment from the perspective of global and hierarchical thinking. Ben Saied Y's approach requires a centralized authority certification, while Samaniego, M's approach is a hierarchical mining technique by introducing blockchain techniques [26].

4 Future Research Trends

Nowadays, the application of zero-trust network is more and more extensive. In order to provide some research ideas for researchers in related fields in the future, in this section, several problems that need to be solved in the current zero-trust network are pointed out.

How to effectively deploy a zero-trust network in a larger and more complex internet environment is an urgent issue. With the development of technologies, such as smart cities, car networking, etc., the security requirements for fog computing are becoming higher and higher. Compared with cloud computing, fog computing can provide more users with lower latency services. However, there are two problems here. The environment in which fog calculation is performed is more complicated, such as more access users and more heterogeneous network environments. These factors lead to many security risks in fog calculation. And the server capacity of fog computing is far less than the cloud computing server, which limits the application of some high-precision algorithms. Therefore, how to design a lighter-weight zero-trust security system for fog calculation is worth studying.

The development of next-generation network technologies requires zero-trust network technology to provide security support. IPV6 solves the problem of shortage of network address resources, but there are problems in how to efficiently manage more types of access devices. Zero-trust networks require centralized management of network resources and users. SDN is a technology that simplifies network management through centralized control. It is a networking solution that fits perfectly with zero-trust networks.

In the process of building a zero-trust network model, how to accurately and quickly classify and authorize data is a difficult problem when faced with huge amounts of complex and multi-featured data. Combining AI(artificial intelligence) technology is one way to solve this problem. Machine learning or deep learning has advantages in extracting features and classifying clustering problems. How to use machine learning to improve the efficiency of data classification and classification of the whole zero-trust network system is a good research direction. Similarly, modules such as identity authentication and access control in a zero-trust network can be combined with AI.

5   Conclusion

This paper reviews the zero-trust network security system. Firstly, the paper expounds design principles and architecture ideas of the zero-trust network. Second, the key technologies of the current zero-trust network are analyzed. Several application scenarios such as the Internet of Things, cloud platform and big data are selected to introduce the deployment method of the zero-trust network. At the end of the article, several research directions of zero-trust network are proposed, which can help readers understand the development of zero-trust network and find some interesting and challenging research topics worthy of attention.

References

1. Cisco Institution.: Cisco 2017 annual cybersecurity report. Cisco, Technical Report (2017)
2. Zuo, Y.N.: Zero trust architecture: a new paradigm for network security. Electron. Fin. **2018**(11), 50–51 (2018). (In Chinese)
3. Mikko, H., Tomi, T.: F-Secure 2017 State of Cybersecurity report. F-Secure, Technical Report (2017)
4. Honeycutt, D., Grumman, N.: Developing a Framework to Improve Critical Infrastructure Cybersecurity (2013)
5. Gilman, E.: Zero Trust Networks: Building Secure Systems in Untrusted Networks (2016)
6. Ward, R., Beyer, B.: Beyondcorp: a new approach to enterprise security. Login **39**(6), 6–11 (2014)

7. Osborn, B., McWilliams, J., Beyer, B., et al.: BeyondCorp: design to deployment at google. Login **41**(1), 28–34 (2016)
8. Beske, C.M.C., Peck, J., Saltonstall, M.: Migrating to BeyondCorp: maintaining productivity while improving security. **42**(2), 49–55 (2017)
9. Escobedo, V.M., Zyzniewski, F., Saltonstall, M.: BeyondCorp: The User Experience (2017)
10. King, H., Janosko, M., Beyer, B., et al.: BeyondCorp: building a healthy fleet. Login **43**(3), 2–64 (2018)
11. Ding, J.: Why to say zero-trust will become one of the popular frameworks of network security. Comput. Netw. **44**(04), 54–55 (2018)
12. Chaffetz, J., Meadows, M., Hurd, W.: The OPM Data Breach: How the Government Jeopardized Our National Security For More Than a Generation. Oversight and Government Reform. Technical Report (2016)
13. Eidle, D., Ni, S.Y., DeCusatis, C., et al.: Autonomic security for zero trust networks. In: 2017 IEEE 8th Annual Ubiquitous Computing, Electronics and Mobile Communication Conference (UEMCON), pp. 288–293. IEEE (2017)
14. DeCusatis, C., Liengtiraphan, P., Sager, A.: Advanced Intrusion Prevention for Geographically Dispersed Higher Education Cloud Networks. In: Auer, M.E., Zutin, D.G. (eds.) Online Engineering & Internet of Things. LNNS, vol. 22, pp. 132–143. Springer, Cham (2018). https://doi.org/10.1007/978-3-319-64352-6_13
15. Stoneburner, G., Goguen, A., Feringa, A.: Risk Management Guide for Information Technology Systems. 800–300. NIST Special Publication (2002)
16. Boyd, J.: OODA Model Summary. https://www.valuebasedmanagement.net/methodsboyd-oodaloop.html. Accessed 15 July 2017
17. Compastié, M., Badonnel, R., Festor, O., et al.: A software-defined security strategy for supporting autonomic security enforcement in distributed cloud. In: 2016 IEEE International Conference on Cloud Computing Technology and Science (CloudCom), pp. 464–467. IEEE (2016)
18. Saxena, A., Lacoste, M., Jarboui, T., Lücking, U., Steinke, B.: A Software Framework for Autonomic Security in Pervasive Environments. In: McDaniel, P., Gupta, S.K. (eds.) ICISS 2007. LNCS, vol. 4812, pp. 91–109. Springer, Heidelberg (2007). https://doi.org/10.1007/978-3-540-77086-2_8
19. Marchal, S., Jiang, X., State, R., et al.: A big data architecture for large scale security monitoring. In: 2014 IEEE International Congress on Big Data, pp. 56–63. IEEE (2014)
20. Sirisha, N., Kiran, K.: Authorization of data in hadoop using apache sentry. Int. J. Eng. Technol. **7**(2018), 234 (2018)
21. Tao, Y., Lei, Z., Ruxiang, P.: Fine-grained big data security method based on zero trust model. In: 2018 IEEE 24th International Conference on Parallel and Distributed Systems (ICPADS), pp. 1040–1045. IEEE (2018)
22. Zissis, D., Lekkas, D.: Addressing cloud computing security issues. Fut. Gener. Comput. Syst. **28**(3), 583–592 (2012)
23. Li, J., Li, B., Wo, T., et al.: CyberGuarder: a virtualization security assurance architecture for green cloud computing. Fut. Gener. Comput. Syst. **28**(2), 379–390 (2012)
24. Hui, H.W., Zhou, C.C., Xu, S.G., Lin, F.H.: A novel secure data transmission scheme in industrial internet of things. China Commun. **17**(1), 73–88 (2020)
25. Ben Saied, Y., Olivereau, A., Zeghlache, D., et al.: Trust management system design for the Internet of Things: a context-aware and multi-service approach. Comput. Secur. **39**, 351–365 (2013)
26. Samaniego, M., Deters, R.: Zero-trust hierarchical management in IoT. In: 2018 IEEE International Congress on Internet of Things (ICIOT), pp. 88–95. IEEE (2018)
27. Saleh, A.S.A., Hamed, E.M.R., Hashem, M.: Building trust management model for cloud computing. In: 2014 9th International Conference on Informatics and Systems. IEEE (2014)

28. Su, J.T., Lin, F.H., Zhou, X.W., Lu, X.: Steiner tree based optimal resource caching scheme in fog computing. China Commun. **12**(8), 161–168 (2015)
29. Dou, Z., Xu, G., Chen, X.B., Yuan, K.G.: Rational non-hierarchical quantum state sharing protocol. Comput. Mater. Continua **58**(2), 335–347 (2019)
30. Zhao, G.D., Zhang, Y.W., Shi, Y.Q., Lan, H.L., Yang, Q.: The application of BP neural networks to analysis the national vulnerability. Comput. Mater. Continua **58**(2), 421–436 (2019)
31. Long, M., Zeng, Y.: Detecting iris liveness with batch normalized convolutional neural network. Comput. Mater. Continua **58**(2), 493–504 (2019)

A Novel Consensus Algorithm for Alliance Chain

Huijuan Wang[✉], Jiang Yong, Xiaofeng Wang, and Xiaotian Yin

The Information Security Department of the First Research Institute of the Ministry of Public Security of P.R.C, Beijing, China
whj409@163.com

Abstract. Block-chain is a decentralized billing technique. It has the advantages of: no corrupted, enhanced security, distributed ledgers, having consensus, and faster settlement. There are lots of application using this technique to deal with various problems. There are three kinds of block-chain which are public blockchain, alliance block-chain, and private block-chain. From other researchers' statements, we get that the note in the alliance chain need rules to limit write permissions. Alliance chain can provide security management functions, and these functions can meet the management between the members, certification, authorization, monitoring, auditing. So the consensus algorithm is the main technical implementation of the alliance chain. This paper mainly analyzes some requirements realization which applies to the alliance chain. It mainly includes the following parts: local data sharing, work order decentralizing transaction consensus, and regulatory compliance.

Keywords: Alliance chain · Consensus algorithm · Data local sharing

1 Introduction

Security and resource allocation are important parts in each network [15–17]. The block-chain is a new way to solve this problem. The essence of the block-chain is a kind of decentralized secure data storage, and its technology realizes the technical difficulties of being open, safe, trustworthy and distributed sharing in the data storage inter-action. The block-chain can also be said that the block-chain is essentially a secure, trusted distributed database, or defined as a shared but cannot change the distributed billing system. Block-chain technology is a collection of several well-established computer technologies that enable distributed decentralized point-to-point transactions, coordination and collaboration among un-trusted nodes through the use of data encryption, time-stamping and distributed consensus. The technical characteristics of the block-chain are decentralized secure distributed storage database. The data application to be solved in the block-chain is to complete the spontaneity of data exchange under the condition that each node needs to write the peer rights and needs to supervise each other, security, anonymity, traceability.

For the participation of node block conditions and business needs, can be divided into public chain, private chain, alliance chain. Participating nodes of the public chain

© Springer Nature Singapore Pte Ltd. 2020
X. Sun et al. (Eds.): ICAIS 2020, CCIS 1252, pp. 61–69, 2020.
https://doi.org/10.1007/978-981-15-8083-3_6

are any nodes of the whole network. Any computer and computing server can participate voluntarily, and can be regarded as a node of the public chain, such as a bit-coin system. Private chain is an application in a small area of the block-chain. The nodes in the private chain run only according to the private organization rules. Currently, the application of the private chain is generally defined within the enterprise or government to solve some database management and audit work, the security requirements of the block-chain is relatively low, more demand is spontaneous data reading and writing and interaction. Most businesses and departments now use affiliate links, which are nodes that participate in joining among affiliates. Different from the private chain, participants in the coalition chain are interactive writes between different departments, and the private chain is written interactively within the department. The rules of read and write permissions on the alliance chain are based on the agreements among alliance members. The nodes participating in the alliance chain need to implement the rules and protocols and complete the data reading and writing and interaction of the block-chain according to the rules and protocols.

Public chain, private chain, alliance chain business operations must rely on consensus algorithms to achieve. This paper analyzes in detail the method of consensus realization of alliance chain in business requirements

Section 1 of this paper introduces the block-chain and briefly introduces the concept of public chain, private chain, and alliance chain. Section 2 summarizes how consensus lines are actually implemented in real business. Section 3 summarizes the full text, and points out that the algorithms need to be perfected, put forward ideas and explore the future research direction of the model.

2   Prepare Consensus Algorithm

There are many consensus algorithms for the current block chain system, including: POW proof of work; PO* credential-type consensus algorithm; Byzantine fault tolerance algorithm; a consensus algorithm combined with a trusted environment. Consensus algorithms of POW mainly include POW consensus adopted by bit-coin, the originator of block chain, and POW variants of some similar projects. The core idea of POW is that all nodes compete for bookkeeping rights, and each bookkeeping is given a problem, requiring only the nodes that can solve the problem to dig out the block is valid. At the same time, all nodes continue to generate their own blocks by trying to solve problems, but only the longest chain in the network is recognized as legitimate and correct. Generally, the difficult problem designed by the consensus algorithm of POW class is that the nodes need to do a lot of calculations to be able to solve. To ensure that the nodes are willing to do so many calculations to continue the growth of the block chain, such systems will reward the generator of each effective block. The computational overhead brought by POW algorithm to participating nodes is meaningless except for the continuation of block continuous growth, but it consumes huge energy.

In view of the shortcomings of POW, some alternatives to pow, PO* class algorithms, have been proposed. These algorithms introduce the concept of credential, according to some attributes of each node, define the difficulty or priority of each node to carry out the report block, and take the node of the best order of credential, to carry out the next period of accounting report block. This kind of consensus algorithm can reduce the overhead of the overall work block to some extent and allocate the work block resources selectively. However, the introduction of vouchers improves the degree of algorithm centralization, which goes against the idea of block continuous decentralization to some extent. Moreover, the motivation of miners in some algorithms is not clear enough, and nodes lack the motivation to participate in this kind of consensus.

The central idea of both the POW algorithm and the PO* algorithm is to treat all nodes as competitors, and each node needs to do some calculations or provide some credentials to compete for the rights of the jobs. The Byzantine algorithm takes a different approach. It wants all nodes to work together and negotiate to produce blocks that can be recognized by all nodes. Byzantine fault-tolerant problem was first proposed by Leslie Lamport and other scholars in 1982, mainly describing the fault-tolerant problem of distributed network node communication. Subsequently, a number of algorithms were proposed to solve this problem, which are called Byzantine algorithms. The practical BFT algorithm was proposed by Miguel Castro and Barbara Liskov in 1999. PBFT is widely used in the actual distributed network. With the rapid development of block interconnection, many optimized BFT algorithms for specific scenarios keep emerging.

In addition to the consensus algorithms for these three types of storage software, there are also algorithms that leverage hardware, such as those for Trusted execution environments that combine hardware and software. The trusted execution environment can be used to limit the nodes participating in the consensus in the block connection system, which can largely eliminate the non-standard and malicious operation of the malicious nodes and improve the performance of the consensus algorithm.

The main technical core of the block-chain is the consensus mechanism. Consensus mechanism using block-chain has many consensus mechanisms such as POW, POS, DPOS, raft and ripple. Although different consensus mechanisms have some outstanding features in one aspect, there is not a perfect block-chain consensus algorithm that can comprehensively solve the business needs. Some alliance chains and private chains use the Byzantine consensus algorithm to identify participating nodes. However, the Byzantine fault-tolerant algorithm expands slowly. When the number of nodes increases by more than twenty or thirty, the performance of block-chain read-write decreases rapidly. Other attributes of consensus algorithms are throughput and security, and these are all important criteria for consensus algorithms.

Alliance chain in the actual business applications generally need to have these features: data is not necessarily global sharing, only to meet the legitimate needs of the party to access the data; without centralized control can arrange the work order; for each data processing can form a consensus.

The core technology of the block-chain function is the consensus algorithm and the password algorithm. The following briefly introduces the consensus algorithms and the password algorithms that are required to apply these functions. Some consensus algorithms are analyzed on the common business requirements of the current alliance chain.

2.1 Local Data Sharing

In the alliance chain, participating organizations are generally based on credible basis, but it does not mean that interactive information can be shared. Alliance chain in the application of information trading permissions and data sharing is not necessarily the whole chain, only to meet the compliance needs of the parties to access the data. To meet the local data sharing capabilities, we can take advantage of the digital identity authentication protocol added to the block-chain. To achieve need three questions:

- Confirmation of the scope of data exchange nodes: How to determine interactive data nodes spontaneously.
- Data Security Interaction: How to finalize the security interaction between nodes.
- Change the permission node selection: If the transaction process needs to be changed, such as process adjustments, how to select the node with the right to change.

For these three issues, given the following solution:

- The Scope of Data Exchange Nodes to Determine

Consensus data sharing algorithm, the need to spontaneously pick out the trusted nodes involved in the transaction.

- Trusted nodes of the transaction, which can be borne by the initiating node;
- The initiating node can define the scope of the data exchange node and notify the terminating node whether all the trading nodes have been included, and if yes, the transaction starts;
- If not, the initiating node hands over the authority to the next node;
- The next node to determine the scope of the transaction, and broadcast again until all participating nodes agree to start trading.

2.2 To Decentralize the Work Order

- Union chain work in the trusted node, the workflow will change, without centralized control can be arranged Union members of the work order is the block-chain to meet the function. The order of work among trusted nodes in the coalition chain can also ensure the security of transactions between nodes. The work sequence of nodes can also ensure the consistency, accuracy and binding of data transactions.

- Data Security Exchange

There are many digital authentication protocols. The elliptic curve public key algorithm for the user address of Bitcoin block-chain can be applied to the authentication of read and write permissions between alliance chain nodes. Using the elliptic curve public key encryption algorithm, the trusted node that initiates the transaction generates the public key and the secret key to distribute, generate the public key, and encrypts the trusted nodes in the affiliate chain that need to interact with each other. Then, the trusted nodes participating in the data exchange mutual authentication according to the distributed key, and continue the data exchange after the verification is successful, otherwise, the user exits.

- Change the Permission Node Selection

According to the Raft agreement election leader consensus agreement [5] plus key verification to determine the electoral node compliance. Raft. The Raft protocol was originally used to manage recovery logs and was a strong consensus protocol reached between nodes. The leader election process in the Raft protocol (Shown in Fig. 1) is:

- Specifies that any trusted node has three states: candidate, follower, and leader;
- Adjusted to a candidate in any trusted node, the encryption key to other nodes follower to send their own election request;
- If nodes agree, feedback passed, start voting, elect votes to encrypt the broadcast;
- Leader: Participation node to get the election results, radio, verify the agreement, choose leader;
- Other nodes change back follower, follow the leader command;
- If you need to change from the first steps.
- Achieve decentralized layout requires the following two conditions:

1. Arrange the work node: let the work node know each other so as to achieve the follow-up work order certification;
2. Serial number assignment and response: Arrange the work order and confirm the work flow.

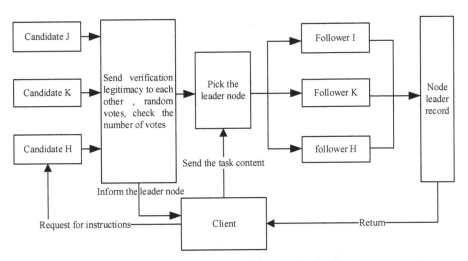

Fig. 1. Changing the permissions node selection

Arrange work node can use UNL (unique node list) [3] UNL configures a list of trusted nodes for each node participating in the work. The node on the list broadcasts the authentication protocol, confirms the number of nodes on the list, and the node address (Shown in Fig. 2). Upon completion of the UNL, the Shamir key sharing algorithm in the ants consensus mechanism can be considered [3].

The serial number assignment response mechanism can be implemented by a practical Byzantine fault-tolerant system (PBFT). PBFT is a type of fault tolerant technology in the field of distributed computing. It is used in the confederation chain and private chain requiring strong consistency to maintain the consistency of data interaction and the correctness of the consensus agreement.

The steps to decentralize the work order are as follows:

- Determine the node and permission nodes involved in the work;
- Using Shamir's key distribution algorithm, nodes broadcast identities and determine the compliance and address of other nodes involved;
- Permission node broadcast sequence number assignment message and the client's request task message;
- Each node receives the message sent by the right node and broadcasts it to other nodes;
- Each node on the request and the order of verification, the broadcast confirmation message;
- Meet a certain number of the same response, the task continues, or a step by step.

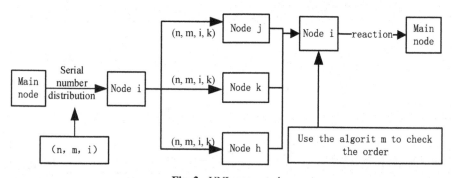

Fig. 2. UNL generated

2.3 Transaction Consensus

One of the main functions of block-chain is to form a consensus on the transaction, to form a consensus on each transaction, and to quickly check the transaction. Transaction consensus can be used PBFT agreement, Ripple agreement, raft agreement to achieve. Ripple consensus protocol [9], the transaction initiated by the client, through the tracking node or the authentication node to broadcast the transaction to the entire network. The main task of tracking nodes is to send transaction information and respond to the client's account request. The verification node can add new transaction records in addition to all the functions of the tracking node. Raft protocol is also a distributed consistency algorithm, which can meet the strong consistency requirement of consensus algorithm and has high consensus efficiency. It is a consensus strong consensus protocol for non-Byzantine failure.

In fact, the realization of the transaction consensus application, the transaction log verification is also a key transaction consensus algorithm. Ethereum has implemented an improved Markle tree algorithm for quick verification of transaction details in transaction verification. The Markle-tree algorithm in bitcoin [6] enables fast authentication of transactions but cannot verify transaction-specific information such as data hold, address registration, transaction status, and so on. In order to verify the details of the transaction, Ethereum algorithm of a Merkle tree in the bitcoin system states that 3 trees are written into the algorithm [1], including:

- Transaction tree
- Data Association Record Tree
- Data state record tree

The addition of these three tree roots to the head of the block will not only enable rapid verification of transaction records and transfer of detailed records, but also display detailed entries for data stubs that can be used for data forensics.

2.4 Regulatory Compliance

The block chain should be designed to support supervisor supervision and compliance monitoring. In addition how to ensure the authenticity of the data is also a problem to be solved, a lot of block-chain above the data is derived from offline, and offline data how to go to the chain above is a big problem [19]. The clear connection between the data and the legal documents written in written language is also a technical difficulty to be considered in realizing the rational regulatory function of the block chain.

- Trading regulation

The authority to federate chain and private chain supervision can be written directly into the creator block, and trusted credence can be added to grant supervisory authority to the supervising node [18]. A brief description of the steps to be taken in the supervision of credible proof: Regulatory node A needs to supervise transaction B, and transaction A is required to provide proof of legitimacy without needing to know the transaction's detailed record.; Transaction B needs regulatory authority A to automatically broadcast the entire network to prove that transaction B is legal (automatically issue a certificate); B need to use zero-knowledge proof to let A know the legitimacy of the contents of the file.

File verification is valid, but how to achieve A automatically to the file B, the literature [5] to introduce a solution algorithm:

```
Encrypt X with random password K, Ex = AES(X, K),
Then, build the program:
Program(K, Ex, H()) =>[Ex, Hk, Y]
{
  Hk = SHK-256(K);
  Y = H(UNAES(Ex, K));
  RETURN[Ex, Hk, Y];
}
```

Since this algorithm is too theoretical, it needs to be rewritten in practice, so this scheme is not widely used.

- Data authenticity

The data uploaded to the block-chain is time-stamped and jointly verified and recorded by the consensus nodes. It cannot be tampered with and forged. These technical rules can satisfy the application of block-chain to various data notary and audit scenarios. However, how to ensure the authenticity and validity of the data uploaded to the block-chain is the aspect that needs to be studied now. Some engineers suggest writing code to the block-chain using its scripts and data bindings after turning many contracts into executable code [20].

3 Conclusion

The widespread concern of block-chain technology has led many departments and industries to consider using block-chain to solve some data security problems, but the development of block-chain is not yet mature. Block-chain now the main problem is the calculation of the data stored in the process of communication problems. Due to the design of block-chain security and the limitation of open source code writing of the original bit-coin system, the currently applicable block-chain can only store data hash. On the other hand, block-chain has some problems in practical application and deployment. Some code on the participating nodes also has some problems, mainly because the block-chain code is difficult to develop and skilled architects are needed in the deployment of block-chain operate. This article mainly analyzes some consensus algorithms in the coalition chain, and proposes a new consensus algorithm for the coalition chain. As more and more applications of the block-chain, the block-chain consensus algorithm will be more perfect for the more applications of the block-chain.

References

1. Nakamoto, S.: Bitcoin: a peer-to-peer electronic cash system (2008). https://bitcoin.org/bit coin.pdf
2. Gervais, A., Karame, G.O., Wust, K.: On the security and performance of proof of work block chains. In: Proceedings of the 2016 ACM SIGSAC Conference on Computer and Communications Security, pp. 3–16. ACM, Australia (2016)

3. King, S., Nadal, S.: PPcoin: peer-to-peer crypto-currency with proof-of-stake. Self-Published Pap. **19**(8), 1–6 (2012)
4. Duong, T., Fan, L., Zhou, H.S.: 2-hop blockchain: combining proof-of-work and proof-of-stake securely (2016)
5. Croman, K., et al.: On scaling decentralized blockchains. In: Clark, J., Meiklejohn, S., Ryan, P.Y.A., Wallach, D., Brenner, M., Rohloff, K. (eds.) FC 2016. LNCS, vol. 9604, pp. 106–125. Springer, Heidelberg (2016). https://doi.org/10.1007/978-3-662-53357-4_8
6. Kiayias, A., Panagiotakos, G.: Speed-security tradeoffs in block chain protocols. IACR Cryptol. ePrint Arch. **2015**, 1019 (2015)
7. Luu, L., Narayanan, V., Zheng, C.: A secure sharding protocol for open block chains. In: Proceedings of the 2016 ACM SIGSAC Conference on Computer and Communications Security, pp. 17–30. ACM, Australia (2016)
8. Forte, P., Romano, D., Schmid, G.: Beyond bit-coin—part II: block-chain-based systems without mining. IACR Cryptol. ePrint Arch. **2016**, 747 (2016)
9. Garay, J., Kiayias, A., Leonardos, N.: The bitcoin backbone protocol: analysis and applications. In: Oswald, E., Fischlin, M. (eds.) EUROCRYPT 2015. LNCS, vol. 9057, pp. 281–310. Springer, Heidelberg (2015). https://doi.org/10.1007/978-3-662-46803-6_10
10. Moore, T., Christin, N.: Beware the middleman: empirical analysis of bitcoin-exchange risk. In: Sadeghi, A.-R. (ed.) FC 2013. LNCS, vol. 7859, pp. 25–33. Springer, Heidelberg (2013). https://doi.org/10.1007/978-3-642-39884-1_3
11. Reid, F., Harrigan, M.: An analysis of anonymity in the bitcoin system. In: Altshuler, Y., Elovici, Y., Cremers, A., Aharony, N., Pentland, A. (eds.) Security and Privacy in Social Networks, pp. 197–223. Springer, NewYork (2013). https://doi.org/10.1007/978-1-4614-4139-7_10
12. Biryukov, A., Pustogarov, I.: Bitcoin over Tor isn't a good idea. In: 2015 IEEE Symposium on Security and Privacy(SP), pp. 122–134. IEEE, NewYork (2015)
13. Wijaya, D.A., Liu, Joseph K., Steinfeld, R., Sun, S.-F., Huang, X.: Anonymizing bitcoin transaction. In: Bao, F., Chen, L., Deng, Robert H., Wang, G. (eds.) ISPEC 2016. LNCS, vol. 10060, pp. 271–283. Springer, Cham (2016). https://doi.org/10.1007/978-3-319-49151-6_19
14. Groth, J., Kohlweiss, M.: One-out-of-many proofs: or how to leak a secret and spend a coin. In: Oswald, E., Fischlin, M. (eds.) EUROCRYPT 2015. LNCS, vol. 9057, pp. 253–280. Springer, Heidelberg (2015). https://doi.org/10.1007/978-3-662-46803-6_9
15. Hui, H.W., Zhou, C.C., Xu, S.G., Lin, F.H.: A novel secure data transmission scheme in industrial Internet of Things. China Commun. **17**(1), 73–88 (2020)
16. Lin, F.H., Zhou, X.W., An, X.S.: Fair resource allocation in an intrusion-detection system for edge computing: ensuring the security of Internet of Things devices. IEEE Consum. Electron. Mag. **7**(6), 45–50 (2018)
17. Su, J.T., Lin, F.H., Zhou, X.W., Lu, X.: Steiner tree based optimal resource caching scheme in fog computing. China Commun. **12**(8), 161–168 (2015)
18. Dou, Z., Xu, G., Chen, X., Yuan, K.: Rational non-hierarchical quantum state sharing protocol. Comput. Mater. Continua **58**(2), 335–347 (2019)
19. He, Q., et al.: A weighted threshold secret sharing scheme for remote sensing images based on chinese remainder theorem. Comput. Mater. Continua **58**(2), 349–361 (2019)
20. Long, M., Zeng, Y.: Detecting iris liveness with batch normalized convolutional neural network. Comput. Mater. Continua **58**(2), 493–504 (2019)

A Novel Thematic Network Data Collector Based on Simulated Annealing Hybrid Genetic Algorithm

Xiaofeng Wang[1](✉), Xiaoxue Yu[2], Shaohui Ma[3], and Huijuan Wang[1]

[1] The Information Security Department of the First Research Institute of the Ministry of Public Security of P.R.C., Beijing, China
wxf_tju@126.com
[2] Information Technology Department of the People's Insurance Company (Group) of China Limited, Beijing, China
[3] The 304 Research Institute of China Aerospace Science & Industry Corp., Beijing, China

Abstract. In the age of big data, the value of data has been paid more and more attention. How to get data efficiently and accurately is one of the fundamental study. Data collector is such a tool. Compared with the normal data collector, the Topic-focused network data collectors pay more attention to web pages related to pre-set topics. This paper designs and implements a network data collector and in order to improve the search efficiency, this paper uses annealing genetic algorithm by studying the hybrid genetic algorithm based on simulated annealing. The result indicated the hybrid algorithm can increase page coverage and crawling efficiency.

Keywords: Genetic algorithm · Simulated annealing algorithm · Hybrid algorithm · Network data collector · Web Crawler

1 Introduction

With the large-scale popularization of the Internet and the improvement of informationization, the scale of the accumulation of information resources has grown rapidly. In the age of big data [1], the value of data has been paid more and more attention by people. How to get data efficiently has become the current research hotspot.

The network data collector, also known as Web Crawler [2] and Web Spider, is a program that can automatically extract the information of web pages. It emulates the browser's access to network resources to obtain the Information that the user needs [3]. A traditional network data collector generally collects web pages as much as possible and does not care about the order of page collection and topic relevance [4]. This not only consumes network bandwidth, generates a large amount of extraneous data, also consumes a large amount of computing resources to deal with the collected data. Topic-focused network data collectors [5] pay more attention to web pages related to pre-set topics, thereby increase page coverage and utilization [29]. This results further can guide the resource management [26, 27, 31].

© Springer Nature Singapore Pte Ltd. 2020
X. Sun et al. (Eds.): ICAIS 2020, CCIS 1252, pp. 70–80, 2020.
https://doi.org/10.1007/978-981-15-8083-3_7

Genetic algorithms (GA) [6] was first proposed by John Holland of the University of Michiga and his colleagues in the study of cellular automata in 1975. It is a search algorithm for optimization [7] and developed from Darwin's evolutionary theory in biology and Mendel's genetic theory mechanism [28]. It can automatically acquire and accumulate knowledge about the search space during the search process, and control the search process adaptively to get the best solution [8]. However, the basic genetic algorithm will appear too precocious and the local search ability is insufficient.

Simulated Annealing (SA) [9] is a traditional probabilistic algorithm invented by S. Kirkpatrick, CD Gelatt, and MP Vecchi in 1983 [10]. It has strong ability of local optimum and can probability jumps out of the local optimal solution to obtain a global optimal solution. However, the computational efficiency of this algorithm is not high [11, 12].

This paper designs and implements a network data collector based on annealing genetic algorithm by studying the hybrid genetic algorithm based on simulated annealing [19, 20].

2 The Traditional Algorithms

2.1 Traditional Genetic Algorithm (GA)

The traditional genetic algorithm uses the laws of biological evolution for reference. The main algorithm steps are:

1. Generate population: generate a character string randomly;
2. Calculate the fitness value of each individual in the population;
3. Select, crossover, and mutation to generate the next generation;
4. Iterate steps 2 and 3 until the stop rule is satisfied;
5. Generations of the next generation.

The pseudo code is shown in Algorithm 1 [12].

2.2 Simulated Annealing Algorithm (SA)

The principle of the simulated annealing algorithm is similar to the principle of metal annealing. f(i) is the energy at state i. The main steps are:

1. Generate initial solution k randomly, calculate energy f(k);
2. Transfer state k to k' and calculates the new energy f(k');
3. Calculate the D-value as the following formula:

$$\Delta f = f\left(k'\right) - f(k) \tag{1}$$

If $\Delta f \leq 0$, the new solution is accepted:

$$k = k', f(k) = f(k') \tag{2}$$

1. If $\Delta f > 0$, then according to the Metropolis criterion, accept with probability, where K is the Boltzmann constant and T is the temperature of the solid;
2. Determine whether it reaches the number of iterations, if it is reached, proceed to step 6, otherwise proceed to step 2;
3. Determine whether the terminating condition is reached, and if so, return the optimal solution.

Table 1. Algorithm 1: The traditional genetic algorithm

```
begin
   initialize P(0)
   t=0              //t is current generations
                    while(t<=M):  //M is target generations
      for i=1 to T:          //T is the number of the population
        evaluate fitness of P(t)       // Calculate the fitness value of P(t)
        end for
        for i=1 to T:
          select operation to P(t)      //the operation of select
  end for
        for i=1 to T/2:
          crossover operation to P(t)      // the operation of crossover
  end for
  for i=1 to T:
        mutation operation to P(t)   // the operation of mutation
  end for
  for i=1 to T:
           P(t+1)=P(t)             //get the new population
        end for
        t++
  end while
  end
```

2.3 Simulated Annealing Hybrid Genetic Algorithm (SHGA)

Since the genetic algorithm is good at grasping the global trend, the ability to obtain a local optimal solution is weak [12], while the simulated annealing algorithm has strong ability to obtain a local optimal solution. Combining the two algorithms, and learn from each other, the new algorithm can get higher efficiency and accuracy. Reference literature [13] proposes a hybrid genetic algorithm that incorporates an improved SA algorithm in GA operation.

The simulated annealing hybrid genetic algorithm uses the improved SA algorithm as an independent operator of the GA algorithm to participate in the execution of the genetic algorithm. The specific steps are as follows:

1. Initialize operation, set various parameters;
2. Generates M individuals satisfying the constraints to form the initial group P(t);
3. Calculate the fitness of P(t);
4. Sort all individuals in the population according to their fitness and do the selection operation.
5. Do cross operation as the probability Pc. After X_A^t and X_B^t are crossed, two new individuals X_A^{t+1} and X_B^{t+1} are obtained, t is the current generation.
6. Do mutation operation as probability Pm. The individual fitness value after mutation is $P'(X_A^t)$, and if $P'(X_A^t) > P(X_A^t)$, the individual after mutation is accepted;
7. Simulated annealing is performed to obtain a new population P'(t). To facilitate the implementation of the algorithm, reference literature [13] proposes to use the current evolutionary generation of the genetic algorithm as the annealing time;
8. Combine P(t) and P'(t) to obtain new population P''(t);
9. Sort P''(t) according to the fitness value and take the first M as the t-th generation result;
10. Determine whether the terminating condition is satisfied, and if it is satisfied, the calculation is terminated and the result is output; if not, $t \leftarrow t + 1$ and repeat step 3.

3   Design of Network Data Collector

3.1   Architecture Design

Compared with the traditional network data collector, the theme-based collector calculate the relevance of the topic and adds the theme-related URLs to the URL database to be crawled. The network data collector designed in this paper uses simulated annealing hybrid genetic algorithm to calculate the topic relevance [14]. There are three main modules in the system, as shown in Fig. 1:

3.2   Determination of the Initial Seed Set

There are mainly three ways to determine the initial seed set: manual formulation, automatic generation, and mixture of both [15]. Because the network data collector is based on the initial seed, the importance of the URL is determined and other operations are performed. Therefore, the quality of the initial seed set is very important. Therefore, the paper adopts a hybrid mode, which uses the search engine and artificial experience to select the topic-related URL as the initial seed set.

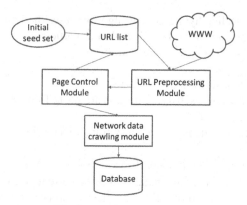

Fig. 1. Architecture diagram

3.3 URL Pre-processing Module

The URL preprocessing module mainly focuses on URLs in the seed set, and carries out normalization, de-duplication, and other operations. URL normalization is a process of converting a URL into a standard equivalent URL [16], determining the equivalent URLs and deleting the duplicated URL, thereby reducing the repeated crawling of the page. The normalization process is:

1. Convert the URL host name and protocol name to lower-case, and replenish the domain name for the URLs whose domain name is missing;
2. Because the escape sequence is case sensitive, convert the escape sequence to uppercase;
3. Delete the "#" after the URL;
4. Delete the "?" of the empty query string;
5. Delete the default suffix;
6. Remove the extra dot modifiers;
7. Delete the variable with the default value.

3.4 Page Control Module [17]

This module mainly uses the simulated annealing genetic algorithm in 3.2 to calculate the relevance of each URL, and compares it with the correlation threshold r0. If it is less than r0, then delete the URL, select, cross, and inherit the new URL list. Determine if the new URL list is empty, if it is not empty, the relevance degree is calculated for the new list and the subsequent steps are repeated. The flow chart is shown in the Fig. 2.

3.5 Network Data Crawling Module

The network data crawling module selects a higher priority [18] URL with from the URL waiting queue and crawls the data on the page. When the collector crawls a page at high concurrency times and high frequencies, it will bring a lot of pressure on the site being crawled [30], or even be forbidden to visit. Therefore, the network data collector implemented in this paper sets the number of parallel requests to 8, and the download delay to 2 s to ensure its normal operation.

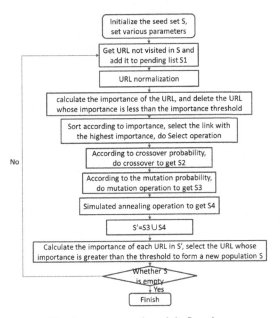

Fig. 2. Page control module flowchart

4 Implement of the Thematic Network Data Collector

The network data collector is written by Python on Linux. The machine configuration is CPU i7-3840QM, memory 8G, hard disk 128G SSD, operating system is CentOS 6.9. The system screenshot is shown in Fig. 3.

Fig. 3. System screenshot

We selected "2019 Beijing world expo" as the theme for testing. The topic words are "2019", "beijing", "expo" and their weight were put in an array as [1, 2, 5]. Select 30 out of the top 60 urls obtained by searching this keyword on baidu as the initial URL, and the number of system threads is 6. Threshold r0 = 0.005, mutation probability Pm = 0.2, crossover probability PC = 0.8. Comparison was made between the search results of common data crawler and crawler based on traditional genetic algorithm (GA). Table 1 shows the experimental results. The total number of urls is respectively 1000, 2000, ... 6000, the number of urls match the topic using three different algorithms. It can be clearly seen from Fig. 4 that more URLs matched the topic can be obtained by using SHGA and GA algorithm.

Table 2. Experimental results

Algorithm	The amount of URLs related to the Theme					
	Total = 1000	Total = 2000	Total = 3000	Total = 4000	Total = 5000	Total = 6000
SHGA	589	1032	1971	2467	3338	3895
GA	718	1437	2006	2382	2530	2876
Normal	482	731	898	1002	1494	1733

Table 2 shows the comparison of the three algorithms.

Number of total URLs	Based on SHGA			Based on GA			Normal		
	Precision	Recall	F-score	Precision	Recall	F-score	Precision	Recall	F-score
1000	71%	59%	0.645	87%	72%	0.786	58%	48%	0.528
2000	66%	52%	0.579	92%	72%	0.807	47%	37%	0.410
3000	77%	66%	0.708	78%	67%	0.721	35%	30%	0.323
4000	83%	62%	0.707	80%	60%	0.683	34%	25%	0.287
5000	86%	67%	0.750	65%	51%	0.569	38%	30%	0.336
6000	92%	65%	0.761	68%	48%	0.562	41%	29%	0.339

$$Precision = \frac{Amount\ which\ data\ collector\ get}{Amount\ of\ real\ urls\ topic-related} \tag{3}$$

$$Recall = \frac{Amount\ which\ data\ collector\ get}{Amount\ of\ total\ urls} \tag{4}$$

$$F-score = \frac{2 * Precision * Recall}{Precision + Recall} \tag{5}$$

The higher the F-score, the better the algorithm. According to Table 2, we can know that SHGA and GA both perform better than normal data collector. When the number of URL is small-less than 3000, GA performs better. As the number of total URL increased, SHGA is better and better. Therefore, the advantage of using algorithms becomes more obvious when the url's number is larger, and the data collector based on SHGA is more efficient.

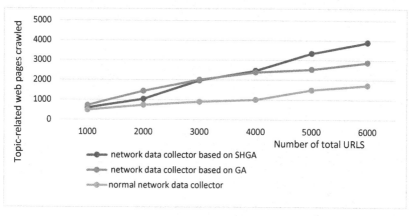

Fig. 4. The number of URLs getted by collector based on different algorithm

5 Conclusions and Future Work

The data collector is a tool to obtain network data and the basis of data analysis. The quality of the page can directly affect the performance of the data collector. In this paper, we design a thematic network data collector. In order to identify whether the web page is related to the theme, SHGA algorithm is proposed to improve the recognition efficiency in view of the shortcomings of traditional GA algorithm. This idea is also verified by experiments. The subsequent research will focus on improving the algorithm complexity, and according to the efficiency and characteristics of different algorithms, establish a mathematical model, and study the relationship between the number of collected urls and algorithm selection.

Acknowledgement. This work is supported by the 13th Five-year Plan on Technology and Innovation. No. 2018YFC0807000.

References

1. Lin, F., Su, J.: Multi-layer resources fair allocation in big data with heterogeneous demands. Wireless Pers. Commun. **98**(2), 1719–1734 (2017). https://doi.org/10.1007/s11277-017-4941-5
2. Dikaiakos, M.D., Stassopoulou, A., Papageorgiou, L.: An investigation of Web crawler behavior: characterization and metrics. Comput. Commun. **28**(8), 880–897 (2005)
3. Guo, L.: Python-based Web crawler design. Electron. Technol. Softw. Eng. **23**, 248–249 (2017)
4. Liu, J.H., Lu, Y.L.: Survey on topic-focused Web crawler. Appl. Res. Comput. **24**(10), 26–29 (2007)
5. Ahmadi-Abkenari, F., Selamat, A.: An architecture for a focused trend parallel Web crawler with the application of clickstream analysis. Inf. Sci. **184**(1), 266–281 (2012)
6. Maulik, U., Bandyopadhyay, S.: Genetic algorithm-based clustering technique. Pattern Recogn. **33**(9), 1455–1465 (2000)
7. Wikipedia: Genetic Algorithm. https://en.wikipedia.org/wiki/Genetic_algorithm. Accessed 15 May 2019
8. Wikipedia: Genetic Algorithm. https://zh.wikipedia.org/wiki/%E9%81%97%E4%BC%A0%E7%AE%97%E6%B3%95. Accessed 19 June 2018
9. Genetic Algorithm (GA). https://www.tutorialspoint.com/genetic_algorithms/genetic_algorithms_introduction.htm. Accessed 15 Aug 2018
10. Detailed Genetic Algorithm (GA). https://blog.csdn.net/u010451580/article/details/51178225. Accessed 19 June 2018
11. Bertsimas, D., Tsitsiklis, J.: Simulated annealing. Stat. Sci. **8**(1), 10–15 (1993)
12. Wikipedia: Simulated Annealing Algorithm. https://zh.wikipedia.org/wiki/%E6%A8%A1E6%8B%9F%E9%80%80%E7%81%AB. Accessed 2 Sept 2018
13. Yu, H.M., Yao, P.J., Yuan, Y.: A combined genetic algorithm/simulated annealing algorithm for large scale system energy integration. Comput. Chem. Eng. **24**(8), 2023–2035 (2000)
14. Zhou, L., Sun, S.D.: Genetic Algorithm Theory and Applications. National Defense Industry Press, Beijing (2001)
15. Simple explanation of genetic algorithm, dialysis GA essence. http://www.bkjia.com/Cyy/492750.html. Accessed 19 June 2018
16. Zhou, L.H., Su, Z.: Study of hybrid genetic algorithm based on simulated annealing. Appl. Res. Comput. **9**, 72–76 (2005)
17. Liu, H., Milios, E.: Probabilistic models for focused Web crawling. Comput. Intell. **28**(3), 289–328 (2012)
18. Zhao, H.J., Sun, W.H.: Unit test method based on annealing genetic algorithm. Comput. Eng. **39**(1), 49–53 (2013)
19. Zhang, H.L., Yuan, D.H.: Focused crawling based on genetic algorithms. Comput. Technol. Dev. **22**(8), 48–52 (2012)
20. Hernández, I., Rivero, C.R., Ruiz, D., Corchuelo, R.: An architecture for efficient Web crawling. In: Bajec, M., Eder, J. (eds.) CAiSE 2012. LNBIP, vol. 112, pp. 228–234. Springer, Heidelberg (2012). https://doi.org/10.1007/978-3-642-31069-0_20
21. Pu, Q.M.: The design and implementation of a high-efficiency distributed Web crawler. In: 2016 IEEE 14th International Conference on Dependable, Autonomic and Secure Computing, 14th International Conference on Pervasive Intelligence and Computing, 2nd International Conference on Big Data Intelligence and Computing and Cyber Science and Technology Congress (DASC/PiCom/DataCom/CyberSciTeCh), pp. 100–104. IEEE (2016)
22. Li, X.-G., Wei, X.: An improved genetic algorithm-simulated annealing hybrid algorithm for the optimization of multiple reservoirs. Water Resour. Manage. **22**(8), 1031–1049 (2008). https://doi.org/10.1007/s11269-007-9209-5

23. Mahfoud, S.W., Goldberg, D.E.: Parallel recombinative simulated annealing: a genetic algorithm. Parallel Comput. **21**(1), 1–28 (1995)
24. Wijaya, D.A., Liu, J.K., Steinfeld, R., Sun, S.-F., Huang, X.: Anonymizing bitcoin transaction. In: Bao, F., Chen, L., Deng, R.H., Wang, G. (eds.) ISPEC 2016. LNCS, vol. 10060, pp. 271–283. Springer, Cham (2016). https://doi.org/10.1007/978-3-319-49151-6_19
25. Groth, J., Kohlweiss, M.: One-out-of-many proofs: or how to leak a secret and spend a coin. In: Oswald, E., Fischlin, M. (eds.) EUROCRYPT 2015. LNCS, vol. 9057, pp. 253–280. Springer, Heidelberg (2015). https://doi.org/10.1007/978-3-662-46803-6_9
26. Su, J.T., Lin, F.H., Zhou, X.W.: Steiner tree based optimal resource caching scheme in fog computing. China Commun. **12**(8), 161–168 (2015)
27. Hui, H.W., Zhou, C.C., Xu, S.G., Lin, F.H.: A novel secure data transmission scheme in industrial Internet of Things. China Commun. **17**(1), 73–88 (2020)
28. Luo, M.H., Wang, K., Cai, Z.P.: Using imbalanced triangle synthetic data for machine learning anomaly detection. Comput. Mater. Con. **58**(1), 15–26 (2019)
29. Zhao, G.D., Zhang, Y.W., Lan, H.Y.: The application of BP neural networks to analysis the national vulnerability. Comput. Mater. Con. **58**(2), 421–436 (2019)
30. Chen, W.J., Feng, G., Zhang, C., Liu, P.Z.: Development and application of big data platform for garlic industry chain. Comput. Mater. Con. **58**(1), 229–248 (2019)
31. Lin, F.H., Zhou, X.W., An, X.S.: Fair resource allocation in an intrusion-detection system for edge computing: ensuring the security of Internet of Things devices. IEEE Consum. Electron. Mag. **7**(6), 45–50 (2018)

The Study of Fog Computing Security Situation Prediction in Industrial Internet

Xing-Shuo An[1]([✉]), Lei Cai[1], and Yanyan Zhang[2]

[1] North China Institute of Computing Technology, NCI,
Beijing 100083, People's Republic of China
axsdhh@163.com
[2] Beijing Economic and Technological Development Area, Beijing 100176,
People's Republic of China

Abstract. The industrial Internet needs fog computing to activate its potential. But the security threat of fog computing applied to industrial Internet is a problem that cannot be ignored. Security situation prediction is an effective method to predict the possible security threats in the network. Therefore, this paper focuses on the security problems of fog computing in industrial Internet and proposes a model for measuring the security situation of industrial fog Internet. In this paper, ELM algorithm is adopted to verify the proposed model. The result shows the effectiveness of the model, and ELM has a good performance in the prediction effect.

Keywords: Fog computing · Industrial Internet · Security situation prediction

1 Introduction

Fog computing expands cloud computing and storage resources closer to users to provide low-latency services for users in the network. Since fog computing was proposed, it has been widely used in many fields, especially industrial Internet [1–3].

In the industrial Internet, the fog node in the industrial Internet usually consists of servers deployed in the factory. As the data center of the factory, the cloud server is responsible for providing centralized services and managing and monitoring fog nodes. We define the network form combining fog computing and industrial internet as Industrial fog network, and its network structure is shown in Fig. 1.

While serving the factory, the fog node connects with the Internet and exchanges data with the outside world [4]. While fog computing brings benefits to industrial Internet, it also makes industrial control system related to production security easily exposed to the Internet [5, 6]. The security of Industrial fog network is challenged from all levels [7, 8]. Therefore, how to effectively prevent the security threats in Industrial fog network in Industrial Internet has become a common concern of industry and academia [9–11].

Different from traditional detection technology, security situational awareness technology can, on the basis of obtaining system data information, fuse data by analyzing the correlation between information, obtain macro security situation, accurately judge whether the system is attacked, identify the attack type, and give the current security state of the system.

© Springer Nature Singapore Pte Ltd. 2020
X. Sun et al. (Eds.): ICAIS 2020, CCIS 1252, pp. 81–89, 2020.
https://doi.org/10.1007/978-981-15-8083-3_8

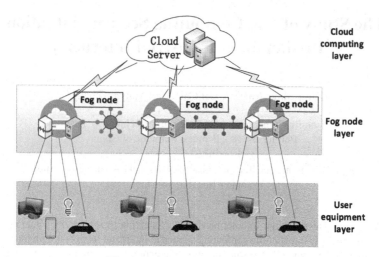

Fig. 1. Fog computing architecture

In the study of Industrial fog network security situation awareness, it is first necessary to study and construct the security situation evaluation index suitable for fog computing. Secondly, the accuracy of security situation is also an important Angle. In view of the characteristics of fog computing, this paper firstly proposes an agent-based situation prediction model for deployment in Industrial fog network. Secondly, we constructed the security situation evaluation model of Industrial fog network and proposed the security situation prediction model of Industrial fog network based on ELM. Simulation results show that the proposed model has high accuracy.

2   Industrial Fog Network Based on Security Situation Awareness Agent

This paper proposes a security situational awareness Agent applicable to Industrial fog network [12]. Agent is divided into three layers, namely Data Layer, Characteristic Layer and Situation Layer. The working principle of Agent is shown in the Fig. 2.

Data Layer: the main function of the Data Layer is Data collection. First, data from the user's device layer is transmitted over the network to the fog node. The Agent data acquisition module deployed in fog node collects real-time network data from the outside of fog node and local data of fog node. Information including CPU, memory, network traffic, port, registry, system process, etc. will be synchronized and fed back to the data preprocessing module [13].

Characteristic Layer: Characteristic Layer features extraction and processing of security situation with the Data Layer's Data processing results. Network security situation can be obtained at multiple abstraction levels. Currently, methods to obtain network security situation at low abstraction levels mainly include situational awareness and alarm correlation, vulnerability analysis, correlation analysis, etc.

Situation Layer: in the Situation Layer, security Situation results can be understood and concerned by managers through further processing of Situation data. The acquisition

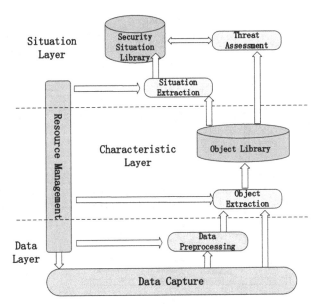

Fig. 2. Workflow of the situational awareness Agent

of network security situation at a higher level of abstraction relies more on the automatic analysis of data, such as big data technology, artificial intelligence and machine learning.

Resource Management: due to the resource-limited characteristics of fog nodes, Resource Management is necessary in the design of security situation Agent. The Resource Management module is executed across layers. Its function is mainly responsible for balancing the load proportion of resources occupied by the security situational awareness Agent on the fog node and resources occupied by other business services.

The functional modules of the security situation Agent can be decoupled and flexibly deployed in the Industrial fog network. Figure 3 shows the working process of the Agent module in the Industrial fog network. Industrial field produces a large amount of data, most of which comes from industrial controllers and CNC machine tools. The fog node collects data from the industrial field layer through the probe and calls the Agent's data preprocessing module. The Agent deployed locally in fog node stores the feature library of security situational awareness. Agent of fog node calls feature library to perform initial situation information processing. The weak decision of primary security situation result can be executed on the fog node. The fog node will transmit the difficult situation information to the cloud server, which will conduct the global security situation calculation.

3 Industrial Fog Network Security Situational Awareness Model and Algorithm

Industrial fog network is quite different from other traditional networks. Fog node provides network services for heterogeneous user devices, and the collected data may face

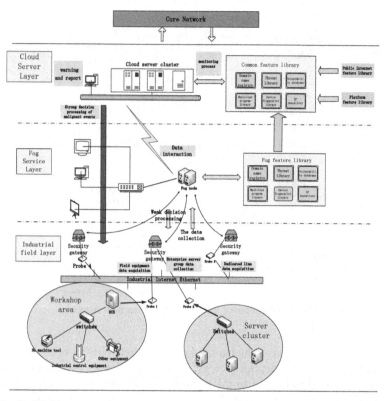

Fig. 3. Working process of the security situation Agent in the Industrial fog network

problems such as field disunity and field missing. In addition, the network environment of Industrial fog network is highly dynamic and requires high real-time situational awareness. Therefore, in this paper, factors such as accuracy in traditional security situational awareness are included in the measurement range, and a new situational awareness measurement model is proposed to measure its performance and effection in Industrial fog network environment.

First, we define indicators that reflect situational awareness accuracy. Suppose there are M samples in the test sample space and the number of categories is C. There are usually three types of errors in the judgment result of security situational awareness: 1) omission: an input sample is an intrusion, while the judgment result of situational awareness is a normal behavior; 2) false alarm: an input sample is a normal behavior, but the result of situational awareness discrimination is an invasion; 3) false positives: the intrusion type of an input sample is C_j, and the situational awareness discrimination result is other intrusion types except C.

Assume that, in the situational awareness result, the actual number of invasion samples output is. Where, the number of omitted report is P_l, and the number of false report is P_f. The alarm rate and false alarm rate can be expressed as.

$$P_l = \frac{\text{The number of missing reports in situation awareness}}{\text{Number of real intrusion samples in test samples}} = \frac{l}{q + l - f} \quad (1)$$

$$P_f = \frac{\text{The number of false reports in situation awareness}}{\text{Number of real intrusion samples in test samples}} = \frac{f}{q + l - f} \quad (2)$$

$$P_w = 1 - \frac{1}{C} \sum_{j=1}^{C} \frac{\text{Output result correctly identified as } C_j}{\text{Sample number of } C_j \text{ in the test sample}} \quad (3)$$

Based on the above three indicators, the utility function to measure the accuracy of situational awareness is given in this paper:

$$UF_a = r_1(1 - P_l) + r_2(1 - P_f) + r_3(1 - P_w) \quad (4)$$

where r1, r2, r3 represent utility parameters in three types of error cases, $\sum_{i=1}^{3} r_i = 1$.

Secondly, aiming at the challenge of high network complexity faced by fog node, the detection survival space of fog node situational awareness was defined. Assuming the data dimension of the original test sample is V, the situational awareness accuracy of the original test sample is P_a, $P_a = (1 - P_w)$. In the process of V's going down, P_a is definitely to go down. However, the existence of V', make $\frac{V'}{V} \geq \eta$, $\eta \leq P_a$. This chapter define V' as the survival threshold of situational awareness, that is to detect the data dimension where the security of the system can be guaranteed when the detection accuracy declines to η. It can be calculated by iterative method, the pseudo-code of the algorithm is as follows.

Algorithm 1
_____

Input: data dimension, available detection accuracy, detection accuracy

Output: survival threshold V'

Situational awareness function (V, P_a, η)

While True:

    if $P_a \leq \eta$:

        $V' = V$

        return V'

    P_a = situational awareness function _ $(-- V, P_a)$

The premise of the significance of Calculating V' is that each field in the sample library is equally important. Represents the survival threshold of fog computing for situational awareness. In order to facilitate the inclusion of the description of situational awareness measurement model, the survival space of situational awareness is defined as V = v − v'. Survivable space V reflects the survivable space of situational awareness algorithm when the dimension of sample data is reduced or the collected data is incomplete.

Finally, combined with the training time of the sample, the measurement model of situational awareness in fog computing can be given

$$MF = \frac{\omega_1 \cdot UF_a + \omega_2 \cdot \triangle V}{\omega_3 \cdot \sum_{i=1}^{L} t_i(J)} \tag{5}$$

Among them is the measurement parameter of each index. Due to the difference of dimension and order of magnitude of each index, it is necessary to carry out data standardization processing for each index. The data standardization process has been included in the calculation. Standardized treatment is as follows:

$$\frac{\triangle V - Min \triangle V}{Max \triangle V - Min \triangle V} = \frac{\triangle V}{V} \tag{6}$$

For the standardization of time, Sigmoid transformation function is adopted in this paper to transform the time parameter into an interval from 0 to 1.

$$Sigmoid(t) = \frac{\omega_3}{1 + e^{-\sum_{i}^{L} t_i(J)}} \tag{7}$$

According to (4–5), (4–6) and (4–7), the expression of fog computing situational awareness measurement model can be obtained as follows:

$$MF = \frac{1}{\omega_3}[1 + e^{-\sum_{i}^{L} t_i(J)}](\omega_1 \cdot UF_a + \omega_2 \cdot \frac{\triangle V}{V}) \tag{8}$$

4 Simulation

This paper adopts extreme learning machine as the detection algorithm of situational awareness. ELM was first proposed by Huang. The principle of ELM algorithm will not be given in this paper. Detailed introduction of the principle is shown in [14]. The calculation structure of ELM is shown in Fig. 4.

The experiment is simulated in the Windows 7 operating system (i7-2760QM, 2.4 GHz CPU, 8.00 GB RAM), and the ELM algorithm is implemented using Matlab 2014a. In our previous research, the calculation method of the security threat value of fog nodes has been given. This paper combines the reference [15] and the situation awareness model proposed in this paper to calculate the security situation value of fog nodes. We take two fog nodes deployed in Industrial fog network as the research object to calculate the security situation value. The calculated value of security situation is shown in Fig. 5.

Based on ELM, this paper predicts the generated security situation and calculates the accuracy of the predicted result and the security situation. The simulation results are shown in Fig. 6 and Fig. 7.

The security situation of 80 data samples has been simulated. According to the results in Fig. 6 and Fig. 7, the prediction result of ELM has little difference from the actual

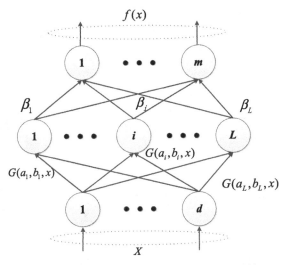

Fig. 4. Neural network model structure of extreme learning machine

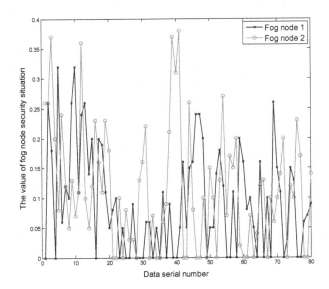

Fig. 5. Security situation value of two fog nodes

security situation. In fog node 1, 5 predicted security situation values deviated from the actual values, and the accuracy of security situation prediction of fog node 1 was 93.75%. In fog node 2, 4 data deviated, and the prediction accuracy of security situation of fog node reached 95%. Therefore, we can conclude that ELM performs well in the security situation prediction of Industrial fog network.

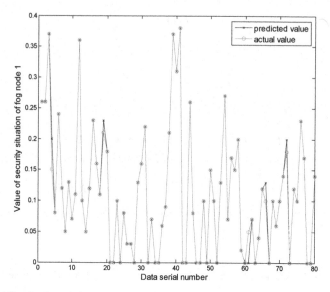

Fig. 6. Comparison of predicted value and actual value of fog node 1

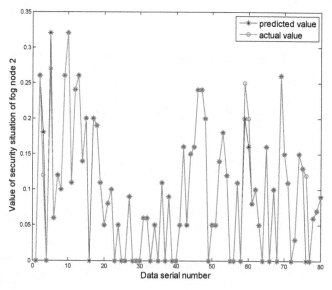

Fig. 7. Comparison of predicted value and actual value of fog node 2

5   Conclusion

The security threat of fog computing in industrial Internet is the problem that this paper tries to solve. Firstly, this paper proposes a measurement model for the security of fog calculation in industrial Internet. Secondly, ELM algorithm is adopted in this paper to verify the model. The results show that the proposed model is effective and ELM performs well in prediction.

References

1. Hui, H., Zhou, C., Xu, S., Lin, F.: A novel secure data transmission scheme in industrial Internet of Things. China Commun. **17**(1), 73–88 (2020)
2. Sadeghi, A.R., Wachsmann, C., Waidner, M.: Security and privacy challenges in industrial Internet of Things. In: 2015 52nd ACM/EDAC/IEEE Design Automation Conference (DAC), pp. 1–6. IEEE (2015)
3. Lin, F., Zhou, Y., You, I., Lin, J., An, X., Lü, X.: Content recommendation algorithm for intelligent navigator in fog computing based IoT environment. IEEE Access **7**, 53677–53686 (2019)
4. Khan, S., Parkinson, S., Qin, Y.: Fog computing security: a review of current applications and security solutions. J. Cloud Comput. **6**(1), 1–22 (2017). https://doi.org/10.1186/s13677-017-0090-3
5. Kim, D.-Y., Kim, S.: A data download method from RSUs using fog computing in connected vehicles. Comput. Mater. Cont. **59**(2), 375–387 (2019)
6. Guo, Y., Liu, F., Xiao, N., Chen, Z.: Task-based resource allocation bid in edge computing micro datacenter. Comput. Mater. Con. **61**(2), 777–792 (2019)
7. Wei, Y., Wang, Z., Guo, D., Richard Yu, F.: Deep Q-learning based computation offloading strategy for mobile edge computing. Comput. Mater. Cont. **59**(1), 89–104 (2019)
8. Su, J., Lin, F., Zhou, X., Lu, X.: Steiner tree based optimal resource caching scheme in fog computing. China Commun. **12**(8), 161–168 (2015)
9. Bonomi, F., Milito, R., Zhu, J., et al.: Fog computing and its role in the Internet of Things. In: Proceedings of the First Edition of the MCC Workshop on Mobile Cloud Computing, pp. 13–16. ACM (2012)
10. Hu, W., Li, J., Chen, X., Jiang, X.: Network security situation prediction based on improved adaptive grey Verhulst model. J. Shanghai Jiaotong Univ. (Sci.). **15**(4), 408–413 (2010). https://doi.org/10.1007/s12204-010-1025-z
11. Zhang, Y., et al.: Network security situation awareness approach based on Markov game model. J. Softw. **22**(3), 495–508 (2011)
12. Bijani, S., Robertson, D.: A review of attacks and security approaches in open multi-agent systems. Artif. Intell. Rev. **42**(4), 607–636 (2014). https://doi.org/10.1007/s10462-012-9343-1
13. Lin, F., Zhou, Y., An, X., You, I., Choo, K.-K.R.: Fair resource allocation in an intrusion-detection system for edge computing: ensuring the security of Internet of Things devices. IEEE Consum. Electron. Mag. **7**(6), 45–50 (2018). https://doi.org/10.1109/MCE.2018.2851723
14. Huang, G.-B., Zhu, Q.-Y., Siew, C.-K.: Extreme learning machine: theory and applications. Neurocomputing **70**(1–3), 489–501 (2006)
15. An, X., Lü, X., Yang, L., Zhou, X., Lin, F.: Node state monitoring scheme in fog radio access networks for intrusion detection. IEEE Access **7**, 21879–21888 (2019). https://doi.org/10.1109/ACCESS.2019.2899017

A Novel Keypoints-Based Image Registration Method with Fully Convolutional Neural Network

Xiaodong Yang[1] ⓘ, Daping Li[1], Qiaolin He[2], Zhu Wang[3], Ying Fu[1], Jiliu Zhou[1], and Jinrong Hu[1](✉)

[1] Chengdu University of Information Technology, Chengdu, China
dongxiaoyang1015@foxmail.com, ldp01@vip.qq.com,
{Chinafuying,zhoujl,hjr}@cuit.edu.cn
[2] College of Mathematics, Sichuan University Chengdu, Chengdu, China
qlhejenny@scu.edu.cn
[3] Law School, Sichuan University Chengdu, Chengdu, China
wangzhu@scu.edu.cn

Abstract. Image registration plays an important role in image processing. The key-points based registration technology is a research hotspot. However, the quality of key-points detection will greatly affect the performance of image registration. In this paper, we use the fully convolutional neural network to perform key-points detection and feature extraction on the image, which is applied to the registration. Experiments show that the proposed method achieves better performance and is superior to the traditional key-points based registration method.

Keywords: Image registration · Fully convolution network · Key-points detection

1 Introduction

Image registration has generally divided into two methods: image registration based on gray information and key-points. The gray-based image registration method is the earliest proposed algorithm. In 1972, Leese [25] and others applied the mutual information algorithm to the remote sensing image, which uses the statistical map to register the infrared image with the ordinary camera, excellent results have been achieved. Silverman [26] et al. proposed improvements to the above cross-correlation method to improve the registration speed, but could not overcome the effect of noise on the image. Viola [27] et al. used the maximum cross-correlation algorithm to achieve scene registration, and applied the registration technology to medical images for the first time, completing the fusion of medical images. However, the image registration of gray information is sensitive to noise anomaly, and multiple images need to have a large number of overlapping regions. The calculation cost is high, which cannot meet the efficiency requirement in practical applications.

X. Sun et al. (Eds.): ICAIS 2020, CCIS 1252, pp. 90–101, 2020.
https://doi.org/10.1007/978-981-15-8083-3_9

Key-points based image registration algorithm is a mature and widely used algorithm in image processing. It mainly uses key-points extracted from multiple images as matching primitives, so it is not sensitive to care transformation and noise. More stable. In 2004, Lowe [8] perfected the scale-invariant feature transform algorithm and used the pyramid model to calculate the extreme points of the image difference in the Gaussian scale-space to obtain the key-points. However, SIFT key-points have sizeable computational complexity and key-points redundancy in the registration algorithm. On this basis, Bay H [28] et al. proposed the SURF algorithm to improve the operation speed of SIFT, but it is robust to rotation and scale. Slightly worse. Montiel et al. proposed the ORB [23] algorithm, which is more robust to the rotation of the object, but the feature matching accuracy is low. The key-points-based algorithm is much faster in image registration, but how to maintain the independence of the key-points in the image registration, rotation invariance, and robustness is still a technical difficulty.

2 Related Work

Convolutional neural networks have proven to be superior to hand-craft representations on all tasks that require images as input. The fully convolutional network that predicts 2D key-points has been studied in depth for various tasks, such as human pose estimation [14], object detection, and room layout estimation [29]. At the heart of these technologies are a large number of 2D image real key-point datasets that are manually labeled. But there are many problems in translating key-point detection into supervised machine learning problems and using convolutional neural networks to train them. For example, training networks are detecting body parts such as joints and noses. The concept of key-points detection is semantical, not clear. Because this paper uses a self-supervised learning method to train convolutional neural networks to detect key-points [17–19].

Instead of using human annotation to define key-points in real images, this article uses a self-supervised solution. We first generate several synthetic shape datasets [6], which are composed of simple geometric shapes, so there is no ambiguity in the position of the key-points. By training the key-point detector through this synthetic datasets, the uncertainty on the key-points label can be avoided, and the trained detector is applied to the natural image or the medical image as the initial pseudo-ground-truth of the training, through multiple epochs. Training makes the key-points detector work well in real images. In combination with data enhancement, the key-points detector can be made to have rotational scale invariance. After detecting a key-points, a standard method is to abstract the grayscale information in the key-points domain into a fixed-dimensional descriptor, so that a higher-level semantic task can be performed. Therefore, this paper combines the detected key-points with the descriptor network, and performs key-points extraction and descriptor generation synchronously, so that the descriptor can better characterize the key-points. There can be more superior performance in the subsequent registration tasks.

Image registration based on key-points has become the research direction of scholars. It does not focus on the global information of known images, but finds the more significant local features in the image through the algorithm, and finds the corresponding relationship of multiple images through local feature comparison. This way of finding the representative information significantly reduces the amount of calculation of the registration method, and can also be robust to images with large differences in gray scale. The key-points are generally corner points, high curvature points, etc., that is, points where the gray value of the neighborhood is greatly transformed. The key-points are mostly stable points and play a very important role in the image. According to statistics, only 0.05% of the image pixels represent all the important information of the image. Harris corner points [13], SIFT, SURF and ORB extract key-points have their own good characteristics.

Image registration based on key-points has become the research direction of scholars. It does not focus on the global information of known images, but finds the more significant local features in the image through the algorithm, and finds the corresponding relationship of multiple images through regional feature comparison. This way of finding the representative information significantly reduces the amount of calculation of the registration method, and can also be robust to images with significant differences in grayscale. The key-points are generally corner points, high curvature points, etc., that is, points where the gray value of the neighborhood is much transformed. The key-points are mostly stable and play a vital role in the image. According to statistics, only 0.05% of the image pixels represent all the essential information of the images. Harris corner points [11], SIFT, SURF, and ORB extract key-points have their excellent characteristics.

The SIFT proposed by Lowe [8] has attracted the attention of researchers because of its excellent characteristics of key-points extraction and description. Bhargavi et al. [21] performed sparse coding based on the SIFT key-points method, and used the spatial pyramid matching kernel to retrieve the data objects, and proved the feasibility of the improved algorithm through experiments. G. Ramu [22] and so on using the SIFT Key-points method, combined with RANSAC technology, for authenticity detection of a given image. Compared with other detection methods, the authenticity detection result of the algorithm is more accurate. The image matching algorithm based on SIFT key-points is considered to be one of the best matching methods. It has good stability to the rigid body transformation, illumination fitness, noise intensity, and scale change of objects in the image. The literature compares the matching time based on SIFT key-points. Experiments show that the extraction time of SIFT key-points accounts for 30%–40% of the total image matching time. The extraction of unstable edge points leads to an increase in matching time, making it difficult to apply in real-time. Therefore, how to reduce instability or find a technology that can replace SIFT key points is a hot topic in today's research field.

For Moravec corner points sensitive to the edge region, the sliding window is easily interfered with by other factors, and there is a strong dependence on the direction of the operator. Harris and Tomasi [21] respectively improved it. Harris corners are invariant features such as illumination, rotation, etc. Still, there are some shortcomings in applying Harris corners to image matching, and registration: (1) Harris corners have no spatial multi-scale. In multiple images in the same scene, the object will change the scale due to the difference of the image acquisition distance and the resolution. The lack of multi-scale will seriously affect the image matching and registration accuracy. (2) The number of key-points extracted by Harris corner points is small. The number of key-points extracted by SIFT is approximately two to three times the number of jobs associated with Harris

Corner 2. Key-points are the representation and embodiment of crucial information in the image. The insufficient number of key-points may result in the loss of image information and reduce the accuracy of matching. 3) The algorithmic judgment of the Harris corner is determined by the difference gray value of the edge and the corner point. If there are weak edges in the image, the Harris corner algorithm cannot be accurately extracted, which may cause some essential information to be lost, and further reduce the number of key-points extracted. Since the Harris corner is sensitive to images with weak edges and the number of extracted key-points is far less than the SIFT key-points algorithm, the matching and registration are not accurate. How to find a reliable and effective edge extraction method and increase the number of extracted key-points at the same time is the focus of the improvement of a key-points algorithm.

Traditional methods of key-points detection have many drawbacks so that key-points detection through convolutional neural networks has become a research trend. FAST was the first method to use machine learning to detect key-points. There are many ways to improve FAST and add descriptor and direction estimates for FAST, which also has an impact on CNN-based methods. TILDE [7] trains multiple piecewise linear regression models to identify the key-points of robustness under different weather and illumination variations. LIFT [4] implements an end-to-end framework for key-points detection and descriptor generation, including direction estimates for each key-points. Quad-networks uses a quadruple image block and points response method as a loss function, training a key-points detector. Lf-net estimates the position, scale, and scale of the feature by jointly optimizing the detector and descriptor. Direction. These neural network-based key-points detectors are based on image blocks and are relatively shallow networks that do not take advantage of the fully convolutional neural network. MagicPoint uses a self-supervised learning method to generate a special integer point detector, which is extended to Superpoint by corresponding parameter transformation between images, which includes key-points detection and descriptors. Key-points detection [3, 4, 6, 15] and feature extraction are still a research hotspot using full convolution.

The method proposed in this paper is similar to Superpoint's self-supervised way. It trains a simple key-points detector through synthetic data, avoids the ambiguity of manually marking key points, and adaptively creates labels based on the learned detectors, on real images. And finally, key-points detection and feature extraction for full-size images used for image registration.

3   Method

This paper uses a structure of a fully convolutional neural network that runs on a full-scale image, detects key-points and fixed-length descriptors, and then estimates the transformation parameters between the two images by matching the key-points, finally the task of registration is completed. This section will introduce the registration method proposed in this paper from four aspects: key-points detection, descriptor generation, key-points matching, and fitting transformation (registration).

3.1 Key-Points Detection and Descriptor Generation

The key-points detection and descriptor survival used in this paper is to detect the full-size image through the fully convolutional neural network. First, the size of the image is reduced by a VGG-like encoder. The encoder consists of convolution, pooling, and nonlinear activation. The size of the full-size image is down sampled from H × W to H' = H/8, W' = W/8 by three consecutive encoder structures. The encoder maps the full-size input image to an image with a smaller size and a broader channel depth. The small-size image contains more general advanced image information, and these small-sized images are used to map key-points.

For key-points detection, each pixel of the output corresponds to the probability that the pixel is a key-points in the input image. A network for dense prediction requires a pair of encoder-decoder structures in which the spatial resolution is passed through the encoder and then restored to full size by the decoder. There are many ways to do this. The SigNet [19] uses up sampling to full-size resolution, but the up sampling layer tends to add a lot of computation and can cause undesirable checkerboard effects. So this article uses a shared encoder to process and reduce the size of the input image. After the encoder, it splits into two decoder heads for specific learning tasks, one for key-points detection and one for key-points description. Most of the parameters are shared between these two tasks, which is different from the traditional method of detecting key points first in the calculation.

The key-points detection head uses H' × W' × 64, and the tensor output dimension is H × W, where every 8 × 8 non-overlapping grid areas represent a key-points position. The encoder is decoded into the original picture 1/8 size, the original image is sampled to H*W by subpixel convolution, wherein the channel is used as a softmax to map the probability value of the position as a key-point. Finally, the full-size image is detected by the encoder-decoder step to identify the location of the key-points. Screen out the appropriate key points by non-maximal inhibition.

The descriptors and key points of the key points are generated synchronously, and H × W × D is generated by the size of the descriptor header H' × W' × D. In order to normalize the length of the descriptor's length descriptor, this article uses a similar UCN to directly up sample the image to a fixed length, which reduces training parameters and is easy to handle.

The final loss function consists of two parts: one is the key-points detector Lp, and the other is the descriptor detector Ld. To make the detector's key points and descriptors have rotation invariance, this paper will use paired images for training, they have the basis of pseudo key points, and transform parameters so that the key-points of the two images can correspond. By training a given pair of images, the two-loss functions can be optimized at the same time. Different coefficients are given to different losses to balance for optimize network training

$$L\left(X, X^{'}, D, D^{'}\right) = L_p(X, Y) + L_p\left(X^{'}, Y^{'}\right) + \lambda L_d\left(D, D^{'}\right)$$

The loss function pseudo-Lp of the keypoint detector, specifically the cross-entropy loss of the full convolution on the small unit of each image. For the predicted key position, in the H × W image, each pixel corresponds to the probability of being a key point, that

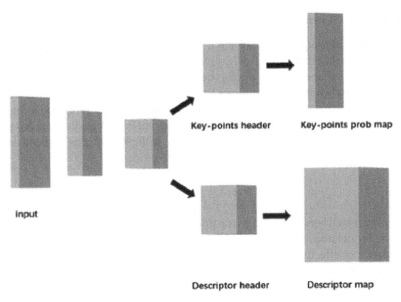

Fig. 1. Proposed framework

is, xhw belongs to HW, and the ground-truth of the corresponding key point is yhw belongs to Y, Y also A probability plot for the key points of the corresponding size of the full map. The specific key-points loss function is as follows:

$$L_p(X, Y) = \frac{1}{H_c W_c} \sum_{\substack{h=1 \\ w=1}}^{H_c, W_c} l_p(x_{hw}; y_{hw})$$

The loss function of the descriptor also uses MSE. We expect the descriptors of the corresponding key points to be as similar as possible. Then, for the key point descriptor D_{hw} of an image belongs to D, another key point of the image can be found through the mapping relationship. The descriptor D'_{hw} belongs to D', then we want their MSE to be as small as possible, that is, the transformed descriptors are still similar, making the descriptors more robust in the face of change [30]. The specific losses are as follows:

$$L_d(D, D') = \frac{1}{H * W} \sum_{\substack{h=1 \\ w=1}}^{H_c, W_c} (D_{hw} - D'_{hw})^2$$

The framework of key-points detection and descriptor generation is introduced above. Robust key points and descriptors are obtained through training. After key points and descriptors are obtained, the first thing to do is key-points matching

3.2 Key-Points Matching

Key point matching requires identifying a subset of key points in one image that is key points in another image. Formally, given the set of key-points descriptors in the reference image, and the set of key-points descriptors in the image to be registered, it is necessary to find a bijection from a subset to a subset. Under a descriptor metric method $m(x, y)$, the members are sorted by their distance from the descriptor. Due to the low computational cost and superior matching performance of Euclidean distance, this paper uses Euclidean distance as m. Let $xx \subset S1$, $yi \subset S$, is the ith and closest member, and the matching score is defined as:

$$socre(x, S_2) = \frac{m(x, y_1)}{m(x, y_2)}$$

When the match between x and y_1 is particularly noticeable, for example, it is closer than any other member, so if it is below a certain threshold, it is considered to match. This method can effectively avoid the mismatch that occurs when the key points are locally similar in medical images.

3.3 Transform Fitting

This paper obtains the corresponding relationship of key points by feature matching of key-points and performs a geometric transformation to fit the image. This paper uses affine transformation, which is mathematically simple enough to register the data in this paper. In the given coordinates, parameters then the affine transformation parameters are:

$$\begin{pmatrix} o' \\ 1 \end{pmatrix} = \begin{pmatrix} A & b \\ o^T & 1 \end{pmatrix} \begin{pmatrix} o \\ 1 \end{pmatrix}$$

This paper fits the affine transformation by linear regression, requiring at least n + 1 matching uniqueness. Some matches will be wrong, so this article rejects outliers by the random sample formula (RANSAC). The transformation is fitted to a subset of the data in an iterative manner to find the transformation with the most points. The final transformation is the affine transformation required in this paper.

The method proposed in this paper is completed under the framework of Tensorflow [20]. It is based on synthetic data to train a key-points detector. The synthesized data is as follows. A key-points detector is trained by automatically annotating key-points in the synthesized data that are not ambiguous. This detector only needs to detect some pseudo-ground-truth for subsequent training of key-points and descriptors. The key-points detector trained by the synthetic data performs the first round of pre-training on the obtained label and complete training on the new real data set, including COCO2014 [12], NPC medical image dataset. These data trainings have enabled us to obtain key-points detectors that have achieved excellent results on both natural and medical images. We use some data enhancement methods, such as rotation, scaling, translation, etc., to get pairs of input images and transformation mode H. In the process of continuous iteration, the network adapts to the data changes, so that the key-points detector and descriptor are both More robust.

4   Experiment

In this section, we present the quantitative results of the proposed method. This paper starts from the direction of image registration based on key-points and takes the superiority of key-points and descriptors as the representative. The following three experiments are set: evaluation of key-point detection quality, evaluation of descriptor matching robustness, and registration performance.

4.1   Key-Points Detection Quality

Key-points matching is often evaluated by stability. [18] proposed the evaluation criteria of key-points detector and matching result. Figures A and B are two images to be matched, and Figure A has a homography to map B. Matrix H1, Figure B maps to Figure A with homography matrix H2, Figure A detects N1 key-points, and Figure B detects N2 key-points. Because images A and B have partial images that do not overlap, A maps are detected. The coordinates of the key-points are calculated from the coordinates of the B map by H1, and the key-points of the unqualified (calculation result exceeds the coordinates of the B image) are removed, and the remaining key-points are recorded as n1; likewise, the key-points of the B map are processed to be left n2 The denominator is $\min(n1, n2)$. If the distance is smaller than the threshold ε, it is considered It is repeated [17]. We compare SIFT, ORB, and the methods proposed in this paper. The experimental results are as follows:

We tested 100 pairs of images and performed illumination, rotation, and other transformation experiments. The proposed method achieves the optimal repetition rate of feature point detection when the threshold ε is set to 1, 3, 5 (Table 1).

Table 1. Detected key-points repeated rates

	$\varepsilon = 1$	$\varepsilon = 3$	$\varepsilon = 5$
SIFT	**0.424**	0.598	0.732
ORB	0.157	0.436	0.582
PROPOSED	0.335	**0.627**	**0.829**

Experiments show that the proposed method achieves the best in the repetition rate of key-points detection. When the threshold ε is set to 1,3, 5, we test 100 pairs of images, respectively, take care, rotation, and other transformations. Excellent.

4.2   Descriptor Matching Robustness

Feature matching is an essential intermediate stage of image registration. The better the performance of feature matching, the better registration is achieved. This article uses a test pair that is completely complete to obtain a standard image. By this method, the accuracy and recall rate of each matching key extraction feature can be independently verified. The offset of the specified point pair within 5 mm is the correct match. The real example is the correct pair of key-points, and the false positive is the key pair of mismatches. The false-negative example is that there is a crucial matching pair but no correct match. Based on these definitions, the standard accuracy and recall rate is calculated as follows:

$$Precision = \frac{true\,positives}{(true\,positives\,+\,false\,positives)}$$

$$Recall = \frac{true\,positives}{(true\,positives\,+\,false\,negatives)}$$

This section is also performed under 100 pairs of test images, randomly rotating, panning, scaling, etc. the image pairs. Experiments set different thresholds (0.6, 0.7, 0.8, 0.9, 1.0) to verify the effectiveness of the three methods. The lower the threshold, the higher the requirement for matching, the better the accuracy. As can be seen from the Fig. 1 the proposed method achieves the best precision and recall under different thresholds, which is better than SIFT and ORB (Fig. 2).

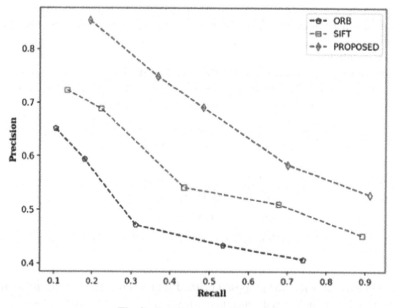

Fig. 2. Descriptor matching result

4.3 Registration Performance

Registration accuracy measures the registration accuracy by the target registration error (TRE), which is the root mean square of the distance error of the test's global coordinate pair. Use the key point position as the coordinates. The TRE is calculated as follows:

$$TRE = \sqrt{\frac{1}{N} \sum_{i=1}^{N} \|P_i - T \cdot P'_i\|_2^2}$$

Where P is the reference position of the key-points, P^l is the key-points on the image to be registered. T is the transformation matrix that estimates the fitted transformation, and N is the number of key-points. The smaller the value of TRE, the lower the coordinate error, the more effective the registration

The results of the registration performance are shown in Table 2. Among them, ORB has the worst performance in registration, and its TRE value is the highest, SIFT is slightly better than ORB. We propose that the method achieves the optimal result and obtains the minimum TRE value. This experiment shows that our proposed method is superior to the other two methods in registration and has better performance.

Table 2. Registration performance result

ORB	SIFT	PROPOSED
6.732	3.428	0.568

5 Conclusion

This paper uses a fully convolutional neural network architecture for training critical point detection and description. Our experiments show that (1) self-labeling and training through synthetic data sets are effective in practice. (2) key points and descriptors obtained based on fully convolutional neural networks are more robust and effective than traditional methods. (3) The quality of the method that based on key-points image registration depends on the effect of key-points detection, and the high-quality key-points have a definite positive impact on the registration result. We will achieve fully automatic key-points registration from the input of the pair of images, the results of the registration, and pre-work for subsequent non-rigid registration in the future. At the same time, the results of key-points detection can be used in the field of more real images, such as three-dimensional reconstruction, target tracking, and the like. Subsequent will further optimize the proposed method and apply it to a wider and broader field.

Acknowledgment. This work is supported by National Science Foundation of China (No. 61602390), National Key RD Program of China: Studies on Key Technologies and Equipment Supporting A High Quality and Highly Efficient Court Trial (2018YFC0830300), Ministry of Education, China: Chunhui Project (No. Z2015108), Supported by Sichuan Science and Technology Program (No. 2018RZ0072, 2019YFG0196).

References

1. Abadi, M., et al.: Tensorflow: a system for large-scale machine learning. In: 12th {USENIX} Symposium on Operating Systems Design and Implementation ({OSDI} 2016), pp. 265–283 (2016)
2. Badrinarayanan, V., Kendall, A., Cipolla, R.: Segnet: a deep convolutional encoder-decoder architecture for image segmentation. IEEE Trans. Pattern Anal. Mach. Intell. **39**(12), 2481–2495 (2017)
3. Barnea, D.I., Silverman, H.F.: A class of algorithms for fast digital image registration. IEEE Trans. Comput. **100**(2), 179–186 (1972)
4. Bay, H., Tuytelaars, T., Van Gool, L.: SURF: speeded up robust features. In: Leonardis, A., Bischof, H., Pinz, A. (eds.) ECCV 2006. LNCS, vol. 3951, pp. 404–417. Springer, Heidelberg (2006). https://doi.org/10.1007/11744023_32
5. Bhargavi, K.N.D., Rani, C.S.: Cbir based on linear SPM using sift sparse codes. In: 2016 IEEE International Conference on Computational Intelligence and Computing Research (ICCIC), pp. 1–3. IEEE (2016)
6. Choy, C.B., Gwak, J., Savarese, S., Chandraker, M.: Universal correspondence network. In: Advances in Neural Information Processing Systems, pp. 2414–2422 (2016)
7. DeTone, D., Malisiewicz, T., Rabinovich, A.: Superpoint: self-supervised interest point detection and description. In: Proceedings of the IEEE Conference on Computer Vision and Pattern Recognition Workshops, pp. 224–236 (2018)
8. Guan, S.Y., Wang, T.M., Meng, C., Wang, J.C.: A review of point feature based medical image registration. Chin. J. Mech. Eng. **31**(1), 76 (2018)
9. Han, X., Leung, T., Jia, Y., Sukthankar, R., Berg, A.C.: Matchnet: unifying feature and metric learning for patch-based matching. In: Proceedings of the IEEE Conference on Computer Vision and Pattern Recognition, pp. 3279–3286. IEEE (2015)
10. Hu, J., et al.: Towards accurate and robust multi-modal medical image registration using contrastive metric learning. IEEE Access **7**, 132816–132827 (2019)
11. Laguna, A.B., Riba, E., Ponsa, D., Mikolajczyk, K.: Key net: keypoint detection by handcrafted and learned CNN filters. arXiv preprint arXiv:1904.00889 (2019)
12. Leese, J.A., Novak, C.S., Clark, B.B.: An automated technique for obtaining cloud motion from geosynchronous satellite data using cross correlation. J. Appl. Meteorol. **10**(1), 118–132 (1971)
13. Lenc, K., Vedaldi, A.: Large scale evaluation of local image feature detectors on homography datasets. arXiv preprint arXiv:1807.07939 (2018)
14. Lin, T.Y.: Microsoft COCO: common objects in context. In: Fleet, D., Pajdla, T., Schiele, B., Tuytelaars, T. (eds.) ECCV 2014. LNCS, vol. 8693, pp. 740–755. Springer, Cham (2014). https://doi.org/10.1007/978-3-319-10602-1_48
15. Liu, W., et al.: SSD: single shot MultiBox detector. In: Leibe, B., Matas, J., Sebe, N., Welling, M. (eds.) ECCV 2016. LNCS, vol. 9905, pp. 21–37. Springer, Cham (2016). https://doi.org/10.1007/978-3-319-46448-0_2
16. Lowe, D.G.: Distinctive image features from scale-invariant keypoints. Int. J. Comput. Vis. **60**(2), 91–110 (2004)
17. Mikolajczyk, K., Schmid, C.: An affine invariant interest point detector. In: Heyden, A., Sparr, G., Nielsen, M., Johansen, P. (eds.) ECCV 2002. LNCS, vol. 2350, pp. 128–142. Springer, Heidelberg (2002). https://doi.org/10.1007/3-540-47969-4_9
18. Mikolajczyk, K., Schmid, C.: A performance evaluation of local descriptors. IEEE Trans. Pattern Anal. Mach. Intell. **27**(10), 1615–1630 (2005)
19. Mur-Artal, R., Montiel, J.M.M., Tardos, J.D.: Orb-slam: a versatile and accurate monocular slam system. IEEE Trans. Robot. **31**(5), 1147–1163 (2015)

20. Ono, Y., Trulls, E., Fua, P., Yi, K.M.: LF-net: learning local features from images
21. Rosten, E., Drummond, T.: Machine learning for high-speed corner detection. In: Leonardis, A., Bischof, H., Pinz, A. (eds.) ECCV 2006. LNCS, vol. 3951, pp. 430–443. Springer, Heidelberg (2006). https://doi.org/10.1007/11744023_34
22. Verdie, Y., Yi, K., Fua, P., Lepetit, V.: Tilde: a temporally invariant learned detector. In: Proceedings of the IEEE Conference on Computer Vision and Pattern Recognition, pp. 5279–5288. IEEE (2015)
23. Viola, P., Wells III, W.M.: Alignment by maximization of mutual information. Int. J. Comput. Vis. 24(2), 137–154 (1997)
24. Wei, S.E., Ramakrishna, V., Kanade, T., Sheikh, Y.: Convolutional pose machines. In: Proceedings of the IEEE Conference on Computer Vision and Pattern Recognition, pp. 4724–4732. IEEE (2016)
25. Yi, K.M., Trulls, E., Lepetit, V., Fua, P.: LIFT: learned invariant feature transform. In: Leibe, B., Matas, J., Sebe, N., Welling, M. (eds.) ECCV 2016. LNCS, vol. 9910, pp. 467–483. Springer, Cham (2016). https://doi.org/10.1007/978-3-319-46466-4_28
26. Zhang, X., Yu, F.X., Kumar, S., Chang, S.F.: Learning spread-out local feature descriptors. In: Proceedings of the IEEE International Conference on Computer Vision, pp. 4595–4603. IEEE (2017)
27. Long, M., Zeng, Y.: Detecting iris liveness with batch normalized convolutional neural network. Comput. Mater. Continua. 58(2), 493–504 (2019)
28. Yu, S., Liu, J., Zhang, X., Shangbin, W.: Social-aware based secure relay selection in relay-assisted D2D communications. Comput. Mater. Continua. 58(2), 505–516 (2019)
29. Zhao, Y., Yang, X., Li, R.: Design of feedback shift register of against power analysis attack. Comput. Mater. Continua. 58(2), 517–527 (2019)
30. Zhang, O., Wei, X.: Online magnetic flux leakage detection system for sucker rod defects based on labVIEW programming. Comput. Mater. Continua. 58(2), 529–544 (2019)

Image Super-Resolution Reconstruction with Dense Residual Attention Module

Li Wang[1], Ziyi Chen[1], Hui Li[1(✉)], Chengwei Pan[2,3], and Dezheng Zhang[2,3]

[1] School of Automation and Electrical Engineering, University of Science and Technology Beijing, Beijing 100083, China
lihui2868@vip.163.com
[2] School of Computer and Communication Engineering, University of Science and Technology Beijing, Beijing 100083, China
[3] Beijing Key Laboratory of Knowledge Engineering for Materials Science, Beijing 100083, China

Abstract. Deep convolutional neural networks have recently achieved great success in the field of image super-resolution. However, most of the super-resolution methods based on deep neural network do not make full use of the multi-level features which extracted from low-resolution images, and do not pay attention to the high-frequency information which needs to be reconstructed in the image, so the performances are relatively poor. Aiming at these problems, we propose a dense residual attention module to improve the image reconstruction performance. The dense residual attention module proposed in this paper makes full use of low-level image feature, and the channel spatial attention mechanism makes the network pay more attention to the high-frequency information that the image needs to be repaired, and uses the sub-pixel convolution to complete the image. Experiments were carried out on five benchmark datasets Set5, Set14, BSD100, Urban100 and DIV2K100. When the magnification was 4, the PSNR and SSIM are 32.47 dB/0.8986, 29.72 dB/0.8004, 27.73 dB/0.7423, 26.63 dB/0.8030, 29.43 dB/0.9023. Compared with other methods, we obtain the expected results.

Keywords: Super-resolution reconstruction · Convolutional neural network · Multi-level features · Channel spatial attention mechanism · Dense residual connection · Sub-pixel convolution

1 Introduction

Super-resolution reconstruction problems, especially single-image super-resolution reconstruction, are intended to infer high-resolution images from low-resolution pictures. Early stage, an interpolation technique based on sampling theory [1–3] was used to solve the problem of super-resolution reconstruction. However, these methods show limitations in predicting detailed, realistic textures. Previous studies have also used natural image statistics [4, 5] to predict the texture information to reconstruct better high-resolution images, but these methods did not achieve better results. Subsequently, a more advanced approach aims to learn the mapping function between low-resolution

X. Sun et al. (Eds.): ICAIS 2020, CCIS 1252, pp. 102–114, 2020.
https://doi.org/10.1007/978-981-15-8083-3_10

images and high-resolution image pairs. These learning methods rely on techniques from neighbor embedding [6–9] to sparse coding [10–13].

With the development of deep learning, super-resolution reconstruction has become an area of computer vision, which has rapid development. Recently, the super-resolution reconstruction method based on convolutional neural network [14, 15] has led the trend in this field. Through several convolutional layers, a better mapping function is obtained. With the introduction of the residual network into the field of super-resolution reconstruction [16, 17, 24, 26], deeper network architecture has used to achieve better performance. In particular, it proves that skipping connections and recursion reduce the computational burden of super-resolution networks. With the advent of the DenseNet [18] architecture, Tong et al. introduced this structure into the super-resolution reconstruction task and built a densely connected network SRDenseNet [19], which achieved superior results through dense connection modules. Different from the above network structure, EDSR [20] improves the performance of the network by deleting some unnecessary modules in the ResNet structure [21], such as the BN layer. Experiments show that the performance of the network is improved after the BN layer is removed.

Although these models have achieved good performance, these models are just stack of convolutional layers and network modules. They do not make good use of the information of each feature layer, and do not distinguish which high-frequency information needs to be recovered. Moreover, as the network deepens, the network parameters are also geometric multiples.

In response to these problems, we combine the structure of ResNet [21] and DenseNet [18], and proposes a new connection between modules, which can make full use of the information between each level. Compared to the above model, a large number of parameters are reduced in the case of the same number of network layers. At the same time, it also introduces an attention mechanism, which makes the network pay more attention to some high-frequency information that needs to be repaired by integrating channel attention and spatial attention mechanism. Finally, a feature reorganization module and a dense residual attention module were built to form the structure of the reconstruction network. Therefore, the super-resolution reconstruction network proposed in this paper makes full use of the characteristics of each feature level. At the same time, the network pays more attention to the image detail information that needs to be repaired. Finally, it greatly reduces the parameters of the network and improves the performance of the network.

In summary, our main contributions are as follows:

1) We proposed the feature reorganization module and the dense residual attention module, which combines the characteristics of each feature level and makes full use of different levels of information by the network.
2) For the super-resolution reconstruction task, a new connection method between modules is proposed, which can improve the performance of the network and reduce a large number of parameters.
3) A fusion attention module is proposed. Through the channel and spatial attention mechanism, the network is more focused on recovering high-frequency information, and selects the image details that need to be repaired adaptively.

2 Network Structure

The network structure proposed in this paper, as shown in Fig. 1, can be roughly divided into three parts: 1) a low-level feature extraction network composed of two convolutional layers; 2) a network main structure composed of feature reorganization modules; 3) A reconstruction module that forms a high-resolution image.

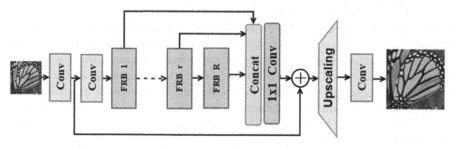

Fig. 1. The network's structure

2.1 Feature Extraction Part

Let I^{LR} and I^{HR} represent the low-resolution image of the input network and the high-resolution image finally generated by the network. First, I^{LR} is input into a low-level feature extraction network composed of two convolutional layers to extract the initial feature mapping required by the subsequent network backbone:

$$F_0 = f_0\left(I^{LR}\right) \tag{1}$$

$$F_1 = f_1(F_0) \tag{2}$$

Where $f_0(\bullet)$ represents the first convolution operation, and the extracted feature map F_0 is sent to the second convolution $f_1(\bullet)$ to obtain the initial feature map F_1. F_0 will be further used for subsequent global residual learning, and F_1 will be used as input for subsequent network backbones. We use $Conv_{w,n}(\bullet)$ to represent the convolution operation of this article, w denotes the convolution kernel size, n denotes the number of filters, then $f_0(\bullet), f_1(\bullet)$ are both $Conv_{3,64}(\bullet)$.

2.2 Network Architecture

Our network backbone consists of multiple feature reorganization modules and the final feature fusion module. The feature reorganization module is composed of dense residual attention modules. We will elaborate the intensive residuals in Sect. 2.2

First, the initial feature F_1 is sent to a network backbone composed of a plurality of feature reorganization modules in series to obtain a feature map F_R:

$$F_R = D_R(D_{R-1}(\ldots D_1(F_1)\ldots)) \tag{3}$$

Where $D_r(\bullet)$ represents the rth feature reassembly module, and then the output F_r of each feature reassembly module will be extracted for subsequent feature fusion operations to obtain the final global feature map F_f:

$$F_f = f_f(H_{ff}(F_1, \ldots F_r \ldots, F_R)) \tag{4}$$

Where $H_{ff}(\bullet)$ means that the output features of each feature reassembly module are merged together, and $f_f(\bullet)$ represents a $Conv_{1,64}(\bullet)$ operation, that is, the convolution kernel is 1, and the merge is obtained. The multi-level feature layers are fused by $f_f(\bullet)$ to obtain a global feature map F_f that fuses multi-level features.

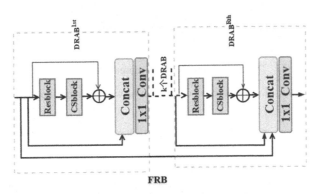

Fig. 2. Feature reorganization module

Connection Between Modules

The feature reorganization module proposed in this paper is shown in Fig. 2. It is composed of multiple dense residual attention modules. The connection method is shown in Fig. 3. It is similar to the connection with DenseNet [18], but we make some improvements towards to the resolution task. There is some difference.

In DenseNet [18], as shown in the dashed box in Fig. 3(a), the input of the next convolutional layer and the active layer is the merging of the feature maps of the outputs of all the previous layers, thereby merging the multi-level feature maps. Information, but there is a problem that this operation will bring a lot of parameters, increase the amount of calculation, and bring a huge computational load. Therefore, we propose a new connection mode between modules. The connection mode of the feature reorganization module is shown in the dotted line box of Fig. 3(b). After the feature image splicing operation, a 1 × 1 convolution operation is added.

The 1 × 1 convolution action is shown in Fig. 4. Through a convolution operation, the feature maps of all levels are linearly weighted to obtain a new feature that fuses the information of all feature layers, because the 1 × 1 convolution kernel has only one parameter. The merged feature layer can be dimensioned by setting the number of output channels, so the number of parameters of the network can be greatly reduced. At the same time, under the premise of keeping the feature map constant, the nonlinear characteristics of the network are greatly increased without the resolution of the loss

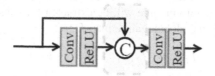

(a)   The connection of DenseNet

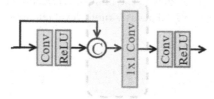

(b)   The connection of feature reorganization module

Fig. 3. The different connection between two modules

feature. The information can be circulated and interacted between different channels, which is extremely helpful for super-resolution reconstruction tasks.

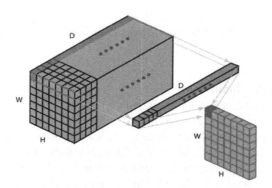

Fig. 4. The concrete operation of 1×1conv

Dense Residual Attention Module

The dense residual attention module contains two small modules: a local residual module and a fusion attention module. The local residual module uses the residual module structure in EDSR [20] to learn the different levels of feature layer information.

The second module is a fusion attention module, as shown in Fig. 5, after the local residual module is connected to the fusion attention module, and F_{r-1} and F_r are the input and output feature of the rth dense residual attention module. Then F_r can be expressed as:

$$F_r = F_{r-1} + f^{FA}(f_{lres}(F_{r-1}))$$ (5)

where $f_{lres}(\bullet)$ represents the output of a local residual module, and $f^{FA}(\bullet)$ represents the operation of fusion attention module.

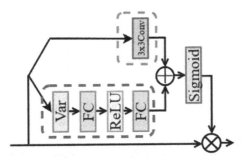

Fig. 5. Fusion attention module

Our fusion attention mechanism is composed of two parts, the channel attention mechanism in the red dotted frame, and the spatial attention mechanism in the green dotted frame. For the channel attention mechanism, we borrowed the structure of SENet [22], but the previous channel attention mechanism simply adopted the popular averaging pooling method in the squeeze process. For high-level computer vision such as image classification and objection detection, the averaging pooling has no problem. However, since the super-resolution reconstruction task is aimed at restoring the high-frequency information of the image, it is more reasonable to use the high-frequency statistics information about the channel to determine the attention feature map. Therefore, we choose to use the variance rather than the average for the pooling method.

$$S_{r-1} = pool_{var}(X_{r-1}) \tag{6}$$

Where $pool_{var}(\bullet)$ represents the variance pooling, $S_{r-1} \in \mathbb{R}^{1 \times 1 \times C}$ is output high frequency statistics, $X_{r-1} = f_{lres}(F_{r-1})$. The remaining activation functions and scaling processes are performed in the same manner as SENet [22], resulting in a channel attention graph M_{r-1}^{CA}.

For the spatial attention mechanism, each channel represents a filter, and different filters are responsible for extracting different features of the image. For example, information from complex filters is more important in extracted edges or complex texture maps. On the other hand, if there is no high frequency information in the image area that needs to be restored, the relatively less detailed information is more important and needs to be noticed. Therefore, we use depth separable convolution here, convolution for each channel feature to get attention map:

$$M_{r-1}^{SA} = conv_{3 \times 3, depth}(X_{r-1}) \tag{7}$$

Where $conv_{3 \times 3, depth}(\bullet)$ represents 3×3 depth separable convolution, $M_{r-1}^{SA} \in \mathbb{R}^{H \times W \times C}$ is the different attention feature map.

Finally, the channel attention map and the spatial attention map are added together, through a Sigmoid function, finally multiplied by the original feature. The recalibrated feature map X_{r-1} can be obtained:

$$\hat{X}_{r-1} = f^{FA}(X_{r-1}) = \sigma\left(M_{r-1}^{CA} \oplus M_{r-1}^{SA}\right) \otimes X_{r-1} \qquad (8)$$

Where the $\oplus$ represents the addition operation, $\otimes$ represents the multiplication operation.

2.3 Image Reconstruction

Image reconstruction refers to the fusion of global feature mapping and global residual learning. After sub-pixel convolution [23], the low-resolution features of the r^2 dimension are reassembled into a high-resolution image, essentially by inserting low-resolution features into a high-resolution image periodically according to a specific location. The insertion method of sub-pixel convolution can be observed by color. Finally, a reconstructed picture is obtained through a convolutional layer:

$$F_{DF} = F_0 + F_f \qquad (9)$$

$$I_{HR} = f_l(f^{sub}(F_{DF})) \qquad (10)$$

where F_0 and F_f are shallow feature map and global feature map respectively, $f^{sub}(\bullet)$ is a sub-pixel convolution operation, that is, image enlargement operation in image reconstruction, and $f_l(\bullet)$ is the last convolution operation $Conv_{64,3}(\bullet)$.

3 Experimental Details

In the experiment, we will analyze the performances of different attention mechanisms on the network, make comparative experiments, and experiment with the performances of different number of feature reorganization modules and dense residual attention modules. Finally, we will compare the network with the mainstream network architecture.

3.1 Implementation Details

In order to construct the input small batch data for training, the high-resolution image is first cropped to a medium size image, for example, the 2040 × 1080 image is cropped to 480 × 480, the cropping step is 240, and then we will randomly crop these medium-sized pictures, get 32 × 32 small pictures, every 16 small pictures as a batch. For data augmentation, we randomly flip and randomly rotate the images (90°, 180°, and 270°) [25]. For the trained picture, all three channels are trained. For each channel, we subtract the pixel mean of the corresponding channel of the entire dataset, this operation is used to maintain the smoothness of the training.

In the network proposed in this paper, except for the local feature fusion and the global feature fusion stage, the convolution kernel size is 1 × 1, and the convolution kernels of all the other convolutional layers are 3 × 3, and the number of filters in each layer of the network is 64. For a convolutional layer with a convolution kernel size of

3×3, we zero-fill each side of the input feature map to preserve the edge information of the image. We used the L1 loss function instead of the traditional L2 loss function. In this paper, the Adam optimsizer is selected, and the parameters are set as follows: $\beta_1 = 0.9$, $\beta_2 = 0.999$, $\epsilon = 10^{-8}$

We trained the super-resolution model on four NVIDIA GeForce GTX 1080ti GPUs with a learning rate of 0.002 and a total training round of 100 k. To ensure convergence of the model, we reduced the learning rate by 70 k and 90 k. We build the super-resolution network model on the Pytorch deep learning framework.

3.2 Ablation Experiments

Selection of the Number of Modules

In this section we will explore the number of modules, the number of feature reorganization modules (represented by F below) and the number of dense residual attention modules (represented by D below).

The indicators are shown in Table 1, where F4D4 represents four feature reorganization modules in the network, and each feature reorganization module has four dense residual attention modules. The test indicator is selected as the PSNR(/dB). It can be seen that as the network model increases, the value of PSNR continues to rise. We find that the parameter amount of F8D4 is only 0.1 M more than F4D8, but it is much higher in PSNR index, and compared with F8D8, the parameters are nearly half the size, but the performance is only a little worse. Therefore, considering the model performance and model size, we chose the F8D4 model. There are four feature recombination modules, and there are 8 dense residual attention modules in each feature reorganization module. In subsequent experiments, we will choose F8D4 model.

Table 1. Module number analysis.

Dataset	Scale	F4D4	F4D8	F8D4	F8D8
Set 5	×2	38.11	38.16	38.18	**38.20**
	×3	34.43	34.55	34.62	**34.65**
	×4	32.20	32.31	32.43	**32.45**
Parameters		1.8 M	3.3 M	3.4 M	**6.6 M**

Module Simplification Experiment

In the model simplification experiment, we will explore the performance of our model with different attention mechanisms to prove the superiority of the fusion attention mechanism. CA represents the channel attention, SA represents the spatial attention mechanism, and CSA represents the fusion attention mechanism.

From Table 2, it can be seen that both the channel attention mechanism and the spatial attention mechanism added to the model, the performance of the model is improved.

Table 2. Attention mechanisms analysis.

Dataset	Scale	F8D4	+CA	+SA	+CSA
Set 5	×2	38.18	38.23	38.22	**38.25**
	×3	34.62	34.63	34.62	**34.65**
	×4	32.41	32.43	32.43	**32.47**
Parameters		1.8 M	3.4 M	3.5 M	3.7 M

After adding the fusion attention mechanism, the performance is best. From the point of view of the parameter quantity, the addition of the channel attention mechanism and the spatial attention mechanism are extremely small for the increase of the parameter quantity, so there is not much influence on the speed of the model.

Module Benchmark

We compare the network structure proposed in this paper with some traditional methods and several popular network structures, such as Bicubic, A + [12], SRCNN [14], VDSR [17], SRDenseNet [19], EDSR [20]. The advantages of our network are demonstrated by comparing the Peak Signal to Noise Ratio (PSNR) and Structural Similarity Index (SSIM) and the parameter quantities of the model structure. The training set of the model, the selection of the optimizer, the parameter settings of the optimizer and the learning rate setting strategy are the same as the EDSR [20].

The scaling scale selects three scales of ×2, ×3, and ×4. The results are shown in Table 3. It can be seen that the proposed method compares with some classical methods and the popular super-resolution models. Our model has a certain improvement in both RSNR and SSIM. Compared with EDSR [20], although the improvement is not a lot, our method wins less than the model parameters, only one-tenth of the EDSR [20], so our method is faster than EDSR. On the Set14 dataset, when the scaling scale is ×4, compared to Bicubic, A + [12], SRCNN [14], VDSR [17], SRDenseNet [19], EDSR [20], our method increased by 3.72 dB, 2.40 dB, 2.22 dB, 1.71 dB, 1.22 dB, 0.92 dB on the RSNR indicator. On the SSIM indicator, our method increased by 9.77, 5.13, 4.19, 3.3, 2.22, and 1.28 percentage points respectively. As shown in the Fig. 6, the better visual performance has been shown compared to other methods.

Table 3. Module benchmark analysis.

Dataset	Scale	Bicubic	A+	SRCNN	VDSR	SRDenseNet	EDSR	Ours
Set 5	×2	33.66/0.9299	36.54/0.9544	36.66/0.9542	37.53/0.9587	–/–	38.11/0.9602	**38.25/0.9612**
	×3	30.39/0.8682	32.58/0.9088	32.75/0.9090	33.66/0.9213	–/–	**34.65**/0.9282	**34.65/0.9289**
	×4	28.42/0.8104	30.28/0.8603	30.48/0.8628	31.35/0.8838	32.02/0.8934	32.46/0.8968	**32.47/0.8986**
Set 14	×2	30.24/0.8688	32.28/0.9056	32.42/0.9063	33.03/0.9124	–/–	33.92/0.9195	**34.55/0.9196**
	×3	27.55/0.7742	29.13/0.8188	29.30/0.8215	29.77/0.8314	–/–	30.52/0.8462	**31.34/0.8488**
	×4	26.00/0.7027	27.32/0.7491	27.50/0.7513	28.01/0.7674	28.50/0.7782	28.80/0.7876	**29.72/0.8004**
BSD100	×2	29.56/0.8431	31.21/0.8863	31.36/0.8879	31.90/0.8960	–/–	**32.32**/0.9013	**32.32/0.9015**
	×3	27.21/0.7385	28.29/0.7835	28.41/0.7863	28.82/0.7976	–/–	**29.25/0.8093**	29.24/0.8083
	×4	25.96/0.6675	26.82/0.7087	26.90/0.7101	27.29/0.7251	27.53/0.7337	27.71/0.7420	**27.73/0.7423**
Urban100	×2	26.88/0.8403	29.20/0.8938	29.50/0.8946	30.76/0.9140	–/–	**32.93**/0.9351	32.92/**0.9352**
	×3	24.46/0.7349	26.03/0.7973	26.24/0.7989	27.14/0.8279	–/–	**28.80/0.8653**	28.78/0.8649
	×4	23.14/0.6577	24.32/0.7183	24.52/0.7221	25.18/0.7524	26.05/0.7819	**26.64/0.8033**	26.63/0.8030
DIV2K100	×2	31.01/0.9393	32.89/0.9570	33.05/0.9581	33.66/0.9625	–/–	35.03/0.9695	**35.67/0.9703**
	×3	28.22/0.8906	29.50/0.9116	29.64/0.9138	30.09/0.9208	–/–	31.26/0.9340	**31.62/0.9361**
	×4	26.66/0.8521	27.70/0.8736	27.78/0.8753	28.17/0.8841	–/–	29.25/0.9017	**29.43/0.9023**
Parameters		–/–	–/–	0.6 M	6.66 M	20 M	43 M	3.7 M

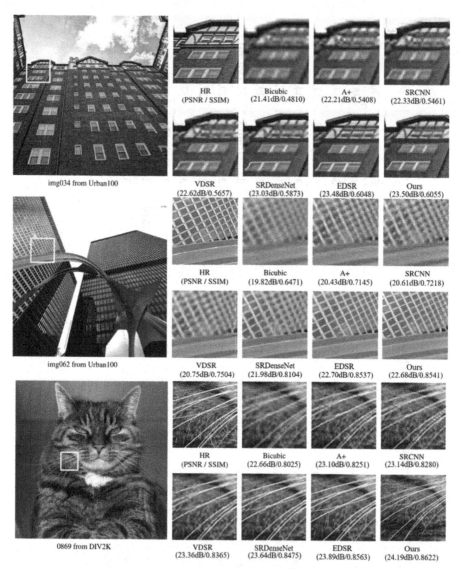

Fig. 6. Qualitative comparison of our model with other works (Scaling × 4)

4   Conclusion

This paper proposes a super-resolution reconstruction model that combines the attention of dense residuals. It is mainly used to solve the problem that the existing models do not make full use of multiple feature layers and do not pay attention to the details of the images that need to be repaired. This paper solves these two problems by proposing a dense residual module and a attention fusion module.

For dense residual modules, it combining the advantages of residual connections and dense connections to learn multi-layer feature map information from the input image. We use 1×1 convolution to fuse the information of each feature layer, which also greatly reducing the number of parameters and improving the speed of the model. For the attention fusion module, the channel attention mechanism and the spatial attention mechanism are combined to make the model focus on the detailed information. The dense residual module and the fusion attention module are combined to form a feature reorganization module, which finally constitutes the overall structure of the network model.

The experimental results show that compared with other methods, our method certain improvements in both RSNR and SSIM, which have better visual performance.

Acknowledgment. This work was supported by: Ningxia Hui Autonomous Region Key R&D Plan Projects: Research and Demonstration Application of Key Technologies of Spatial Planning Intelligent Monitoring Based on High Score Remote Sensing (Item Number: 2018YBZD1629).

References

1. Allebach, J., Wong, P.W.: Edge-directed interpolation. In: Proceedings of 3rd IEEE International Conference on Image Processing, vol. 3, pp. 707–710 (1996)
2. Li, X., Orchard, M.T.: New edge-directed interpolation. IEEE Trans. Image Proc. **10**(10), 1521–1527 (2001)
3. Zhang, L., Wu, X.: An edge-guided image interpolation algorithm via directional filtering and data fusion. IEEE Trans. Image Proc. **15**(8), 2226–2238 (2006)
4. Tai, Y.W., Liu, S., Brown, M.S., Lin, S.: Super resolution using edge prior and single image detail synthesis. In: 2010 IEEE Computer Society Conference on Computer Vision and Pattern Recognition, pp. 2400–2407 (2010)
5. Sun, J., Xu, Z., Shum, H.Y.: Image super-resolution using gradient profile prior. In: 2008 IEEE Conference on Computer Vision and Pattern Recognition, pp. 1–8 (2008)
6. Chang, H., Yeung, D.Y., Xiong, Y.: Super-resolution through neighbor embedding. In: Proceedings of the 2004 IEEE Computer Society Conference on Computer Vision and Pattern Recognition, 2004. CVPR 2004, vol. 1, p. I-I (2004)
7. Bevilacqua, M., Roumy, A., Guillemot, C., Morel, M.L.A.: Low-complexity single-image super-resolution based on nonnegative neighbor embedding (2012)
8. Gao, X., Zhang, K., Tao, D., Li, X.: Image super-resolution with sparse neighbor embedding. IEEE Trans. Image Proc. **21**(7), 3194–3205 (2012)
9. Roweis, S.T., Saul, L.K.: Nonlinear dimensionality reduction by locally linear embedding. Sci. **290**(5500), 2323–2326 (2000)
10. Yang, J., Wright, J., Huang, T.S., Ma, Y.: Image super-resolution via sparse representation. IEEE Trans. Image Proc. **19**(11), 2861–2873 (2010)
11. Yang, J., Wang, Z., Lin, Z., Cohen, S., Huang, T.: Coupled dictionary training for image super-resolution. IEEE Trans. Image Proc. **21**(8), 3467–3478 (2012)
12. Timofte, R., De Smet, V., Van Gool, L.: A+: adjusted anchored neighborhood regression for fast super-resolution. In: Asian Conference on Computer Vision, pp. 111–126 (2014)
13. Zeyde, R., Elad, M., Protter, M.: On single image scale-up using sparse-representations. In: International Conference on Curves and Surfaces, pp. 711–730 (2010)

14. Dong, C., Loy, C.C., He, K., Tang, X.: Learning a deep convolutional network for image super-resolution. In: Fleet, D., Pajdla, T., Schiele, B., Tuytelaars, T. (eds.) ECCV 2014. LNCS, vol. 8692, pp. 184–199. Springer, Cham (2014). https://doi.org/10.1007/978-3-319-10593-2_13

15. Dong, C., Loy, C.C., Tang, X.: Accelerating the super-resolution convolutional neural network. In: Leibe, B., Matas, J., Sebe, N., Welling, M. (eds.) ECCV 2016. LNCS, vol. 9906, pp. 391–407. Springer, Cham (2016). https://doi.org/10.1007/978-3-319-46475-6_25

16. Kim, J., Kwon Lee, J., Mu Lee, K.: Accurate image super-resolution using very deep convolutional networks. In: Proceedings of the IEEE Conference on Computer Vision and Pattern Recognition, pp. 1646–1654 (2016)

17. Tai, Y., Yang, J., Liu, X.: Image super-resolution via deep recursive residual network. In: Proceedings of the IEEE Conference on Computer Vision and Pattern Recognition, pp. 3147–3155 (2017)

18. Huang, G., Liu, Z., Van Der Maaten, L., Weinberger, K.Q.: Densely connected convolutional networks. In: Proceedings of the IEEE Conference on Computer Vision and Pattern Recognition, pp. 4700–4708 (2017)

19. Tong, T., Li, G., Liu, X., Gao, Q.: Image super-resolution using dense skip connections. In: Proceedings of the IEEE International Conference on Computer Vision, pp. 4799–4807 (2017)

20. Lim, B., Son, S., Kim, H., Nah, S., Mu Lee, K.: Enhanced deep residual networks for single image super-resolution. In: Proceedings of the IEEE Conference on Computer Vision and Pattern Recognition Workshops, pp. 136–144 (2017)

21. He, K., Zhang, X., Ren, S., Sun, J.: Deep residual learning for image recognition. In: Proceedings of the IEEE Conference on Computer Vision and Pattern Recognition, pp. 770–778 (2016)

22. Hu, J., Shen, L., Sun, G.: Squeeze-and-excitation networks. In: Proceedings of the IEEE Conference on Computer Vision and Pattern Recognition, pp. 7132–7141 (2018)

23. Shi, W., et al.: Real-time single image and video super-resolution using an efficient sub-pixel convolutional neural network. In: Proceedings of the IEEE Conference on Computer Vision and Pattern Recognition, pp. 1874–1883 (2016)

24. Guo, Y., Cui, Z., Yang, Z., Xi, W., Madani, S.: Non-local DWI image super-resolution with joint information based on GPU implementation. Comput. Mater. Continua 61(3), 1205–1215 (2019)

25. Pan, L., Qin, J., Chen, H., Xiang, X., Li, C., Chen, R.: Image augmentation-based food recognition with convolutional neural networks. Comput. Mater. Continua 59(1), 297–313 (2019)

26. Zou, J., Li, Z., Guo, Z., Hong, D.: Super-resolution reconstruction of images based on microarray camera. Comput. Mater. Continua 60(1), 163–177 (2019)

GF-2 Image Blue Roof Building Extraction Method Based on Object-Oriented Classification Technology

Dezheng Zhang[1,2], Xinyu Yin[1,2], Yonghong Xie[1,2], Zheyu He[1,2], and Li Wang[3(✉)]

[1] School of Computer and Communication Engineering,
University of Science and Technology Beijing, Beijing 100083, China
[2] Beijing Key Laboratory of Knowledge Engineering for Materials Science, Beijing 100083, China
[3] School of Automation and Electrical Engineering,
University of Science and Technology Beijing, Beijing 100083, China
wl3927@126.com

Abstract. Remote sensing image classification method is the focus of current academic field. Most studies use complex machine learning and deep learning methods to extract ground object, but lack simple and effective methods to extract ground object with distinctive features. In this paper, using rule-based object-oriented classification technology, through remote sensing image preprocessing, multi-scale segmentation, extraction rule formulation and other steps, using object-oriented classification method, taking Jinfeng District, Xixia District and Xingqing District of Yinchuan City as an example, The blue roof buildings in the range were extracted, and the results showed that the method can effectively extract the target features.

Keywords: Object-oriented · Multi-scale segmentation · Image preprocessing · Rules · Ground object extraction

1 Introduction

Since the 1960s, remote sensing technology has continued to develop. Because remote sensing technology can detect and identify various scenes on the ground, it has the characteristics of fast acquisition speed and large acquisition. Therefore, remote sensing technology is widely used in many fields such as resource survey and map surveying. At the same time, remote sensing technology has also attracted widespread attention in the academic community. At present, remote sensing image classification is the focus of academic research. There are mainly remote sensing image classification methods based on machine learning and deep learning. However, these methods often need to select sample sets and training models, and the process is more complicated. So is there a simple extraction method for objects with distinctive features? In view of this problem, this paper takes the blue roof buildings in Jinfeng District, Xixia District and Xingqing District of Yinchuan City as the research object, and draws on the ideas of

© Springer Nature Singapore Pte Ltd. 2020
X. Sun et al. (Eds.): ICAIS 2020, CCIS 1252, pp. 115–127, 2020.
https://doi.org/10.1007/978-981-15-8083-3_11

object-oriented remote sensing image classification to formulate specific rules, in order to explore a simple and effective extraction method.

Researchers have successively carried out research on remote sensing image classification, and applied object-oriented remote sensing image classification methods to forest areas [1], urban water bodies [2], mining areas [3, 4], urban green spaces [5] and other areas, and achieved good results. Some studies have shown that object-oriented remote sensing image classification technology can fuse spectral features, shape features, texture features, etc., and can solve the problem of homologous and homoplasmic foreign objects in the classification process to a certain extent [6], and it can also have a better classification ability in the area with complex land use [7]. Moreover, the object-oriented classification method can improve the accuracy by 3%–10% compared with the pixel-based classification method [8]. The most important step in the object-oriented classification method is image segmentation [9]. Image segmentation under the optimal segmentation scale can avoid the phenomenon of "under-segmentation" and "over-segmentation", which can effectively improve the accuracy of remote sensing image classification [10]. The optimal segmentation scale is affected by regional topography, geomorphology and other factors [11]. It is necessary to formulate corresponding optimal segmentation scales according to different research areas and objects. The researchers used the trial and error method [12, 13], the local variance method [14, 15], and the correlation index construction function [16] to determine the optimal segmentation scale, and achieved good results.

2 Research Area Overview

This paper takes the three districts of Xingqing District, Xixia District and Jinfeng District of Yinchuan City in Ningxia Hui Autonomous Region as the research area. Yinchuan City is the capital of Ningxia Hui Autonomous Region and an important central city in the Northwest. Yinchuan has an area of 9025.38 km^2 and a built-up area of 170 km^2. It has jurisdiction over Xingqing District, Jinfeng District, Xixia District, Yongning County, Helan County and Lingwu City. At the end of 2018, the total population of the city was 2,250,600, radiating more than 21 million people in 13 prefecture-level cities in the neighboring areas of Ningxia Hui Autonomous Region, Inner Mongolia, Shaanxi and Gansu. It has won the honors of national civilized city, national historical and cultural city, national ecological garden city, national happy city, China tourism and leisure demonstration city, international wetland city, and China's leading smart city. Yinchuan has a unique geographical location, with ditches and idyllic landscapes. It has more than 200 wetland lakes with an area of more than 530 km^2. Yinchuan has an advantageous economic location and is also an important energy and chemical base in China, a new industrialized production demonstration base, an important commodity grain production base in the country, and a service industry initiative and reform pilot city. Yinchuan adheres to the urban development concept of "green, high-end, harmonious and livable" and vigorously develops relevant industries.

Yinchuan City contains many ecological protection areas, permanent basic farmland and nature reserves. At the same time, Yinchuan Municipal Government also regards the protection of ecological environment and sustainable development as the starting point

Fig. 1. Overview of the study area

for implementing policies and regulations. Xingqing District, Jinfeng District and Xixia District of Yinchuan City are three representative areas, and are also the experimental areas of Ningxia Remote Sensing Survey and other departments. These areas include a variety of city types and land use types, with good representation (Fig. 1).

The research data used in this paper is the 2015 GF-2 remote sensing image in Jinfeng District, Xingqing District and Xixia District of Yinchuan City. The data source is Ningxia Remote Sensing Survey. In 2015, the GF-2 remote sensing image contained three bands of red, green and blue, and the image resolution was 1 m.

3   Object-Oriented Classification Technology Based on Multi-scale Segmentation

3.1   Multi-scale Segmentation Technique

Multi-scale segmentation is a top-down segmentation method that divides the image into several parts to ensure that the edge of the segmented object is accurate and the internal heterogeneity is low, corresponding to the shape of the feature in the real world [17]. Each feature has a corresponding optimal segmentation scale. The segmentation and extraction of the feature at the optimal segmentation scale can ensure that the segmentation object is as close as possible to the real object shape, and the shape feature of the segmented object can better represent the shape feature of the real object. Subsequent analysis using the object obtained at the optimal segmentation scale can give better results. Multi-scale segmentation has a good effect in the face of complex remote sensing images.

In the multi-scale segmentation process, the most important is to determine the optimal segmentation parameters, including scale parameters, band weights, color parameters, and shape parameters. The scale parameter defines the maximum standard deviation of the uniformity criterion of the weighted influence layer of the image object result [18]. The larger the scale parameter value, the larger the image result obtained by the segmentation. The band weight defines the weight of the different bands of the remote sensing image during the segmentation process. If the feature to be extracted has a unique value in a certain band, the weight of this band can be increased to optimize the extraction result. The color parameter defines the proportion of spectral features in the segmentation process. Shape parameters, including smoothness and compactness, define the texture consistency of the image object's results. Smoothness uses shape criteria, considers smooth edges, and optimizes the results of image objects; compactness uses shape criteria to consider overall compactness and optimize image object results (Fig. 2).

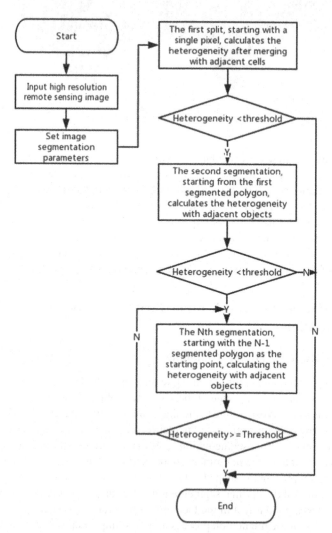

Fig. 2. Multi-scale segmentation flow chart

3.2   Object-Oriented Remote Sensing Image Classification Technology

Remote sensing image classification methods are various, and can be divided into pixel-oriented classification methods and object-oriented classification methods according to different analysis objects. According to different analysis methods, it can be divided into image classification methods based on machine learning and deep learning, and rule-based image classification methods. The pixel-based classification method uses pixels as the object of analysis. According to the classification rules learned from the training set, the model judges and classifies each pixel one by one in the image, and the final result is composed of one pixel. There is no boundary information for the object. If you want to get the boundary information of the object, you need to add extra steps to re-aggregate the pixels into objects [19]. The object-oriented classification method is based on the image segmentation as the basic unit of analysis. According to the classification rules, the model judges and classifies each object object in the image one by one, and the final result is composed of one object. The boundary information of the object is relatively complete.

At present, the classification effect of pixel-based remote sensing image classification technology is better, which is the classification method of machine learning and deep learning methods. But both machine learning and deep learning require the selection of a sample area to create a training set. At the same time, the selection of the sample area also has certain requirements. If the sample area is not properly selected, the final classification effect of the model will not be good. The object-oriented remote sensing image classification method can utilize the spectral features and shape features of the object, and if the feature differentiation between the models is large, no complicated model is needed, and different categories can be distinguished only by setting corresponding thresholds. The process of classification is easier.

The object-oriented remote sensing image classification process is divided into three steps: Firstly, the image segmentation technology is used to segment the remote sensing image to obtain the object. Then add feature attributes such as spectral features and shape features to the object. Finally, according to the characteristics of different land types, different feature attributes are used to distinguish, and corresponding classification rules are formulated to complete the feature extraction.

4   Blue Roof Building Extraction Based on Object-Oriented Classification Technology

4.1   Remote Sensing Image Preprocessing

Since satellites are affected by various aspects during the shooting process, such as atmospheric influences and light effects, there are inevitably some problems in the original images generated by remote sensing satellites. This causes problems such as noise and geometric distortion in the resulting remote sensing image. These problems in the original remote sensing image will affect the quality of the image. If the research is carried out on the problematic image, the final result is likely to be unavailable due to excessive error. Therefore, preprocessing of the original remote sensing image is necessary. Commonly used remote sensing image preprocessing methods include geometric correction (geographic positioning, geometric fine correction, image registration, orthorectification, etc.), atmospheric correction, image fusion, image mosaic, image cropping and other links (Fig. 3).

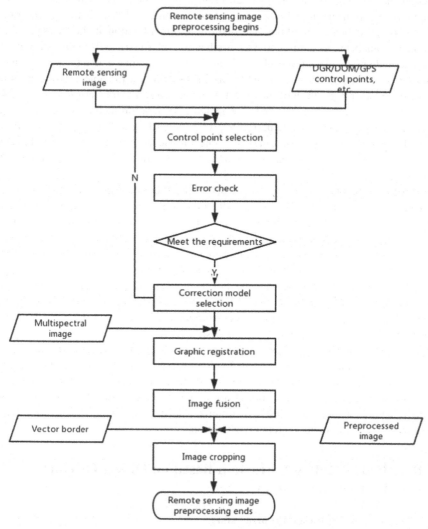

Fig. 3. General procedure for remote sensing image preprocessing

Geometric Precision Correction and Image Registration

Image geometry correction includes geocoding, georeferencing, and partial image registration. The general steps include the selection of GCP (ground control points), the establishment of geometric correction models, and image resampling.

Ground control point selection is the most important step in geometric correction. The topographic map can be used as a reference for control selection, or it can be obtained by field GPS measurements, or obtained from corrected images. The selected control points have the following characteristics:

1) The ground control points have obvious and clear points on the image, such as road intersections and river intersections.
2) The ground objects on the ground control points do not change with time.

Requirements for the number of control points. The auxiliary data provided by the satellite can establish a rigorous physical model, which requires only 9 control points. For a rational polynomial model, generally no less than 30 control points are required for each scene, and points are appropriately added in difficult areas; the geometric polynomial model will be determined according to the terrain. It requires more control points than the above models. Usually, each scene requires 30–50 or so, especially for mountain areas.

After the ground control point is determined, a reasonable coordinate transformation function (i.e., correction model) is selected by using the pixel coordinates (x, y) on the image and its reference geographic coordinates (X, Y), and the transformation function is derived. Recalculate the control points to get (X', Y'), use (X, Y) and (X', Y') to calculate the error of the control point, i.e. RMS, if the RMS is too large, you need to re-adjust the control point. Repeat this process to get a more accurate transformation function and apply to the entire image.

The relocated cells are unevenly distributed in the original image. Therefore, according to the position of each pixel on the output image in the input image, the original image is resampled according to a certain rule, and the interpolation of the luminance value is performed to establish a new image matrix. Commonly used interpolation methods are nearest neighbor method, bilinear interpolation method, and cubic convolution interpolation method. The nearest neighbor method helps maintain the gray level in the original image, but it is more damaging to the geometry in the image. Although the latter two methods approximate the pixel values, they also largely retain the original geometric structure of the image, such as road network, water system, and feature boundary.

Image Fusion and Image Mosaic Cutting

Image fusion is an image processing technique that resamples low-resolution multi-spectral images and high-resolution single-band images to generate a high-resolution multi-spectral image remote sensing image, so that the processed image has high spatial resolution. The rate has multi-spectral characteristics.

When the remotely sensed image obtained by a single shot cannot cover the target area, or part of the image information is missing due to the occlusion of the cloud layer, the image needs to be cropped and inlaid, and splicing remote sensing images from multiple periods, and finally, the remote sensing image with the information that can cover the entire target area without the occlusion of the cloud layer is obtained.

4.2 Multi-scale Segmentation

This paper uses the multi-scale segmentation module provided by eCognition, a remote sensing image analysis and processing software, to perform multi-scale segmentation operations on the study area. In the multi-scale segmentation process, the most important is to determine the optimal segmentation scale, including scale parameters, band weights, color parameters, and shape parameters. By using the optimal segmentation scale for segmentation, a segmentation object with a higher degree of coincidence with the real object can be obtained, so that the extraction effect on the target feature is improved.

Determining the Optimal Segmentation Scale

In this paper, the mean variance method is used to determine the optimal segmentation scale. The optimal segmentation scale can make the heterogeneity between objects of the same category as small as possible, and the heterogeneity between different classes of objects is as large as possible. When the number of mixed objects in the image increases, the spectral heterogeneity between different objects and adjacent objects decreases, and the mean variance of all objects in the image becomes smaller; when the mixed objects in the image increase, between different objects and adjacent objects spectral heterogeneity increases and the mean variance of all objects in the image increases. Therefore, the optimal segmentation scale may appear at the peak of the mean variance.

In order to select a better segmentation scale, this paper sets the band weight used in the segmentation process to 1:1:1, the color parameter to 0.2, and the scale parameter to 0.8. The tightness and smoothness are both set to 0.5. The segmentation scale is set to 10 to 170, and image segmentation is performed every 5 using the current segmentation scale. And the segmentation result is exported to EXCEL, and the mean variance of all objects in the study area is calculated. The line graph is used to describe the trend of the mean variance of objects at different segmentation scales. The calculation results of the mean variance corresponding to different segmentation scales are shown in Fig. 4. In the figure, the abscissa is a different segmentation scale, and the ordinate is the calculated value of the mean variance of all the segmentation objects at the current segmentation scale.

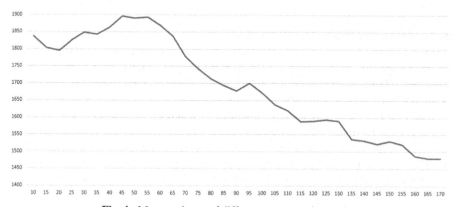

Fig. 4. Mean variance of different segmentation scales

It can be seen from the mean variance line graph corresponding to different segmentation scales that the preferred segmentation scale for blue roof buildings is 10, 30, 45, 55, 95, 125, 150.

Determine the Best Segmentation Scale and Segment the Image

In this paper, the optimal segmentation scale of blue roof buildings is selected from the optimal segmentation scales by artificial visual comparison.

The study area is segmented using the determined superior segmentation scale. Through the manual visual interpretation method, the segmentation results of the study area are compared and observed, and the number of map spots, the shape of the spot and the boundary of the different segmentation scales are compared with the real blue roof buildings. The segmentation scale with complete segmentation and moderate number of segmentation objects is selected as the optimal segmentation scale for the blue roof building category. After manual visual comparison, this paper finally chose 55 as the best segmentation scale for blue roof buildings. The band weight is set to 1:1:1, the color parameter is set to 0.6, and the scale parameter is set to 0.4. The tightness and smoothness are both set to 0.5.

The multi-scale segmentation of the study area is performed using the optimal segmentation parameters to obtain multiple segmentation objects. The multi-scale segmentation results are shown in the Fig. 5.

Fig. 5. Multi-scale segmentation results

4.3   Blue Roof Building Extraction Based on Object-Oriented Method

Add Features to the Segmented Object

After obtaining different object objects, it is necessary to distinguish the target land class from other land classes according to the spectral features, shape features, and the like of the object. By observing the characteristics of the blue, green and red bands of the features, it is found that the blue roof buildings have higher values in the blue band, lower values in the red band, and significant differences between the red and blue bands. Therefore, the difference in red and blue band values can be used to distinguish blue roof buildings. At the same time, it is found that some building shadows also have similar spectral features. The shaded areas have low brightness, and the shape is usually elongated and has a large aspect ratio. Therefore, the shadow area can be removed by using the two characteristics of brightness and aspect ratio, and the blue roof building object is retained. Therefore, in order to highlight the difference between the two bands of red and blue, this paper constructs the red-blue band difference ratio parameter (blue_ratio), which is calculated as shown in formula (1).

$$blue\_ratio = (B - R)/R \tag{1}$$

In the formula

B – Split object blue band mean;
R – Split object red band mean.

This article also adds two features, Brightness and Aspect Ratio (L_W), to remove shadow areas from the extraction results. The brightness parameter is calculated as shown in formula (2), and the aspect ratio parameter is calculated as shown in formula (3).

$$Brightness = (B + R + G)/3 \tag{2}$$

In the formula

B – Split object blue band mean;
R – Split object red band mean;
G – Split object green band mean.

$$L\_W = L/W \tag{3}$$

In the formula

L – The length of the smallest circumscribed rectangle of the split object;
W – Split the width of the smallest bounding rectangle of the object.

Develop Blue Roof Building Extraction Rules

According to the difference of the blue roof building in the red-blue band difference ratio parameter and other land types, this paper sets the extraction rule of blue_ratio > 0.395. At the same time, according to the difference of the shadow area in the brightness and aspect ratio characteristics and the blue roof building, this paper sets two extraction rules of Brightness > 90 and L_W > 10. With the three extraction rules set, the blue

Fig. 6. Original remote sensing image of the study area (Color figure online)

Fig. 7. Extraction results of blue roof buildings in the study area (Color figure online)

roof building object can be better extracted from the segmentation result. The extraction results are shown in the Figs. 6 and 7.

5 Conclusion

This paper studies the simple extraction method of blue roof buildings with distinctive features in spectrum and shape. This paper takes the three districts of Jinfeng District, Xixia District and Xingqing District of Yinchuan City as the research area, and takes the blue roof architecture within the three districts as the research object. According to the spectral characteristics and shape characteristics of blue roof buildings, the rules of extraction were established, and the blue roof buildings were extracted by object-oriented remote sensing image classification technology. Compared with other remote sensing image classification methods, the object-oriented remote sensing image classification method used in this paper can preserve the boundary shape features of the object objects as much as possible. According to the spectral shape characteristics of the object, the corresponding classification rules are formulated in the classification process. It is not necessary to make a sample set and model training, and the blue roof building can be effectively extracted by simple classification rules. When the extraction target has distinctive features such as spectrum and shape, the target can be effectively extracted according to the feature, without complicated operations such as selection of the model and training of the model. The related research in this paper provides a new solution for extracting feature objects with distinctive features from GF-2 remote sensing image.

Acknowledgments. This work was supported by: Ningxia Hui Autonomous Region Key R&D Plan Projects: Research and Demonstration Application of Key Technologies of Spatial Planning Intelligent Monitoring Based on High Score Remote Sensing (Item Number: 2018YBZD1629).

References

1. Liping, C., Yujun, S.: Classification and comparison of remote sensing imagery in object-oriented forest areas based on different decision trees. Chin. J. Appl. Ecol. **29**(12), 3995–4003 (2018)
2. Junhai, W., Renzong, Z., Ying, C., Peng, L.: Water extraction of object-oriented city based on high score 2. Geospatial Inf. **16**(09), 34–37 + 40 + 10 (2018)
3. Linlin, C., Xuemei, D., Jiaqi, Z., Ye, Z.: Classification of wetlands in coal mining subsidence area based on object-oriented GF-1 remote sensing image. Trans. Chin. Soc. Agric. Eng. **34**(09), 240–247 (2018)
4. Hang, C., Shaogang, L.: Analysis of artificial vegetation extraction and reconstruction based on object-oriented mining area. J. Arid Land Res. Environ. **32**(07), 98–103 (2018)
5. Mengya, L., Xiaoping, Z., Xiaofeng, J.: Using object-oriented high resolution remote sensing data to extract urban green space. Beijing Surv. Mapp. **33**(02), 196–200 (2019)
6. Sen, Z., Jianfei, C.: Discussion on decision tree method of object-oriented classification–taking landsat-8OLI as an example. Sci. Surv. Mapp. **41**(06), 117–121 + 125 (2016)
7. Qian, C., Jin-feng, C.: Study on the method of extracting land cover information based on coastal land south bank of Hangzhou Bay based on high score No.1. J. Nat. Res. **30**(02), 350–360 (2015)

8. Fu, B., et al.: Comparison of object-based and pixel-based Random Forest algorithm for wetland vegetation mapping using high spatial resolution GF-1 and SAR data. Ecol. Indic. **73**, 105–117 (2017)
9. Hay, G.J., Castilla, G.: Geographic Object-Based Image Analysis: A New Name for a New Discipline, pp. 75–90. Springer-Verlag, Berlin Heidelberg (2008)
10. Hua, Z., Gaigai, Z.: Objective-oriented multi-scale segmentation of GF-1 remote sensing image. J. Gansu Agric. Univ. **53**(04), 116–123 (2018)
11. Hengkai, L., Jiao, W., Xiuli, W.: Classification of object-oriented land use in Dongjiang River Basin based on GF-1 image. Trans. Chin. Soc. Agric. Eng. **34**(10), 245–252 (2018)
12. Qin, L., Xi-zhang, G., Tao, Z., Wei, L., Jian-ming, G.: Experimental analysis of multi-level remote sensing object classification based on optimal segmentation scale. J. Geo-Inf. Sci. **13**(03), 409–417 (2011)
13. Meng, Y., Shuwen, Y., Wanling, Y., Shan, Z.: Shadow multiscale segmentation method for integrated feature components. Remote Sens. Inf. **32**(01), 109–114 (2017)
14. Woodcock, C.E., Strahler, A.H.: The factor of scale in remote sensing. Remote Sens. Environ. **21**, 311–332 (1987)
15. Yan, T., Yubo, X., Wenzhong, S., Furen, P., Jian, L.: Multi-resolution image segmentation based on local variance. Syst. Eng. Electron. **12**, 1922–1926 (2006)
16. Min, H., Wen-jun, Z., Wei-hong, W.: Object-oriented optimal segmentation scale calculation model. J. Geodesy Geodyn. **29**(01), 106–109 (2009)
17. Wu, H., Liu, Q., Liu, X.: A review on deep learning approaches to image classification and object segmentation. Comput. Mater. Continua **60**(2), 575–597 (2019)
18. Wu, Q., Li, Y., Lin, Y., Zhou, R.: Weighted sparse image classification based on low rank representation. Comput. Mater. Continua **56**(1), 91–105 (2018)
19. He, Q., et al.: A weighted threshold secret sharing scheme for remote sensing images based on chinese remainder theorem. Comput. Mater. Continua **58**(2), 349–361 (2019)

Optimization and Parallelization of the Cosmological N-Body Simulation on Many-Core Processor

GuiYing Zhang[1], Hao Yang[1,2(✉)], and ZhiNi Li[1]

[1] School of Computer Science, Chengdu University of Information Technology, Chengdu, China
vhaoyang@gmail.com
[2] School of Information and Software Engineering, University of Electronic Science and Technology of China, Chengdu, China

Abstract. N-body numerical simulation can solve the formation and evolution of large-scale structure in space, and then help to study the essence of the most essential problems, including the distribution of matter in the universe, the formation of galaxies, dark matter and dark energy, etc. [1]. Thus, the transplantation and application of the N-body simulation software on the Sunway TaihuLight platform are of great significance. In order to enhance the entire performance of the N-body simulation software photoNs 2.0, a variety of methods were utilized to achieve it, such as using Athread thread library to exploit the potential capability of the many-core node of sw26010 system, tuning compile options, rewriting the transcendental function with lookup table (LUT) and leveraging the vectorization optimization instruction provided by Sunway TaihuLight. In addition, we extended the application to run with a mode of host and slave working simultaneously. A detailed performance evaluation was performed and the results showed that the proposed parallelization method achieve good accelerated effect of 13x when evaluating up to 512 MPI processes on Sunway TaihuLight, and correspondingly the calculation of P2P kernel of fast multipole method was tremendously improved by the strategies mentioned in this paper.

Keywords: Fast Multipole Method · Particle mesh method · N-body simulations · Sunway TaihuLight · Many-core computing · Heterogeneous computing

1 Introduction

N-body problem is one of the basic problems of celestial mechanics and general mechanics, it determined the motion of N particles which interact with a force, such as gravitation or electrostatics [19]. Astrophysical N-body simulations played a very significant role in the study of nonlinear structure formation in the universe. Such simulations are usually called as cosmological N-body simulations, which simulate each single particle's move according to the interaction of all the other particles in the simulative system [2].

© Springer Nature Singapore Pte Ltd. 2020
X. Sun et al. (Eds.): ICAIS 2020, CCIS 1252, pp. 128–140, 2020.
https://doi.org/10.1007/978-981-15-8083-3_12

The most straightforward algorithm of N-body simulation is direct summation, which calculate the acceleration of a particle according to the forces given by the rest of the particles in the system. Assuming that a simulative system contains N particles, while N is large $(N > 10^6)$, this method appears to bring unaffordable $O(N^2)$ computations [1]. It boils down to that faster, better algorithms with some approximation are needed to alleviate the computation. One of the most famous algorithms is the Fast Multipole Method (FMM), which is derived from tree code and widely used in cosmological N-body simulations [22]. The basic idea of this method is organizing all the particles in the simulative system into a hierarchical tree structure. Other algorithms like particle mesh (PM) method is also widely used, which aim at reduce memory usage and improve the computational efficiency [3]. On the one hand, benefiting from the fast Fourier transform (FFT) libraries, such as FFTW3, the speed is quite high, on the other hand, the load-balancing problem is well-addressed because the distribution of particle is rather homogeneous. Some famous N-body simulation software like GADGET, Barnes-Hut simulation, ExaFMM, Puma-EM and some analogues like them are developed base on the FMM or PM algorithm. The photoNs 2.0 combined those two methods, it is, the PM algorithm handle the long-range gravitation, while the FMM algorithm deal with the short-range gravitation.

During the past decade, with the rapid development of supercomputers, on the one hand, a variety of fields are apply these supercomputer to achieve their purpose more effectively [23–26], one the other hand, methodologies and techniques to exploit higher performance of numerical simulations on state-of-the-art supercomputers is extraordinary needed [4]. Some kernel like N-body simulation is of great significance to port onto those supercomputers. This is especially true for the Sunway TaihuLight supercomputer, which was released on June, 2016 as the first supercomputer with over 100 PFLOPS peak performance. It uses the many-core SW26010 processor with a relatively high aggregated performance and a relatively low memory bandwidth [5]. Taking account of the fact that photoNs is a compute-intensive program, there existing a great potential to porting the program on the Sunway TaihuLight and to optimize it.

This paper introduces the methods to port photoNs 2.0 onto Sunway TaihuLight,and illustrate the prime algorithms and several techniques we used, including the load balance of computation task, rewrite of the transcendental function, the decoupling between communication and computation, the parallelization of PM algorithm and FMM algorithm, and the vectorization of transcendental function. Following those methods, the result of performance enhancement of the many-core acceleration is also provided.

2 Platform Overview and Problem Description

2.1 Platform Overview

The Sunway TaihuLight is designed as a supercomputer with heterogeneous architecture base on SW26010 processor [6], which comprise of connected 40960 nodes, as show in Fig. 1, each node has one SW26010 processor. The processor consists of four "core groups" (CGs), one CG including a management processing element (MPE) and a computing processing element (CPE) cluster with 64 CPEs organized as an 8 by 8 mesh network. Both the MPE and CPEs are 64-bit RISC processors and have almost the

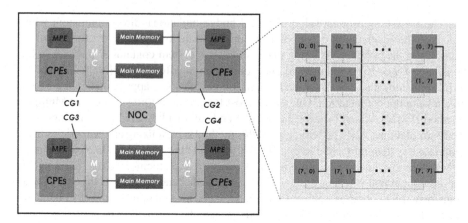

Fig. 1. The architecture of SW26010 processor

same architecture [7]. Both MPE and CPEs have instruction caches. MPE has L1 and L2 data caches, while each CPE only has local data memory (LDM, 64 KB) and no cache memory [7]. Each CPE can still perform load/store operations to the main memory, and they can also issue DMA transfers between LDM and the main memory [7]. The need for explicit control of data movement between LDM and main memory makes the porting of the existing codes rather complicated. On the other hand, the possibility of explicit control makes performance tuning relatively straightforward [7].

Due to the fact that the operation system and user program both run in the MPE, we need use the OpenACC or Athread to utilize the CPEs, the former one is easily used by add compile directive in the code, while the latter one must be used elaboratively to design a new program or port an existed program onto the Sunway TaihuLight.

Both of MPE and CPEs are run with a clock speed of 1.45 GHz. Benefitting from the 256-bit wide vector registers provided by SW26010, the MPE and CPEs can perform four double-precise multiply-and-add operations simultaneously in one clock cycle. It means that the theoretical peak performance of one processor is 3.016 TFlops, thus, that of the entire machine with 40960 nodes is 123.5 PFlops. The bandwidth of 8 GB DDR3 memory of each CG only reached 34 GB/s, it is relatively lower than the computation of processors. Thus, it is crucial to improve the ratio of computation to memory access [7].

2.2 Problem Description

The PM algorithm and FMM algorithm constitute the main body of photoNs. Figure 2 portray the main idea of those two methods. In this section, we will introduce those two algorithms.

The main idea of PM algorithm is to create a grid on the box, each grid cell has a grid point, solve the potential at the grid point, and then calculate the potential gradient to get the force at each grid cell [8]. For far field, the principle steps of the mesh calculation are as follows:

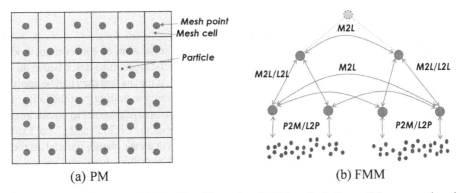

Fig. 2. PM method and FMM algorithm illustration. In PM method, the particles are portioned to each single box. And in FMM algorithm, particles are organized into the leaves of a tree.

1. Assign "mass" to the mesh ("particle mass" becomes "grid density"),
2. Solve the field potential equation (e.g. Poisson's) on the mesh,
3. Calculate the force field from the mesh-defined potential,
4. Interpolate the force on the grid to find forces on the particles.
5. Now like the PP: integrate the forces to get particle positions and velocities.
6. Update the time counter.

For step 2, the PM method solves the Poisson equation:

$$\nabla^2(\varphi) = \pi G \rho$$

where G is Newton's constant and ρ is the density (number of particles at the mesh points). the gravitational potential φ is trivial to solve by using the FFT technique [8, 9]. The transform is computed by multiplication with a suitable Green's function for the Poisson equation which contains a spatially-varying part of the mass density field. Periodic boundary conditions are usually used to simulate an "infinite universe" [8–11, 18, 21].

The Fast Multipole Method (FMM) is a tree code method that uses two representations of the potential field, the far field (multipole) and local expansions [14, 15, 20].

This FMM calculate the potential filed extremely fast. From basic physics that the force is just the negative of the gradient of the potential, it indicates that the force is a vector while the potential φ (x, y, z) is a scalar. It's computationally easier to deal with the potential than that of the force [12–16].

In this method, the particles are organized into a k-dimensional (k-d) tree, whose leaves are package of particles while each one of nodes store two multipoles M and L. The leaf accepting the effect from other leaves is called target leaf, and the leaf applying impact on other leaves is refer to as source leaf. Via this structure, the calculation of forces among those particles are convert into the interaction of those multipoles. There are six operators in FMM: particle to multiple (P2M), multipole to multipole (M2M), multipole to local (M2L), local to local (L2L), local to particle (L2P) and particle to particle (P2P). M2L and P2P are hotspots of computation among these operators.

3 Parallel Algorithms

In order to balance the performance and generality, the separation of concerns method was used to implement the following algorithms. Because the algorithms described in this section are not involving much architecture characteristic, it means that they can be apply to next generation and other similar platform. The algorithms including port the hotspot function to CPEs, calculate the number of tasks before perform p2p kernel to obtain load balance, and rewrite the exponential function to avoid global store (GST) and global load (GLD), Uncouple the communication and computation via a task queue, parallelize the PM and FMM algorithm by making MPE and CPEs work simultaneously, and vectorize the exponential function by means of the vector registers provide by SW26010.

3.1 Porting the P2P on CPEs

Sunway TaihuLight is typical accelerator-rich system, the overwhelming part of computing power of it is gained by the CPEs. Thus, CPEs' utilization is key point of attain good performance. Thus, it's essential to take advantage of the CPEs to handle the heavy computation task of p2p. The origin version of p2p adopt a straightforward pattern which firstly traverse the k-d tree, and then judge if two leaves are interact with each other, if so, finally apply p2p operation on them. This is fine for MPE, but taking account for CPEs, the situation might become much tougher, if CPEs want to take the same pattern of MPE, the traversal of k-d tree has to elaborately redesign to accommodate to the CPEs' characteristic, which means it will greatly increase the complexity of programming. the P2P kernel is the computation between two leaves, the maximal particles in a leaf is 16, thus, another solution seems is assign the computation between two leaves to 64 CPEs. However, single P2P operation might not enough to distribute to 64 CPEs, meanwhile the overhead of thread scheduling is too expensive. Instead of the two former methods, as the pseudocode show in Algorithm.1, we employ a strategy, which firstly traverse the tree to collect the information required by all p2p computation, then assign the computational task to CPEs, finally complete these tasks and store the results. The data structure is show in Fig. 3, the ileaf denote target leaf while the jleaf denote source leaf.

Algorithm 1 . TRAVERSE P2P BETWEEN LEAVES

Input: A k-dimensional tree T ; a empty lists $(L_1, L_2, L_3, ..., L_n)$
Output: Lists $(L_1, L_2, L_3, ..., L_n)$ of interaction leaves of each leaf

```
 1: FOR MPE:
 2: initialize: organize particles to k-dimensional tree T
 3: for all ileaf in T  do
 4:     Initialize the L_i
 5:     for all jleaf in T  do
 6:         if jleaf interact with ileaf then
 7:             add jleaf to L_i
 8:             i++
 9:         end if
10:     end for
11: end for
12:
13: FOR CPEs:
14: initialize: get corresponding data of target leaf from MPE by the id of CPEs
15: for ileaf from ¯rst_leaf to last_leaf  do
16:     get the L_i according to ileaf
17:     for all jleaf in T  do
18:         p2p(ileaf,jleaf)
19:     end for
20: end for
```

There is a phenomenon that first we port the p2p to CPEs, the performance was greatly decreased. By analysis the assembly code, we found too many GLD/GST instructions was generated, so the DMA technique was used to avoid the long latency of memory access between MPE and CPEs. Specifically, the particles' information store in memory on MPE is a kind of array of structure (AOS), instead access directly, we use the MPE to make the AOS to structure of array, in other word, putting particles' information, such as position, velocity, and so on, into several array store in MPE and then it can be

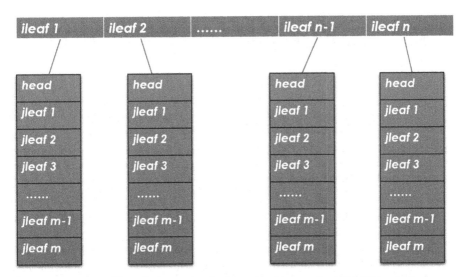

Fig. 3. The pattern of how the leaves in a k-dimensional tree perform the P2P operation, every target ileaf was interact with its source of jleafs

accessed expediently by CPEs via DMA. The AOS to SOA operation, which traverse all the particles, is processed on MPE, so it cost some time, but for the sake of the DMA are much faster with continuously memory access, the entire performance is improved.

By using such a strategy, the computation was centralized, so the utilization efficiency of CPEs are greatly increased.

3.2 Load Balance

Since the number of interactive leaves is not equal of each target leaf and the calculated amount is determined by both the source leaf and target leaf, so distributing the target leaves to 64 CPEs evenly can bring a load imbalance among those CPEs. Because of there is a barrier among all the them, the wall time of computation of P2P kernel on CPEs is determined by the CPE with longest time, thus, the uneven task distribution among CPEs becomes a big obstacle. We applied the following simple strategy to handle this problem.

1. Calculate the average amount of target leaves a CPE should handle.
2. Identify the lists of source leaves corresponding to the average target leaves
3. Assign these tasks to the CPEs

By doing so, as show in Fig. 4, the tasks were evenly distributed to CPEs.

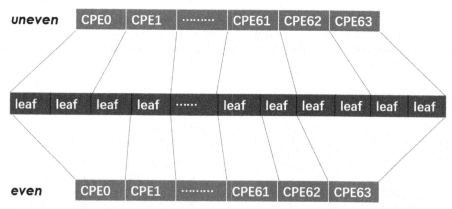

Fig. 4. Load balance of CPEs, the "leaf" is the source leaf, its interactive leaves (it's not show in the picture) is not equal. The "uneven" means the task distribution is not fair for 64 CPEs, the even means task distribution is approximately even for 64 CPEs.

Although the number of particles in a leaf is always not equal, but the difference is very small, so this algorithm works quiet well.

There also exists a method, which distribute the successive 64 leaves from first leaf to last leaf to 64 CPEs until all leaves get processed, it is feasible, but it consequently increases the GLD operations. The memory accesses of GLD operations are serialized when issued from multiple CPEs simultaneously, leading to the high latency (~5376 cycles if n = 64) and poor bandwidth [17].

3.3 Rewrite the Exponential Function

Lots of exponential function are used in the P2P operation, it cost most of the time. In the origin implement of exponential function on the Sunway TaihuLight, it takes the method of look-up table, which store results of the function in memory. Unfortunately, the local date memory (LDM) is quite small with the size of 64 KB, so the table is store at the main memory. Every time the CPE call the exponential function will lead a GLD, as mentioned in [16], the latency is extremely high comparing with the direct memory access (DMA). So, we rewrite the function as follows:

$$e^x = e^{p*ln2} = 2^p * e^q$$

For the term 2^p , we can set p as exponential of a float point number, while the e^q can be approach by polynomial P(x), the polynomial is calculate with LUT, which store in LDM. By eliminating the GLD, the performance is largely improved.

3.4 Porting the P2P Among Processors on CPEs

The inter-processors P2P operation is not the same as in-processor P2P operation illustrated above. Because the inter-processor P2P only happened when two leaves belong to different processor and close enough, one can infer that not all leaves engage in the p2p operation. So, it is not feasible to apportion the target leaves to CPEs, there is a need to change the strategy of task distribution, it is, as show in Algorithm 2, we collect the all leaf pairs that apply the P2P operation by the order they happened, and then distribute them to the CPEs. For one collection, the number of pairs might less than 64, in this case, we directly compute them on MPE. In algorithm 2, the $TREE_{rs}$ is the trees receive from other processor, the LETs are abbreviation for Local Essential Tree, which store the information of particles that may involve in inter-processor p2p operation.

Algorithm 2 . P2P_EX

Input: $TREE_{rs}$ which receive LETs , TASK[n] which store the leaves pairs

Output: None

```
 1: initialize: Set i = 0
 2: for all TREEr in TREErs do
 3:     for all ileaf in TREEr do
 4:         for all jleaf in TREEr do
 5:             if jleaf interact with ileaf then
 6:                 add (ileaf,jleaf) to TASK[i]
 7:                 i++
 8:             end if
 9:         end for
10:     end for
11:     if (i< 64) then
12:         MPE handle task[ ]
13:     else
14:         assign TASK[ ] to CPEs
15:     end if
16: end for
```

Like task assignment, the DMA access also quite different with the in-processor p2p. The in-processor p2p operation can traverse all particles to put all the information that CPEs needed to several array, while the inter-processors p2p operation is make by small amount of the particles, it indicates the traverse operation might spend more time than that of in-processor p2p operation. We also notice that two leaves involved in inter-processors p2p operation is adjacent in logical index. And combining the fact that the particles' in information are continuously stored in memory, as a trade-off, we choose to leverage DMA channel to transfer the structures to CPEs for p2p operation, which transfer lots of useless data in these structures, but it is still much faster than the SOA to AOS operation on MPE.

3.5 Uncouple the Communication and Computation

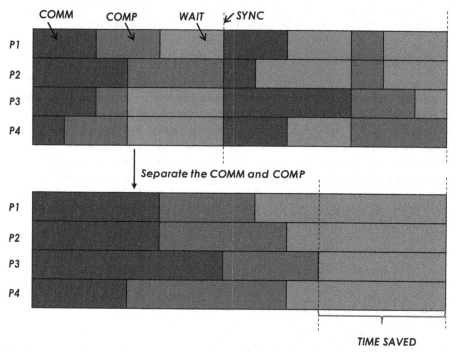

Fig. 5. The figure illustrates the behavior of send and receive LETs and inter-processor P2P kernel. P1, P2, P3, P4 represent four processors, and the "COMM" means communication, "COMP" means computation base on the data received LETs, "WAIT" means wait for synchronization, "TIME SAVED" means the time lessened after separate the communication and computation.

In the initial implement of inter-processor P2P operation, in order to apply P2P operation on the leaf belongs to other processor, the MPE must sent and receive a local essential tree (LET) to other processors, as illustrate in the upper half part of Fig. 5, the communication and computation are alternately processed, and the data dependency exists between communication and computation, the computation must resumed after receive the LETs and the communication among MPEs have a synchronization, therefore, even P1, P3 or P4 have already finish their computational job, it must wait P1 end its computation. The circumstance gets more terrible when MPI processors increased, as a result, the performance was greatly declined by waiting each other to end computation. Rather than communication and computation processing alternately, we split it individually. Specifically, all MPE firstly receive the LETs from other processors, meanwhile, use a queue data structure to store the information of computation task generate by the LETs, then after the communications are finished, the computation task in the task queue can be handled.

3.6   Parallelize the PM and FMM Algorithm

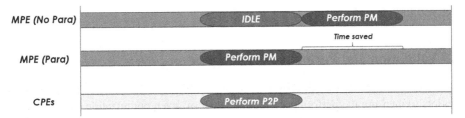

Fig. 6. MPE CPEs parallel

For the Sunway TaihuLight, the common schema of the MPE and CPEs is that MPE assign work to CPEs and wait for the CPEs finish their work. During the period of waiting the MPE wait for the CPEs finish, the MPE is do nothing but blocked in joining the thread. Given that there is no data dependence between PM and FMM algorithm, we utilize the MPE to handle PM algorithm rather than idle waiting for CPEs get the FMM done. As show in Fig. 6, the PM algorithm takes relatively little time compared with FMM, thus, the time of PM is completely hidden.

3.7   Vectorize the Exponential Function

The exponential function is still a hotspot after rewrite it, thus, we take full advantage of the vector instruction provided by SW26010 to vectorize the exponential function. But using the vectorized exponential function directly is inefficient, because of the number of particles in a leaf is less than 16, it's means that many scalar computations will be performed. Thus, we devise a collect-compute-replace strategy as show in Algorithm 3 to efficiently exploit the vectorization component of SW26010.

```
Algorithm 3 . VECTORILIZE P2P
────────────────────────────────────────────
Input: ileaf, jleaf
Output: None
 1: initialize: Set i = 0
 2: for all particle1 in ileaf do
 3:     for all particle2 in jleaf do
 4:         collect x which x perform exp(x) to data[ ]
 5:     end for
 6: end for
 7: result[ ]= vec_exp(data[ ])
 8: for all particle1 in ileaf do
 9:     for all particle2 in jleaf do
10:         put result[ ]
11:     end for
12: end for
```

4 Validation and Performance Analysis

To evaluate the effects of the many-core acceleration, we use 4,16,128 SW26010 processors to measure the performance improvement of seven optimization versions. The number of particles of one MPI processor is 32768, thus, the total number of 8, 64, 512 MPI processors is 262144, 2097152, 16777216 respectively. The results are presented below.

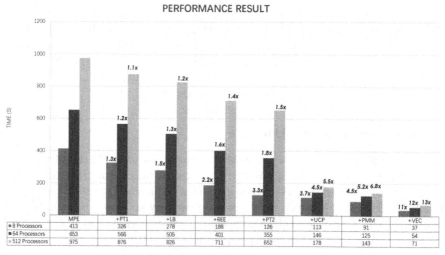

PERFORMANCE RESULT

	MPE	+PT1	+LB	+REE	+PT2	+UCP	+PMM	+VEC
■ 8 Processors	413	326	278	188	126	113	91	37
■ 64 Processors	653	566	505	401	355	146	125	54
▨ 512 Processors	975	876	826	711	652	178	143	71

Fig. 7. Performance result. MPE is the baseline, the PT1 means the porting of P2P, the LB means load imbalance, REE rewrite exponential function, PT2 means porting of remote P2P, UCP means uncouple the communication and computation, PMM means parallelize the FMM and PM. VEC means vectorize the exponential function.

By analyzing Fig. 7, a basic CPEs parallelization of P2P kernel only leads to the speedups of 1.26x, 1.2x, 1.1x of 8, 64, 512 processors respectively, after solving the load imbalance among CPEs, speedups of 1.3x, 1.2x, 1.1x of 8,64,512 processors are achieved separately. By using the CPE version of exponential function which we rewritten, the speedups ascend to 2.19x, 1.2x, 1.1x of 8, 64, 512 processors separately. A further 3.3x, 1.2x, 1.1x of 8, 64, 512 processors improvement of performance is achieved respectively results from the parallelization of remote P2P kernel on CPEs. For the method of uncoupling the communication and computation, the speedups of 8, 64, 512 processors are 3.7x, 4.5x, 6.8x respectively, which are not approximate to that of the pervious method mentioned, this is because the further quantity of MPI processors will leads more communication waiting, by utilizing uncoupling of communication and computation, the efficiency of was greatly enhanced. In addition, by taking full advantage of the MPE, we arrange the PM task to it when CPEs handle the FMM task, it brings speedups of 4.5x, 1.2x, 1.1x of 8, 64, 512 processors separately. Finally, an impressive speedup of 11.1x, 1.2x, 1.1x of 8,64,512 processors are sustained respectively by means of the 256-bit wide vector registers of SW26010.

5   Conclusion Remarks

In this paper, we have expounded the details for efficiently accelerating the processes stem from the cosmological N-body simulations on the gradually mature Sunway TaihuLight platform. By conducting the optimization from details of code to the algorithm, we gain a good performance consequently. In the future, we intend to go deeper of the N-body simulation and we hope these algorithms we proposed in this paper can be generalized to more areas.

Acknowledgments. This source code comes from the photoNs2 developed by National Astronomical Observatories of China (NAOC). we also got a lot of help of the National supercomputer center in Wuxi and the scientific researcher Wang Qiao of NAOC. This study was supported by the Scientific Research Foundation (KYTZ201718) of CUIT.

References

1. Springel, V., Yoshida, N., White, S.D.M.: GADGET: a code for collisionless and gasdynamical cosmological simulations. New Astron. **6**(2), 79–117 (2000)
2. Ishiyama, T., Nitadori, K., Makino, J.: 4.45 Pflops Astrophysical N-body simulation on K computer–The gravitational trillion-body problem. In: The SC 2012 Proceedings of the International Conference on High Performance Computing, Networking, Storage and Analysis, 2012. ACM, New York (2012)
3. Yu, H.R., Pen, U.L., Wang, X.: CUBE: an information-optimized parallel cosmological N -body algorithm. Astrophys. J. Supp. Series **237**(2), 24 (2017)
4. Asanovic, K., et al.: A view of the parallel computing landscape. Commun. ACM **52**, 56–67 (2009)
5. Fu, H., et al.: The sunway taihulight supercomputer: system and applications. Sci. China Inf. Sci. **59**(7), 1–16, June 2016
6. Ao, Y., Yang, C., Wang, X., et al.: 26 PFLOPS stencil computations for atmospheric modeling on sunway TaihuLight. In: IEEE International Parallel & Distributed Processing Symposium (IPDPS 2017). IEEE (2017)

7. Iwasawa, M., Wang, L., Nitadori, K., et al.: Global simulation of planetary rings on sunway TaihuLight (2018)
8. Bertschinger, E., Gelb, J.M.: Cosmological N-body simulations. Comput. Phys. **5**(2), 164–179 (1991)
9. Hockney, R.W., Eastwood, J.W.: Computer Simulation Using Particles. Institute of Physics Publishing, Bristol (1988)
10. Melott, A.L.: Comment on "nonlinear gravitational clustering in cosmology". Phys. Rev. Lett. **56**, 1992 (1986)
11. Peebles, P.J.E., Melott, A.L., Holmes, M.R., Jiang, L.R.: A model for the formation of the local group. Ap. J. **345**, 108 (1989)
12. Elliott, W.D., Board Jr, J.A.: Fast fourier transform accelerated fast multipole algorithm. SIAM J. Sci. Comput. **17**(2), 398–415 (1996)
13. Greengard, L.: The numerical solution of the N-body problem. Comput. Phys. **4**(2), 142–152 (1990)
14. Greengard, L., Rokhlin, V.: A fast algorithm for particle simulations. J. Comp. Phys. **73**(2), 325–348 (1987)
15. Greengard's 1987 Yale dissertation "The Rapid Evaluation of Potential Fields in Particle Systems" won an ACM Distinguished Dissertation Award
16. McMillan, S.L.W., Aarseth, S.J.: An O(NlogN) integration scheme for collisional stellar systems. Astrophys. J. **414**, 200–212 (1993)
17. Xu, Z., Lin, J., Matsuoka, S.: Benchmarking SW26010 many-core processor. In: 2017 IEEE International Parallel and Distributed Processing Symposium Workshops (IPDPSW). IEEE (2017)
18. Klypin, A., Holtzman, J.: Particle-mesh code for cosmological simulations. Physics **145**(1), 1–13 (1997)
19. Moscardini, L., Dolag, K.: Cosmology with numerical simulations (2011)
20. Singh, J.P., Holt, C., Hennessy, J.L., et al.: A parallel adaptive fast multipole method. In: Supercomputing 1993. Proceedings. IEEE (1993)
21. Hellwing, W.A.: Short introduction to numerical methods used in cosmological N-body simulations. Introduction to Cosmology (2015)
22. Ambrosiano, J.: The fast multipole method for gridless particle simulation. Comput. Phys. Commun. **48**(1), 117–125 (1988)
23. Li, Y., et al.: A distributed ADMM approach for collaborative regression learning in edge computing. Comput. Mater. Continua **59**(2), 493–508 (2019)
24. Hsu, I.-C.: XML-based information fusion architecture based on cloud computing ecosystem. Comput. Mater. Continua **61**(3), 929–950 (2019)
25. Zhang, S., et al.: Quantum communication networks and trust management: a survey. Comput. Mater. Continua **61**(3), 1145–1174 (2019)
26. Li, S., Liu, F., Liang, J., Cai, Z., Liang, Z.: Optimization of face recognition system based on azure iot edge. Comput. Mater. Continua **61**(3), 1377–1389 (2019)

Parallel Optimization of Stencil Computation Base on Sunway TaihuLight

YunBo Tang[1], Mingdong Li[2], Zifang Chen[1], Chen Xue[1], Changming Zhao[1(✉)], and Hao Yang[1]

[1] School of Computer Science, Chengdu University of Information Technology, No 24 Block 1, Xuefu Road, Chengdu 610225, China
zcm84@cuit.edu.cn

[2] Wuhan GreeNet Information Service Co., Ltd., Room 603, CLP Information Building, No. 6 Zhonguancun South Street, Haidain District, Beijing, China

Abstract. Stencil computation is a kind of memory intensive computing core widely used in image and video processing, large-scale science and engineering calculation, which has been taken as the object of performance optimization by many scientific researchers, including parallel acceleration, communication optimization, load balance, while the memory access optimization of stencil computation needs further research [1, 2]. Based on the self-developed supercomputer "Sunlight", this paper proposes an efficient parallel optimization method for the stencil algorithm. It includes multi-level optimization accelerated by MPI + multi-core, efficient DMA transmission, mutual concealment of communication and calculation, data reuse and other parallel optimization strategies. Experiments on Sunway platform show that the strategy proposed in this paper greatly improves the efficiency of the algorithm and the performance of the algorithm.

Keywords: Sunlight · Parallel optimization · Intensive memory access · Stencil computation

1 Instruction

Stencil computation [3] is a kind of important computing core widely used from image and video processing to large-scale scientific and engineering simulation and computing fields, including image processing [4–6], structured grid computing [7], explicit and implicit PDE solver [8], Jacobi [9] and Gauss Seidel [10] methods in computational fluid dynamics. At present, Stencil codes in the real world usually need manual adjustment and optimization to provide a variety of stencil codes suitable for specific applications and platforms, which often requires a lot of engineering work. Therefore, simplifying the construction of high-performance stencil computation has become an important research topic.

There are two significant characteristics of stencil computation access: ① low computing access ratio and high request for access bandwidth; ② discontinuous memory access, which is easy to cause cache loss. Therefore, stencil computation is recognized as the core of computing intensive and memory intensive engineering applications, and the computing time and memory consumption will increase linearly with the number of array elements, so the parallel implementation and optimization of stencil code on multiple platforms has become a research hotspot. Due to the tight coupling of the calculation and the low ratio of memory access, the optimization of stencil calculation is full of challenges. Nowadays, there are many optimization methods for stencil computing, such as objective [11], timeskew [12], loop tiling [13], etc., but there are many problems, such as data block difficulty, load imbalance, complex boundary processing and so on.

In this paper, we use a variety of platform tools to analyze the performance of the algorithm in detail, and design and implement an efficient parallel optimization method:

1. Asynchronous MPI parallel communication algorithm conceals communication delay.
2. Use accelerated thread library(Athread) to reconstruct the original algorithm, load the core computing part into the whole column from the core, and realize the multi-level parallel method of MPI + multi-core acceleration.
3. Divide the data from the core reasonably to balance the load of the slave core array and reduce the cost of memory access.
4. The scheme of asynchronous DMA transmission can realize the mutual concealment of calculation and memory access time.

Through these ways, the program performance has been greatly improved.

The rest of this paper is arranged as follows: the second section investigates the traditional processing scheme of stencil computation and its analysis deficiencies, the third section describes the platform and architecture features of this experiment, the fourth section introduces the optimization methods proposed in our experiment, the fifth section discusses and analyzes the results of the experiment, and the last section is our summary and some prospects.

2 Algorithm Introduction

Stencil computation is a kind of iterative core code that updates the value of array elements through a fixed pattern. For a simple example, the heat conduction equation is solved in the homogeneous anisotropic heat conduction medium, and the temperature distributed in three-dimensional space and changing with time is expressed in the form of discrete grid. The temperature of a point at the next time is calculated according to the thermometers of several points near the point at the previous time. The algorithm is as follows:

```
Int count
//3D space size nx*ny*nz
Real a1[nx][ny][nz],a2[nx][ny][nz]
//coefficient
Real zzz, nzz, pzz, znz, zpz, zzn, zzp
//Time cycle performs count iterations
Repeat count times
```

```
//Update all points in A2 by A1
For(x,y,z) in nx*ny*nz
//7-points stencil computation and boundary treatment
a2[x,y,z] = zzz*a1[x,y,z] \
+nzz*a1[x-1,y,z]\
+pzz*a1[x+1,y,z]\
+znz*a1[x,y-1,z]\
+zpz*a1[x,y + 1,z]\
+zzn*a1[x,y,z-1]\
+zzp*a1[x,y,z + 1]
End for
Swap(a1,a2)
End repeat
```

In addition, the finite difference equation, Jacobian iteration and Gauss Seidel method are also used to design the stencil calculation. The most common stencil is 2D von Neumann stencil commonly used in JM (Jacobi method) [14] code, 3D von Neumann stencil commonly used in LBM (lattice Boltzmann methods) [15] or TLBM (thermal lattice Boltzmann methods) [16] code. In addition, other types of stencils can be found in many natural science simulation programs, such as linear processing, seismic wave propagation simulation [17], etc. For the treatment of boundary value in stencil computation, most cases are to keep the boundary value unchanged, and some cases in order to maintain the equivalence of each element, these boundary values will also make corresponding adjustments. Stencil computation is a classic problem of high-performance computing. There are many solutions, such as explicit, loop tiling, timeskew, etc.

The objective algorithm (as shown in Fig. 1) is to divide the scale of the problem re cursively. When it is divided to a threshold, it can be calculated again. This method has nothing to do with buffer, so there is no need to tune the cache. This method is simple to implement, but its performance is poor.

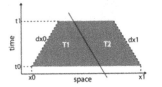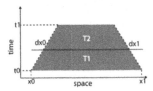

Fig. 1. Schematic diagram of oblivious algorithm

Loop tiling (as shown in Fig. 2) is a common technology to improve data reuse by using time locality and space locality in cache architecture. It is an inevitable choice to increase the memory access locality of stencil computation, but how to choose the block size on multi-core multi-level cache processor becomes the key to optimization. In addition, due to the data correlation between adjacent time steps in stencil computing, the parallelization of stencil computation using only cyclic block can only exist in a single time step, the overall parallelization costs a lot, and the reuse data between adjacent blocks cannot be explored (Fig. 3).

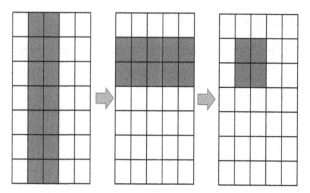

Fig. 2. Schematic diagram of loop tiling algorithm

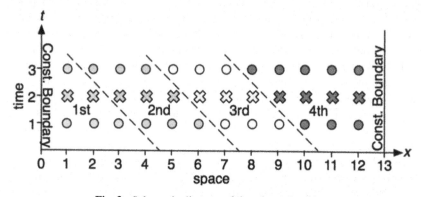

Fig. 3. Schematic diagram of timeskew algorithm

Timeskew method is to divide the time dimension obliquely. It can reuse the data calculated before in cache, which is beneficial to the improvement of performance. For each later T, the data that needs to be used up to the previous time has been cached in the cache, which will improve the performance of the algorithm. However, there are some disadvantages, such as unbalanced parallel load, inefficient use of reused data, complex boundary processing and difficult to implement.

3 Introduction of Experimental Platform

SW26010 heterogeneous multi-core processor consists of four core groups, a total of 260 cores. Each core group contains an operation control core (hereinafter referred to as the main core) and an operation core array. The operation core array consists of 64 operation cores (hereinafter referred to as the slave core). As a general processor core, the main core can perform communication, IO, computing and other operations. 64 slave cores are used to speed up the computation intensive part of the code [18]. It is easy to understand that the heterogeneous computing platform built by x86 processor + GPU can be used for comparison. From the functional point of view, the main core of sw26010 can correspond to the general processor core (CPU) of X86 platform, and 64 slave cores can correspond to the GPU acceleration card in it, which is used to assist in computing acceleration (Fig. 4).

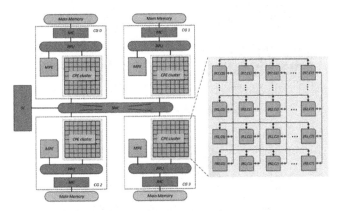

Fig. 4. The general architecture of the SW26010 processor

The main core frequency of sw26010 processor is 1.45 ghz, the memory of each core group is 8 GB, the L1cache size is 32 KB, and the L2cache size is 256 Kb. The main frequency of the slave core is 1.45 ghz, which can be accessed by GLD/GST directly and discretely, or by DMA in batch. The slave core array uses register communication mode to communicate with each other. The local storage space of the slave core is 64 KB, and the instruction storage space is 16 KB. The main basic programming languages of the system are C language (supporting C99 standard), C++ language (supporting C++ 03 Standard and providing SWGCC compiling environment supporting C++ 11 standard), FORTRAN language (supporting main functions in FORTRAN 2003 standard). The master-slave parallel computing mode includes: master-slave accelerated parallel computing mode, master-slave collaborative parallel computing mode, master-slave asynchronous parallel computing mode [19] (Fig. 5).

The code of this experiment is written in C language + MPI + Athread. On Sunway system, the main core code and the slave core code are compiled separately, and then they are linked together. For example

(1) compilation of main core file
    sw5cc -host -c master.c
(2) compiling from nuclear documents:
    sw5cc -slave -c slave.c
(3) hybrid link:
    sw5cc -hybrid master.o salve.o -o main

Finally, the generated executable files are submitted to the queue through bsub.

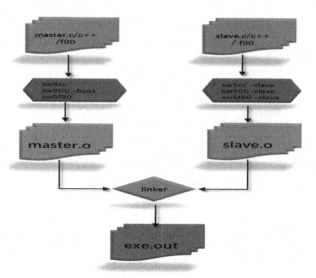

Fig. 5. The process of compiling connection for Sunway heterogeneous processor

4 Parallel Optimization Method

4.1 Master Slave Asynchronous Mode Optimization

In SW26010 processor, there are three computing modes for the master and slave cores: master-slave synchronous mode, master-slave asynchronous mode and master-slave cooperative mode. In the three modes, the program is entered by the main core, and then called by the main core to accelerate from the core. this paper adopts asynchronous mode. In asynchronous mode, MPI and Sunway's unique accelerated thread library (Athread) are used. After the main core loads the code on the slave core, it does not wait for the completion of the return from the core calculation, but directly continues the following calculation tasks, and loads the core calculation part into the whole column from the core. All the calculations are put into the slave core, and the 64 operation cores of the slave core are used to accelerate the calculation to realize the multi-level parallel of MPI + multi-core acceleration. In the design of data block, this method also refers to the idea of loop tiling algorithm, and comprehensively considers three factors that affect the performance of the program: the number of MPI communications, the continuity of data, and the size of each block of data, which increases the memory access locality of the stencil computation (Fig. 6).

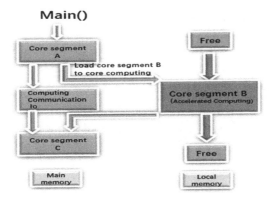

Fig. 6. Master-slave kernel asynchronous mode

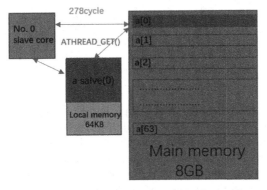

Fig. 7. Accelerate thread library working mode

4.2 DMA Optimization

Because the calculation of stencil needs to iterate many times, each cycle needs to call the slave core. When the slave core finishes the calculation of the core part, it writes back to the master core. When the next cycle iteration is going on, the slave core copies the data from the master core, so there is frequent and large amount of data exchange between the master and slave cores. In this case, DMA (direct memory access) is used to exchange data between master and slave cores. Because under the same level of processor burden, DMA is a fast way of data transmission (Fig. 8).

Figure 7 shows the storage hierarchy of sw26010. It can be seen that the storage hierarchy between the main core and the main memory is very similar to that of other processors. There are L1cache and L2cache in the middle, but the storage hierarchy of the slave core is slightly special. The slave core can access the main memory directly and discretely through (GLD/GSD), or by first accessing LDM and then accessing the main memory in batches through DMA. The delay of accessing main memory from the first way of core (GLD/GSD) is very large, so it should be avoided in the program as much as possible, otherwise the performance of the program will be greatly reduced. In the second

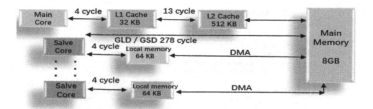

Fig. 8. Storage hierarchy of SW26010

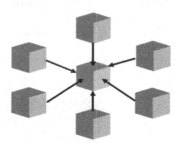

Fig. 9. 3D-7P stencil calculation

way, DMA accesses main memory in two steps. In the first step, the delay of accessing LDM from the core is very small. Therefore, if the program can get the data required by the calculation from the core to LDM in batch through LDM, and then directly access the data required by LDM when the subsequent calculation is done from the core, it is possible to greatly reduce the delay of accessing memory and ensure the performance of the program. Through this strategy, when the master-slave core data exchange, we can simultaneously carry out the calculation independent of the transmitted data, so as to realize the overlap of calculation and communication, and improve the program performance.

4.3 LDM Optimization

The 64 slave cores of SW26010 processor can directly access the main core's memory, but the direct access to memory is very slow, and the memory of 64 slave cores accessing the main core at the same time will be congested, which greatly increases the access delay. Each slave core has its own private programmable memory LDM (local data memory) [20, 21], and each LDM has 64 KB of storage space. In this paper, the frequency of accessing the main core memory from the slave core is reduced by using the LDM of the slave core. Some data commonly used in the calculation are loaded into the LDM of each slave core when the slave core is started by building the structure, so that the data can be reused once loaded, and then the frequency of accessing the main core memory space from the slave core is reduced. Secondly, through repeated calculation, every DMA transfer as much data as possible from the core, making full use of the limited storage space of LDM, reducing the number of DMA communication, so as to improve the program performance. This method simplifies the control overhead of the traditional cache implementation, can realize the accurate use of space, reduce the Miss traffic caused by cache, and avoid the design complexity and performance degradation caused by the consistency processing among many computing cores.

4.4 Communication Optimization

Communication optimization is divided into two parts: MPI communication optimization and DMA communication optimization.

For MPI communication optimization, in Sect. 4.1, the data is divided according to the three directions of X, Y, Z, and the data is exchanged with MPI_Sendrecv() function. Through repeated tests, combined with the characteristics of stencil computing code itself, we find that dividing data according to Z direction can not only ensure the continuity of data, but also improve the amount of data transmitted each time and reduce the number of MPI communications. In addition, a more advanced MPI function is used, which uses non blocking communication MPI_Isend() and MPI_Irecv(), so as to overlap computation and communication and improve program performance.

For DMA communication optimization, it is found in repeated tests that DMA communication time is far less than slave core calculation time. So by changing the data traffic of DMA, we realize the mutual concealment of DMA communication time and slave computing time. Improved program performance.

4.5 Data Reuse

In the iteration of the stencil calculation cycle, the calculation of each point depends on its surrounding points, such as the 3d-7p stencil calculation [22]. The calculation of a point requires the value of six points around it. Many data can be used repeatedly in the experiment.

For example, there are four layers of data in Z direction: A, B, C, D. when calculating B layer, we use the data of a layer and C layer. However, when calculating the C layer, we only need to copy the D layer data from the main core. The B layer data already exists in LDM. Therefore, on the basis of Sects. 4.2 and 4.3, referring to the idea of timeskew algorithm, we define a circular array, and reuse the data by the way of pointer, which can reduce the times of DMA communication, reduce the time of communication, make better use of LDM, and improve the performance of the program.

5 Experimental Results and Analysis

The experimental results and sub-systems in this paper are 7-point $512 \times 512 \times 512$ and 27 point $512 \times 512 \times 512$ scale stencil computation. Aiming at the special architecture of domestic CPU SW26010, we make full use of the slave core resources of SW26010 processor to parallelize the stencil algorithm with many cores. The implementation results are as shown in the figure.

As can be seen from Fig. 10 and Fig. 11, the optimization method proposed in this paper greatly improves the performance of the algorithm. Among them, the initial time of 7-point stencil computation is 172.98014 s, the final optimization time is 0.512192 s,

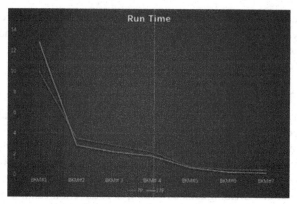

Fig. 10. The diagram is a line chart of the running time of the program, in which the blue broken line is calculated by 7 points' stencil, the orange broken line is calculated by 27 points' stencil, the horizontal axis is the optimization method proposed by us, and the vertical axis is the running time.

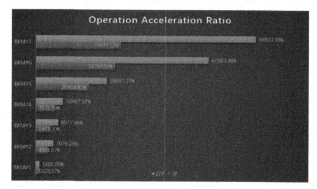

Fig. 11. The diagram shows the run-time speedup of the program. Where blue is the acceleration ratio calculated by the 7-point stencil, and orange is the acceleration ratio calculated by the 27-point stencil (Color figure online)

the acceleration ratio is 33672.52%, the initial time of 27 points' stencil computation is 203.31153 s, the final optimization time is 0.23476 s, and the acceleration ratio is 86503.99%. Using accelerated thread library(Athread) to reconstruct the original algorithm structure, load the core computing part into the slave core array, and realize the multi-level optimization of MPI + multi-core acceleration. From the analysis of Fig. 9 and Fig. 10, it can be concluded that the above method has better effect on the optimization of larger scale stencil. Because this paper adopts the idea of mutual concealment of computation and communication, and adopts the efficient DMA communication mode, the communication time of 7-point stencil and 27 points' stencil is almost the same. For the calculation of 27 points' stencil, the calculation of its core part will be more intensive than that of 7 points' stencil, that is to say, the calculation time can completely cover the communication time. In each cycle iteration, 27 points' stencil does not need to wait for the end of data exchange to start the calculation, because in the last iteration, the data has been successfully exchanged and does not need to wait for the end of communication. Therefore, the above optimization method is more effective for the dense stencil calculation, and is suitable for the larger scale stencil access mode.

6 Conclusion and Prospect

In this paper, through Sunway platform, we make full use of the heterogeneous architecture of Sunway TaihuLight, improve the traditional optimization method of stencil computation, load the computing data to the core array for efficient acceleration computing, design and implement the optimization method closely combined with the sw26010 processor architecture, and get more than 800 times of the acceleration effect. It provides a new solution for the acceleration of the application with intensive stencil access mode.

Acknowledgment. This work is supported by National Major Project (No. 2017ZX03001021-005).

References

1. Dong, Y.: Optimizations of memory-access for stencil computations on sharedmemory multi-core processor. University of Science and Technology of China, December 2015
2. Hi Stencils [EB/OL]. http://www.exastencils.org/histencils/. Accessed 1 Nov 2015
3. Wikipedia. Stencil code [EB/OL], February 2 2015. http://en.wikipedia.org/wiki/Stencil_code. Accessed 1 Nov 2015
4. Ma, W., Qin, J., Xiang, X., Tan, Y., Luo, Y., Xiong, N.N.: Adaptive median filtering algorithm based on divide and conquer and its application in captcha recognition. Comput. Mater. Continua **58**(3), 665–677 (2019)
5. Zhang, J., Li, Y., Niu, S., Cao, Z., Wang, X.: Improved fully convolutional network for digital image region forgery detection. Comput. Mater. Continua **60**(1), 287–303 (2019)
6. Wu, X., Luo, C., Zhang, Q., Zhou, J., Yang, H., Li, Y.: Text detection and recognition for natural scene images using deep convolutional neural networks. Comput. Mater. Continua **61**(1), 289–300 (2019)
7. Zhu, Z., Li, J.: Grid generation method in CFD and its application. Acta Aeronautica ET Astronautica Sinica **19**(2), 25–31 (1998)
8. Bernal, F., Reis, G.D., Smith, G.: Hybrid PDE solver for data-driven problems and modern branching. Papers (2017)
9. Jeong, W.K., Fletcher, P.T., Tao, R., et al.: Interactive visualization of volumetric white matter connectivity in DT-MRI using a parallel-hardware hamilton-jacobi solver. IEEE Trans. Vis. Comput. Graph **13**(6), 1480–1487 (2007)
10. Hu, C., Zhang, J., Wang, J., et al.: Parallel iteration space alternate tiling Gauss-Seidel solver. In: IEEE International Conference on Cluster Computing, pp. 440–445 (2007)
11. Frigo, M., Strumpen, V.: Cache oblivious stencil computations. In: ACM International Conference on Supercomputing, pp. 361–366 (2005)
12. Solar-Lezama, A., Arnold, G., Tancau, L., et al.: Sketching stencils. In: ACM SIGPLAN Conference on Programming Language Design & Implementation, pp. 167–178. ACM (2007)

13. Bondhugula, U., Bandishti, V., Pananilath, I.: Diamond tiling: tiling techniques to maximize parallelism for stencil computations. IEEE Trans. Parallel Distrib. Syst. **28**(5), 1285–1298 (2017)
14. Fan, E., Zhang, J.: Applications of the Jacobi elliptic function method to special-type nonlinear equations. Phys. Lett. A **305**(6), 383–392 (2002)
15. Ho, M.Q., Obrecht, C., Tourancheau, B., et al.: Improving 3D lattice boltzmann method stencil with asynchronous transfers on many-core processors. In: Performance Computing & Communications Conference (2018)
16. Demuth, C., Mendes, M.A.A., Ray, S., et al.: Performance of thermal lattice Boltzmann and finite volume methods for the solution of heat conduction equation in 2D and 3D composite media with inclined and curved interfaces. Int. J. Heat Mass Transf. **77**, 979–994 (2014)
17. Micikevicius, P.: 3D finite difference computation on GPUs using CUDA. In: Proceedings of 2nd Workshop on General Purpose Processing on Graphics Processing Units ACM, pp. 79–84 (2009)
18. Yang, G.W., Zhao, W.-l., Ding, N.: "Sunway TaiHuLight" and its application system. Science **69**(3), 12–16 (2017)
19. Yao, W.J.: Implementation and optimization of molecular dynamics application on Sunway TaihuLight supercomputer. University of Science and Technology of China A dissertation for master's degree (2017)
20. Liu, F.F., Yang, C., Yuan, H.X., et al.: General SpMV implementation in many-core domestic sunway 26010 processor. J. Softw. **29**(12), 331–342 (2018)
21. Yao, W.J., Chen, J.S., Zhi-Chao, S.U., et al.: Porting and optimizing of NAMD on SunwayTaihuLight system. Comput. Eng. Sci. (2017)
22. Cai, Y., Yang, C., Ma, W., et al.: Extreme-scale realistic stencil computations on Sunway TaihuLight with ten million cores. In: 2018 18th IEEE/ACM International Symposium on Cluster, Cloud and Grid Computing (CCGRID). ACM (2018)

Chinese News Data Extraction System Based on Readability Algorithm

Tianhao Xu⬡, Ao Feng(✉)⬡, Xinyu Song⬡, Zhengjie Gao⬡, and Xinke Zeng⬡

Chengdu University of Information Technology, Chengdu, China
kylex@foxmail.com, abraham.feng@gmail.com, songxinyu17@gmail.com,
gaozhengj@foxmail.com, 1822042799@qq.com

Abstract. In this era of data explosion, the number of Chinese news has increased exponentially. We need an efficient way to collect data to support the data analysis industry or to meet the data needs of artificial intelligence domain model training. The purpose of this article is to build an efficient data extraction system for Chinese news data collection. First, we will introduce the development of the field of network data collection, review the previous research routes and ideas, then we choose the Readability algorithm to extract the text data, improve some of the rules, and add the consideration of text data sparsity to make it more suitable for Chinese news data. The system is based on the Scrapy framework to facilitate large-scale Crawling. By comparing the basic readability algorithm with the experimental results, the improved crawling system can extract Chinese news data more accurately and efficiently.

Keywords: Web data extraction · Web mining · Readability algorithm

1 Introduction

In recent years, with the popularity of the mobile Internet, traditional paper media has been greatly impacted. The Internet has become the main way for users to obtain information [1]. In addition to the traditional four portal websites (Sina Netease Sohu Tencent), Headlines Today and other news aggregation APP users have also experienced explosive growth, and Internet giants are also beginning to enter this field. Alibaba has become the major shareholder of Sina Weibo, and Baidu has begun to build the "Baijiahao" ecosystem with the help of their search engines.

A large amount of news has provided a sufficient data foundation for the development of other fields. It can be seen from the development of deep learning in recent years that the increase in the amount of data has greatly contributed to the overall improvement of the model, and the prediction results in many fields are new state-of-the-art. Therefore, how to efficiently acquire data and make effective use is an issue worthy of consideration and attention [2].

There is a lot of redundant information on the pages of the news website, including the navigation bar at the top, the information bar at the bottom, the thumbnails of the sidebar, and advertisements. How to remove this information to obtain the body content

© Springer Nature Singapore Pte Ltd. 2020
X. Sun et al. (Eds.): ICAIS 2020, CCIS 1252, pp. 153–164, 2020.
https://doi.org/10.1007/978-981-15-8083-3_14

of the news efficiently is the main problem that the news extraction algorithm needs to solve [3]. The system constructed in this paper is based on the readability algorithm, considering the sparseness of text features, such as the aggregation of text blocks and the density of punctuation, to determine the distribution of text data, and thus extract the data.

There are many methods for extracting web content, including tree-based techniques, web wrappers, and more complex hybrid systems, which have been applied in many fields. In the next chapter, we will first introduce and analyze the development of existing methods and applications. In the third chapter, the basic principles and improvements of the extraction algorithm we use are introduced. The fourth chapter describes the implementation process of the system in detail. Finally, the extraction effect of the system is analyzed and the conclusion is given.

2 Related Work

The most utilized in web data extraction is the semi-structured nature of web pages. The web page can be naturally converted into a tagged ordered root tree, where the tags are the appropriate tags for the HTML markup language grammar and the tree hierarchy represents the different nesting levels of the elements that make up the web page.

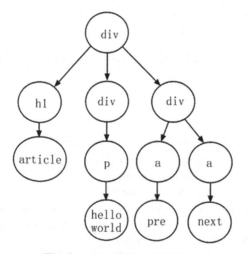

Fig. 1. An example of DOM tree

A tagged ordered root tree for a web page is often referred to as a DOM (Document Object Model). The general idea behind the document object model is that HTML pages are represented in plain text, which contains HTML tags, which are defined in a markup language and can be interpreted by the browser to represent specific Web elements. Pages (for example, hyperlinks, buttons, images, etc.), such as free text. HTML tags can be nested together to form a hierarchy. This hierarchy is captured in the DOM by the document tree whose nodes represent HTML tags. The document tree (also referred to below as the DOM tree) has been successfully used for web data extraction purposes through various techniques discussed below.

2.1 Path-Based Extraction Method

There are two ways to use XPath: (i) identify a single element in the document tree, or (ii) respond to multiple occurrences of the same element. For the purpose of Web data extraction, the possibility of using this powerful tool is extremely important: XPath has been widely used as a tool for solving web page elements in the literature. The main disadvantage of XPath is the lack of flexibility: each XPath expression is strictly related to the structure of the Web page, which has been defined at the top of the Web expression. However, this limitation has been partially mitigated by introducing relative path expressions in the latest version. Often, even minor changes to the structure of a Web page can corrupt the proper functionality of XPath expressions defined on previous versions of the page.

In order to maintain the functionality of the web data extraction process, the expression should be updated when any changes are made to the underlying page generation model. Such operations require a high manpower input, so the cost may be too high. To this end, some authors [8, 9] introduced the concept of package robustness: they proposed a strategy to find XPaths that are less affected by potential changes in all XPath expressions that can extract the same information from a Web page. expression. In the structure of the page, such an expression identifies a more robust wrapper.

2.2 Tree-Based Extraction Method

Because of the hierarchical structure of web pages, the research on extraction algorithm based on tree matching is the first area to be concerned. Several researches on tree matching algorithms are introduced below.

Tree Edit Distance Matching Algorithms. The first technique we describe is called tree edit distance matching. The problem of calculating the tree edit distance between trees is a variant of the classic string edit distance problem. Given two ordered root trees A and B with labels, the problem is to find a match that converts A in B with the least number of operands (and vice versa). This set of possible operations includes node deletion, insertion or replacement. Costs can be incurred in each operation, in which case the task has a problem of minimizing costs (ie finding the smallest cost of the sequence of converting A to B).

The above reasoning is formally defined in the mapping definition proposed in [19]. The mapping M between two trees A and B is defined as an ordered pair (i, j), and each pair has a pair, which satisfies the following conditions: (i1, j1), (i2, j2) in M.

Based on this idea, many techniques have been proposed to solve this problem [7, 27]. These methods support all three types of operations on the node (i.e., node deletion, insertion, and replacement), but suffer from high computational cost. It has also been shown that the formula for the unordered tree is NP-complete [30].

The Simple Tree Matching Algorithm. The simple tree matching algorithm [24] and its variants provide an efficient computational solution for tree editing distance matching problems. This optimized strategy comes at a price: node replacement is not allowed during the matching process.

The computational cost of a simple tree match is O(nodes(A).nodes(B)), where nodes(T) are functions that return the number of nodes in the tree (or sub-tree) T. Low cost ensures excellent performance when applied to HTML trees that may contain a large number of nodes.

But there are two main limitations to this algorithm:

- It cannot match the arrangement of nodes;
- Cross-level is not allowed (it is not possible to match nodes at different levels).

Despite these inherent limitations, this technique seems to be well suited for the purpose of matching HTML trees in the context of a Web data extraction system. In fact, it has adopted [10–12, 17, 28, 29, 31] in several cases. One of the first Web data extraction methods based on the tree edit distance algorithm was proposed by Reis et al. [22].

The Weighted Tree Matching Algorithm. Weighted tree matching. It adjusts the similarity values provided by the original simple tree matching by introducing a renormalization factor. The pseudo-codify of the weighted tree matching, recently presented in [10].

The advantage of weighted tree matching is that it better reflects the similarity between the two trees. In the simple tree matching algorithm, the assigned matching value is always equal to 1, and the weighting tree matching algorithm assumes that the tree structure changes are less important (i.e., the weight is lower) when the tree structure changes occur in the deeper sub-levels. Such changes may be the addition or removal of leaf nodes, truncation or addition of branches, and so on. Moreover, when changes occur in sub-levels with multiple nodes, the weights are reduced. The weighted tree matching algorithm returns the value in the interval [0, 1]. The closer the final value is to 1, the more similar the two input trees are.

2.3 Wrapper-Based Method

First we give the definition of a *Wrapper*, it's a process that can implement one or more algorithms to find and retrieve the data needed by human users, extracting data from unstructured (or semi-structured) Web resources. And then convert it to structured data, merge and unify this information for further processing in a semi-automatic or fully automated way.

This section we will introduce *regular expressions, wrapper programming languages* and *partial tree alignment*.

Regular Expressions. One of the most common methods is based on regular expressions, a powerful formal language for identifying strings or patterns in unstructured text based on certain matching criteria. Rules can be complex, so writing them manually can take a lot of time and expertise: a regular expression-based wrapper dynamically generates rules to extract the required data from a web page. W4F is a well-known tool for implementing regular expression-based extraction [23].

Wrapper Programming Languages. An example of a powerful language developed for data extraction purposes comes from the Web-specific wrapper programming language. A tool based on the wrapper programming language treats a web page not only as a text string, but also as a semi-structured tree document, while the DOM of a web page represents its structure, where the node has both its attributes and its content characteristics. Elements. The advantage of this approach is that you can define a wrapper programming language to take full advantage of the semi-structured nature of Web pages and their content - the lack of the former in regular expression-based systems. The first powerful wrapping language has been formalized by Gottlob and Koch [14]. The information extraction function implemented by this wrapper language relies on single-subdata records on the tree [15]. The first implementation of this wrapping language in the actual scenario was due to Baumgartner et al. [4, 5].

Partial Tree Alignment. The last technique discussed in this section is related to the generation of wrappers, called partial tree alignment. Zhai and Liu [28, 29] recently formalized it, and the author also developed a Web data extraction system based on it. This technique relies on the idea that information in a web document is typically collected in a contiguous area of the page (referred to as a data recording area). The strategy of partial tree alignment is to identify and extract these areas. In particular, the authors obtained inspiration from the tree matching algorithm by using the tree edited distance matching already discussed.

2.4 Machine Learning

Machine learning techniques are ideal for extracting domain-specific information from Web resources because these models require knowledge of the relevant fields through the training process. The machine learning method requires a training step in which the domain specialist provides some manually tagged web pages that can be obtained from different websites or from the same website. Special attention should be paid to providing examples of web pages that belong to the same domain but present different structures. This is because, even in the same domain scenario, the templates that are typically used to generate dynamic content web pages will be different, and the system should be able to learn how to extract information in those contexts. A statistical machine learning system has also been developed that relies on conditional models [21] or adaptive searches [26] as an alternative solution to human knowledge and interaction.

Web data extraction methods currently relying on machine learning algorithms are WIEN [26], Rapier [6, 18], WHISK [20], SRV [25], SoftMealy [13], STALKER [16].

3   Readability Algorithm Based on Feature Sparsity

3.1   Basic Readability Algorithm

The Readability algorithm performs content analysis by filtering and weighting the tags by the textual characteristics of the <p> tag and the defined regular expression. The regular expression is shown in Table 1.

Table 1. Regular expression matching.

Name	Regular expression	Use for
unlikely_Candidates	combx|comment|disqus|foot|header|menu| meta|nav|rs|shoutbox|sidebar|sponsor	Filtering nodes with low probability of text
positive	article|body|content|entry|hentry|page| pagination|post|tex	add points(+25)
negative	ombx|comment|contact|foot|footer|footnote| link|media|metapromo|related|scroll| shoutbox|sponsor|tags|widge	lose point(-25)

Algorithm Steps:

Step 1 HTML parsing. As shown in Fig. 1, the HTML is parsed into a DOM tree, and the HTML tag is manipulated by traversing the tree nodes.

Step 2 Filter. Iterate through the label nodes and extract their class and id attributes for regular matching. In Table 1, the unlikely _Candidates is used for filtering the nodes, indicating that the content of the node is unlikely to be the body. Only when the text extraction result is empty, choose not to filter the nodes for secondary extraction.

Step 3 Determine the main block of the body. Score the parent and grandparents for the paragraph label p tag. The scoring factor includes the length of the text contained in the p tag, the number of punctuation, and the node tag name. If the p tag text is up to standard ($>$ 25), add its parent and grandparents to the list of candidate nodes. Finally, by traversing the candidate nodes, the label node with the highest score is selected as the main block node of the text in combination with the plain text ratio.

Step 4 Generate the body block. Traversing the sibling node of the main block node of the body to determine whether it is a body node. First, the node score is evaluated. If the node score is up to standard, it is marked as the body node. Otherwise, it is judged whether it is a p tag node. If it is a p tag node and its text characteristics are up to standard, it is also marked as a body node. Finally, a container node is created as a text block node, and the filtered body node and the body main block node are spliced into the body block node.

Step 5 Pruning. Clears the specific tags in the block node, traverses the *div*, *table*, *ul* tag nodes, and clears the tags according to factors such as node weight, number of tags, and plain text ratio. The effect of noise. Among them, positive and negative are positively matched by the tag attribute of the node to generate node weight.

3.2 Improvement Based on Feature Sparsity

Partial Tree Alignment. In order to avoid losing the body information, the improved algorithm will simultaneously evaluate the text characteristics of the non-<p> tag nodes, taking the plain text ratio and the text length as text property parameters. At the same time, in order to effectively filter the web page noise whose partial text characteristics are similar to the main text, according to the close concentration of the text information on the web page distribution, the relative distance at the node is used as the evaluation factor of the text node.

Text Density and Symbol Density. After the first step of improvement, the model has a good extraction effect, but hope to further improve the correct rate of text extraction. After studying a lot of web pages, I found that there are basically punctuation marks in the body, and webpage links, advertising information, because there is usually no punctuation, the S_bD_i is the symbol density of a paragraph of text.

$$S_bD_i = (T_i - LT_i)/(Sb_i + 1) \tag{1}$$

The symbol density is the ratio of the number of words to the number of symbols. According to our experience, the S_bD_i of the body is usually larger than the non-text. Non-text may not have symbols, and since non-text is usually less words, it may be some navigation information, so its S_bD_i will be smaller than the body in the same number of words. So we use the function (2) as the core function to extract the content of the page.

$$Score = \log SD \times ND_i \times \log_{10}(PNum_i + 1) \times \log S_bD_i \tag{2}$$

SD is the standard deviation of the node text density, ND is the text density of node i and $PNum_i$ is the number of p-tags of node i.

4 System Implementation

This part introduces part of the system implementation, because the overall system design is too complicated to be comprehensively summarized, so choose some content worthy of attention to explain, first introduce the system flow based on the scrapy framework, and then introduce the factors that affect the system efficiency - agent pool The construction of the multi-threaded, and finally introduced the Bloom filter and Redis database to avoid repeated data collection.

4.1 Scrapy Platform

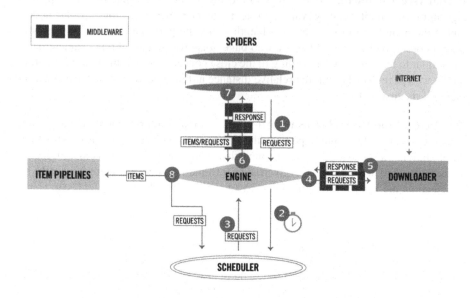

Fig. 2. Scrapy data flow

Data Flow. The data flow in Scrapy is controlled by the execution engine. The process is as follows (Fig. 2):

1. The engine opens a website (open a domain), finds the Spider that handles the website, and requests the spider for the first URL(s) to crawl.
2. The engine gets the first URL to crawl from the Spider and dispatches it in the scheduler (Scheduler).
3. The engine requests the scheduler for the next URL to crawl.
4. The scheduler returns the next URL to be crawled to the engine, which forwards the URL to the down-loader via the download middle-ware (request direction).
5. Once the page is downloaded, the down-loader generates a Response for the page and sends it to the engine via the download middle-ware (response direction).
6. The engine receives the Response from the down-loader and sends it to the Spider for processing via the Spider middle-ware (input direction).
7. The Spider processes the Response and returns the crawled Item and the (followed) new Request to the engine.
8. The engine will (for the Spider returned) the item to the Item Pipeline and the (Spider returned) Request to the scheduler.
9. (From the second step) repeat until there are no more requests in the scheduler, the engine closes the site.

4.2 Proxy Pool

We use the open source tool ProxyBroker, which can asynchronously look up public agents from multiple sources and check their validity at the same time. The tool is small and easy to extend, does not require third-party dependencies such as redis, and has many features:

- Finds more than 7000 working proxies from 50 sources.
- Support protocols: HTTP(S), SOCKS4/5. Also CONNECT method to ports 80 and 23 (SMTP).
- Proxies may be filtered by type, anonymity level, response time, country and status in DNSBL.
- Work as a proxy server that distributes incoming requests to external proxies. With automatic proxy rotation.
- All proxies are checked to support Cookies and Referer (and POST requests if required).
- Automatically removes duplicate proxies.
- Is asynchronous.

4.3 Efficiency Improvement

Scrapy is based on the twisted asynchronous IO framework, and the down-loader is multithreaded. However, since Python uses GIL (Global Interpreter Lock, which guarantees that only one thread is using an interpreter at the same time), this greatly limits parallelism, and Python's multithreading is poor when dealing with computationally intensive programs, and if Python's multithreading can make a bigger difference when opening multiple threads for time-consuming IO operations. (Because Python will release GIL when performing long-term IO operations) So, simply, Scrapy is multi-threaded and must not be set up. Due to the current version of Python, multithreading is not very complete, but the actual test Scrapy efficiency is acceptable.

So, the way to improve scrapy crawling efficiency is:

- Set DOWNLOADDELAY to a smaller value in settings.py (guarantee that IP is not blocked)
- Increase the number of concurrency (CONCURRENTREQUESTS)
- The bottleneck is in IO, so it is very likely that the IO is full, but the CPU is not full, so it is not valid to use the CPU to speed up the crawl. It's better to run a few processes, so the CPU is full.
- In setting.py, you can change the number of concurrent threads of single IP or single domain to 16 or higher. 16 threads are no problem for general websites, and Scrapy's own scheduling and retry system can guarantee every Pages are successfully crawled
- Dynamic page is best to find the json data transmitted by Ajax, and then grab the content that needs it.

5   Experiments and Results

5.1   Evaluation Method

The precision R and the recall ratio P were used to evaluate the feasibility of the algorithm, and the score for (2) is also considered.

$$R = LCD(a, b).length/a.length \qquad (3)$$

$$P = LCS(a, b).length/b.length \qquad (4)$$

where a is extracted body content and b is the body content of the standard, the *LCS* function is using for calculate the longest common subsequence.

Because there is no public data set for judging the accuracy of Chinese news, we used the crawler technology to download the pages of ifeng.com, Netease, Sina, and Tencent News. Each website downloads 2000 web pages. At the same time, regular text expression matching is used for each web page to save the body content seen by the human eye, and then the same content is collected using the extraction algorithm of the present article to obtain accuracy. 90.6% 92.2% 88.7% 91.1% 85.2% 90.8%.

5.2   Results

Table 2. Experiment results.

Website	P-basic	P-new	R-basic	R-new	Score-basic	Score-new
http://www.ifeng.com/	95.6%	97.2%	96.5%	98.3%	93.2%	95.8%
https://www.163.com/	93.1%	95.6%	94.2%	96.4%	91.2%	94.8%
https://finance.sina.com.cn/	87.1%	90.9%	85.5%	88.3%	81.2%	87.1%
https://www.qq.com/	90.6%	92.2%	88.7%	91.1%	85.2%	90.8%

It can be seen from the results that the improved algorithm is superior to the basic readability algorithm in the recall rate and precision rate, and has achieved a relatively high accuracy rate, which has reached the project usable level (Table 2).

6   Experiments and Results

This article first reviews and introduces the development of the network data extraction field, and explains the development process and ideas of the previous technology. Based on this knowledge and the characteristics of Chinese news, we have improved the readability algorithm to apply to the Chinese news data. This paper introduces some improvements to the algorithm, as well as some points that need to be paid attention to in the engineering implementation. Finally, the experiment has shown that the accuracy of the Chinese news text extraction has exceeded the basic readability algorithm and achieved a good effect, the future can continue to develop on this basis.

Acknowledgment. Supported in part by the Research Innovation Team Fund (Award No. 18TD0026) and Youth Technology Fund (Award No. 2017JQ0030) from the Department of Education, and in part by the Seedling Project of Science and Technology Innovation (Project No. 2018115) from the Science Technology Department, Sichuan Province.

References

1. Akyol, K., Şen, B.: Modeling and predicting of news popularity in social media sources. Comput. Mater. Con. **61**(1), 69–80 (2019)
2. Yin, L., Meng, X., Li, J., Sun, J.: Relation extraction for massive news texts. Comput. Mater. Con. **60**(1), 275–285 (2019)
3. Yang, Z., Huang, Y., Li, X., Wang, W.: Efficient secure data provenance scheme in multimedia outsourcing and sharing. Comput. Mater. Con. **56**(1), 1–17 (2018)
4. Baumgartner, R., Flesca, S., Gottlob, G.: The Elog web extraction language. In: Nieuwenhuis, R., Voronkov, A. (eds.) LPAR 2001. LNCS (LNAI), vol. 2250, pp. 548–560. Springer, Heidelberg (2001). https://doi.org/10.1007/3-540-45653-8_38
5. Baumgartner, R., Flesca, S., Gottlob, G.: Visual web information extraction with lixto (2001)
6. Califf, M.E., Mooney, R.J.: Bottom-up relational learning of pattern matching rules for information extraction. J. Mach. Learn. Res. **4**, 177–210 (2003)
7. Chen, W.: New algorithm for ordered tree-to-tree correction problem. J. Algorithms **40**(2), 135–158 (2001)
8. Dalvi, N., Bohannon, P., Sha, F.: Robust web extraction: an approach based on a probabilistic tree-edit model. In: Proceedings of the 2009 ACM SIGMOD International Conference on Management of Data, pp. 335–348. ACM (2009)
9. Dalvi, N., Kumar, R., Soliman, M.: Automatic wrappers for large scale web extraction. Proc. VLDB Endow. **4**(4), 219–230 (2011)
10. Ferrara, E., Baumgartner, R.: Automatic wrapper adaptation by tree edit distance matching. In: Hatzilygeroudis, I., Prentzas, J. (eds.) Combinations of Intelligent Methods and Applications. SIST, vol. 8, pp. 41–54. Springer, Heidelberg (2011). https://doi.org/10.1007/978-3-642-196 18-8_3
11. Ferrara, E., Baumgartner, R.: Design of automatically adaptable web wrappers. arXiv preprint arXiv:1103.1254 (2011)
12. Ferrara, E., Baumgartner, R.: Intelligent self-repairable web wrappers. In: Pirrone, R., Sorbello, F. (eds.) AI*IA 2011. LNCS, vol. 6934, pp. 274–285. Springer, Heidelberg (2011). https://doi.org/10.1007/978-3-642-23954-0_26
13. Freitag, D.: Machine learning for information extraction in informal domains. Mach. Learn. **39**(2–3), 169–202 (2000). https://doi.org/10.1023/A:1007601113994
14. Gottlob, G., Koch, C.: Logic-based web information extraction. ACM SIGMOD Rec. **33**(2), 87–94 (2004)
15. Gottlob, G., Koch, C.: Monadic datalog and the expressive power of languages for web information extraction. J. ACM (JACM) **51**(1), 74–113 (2004)
16. Hsu, C.-N., Dung, M.-T.: Generating finite-state transducers for semi-structured data extraction from the web. Inf. Syst. **23**(8), 521–538 (1998)
17. Kim, Y., Park, J., Kim, T., Choi, J.: Web information extraction by HTML tree edit distance matching. In: 2007 International Conference on Convergence Information Technology (ICCIT 2007), pp. 2455–2460. IEEE (2007)
18. Kushmerick, N.: Wrapper induction: efficiency and expressiveness. Artif. Intell. **118**(1–2), 15–68 (2000)

19. Liu, B.: Structured data extraction: wrapper generation. In: Web Data Mining. DCSA, pp. 363–423. Springer, Heidelberg (2011). https://doi.org/10.1007/978-3-642-19460-3_9

20. Mooney, R.: Relational learning of pattern-match rules for information extraction: In: Proceedings of the Sixteenth National Conference on Artificial Intelligence, vol. 334 (1999)

21. Phan, X.-H., Horiguchi, S., Ho, T.-B.: Automated data extraction from the web with conditional models. Int. J. Bus. Intell. Data Min. 1(2), 194–209 (2005)

22. de Castro Reis, D., Golgher, P.B., Silva, A.S., Laender, A.F.: Automatic web news extraction using tree edit distance. In: Proceedings of the 13th International Conference on World Wide Web, pp. 502–511. ACM (2004)

23. Sahuguet, A., Azavant, F.: Building light-weight wrappers for legacy web data-sources using W4F. In: VLDB, vol. 99, pp. 738–741 (1999)

24. Selkow, S.M.: The tree-to-tree editing problem. Inf. Process. Lett. 6(6), 184–186 (1977)

25. Soderland, S.: Learning information extraction rules for semi-structured and free text. Mach. Learn. 34(1–3), 233–272 (1999). https://doi.org/10.1023/A:1007562322031

26. Turmo, J., Ageno, A., Català, N.: Adaptive information extraction. ACM Comput. Surv. (CSUR) 38(2), 4 (2006)

27. Wang, J.T.-L., Shapiro, B.A., Shasha, D., Zhang, K., Currey, K.M.: An algorithm for finding the largest approximately common substructures of two trees. IEEE Trans. Pattern Anal. Mach. Intell. 20(8), 889–895 (1998)

28. Zhai, Y., Liu, B.: Web data extraction based on partial tree alignment. In: Proceedings of the 14th International Conference on World Wide Web, pp. 76–85. ACM (2005)

29. Zhai, Y., Liu, B.: Structured data extraction from the web based on partial tree alignment. IEEE Trans. Knowl. Data Eng. 18(12), 1614–1628 (2006)

30. Zhang, K., Statman, R., Shasha, D.: On the editing distance between unordered labeled trees. Inf. Process. Lett. 42(3), 133–139 (1992)

31. Zhang, Z., Zhang, C., Lin, Z., Xiao, B.: Blog extraction with template-independent wrapper. In: 2010 2nd IEEE International Conference on Network Infrastructure and Digital Content, pp. 313–317. IEEE (2010)

Parallel Acceleration Improvement of Physical Quantity Gradient Algorithm Based on CFD

Jiaming Zhang[1], Tao Wu[1(✉)], Hao Yang[1], Jie Tan[1], and Xi Chen[2]

[1] School of Computer Science, Chengdu University of Information Technology, Chengdu 610225, China
wut@cuit.edu.cn

[2] School of Computer Science and Technology, Southwest Minzu University, Chengdu 610041, China

Abstract. In order to solve the problem that the physical quantity gradient algorithm consumes a lot of time in the calculation process, the algorithm is improved by parallel acceleration. In computational fluid dynamics (CFD), the key to the discretization of viscous terms is to calculate the gradient of various physical quantities (such as velocity, temperature, etc.) at the interface. By gauss-green formula, the gradient of each physical quantity in the center of the unit can be obtained by integrating the value of the center of the plane. In this paper, the gradient algorithm is optimized based on the application software PHengLEI, which will solve the gradient of four physical quantities on the "unit interface" successively from three directions. In order to solve the interface gradient more efficiently and improve the program execution efficiency and software performance, this paper will make use of diversified methods to optimize the performance of software PHengLEI, including using C++ class template to expand and vectorize, using Openmp to create multi threads for independent 'for' loop, using static scheduling method to reduce scheduling overhead and exchange loop sequence and so on. After many tests and verification, under the condition that the results are correct, the optimization effect has been significantly improved, reaching an acceleration ratio of 5666.67%.

Keywords: CFD · Gradient · PHengLE · Vectorization · Openmp · Static scheduling

1 Introduction

CFD, short for computational fluid dynamics, is a new interdisciplinary subject that integrates fluid mechanics and computer science [1]. It starts from the calculation method and uses the fast computing power of computer to get the approximate solution of the fluid control equation [2]. Because computational fluid dynamics belongs to the subject of intensive scientific calculation, it is very dependent on the development of high-performance parallel computing. Due to the small amount of calculation in the early CFD, most of the scientific calculation is carried out in the form of serial calculation

© Springer Nature Singapore Pte Ltd. 2020
X. Sun et al. (Eds.): ICAIS 2020, CCIS 1252, pp. 165–174, 2020.
https://doi.org/10.1007/978-981-15-8083-3_15

method, the calculation method is relatively simple, and the simulation shape can only simulate the simpler geometric model.

Since the 1990s, CFD has made great progress in computational methods and turbulence models, and other aspects. With the continuous improvement of spatial and temporal resolution, the development of grid generation technology has also made the simulation of geometric configurations more and more realistic [3]. However, with the continuous expansion of the scale of calculation, the amount of calculation also increases on a geometric scale [4]. In recent ten years, due to the continuous upgrading of computer hardware and the development of high-performance parallel computing technology, CFD software has realized large-scale numerical simulation through code parallelization [5]. In the parallel field, parallel programming methods represented by Openmp and MPI [6, 7] have been widely applied in CFD practical applications.

In today's practical application of computational CFD, calculation is usually carried out by dividing the three-dimensional space to be calculated into scattered grids. The decentralized grid will be more conducive to parallelization and structure [8–10]. Because the existing CFD applications are basically based on spatial model decomposition, that is, the grid of the whole computational space is divided into different scattered grids, so MPI method can be adopted. That is to say, different MPI processes are executed on each grid block, and MPI communication is carried out among each grid block. Due to the different complexity of spatial simulation of each grid block, the time consumed by different MPI processes is not the same. Therefore, in order to improve the application efficiency and better parallelization, it is necessary to balance the calculation amount and complexity of each grid with the method of load balancing [11].

In this paper, parallel computation and performance optimization of PHengLEI software framework are realized by means of solving the CFD based physical quantity gradient algorithm on Intel Xeon processor, and combining MPI, Openmp, unrolling C++ class template, static scheduling, exchanging cycle sequence and AVX256 and AVX512 vectorization programming interfaces provided by Intel. In addition, the performance test and optimization comparison between the results of parallel optimization and the original application results are made, and the specific optimization part and process are evaluated.

2   Introduction to Application and Algorithm

2.1   PHengLEI Introduction

PHengLEI is a large-scale parallel computing CFD software platform developed by China Aerodynamic Research and Development Center on the basis of several existing structural and non-structural in-house codes, which is suitable for structure grid, non-structure grid and overlapping grid at the same time. PHengLEI not only provides a large number of application weather data but also provides a unified grid, parallel API interface, mathematical library interface and so on [12–14]. PHengLEI has also designed an efficient parallel computing framework, which adopted a hierarchical structure, from top to bottom: parallel API interface layer, interface data layer, data bottom layer and MPI communication layer, respectively corresponding to secondary developer layer, geometric layer, database layer and MPICH layer [15–17] (Fig. 1).

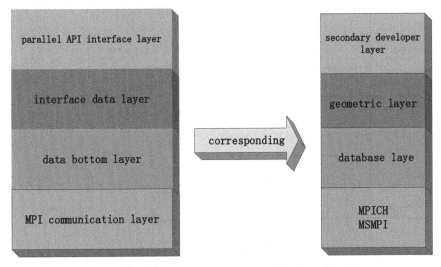

Fig. 1. Relationships among processes, grid blocks, and interfaces

2.2 Introduction to CFD Physical Quantity Gradient Solving Algorithm

In this project, the part of solving the gradient in computational fluid dynamics is to calculate the discretization of viscous terms in CFD, and the key to calculate the discretization of viscous terms is to calculate the gradient of physical quantities in the interface, among which Gauss-Green formula plays an important role.

$$\int_v N\nabla Q dV = \iint_{\partial v} Q n dS$$

That is to say, the gradient of each physical quantity in the center of a unit can be obtained by integrating the value of the center of the mesh.

$$(\nabla\phi)_{i,j,k} = \frac{(\phi S)_{i+1/2,j,k} - (\phi S)_{i-1/2,j,k} + (\phi S)_{i,j+1/2,k} - (\phi S)_{i,j-1/2,k} + (\phi S)_{i,j,k+1/2} - (\phi S)_{i,j,k-1/2}}{V_{i,j,k}}$$

The approximate process is: The practical application of this project has three planes, each plane has three directions of x, y, z, taking the X direction at the bottom left as an example, by multiplying the normal vector in the X direction at the bottom left and the area of the corresponding area, the result is multiplied by the storage flow field in the center of the unit, and then an intermediate quantity is obtained. The inverse of the intermediate quantity is multiplied by the reciprocal of the grid cell volume.

The interface gradient value of the corresponding physical quantity in the x direction will be obtained, this value will be used for the calculation of the viscous flux, after that, the interface gradient value in the next direction will be re-assigned to 0 (Fig. 2).

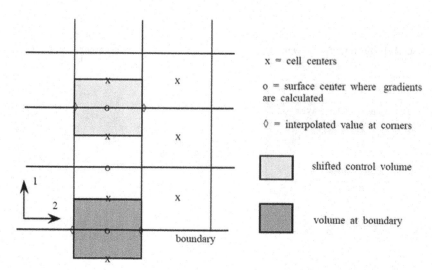

Fig. 2. Two-dimensional diagram

3   Parallel Optimization Method

3.1   Hot Spot Analysis

Firstly, the hot spot of this application is analyzed by means of vtune tool. Through the analysis, it is found that the main time-consuming part calculates the gradient part of each physical quantity in each direction of three planes in the main function, namely the maximum three iterations. Many of the C++ class templates in the three iterations are also time-consuming. These class templates are used to describe these physical quantities, such as the normal vector, area of zone, storage flow field in the center of the unit, interface gradient value and others.

3.2   The Optimized Content

MPI Communication

Because CFD is a spatial model divided by grid partition, the original grid can be divided into sub grid, and then these sub grid can be allocated to each process for calculation, but the data of the interaction surface between the grids will be leak, so the method of MPI communication should be used to communicate the variables on the interaction surface to ensure the correctness of the results [18–20] (Fig. 3).

Communication Masking

Because there are 3 iterations in the application, MPI communication should be carried out in each iteration, and MPI communication should be carried out before the calculation gradient of each iteration, so communication masking can be used. When the calculation gradient of this iteration is carried out, MPI communication of the next iteration can be carried out too, so the time of MPI communication is covered (Fig. 4).

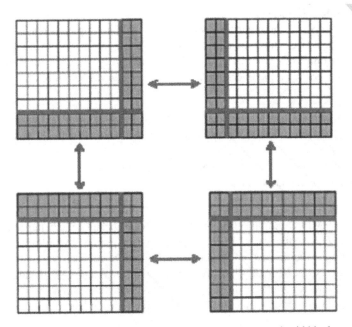

Fig. 3. Interface and communication between subgrid blocks

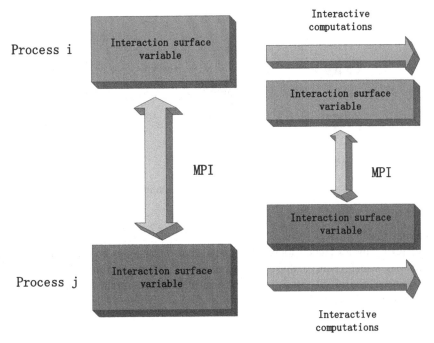

Fig. 4. Communication masking process

C++ Class Template Expansion

After in-depth analysis of the algorithm, we find that a class template such as XXX(I, J, K, M) can be converted into a quadruple for loop, while the I, J, K, M range of the four-tier for is the range of XXX class I, J, K, M. Because only when the class template is expanded into a loop, can the operation of Openmp be carried out more efficiently.

Vectorization

After the C++ class template is expanded, because there are a lot of double precision floating-point variables that need to be calculated in the expanded cycle, the calculation process in the expanded cycle can use the interface of avx512 and avx256 provided by Intel to calculate eight or four double precision floating-point variables at one time, greatly reducing the calculation time.

Openmp

Because the single MPI communication optimization can't achieve the better optimization effect, so we choose the way of MPI and Openmp fine-grained hybrid parallel, that is to use Openmp parallel in each node, and use MPI parallel between nodes to achieve the purpose of two-level parallel. First, we use Openmp to create multithreads for the independent loop, and use multiple threads to calculate the hotspot part at the same time. Then we use Openmp's collapse statement to merge the independent loops, and set the scheduling mode to static, which can reduce the scheduling overhead (Fig. 5).

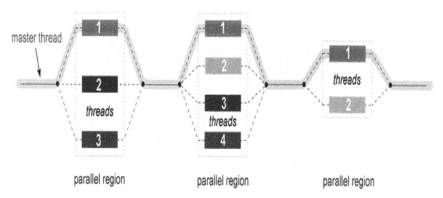

Fig. 5. Openmp multithreaded computing model

Exchange Cycle Order

By analyzing the expanded loops, it is found that many loops are calculated across dimensions, which greatly reduces the calculation efficiency. Therefore, by exchanging the loop order, the calculation is increased according to the correct dimensions and the calculation time is reduced.

3.3   Performance Analysis

In order to evaluate the effect of optimization, we compare it with the original serial program. The hardware environment we adopted is Intel Xeon processor Gold 6140

2.30 ghz. Under the condition of 4 processes and 36 threads derived from Openmp, the time is successfully reduced from 102 s of the benchmark time to the final 1.8 s, reaching an acceleration ratio of 5666.67%. The time is greatly reduced, and the performance of the algorithm is significantly improved (Table 1, Fig. 6).

Table 1. Acceleration ratio table

Optimization method	Acceleration
MPI communication	275.67%
Communication masking	497.56%
C++ class template expansion	816.00%
Vectorization	1214.28%
Openmp	5368.42%
Exchange cycle order	5666.67%

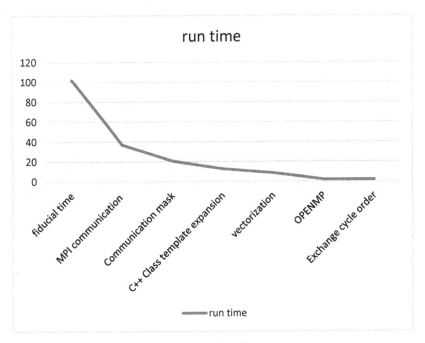

Fig. 6. Run-time diagram

Under the condition of 16 processes and 36 threads derived from Openmp, the time of MPI communication also increases with the increase of the number of processes. The running time decreases from 37 s of the benchmark time to 0.76 s, reaching 4868.42% acceleration ratio, which is less than the acceleration ratio of 4 processes, indicating that the method of traffic concealment does not achieve the desired effect (Fig. 7).

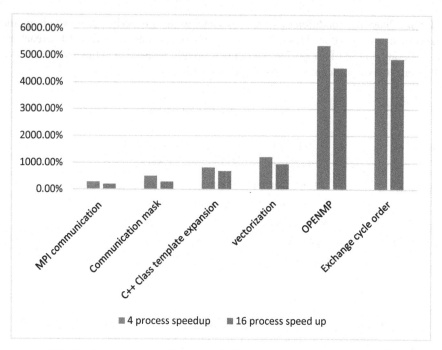

Fig. 7. Compare the acceleration ratio between process 4 and process 16

It can be seen from the analysis of acceleration ratio data that the communication effect of MPI is weakened after increasing the process, because the communication time is increased, but the method of communication mask does not have an ideal effect, which may be due to the less computation and less computation time, resulting in the incomplete masking of communication time. Therefore, we adjusted the experimental objects and re-compared the three sets of acceleration ratio data under the communication masking method. One group is that under the condition of 16 processes, the scale of spatial grid is further expanded and the calculation amount is increased. The other two groups are that in 4 processes and 16 processes, the calculation amount is not increased. By comparison, we found that the acceleration ratio under the communication masking method in 16 processes with the increased calculation amount reached 672.98%, which achieved a desired effect (Fig. 8).

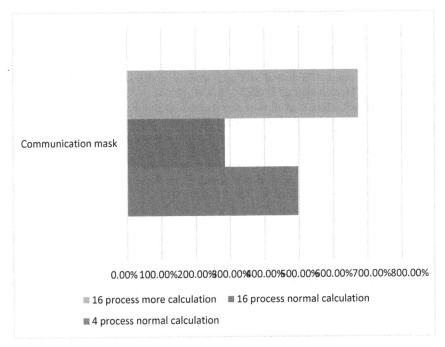

Fig. 8. Comparison of acceleration ratio of communication mask

4 Conclusion

This paper introduces a parallel optimization method based on CFD physical quantity gradient solution algorithm in PHengLEI, analyzes and optimizes the hot spot of gradient solution algorithm in this application, greatly reduces the time of this algorithm in practical application, achieves considerable acceleration ratio and optimization effect, and improves the performance and efficiency of this application, because the physical quantity gradient solution algorithm is widely used in many CFD fields, so it is necessary to adopt the parallel optimization method used in this paper to improve the efficiency of practical application.

References

1. Milovan, P.: Flow simulation using control volumes of arbitrary polyhedral shape. ERCOF-TAC Bull. **62**, 25–29 (2004)
2. Mani, M., Ladd, J.A., Cain, A.B., et al.: An assessment of one and two-equation turbulence models for internal and external flows. In: AIAA-97-2010 (1997)
3. Tran, T.D., Thai, C.H., Nguyen-Xuan, H.: A size-dependent functionally graded higher order plate analysis based on modified couple stress theory and moving Kriging meshfree method. Comput. Mater. Continua **57**(3), 447–483 (2018)
4. Zhao, Z., Zhang, L.P.: PHengLEI: a large scale parallel CFD framework for arbitrary grids. Chin. J. Comput. **42**, 41–91 (2018)

5. Zhang, X., Li, Z., Liu, G., Jiajun, X., Xie, T., Nees, J.P.: A spark scheduling strategy for heterogeneous cluster. Comput. Mater. Continua **55**(3), 405–417 (2018)
6. Zhao, C., Wang, T., Yang, A.: A heterogeneous virtual machines resource allocation scheme in slices architecture of 5G edge datacenter. Comput. Mater. Continua **61**(1), 423–437 (2019)
7. Qin-gu, J., Zhi-yan, J.: The hybrid MPI and Openmp parallel scheme of GRAPES global model. J. Appl. Meteorological Sci. **25**(5), 581–591 (2014)
8. He, X., Zhang, L.P., Zhao, Z., et al.: Research of general large scale CFD software architecture and data structure. Acta Aerodynamica Sinica **30**(5), 557–565 (2012). (in Chinese)
9. Slotnick, J., et al.: CFD vision 2030 study: A path to revolutionary computational aerosciences. In: NASA/CR–2014-218178 (2014)
10. Baker, T.J.: Mesh generation: art or science? Progress Aerosp. Sci. **41**, 29–63 (2015)
11. Tonks, M., Gaston, D.: An object-oriented finite element framework for multiphysics phase field simulations. Comput. Mater. Sci. **51**(1), 20–29 (2012)
12. Zhang, L.P., Chang, X.H., Zhao, Z.: Mesh Generation Techniques in Computational Fluid Dynamics, Science Press, Beijing (2017). (in Chinese)
13. He, X., Zhao, Z., Ma, R., Wang, N., Zhang, L.: Validation of HyperFLOW in subsonic and transonic flow. Acta Aerodynamica Sinica **34**(2), 267–275 (2016)
14. Zhao, Z., He, L.: Large scale grid generation techniques based on global mesh refinement. In: China Aerodynamics Research and Development Center, Mianyang, China, 201710655494. (in Chinese)
15. He, X., Zhao, Z., Zhang, L.P.: Validation of the structured/unstructured hybrid CFD software HyperFLOW. In: Proceedings of the 15th Conference on Computational Fluid Dynamics, Yantai, China, pp. 1282–1287 (2012). (in Chinese)
16. Zhao, Z., He, X., Zhang, L.P.: Numerical research of NASA high-lift trap wing model based on HyperFLOW. Acta Aerodynamica Sinica **33**(5), 594–602 (2015). (in Chinese)
17. Schloegel, K., Karypis, G.: Multilevel k-way partitioning scheme for irregular graphs. J. Parallel Distrib. Comput. **48**(1), 96–129 (1998)
18. Guo, H., Mo, Z.Y., Zhang, A.Q.: A parallel module for the multiblock structured mesh in JASMIN and its applications. Comput. Eng. Sci. **34**(8), 69–74 (2012). (in Chinese)
19. Sun, Y., Sun, L.: Isoparametric element algorithm framework design based on Jaumin. Comput. Aided Eng. **24**(1), 63–67 (2015). (in Chinese)
20. He, X., Zhao, Z., Zhang, L.P.: The research and development of structured-unstructured hybrid CFD software. Trans. Nanjing Univ. Aeronaut. Astronaut. **30(sup)**, 116–126 (2013)

Using Process Visualization and Early Warning Based on Learning Analytics to Enhance Teaching and Learning

MaoYang Zou[1,2(✉)] ⓘ, Ting Wang[1], Hong Xu[1], XiaoJie Li[1], and Xi Wu[1]

[1] Chengdu University of Information Technology,
No. 24 Block 1, Xuefu Road, Chengdu 610225, China
zoumy@cuit.edu.cn
[2] Chengdu Institute of Computer Application, University of Chinese Academy of Sciences,
No. 9 the 4th Section of South Renmin Road, Chengdu 610041, China

Abstract. With the rapid development of educational big data, learning analytics (LA) has been put forward. Without a commercial system which need numerous resources to construct, our study makes full use of the data from existing learning management system, exercises & examination system, and then makes analysis and prediction, finally optimizes the teaching and learning. Specifically, the visualized data can be presented timely to students and teachers, which can enable them to rethink and solve the problem. Logical regression, naive bayes classifier (NBC), support vector machine algorithm (SVM), K-means and artificial neural network (ANN) are used to predict the students' risk of failure, and NBC has the best prediction effect on our dataset. The early warning is issued, so that the personalized preventive measures can be taken. According to the results of the comparative experiment, the scores of learning analytics group are more than 8% higher than those of the traditional group. Overall, it is easy to implement, and has high cost performance and certain reference value.

Keywords: Learning analytics · Educational big data mining · Learning process visualization · Early warning

1 Introduction

In the 1990s, researchers began to use data analysis to aid teaching, such as intelligent tutoring system (ITS). Nowadays, data analysis is developed rapidly, which makes educational policy more reliable and teaching service more accurate.

United States Department of Education published the report of "Enhancing Teaching and Learning through Educational Data Mining and Learning Analytics" in 2012. In this report, two important concepts are pointed out: educational data mining (EDM) and learning analytics (LA) [1]. The International Educational Data Mining Society defines EDM as follows: EDM "is an emerging discipline, concerned with developing methods for exploring the unique and increasingly large-scale data that come from educational settings and using those methods to better understand students, and the settings which

© Springer Nature Singapore Pte Ltd. 2020
X. Sun et al. (Eds.): ICAIS 2020, CCIS 1252, pp. 175–183, 2020.
https://doi.org/10.1007/978-981-15-8083-3_16

they learn in" [2]. "According to the definitions introduced during the 1st International Conference on Learning Analytics and Knowledge (LAK), LA is the measurement, collection, analysis and reporting of data about learners and their contexts, for purposes of understanding and optimizing learning and environments in which it occurs" [3]. Based on the results of 402 studies, Aldowah et al. [4] propose that "applying EDM and LA in higher education can be useful in developing a student-focused strategy". Ray et al. [5] present how EDM and LA techniques are used to analyze the learning process of students and assess their performance.

At present, there are two common problems in higher education. Firstly, some students have not correct self-awareness of their own learning, and teachers are also unable to evaluate the learning status of the whole class and each student in real time, so that the problem cannot be predicted and the preventive measures cannot be taken; Secondly, students' personalized learning is difficult to implement without the support of data mining.

In response to above problems, our team has done research and practice for two years. Compared with EDM, LA is more driven by learning demand and aims at solving educational problems, so our focus is on LA. "The objective of LA is to analyze the large dataset and provide feedbacks that have an impact directly on the students, the instructors and the details of the learning process" [5]. For our team, the dataset is collected and mined, and then visualized analytic result can be presented to students and teachers to promote reflection. By using algorithm, such as logical regression, naive bayes classifier (NBC), support vector machine (SVM), artificial neural network (ANN) and K-means algorithm, students' grades are predicted in two categories, so early warning is carried out in time.

The contribute of this work is that:

(1) If a commercial learning analysis system is used, it requires a lot of financial and human resources such as purchasing, building and data migration. To take effective solution for learning problem without the above, we makes full use of the data of existing system to mining, which has high cost performance for promoting personalized learning.
(2) The early warning accuracy of the five algorithms is compared, and NBC has the highest accuracy for students at risk of failure. The reason is analyzed for the dataset from the learning management system and the testing system.
(3) The data mining is driven by learning rather than technology, and the result of applying those approach in the course show that this is feasible and efficient for enhancing the learning and teaching. Therefore, this is a reference for the peers.

2 Related Work

There are five common approaches of educational data analysis: prediction, clustering, relationship mining, distillation of data for human judgement and discovery with model [6]. The prediction can be used for learning early warning. The variables, such as students' score, is predicted by building models with population data, learning historical data, learning dynamic data and so on. Table 1 shows the algorithms commonly used for early warning. According to statistics [7], two algorithms most commonly used in the past are linear regression and logical regression.

Table 1. Algorithm for early warning.

Category	Algorithm	Description(come from Wikipedia partly)
Classification	Linear regression	It is a linear approach to model the relationship between a scalar response (or dependent variable) and one or more explanatory variables. It is used usually to predict continuous variables
	Logistic regressive	It uses a logistic function to model a binary dependent variable. It is used usually for the classification of discrete variables
	Decision tree	A decision tree (as a predictive model) goes from observations about an item (represented in the branches) to conclusions about the item's target value (represented in the leaves). The results of decision tree algorithm are easy to understand, but sensitive to missing data
	NBC	NBC assumes that the data set attributes are independent of each other, so the logic of the algorithm is very simple, and the algorithm is stable and robust
	SVM	SVM is supervised learning model that analyzes data used for classification and regression analysis. SVM has good technical performance, but it is sensitive to missing data
	ANN	ANN is a computing system vaguely inspired by the biological neural networks that constitute animal brains. The process of algorithm is a black box
Cluster	K-means	K-means is the most simple and efficient clustering algorithm. Initially, the K initial Centroids is specified by the user, and the algorithm iterates until convergence

For learning process visualization, various learning analytics dashboard (LAD) are popular at present. LAD "realizes the visualization of knowledge generation and educational data mining results, which can support students' self-cognition, self-evaluation, self-motivation and social awareness, and optimize the learning environment of future wisdom [8]". The "Course Signals" system created by Purdue University, which was deployed in 2008, caused a stir. It extracted data for analysis and provided students and teachers with a dashboard to track the situation of students [9]. In 2014, the Nottingham Trent University in the United Kingdom also launched a learning dashboard throughout the university, and after a period of promotion, the attendance rate of students increased. The Maryland University has developed a "Check My Activity" system. In the 131 courses, BlackBoard platform with the Check My Activity system is used to significantly reduce the number of students who get a D or F, the value of providing corresponding feedback to improve the learning efficiency is fully presented [10].

For early warning, the data mining technology that has arisen in recent years has promoted it [11]. Romero-Zaldivar et al. [12] monitor the learning activities occurring in a student personal workspace using virtual appliances, and then they use the recorded data for the prediction of student score in a course. To enhance the teaching and learning process, Ganesan Kavitha et al. [13] collect data from a large number of student assessment to identify the students at risk and provide suggestions for improvement. Macfadyen et al. [14] investigate which online activities on Blackboard can accurately predict score, and generate a predictive model for a course. Zhao Huiqiong et al. [15] used the multiple regression analysis to issue early warning. Other related studies also include the literature [16–24].

In order to achieve a better result, some pre-processing tasks are important, such as filtering, discretization, or retargeting, without an algorithm that can obtain the best accuracy in all cases (for all datasets). Which algorithm can obtain the best accuracy for the dataset from the learning management system and the testing system? This is a question that needs to be studied and the best prediction algorithm should be applied in our system.

3   Dataset and Data Preprocessing

This study has experimented with 682 students. The students are divided into two groups: group A is learning analytics group and group B is traditional group. There are two sources of experimental data: historical learning data and current dynamic learning data. The data must be cleaned because of the complexity and heterogeneity. Which data should be analysed? Our idea is that data should be more education-driven, rather than being driven by the data mining technology, and the results should be used to solve realistic educational problems. Therefore, the structural data with learning value, such as learning motivation, should be analysed. Furthermore, Hu et al. [25] propose that time-dependent variables extracted from learning management system are critical factors for online learning, so time-dependent variables are specially collected.

The data is selected as follows:

(1) Historical learning data: the score of entrance examination; grade point average (GPA) of the last year.
(2) Current dynamic learning data is as follows:

- Data from learning management system:

  Login information: login/exit time; online time, etc.
  Content usage: time and times for studying course video; degree of completion of learning (completion/skipping/abandonment); number of downloads for various learning materials, etc.
  Interactive data: number of discussion posts, number of replies to discussion posts; total number of words posted; number of votes received by the main post/reply post.
  Evaluation: times of checking regular grade; times for checking evaluation.

The data of login, content usage and evaluation are helpful to the analysis of learning habits, learning engagement, and interactive data are helpful to the analysis of group learning participation.

- Data from exercise & examination system.

  Basic information of each week's exercise: online time for each exercise; the time to do each question; times of uploads for each question; scores of each question.

The data from the exercise & examination system is helpful to the analysis of knowledge level and learning engagement.

4 Application of Learning Analysis

There are two aspects for learning analysis and intervention: learning process visualization and learning grade prediction for early warning. The following is a description of our approaches in these two aspects.

4.1 Learning Process Visualization

The benefits of learning process visualization are obvious, it can create conditions for learning to learn by providing students with feedback on learning behavior, learning content, learning activities and learning communities [26]. In our study, visualization of learning process assists in the hierarchical learning which has three steps: self-awareness, self-reflection, reflection-sensemaking-impact. In particular, our team visually presents task processes and summaries, such as task schedule, learning spider charts of the course (see Fig. 1), trend map of learning engagement (see Fig. 2), overview of knowledge level, etc. The learning spider charts explains the students' learning habits, learning engagement, learning ability, initiative to widen horizons and knowledge level in the process of learning (see Fig. 1). It is clear from this figure how the student's learning status is, what his level is in the team, and what learning advice should be given him. The trend map of learning engagement shows the student's learning engagement online at each knowledge point, and the area formed by the upper curve and the lower curve is the learning engagement of the students in the middle of 80%, where 1 represents the mean (see Fig. 2).

4.2 Predicting the Grade

A few years ago, the early warning system for learning has some problems, such as single indicator, available with a lag and so on. With the development of machine learning, the prediction result and real-time are improved.

The students' grades are predicted into two classification, and 0–60 is classified as F, 61–100 as A. In terms of cleaning data, inspired by Lee et al. [27] and Chen et al. [28], the first 3 weeks of testing scores are removed. Whereafter, we use the Pearson correlation

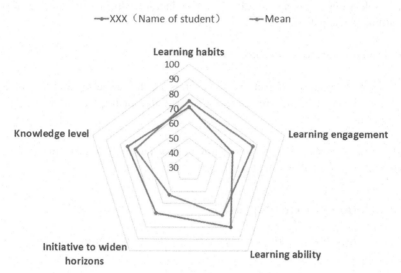

Fig. 1 Learning spider charts

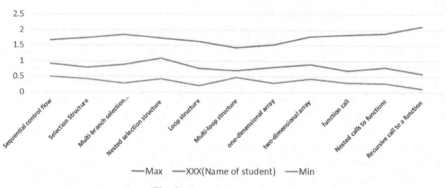

Fig. 2. Learning engagement

coefficient between variables and score to sort. The greater the coefficient, the stronger the correlation between the variable and the score. We select the first 20 variables for classification. Finally, the logical regression, NBC, SVM, K-mean and ANN are used to classification respectively. The original data is divided into training set and verification set, and ten-fold cross validation is used. The results are shown in the Table 2. As a result, NBC has the best prediction effect for students at risk of failure.

According to the principle, the classification error is caused by deviation and variance. Simple models, such as logistic regressive, have higher deviation. More complex models such as ANN have higher variance. In our study, NBC obtains the highest correct rate of students at risk of failure because of the low number and proportion of students at risk of failure in the course. In addition, NBC model structure is simpler than ANN,

Table 2. The results of classification.

	Logistic regressive	NBC	SVM	K-mean	ANN
Accuracy of pass	0.910	0.885	0.891	0.931	0.924
Accuracy of fail	0.592	0.862	0.750	0.406	0.693

SVM, etc. In the case of low sample size, simple models with high deviation and low variance (such as NBC) have advantages over complex models with low deviation and high variance.

5 Investigation on the Application of LA

We analyze the effectiveness of LA in terms of test scores. The scores are shown in Table 3.

Table 3. The average scores

Year	Group A		Group B	
	Mean	Standard deviation	Mean	Standard deviation
First year	71.92	9.27	66.12	10.09
Second year	68.09	8.53	61.24	10.87

The average scores of the students in group A were 8.06% higher than those in group B in first year, and 10.06% higher in the second year, Besides, the standard deviation of group A students' scores was smaller than that of group B students' scores. so those prove application of LA is helpful to the learning. In addition, it can be seen from dataset that the students who ranked in the middle of the middle are more profitable in application of LA.

6 Conclusion

For a few years of practice, we have achieved some results in the research of LA. Through the application of data mining, such as learning process visualization and early warning, the students take more active learning, and the teaching design of teachers and the individualized evaluation for students are optimized. The data mining technology has enhanced the teaching and learning.

References

1. Bienkowski, M., Feng, M., Means, B.: Enhancing teaching and learning through educational data mining and learning analytics: an issue brief. Department of Education, Office of Educational Technology. Technical report, Washington, D.C., US (2012)
2. Educational data mining, July 2011. http://www.educationaldatamining.org/
3. Papamitsiou, Z., Economides, A.A.: Learning analytics and educational data mining in practice: a systematic literature review of empirical evidence. J. Educ. Technol. Soc. 17(4), 49–64 (2014)
4. Aldowah, H., Al-Samarraie, H., Fauzy, W.M.: Educational data mining and learning analytics for 21st century higher education: a review and synthesis. Telematics Inform. 37, 13–49 (2019)
5. Ray, S., Saeed, M.: Applications of educational data mining and learning analytics tools in handling big data in higher education. In: Alani, M.M., Tawfik, H., Saeed, M., Anya, O. (eds.) Applications of Big Data Analytics, pp. 135–160. Springer, Cham (2018). https://doi.org/10.1007/978-3-319-76472-6_7
6. Yu, L., Yang, Q.Y., Nan, Z.: Model driven educational big data mining for enhancing teaching and learning: an interview with Dr. Mimi Recker from Utah state university. Open Educ. Res. 1, 4–9 (2018)
7. Xiao, W., Ni, C.B., Li, R.: Research on learning early warning based on data mining abroad: review and prospect. Distance Educ. China 2, 70–78 (2018)
8. Jiang, Q., Zhao, W., Li, Y.F., et al.: Research on learning analytics dashboard based on big data. China Educ. Technol. 1, 112–120 (2017)
9. Arnold, K.E., Pistilli, M.D.: Course signals at Purdue. In: Proceedings of the 2nd International Conference on Learning Analytics and Knowledge, pp. 267–270 (2012)
10. Hu, Y.L., Gu, X.Q., Luo, J.T.: An analysis of education-decision support oriented by educational effectiveness: from the perspective of learning analytics. Mod. Distance Educ. Res. 6, 41–47 (2014)
11. Xiao, W., Ni, C.B., Li, R.: Research on learning early warning based on data mining in foreign countries: review and prospect. Distance Educ. China 2, 70–78 (2018)
12. Romero-Zaldivar, V.-A., Pardo, A., Burgos, D., Kloos, C.D.: Monitoring student progress using virtual appliances: a case study. Comput. amp Educ. 58(4), 1058–1067 (2012)
13. Kavitha, M.G., Raj, L.: Educational data mining and learning analytics - educational assistance for teaching and learning. Int. J. Comput. Organ. Trends (IJCOT) 41(1) (2017)
14. Macfadyen, L.P., Dawson, S.: Mining LMS data to develop an early warning system for educators: a proof of concept. Comput. Educ. 54(2), 588–599 (2010)
15. Zhao, H.Q., Jiang, Q., Zhao, W., et al.: Empirical research of predictive factors and intervention countermeasures of online learning performance on big data-based learning analytics. E-educ. Res. 1, 62–69 (2017)
16. Popoola, S.I., Atayero, A.A., Badejo, J.A., John, T.M., Odukoya, J.A., Omole, D.O.: Learning analytics for smart campus: data on academic performances of engineering undergraduates in Nigerian private university. Data Brief 17, 76–94 (2018)
17. Mishra, A., Bansal, R., Singh, S.N.: Educational data mining and learning analysis. In: International Conference on Cloud Computing, Honolulu, HI, US (2017)
18. Kop, R.: The design and development of a personal learning environment: researching the learning experience. Media Inspirations for Learning: What Makes the Impact? Technical report, Canada (2010)
19. Marbouti, F., Diefes-Dux, H.A., Madhavan, K.: Models for early prediction of at-risk students in a course using standards-based grading. Comput. Educ. 103, 1–15 (2016)
20. He, W., Yen, C.J.: Using data mining for predicting relationships between online question theme and final grade. J. Educ. Technol. Soc. 15(3), 77–88 (2012)

21. Pardo, A., Han, F., Ellis, R.A.: Combining university student self-regulated learning indicators and engagement with online learning events to predict academic performance. IEEE Trans. Learn. Technol. **10**(1), 82–92 (2017)
22. Yang, Y.Q., Zhou, D.Q., Yang, X.J.: A multi-feature weighting based k-means algorithm for MOOC learner classification. Comput. Mater. Continua **59**(2), 625–633 (2019)
23. Xi, X.F., Sheng, V.S., Sun, B.Q.: An empirical comparison on multi-target regression learning. Comput. Mater. Continua **56**(2), 185–198 (2018)
24. Wang, T.J., Wu, T., Ashrafzadeh, A.H.: Crowdsourcing-based framework for teaching quality evaluation and feedback using linguistic 2-tuple. Comput. Mater. Continua **57**(1), 81–96 (2018)
25. Hu, Y.H., Lo, C.L., Shih, S.P.: Developing early warning systems to predict students online learning performance. Comput. Hum. Behav. **36**, 469–478 (2014)
26. Zhang, Z.H., Liu, W., Zhi, H.: Learning dashboard: a novel learning support tool in the big data era. Mod. Distance Educ. Res. **3**, 100–107 (2014)
27. Lee, U.J., Sbeglia, G.C., Ha, M., Finch, S.J., Nehm, R.H.: Clicker score trajectories and concept inventory scores as predictors for early warning systems for large stem classes. J. Sci. Educ. Technol. **24**(6), 848–860 (2015)
28. Chen, Z.J., Zhu, X.L.: Research on prediction model of online learners academic achievement based on educational data mining. China Educ. Technol. **371**(12), 75–81 (2017)

Research Progress of Knowledge Graph Embedding

Chengyuan Duan[1][(✉)], Hongliang You[1], Zhiping Cai[2], and Ziwei Zhang[3]

[1] Academy of Military Sciences, Beijing, China
chengyuan_duan@163.com
[2] National University of Defense Technology, Changsha, China
[3] 31131 Troop of People's Liberation Army of China, Nanjing, Jiangsu, China

Abstract. As an effective and efficient approach for describing real-world entities with relations, Knowledge graph (KG) technology has received a lot of attention in recent years. KG embedding technology becomes one hot spot in KG research in terms of its efficiency in KG completion, relationship extraction, entity classification and resolution, etc. KG embedding is to embed KG entities and relations as vectors into the continuous spaces, aims at simplifying the operation, also retaining the inherent structure of the KG. In this paper, we focus on the progress of KG embedding in recent these years and summarize the latest embedding methods systematically into a review. We classify these embedding methods into two broad categories based on the type of information in the KG used in this review. We started at introducing models that only use the fact information in the KG followed by briefly review of previous models, focusing on the new models and the improved models based on the previous models. We describe the core ideas, implementation methods, the advantages and disadvantages of these technologies. Then, models incorporate additional information, including entity types, relational paths, textual descriptions, and the use of logical rules will be also included.

Keywords: Knowledge graph embedding · Embedded vector · Relational learning

1 Introduction

KGs are designed to describe the various entities, concepts with relations that exist in the real world. KG constitutes a huge semantic network graph, encodes nodes with entities or concepts, makes the edges consisting attributes or relationships [1]. A KG is a collection of multiple triples, with individual triple consists of a head entity, a tail entity and relations [2]. The store form of a triple is *(head entity, relation, tail entity)*, noted as (s, r, o) this store formation indicates a triple is a fact, and two entities are connected by a specific relation [3]. This representation of information empowers navigation across information and provides an effective utilization of encoded knowledge [4]. However, volume of knowledge existing in the real world, makes capturing all information is invisible, makes KGs are usually failed owing to incomplete. KG embedding is an elegant solution to fill

© Springer Nature Singapore Pte Ltd. 2020
X. Sun et al. (Eds.): ICAIS 2020, CCIS 1252, pp. 184–194, 2020.
https://doi.org/10.1007/978-981-15-8083-3_17

the gap of the incompleteness of KG. The main idea of KG embedding is to embed KG components, including transforming entities and relationships into continuous vector spaces to simplify operations while preserving KG's inherent structure. Embeddings utilize likelihood estimation for evaluating the triple to be true or not [5]. Various score function is defined in different vector spaces. Therefore, KG embedding technology occupies an essential position in the KG, and has a broad application prospect in KG completion relationship extraction, entities classification and entity analysis [6].

Most embedding methods focus on the observed facts, represent the entities and relationships in a KG in the continuous vector space, define a scoring function to calculate the vectors of each fact, and then obtain the relationship embedding by maximizing the total credibility [7]. In the whole process, embedding relationships only need to be compatible with individual facts, which may be difficult to meet the needs of practical applications. Therefore, it is particularly important to study the embedding method of KG by integrating other KG related information [8], such as entity type, relational path, text description, logical rules, etc. In recent two years, researchers have proposed many new methods for predictive embedding of KG.

In this article, we review the development of KG embedding technology in recent years comprehensively and systematically, Quan Wang et al. reviewed relevant models of KG embedding. We used their classification criteria for reference to classify according to the types of information used by these models [8]. We introduce the models that use only the facts observed in KG, and divide such models into models based on distance translation and models based on semantic matching. Then, we introduce the models that incorporates additional information, which are mainly divided into entity types, associated paths, text descriptions, and logical rules. For each type of models, we first review the representative models, and then summarize in detail the new models with good performance in the past two years.

The rest of this article is structured as follows. Section 2 reviews embedding models that use only the observed facts in KG, starting with a brief introduction to the previous models, and then focusing on new technologies that have emerged in recent two years. Section 3 discusses embedding techniques that incorporate additional information. We focus on the use of entity types, relation paths, textual descriptions, logical rules, and other information. Finally, we present our conclusion in Sect. 4.

2   KG Embedding Merging Facts

The purpose of KG embedding is to embed entities and relationships into a low-dimensional continuous vector, thus simplifying operation and facilitating calculation [9]. KG embedding generally involves three steps. First, entities and relationships are expressed as a continuous vector, entities are usually expressed as vectors, and relationships are expressed as operational vector spaces, which can be expressed as vectors, matrices, tensors, gaussian distributions. Second, a scoring function $f_r(h, t)$ is defined in each fact (h, r, t) to measure the rationality of the facts, in which the observed facts tend to receive higher scores than the unobserved facts. Finally, learn about these entities and relationships. According to the differences of scoring functions, the KG embedding technologies that fuse fact information can be roughly divided into two categories, namely translation distance models and semantic matching models [8]. The translation distance models use a distance-based scoring function to measure the rationality of facts by the distance between two entities. Semantic matching models utilize scoring function based on similarity. They measure the credibility of the fact by matching the underlying semantics of the entities and the relationships contained in the vector space representation.

2.1 Translation Distance Models

In recent years, researchers have proposed many KG embedding techniques based on translation distance models. TransE is one of the most typical of these approaches. It assumes that a head entity can be transformed into a tail entity through a relationship. Compared with traditional translation methods [1], TransE can well balance the effectiveness and efficiency of translation, while the over-simplified translation hypothesis limits the performance of translation when dealing with complex relations. To correct this deficiency, some improved models were proposed. TransA sets different weights on different axes to find the most relevant relationship between two entities [3]. TansH projects each entity into a specific hyperplane that is perpendicular to the relationship embedding. TransD and TransR use TransH's principle to project entity to a specific space to deal with complex relations. KG2E uses the Gaussian distribution to express the relationship and entity, and the covariance of the Gaussian distribution to express the uncertainty of the entity or relationship [4]. TransG uses Gaussian mixture model to solve the problem that a relationship corresponds to multiple semantics. Theoretical and experimental results show that the performance of TransE depends to a large extent on the loss function. TransEAML uses Adaptive Margin Loss (AML) as loss function, which is inspired by Margin Ranking Loss (MRL), to solve the problem that the performance of TransE depends to a large extent on the loss function [1]. TransEAML sets a boundary (two variables) between positive samples and negative samples to separate them. TransEAML proposes two independent loss functions to obtain the margin automatically, one for expansion and the other for contraction, and in this way, TransEAML has higher precision than TransE.

The typical models such as TransE, TransH, and TransR based on translating distance map different relations into vector space, and ignore the internal correlation of these relations. In experiment and application, it is found that the correlation of KG is of low rank structure on the embedded relation matrix. TransCoRe characterizes the low rank structure by decomposing the embedding relation matrix into the product of two low dimensional matrices, so as to enhance the correlation of relations in vector space and improve the performance of translation distance model [2].

TransE regularizes the entity, forcing it to be embedded on the sphere of the embedded space. This approach, while ensuring that the embedded system does not diverge indefinitely, distorts the embedded system and conflicts with TransE's principle. TorusE model proposes to replace the sphere embedded in space with torus, which avoids regularization and ensures that the embedding will not diverge indefinitely [3].

TorusE replaces the embedded space with a compact space from an open popular space, replaces the embedded space sphere with a torus, satisfies the principles of TransE embedding, such as differentiability, Calculation possibility, and Definability of a scoring function. TorusE designed the distance function and scoring function suitable for the torus. However, torus can only achieve link prediction on triples, and how to achieve more general prediction is a problem worth studying. In addition, torus still has difficulties in combining with other methods, which needs further study.

The performance of the embedding models based on translation distance depend largely on the choice of the embedded vector geometry space, and a KG as a scale-free network can be naturally represented by hyperbolic space. HyperKG introduces hyperbolic space into translational distance models, which better reflects the topological characteristics of KG and significantly reduced the performance differences between the translational distance models and the bilinear models [7]. In HyperKG, the translational models were extended by learning embeddings of KG entities and relations in the Poincare-ball model of hyperbolic geometry. The confidence of a fact is measured by the hyperbolic distance between the constituent vector representation of its entity and the learned relation vector. In addition, Hyper adds many constraints in hyperbolic space, such as regularization, vector constraints, etc. In fine-grained tasks, HyperKG has made good progress.

Hyperbolic space is not a perfect embedding vector geometric space. HyperKG adopts regularization method to deform the mapping between entities and relations, which may reduce the accuracy of relation prediction. In addition, HyperKG does not significantly improve the performance of KG embedding compared to other methods for tasks with less fine-grained hyperparameter tuning. However, like TorusE, HyperKG is an interesting attempt to replace the embedded space of translational distance models and is a promising research direction.

2.2 Semantic Matching Models

Semantic matching model utilizes similarity-based scoring models. The credibility of facts is generally measured by the relationships contained in vector space representations and the underlying semantics between entities. Semantic matching models include bilinear models and neural-network-based models [8]. RESCAL represents the relationship in the KG as a matrix. Relational matrices model paired interactions in potential factors and evaluate the credibility of facts with a bilinear scoring function. However, RESCAL has problems of over-fitting and high calculation cost [9]. DistMult simplifies RESCAL by limiting the relational matrix to diagonal matrices. But this oversimplified model can only deal with symmetry. HolE scores the facts by matching the combination vector to the relationship representation. The HolE model combines the expressiveness of RESCAL with the efficiency and simplicity of DistMult [10]. ComplEx introduced the plurality into DistMult. Complex numbers improve the symmetric matrix in DistMult so that the scoring function is no longer symmetric and can better model asymmetric spaces. SME adopts neural network structure for semantic matching. SME projects entities and relationships onto embedded vectors in the input layer, and then scores the facts based on their dot product. NTN is another neural network structure. NTN projects entities to embedded vectors in the input layer, then combines two entities with a relational-specific tensor and maps them to a nonlinear hidden layer [11]. Finally, a relational - specific layer of linear output is scored. NTN needs to store a large number of parameters and cannot handle large KGs easily and efficiently. In addition, MLP and NAM are commonly used neural network-based embedding methods.

Bilinear Models. Tensor factorization is one of the best methods of KG embedding. KG can be expressed as a three-order binary tensor, and each element corresponds to a fact triad. CP decomposition model introduces an inverse triad for each existing triad to realize the performance equivalent to that of other bilinear models in KG embedding. However, the CP model needs to maintain a large number of 32-bit (entity) and 64-bit (relation) value vectors, and this huge memory consumption seriously affects the further development of CP model. The B-CP model introduces a quantization function on the basis of CP [9]. This quantization function forces binarization of embedded vectors, which can replace the original floating-point numbers after optimization, greatly reducing the memory seizure of the model. In addition, B-CP uses the bit operation method to reduce the time required to calculate the reliability of triad.

B-CP is a meaningful attempt to introduce the quantization technique used in the neural network into tensor decomposition algorithm for the first time. Moreover, the memory space required by the binarized CP model is greatly reduced. B-CP accelerates the calculation of fractions by bit operation. However, time overhead is still a disadvantage of B-CP. Forcing the vector represented by floating-point into the bit binary vector increases the time cost of the model, and the time of training the model is not accelerated by the way of the bit operation.

SimplE is a simple enhancement to CP (Canonical Polyadic). SimplE, as an enhancement to CP, allows two embeddings of each entity to be learned independently, solving the problem of independence between two embedding vectors of an entity. It can be weighted to incorporate certain types of background knowledge into the embedded space. SimplE is not only a fully expressed model, but also an interpretable model. In addition, the complexity of SimplE increases linearly with the size of the embeddings, which is a very potential knowledge graph embedding model [10].

However, SimplE, as a fully expressed model, cannot provably respect sub-class and sub-property information, so there is still room for improvement. SimplE+ , improved based on SimplE, has better performance than SimplE. SimplE+ adds a nonnegative constraint to the entity embeddings of SimplE. SimplE+ forces the inclusion of classification information as sub-classes and sub-attributes into the relational embedding model [12]. In this way, SimplE+ not only has the advantage of SimplE full expression, but also implements mandatory inclusion, which greatly improves embedding performance [13]. Although it is effective to integrate the background classification information into the tensor decomposition models, it also increases the workload of extracting the background classification information.

QuatE uses quaternion embedding (hypercomplex-valued embeddings with three imaginary components) to represent entities. Relationships are modeled as rotations in quaternions [14]. Quaternions rotate in a four - dimensional space and are more flexible than in a complex plane. In addition, quaternion is an extension of complex, and its flexibility and expressive ability can more easily express the relations of symmetry, anti-symmetry and inversion. QuatE uses Hamilton product to realize quaternion rotation when calculating inner product, and expresses all potential interactions between all relations, which is a highly expressed model.

Although QuatE has the advantages of strong modeling ability, high expression freedom and strong generalization ability, using quaternion rotation causes efficiency loss. In addition, QuatE expresses the potential interactions of all relationships, which makes information redundant.

Neural-Network-Based Models. The expression ability of shallow fast models is not as good as that of deep multilayer models. ConvE based on multilayer convolutional network is an efficient model. ConvE increases the interaction points between embeddings by using a 2D convolution to obtain more interaction times, which increases the expressiveness of the model [11]. ConvE is composed of a single convolution layer, a projection layer of embedded dimension and an inner product layer. 1-N scoring system is adopted to improve the training speed. In addition, ConvE solves the overfitting problem by using efficient and fast parameter operators that can form deep network to increase the robustness of the model.

ConvE has good performance on data sets with high relation to specific degree and has high parameter efficiency. However, ConvE does not perform well on low-relational datasets. And the interpretability of ConvE also is a problem.

2.3 Other Models

In addition to the above methods, there have been many methods or opinions observed which rely on factual information of KGs in the past two years. Group representation theory is one of them. Group representation theory holds that symmetry/anti-symmetry, flipping and combining in relational modeling have a natural correspondence with concepts in group theory [15]. Various model relationships can be represented by modeling the relationship as a group element to rotate. However, group theory cannot model uncertainty, sub-relationships and complex relationships, which limits the group theory of relational modeling. TransGate is a cross-gate model for the inherent correlation between relationships. Two shared gates are set for the head and tail entities respectively [16]. The translation between the head and tail identification information is established, and the score function is used to determine whether the triple is valid. TransGate reduces computational complexity of the model by reconstructing standard gates and parameter sharing using weight vectors. The dihedral symmetry group model represented by the dihedral and dihedral groups in KG is intended to solve the problem of lack of interpretability of KG reasoning. The elements in the dihedral symmetry group model are composed of rotation and reflection operations on a two-dimensional symmetric polygon, which is fully expressive and enhances the interpretability of the relational embedding space. NTransGH combines the translation distance model and neural network to improves the ability of expressing complex relationships [17]. The design idea of NTransGH is to project relations and entities into a generalized hyperplane space, and then use a neural network to obtain complex relation patterns. NTransGH follows the principle of TransH. It uses a set of base vectors to determine a hyperplane space. The basic idea of NTransGH is that for a given triplet, in translation phrase, NTransGH firstly projects two entity embeddings on the generalized hyperplane with a set of basis vectors respectively. Then it conducts translation operation with a transfer matrix for getting the triplet representation. NTransGH can express the generalization ability and mapping ability of complex relation facts.

3 Incorporation Additional Information

Incorporating additional information into the embedding models can improve the embedding performance [8]. The additional information includes entity types, relation paths, textual descriptions, and logical rules. The relevant models are described below.

3.1 Entity Types

An entity type, that is, a semantic category to which an entity belongs, is usually encoded by a specific relationship and stored in the form of a triple. TKRL is a translational distance model with a specific type of solid projection [8]. It can handle hierarchical entity categories and multiple category labels with better performance. However, TKRL associates each category with a specific projection matrix with a high spatial complexity.

Traditional embedding methods encode concepts and instances as entities equally in low-dimensional semantic spaces, ignoring the differences between concepts and instances. TransC divides entity types into concepts and instances [18]. Each concept is encoded as a sphere, and each instance is encoded as a vector in the same semantic space. TransC uses relative positions to represent relationships between concepts and instances, by defining loss functions to measure relative position and to optimize KG embedding.

TransC combines entity types with distance-based translation models, which increases the expressiveness of KG embedding and improves embedding performance. However, the sphere is a simple conceptual representation model of semantic space. It has weak expressive power and cannot fully reflect the relationship between instances and concepts. In addition, a concept may have different meanings in different triples. How to use entity vectors to represent the different meanings of concepts is a problem that needs to be studied.

An entity may involve multiple types, so just considering all entities in a semantic space is not a logical way to build an effective model. TransET maps each entity according to the types of each entity, explicitly defining the role of the entity types in the relationship [19]. In TransET, the mapping matrix is designed by considering the entity types. For each relationship, the entity maps based on types and relationships.

TransET only considers the basic types of entities and can be easily combined with translation-based distance models to improve performance without increasing complexity. TransET uses negative sampling to classify entities, and entities of the same type tend to aggregate and form clusters, which can lead to errors.

3.2 Relation Paths

The relation path, that is, the multi-hop relationship between entities, contains rich semantic cues, which is very useful for the completion of KGs. The path sorting algorithm directly uses the paths connecting the two entities as feature vectors to predict possible associations between them [8]. PTransE combines the path between entities and the vector of constituent relationships to improve the performance of TransE. In addition, the use of entities not only connected to the relationship, but also connected with the relation path to improve the performance of the model has a good effect. However, a large number of paths increase the complexity of models, which is the main problem faced by the associated path model.

The multi-step relationship path methods that minimize the loss function based on the general margin shared by all relation paths cannot consider the differences between the different relationship paths. In response to this problem, PaSKoGE uses a loss function based on a specific path margin to perform KG embedding. PaSKoGE adaptively determines its edge-based loss function by encoding the correlation between any given pair of entities and the relationships between the multi-step relationship paths [20]. This method takes full account of the differences between the paths. For any one path, PaSKoGE defines the margin of each arbitrary length path by simply encoding the relationship between any given pair of entities and the relationship between the multi-step relationship paths. However, the time and space complexity of this method is a problem to be considered.

3.3 Textual Descriptions

Entities with rich semantic information usually have concise descriptions. Textual descriptions are to embed text information into KGs. Textual descriptions are not only stored in KGs, but can be extended to incorporate more general text information. The joint model aligns the given KG with the auxiliary text corpus and then combines KG embedding and word embedding [8]. This method combines entities, relationships, and words in the same vector space, combining structured triples and unstructured textual information to improve the embedding performance of the model. DKRL combines knowledge descriptions with TransE. This model relates entities with two vectors that capture triplet information and capture textual information represented by entity descriptions, which is superior to TransE [21]. TEKE is also a text-enhanced KG embedding model. For a given KG and a text corpus, TEKE first annotates the entities of the corpus to form a network of entities and words [12]. Then, words and entities in the text corpus that are frequently co-occurring with entities are defined as neighborhoods. TEKE combines text context embedding into traditional methods with greater expressive power.

KSR is an unsupervised KG embedding model based on multi-view clustering framework. It uses two-level split generation process for semantic knowledge representation. First, the first layer process generates a large number of knowledge views with different semantics. Then, the second layer process groups the triples according to the corresponding semantic views [22]. Finally, KSR constructs the semantic representation of the knowledge elements according to the cluster identifier of each view. Because the semantic representation is a vector of probability distributions, and the knowledge views are potential concepts, KSR uses the textual description of KG to map potential views and clusters into words that humans can understand. The specific method is to embed the knowledge elements and the textual description in the same semantic space, and then uses a query as a word sequence to predict the corresponding entity through semantic matching. This is a novel unsupervised embedding paradigm, but with a high degree of time and space complexity.

3.4 Logical Rules

The logic rules in KGs contain rich background information, which can effectively improve the performance of the embedding models. KALE is a framework that combines basic atoms with logical conjunctions to construct a complex formula [8]. The embedding learning is not only compatible with facts, but also compatible with rules, which can more effectively acquire and reason knowledge. However, this method is less efficient in time and space.

Recently, progress has been made in using logic rules to add simple constraints to KG to improve KG embedding. In the KG embedding, non-negative constraints on the representation of the entities and approximate implication constraints on the representation of the relationships are introduced. The former helps to learn the compact and interpretable representations of the entities. The latter further encodes the logically inevitable laws between relationships into their distributed representations. These constraints impose a priori information on the structure of the embedded space, which is beneficial for embedded prediction without significantly increasing the complexity of time and space. In addition, RUGE based on soft rules iteration guidance is a new paradigm in the logical rule models. RUGE believes that the specification can better enhance KG embedding in an iterative manner [23]. It can simultaneously learn from the markup triples directly observed in a given KG, the unlabeled triples whose names are to be iterated, and the soft rules that automatically extract various confidences from the KG. RUGE uses the currently learned embedding and soft rules to predict the soft tags of unlabeled triples, and substitutes the soft rules in the trusted prediction into the model for iteration. After such iterations, the knowledge contained in the logical rules can be better transferred to the embedded learning. Although this method is flexible, it has uncertainty and is highly dependent on the scoring function. R-MeN uses a relational memory network to model a relational triplet, which represents a triplet as a sequence of three input vectors that recursively interact with the relational memory network [24]. In the memory network, R-MeN uses a self-attention mechanism to integrate new information, and the output three vectors form a new vector, which improves the embedding performance by using the correlation between entities.

4 Conclusion

KG embedding technology embeds entities and relationships into a continuous vector space, and evaluates the relationships between them to obtain credible new entities and relationships. KG embedding technology has a broad application space in KG completion, relationship extraction, entity classification and resolution, etc. This article systematically evaluates the new technologies proposed in the recent two years. Based on the previous embedding models, focusing on the development of the past two years, this paper focuses on the new models and viewpoints on the KG embedding. The article classifies the model according to the type of information used in KG embedding. First, models that use only the information observed by facts are introduced, and the core ideas, implementation methods, advantages and disadvantages are briefly described. Then, models that fuse additional information are introduced and classified according to the kinds of additional information. We hope this short review can contribute a little to the development of KG embedding.

References

1. Nayyeri, M., Zhou, X., Vahdati, S., Yazdi, H.S., Lehmann, J.: Adaptive Margin Ranking Loss for Knowledge Graph Embeddings via a Correntropy Objective Function, pp. 1–7 (2019)
2. Zhu, J.-Z., Jia, Y.-T., Xu, J., Qiao, J.-Z., Cheng, X.-Q.: Modeling the correlations of relations for knowledge graph embedding. J. Comput. Sci. Technol. **33**(2), 323–334 (2018). https://doi.org/10.1007/s11390-018-1821-8
3. Ebisu, T., Ichise, R.: TorusE: knowledge graph embedding on a lie group. In: 32nd AAAI Conference Artificial Intelligence, AAAI 2018, pp. 1819–1826 (2018)
4. Niu, B., Huang, Y.: An improved method for web text affective cognition computing based on knowledge graph. Comput. Mater. Contin. **59**, 1–14 (2019). https://doi.org/10.32604/cmc.2019.06032
5. Li, D., Wu, H., Gao, J., Liu, Z., Li, L., Zheng, Z.: Uncertain knowledge reasoning based on the fuzzy multi entity Bayesian networks. Comput. Mater. Contin. **61**, 301–321 (2019). https://doi.org/10.32604/cmc.2019.05953
6. Lu, W., et al.: Graph-based Chinese word sense disambiguation with multi-knowledge integration. Comput. Mater. Contin. **61**, 197–212 (2019). https://doi.org/10.32604/cmc.2019.06068
7. Kolyvakis, P., Kalousis, A., Kiritsis, D.: HyperKG: hyperbolic knowledge graph embeddings for knowledge base completion (2019)
8. Wang, Q., Mao, Z., Wang, B., Guo, L.: Knowledge graph embedding: a survey of approaches and applications. IEEE Trans. Knowl. Data Eng. **29**, 2724–2743 (2017). https://doi.org/10.1109/TKDE.2017.2754499
9. Kishimoto, K., Hayashi, K., Akai, G., Shimbo, M., Komatani, K.: Binarized knowledge graph embeddings. In: Azzopardi, L., Stein, B., Fuhr, N., Mayr, P., Hauff, C., Hiemstra, D. (eds.) ECIR 2019. LNCS, vol. 11437, pp. 181–196. Springer, Cham (2019). https://doi.org/10.1007/978-3-030-15712-8_12
10. Kazemi, S.M., Poole, D.: Simple embedding for link prediction in knowledge graphs. In: Advances in Neural Information Processing System, pp. 4284–4295 (2018)
11. Dettmers, T., Minervini, P., Stenetorp, P., Riedel, S.: Convolutional 2D knowledge graph embeddings. In: 32nd AAAI Conference on Artificial Intelligence AAAI, pp. 1811–1818 (2018)
12. Ding, B., Wang, Q., Wang, B., Guo, L.: Improving knowledge graph embedding using simple constraints. In: ACL 2018 - 56th Annual Meeting Association Computer Linguistic Proceedings Conference, Long Paper, vol. 1, pp. 110–121 (2018). https://doi.org/10.18653/v1/p18-1011
13. Fatemi, B., Ravanbakhsh, S., Poole, D.: Improved knowledge graph embedding using background taxonomic information. In: Proceedings of the AAAI Conference on Artificial Intelligence, vol. 33, pp. 3526–3533 (2019)
14. Zhang, S., Tay, Y., Yao, L., Liu, Q.: Quaternion knowledge graph embedding. In: Advances in Neural Information Processing Systems, pp. 1–12 (2019)
15. Cai, C.: Group Representation Theory for Knowledge Graph Embedding (2019)

16. Yuan, J., Gao, N., Xiang, J.: TransGate: knowledge graph embedding with shared gate structure. In: Proceedings of the AAAI Conference on Artificial Intelligence, vol. 33, pp. 3100–3107 (2019). https://doi.org/10.1609/aaai.v33i01.33013100
17. Zhu, Q., Zhou, X., Zhang, P., Shi, Y.: A neural translating general hyperplane for knowledge graph embedding. J. Comput. Sci. **30**, 108–117 (2019). https://doi.org/10.1016/j.jocs.2018.11.004
18. Lv, X., Hou, L., Li, J., Liu, Z.: Differentiating Concepts and Instances for Knowledge Graph Embedding, pp. 1971–1979 (2019). https://doi.org/10.18653/v1/d18-1222
19. Rahman, M.M., Takasu, A.: Knowledge graph embedding via entities' type mapping matrix. In: Cheng, L., Leung, A.C.S., Ozawa, S. (eds.) ICONIP 2018. LNCS, vol. 11303, pp. 114–125. Springer, Cham (2018). https://doi.org/10.1007/978-3-030-04182-3_11
20. Jia, Y., Wang, Y., Jin, X., Cheng, X.: Path-specific knowledge graph embedding. Knowl.-Based Syst. **151**, 37–44 (2018). https://doi.org/10.1016/j.knosys.2018.03.020
21. Ma, L., Sun, P., Lin, Z., Wang, H.: Composing Knowledge Graph Embeddings via Word Embeddings (2019)
22. Xiao, H., Chen, Y., Shi, X.: Knowledge graph embedding based on multi-view clustering framework. IEEE Trans. Knowl. Data Eng., 1 (2019). https://doi.org/10.1109/tkde.2019.2931548
23. Guo, S., Wang, Q., Wang, L., Wang, B., Guo, L.: Knowledge graph embedding with iterative guidance from soft rules. In: 32nd AAAI Conference on Artificial Intelligence, AAAI 2018, pp. 4816–4823 (2018)
24. Nguyen, D.Q., Nguyen, T.D., Phung, D.: Relational Memory-based Knowledge Graph Embedding (2019)

A Robust Framework for High-Quality Voice Conversion with Conditional Generative Adversarial Network

Liyang Chen[1,3], Yingxue Wang[1,2(✉)], Yifeng Liu[2], Wendong Xiao[3], and Haiyong Xie[1,2]

[1] Advanced Innovation Center for Human Brain Protection, Capital Medical University, Beijing 100054, China
wangyingxue@csdslab.net
[2] National Engineering Laboratory for Public Safety Risk Perception and Control by Big Data (NEL-PSRPC), Beijing, China
[3] University of Science and Technology Beijing, Beijing, China

Abstract. The deep neural network (DNNs) has been applied in voice conversion (VC) system successfully. DNN shows its effectiveness especially with a large scale of training speech data, but on a small dataset, DNN suffers from the overfitting problem, resulting in performance degradation. Recently, many generative adversarial network (GAN) based VC methods have been developed, which prove to be a promising approach. However, the quality and similarity of generated speech are not entirely satisfactory. The converted speech usually consists of vague contents with buzzy noise and sounds robotic. In this paper, we study and make modification to the basic conditional generative network (cGAN). Focusing on establishing a robust framework for high-quality VC, the proposed method uses a cGAN with a L1 loss and a less explicit constraint, an identity loss. These constraints cooperate to generate speech of higher quality and similarity. We test our method on non-parallel datasets. An objective evaluation demonstrates that this approach achieves better performance and robustness than other GAN-based methods on the intra-gender task. A subjective evaluation shows that the naturalness and similarity are improved.

Keywords: Voice conversion · Generative adversarial network · Conditional generative adversarial network

1 Introduction

Voice conversion is a technique to convert the voice characteristics from one person to another, which means changing the non-linguistic information of speech but preserving the linguistic information. This technique can be applied to text-to-speech (TTS) synthesis [1], speech-to-speech translation [2], speaking assistant, mimicking voice, speech processing [3] and many entertainment areas like movie or game dubbing.

© Springer Nature Singapore Pte Ltd. 2020
X. Sun et al. (Eds.): ICAIS 2020, CCIS 1252, pp. 195–205, 2020.
https://doi.org/10.1007/978-981-15-8083-3_18

Since Kersta raised the concept of voice-print [4] in the 1970s, many voice conversion (VC) frameworks have been proposed. In the 1980s, when nonparametric models were popular, Masanobu proposed a VC method using vector quantization [5]. In the 1990s, the Gaussian mixture models [6, 7] were introduced into voice conversion and achieved great success. Recently, plenty of methods based on neural networks (NNs) have also been proved effective, such as artificial NN (ANN) [8], deep NN (DNN) [9], convolutional NN (CNN) [10], recurrent NN (RNN) [11], long short-term memory (LSTM) [12, 13], and generative adversarial networks (GANs) [10, 14–16].

These approaches mentioned above usually have one problem that the speech generated by the converter tends to be mingled with buzzy noise because of the over-smoothed acoustic features. The similarity of different acoustic features is commonly specified as mean square error (MSE), which probably causes the generated feature over-fitting. Hence, the problem of buzzy noise will always exist as long as the reconstruction loss (e.g., MSE) is introduced manually. Some attempts that use global variance [17] or modulation spectrum [18] have been made to mitigate this problem. Another powerful framework that fundamentally solves this problem involves GAN, because GAN offers a discriminator instead of a particular similarity loss to estimate if the generated speech is natural enough. Inspired by GAN's remarkable performance in image processing [19, 20] and signal processing [21], variants of GANs [10, 14] have been applied to voice conversion. However, the quality of the converted speech varies greatly due to the instability of GAN [22, 23]. At the same time, the converted speech is sometimes presented to be slurred and disfluent with vague pronunciation, since a defective data distribution might be learned when there're many mappings that can satisfy the GAN.

To overcome the limitations of existing methods and improve the quality and similarity of the converted speech, this paper proposes a VC method, using a conditional generative adversarial network (cGAN). This method, called cGAN-VC, contains two stages: training and conversion. In training the cGAN, the generator and discriminator keep updating their parameters when feature sequences from the source and target speech are extracted and then fed into the cGAN network. The L1 loss and identity loss cooperate to help constrain the cGAN to be optimized to a proper mapping. At the conversion stage, the synthesizer produces speech based on the feature sequences which are converted by the pretrained generator that has learned the target data distribution.

Although many GAN based methods have been studied to implement voice conversion, to the best of our knowledge, it's the first time to apply the conditional GAN to voice conversion.

This paper is organized as follows. In Sect. 2, related works about GAN based methods are demonstrated. Section 3, 4 present the basic GAN and cGAN. The proposed cGAN is described in Sect. 5. In Sect. 6, experiments are carried out to estimate the proposed method and compare it with other methods. In Sect. 7, we summarize this paper and illustrate our future work.

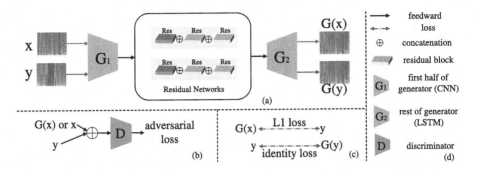

Fig. 1. The proposed pipline of cGAN. Given two speech utterances from the source speaker x and the target speaker y, the generator produces G(x) and G(y) respectively. As shown in (a), the inputs are fed into G1 which is constructed with 1-D CNNs and then through G2 which is stacked with LSTM. The traditional adversarial loss is shown in (b). We introduce L1 loss and identity loss to for optimization as illustrated in (c). All of the notations are listed in (d).

2   Related Works

In recent two years, GANs have been studied vigorously and many voice conversion methods have been proposed based on GANs [10,14–16]. One method [10] that involved GAN used the hidden layer feature derived from the discriminator to describe similarity between the target and converted speech, which proved to be a reasonable idea. A method [14] combined a conditional variational autoencoder (CVAE) and Wasserstein GAN (WGAN), where the WGAN was designed to synthesize speech. However, there is still a discernible similarity gap between the converted voice and the target with these two methods. A variant of GAN, called cycleGAN, recently has been proposed [15,16] and gained impressive improvement. By establishing a cycle consist model, it successfully separated the speaker characteristics from speech. The speech generated by [15] sounds quite like the target, but some speech is not clear enough to accurately identify the speech contents.

Drawing ideas from the methods above, our work focuses on building a more accurate model for non-linguistic information and linguistic contents in speech by integrating the cGAN with two specified constraints. We modified the original cGAN and found that the cGAN could be a more effective model for the VC task, which has not been considered in earlier VC studies.

3   Generative Adversarial Networks

Generative adversarial network was proposed by Goodfellow [22] in 2014, which aims to train deep generative models. The goal of GAN is to let the generator G learn a mapping from random noise vector z to output y, as well as the discriminator D distinguish between real y and fake $G(z)$. The objective of GAN [22] can be expressed as

$$\mathcal{L}_{GAN}(G, D) = \mathbb{E}_{x \sim p_{data}(x)}[\log D(x)] + \mathbb{E}_{z \sim p_z(z)}[\log(1 - D(G(z)))], \quad (1)$$

where $D(x)$ or $D(G(z))$ represents the probability that x or $G(z)$ comes from the real data distribution or fake data. $P_{data}(x)$ and $P_z(z)$ denote the distribution of real data and noise. In the process of training, the generator G tries to minimize this objective, while the discriminator D tries to maximize it, like a minimax two-player game.

4   Conditional Generative Adversarial Networks

The original GAN is under no condition and its output cannot be predicted and controlled. The conditional GAN [24] is a variant of GAN, whose goal is to let G learn a mapping from the condition x and random noise vector z to output y, while D needs to correctly classify (x, y) as real pair and $(x, G(x, z))$ as fake pair. The objective [25] is written as

$$\mathcal{L}_{cGAN}(G, D) = \mathbb{E}_{x,y}[\log D(x, y)] + \mathbb{E}_{x,z}[\log(1 - D(x, G(x, z)))], \quad (2)$$

where the condition x could denote class labels or other data modalities and it is fed into both the generator and the discriminator. The condition x is introduced to direct the generation process, producing certain results as well as significantly improve the quality of outputs.

Besides the adversarial loss $L_{cGAN}(G, D)$ in cGAN, previous research [26] indicated that it's beneficial to mix the cGAN objective with a manual loss, such as L1 distance:

$$\mathcal{L}_{L1}(G) = \mathbb{E}_{x,y,z}[\|y - G(x, z)\|_1], \quad (3)$$

which gives the network an explicit direction to converge.

5   Conditional Adversarial Network for Voice Conversion

The voice conversion task can be considered as learning a mapping from the source speaker $x \in X$(X:source speaker) to the target speaker $y \in Y$(Y:target speaker). Our method, as shown in Fig. 1, modifies the original cGAN for meeting the requirement of speech signal processing and VC system.

A common problem regarding regular GANs is that the traditional adversarial loss in Eq. (2) will lead to gradients vanishing and instability, and therefore this paper adopts the least squares loss function [27]. In the meantime, the random noise vector z is abandoned for showing no effectiveness in our experiments. In order to use the same tool to optimize G and D, we split the adversarial loss into two parts $\mathcal{L}_{cGAN}(G)$ and $\mathcal{L}_{cGAN}(D)$ and transform both of them into the problem of minimum:

$$\mathcal{L}_{cGAN}(G) = \mathbb{E}_x[(D(x, G(x)) - 1)^2], \tag{4}$$

$$\mathcal{L}_{cGAN}(D) = \mathbb{E}_y[(D(x, y) - 1)^2] + \mathbb{E}_x[D(x, G(x))^2], \tag{5}$$

$$\mathcal{L}_{cGAN}(G, D) = \mathcal{L}_{cGAN}(G) + \mathcal{L}_{cGAN}(D). \tag{6}$$

If there're no other constraints to be introduced besides the adversarial loss, cGAN tends to produce blurry results. For this reason, apart from the $\mathcal{L}_{L1}(G)$ mentioned in last section, a less explicit constraint is introduced:

$$\mathcal{L}_{id}(G) = \mathbb{E}_y[\|G(y) - y\|_1]. \tag{7}$$

This identity loss ensures that when real y is fed into the G, the output of G keeps unchanged, referred from the idea of cycleGAN [16].

Thus the full objective to be minimized is given as

$$\mathcal{L}_{full} = \mathcal{L}_{cGAN}(G, D) + \lambda_{L1}\mathcal{L}_{L1}(G) + \lambda_{id}\mathcal{L}_{id}(G), \tag{8}$$

where λ_{L1} and λ_{id} separately weigh the importance of the L1 loss and the identity loss. In this equation, λ_{L1} enforces correctness of speech contents while λ_{id} encourages the speech timbre.

6   Experiments

6.1   Implementation of the Proposed Method

The process of voice conversion is composed of three phases: feature extraction, feature conversion and speech synthesize. The Fig. 2 shows the framework of the approach we have proposed.

In this paper, three features [12], which are widely used in VC areas, have been extracted from speech data: mel-cepstral coefficients(MCEPs), logarithmic fundamental frequency($\log F0$) and aperiodic components(APs). These three features are converted separately. MCEPs represent the distribution of speech signal energy in different frequency ranges, based on known variation of the human ear's critical bandwidth [28]. MCEPs are transformed with the modified cGAN, where the MCEPs of 24 dimensions from the source speaker are considered as the condition x and those of the target speaker as y. The $\log F0$ is converted according to the linear transformation [29] as indicated in the Eq. (9) below:

$$\log(f0_{conv}) = \mu_{tgt} + \frac{\sigma_{tgt}}{\sigma_{src}}(\log(f0_{src}) - \mu_{src}), \tag{9}$$

where μ_{src} and σ_{src} denote the mean and variance of the logarithmic fundamental frequency for the source speaker, $f0_{src}$ and $f0_{conv}$ are the fundamental frequency for the source speech and the converted speech. The APs remain

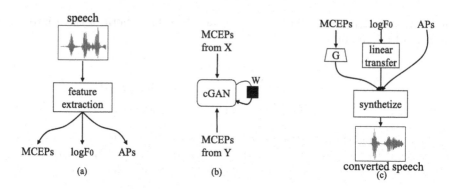

Fig. 2. Framework of cGAN-VC. Three features are extracted from speech as shown in (a). With the MCEPs extracted from the source speaker X and target speaker Y, the cGAN updates the parameters as illustrated in (b). Three features are converted respectively and synthetized to the final converted speech. The MCEPs are converted by the generator (G) in cGAN as shown in (c).

unchanged because the previous study has shown they make little significant difference on the synthesized speech [30].

Once we obtain the converted MCEPs, log $F0$ and APs, we can reconstruct a time-domain signal using the WORLD [31], which is a famous speech synthesis system.

6.2   Network Architecture

The generator and discriminator architectures are adapted from CNN and LSTM. The generator, structurally similar to an encoder-decoder network, is designed using one dimensional CNNs (1-D CNNs) and LSTM, which have been widely used for sequence models. In the first half of G, the input is passed through a series of convolutional and pooling layers that progressively downsample and capture the relationship among feature sequences. The rest of G uses upsampling layers [32] followed with LSTM nets to restore the tensor dimension for reconstructing feature sequences. Residual Networks are introduced to connect the generator, which prove to improve the generation performance. The inputs of D are pairs of (x, y) and $(x, G(x))$, where feature sequences from the source speech as x, those from the target speech as y and those from the generated speech as $G(x)$. The input pair needs to be concatenated at the dimension of feature rather than batch size. The discriminator is constructed with stacks of LSTM to give a probability, trying to distinguish between real (x, y) and fake $(x, G(x))$ pair. The discriminator constructed with LSTM shows higher stability and faster convergence in training compared with CNNs.

6.3   Experimental Setup

To explore the performance of cGAN-VC, the proposed method is evaluated on the corpus including the datasets of Voice Conversion Challenge 2016 and 2018 [33]. The datasets contain parallel data from 5 male speakers and 5 female speakers, and we choose SF1 and SM1 as the female-to-male (inter-gender) test while TF2 and SF1 as the female-to-female (intra-gender) test. For each speaker, 192 utterances as training data and 59 utterances as evaluation data are provided. The speech data is sampled at 16 kHz, and 24 MCEPs, $\log F0$ and APs are extracted every 5 ms by WORLD [31]. To optimize the networks, we followed the standard approach in [22], alternating between G and D. The Adam solver was applied in training with a learning rate of 0.0002, and momentum parameters $\beta_1 = 0.5$, $\beta_2 = 0.999$. We set $\lambda_{L1} = 1$ and $\lambda_{id} = 10$ to ensure the quality of voice as well as avoid buzzy noise. The number of training epochs was 150.

Table 1. Comparison of MCD and LPCCs distance.

	MCEPS		LPCC	
Method	SF1-SM1	TF2-SF1	SF1-SM1	TF2-SF1
cGAN	**8.52**	**7.44**	**0.48**	**0.40**
cycleGAN	8.46	7.64	0.50	0.43
WGAN	9.61	9.44	0.82	0.88
GAN	12.32	11.45	1.02	1.10

Since GAN-based works are the state-of-the-art VC techniques, we compare our approach with methods based on GAN, WGAN and cycleGAN proposed in [15], and all methods are tested on inter-gender and intra-gender tasks.

6.4   Objective Evaluation

Mel-cepstral distortion (MCD) is a common objective evaluation method to compute the spectral distortion between the converted speech and the target speech, given by the following equation:

$$MCD[dB] = \frac{10}{\ln 10} \frac{1}{T} \sum_{t=0}^{T} mcd(t), \tag{10}$$

$$mcd(t) = \sqrt{2 \sum_{d=1}^{24} \|mc_{tgt}(t,d) - mc_{conv}(t,d)\|_2}, \tag{11}$$

where $mc_{tgt}(t,d)$ and $mc_{conv}(t,d)$ denote the dth coefficient at the t frame index of the target and the converted mel-cepstra, respectively. We apply the dynamic time warping (DTW) algorithm before computing MCD to reduce interference of different pronunciation habits. Similarly, the distance of linear predictive cepstral coefficients (LPCCs) between the target and the converted speech is also calculated.

As shown in Table 1, the proposed cGAN-VC outperforms the GAN and WGAN which rarely produce effective results. It can be observed that on the intra-gender task, the MCD has been reduced to 7.44, 0.2 dB lower than cycleGAN. In the aspect of LPCC distance, our method achieves lower grades in both inter-gender and intra-gender task compared with cycleGAN. In the progress of training, we found a tendency that the increasement of λ_{L1} could reduce the MCD however make the speech sound less natural. We also show the selected envelopes of MCEPs sequences in Fig. 3, while the curve of GAN is omitted because of its weak performance. It indicates that the MCEPs curves generated by our method are sometimes closer to the target.

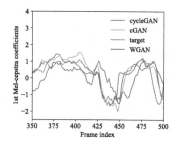 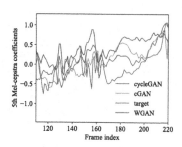

Fig. 3. 1st and 5th MCEPs sequences from SM1 to SF1.

6.5 Subjective Evaluation

To measure the quality and similarity of the converted speech, the mean opinion score (MOS) tests are conducted. Ten well-educated people participated in the tests and they were asked to give points scaled form 5 (top) to 1 (worst) on 10 sentences generated by each method.

As shown in Table 2, either in the inter-gender or intra-gender test, our method and cycleGAN have significant advantages, since speech generated by the other two methods have plenty of glitches between pronunciation.

In terms of the quality evaluation, listeners considered that cGAN-VC provided the most natural samples of all methods, which sounded more clear and coherent with less buzzing noise. The quality of WGAN and GAN outputs vary greatly in different speech. In the evaluation of similarity, cGAN-VC has obvious enhancements in the inter-gender task, but achieves lower grades than cycleGAN when converting voice between females.

The objective and subjective evaluation almost reach the consistent conclusion that cGAN-VC has gained significant improvement with speech of higher

Table 2. MOS for quality and similarity of converted speech.

Method	Quality		Similarity	
	Inter-gender	Intra-gender	Inter-gender	Intra-gender
cGAN	**3.1**	**3.2**	**2.8**	**2.5**
cycleGAN	3.1	3.0	2.7	2.8
WGAN	2.4	2.5	1.4	2.0
GAN	1.5	1.4	1.1	1.3

quality and similarity. Furthermore, it's noteworthy that in the training, cGAN-VC is so controllable and robust that the quality and similarity of the speech can be adjusted with the L1 and identity loss.

7 Conclusions and Future Work

We have proposed a voice conversion framework based on the conditional GAN. The network learns a reliable and robust mapping from the source speaker to the target speaker. With a L1 loss and identity loss to be introduced, the quality and naturalness of converted speech is ensured while the characteristic and similarity of voice is encouraged correctly. The objective evaluation indicates that the speech obtained by our method proves to be closer to the target. The subjective evaluation confirms that cGAN-VC produces speech of higher quality and outperforms other GAN based methods in the evaluation of similarity.

In this paper, the network mapping is only applied to the MCEPs, while $\log F0$ is transformed arithmetically and APs are preserved. To improve the similarity of conversion, we plan to develop a integrated system to convert all the three elements.

Acknowledgements. This research is supported in part by the National Science and Technology Major Project for IND (investigational new drug) (Project No. 2018ZX09201-014), National Key Research and Development Project (Grant No. 2017YFC0820504), and the CETC Joint Advanced Research Foundation (Grant No. 6141B08080101, 6141B08010102).

References

1. Jia, Y., Zhang, Y., Weiss, R., et al.: Transfer learning from speaker verification to multispeaker text-to-speech synthesis. In: Advances in Neural Information Processing Systems, pp. 4480–4490 (2018)
2. Jia, Y., Weiss, R.J., Biadsy, F., et al.: Direct speech-to-speech translation with a sequence-to-sequence model (2019). arXiv preprint arXiv:1904.06037
3. Zhao, Y., Yue, J., Song, W., et al.: Tibetan multi-dialect speech and dialect identity recognition. Comput. Mater. Continua **60**(3), 1223–1235 (2019)
4. Kersta, L.G.: Voiceprint identification. J. Acoust. Soc. Am. **34**(5), 725–725 (1962)

5. Abe, M., Nakamura, S., Shikano, K., et al.: Voice conversion through vector quantization. J. Acoust. Soc. Jpn (E) **11**(2), 71–76 (1990)
6. Stylianou, Y., Cappé, O., Moulines, E.: Continuous probabilistic transform for voice conversion. IEEE Trans. Speech Audio Process. **6**(2), 131–142 (1998)
7. Chen, Y., Chu, M., Chang, E., et al.: Voice conversion with smoothed GMM and MAP adaptation. In: Eighth European Conference on Speech Communication and Technology (2003)
8. Desai, S., Black, A.W., Yegnanarayana, B., et al.: Spectral mapping using artificial neural networks for voice conversion. IEEE Trans. Audio Speech Lang. Process. **18**(5), 954–964 (2010)
9. Mohammadi, S.H., Kain, A.: Voice conversion using deep neural networks with speaker-independent pre-training. In: IEEE Spoken Language Technology Workshop (SLT), pp. 19–23 (2019)
10. Kaneko, T., Kameoka, H., Hiramatsu, K., et al.: Sequence-to-sequence voice conversion with similarity metric learned using generative adversarial networks. In: INTERSPEECH, pp. 1283–1287 (2017)
11. Tobing, P.L., Wu, Y.C., Hayashi, T., et al.: Voice conversion with cyclic recurrent neural network and fine-tuned Wavenet vocoder. In: ICASSP 2019–2019 IEEE International Conference on Acoustics, Speech and Signal Processing (ICASSP), pp. 6815–6819. IEEE (2019)
12. Sun, L., Kang, S., Li, K., et al.: Voice conversion using deep bidirectional long short-term memory based recurrent neural networks. In: 2015 IEEE International Conference on Acoustics, Speech and Signal Processing (ICASSP), pp. 4869–4873. IEEE (2015)
13. Sun, L., Li, K., Wang, H., et al.: Phonetic posteriorgrams for many-to-one voice conversion without parallel data training. In: 2016 IEEE International Conference on Multimedia and Expo (ICME), pp. 1–6. IEEE (2016)
14. Hsu, C.C., Hwang, H.T., Wu, Y.C., et al.: Voice conversion from unaligned corpora using variational autoencoding wasserstein generative adversarial networks (2017). arXiv preprint arXiv:1704.00849
15. Fang, F., Yamagishi, J., Echizen, I., et al.: High-quality nonparallel voice conversion based on cycle-consistent adversarial network. In: 2018 IEEE International Conference on Acoustics, Speech and Signal Processing (ICASSP), pp. 5279–5283. IEEE (2018)
16. Kaneko, T., Kameoka, H., Tanaka, K., et al.: CycleGAN-VC2: improved CycleGAN-based non-parallel voice conversion. In: ICASSP 2019–2019 IEEE International Conference on Acoustics, Speech and Signal Processing (ICASSP), pp. 6820–6824. IEEE (2019)
17. Silén, H., Helander, E., Nurminen, J., et al.: Ways to implement global variance in statistical speech synthesis. In: Thirteenth Annual Conference of the International Speech Communication Association (2012)
18. Takamichi, S., Toda, T., Black, A.W., et al.: Postfilters to modify the modulation spectrum for statistical parametric speech synthesis. IEEE/ACM Trans. Audio Speech Lang. Process. (TASLP) **24**(4), 755–767 (2016)
19. Creswell, A., White, T., Dumoulin, V., et al.: Generative adversarial networks: an overview. IEEE Sig. Process. Mag. **35**(1), 53–65 (2018)
20. Li, C., Jiang, Y., Cheslyar, M.: Embedding image through generated intermediate medium using deep convolutional generative adversarial network. Comput. Mater. Continua **56**(2), 313–324 (2018)

21. Tu, Y., Lin, Y., Wang, J., Kim, J.-U.: Semi-supervised learning with generative adversarial networks on digital signal modulation classification. Comput. Mater. Continua **55**(2), 243–254 (2018)
22. Goodfellow, I., Pouget-Abadie, J., Mirza, M., et al.: Generative adversarial nets. In: Advances in Neural Information Processing Systems, pp. 2672–2680 (2014)
23. Arjovsky, M., Chintala, S., Bottou, L.: Wasserstein generative adversarial networks. In: International Conference on Machine Learning, pp. 214–223 (2017)
24. Mirza, M., Osindero, S.: Conditional generative adversarial nets (2014). arXiv preprint arXiv:1411.1784
25. Isola, P., Zhu, J.Y., Zhou, T., et al.: Image-to-image translation with conditional adversarial networks. In: Proceedings of the IEEE Conference on Computer Vision and Pattern Recognition, pp. 1125–1134 (2017)
26. Pathak, D., Krahenbuhl, P., Donahue, J., et al.: Context encoders: feature learning by inpainting. In: Proceedings of the IEEE Conference on Computer Vision and Pattern Recognition, pp. 2536–2544 (2016)
27. Mao, X., Li, Q., Xie, H., et al.: Least squares generative adversarial networks. In: Proceedings of the IEEE International Conference on Computer Vision, pp. 2794–2802 (2017)
28. Muda, L., Begam, M., Elamvazuthi, I.: Voice recognition algorithms using mel frequency cepstral coefficient (MFCC) and dynamic time warping (DTW) techniques (2010). arXiv preprint arXiv:1003.4083
29. Liu, K., Zhang, J., Yan, Y.: High quality voice conversion through phoneme-based linear mapping functions with STRAIGHT for mandarin. In: Fourth International Conference on Fuzzy Systems and Knowledge Discovery (FSKD 2007), vol. 4, pp. 410–414. IEEE (2007)
30. Ohtani, Y., Toda, T., Saruwatari, H., et al.: Maximum likelihood voice conversion based on GMM with STRAIGHT mixed excitation (2006)
31. Morise, M., Yokomori, F., Ozawa, K.: WORLD: a vocoder-based high-quality speech synthesis system for real-time applications. IEICE Trans. Inf. Syst. **99**(7), 1877–1884 (2016)
32. Zhao, Y., Li, G., Xie, W., et al.: GUN: gradual upsampling network for single image super-resolution. IEEE Access **6**, 39363–39374 (2018)
33. Lorenzo-Trueba, J., Yamagishi, J., Toda, T., et al.: The voice conversion challenge 2018: Promoting development of parallel and nonparallel methods (2018). arXiv preprint arXiv:1804.04262

Effective Android Malware Detection Based on Deep Learning

Yueqi Jin[1,2,3], Tengfei Yang[1(✉)], Yangyang Li[1], and Haiyong Xie[1,3]

[1] National Engineering Laboratory for Public Safety Risk Perception and Control by Big Data (NEL-PSRPC), Beijing, China
yangtengfei1@cetc.com.cn
[2] Key Laboratory of Electromagnetic Space Information, Chinese Academy of Sciences, Beijing, China
[3] University of Science and Technology of China, Hefei, China

Abstract. Android, the world's most widely used mobile operating system, is the target of a large number of malwares. These malwares have brought great trouble to information security and users' privacy, such as leaking personal information, secretly downloading programs to consume data, and secretly sending deduction SMS messages. With the increase of malwares, detection methods have been proposed constantly. Especially in recent years, the malware detection methods based on deep learning are popular. However, the detection methods based on static features have a low accuracy, and others based on dynamic features take a long time, all this limits its scope.

In this paper, we proposed a static feature detection method based on deep learning. It extracts specific API calls of applications and uses DNN network for detection. With the dataset composed about 4000 applications and extremely short time, it can achieve an accuracy rate of more than 99%.

Keywords: Android security · Deep learning · Malware detection

1 Introduction

Mobile phones are now an integral part of our lives, and the most widely used mobile operating system is Android, which accounts for about 85% of the world [1]. Android is used not only on mobile phones, but also on various mobile platforms, such as tablets. Obviously, these mobile devices store a huge amount of users' personal information and even money, so they need to be protected carefully. Is different from the PCs, however, only few years, the popularity of mobile devices in security is not popularized the decades of the PCs, which leads to more and more malwares aimed at the android. According to the report by Symantec [2], 20% Android apps are malwares.

Initially, the idea was to use signature files for detection. But with the outbreak of malwares, this kind method witch depends on huge signature library

© Springer Nature Singapore Pte Ltd. 2020
X. Sun et al. (Eds.): ICAIS 2020, CCIS 1252, pp. 206–218, 2020.
https://doi.org/10.1007/978-981-15-8083-3_19

has gradually become ineffective. Later, people tried running applications with virtual machines to monitor applications' malicious behavior directly ([3,4]). Obviously this method is the most direct, but there may be missing information, and takes a long time. And new malwares increased the delay time in starting up or even directly detect the virtual machine environment for counter-monitoring. Around 2010, the concept of machine learning emerged, and a series of detection methods using machine learning classifier appeared, such as support vector machine(SVM). It extracts some static feature codes in the application or feature logs generated by runtime, and uses various classifier of machine learning to discriminate malwares. This method also achieved great results.

Deep learning is the strengthening of the machine learning. The concept of using deep learning networks to detect Android malware was first proposed in 2014. With AlphaGo beat Sedol Lee in 2016, the value of deep learning was seen by more people, and detection methods based on deep learning were constantly proposed. In general, the effect of deep learning is closely related to features and network.

Our Contribution: We used 1092 sensitive system API calls as features and Deep Neural Network for training. When tested in a dataset consisting of about 4,000 applications, the accuracy was consistently over 99% with minimal time consumption.

The Reminder of the Paper Is Organized as Follows: Section 2 reviews previous work on android malware detection. Section 3 introduces the application features and DNN network related preliminaries. Section 4 and Sect. 5 gives the implementation details of our experiments and results with evaluation.

2   Related Work

2.1   Static-Feature Detection

The earliest tests using completely static features were published in 2016 ([5–7]). The first two papers are similar in that they use DBN to learn using the permissions requested by applications and the APIs called as features. [7] introduced the concept of API-blocks and achieved 96% accuracy. In 2017, [8] was the first to introduce CNN, which reshaped feature vectors into matrices and trained them by image recognition. This idea also appeared in [9] and [10] of the same year, achieving nearly 100% accuracy.

The biggest drawback of CNN and DBN is the high time complexity, which is not suitable for real-time scanning. In 2018, [11] first used DNN to train the static permissions-api feature, which is also the most similar to our work. The DNN network had a significant speed advantage on the (relative to the image) low-dimensional feature set, and they had a 95.67% F1-score.

```
.method public constructor <init>()V
    .registers 1

    .prologue
    .line 17
    invoke-direct {p0}, Ljava/lang/Object;->:<init>()V

    return-void
.end method
```

Fig. 1. Smali code

2.2 Dynamic-Feature Detection

Detection that relies entirely on dynamic features is less frequent because it takes a long time. In 2016 and 2017, [12] adopted the method of emotional analysis to realize malware identification by monitoring system calls and treating system call sequence as text. [13] used Stacked Autoencoders (SAEs) to scan malware and identify new malwares according to the graphical representation of extracted system calls in Linux.

2.3 Hybrid-Feature Detection

[14] in 2014 was the first attempt to apply deep learning to android malware detection. It extracted permissions and sensitive API calls as static feature, used actions monitored by running applications in sandbox as dynamic features, and used DBN for training. This method obtained a good accuracy about 93.5%. In [15], a detection method based on HADM is proposed, which uses Self-Encoder to study the features of applications, and then uses SVM for classification, achieving 95% accuracy. [16] extracts the dynamic and static features, then uses LSTM to analyze, and good results has been achieved.

3   Our Method Description

3.1 Feature Extraction

We can get the "smali" code by decompiling the application file, as Fig. 1. The function calls in the smali code have a format similar to *Ljava/long/Object;->*<*init*>*()V*. What we care about is which system sensitive APIs the application calls. For example, *SmsManager;->sendTextMessage* is used to send text messages, *ITelephony$Stub$Proxy;->call* is used to make phone calls. Of course, these APIs are called in benign applications, so we want to use neural networks to help us analyze the underlying information between these calls.

- **Step1:** After decompressing the Apk file to get the "classes.dex" file, we decompile it using the "baksmali" program to get the smali code.
- **Step2:**[1] Document all statements in smali code that contain ";->".

---

[1] Step 2 is not necessary, but it improves the efficiency of the search in step 3.

– **Step3:** Using our list of sensitive APIs, we organize the application's corresponding smali code into boolean vectors.

Here we will explain step 3. Assumes that our list of sensitive APIs contains n values, in order $[f_1, f_2, ..., f_n]$, so our Boolean vector from step 3 should have n dimensions, let's call that $[x_1, x_2, ..., x_n]$. For each $i \in \{1, 2, ..., n\}$, $x_i = 1$ if and only if f_i appears in the smali code. In other words, the program calls the API f_i. For example, smali code contains f_1 and f_3, not f_2, so the corresponding boolean vector is $[1,0,1,...]$. We don't care about the order or time of API calls here, just whether they appeared in the smali code.

3.2 Sensitive API List

The core of our results is a more typical sensitive API list. These APIs are selected from the PSCout dataset [17], which contains a large number ofs system APIs and their corresponding permissions. We counted how often these APIs appeared in thousands of benign applications and malwares (The application dataset used here is completely different from the experimental dataset in next Section). We find APIs that appear more frequently in malwares and less frequently in benign applications that make up this list[2]. Compared with other similar methods, we dropped the less distinguishing features of permission and expanded the list of API features in selecting features. These APIs perfectly represent the malicious nature of the program. Based on this list, we can steadily improve the accuracy rate to 99%. At the same time, we can use a simpler network than other methods, thus reducing its running time while maintaining accuracy.

3.3 Training DNN Model

DNN training process, like other networks, is divided into forward propagation and back propagation.

Forward Propagation. For each neuron in each hidden layers in Figure ??, we can think of it as a perceptron like Fig. 2. Its output is the following:

$$b_{in} = \sum_{i=1}^{m} w_i a_i$$

m is the number of neurons in the upper layer. Unlike perceptrons, its output can only be used as the input of the next layer by introducing nonlinear factors through activation function. The RELU function is used in our network. So the output of the neurons in each of the hidden layers of DNN is

$$b_{out} = relu(b_{in}) = relu(\sum_{i=1}^{m} w_i a_i)$$

---

[2] In appendix, we will show part of this list.

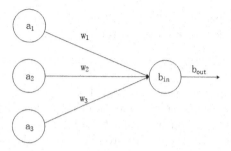

Fig. 2. Propagation

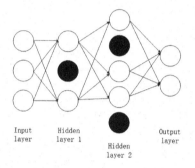

Fig. 3. Dropout

Input the n-dimensional vector obtained in the previous step into the input layer, the output of the output-layer is calculated layer by layer, which completes forward propagation.

Back Propagation. Forward propagation is to sum the output of the upper layer by the weight of edges to get the input of the next layer. Backpropagation is the process of updating the weight of each edge, so that the final value obtained by forward propagation is close to the actual label. The function that measures this approximation is called the loss function. The purpose of back propagation is to reduce the value of loss function. Our network uses the cross entropy loss function. To achieve this goal, we need to use the gradient descent method to change the weight of each edge iteratively. The specific calculation of back propagation is relatively complex, which can be referred to the paper, but will not be described here.

3.4   Dropout

Overfitting is a common problem in deep learning. The specific manifestation of overfitting is that the trained model has a higher accuracy in the training set, but a lower accuracy in the test set. In order to solve this problem, Hinton proposed *Dropout* in 2012 [18], which can effectively alleviate the overfitting phenomenon.

Dropout simply means that during the forward propagation, some neurons stop working at a certain probability (i.e., output value is 0). Compared with Figure ??, black neurons shown in Fig. 3 are inactive. In this way, the generalization performance of the model is stronger and it is less likely to be overly dependent on some localb features. During the training, we set a probability to prevent overfitting, and the difference in accuracy in the test set can be clearly seen during the test. (See next section for details)

4   Experiment Result and Evaluation

4.1   Application Dataset

We selected a dataset composed of about 4,000 applications. Among them, about 2,000 samples of benign applications are from XiaoMi-APPStore (after scanning by anti-virus software, there may still be malwares in them, but we temporarily consider this dataset reasonable), about 2000 malwares come from the Drebin Dataset ([19,20]). We selected almost all kinds of applications and made sure there were no duplicate elements in our dataset. We take 600 applications (300 in each case) as the test set and the rest as the training set.

4.2   Sensitive API List

The list of sensitive APIs refers to the PSCout Dataset [17], which contains about 35000 system APIs and their corresponding permissions in the latest version. We have selected 1092 representative ones for our sensitive API list.

4.3   Runtime Environment

In order to prove that our model is efficient, we did not adopt a more efficient GPU, instead, model training was done using a PC CPU. Our experiment ran in Windows 10, and hardware setting are 4 GB DDR4 RAM and Intel(R) Core(TM) i5-3470 CPU.

4.4   Experimental Results Under Different Parameters

Compared to other papers, we only selected the static feature of API calls, but we chose a larger list of sensitive APIs than others. Here we test three metrics: precision, recall, accuracy, and time consumption.

- **Precision:** Currently classified into positive sample categories, the proportion correctly classified.
- **Recall:** The percentage of all positive samples that are currently assigned to a positive sample category.
- **Accuracy:** The ratio of correctly predicted samples to the total predicted samples.

Table 1. Results with different network model

Malware/Benign = 1 : 1, Train : Test = 3400 : 600, Epochs = 200					
Network	Learning rate	Precision(%)	Recall(%)	Accuracy(%)	Time cost(s)
[500]	0.008	99.67	99.33	99.5	67
[1000, 100]	0.005	99.01	99.67	99.33	114
[1000, 500, 100]	0.0005	99.33	99.67	99.5	155
[1000, 600, 200, 50]	0.00005	98.36	100	99.167	176

Network [500] represents a network with only one hidden layer of 500 neurons, others in a similar way

Table 2. Results with different network model

Malware/Benign = 1 : 1, Train : Test = 3000 : 1000, Epochs = 200					
Network	Learning rate	Precision(%)	Recall(%)	Accuracy(%)	Time cost(s)
[500]	0.008	99.2	99.6	99.4	51
[1000, 100]	0.005	99.4	99.4	99.4	99
[1000, 500, 100]	0.0005	99.01	99.8	99.4	144
[1000, 600, 200, 50]	0.00005	99.2	99	99.1	169

Because the accuracy of the experiment may fluctuate slightly, in this section, we give the most common accuracy in the experiment and its corresponding precision and recall. In appendix 2, we give the accuracy list of 10 consecutive experiments under different conditions.

Table 1 describes the influence of network depth on the results when the number of positive and negative examples is equal. It can be seen from the table that all networks can achieve good results. Our training set has about 3400 samples. When the *BATCH_SIZE* is set to 50, there are about 65 iterations per epoch. In fact, our algorithm has basically converged after the first few iterations of the first epoch, and Fig. 4 below shows the accuracy curve of the first epoch. It can be seen that the accuracy rate after a epoch has been basically stable, and the iteration time of a epoch only takes a few seconds, which is almost negligible.

In the above experiment, Train: Test is 34:6. Next, we adjust this ratio to 3:1. Take 1000 samples as the test set, and the rest as the training set. Also use the above several networks for training. Table 2 shows the experimental results. It can be seen that under such conditions, all networks can still maintain an average accuracy rate above 99%.

In practice, the number of benign applications is obviously greater than that of malwares, so we reduced the proportion of malwares in the training set to conduct training. In the following experiments, *Malware : Benign* = 1 : 2, and the number of samples in the test set is 600. Table 3 shows the experimental results. From the results, the network accuracy rate of 2 or 3 hidden layers is stable at 99%–99.5%.

In Table 4, we further reduce the proportion of malicious programs and set *Malware : Benign* = 1 : 5. It can be seen from the results that the accuracy

Table 3. Results with different network model

Malware/Benign = 1 : 2, Train : Test = 2550 : 600, Epochs = 200

Network	Learning rate	Precision(%)	Recall(%)	Accuracy(%)	Time cost(s)
[500]	0.008	99.33	99.67	99.5	50
[1000, 100]	0.005	99.01	99.67	99.33	99
[1000, 500, 100]	0.0005	99.33	99.67	99.5	148
[1000, 600, 200, 50]	0.00005	98.03	100	99	159

Table 4. Results with different network model

Malware/Benign = 1 : 5, Train : Test = 2040 : 600, Epochs = 200

Network	Learning rate	Precision(%)	Recall(%)	Accuracy(%)	Time cost(s)
[500]	0.008	100	98.67	99.33	41
[1000, 100]	0.005	99.33	99	99.167	79
[1000, 500, 100]	0.0005	99.01	99.67	99.33	123
[1000, 600, 200, 50]	0.00005	97.39	99.67	98.5	138

rate is maintained at 98%–99%. In this experiment, due to the low proportion of malwares, the accuracy of the model trained from scratch fluctuates to a certain among. In general, increasing the proportion of benign procedures in training concentration will have a negative impact on the training effect, but the impact is limited.

In addition, we tested the accuracy of the test set after the model was trained from scratch with 20 epochs under various parameters. Table 5, 6, 7, 8 and 9 shows the results of 10 consecutive experiments under each parameter. The experiment of Table 5 uses networks like other tables but without the dropout layer. We can see that after removing the Dropout layer network is not stable. To see from the table, the new model, the minimal number of epochs can achieve good accuracy. This shows that our model can be retrained according to the updated training set at any time without consuming too much time (20 epochs take only a few seconds). In other words, our approach can add new applications to the training set and optimize our model by retraining.

Table 5. Results with network model without dropout

	Malware/Benign = 1 : 1 Train : Test = 3400 : 600, Epochs = 20									
[500]	97.83	98.33	97.67	98	99.167	98.5	97	98.33	97.5	98
[1000, 100]	99	99.167	98.83	98.83	99	99.167	99.167	98.83	99.33	98.5
[1000, 500, 100]	99	98.67	98	98.83	98.33	99	99.167	98.67	99	98.83
[1000, 600, 200, 50]	96.83	98.67	96.83	99.33	98.5	97.34	98.67	97.83	98.67	98.67

Table 6. Results with different network model

	Malware/Benign = 1 : 1, Train : Test = 3400 : 600, Epochs = 20									
[500]	99.67	99.33	99.17	99.5	99.5	99.167	99.83	99.17	99.33	99.33
[1000, 100]	99.17	99.67	99.5	99.5	98.83	99.67	99.5	99.5	99.33	99.33
[1000, 500, 100]	99.5	99.33	99.67	99.5	99.5	99.5	99.5	99.67	99	99.33
[1000, 600, 200, 50]	99.5	99	98.67	98.83	99.167	99.33	98.5	98.5	98.67	99.5

Table 7. Results with different network model

	Malware/Benign = 1 : 1, Train : Test = 3000 : 1000, Epochs = 20									
[500]	99.30	99.30	99.40	99.40	99.50	99.20	99.40	99.40	99.30	99.30
[1000, 100]	99.30	99.50	99.30	99.40	99.50	99.50	99.60	99.40	99.10	99.30
[1000, 500, 100]	99.40	99.40	99.40	99.30	99.60	99.30	99.10	99.20	99.50	99.60
[1000, 600, 200, 50]	99.2	98.5	99	98.7	98.9	99.20	99.40	99	98.40	99.10

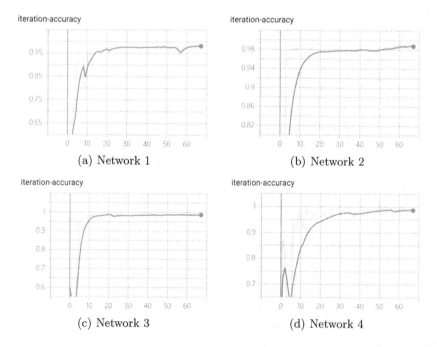

(a) Network 1

(b) Network 2

(c) Network 3

(d) Network 4

Fig. 4. Iteration-accuracy at first epoch (Malware/Benign = 1 : 1 , Train : Test = 3400 : 600)

Table 8. Results with different network model

	Malware/Benign = 1 : 2, Train : Test = 2550 : 600, Epochs = 20										
[500]	99.33	99	99	99.167	99	98.33	98.83	99.5	99.167	98.67	
[1000, 100]	99.33	98.83	99.5	99.83	99.5	99.33	99.67	99.167	99.5	99.33	
[1000, 500, 100]	99.67	99.5	99.67	99.167	99.5	99.5	99.5	99.33	99	99.5	
[1000, 600, 200, 50]	99	99	99.167	97.83	98.67	98.67	99		99.167	99.167	98.83

Table 9. Results with different network model

	Malware/Benign = 1 : 5, Train : Test = 2040 : 600, Epochs = 20										
[500]	98.83	98	98	98.83	99	99	99.33	98.5	97.83	98.33	
[1000, 100]	99.5	99.5	99.5	99.33	99	98.33	99.167	98.83	99.33	99.33	
[1000, 500, 100]	99.33	99.5	99.5	98.83	99.67	99.67	99.5	99.5	99.167	99.167	
[1000, 600, 200, 50]	99.167	98.83	97.83	99.33	99.167	99.33	98.33	99		99.33	98.83

5 Conclusion

In this paper, we use DNN to train feature vectors composed of 1092 sensitive APIs to achieve the purpose of detecting android malwares. Compared with other papers, we did not adopt very complex features, but selected more direct API calls as features. The only difference is that we have expanded the list of sensitive APIs, which gives our method an average accuracy of over 98.5%. To summarize, our approach has the following advantages and disadvantages.

5.1 Advantages

- **Features are simple:** All the features can be extracted by reading the smali code once.
- **Less time consuming:** Both feature extraction and model training take very short time. It only takes several iterations for the model from initial training to stable accuracy.
- **Easy to maintain:** After being put into use in the future, applications can be collected to expand training set, which ensures the feasibility of retraining model at low consumption.

5.2 Disadvantages

- **Being attacked:** Static features are easily disguised to allow malwares to evade detection.
- **Exceptional case:** When the proportion of positive and negative examples in training concentration is too large, the accuracy of the model decreases.
- **Behavioral uncertainty:** Unable to determine the specific malicious behavior.

In general, our approach is satisfactory from the experiment. Aiming at the first disadvantage, our future research direction is to introduce dynamic features to identify malwares after disguising. In addition, the third disadvantage is common to all current deep learning based approaches. To address this shortcoming, we have two ideas that may be implemented in the future. The first, combined with dynamic analysis, is to obtain specific malicious behavior based on the calls of sensitive apis in dynamic analysis. The second is to turn a binary task into a multi-categorization task, which classifies malwares into malicious behaviors, which requires more complex datasets. Finally, we think that our results help to promote the development of the android security.

Acknowledgment. This work was supported by the CETC Joint Advanced Research Foundation (No. 6141B08020101).

1 Appendix. Part of our list

Table 10 lists part of the sensitive apis that we use.

Table 10. Part of our sensitive API list

1	android/media/MediaPlayer;->create
2	android/graphics/Picture;-><init>
3	android/os/Handler;->dispatchMessage
4	android/media/MediaPlayer;->prepare
5	android/media/MediaPlayer;->reset
6	android/os/Looper;->loop
7	android/media/Ringtone;->setStreamType
8	android/webkit/WebView;->capturePicture
9	android/webkit/WebView;->destroy
10	android/view/accessibility/AccessibilityNodeInfo;->getChild
11	android/view/accessibility/AccessibilityNodeInfo;->focusSearch
12	android/view/accessibility/AccessibilityRecord;->getSource
13	android/view/accessibility/AccessibilityNodeInfo;->findFocus
14	android/view/accessibility/AccessibilityNodeInfo;->findAccessibilityNodeInfosByText
15	android/view/accessibility/AccessibilityNodeInfo;->performAction
16	android/view/accessibility/AccessibilityNodeInfo;->getParent
17	junit/framework/TestResult;->endTest
18	com/android/internal/telephony/gsm/SmsMessage;->getSubmitPdu
19	com/android/internal/telephony/gsm/SmsMessage;->calculateLength
20	com/android/internal/telephony/cdma/sms/BearerData;->calcTextEncodingDetails
21	android/view/View;->addFocusables
22	android/webkit/WebView;->reload

(continued)

Table 10. (*continued*)

23	android/webkit/WebView;->stopLoading
24	android/webkit/WebView;->canGoBack
25	android/widget/AbsListView$LayoutParams;-><init>
26	android/webkit/WebView;->goBack
27	android/webkit/WebView;->canGoForward
28	android/webkit/WebView;->goForward
29	android/webkit/WebView;->saveState
30	android/webkit/WebView;->loadData
31	android/webkit/WebView;->loadDataWithBaseURL
32	android/view/View;->focusSearch
33	android/webkit/WebView;->postUrl
34	android/webkit/WebView;->restoreState
35	android/webkit/WebView;->loadUrl
36	android/webkit/WebView;->getProgress
37	android/webkit/WebView;->pauseTimers
38	android/webkit/WebView;->resumeTimers
39	android/webkit/WebView;->getTitle
40	android/widget/AbsoluteLayout$LayoutParams;-><init>

References

1. Smartphone, O.: Market share, 2015 q2 (2016). IDC [on-line].[dostkep 22.08. 2015]. Dostkepny w: http://www.idc.com/prodserv/smartphone-os-market-share.jsp
2. Wood, P., Nahorney, B., Chandrasekar, K., Wallace, S., Haley, K.: Internet security threat report 2015. Symantec, California (2015)
3. Enck, W., et al.: Taintdroid: an information-flow tracking system for realtime privacy monitoring on smartphones. Acm Trans. Comput. Syst. **32**(2), 1–29 (2014)
4. Hornyack, P., Han, S., Jung, J., Schechter, S.E., Wetherall, D.: These aren't the droids you're looking for: retrofitting android to protect data from imperious applications. In: Acm Conference on Computer & Communications Security (2011)
5. Su, X., Zhang, D., Li, W., Zhao, K.: A deep learning approach to android malware feature learning and detection. In: IEEE Trustcom/BigDataSE/ISPA, vol. 2016, pp. 244–251. IEEE (2016)
6. Wang, Z., Cai, J., Cheng, S., Li, W.: Droiddeeplearner: identifying android malware using deep learning. In: IEEE 37th Sarnoff Symposium, vol. 2016, pp. 160–165. IEEE (2016)
7. Hou, S., Saas, A., Ye, Y., Chen, L.: DroidDelver: an android malware detection system using deep belief network based on API call blocks. In: Song, S., Tong, Y. (eds.) WAIM 2016. LNCS, vol. 9998, pp. 54–66. Springer, Cham (2016). https://doi.org/10.1007/978-3-319-47121-1_5
8. Ganesh, M., Pednekar, P., Prabhuswamy, P., Nair, D.S., Park, Y., Jeon, H.: CNN-based android malware detection. In: 2017 International Conference on Software Security and Assurance (ICSSA), pp. 60–65. IEEE (2017)

9. McLaughlin, N., et al.: Deep android malware detection. In: Proceedings of the Seventh ACM on Conference on Data and Application Security and Privacy, pp. 301–308. ACM (2017)

10. Nix, R., Zhang, J.: Classification of android apps and malware using deep neural networks. In: International joint conference on neural networks (IJCNN), 2017, pp. 1871–1878. IEEE (2017)

11. Li, D., Wang, Z., Xue, Y.: Fine-grained android malware detection based on deep learning. In: 2018 IEEE Conference on Communications and Network Security (CNS). IEEE, pp. 1–2 (2018)

12. Martinelli, F., Marulli, F., Mercaldo, F.: Evaluating convolutional neural network for effective mobile malware detection. Procedia Comput. Sci. **112**, 2372–2381 (2017)

13. Hou, S., Saas, A., Chen, L., Ye, Y.: Deep4maldroid: a deep learning framework for android malware detection based on linux kernel system call graphs. In: 2016 IEEE/WIC/ACM International Conference on Web Intelligence Workshops (WIW), pp. 104–111. IEEE (2016)

14. Yuan, Z., Lu, Y., Wang, Z., Xue, Y.: Droid-sec: deep learning in android malware detection. In: ACM SIGCOMM Computer Communication Review, vol. 44, no. 4, pp. 371–372. ACM (2014)

15. Xu, L., Zhang, D., Jayasena, N., Cavazos, J.: HADM: hybrid analysis for detection of malware. In: Bi, Y., Kapoor, S., Bhatia, R. (eds.) IntelliSys 2016. LNNS, vol. 16, pp. 702–724. Springer, Cham (2018). https://doi.org/10.1007/978-3-319-56991-8_51

16. Vinayakumar, R., Soman, K., Poornachandran, P., Sachin Kumar, S.: Detecting android malware using long short-term memory (Lstm). J. Intel. Fuzzy Syst. **34**(3), 1277–1288 (2018)

17. Au, K.W.Y., Zhou, Y.F., Huang, Z., Lie, D.: Pscout: analyzing the android permission specification. In: Proceedings of the 2012 ACM Conference on Computer and Communications Security, pp. 217–228. ACM, 2012

18. Hinton, G.E., Srivastava, N., Krizhevsky, A., Sutskever, I., Salakhutdinov, R.R.: Improving neural networks by preventing co-adaptation of feature detectors (2012). arXiv preprint arXiv:1207.0580

19. Arp, D., Spreitzenbarth, M., Hubner, M., Gascon, H., Rieck, K., Siemens, C.: Drebin: effective and explainable detection of android malware in your pocket. In: Ndss, vol. 14, pp. 23–26 (2014)

20. Michael, S., Florian, E., Thomas, S., Felix, C.F., Hoffmann, J.: Mobilesandbox: looking deeper into android applications. In: Proceedings of the 28th International ACM Symposium on Applied Computing (SAC) (2013)

21. Naway, A., Li, Y.: A review on the use of deep learning in android malware detection (2018). arXiv preprint arXiv:1812.10360

Research on Tampering Detection of Material Gene Data Based on Fragile Watermarking

Shengjie Sun[2,3](✉) (iD), Yabin Xu[1,2,3](✉) (iD), and Zhuang Wu[3] (iD)

[1] Beijing Key Laboratory of Internet Culture and Digital Dissemination Research, Beijing 100101, China
xyb@bistu.edu.cn
[2] Beijing Advanced Innovation Center for Materials Genome Engineering, Beijing Information Science and Technology University, Beijing 100101, China
15532394521@163.com
[3] School of Computer, Beijing Information Science and Technology University, Beijing 100101, China

Abstract. In order to timely and effectively discover the error or falsification of the data in the material gene database, a data tamper detection method based on the fragile watermarking technology is proposed. The method is divided into two stages: embedding and detection of fragile watermarks. In the embedding stage of the watermark, the original data is first grouped and the eigenvalues are extracted. On this basis, the watermark is generated and embedded. In the data tampering detection stage, the data is first grouped and the watermark is extracted, and then the watermark is calculated and detected. The experimental results show that the method can not only effectively detect the situation of data errors or tampering, but also accurately locate a tuple that has been tampered with.

Keywords: Material gene database · Digital watermark · Fragile watermark · Tamper detection

1 Introduction

Material gene database (www.mgedata.cn) is a database/application software integration system platform based on the ideas and concepts of material gene engineering, supported by the national "13th five-year" key research and development plan "material gene engineering key technology and support platform". Material genetic engineering database is a material database without schema storage, which can meet the demand of flexible expansion and data mining of complex and heterogeneous data. Based on the special database of material genetic engineering, the national data sharing and service platform of material genetic engineering will be formed through development and improvement.

Material gene database is characterized by its heterogeneity and complex diversity of data. Its heterogeneity means that the original data table is divided into two forms: two-dimensional table and field table. Two-dimensional table refers to putting all the data into one table, while field table is to divide all the data into several tables according

© Springer Nature Singapore Pte Ltd. 2020
X. Sun et al. (Eds.): ICAIS 2020, CCIS 1252, pp. 219–231, 2020.
https://doi.org/10.1007/978-981-15-8083-3_20

to the content of the data and correlate them with each other according to the data ID. Its complex diversity indicates that it include the data ID, material brand name, material type, chemical composition, raw material information, performance information, pictures, documents, experimental conditions, data collection and review and other data.

Material gene database is the basis and premise of material gene engineering research. When data mining or predictive analysis of material gene data, data stored in the database must be used. In addition, the process and results of the research or experiment on the genetic data of materials will be stored in the database. It can be said that material gene database is the most fundamental and critical part of the whole material gene engineering.

However, material gene database is usually open, so its data security is threatened. There may be cyber attacking, unauthorized tampering or malicious tampering, taking part of the data and claiming personal ownership, and so on. In this way, the credibility and value of the material gene database will be greatly reduced. Therefore, how to ensure the safety of the data in the material gene database is very important.

2   Related Work

The security of database data involves two parts: the security of data transmission, and the security of data storage and access [1]. In this paper, the tamper detection technology mainly detects whether the integrity and authenticity of the data stored and accessed in the material gene database are satisfied. If not, a warning will be issued through some preset mode.

At present, database tamper detection technology mainly includes three categories: digital signature technology, digital fingerprint technology and digital watermark technology. Among them, Tampering detection based on digital signature technology [2, 3] mainly used the method of gathering digital signature and linking. Although this method realizes the correctness and completeness of query results, and consumes less time and space, the detection accuracy is only at the table level. Tampering detection based on digital fingerprint technology [4] is mainly implemented by one-way hash algorithm and "antibody" factor. This method can detect any illegal tampering of sensitive data in the database in a timely and effective manner, but it cannot locate and detect tampered data in real time.

In addition, digital watermarking technology is generally divided into robust watermarking [5, 6], zero watermarking [7] and fragile watermarking [8–17]. But neither of the first two methods can be used to detect tamper attacks.

However, the fragile watermarking technology can realize the detection, location and even recovery of attacks by embedding watermark [8, 9] in the data, extracting zero-vulnerability watermark [10, 11], or saving watermark [12–17] by using tuple sorting. But, the embedding method of watermark will cause some distortion to the data, while the latter two methods are distortion free fragile watermarking and will not have any influence on the data. Therefore, choosing the distortion free fragile watermarking technology can realize the tampering detection of database more accurately and effectively.

In the study of distortion free fragile watermarking, the literature [10] proposed that group watermarks are generated according to the square array and diagonal minor values, and then merged into global watermarks. The global watermarks were encrypted with the safe hash function to form the watermark certificate. Literature [11] proposed to use the algorithms to evaluate and generate various sub-watermarks according to the number, length and range of Numbers in the database. The sub-watermarks were combined and encrypted. After encryption, the watermark and owner ID and timestamp were connected to generate watermark certificates, which were registered in CA.

Literature [12] proposed that the database is sorted by virtual grouping according to classification values. The HMAC function was used to calculate group hash values. Then the group hash values and the number of tuples was used to calculate group watermark and total watermark, and the watermark was embedded by transposing the tuple sequence. Literature [13] proposed to calculate the tuple hash value based on the primary key and all attributes of the tuple, and then combined the key to calculate the group hash value, and merged them into a total watermark. Each tuple adjusted or remains unchanged according to the watermark value.

Literature [14] proposed that after the index was stored in the R tree, one or more of the "minimum tree value, region, perimeter and hash" were used for initial sorting, and the decimal watermark was converted into a factorial form. Then the items in the R tree were moved to the left to embed the watermark according to the watermark value. Literature [15] proposed to perform initial sorting of tuples, such as ordering, and placed the tuples at positions corresponding to the watermark value W_j according to the watermark value W. Literature [16] proposed to calculate integrity verification information according to the standard form (the ranks were sorted according to the attribute name in ascending order) of the key and group, and then rearranged the tuple order by the linear permutation algorithm. Literature [17] proposed to group and sort all data sets, convert the decimal watermark into a factorial form, and reordered the groups according to the corresponding relationship.

To sum up, the literature [10, 11] adopted the fragile zero-watermark scheme, which extracted the fragile watermark information from the data and then stored the watermark information in the third-party authentication center for authentication. However, this method was only aimed at numeric data and did not protect other types of data. Literature [12, 13] used the sequence of the data to save the watermark, but it was targeted at the database with classification attributes and had certain limitations. Literature [14–17] also used sorting to save watermarks, but the detection accuracy of these methods could only be accurate to grouping.

3 Material Genome Database Tampering Detection Process

The principle of the tamper detection process of the material gene database is shown in Fig. 1.

It can be seen from Fig. 1 that the whole process is divided into two stages: embedding and detecting of fragile watermarks.

When fragile watermark embedding is performed, the data is first grouped. On the basis of comprehensive consideration of all types of data in the material gene database, the grouping characteristic values are extracted. Then the watermarking information is generated by grouping eigenvalues. Finally, the watermark embedding algorithm is used

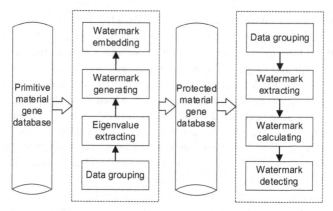

Fig. 1. Schematic diagram of tampering detection process of material gene database.

to reorder the group and the data in the group and realize the embedding of watermark information.

In the detection of data tampering, the data is firstly grouped. Then the watermark information W is extracted by the watermark extracting algorithm, and then the watermark information W' is calculated by the watermark calculating algorithm. The attacked group is determined by judging whether the two-watermark information match or not. For the attacked group, the grouping detection algorithm is used to locate the attacked data tuples.

The innovations of this paper are as follows:

(1) In view of the fact that the fragile watermark only protects the numeric data in the original data tampering detection. A method for extracting the eigenvalues of the material genetic engineering database is proposed. In addition to numerical data, tamper detection of all-important data can be achieved.
(2) In view of the fact that the original data tampering detection can only detect the group level, can't locate the tuple. By the method for saving watermark information into data sorting order by using fragile watermarking technology, not only can be done in a relatively short period of time the watermark embedding and detection, can also be on the premise of no distortion to locate the attacked tuples.

4   Design of Fragile Watermarks

The embedding process of the fragile watermark proposed is mainly divided into four steps: data grouping, team eigenvalue value extraction, watermark generation and watermark embedding.

4.1   Grouping of Data

In order to improve the accuracy of data tampering detection and embed the watermark information into the data sequencing better, the material genetic data need to be grouped twice. Since the data ID can accurately identify each tuple in the material gene database, the tuples are first arranged in ascending order according to the data ID in the first grouping. Then, the number of attributes in the material gene database is counted as γ and take γ tuples at a time to form a team according to the tuple arrangement order, until all tuples are grouped. Thus, t teams are obtained. In the second grouping, the number of teams in each group is n according to formula (1). Then, take n teams at a time in order to form a group until all teams are grouped. Thus, a total of $\lceil t/n \rceil$ groups are obtained. The schematic diagram of data grouping is shown in Fig. 2.

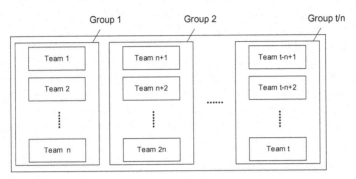

Fig. 2. Schematic diagram of data grouping of material gene database.

$$n = \arg \min_{i \in N} \{i | i * 16 - i! + 1 < 0\} \qquad (1)$$

4.2 Extraction of Eigenvalue from Team

The data tables in the material genetic engineering database that need to be protected by digital watermarking technology are chemical composition table, experimental conditions table and performance information table. The extracting methods of the characteristic values of the three tables are as follows:

(1) Data ID, content, parameter value, temperature and performance value: according to the number and range of different Numbers (0–9), the characteristics of Numbers are characterized, and thus the digital characteristic value W_d is constituted.
(2) Parameter name, unit and performance name: the character of text is represented by the number and length of different fields, which is also the character characteristic W_t.
(3) Composition: according to the number of different elements (according to the position of the element in the periodic table), this element is used to characterize the characteristics of chemical elements, which is also W_c.

Each eigenvalue in the three tables is combined together to form the eigenvalue of team, namely the total eigenvalue $W_r = W_d + W_t + W_c$.

Because the eigenvalue extracted by this method is too long (from the above three categories of attributes, the eigenvalue length can be extracted to 16 bits, 51 bits, 118 bits respectively, a total of 185 digits), so it needs to be compressed. Here, we use hash algorithm to compress. SHA-256 hash algorithm is selected to compress and encrypt the total eigenvalue W_r and form the team eigenvalue E_{W_r} after hash encryption.

4.3   Data Watermark Generation

Because the watermark embedding needs to rearrange the order of the team according to the grouping watermark, and then rearrange the order of the tuple according to the tuple watermark. Therefore, the grouping watermark value and the tuple watermark value need to be calculated first.

First, the highest bit is extracted from each team eigenvalue E_{W_r} calculated before as the watermark value W of the team. The watermark value W_B of each group is the sum of the watermark values W of all teams in the group. Finally, the watermark value W_D of the tuple is composed of several Numbers in the watermark value W selected in order, and the sum of these numbers is consistent with the number of tuples in the team.

4.4   Data Watermark Embedding

In order to improve the accuracy of data tamper detection and shorten the time of tamper detection, the embedding process of watermark should be divided into two parts: the embedding of grouping watermark and the embedding of tuple watermark.

(1)   Grouping watermark embedding: In the group after two groupings, the watermark is embedded by changing the order of the team. In the specific operation, according to the algorithm unrank(n, W_B, π) given in literature [18], the number of teams n in each group, the watermark value W_B of the group and the ranking π of the team need be calculated first. Then, repeat recursively swapping the positions of $\pi[n-1]$ and $\pi[W_B \bmod n]$ depending on the size of n. This method can accurately apply the watermark value to the team ranking order, and the team's ranking corresponding to different watermark values is unique. In this way, all groups can rely on team sequencing's changes to achieve the embedding of group watermark.

(2)   Tuple watermark embedding: When sorting tuples in the team, first calculate the hash encoding of key information of each tuple. Then, according to each digit d in the tuple watermark, the corresponding d tuples in the team are operated in reverse order according to the size relation of hash encoding of key information, until all tuples of all teams are processed. Watermark embedding algorithm is shown in Algorithm 1.

Algorithm 1. Watermark Embedding Algorithm
Input: material gene database after grouping;
Output: material gene database after watermark embedding;
1: Extract the watermark value W based on the grouped material gene database;
2: Extract the group watermark W_B from the watermark value W;
3: Extract the tuple watermark W_D from the watermark value W;
4: **for** each group of material gene database **do**
5:   Sort the group based on the number of teams n, the grouping watermark W_B, and the team sorting π;
6:   **for** each team of group **do**
7:     Sorting tuples according to tuple watermark W_D;
8:   **end for**
9: **end for**

5   Data Tamper Detection

The process of data tampering detection based on fragile watermark is mainly divided into four steps: data grouping, watermark extraction, watermark calculation and watermark detection.

5.1   Data Grouping and Watermark Extraction

Data must be grouped before watermark detection. In order to ensure the correctness of data tampering detection, it is required that the data grouping operation and grouping result must be the same when watermark is embedded and when watermark is detected. Therefore, the grouping process here is exactly the same as when the watermark is embedded.

The watermark extraction is to re-extract the grouping watermark W_{B1} and tuple watermark W_D from the material gene database. In order to ensure that the extracted watermark information is consistent with that generated when the watermark is embedded, so as to accurately detect the location of the attack, the eigenvalue extraction and watermark generation method of fragile watermark embedding are used again.

5.2   Watermark Calculation and Tampering Detection

The watermark calculation is based on the grouping sequence to calculate the grouping watermark W_B. The specific method is to first calculate the number n of team in each group, team sort π and team sort inverse $\pi 1$. The value of $\pi 1$ need be calculated by formula (2).

$$\pi 1[\pi[i]] = i, (i = 0, 1, 2, \ldots, n) \tag{2}$$

Then, according to the rank(n, π, $\pi 1$) algorithm given in literature [18], the specific process of calculating the grouping watermark value W_{B2} is as follows: When n is not equal to 1, switch the position of $\pi[n-1]$ and $\pi[\pi 1[n-1]]$ and the position of $\pi 1[\pi[n-1]]$ and $\pi 1[n-1]$. Then, return $\pi[n-1] + n*rank(n-1, \pi, \pi 1)$. Finally, a recursive call is made to return the calculated grouping watermark value W_{B2}.

In the detection of data tampering, the attacked group should be detected first, and then the attacked team and tuples should be detected in the attacked group. The specific process is as follows:

First, the two grouping watermarks W_{B1} and W_{B2} are compared bit by bit, and the position that failed to match are the attacked group.

Then, in the attacked group, hash codes of key information of each tuple are calculated first. And then for each number d in the tuple watermark W_D, if the corresponding d tuples in the team are in reverse order according to the size of the hash code, the team is not attacked. Otherwise, it indicates that the team is attacked, and the group to which the tuple belongs is the attacked group.

Finally, if the attacked tuples and groups are detected, a warning is issued and the location of the attack is located.

Data tampering detecting algorithm is shown in Algorithm 2.

Algorithm 2. Data Tampering Detecting Algorithm
Input: material gene database after public using;
Output: group F_G, team F_T and tuple F_D under attack;
1: **for** each group of material gene database **do**
2:      Re-extract the grouping watermark value W_{B1} according to the material gene database;
3:      Calculate the grouping watermark value W_{B2} according to the sorting of the groups;
4:      **if** a number B_{n1} in $W_{B1} \neq$ the number B_{n2} of the corresponding position in W_{B2} **then**
5:          Attacked group $F_G = B_{n1}$;
6:           Find the attacked tuple F_D according to the tuple watermark W_D and the order of the tuples in the group;
7:           The attacked team $F_T =$ the team to which the attacked tuple F_D belongs;
8:      **end if**
9: **end for**

---

6 Experiment and Result Analysis

6.1 Experimental Environment and Experimental Data

The experimental environment of this paper is: CPU model is Intel® CoreTM i5-8259U CPU @ 2.3 GHz, memory is 16 GB, operating system is macOS 10.15, development language is Java, development environment is Eclipse, database is MySQL.

I selected a nickel-based superalloy with a large amount of data from a dedicated database of material genetic engineering, including a total of 11,216 data. Among them, the relatively important and necessary protection is the chemical composition table, which contains information items: data ID, chemical element, and ratio.

6.2 Experimental Results and Analysis

The Effect of Different Data Amount on Detection Rate
In order to test the influence of different data amounts on the detection rate of this method, different data amounts are selected respectively and a fixed tamper rate (10%) is selected. Among the 11216 pieces of data, 10%, 25%, 50%, 75% and 100% are selected

for watermark embedding. Then they are simulated attack, and set the attack strength to 10%. Finally, the watermark detection program is run to locate the attacked groups and tuples, and the detection rate of tuple detection and group detection are calculated.

Group detection and tuple detection results under different data amounts are shown in Fig. 3.

As can be seen from Fig. 3, with the continuous increasing of the amount of data, the detection rate of group detection and tuple detection are gradually increasing. At the same time, the detection rate of tuple detection and grouping detection has been kept at a very high watermark. This is because both grouping detection and tuple detection algorithms need to conduct detection and positioning according to the arrangement order of grouping and tuples. With the increase of the amount of data, the sorting of groups and tuples becomes more complicated, which contains more watermark information and makes it easier to detect the groups and tuples that do not conform to the design rules. So, we can draw the following conclusions: the method of this scheme is fully applicable to materials gene databases with different data amounts.

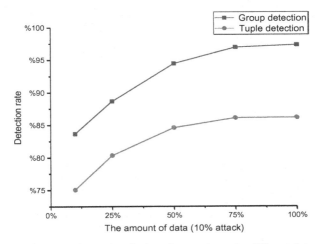

Fig. 3. Grouping detection and tuple detection results under different data amounts.

Influence of Different Tamper Rate on Tuple Detection Performance

In order to test the influence of different tampering rates on the tuples detection of this scheme, a fixed number of 11216 data bars are selected, and the tampering rates are 2.5%, 5%, 7.5%, 10%, 12.5%, 15%, 17.5% and 20%. After watermark embedding is completed, tampering attacks of different degrees are carried out respectively. Then, the watermark detection program is run to calculate the detection rate of the tuple detection by the method under different tamper rates. The experimental results are shown in Fig. 4.

As can be seen from Fig. 4, with the gradual increasing of tamper rate, although the detection rate of tuple detection in this scheme is gradually decreasing, the lowest value of detection rate is over 82%, which can be maintained within a high range. This is because under the premise of a fixed amount of data, with the improvement of tamper rate, the amount of data under attack becomes more and more. At this time, although tuple detection can detect more attacked tuples, there will be more and more errors and misjudgments during detection, so the tuple detection rate will show a downward trend. However, on the whole, the tuple detection rate of this scheme is still very high.

Group Detection and Contrast Experiment

Since the detection accuracy of the literature [10] and the literature [15] can only locate the group, the method proposed in this paper is to locate the detection accuracy to both groups and tuples. Therefore, only the accuracy of grouping detection is compared with literature [10] and literature [15].

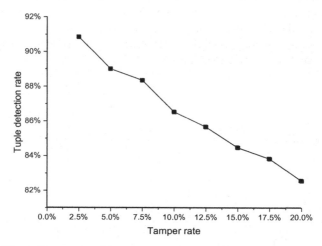

Fig. 4. Test results of the program tuple under different tamper rates.

The data volume in this experiment contains a total of 11216 pieces of data. The tamper rate is set as 2.5%, 5%, 7.5%, 10%, 12.5%, 15%, 17.5% and 20% respectively. After watermark embedding is completed, tamper attacks are carried out in different degrees, and then watermark detection program is run to calculate the detection rates of three methods at different tamper rates.

The detection results of grouping detection of the three methods under different tampering rates are shown in Fig. 5.

As can be seen from Fig. 5, when the modification rate is lower than 10%, the grouping detection rate of this scheme is higher than that of literature [10] and literature [15]. When the modification rate is higher than 10%, the grouping detection rate of literature [15] is higher, but the difference between this scheme and literature [15] is less than 1%. It is indicated that the detection effect of this scheme is the best when the tamper rate is low, and the detection effect of this scheme is equivalent to that of literature [15] when the tamper rate is high.

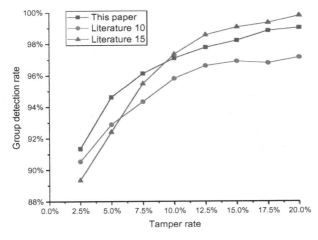

Fig. 5. Detection results of grouping detection by three methods under different tamper rates

Watermark Embedding and Detection Time Comparison Experiment

In order to test the efficiency of the three schemes in the execution of watermark embedding and detecting, the execution time of the watermark embedding algorithm and detection algorithm is compared. The experimental results are shown in Table 1.

Table 1. Watermark embedding and detection execution time of the three methods.

The execution time (ms)	This scheme	Literature [10]	Literature [15]
Watermark embedding	508874	385112	6501427
Watermark detecting	6314	4620	16296

As can be seen from Table 1, when watermark embedding or detection is carried out, the execution time of the proposed method is slightly higher than that in the literature [10]. However, this paper does not only detect groups, but also tuples. In addition, the execution time of watermark embedding in literature [15] is more than ten times that of the method in this paper and literature [10]. Moreover, the execution time of watermark detection in literature [15] is twice as long as that in this paper and three times as long as that in literature [10], with the longest algorithm execution time.

Considering the experimental results in Fig. 5 and Table 1, we can draw the following conclusions: Although the detection rate of literature [15] is higher than that of this scheme when the tamper rate is high, the comprehensive performance of this scheme is higher when the tamper rate is low. In addition, the execution time of the method in this paper for watermark embedding and detection is much lower than that in the literature [15]. Therefore, considering the accuracy and efficiency of the algorithm, the method in this paper is better.

7 Conclusion

In this paper, the material genetic engineering database is studied and tested. The fragile watermarking technology based on no distortion is adopted to effectively solve the problem of data tampering detection in material genetic engineering database. An effective eigenvalue extraction algorithm is presented, which can effectively detect the data tampering attack that may occur to the material genetic database. In addition, by embedding the watermark information into the ordering of the groups and tuples, the positioning accuracy of the attack is innovatively accurate to the tuple. The experimental results show that the time of watermark embedding and detection is relatively short. In the later stage, the algorithm will be further optimized to improve the performance of tuple tamper detection.

References

1. He, J., Wang, M.: Cryptography and relational database management systems. In: Proceedings 2001 International Database Engineering and Applications Symposium, IEEE, pp. 273–284, Grenoble, France (2001)
2. Merkle, Ralph C.: A certified digital signature. In: Brassard, G. (ed.) CRYPTO 1989. LNCS, vol. 435, pp. 218–238. Springer, New York (1990). https://doi.org/10.1007/0-387-34805-0_21
3. Mykletun, E., Narasimha, M. Tsudik, G.: Authentication and integrity in outsourced databases. In: 11th Annual Network and Distributed System Security Symposium, pp. 107–138. ACM, California, USA (2006)
4. Jing, L., Qingsong, H., Jing, Z.: Data tamper detection method based on improved MD5 algorithm. Comput. Eng. Appl. 33, 148–150 (2008)
5. Liu, J., et al.: A novel robust watermarking algorithm for encrypted medical image based on DTCWT-DCT and chaotic map. Comput. Mater. Continua 61(3), 889–910 (2019)
6. Jayashree, N., Bhuvaneswaran, R.S.: A robust image watermarking scheme using Z-transform, discrete wavelet transform and bidiagonal singular value decomposition. Comput. Mater. Continua 58(1), 263–285 (2019)
7. Liu, J., et al.: A robust zero-watermarking based on SIFT-DCT for medical images in the encrypted domain. Comput. Mater. Continua 61(1), 363–378 (2019)
8. Hamed, K., Hassan, R.: A novel watermarking scheme for detecting and recovering distortions in database tables. Int. J. Database Manag. Syst. 2(3), 1–11 (2010)
9. Khanduja, V., Chakraverty, S.: Fragile watermarking of decision system using rough set theory. Arab. J. Sci. Eng. 43(12), 7621–7633 (2018)
10. Camara, L., Junyi, L., Renfa, L., Wenyong, X.: Distortion-free watermarking approach for relational database integrity checking. Math. Probl. Eng. 2014, 1–10 (2014)
11. Aihab, K., Afaq, H.S.: A fragile zero watermarking scheme to detect and characterize malicious modifications in database relations. Sci. World J. 2013, 1–16 (2013)
12. Bhattacharya, S., Cortesi, A.: A distortion free watermark framework for relational databases. In: ICSOFT 2009 - 4th International Conference on Software and Data Technologies, vol. 2, pp. 229–234 (2009)
13. Yingjiu, L., Swarup, V., Jajodia, S.: Tamper detection and localization for categorical data using fragile watermarks. In: The 4th ACM workshop on Digital rights management, pp. 73–82, Washington DC (2004)
14. Kamel, I.: A schema for protecting the integrity of databases. Comput. Secur. 28(7), 698–709 (2009)

15. Kamel, I., Yaqub, W., Kamel, K.: An empirical study on the robustness of a fragile watermark for relational databases. In: International Conference on Innovations in Information Technology, pp. 227–232. IEEE, Abu Dhabi (2013)
16. Guo, J.: Fragile watermarking scheme for tamper detection of relational database. In: International Conference on Computer and Management (CAMAN). IEEE, pp. 1–4. Wuhan (2011)
17. Kamel, I., Kamel, K.: Toward protecting the integrity of relational databases. 2011 World Congress on Internet Security (WorldCIS-2011), pp. 258–261. IEEE, London, UK (2011)
18. Myrvold, W., Ruskey, F.: Ranking and unranking permutations in linear time. Inf. Process. Lett. **79**(6), 281–284 (2001)

Quantitative Evaluation of Promotion of Traditional National Sports Events Based on Probity Multiple Regression Analysis

Zongxian Yu[1(✉)], Li Wu[2], and Jun Yang[3]

[1] School of Physical Education and Health, Aba Teachers University,
Wenchuan 623002, Sichuan, China
`juzhida469644e@163.com`
[2] School of Mathematics and Computer Science, Aba Teachers University,
Wenchuan 623002, Sichuan, China
[3] Chongqing Vocational College of Transportation, Chongqing 402247, China

Abstract. In order to improve the ability of quantitative evaluation of national traditional sports, and to effectively guide the training of traditional national sports, a quantitative evaluation model of national traditional sports promotion based on Probity multiple regression analysis is proposed. Firstly, the information collection and adaptive feature extraction of the quantitative evaluation of traditional national sports are carried out, and the statistical analysis of the quantitative evaluation data of traditional national sports is carried out in combination with the method of segmental sample detection. The stochastic probability density model is used to quantify and decompose the characteristics of national traditional sports evaluation, and the Probity multiple regression analysis method is used to extract the promotive quantitative features of traditional national sports. The unbiased estimation algorithm is used to realize the optimal estimation of the promotive factors of the traditional national sports, so as to realize the quantitative evaluation and decision-making of the promotive nature of the national traditional sports. The simulation results show that the regression and accuracy of the model are good, and convergence performance is better than traditional method in the process of quantitative evaluation.

Keywords: Multiple regression analysis of Probity · Traditional national sports · Quantitative evaluation · Unbiased estimation

1 Introduction

National traditional sport is an important part of human sports culture. It is not only a manifestation of cultural form with national characteristics, but also a cultural form with rather traditional color. It is not only a component of human sports culture, but also an important content of national traditional history and culture. As a comprehensive form of national culture, traditional national sports have always been closely related to other cultural systems in the surrounding environment. Become a kind of open system of

© Springer Nature Singapore Pte Ltd. 2020
X. Sun et al. (Eds.): ICAIS 2020, CCIS 1252, pp. 232–243, 2020.
https://doi.org/10.1007/978-981-15-8083-3_21

culture that exchanges material and information freely with the outside world. National traditional sports are an important part of each nation's traditional culture. It is not only the understanding of human body itself, but also the body-building and entertainment activities in which the body movement is the main content. It is also a kind of special education way that people use to seek to enhance physique skill training. Traditional national sports have a good promotion to the formation of sports culture. In order to quantitatively analyze the promotive effect of national traditional sports on physical education, it is necessary to study the quantitative evaluation of national traditional sports. Combined with mathematical model construction and statistical regression analysis, this paper analyzes the quantitative evaluation model of national traditional sports promotion, and the promotive prediction of national traditional sports events are realized [1].

Traditionally, the methods of promoting quantitative evaluation of traditional national sports include particle swarm optimization model, fuzzy PID model and self-adaptive inversion integral quantitative evaluation mathematical model, etc. [2–5]. By collecting the characteristic parameters of the traditional national sports events and analyzing the characteristics of the traditional national sports events, combining with the corresponding control theory, the above methods achieve the promotive planning of the national traditional sports events, and obtain certain research results, among which, In the literature [5], a quantitative evaluation model for the facilitation of sports events with parallel micro-balanced scheduling is proposed, which takes the promotive nature of traditional national sports events as the load balancing index of each node. Based on the principle of roughly equal cost, a domain is divided into several sub-domains, which makes the load change of the quantitative evaluation of national traditional sports is relatively smooth, thus improving the accuracy of quantitative evaluation of traditional national sports. In literature [6], a quantitative evaluation model of traditional national sports events based on Small-World model was proposed, and the promotive factors of traditional national sports events were obtained by weighted average of intrinsic modal function. Combining the correlation detection method to realize the promotion quantitative evaluation of sports events, this method is easy to fall into local convergence in the quantitative evaluation of traditional national sports events [7].

Aiming at the above problems, a quantitative evaluation model of national traditional sports promotion based on Probity multiple regression analysis is proposed. Firstly, the information collection and adaptive feature extraction of the quantitative evaluation of traditional national sports are carried out, and the statistical analysis of the quantitative evaluation data of traditional national sports is carried out in combination with the method of segmental sample detection [8]. The stochastic probability density model is used to quantify and decompose the characteristics of national traditional sports evaluation, and the Probity multiple regression analysis method is used to extract the promotive quantitative features of traditional national sports [9–12]. The unbiased estimation algorithm is used to realize the optimal estimation of the promotive factors of the traditional national sports, so as to realize the quantitative evaluation and decision-making of the promotive nature of the national traditional sports. The simulation is taken, finally, the simulation analysis is carried out, which shows the superiority of this method in improving the ability of quantitative evaluation of national traditional sports [13–16].

2 Analysis of Constraint Parameters and Construction of Statistical Model for the Quantitative Evaluation of the Promotion of Traditional National Sports Events

2.1 Analysis of Constraint Parameters for the Quantitative Evaluation of Promotion of Traditional National Sports Events

In order to realize the quantitative evaluation of the national traditional sports, the constraint parameter model of the quantitative evaluation of the national traditional sports is constructed, and the characteristics of the national traditional sports are classified and processed [16–18]. The SVM classifier is used to classify the characteristics of traditional national sports, and the standard support vector machine solution is assumed as follows [18–22]:

$$\min_{0 \le \alpha_i \le c} W = \frac{1}{2} \sum_{i,j=1}^{l} y_i y_j \alpha_i \alpha_j K(x_i, x_j) - \sum_{i=1}^{l} \alpha_i + b\left(\sum_{i=1}^{l} y_j \alpha\right) \tag{1}$$

Where, (x_i, x_j) indicates that the characteristic sample of traditional national sports events, b is the feature classification attribute of national traditional sports events. SVM training sample set is [23–32]:

$$S = \{(x_1, x_1), \cdots, (x_l, x_l)\} \tag{2}$$

Under different network structure, the characteristic components of traditional national sports are controlled, and the statistical regression analysis model is established to classify the traditional national sports [8]. The SVM clustering center of traditional national sports classification is obtained as follows [26–32]:

$$G_i = \sum_j \alpha_j y_i y_j K(x_i, x_j) + y_i b - 1 \tag{3}$$

According to convex optimization clustering constraint conditions, the constraint rules for quantitative evaluation of the promotive factors of traditional national sports events are expressed as follows [33]:

$$\min(f) = \sum_{i=1}^{m} \sum_{j=1}^{n} C_{ij} X_{ij} \tag{4}$$

$$\text{s.t} \begin{cases} \sum_{j=1}^{m} X_{ij} = a_i, i = 1, 2 \cdots m \\ \sum_{i=1}^{m} X_{ij} = b_i, j = 1, 2 \cdots n \\ X_{ij} \ge 0, i = 1, 2 \cdots m, j = 1, 2 \cdots n \end{cases} \tag{5}$$

In order to accelerate the local optimization ability of particles in the feature detection training of traditional national sports events using support vector machine, the n samples in the set S_s are decomposed, and the expression of feature decomposition is obtained as:

$$Q' = \begin{bmatrix} 0 & y_1 & \cdots & y_n \\ y_1 & Q_{11} & \cdots & Q_{1n} \\ \vdots & \vdots & \ddots & \vdots \\ y_n & Q_{n1} & \cdots & Q_{nn} \end{bmatrix} \overset{def}{=} \begin{bmatrix} 0 & y^T \\ y & Q \end{bmatrix} \tag{6}$$

Where, the classification attribute matrix Q of traditional national sports is positive definite, and there exists inverse matrix Q of Q^{-1}. By introducing Probity multivariate regression test method, the statistical analysis of multi-parameter constraint of traditional national sports is realized. The output of the statistical characteristic parameters is obtained as follows:

$$X_1 = \left(\alpha_c^{[1]}, \alpha_c^{[2]}, \alpha_c^{[3]}, \cdots \right) \tag{7}$$

$$X_2 = \left(g_c^{[1]}, g_c^{[2]}, g_c^{[3]}, \cdots \right) \tag{8}$$

$$X_3 = \left(W^{[1]}, W^{[2]}, W^{[3]}, \cdots \right) \tag{9}$$

The statistical distribution parameter model of the quantitative evaluation of traditional national sports is calculated, and the statistical analysis method of sample test is adopted to improve the accuracy of the quantitative evaluation [34].

2.2 Construction of Statistical Model

On the basis of constructing the constraint parameter model of the national traditional sports promotion quantitative evaluation, the statistical analysis model of the national traditional sports promotion quantitative evaluation is constructed, and the statistical characteristic quantity is obtained:

$$\begin{cases} c_1 = c_{1ini} - (c_{1ini} - c_{1fin})\,(t/T\text{max}) \\ c_2 = c_{2ini} + (c_{2fin} - c_{2ini})\,(t/T\text{max}) \end{cases} \tag{10}$$

Where, c_{1ini}, c_{2ini} represent the information classification learning factor of traditional national sports, t indicates the distance from extremum to non-inferior solution [35], and T_{max} denotes the maximum iteration number. Under the condition of confidence, the formula of equilibrium measure factor DM for quantitative evaluation of sports events is obtained as follows [36]:

$$DM = \frac{d_e + d_b + \sum_{i=1}^{n-1} \left| d_i - \frac{\sum_{i-1}^{n-1} d_i}{n-1} \right|}{d_e + d_b + (n-1)\frac{\sum_{i=1}^{n-1} d_i}{n-1}} \tag{11}$$

On the basis of the autocorrelation statistical feature analysis method, the optimization problem of the quantitative evaluation of the national traditional sports promotion is described as follows:

$$\max_{xi,yi,j} \max_{xi,yi,j} TP = \frac{1}{tp}, i,j \in \{0, 1, \ldots, v+1\} \tag{12}$$

Where

$$tp = \max\left\{\max_{i \in V} \max_{i \in V}(x_i \cdot \frac{si}{\eta p} \sum_{i \in V} x_i), \max_{(i,j) \in E} \max_{(i,j) \in E}(\frac{d_{i,j}(x_i - x_j)^2}{y_{i,j}})\right\} \tag{13}$$

The average level of confidence is:

$$k = Int(\frac{n\overline{Q}}{1 - \overline{Q}}) + 1 \tag{14}$$

In the formula, $\overline{Q}$ is the explained variable, and the limited set of quantitative evaluation of traditional national sports is as follows:

$$\begin{aligned} f_{lg-M}(z) &= (f_{lg}(z), f_{lg-x}(z), f_{lg-y}(z)) \\ &= (f_{lg}(z), h_x * f_{lg}(z), h_y * f_{lg}(z)) \end{aligned} \tag{15}$$

In the upper expression, $f_{lg}(z)$ represents the finite set of a set of statistical characteristic quantities. Based on the above analysis, the statistical analysis of the quantitative evaluation data of traditional national sports is carried out with the method of segmental sample detection.

3 Quantitative Evaluation Model Optimization

3.1 Probity Multiple Regression Analysis

In this paper, a quantitative evaluation model of national traditional sports promotion based on Probity multiple regression analysis is proposed. The characteristic function of promotive factors of traditional national sports events is calculated by using time average, and the output of multivariate regression test statistics is obtained as follows:

$$\hat{r}_x(\tau) = \sum_{i=1}^{L} (A_i^2/2)\cos(\omega_i\tau) + \sigma^2 \sum_{j=0}^{\infty} h^2(j) \tag{16}$$

Where, σ^2 is the variance of the constraint correlation $w(n)$ for national traditional sports. Statistical sequence is $\{x(t_0 + i\Delta t)\}, i = 0, 1, \cdots, N - 1$, the Probity multiple regression analysis model is constructed as follows:

$$\begin{cases} u_{tt} - \Delta u + |u|^4 u = 0, \\ (u, \partial_t u)|_{t=0} = (u_0, u_1) \in \dot{H}_x^{S_c} \times \dot{H}_x^{S_c-1} \end{cases} \tag{17}$$

Where, $u : I \times IR^d \to IR$ is the fusion quantitative parameter of national traditional sports promotion, and the statistical characteristic distribution is as follows:

$$
\begin{cases}
v_k \sim t_{\tilde{v}_k}\left(\tilde{u}_{v,k}, \tilde{\Sigma}_{vv,k}\right) \\
e_k \sim t_{\tilde{v}_k}\left(\tilde{u}_{e,k}, \tilde{\Sigma}_{ee,k}\right)
\end{cases}
\tag{18}
$$

The piecewise sample estimation method, the unbiased estimators of Probity multivariate regression analysis are obtained as follows:

$$
p(e_k|v_k) \sim t_{(\tilde{v}_k+d_e)}(\tilde{u}_{e|v,k}, \tilde{\sum}_{e|vk})
\tag{19}
$$

The promotive factors of traditional national sports are described in the form of triples [12–14], and the control functions of the promotive estimation are obtained as follows:

$$
V_0(k) = \begin{cases}
\boldsymbol{\gamma}(1)\boldsymbol{\gamma}^T(1), & k = 1 \\
\frac{[\rho V_0(k-1)+\boldsymbol{\gamma}(k)\boldsymbol{\gamma}^T(k)]}{1+\rho}, & k > 1
\end{cases}
\tag{20}
$$

Where, $\boldsymbol{\gamma}(k)$ and $\hat{x}(k|k-1)$ are traditional sports promotion quantitative analysis of the detection statistics, the load is:

$$
\tilde{y}(t) = \iint_{\tau\varphi} b(\tau, \varphi)\exp[j2\pi\varphi t]\tilde{f}(t-\tau)dtd\varphi
\tag{21}
$$

Combined with least square fitting and Probity multiple regression analysis, the accuracy and confidence of promotive evaluation of traditional national sports events are improved.

3.2 Optimal Estimation of Promotive Factors in Traditional National Sports

The Probity multiple regression analysis method is used to extract the promotive quantitative features of traditional national sports events. Combined with the fuzzy decision method, the optimized combination function is described as follows:

$$
\begin{aligned}
minimize \quad & \frac{1}{2}\|w\|^2 + C\sum_{i=1}^{n}(\xi_i + \xi_i^*) \\
subject\ to \quad & y_i - (w'\Phi(x_i) + b) \le \varepsilon - \xi_i \\
& (w'\Phi(x_i) + b) - y_i \le \varepsilon - \xi_i^* \\
& \xi_i, \xi_i^* \ge 0, i = 1, 2, \cdots, n; C > 0
\end{aligned}
\tag{22}
$$

Where, ξ_i and ξ_i^* are detection statistics, C and ε are global extremums, and the global optimization method is used to carry out the quantitative evaluation. The optimal output

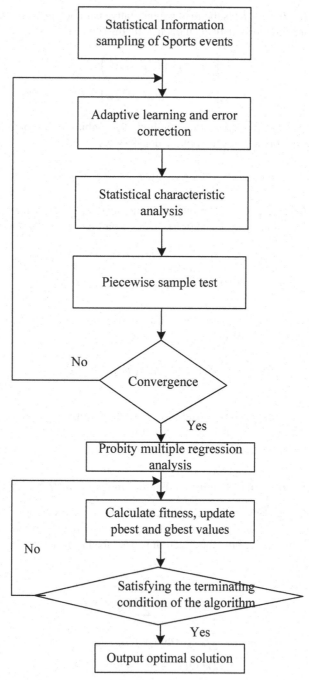

Fig. 1. Quantitative evaluation of national traditional sports promotion based on Probity multiple regression analysis

statistical function of the national traditional sports promotion quantification evaluation is obtained as follows:

$$f(x) = \sum_{i=1}^{n} (\alpha_i - \alpha_i^*) K(x_i, x_j) + b \qquad (23)$$

Where, α_i and α_i^* are bound by a penalty factor, and the adaptive weighted expression for quantifying the evaluation is:

$$K_{\min} = \beta K_{poly} + (1 - \beta) K_{rbf}, \qquad \beta \in (0, 1) \qquad (24)$$

Where, $K_{poly} = [(x \cdot x_i) + 1]^2$ is the control kernel function of the degree of punishment of misdivided samples, the quantitative evaluation of the traditional national sports events based on the Probity multiple regression analysis is realized as shown in Fig. 1.

4   Empirical Data Analysis and Experimental Testing

In order to test the performance of this method in realizing the quantitative evaluation of national traditional sports promotion, the simulation experiment is carried out. The hardware environment of the experiment is a computer with 2. 4 GHz CPU and 1 GB of memory in Intel Core. The national transmission is established by Netlogo software. In the simulation platform of promoting quantitative evaluation of sports events, the simulation parameters are $W_{\min} = 0.4$, $W_{\max} = 0.9$, $C_{\min} = 1.5$, $C_{\max} = 2.0$, the search range of sports vector quantization evaluation is $[0, 1]$ and $[0.1, 100]$, the modified parameter is set to $(\beta, C, \gamma, \varepsilon) = (0.0817, 2.7854, 1.0268, 0.0069)$, and the crossover probability is $0.1 \rightarrow 0.3$. According to the above simulation environment and

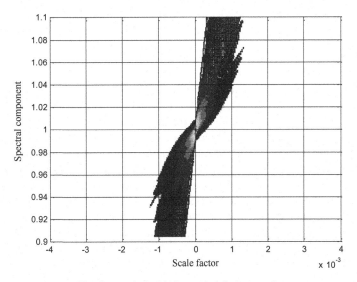

Fig. 2. Statistical information fusion result

parameters are set up. The results of statistical information fusion of promotive factors of traditional national sports are shown in Fig. 2.

Figure 2 shows that by using this method, the promotive parameters of traditional national sports can be effectively integrated and the ability of data fusion can be improved. The quantitative evaluation of traditional national sports is carried out, and the error comparison of evaluation is shown in Fig. 3.

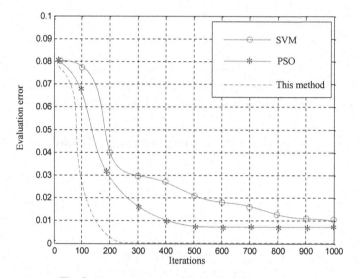

Fig. 3. Error comparison of quantitative evaluation

Figure 3 shows that the method of this paper has lower error and higher level of confidence in the quantitative evaluation of national traditional sports.

5 Conclusions

In this paper, a quantitative evaluation model of national traditional sports promotion based on Probity multiple regression analysis is proposed. Firstly, the information collection and adaptive feature extraction of the quantitative evaluation of traditional national sports are carried out, and the statistical analysis of the quantitative evaluation data of traditional national sports is carried out in combination with the method of segmental sample detection. The stochastic probability density model is used to quantify and decompose the characteristics of national traditional sports evaluation, and the Probity multiple regression analysis method is used to extract the promotive quantitative features of traditional national sports. The unbiased estimation algorithm is used to realize the optimal estimation of the promotive factors of the traditional national sports, so as to realize the quantitative evaluation and decision-making of the promotive nature of the national traditional sports. The simulation results show that the regression and accuracy of the model are good, and convergence performance is better than traditional method in the process of quantitative evaluation, it has very good application value in the national traditional sports training and dissemination.

Fund project:. 1. General project of Hunan Provincial Department of education, project name: Research on the development path of traditional sports in Southwest Hunan under the background of urban and rural co-ordination, subject number: 17C1462

2. The outstanding youth project of Hunan Provincial Department of education, project name: Research on intelligent emergency public opinion event retrieval system based on Ontology field, subject number: 14B163

References

1. Silva, Yasin N., Reed, J., Brown, K., Wadsworth, A., Rong, C.: An experimental survey of MapReduce-based similarity joins. In: Amsaleg, L., Houle, Michael E., Schubert, E. (eds.) SISAP 2016. LNCS, vol. 9939, pp. 181–195. Springer, Cham (2016). https://doi.org/10.1007/978-3-319-46759-7_14
2. Kimmett, B., Srinivasan, V., Thomo, A.: Fuzzy joins in MapReduce: an experimental study. Proc. VLDB Endow. **8**(12), 1514–1517 (2015)
3. Lin, J.: Brute force and indexed approaches to pairwise document similarity comparisons with MapReduce. In: Proceedings of the 32nd International ACM SIGIR Conference on Research and Development in Information Retrieval, pp. 155–162. ACM, New York (2009)
4. Vernica, R., Carey, M.J., Li, C.: Efficient parallel set-similarity joins using MapReduce. In: Proceedings of the 2010 ACM SIGMOD International Conference on Management of Data, pp. 495–506. ACM, New York (2010)
5. Rong, C.T., Lu, W., Wang, X., et al.: Efficient and scalable processing of string similarity join. IEEE Trans. Knowl. Data Eng. **25**(10), 2217–2230 (2013)
6. Lu, X.H., Li, G., Yu, W.: Research management database scheduling algorithm based on fuzzy c means clustering. Comput. Digit. Eng. **44**(6), 1011–1015 (2016)
7. Li, K., Mi, J.: Research on mechanical and electrical control algorithm of bionic robot based on variable structure PID. J. Henan Univ. Eng. (Nat. Sci. Edn.) **28**(2), 32–37 (2016)
8. Pan, J.: Signal detection in strong chaotic interference based on RBF neural network. Comput. Simul. **5**, 136–139 (2010)
9. Yuxiang, Y., Changxiong, X., Wuqin, T.: Estimation of the time varying TDOA and FDOA in GEO-LEO dual-satellites location system. Sig. Process. **28**(10), 1465–1474 (2012)
10. Nguyen, T.C., Shen, W., Luo, Z., Lei, Z., Xu, W.: Novel data integrity verification schemes in cloud storage. In: Lee, R. (ed.) Computer and Information Science. SCI, vol. 566, pp. 115–125. Springer, Cham (2015). https://doi.org/10.1007/978-3-319-10509-3_9
11. Hao, S.G., Zhang, L., Muhammad, G.: A union authentication protocol of cross-domain based on bilinear pairing. J. Softw. **8**(5), 1094–1100 (2013)
12. Sun, S., Wang, S., Fan, Z.: Flow scheduling cost based congestion control routing algorithm for data center network on software defined network architecture. J. Comput. Appl. **36**(7), 1784–1788 (2016)
13. Sehgal, P., Basu, S., Srinivasan, K. et al.: An empirical study of file systems on NVM. In: Proceedings of the 2015 31st Symposium on Mass Storage Systems and Technologies, pp. 1–14. IEEE, Piscataway, NJ (2015)
14. Sha, H.M., Chen, X., Zhuge, Q., et al.: Designing an efficient persistent in-memory file system. In: Proceedings of the 2015 IEEE Non-Volatile Memory System and Applications Symposium, pp. 1–6. IEEE, Piscataway, NJ (2015)

15. Han, D., Chen, X., Lei, Y., Dai, Y., Zhang, X.: Real-time data analysis system based on spark streaming and its application. J. Comput. Appl. **37**(5), 1263–1269 (2017)
16. Zhou, Y., Li, M., Xu, X., Li, M.: A study on dual-load-zone model of overlying strata and evolution law of mining stress. Comput. Mater. Continua **58**(2), 391–407 (2019)
17. Sun, Y., Yuan, Y., Wang, Q., Wang, L., Li, E., Qiao, L.: Research on the signal reconstruction of the phased array structural health monitoring based using the basis pursuit algorithm. Comput. Mater. Continua **58**(2), 409–420 (2019)
18. Zhao, G., Zhang, Y., Shi, Y., Lan, H., Yang, Q.: The application of BP neural networks to analysis the national vulnerability. Comput. Mater. Continua **58**(2), 421–436 (2019)
19. Liu, Z., Xiang, B., Song, Y., Lu, H., Liu, Q.: An improved unsupervised image segmentation method based on multi-objective particle, swarm optimization clustering algorithm. Comput. Mater. Continua **58**(2), 451–461 (2019)
20. Tang, X., Wang, L., Cheng, J., Chen, J., Sheng, V.S.: Forecasting model based on information-granulated GA-SVR and ARIMA for producer price index. Comput. Mater. Continua **58**(2), 463–491 (2019)
21. Long, M., Zeng, Y.: Detecting iris liveness with batch normalized convolutional neural network. Comput. Mater. Continua **58**(2), 493–504 (2019)
22. Shanshan, Y., Liu, J., Zhang, X., Shangbin, W.: Social-aware based secure relay selection in relay-assisted D2D communications. Comput. Mater. Continua **58**(2), 505–516 (2019)
23. Zhao, Y., Yang, X., Li, R.: Design of feedback shift register of against power analysis attack. Comput. Mater. Continua **58**(2), 517–527 (2019)
24. Zhang, O., Wei, X.: Online magnetic flux leakage detection system for sucker rod defects based on LabVIEW programming. Comput. Mater. Continua **58**(2), 529–544 (2019)
25. Kou, L., Shi, Y., Zhang, L., Liu, D., Yang, Q.: A lightweight three-factor user authentication protocol for the information perception of IoT. Comput. Mater. Continua **58**(2), 545–565 (2019)
26. Zhang, S., Karimi, S., Shamshirband, S., Mosavi, A.: Optimization algorithm for reduction the size of Dixon Resultant Matrix: a case study on mechanical application. Comput. Mater. Continua **58**(2), 567–583 (2019)
27. Alabdulkarim, A., Al-Rodhaan, M., Tian, Y., Al-Dhelaan, A.: A privacy-preserving algorithm for clinical decision-support systems using random forest. Comput. Mater. Continua **58**(3), 585–601 (2019)
28. Kaddi, M., Benahmed, K., Omari, M.: An energy-efficient protocol using an objective function & random search with jumps for WSN. Comput. Mater. Continua **58**(3), 603–624 (2019)
29. Santhosh, P.K., Kaarthick, B.: An automated player detection and tracking in basketball game. Comput. Mater. Continua **58**(3), 625–639 (2019)
30. Shen, T., Nagai, Y., Gao, C.: Optimal building frame column design based on the genetic algorithm. Comput. Mater. Continua **58**(3), 641–651 (2019)
31. Liu, Z., Wang, X., Sun, C., Lu, K.: Implementation system of human eye tracking algorithm based on FPGA. Comput. Mater. Continua **58**(3), 653–664 (2019)
32. Ma, W., Qin, J., Xiang, X., Tan, Y., Luo, Y., Xiong, N.N.: Adaptive median filtering algorithm based on divide and conquer and its application in CAPTCHA recognition. Comput. Mater. Continua **58**(3), 665–677 (2019)
33. Wang, B., Kong, W., Li, W., Xiong, N.N.: A dual-chaining watermark scheme for data integrity protection in Internet of Things. Comput. Mater. Continua **58**(3), 679–695 (2019)
34. Feng, X., Zhang, X., Xin, Z., Yang, A.: Investigation on the chinese text sentiment analysis based on convolutional neural networks in deep learning. Comput. Mater. Continua **58**(3), 697–709 (2019)

35. Jin Wang, Yu., Gao, W.L., Wenbing, W., Lim, S.-J.: An asynchronous clustering and mobile data gathering schema based on timer mechanism in wireless sensor networks. Comput. Mater. Continua **58**(3), 711–725 (2019)
36. Long, S., Zhao, M., He, X.: Yield stress prediction model of RAFM steel based on the improved GDM-SA-SVR algorithm. Comput. Mater. Continua **58**(3), 727–760 (2019)

Research on Leisure Sports Activities Based on Decision Tree Algorithm

Qi Li[1(✉)] and Jun Yang[2]

[1] School of Physical Education and Health, Aba Teachers University,
Wenchuan 623002, Sichuan, China
heqidu1984ud@163.com
[2] Chongqing Vocational College of Transportation, Chongqing 402247, China

Abstract. The study of competition pressure of athletes has been in the science circle for many years. However, computer science research as a coping strategy has not been involved in the past. Based on this, data mining was applied to the survey data of sports competition stress in this article. The basic theory of content-based recommendation algorithm was studied, including the idea of algorithm, algorithm description and algorithm implementation. Combining with the characteristics of the stressor data of sports competition, the algorithm was further improved from the perspective of similarity calculation and potential semantic analysis, and then the word frequency of the data was calculated to get the most similar suggestions, and the results obtained were analyzed.

Keywords: Decision tree algorithm · Leisure sports activities · Sports competitions

1 Introduction

With the development of competitive sports in our country, the scale of events and the increase of the number of viewers have also increased the intensity of the competitions in the stadiums [1]. All of these will exert a certain pressure on athletes' psychological pressure. Coping with stress has become an indispensable issue in today's competitive sports. Athletes in order to play a high level in the game, psychological stress are an important factor that must be overcome. Therefore, many scholars and experts pay more and more attention to the field of competition stress [2]. Traditional psychological counseling is usually through the psychological professionals inquiries, or gives some targeted questionnaire to assess the psychological status of athletes [3]. However, these methods are inefficient and do not provide timely counseling advice. By participating in the development of the Athlete Contest Stress Management System under the research program of the General Administration of Sport of China, it is learned that the more traditional way of stress counseling in the field of sports is currently adopted [4]. Applying the methods of data mining to coping with psychological stress can solve the problem of pressure coping with the huge number of athletes and the complex and changing psychological conditions [5]. Therefore, clustering algorithm and content-based recommendation

© Springer Nature Singapore Pte Ltd. 2020
X. Sun et al. (Eds.): ICAIS 2020, CCIS 1252, pp. 244–254, 2020.
https://doi.org/10.1007/978-981-15-8083-3_22

algorithm was proposed to apply competitive stress psychology analysis and recommendation. After the clustering, the corresponding coping strategies of the athletes were given, which improved the psychology of the athletes in the face of the pressure. The athletes were more able to resist the pressure, and the psychological level was improved when the frustration was difficult [6]. Under this background, the evaluation data of psychological questionnaire from the aspects of data mining and recommendation was analyzed and dug, and valuable information was drewto help the psychological experts to make effective psychological diagnosis.

2   Related Work

With the rapid expansion of e-commerce and Web 2.0 technologies, more products are sold on the Internet and more customers are willing to give them the rating or rating they have purchased [7]. This growing amount of information allows companies to tap huge value, create rich benefits, and it is convenient for customers to provide more personalized service. It is in this environment that a personalized recommendation system was born [8]. The proposed algorithm has a long history and has been explored in the mid-1990s as to how to make recommendations from available data [9]. In order to study recommended algorithms, researchers have researched problems from information retrieval and user-modeling techniques, and the relevant technologies for these studies have been successfully deployed in many practical applications. For example, Amazon's book recommendation system, movie recommendation services on Netflix, Lastfin's music recommendation service and YouTube video recommendations. In the past decade, the recommended technology has become an active research topic, scientists studied many algorithms. For example: Some scholars have studied the next generation of recommendation system, elaborated the research direction of recommendation system and bring the influence to people. Since then, other related theoretical studies have focused on a particular recommendation technique, such as collaborative filtering recommendation algorithms, which generate recommendations through ratings of neighbors or merchandise. Later scholars expanded on the basis of their predecessors to synthesize a variety of existing recommendation systems to form a hybrid recommendation system [10].

3   Methodology

3.1   Hierarchical Clustering Algorithm

The results of hierarchical clustering are presented in the form of a tree map, which is used in many fields (e.g., taxonomy, evolutionary theory, etc.). Hierarchical clustering has two kinds of clustering processes. One is to merge any two smaller clusters into larger ones, which are called agglomeration algorithms. One is to divide small clusters into small clusters by splitting them, which is called a segmentation algorithm. The result of the hierarchical clustering algorithm is to get a tree cluster and become a tree map [11]. By cutting the desired level of dendrogram, the relevant levels of clustering can be obtained, which are disjoint. Poly-level algorithm is the most commonly used level algorithm. As shown in the figure, the figure shows that the clustering by the Complete-Link approach is more compact than the Single-Link approach [12]. The clustering generated by the Single-Link is more slender and chain-like. When there is noise data marked with "*" in the data set, this data is likely to be treated as a type of data by Single-Link clustering. However, clusters generated by Single-Link are more versatile. For example, the Single-Link method can extract concentric clusters, but does not use the Complete-Link method [13] (Figs. 1 and 2).

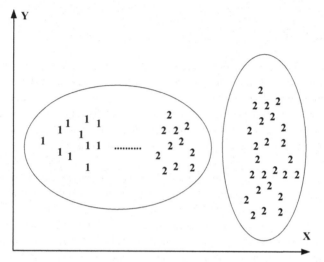

Fig. 1. Single-Link method condenses hierarchical clustering results

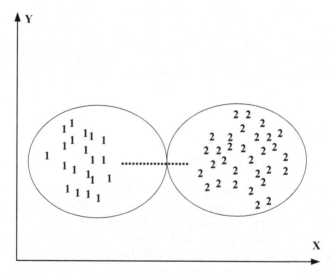

Fig. 2. Complete-Link method condenses hierarchical clustering results

Hierarchical clustering algorithm is more flexible. For example, the Single-Link Hierarchical Clustering algorithm performs well in non-isotropic (non-uniform clusters containing well-separated, chained and concentric clusters) and in non-globular clusters. Aggregation Hierarchical clustering algorithm steps: Each data object as a separate category, calculate the distance between the class and class, they are arranged in a distance between the lists of categories, the list sorted in ascending order; Sort the list in Step 1 to combine classes of different distances, and for each merge, find the closest of the two categories combined as a new category; Calculate the distance between all the old and new categories, still forming a list of distance between the classes until all the data objects are concatenated into a category and stop. Otherwise, repeat steps two and three; the algorithm forms a hierarchy of nested dendrograms, each level can form an abstract view of the data. Based on the method of hierarchical clustering algorithm, the most important of the clustering process is the similarity distance between two objects and the inter-cluster connection rules. The similarity measure method mainly adopts the European distance, the connection rules mainly include: the single connection aggregation rule - the shortest distance:

$$d(o_i, o_k) = \min x \in_{o_i y \in o_k} \|x - y\| \tag{1}$$

Full join aggregation rules - Maximum distance:

$$d(o_i, o_k) = \max x \in_{o_i y \in o_k} \|x - y\| \tag{2}$$

Average link aggregation between clusters - Average link between clusters:

$$d(o_i, o_k) \left(\frac{1}{n_i n_k} \right) = \sum_{x \in o_i} \left(\sum_{y \in o_k} \|x - y\| \right) \tag{3}$$

Intra-cluster average link aggregation - Intra-cluster average link:

$$d(o_i, o_k) = \left(\frac{1}{n_i n_k} \right) \sum_{x \in o_i} \left(\sum_{y \in o_k} \|x - y\| \right) \tag{4}$$

Ward method - dispersion sum of squares:

$$d(o_i, o_k) = (1/C(n_i + n_k, 2)) \sum_{x,y \in (o_i, o_k)} \left(\sum_{y \in o_k} \|x - y\| \right) \tag{5}$$

Clustering algorithms only obtain the division of a data set rather than a data structure shaped like a tree in hierarchical clustering. Due to the large amount of computation when large-scale data sets are used in hierarchical clustering, it is generally used in large data sets to divide algorithms more widely. Clustering is generally divided into clusters by clustering rules. Clustering rules may be locally optimal or globally optimal. However, we cannot find the optimal solution through the choice of clustering criteria. Therefore, clustering algorithms usually run in different initial states multiple times, and then select the best structure to output as the clustering result. The most intuitive and frequently used clustering criterion function in dividing clusters is the square error function. This clustering criterion function is generally used in data sets with well-clustered clustering and large-scale cluster separation. The square error function is as follows:

$$e^2(\aleph, \phi) = \sum_{j=1}^{K} \sum_{i=1}^{n_j} \left\| X_i^{(j)} - C_j \right\|^2 \tag{6}$$

Among them, $\aleph$ is a cluster, ϕ is one of the data, $X_i^{(j)}$ indicates that the i-th data point belongs to the J-th cluster. K-Means algorithm is the simplest and most common algorithm. It chooses random cluster centers as initial values, and then continues to allocate similar data to the same cluster until convergence (the cluster center does not change or the clustering criterion function converges to a certain threshold). K-Means algorithm time complexity is very small. However, K-means algorithm is very sensitive to the initial value, so easy to fall into the local optimal solution. For example, in Fig. 3 and 7 two-dimensional data, if data A, B and C are selected as the initial cluster centers, the output clustering results are "oval" in the figure: {{A}, {B, C}, {D, E, F, G}}. However, we can see that the optimal clustering result is as shown by the square: {{A, B, C}, {D, E}, {F, G}}. Moreover, the value of the square error function of the optimal result set is the minimum globally. If we choose the initial value of ADF, we will produce the clustering result {{A, B, C}, {D, E}, {F, G}}.

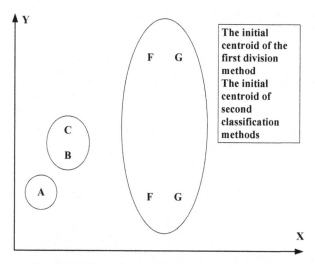

Fig. 3. K-Means algorithm is sensitive to initial value

In order to improve the K-means algorithm easily fall into the local optimum shortcomings, many papers try to change the K-means algorithm, some improvements trying to choose a good initial value makes the algorithm easier to find the global optimal solution; Other improved algorithms try to segment and merge the clusters that have been obtained: In general, a cluster is divided into two clusters when the variance of a cluster in the cluster is higher than the specified closed value. When the centroid distance between two clusters in the clustering result is less than the specified closed value, the two clusters will be merged. These improvements make it possible to get the best clustering results from stochastic initial values. For example, ISODATA algorithm is the use of this technology to merge and split the cluster. In ISODATA, if the initial partition given is in the "oval" partition, the best three partitioned clusters can be generated. ISODATA firstly merges the cluster cages {A} and {B, C} into one cluster because the distance between their centroids is the smallest of all clusters, then for the cluster {D, E, F, G}, it is split into two clusters {D, E} and {F, G}. Still other improved algorithms choose different standard functions. Other improved algorithms, such as dynamic clustering algorithm using maximum likelihood estimation, propose a method to obtain dynamic clustering from data set, and a regular Mahalanobis distance with improved distance measure to obtain super-spherical clustering. The typical partitioning clustering K-Means algorithm is generally used for data sets of the same direction. On the other hand, in terms of time and space complexity, the classification and clustering algorithms have much less time and space complexity than hierarchical clustering algorithms. Therefore, the combination of the advantages of both to develop a hybrid algorithm will have a good clustering effect.

3.2 Decision Tree Algorithm

Decision tree algorithm is a more commonly used recommendation algorithm. Hypothetical: If two users, Ux and Uy, have similar reviews of the same group of products, their consumption behavior or evaluation of other products will be similar. Based on this assumption, by analyzing the history of consumer purchases of goods or the evaluation of goods, the recommendations are made. Algorithms can generally be divided into two categories: memory-based and model-based algorithms. For the model-based collaborative filtering approach, a model is constructed from the user-product scoring matrix to use this model to predict new project ratings. Many techniques of machine learning are used for model-based collaborative filtering. And a memory-based algorithm can be divided into user-based and product-based approaches. Predict this user's rating of a product by gathering some users who are similar to the target user. The recommendation process can be divided into three phases: user (product) rating description, nearest neighbor search, predictive rating and recommendation.

First, is the user (product) rating description, with n * m matrix representation of the user's score. Where n is the number of users, m is the number of items, and the i-th row of the J-th column of the element r is the rating of the user i for the item J. In this matrix, some of the values are empty, indicating that the user did not evaluate them. In most cases, the user-product evaluation matrix is usually a sparse array. Then the nearest neighbor search, this phase select the top similarity of a user as the target user's nearest neighbor set. According to the n * m-level user-project matrix of the previous step, two users i and 1 are defined as n-dimensional vectors corresponding to the i-th and j-th rows of the matrix and then calculating the similarity of the two vectors. Nearest neighbor search is a key step in the algorithm. Then the predictive score, resulting in the recommendation of the nearest neighbor set is determined, the following can be recommended based on the overall rating of neighbors history users. The predicted score ri, j of the target user i for the item J is usually obtained from the aggregated value of the previous historical user's score of the item, which is calculated by the average method:

$$r_{ij} = \frac{1}{N} \sum\nolimits_{i \in n} r_{i,j} \tag{7}$$

Similarity weighted average method:

$$r_{ij} = k \sum\nolimits_{i \in n} sim(i, i') \times r_{i'j} \tag{8}$$

User feedback weighted method:

$$r_{ij} = \overline{r_i} + k \sum\nolimits_{i \in n} sim(i, i') \times (r_{i'j} - \overline{r'})$$ (9)

Among them, k is used for standardization, usually k is calculated as:

$$k = \frac{1}{\sum_{i \in n} sim(i, i')}$$ (10)

$\overline{r_i}$ represents the average of the items that user I has rated. The average method is the simplest method of predictive evaluation; The similarity weighted average method is the most commonly used prediction method; User-feedback weighting is an extension of the second method, which replaces the user rating with the user's dissimilarity with the average. Decision tree algorithm has obvious advantages, it has no special requirements for the recommended content, no matter text or multimedia can be recommended. In addition, it has a good self-learning ability. Before recommending a system to provide recommendations to users, assess whether a project has recommended value or not, and evaluate the system's recommended results according to relevant evaluation indexes such as average absolute error and coverage ratio.

4   Result Analysis and Discussion

In order to verify the effectiveness of the improved algorithm, 111 data were selected in the UCI database, Breast Cancer data and Abalone data for validation. The number of data sets and the number of features are shown in the following table. Experiment in a PC (2.4 GHZ Intel CPU, 2G memory, Windows) for testing, writing language is R language. R language is an open source language and operating environment for statistical analysis and drawing. It is similar to MATLAB commercial software and has syntax similar to C, but has more powerful statistical analysis and data manipulation (more powerful in vector and matrix operations) than C language. In this paper, with its powerful extended language package and matrix arithmetic functions, the algorithm was achieved (Table 1).

Table 1. List of experimental data sets

Dataset name	Data set size	Cluster number
Iris	150	3
Breast Cancer Wisconsin	286	2
Abalone data	4177	29

Then we use the improved hierarchical algorithm to cluster the dataset, and cluster the 22 dimensions such as stress source, social support and athlete burnout to get the final clustering center as shown in the table (Table 2).

Table 2. Final cluster center

Serial number	Final cluster center	Total number of data
1	(0.739 0.125 0.293 0.684 0.800 0.227 0.908 0.624 0.180 0.380 0.317 0.319 0.301 0.085 0.358 0.319 0.219 0.717 0.714 0.733 0.339)	262
2	(0.599 0.110 0.205 0.513 0.570 0.158 0.678 0.412 0.129 0.478 0.435 0.424 0.460 0.108 0.493 0.478 0.418 0.467 0.468 0.523 0.237)	223
3	(0.433 0.874 0.250 0.750 0.667 0.782 0.427 0.760 0.802 0.705 0.091 0.144 0.438 0.882 0.417 0.425 0.617 0.656 0.656 0.573 0.823)	6

Image generated using the algorithm is as follows, as can be seen from the picture, the first category accounted for the largest proportion, the second category followed by the third category. The similarities between the first and the second category are relatively large, some of the attributes are different, while the third category has a smaller proportion, but there is a clear difference with the first and the second category, which means that this part of the athletes psychological level is poor (low overall score, indicating that the source of pressure does not meet, indicating less pressure) (Fig. 4).

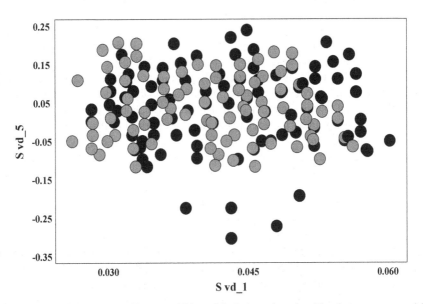

Fig. 4. The distribution map of improved hierarchical clustering algorithm in sports competition pressure data

It can be seen from Fig. 5 that the improved algorithm proposed in this paper has good performance on data analysis. On the whole, there are some conclusions as follows:

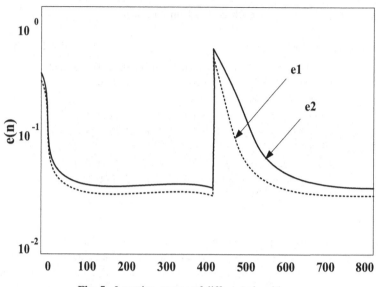

Fig. 5. Learning curves of different algorithms

Among the three types of athletes, the first type of athletes may belong to the "seed" type athletes, the overall athletic quality is higher, and efforts, fitness is good, but the investment is not high enough, need more encouragement; Category 2 athletes, as a whole, are slightly under category 1 and may belong to moderate "diligent" type athletes. Only in certain subtleties, for example: higher burnout, indicating that such athletes usually training more hard, easy to form a burden of psychological, however, due to the fact that the qualifications are not particularly prominent athletes. Therefore, the sense of accomplishment is lower, and the social support is also the lowest, indicating that type 2 athletes tend to form "more than inadequate, more than under" anxiety; The third group of athletes accounted for a relatively small proportion of the most stressful type, in many aspects of the mentality are poor, although the enthusiasm for sports higher, but may not be as good as the former two types of athletes, so prone to burnout, and even easy to question boycott training; In addition, category 3 athletes may not have as much chance of playing in major events as in the previous two categories, resulting in some pressure on such athletes and may be more hopeful of trying to prove themselves, or of total resistance to the extreme emotions of the sport, although the proportion of such small, the need for coaches pay more attention to individualize, to help athletes mental health development. In summary, for the "seed" type players, we should encourage them to keep them in good physical condition. For "diligent" type athletes, we can give more encouragement and social support in information to enhance their sense of accomplishment, in addition to prevent excessive training lead to unnecessary harm. For the last type of over-pressure athletes, coaches should help them to attribute their causes more reasonably and set sports goals rationally. In addition, coaches should guide more psychologically and avoid negative emotions.

5   Conclusion

At present, with the rapid development of computer technology, it is used in more and more industries. The research of sports was referred in this article. Based on the study of leisure sports activities and decision tree algorithm, in this paper, the sports competition pressure as the source questionnaire was firstly introduced, and the data source of the competition stress was prepared, such as data preprocessing and de-dimensioning; Secondly, aiming at the characteristics of the data sources of sports competition stressors, a new improved hierarchical K-Means algorithm was formed by combining the known algorithm K-Means and decision tree. And compared the performance of the old and new algorithms, and then applied it to the data of stressors in sports competitions to get the result of clustering. Then matched it with the sports competition stress coping strategy text library, and compared. Finally, a recommendation result was formed so as to recommend the coping strategies of the athletes with the corresponding pressure characteristics to assist the physicists to diagnose, so that the athletes can obtain good psychological counseling advice and maintain a healthy state of mind.

Research Program:
Humanities and Social Science Research Base of Sichuan Education Department — Sichuan Leisure Sports Industry Development Research Center, No: XXTYCY2017B01.

References

1. Li, L., Zheng, Y., Sun, X.H., Wang, F.S.: The application of decision tree algorithm in the employment management system. Appl. Mech. Mater. 3082(543), 45–46 (2017)
2. Li, L., Zheng, Y., Sun, X.H., Wang, F.S.: Study on data mining with decision tree algorithm in the student information management system. Appl. Mech. Mater. 3082(543), 37–38 (2016)
3. Akkaş, E., Akin, L., Çubukçu, H.E., Artuner, H.: Application of Decision Tree Algorithm for classification and identification of natural minerals using SEM–EDS. Comput. Geosci. 80, 866–867 (2015)
4. Bichescu, A.: Leisure time sport activities of the students at Resita University. Procedia Soc. Behav. Sci. 117, 1102 (2017)
5. Fujita, H., Selamat, A., Haron, H., Kurematsu, M., Hakura, J., Fujita, H.: A framework for improvement a Decision Tree learning algorithm using K-NN. Front. Artif. Intell. Appl. 265, 56–57 (2016)
6. Lee, M.S., Oh, S.: Alternating decision tree algorithm for assessing protein interaction reliability. Vietnam J. Comput. Sci. 1(3), 23–24 (2017)
7. Georgian, B., Lorand, B.: The influence of leisure sports activities on social health in adults. SpringerPlus 5(1), 1566 (2016)
8. Suknovic, M., et al.: Reusable components in decision tree induction algorithms. Comput. Stat. 27(1), 89–90 (2017)
9. Isbister, G.K., Sibbritt, D.: Developing a decision tree algorithm for the diagnosis of suspected spider bites. Emerg. Med. Australas. 16(2), 12–13 (2016)
10. Andersen, K.L., et al.: Leisure time sport activities and maximal aerobic power during late adolescence. Eur. J. Appl. Physiol. Occup. Physiol. 52(4), 41–42 (2017)
11. Qiong, K., Li, X.: Some topological indices computing results if archimedean lattices l (4,6,12). Comput. Mater. Continua 58(1), 121–133 (2019)

12. Deng, Z., Ren, Y., Liu, Y., Yin, X., Shen, Z., Kim, H.-J.: Blockchain-based trusted electronic records preservation in cloud storage. Comput. Mater. Continua **58**(1), 135–151 (2019)
13. Deng, M., Liu, F., Zhao, M., Chen, Z., Xiao, N.: GFCache: a greedy failure cache considering failure recency and failure frequency for an erasure-coded storage system. Comput. Mater. Continua **58**(1), 153–167 (2019)

Semantic Integrity Analysis Based on Transformer

Mengfan Zhao[1,2], Menglei Li[1,2], Cong Li[1,2], and Xin Liu[1,2(✉)]

[1] Hunan Provincial Key Laboratory of Network and Information Security,
Xiangtan University, Xiangtan, China
[2] The College of Information Engineering, Xiangtan University,
Xiangtan, China
liuxin@xtu.edu.cn

Abstract. At present, text semantic similarity is still a key point in natural language processing tasks. Short texts with complete semantics are more accurate when judging semantic similarity. Aiming at this problem, this paper proposes a semantic integrity analysis method based on Transformer encoder. By judging whether the sentence is semantically complete, the long text is divided into multiple short texts with complete semantics. First of all, the text is segmented, mapped to the corresponding word vector and labeled. Secondly the word vector and the annotation information are processed by the sliding window and the random undersampling. And then they are used as the Transformer input. Next the model is obtained after training. The experimental results show that the method can achieve the accuracy of 85.27%, and provide a basis for the calculation of semantic similarity work. At the same time, it can help the research of question and answer system and machine translation.

Keywords: Semantic integrity · Sequence annotation · Transformer Encoder · Natural language processing

1 Introduction

In recent years, natural language processing has gradually become a research hotspot in the field of computer science and artificial intelligence. The main work of semantic integrity analysis is to judge whether a sentence is semantically complete. It is the preliminary work of natural language processing tasks such as syntax analysis, semantic analysis and machine translation. In the automatic scoring of subjective questions, it is necessary to divide the answers into semantically complete sentences and then match the syntactic and semantic similarity. The reason for the semantic integrity analysis of Chinese is that there is no strict grammatical restriction on the use of punctuation in Chinese. In particular, the use of commas is more arbitrary, it can be used to separate semantically complete fragments, or they can be used when the semantics are incomplete. Therefore, it is of great significance to use the latest natural language processing technology to analyze the semantic integrity of Chinese sentences.

© Springer Nature Singapore Pte Ltd. 2020
X. Sun et al. (Eds.): ICAIS 2020, CCIS 1252, pp. 255–266, 2020.
https://doi.org/10.1007/978-981-15-8083-3_23

There is currently no universally accepted definition of semantic integrity. According to the actual needs of work, we believe that a sentence is semantically complete if it can fully express its meaning without the need for other statements, and no ambiguity. Semantic integrity analysis can help improve the accuracy of application systems such as QA systems, machine translation and automatic scoring and so on.

2   Related Work

Deep learning has developed rapidly and is widely used in speech recognition, computer vision and machine translation. At present, the application of deep learning technology to solve natural language processing (NLP) tasks is a research hotspot. The Transformer Encoder is a feature extraction unit based on the self-attention mechanism. When processing text sequence information, it can link any two words in the sentence without distance limitation, and overcome the long-range dependence problem. At the same time, the Transformer encoder uses a multi-headed attention mechanism to perform multiple calculations on the same sentence to capture more semantic features implicit in the context.

Mikolov T et al. proposed the word vector word2vec by using the convolution neural network (CNN) to train the language model, and then the research on the distributed characteristics of the words is constantly emerging [1]. Alex Graves used CNN to generate text, and proposed a new RNN structure MRNN to improve text generation ability [2]. The gated recurrent unit(GRU) was used for sentiment analysis. Compared with the support vector machine (SVM) and CNN methods on the IMDB and other film evaluation datasets. The accuracy rate increased by about 5% [3]. This paper applied large-scale unlabeled data to improve internal representation of Chinese characters, and used these improved representations to enhance supervised word segmentation and POS tagging models [4]. Xinchi Chen et al. propose a novel neural network model for Chinese word segmentation, which adopts the long short-term memory (LSTM) neural network to keep the previous important information in memory cell and avoids the limit of window size of local context [5]. Google proposed the model of transformer, abandoned the previous CNN and RNN and adopted the attention mechanism, which achieved a better BELU value in the field of machine translation, and greatly reduced the training cost [6].

This paper attempts to apply the Transformer to the Chinese sentence semantic integrity analysis, and changes the sentence semantic integrity analysis into a typical sequence labeling problem.

3   Semantic Integrity Analysis Method

The model is based on Transformer in this paper. And the Transformer encoder is regarded as a feature extractor. The input is the pre-processed word sequence of the original text, which is mapped to the corresponding word vector and labeled. After the process of the cyclic sliding window and under-sampling, the position encoding of each word sequence is added as the input of the Transformer. The connection layer finally outputs the corresponding label probability through the softmax layer. The overall architecture of the model is shown in Fig. 1.

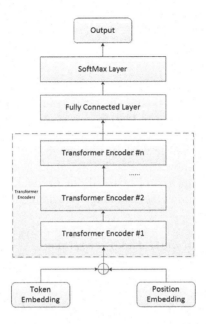

Fig. 1. Transformer-based Semantic integrity analysis method architecture.

3.1 Word Segmentation and Word Vector

Vocabulary is the smallest unit of Chinese language and the atomic structure of Chinese language. So Chinese word segmentation is the basis of natural language processing. The accuracy of word segmentation will directly affect the quality of following part of speech tagging, syntactic analysis, word vector and other related work.

Common word segmentation tools include SnowNLP, PyNLPIR, THULAC, and "jieba". In order to make the word segmentation result more accurate, and the word segmentation can be customized. This paper uses "jieba" for word segmentation, and adds a custom dictionary to identify the unregistered word. The "jieba" is divided into three modes to meet different needs. The mode adopted the precise mode in this paper.

Word vectors are designed to allow computers to understand human natural language. Generally, word vectors are represented in two ways: one-hot representation and distribution representation.

The one-hot representation is simple and easy to realize, but the disadvantage is that the encoding is too sparse, which will lead to a very high dimension. The advantage of distributed representation is that it not only solves the dimensionality disaster problem, but also mines the association attribute between words, each dimension has a specific meaning and contains more information, thus improves the accuracy of vector semantics. In recent years, the popular language model word2vec uses this method to represent word vectors. This paper also uses word2vec to generate word vectors.

3.2   Transformer Encoder

Transformer is widely used in natural language processing, especially in the field of machine translation. It abandons the traditional CNN and RNN, uses the Attention mechanism as the feature processor of the model. Transformer Encoder has two sub-layers, self-attention and feed forward neural network. At the same time, the residual network and normalization are added in each sublayer. The structure is shown in Fig. 2. The multi-headed attention model in the self-attention layer consists of h scaled dot-product attention units. Scaling attention is the basic building block of long attention, and its calculation formula is:

$$Attention(Q, K, V) = softmax(\frac{QK^T}{\sqrt{d_K}})V \tag{1}$$

Here, the attention mechanism is described as a mapping relationship between query (Q) and key-value (K-V). The input dimensions of query and key are d_k dimensions, and value is d_v dimension. Firstly, calculate the dot product of matrix Q and K. Then divid by $\sqrt{k}$ to prevent the value from being too large. Next use Softmax normalization to turn the result into a weight. At last multiply by V to get the vector value.

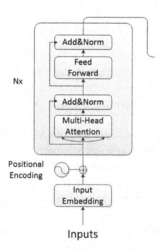

Fig. 2. The structure of Transformer Encoder.

3.3   Transformer for Semantic Integrity Analysis

This paper is based on Transformer to build a semantic integrity analysis model, which is mainly divided into the following three parts.

Input Layer. First, the cleaned data set is segmented. And then labeled with the quaternion set T=S, B, M, E. Label B is defined as the beginning of a semantic complete sentence, M is defined as the middle word of a semantic complete sentence, E is represented as the ending word of a semantic complete sentence, and S is represented as a specific symbol (, : ; etc.) closest to the front and back a word. For example:"物质世界的运动是绝对的 而物质在运动过程中又有某种相对的静止。" The sequence of words corresponding to this semantic complete sentence and the correct label is "物质/B 世界/M 的/M 运动/M 是/M 绝对/M 的/S 而/S 物质/M 在/M 运动/M 过程/M 中/M 又/M 有/M 某种/M 相对/M 的/M 静止/E".

There is a serious category imbalance problem in the number of labels labeled by the quaternary annotation set. And the number of M labels is much larger than that of other labels. We use the random undersampling method to process the M labels. The words with both left and right labels as M are discarded according to a certain ratio. The number of labels before and after processing is shown in Fig. 3. Although label M still accounts for about 50% after processing, the experiment result shows that the random undersampling method can greatly improve the category imbalance problem.

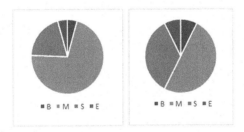

Fig. 3. Statistics before and after sampling of each label.

The word sequence after random undersampling may be underfitting due to changes in context characteristics. In order to preserve the context information that each word should have, this paper proposes using the sliding window to process the sequence data before random undersampling. For the word sequence $T(1:n)$ with n words, a sliding window of size k is used to slide from the beginning to the end, and the subsequence within each window is used as the input of the Transformer. Assuming k value is 5, the subsequence generated by the ith word in the sequence T is represented as $(T_i - 2, T_i - 1, T_i, T_i + 1, T_i + 2)$, where $T_i = T[(n+i)\%n]$.

Transformer with Two Encoder Blocks. We have converted the input word sequence into a word vector at the input layer. In order to capture the sequential feature of each word, we add positional encoding to each word vector. The encoding method uses a randomly assigned form, but the position vector of the same position is still unique. The sliding window used in this paper has a size of 9 and the input word vector is 64 dimensions. A 9*24 matrix will be randomly allocated to generate a unique mapping between each position and the 64-dimensional vector.

The feature vector and position vector of the word sequence are input into Transformer for feature extraction. There are two encoder blocks in total. Each Encoder is composed of multi-head attention and feed forward neural network. The input word vector dimension is 64, the word vector processed in feed forward neural network is 256 dimensions, and the output word vector after normalization layer is finally converted into 64 dimensions (Fig. 4).

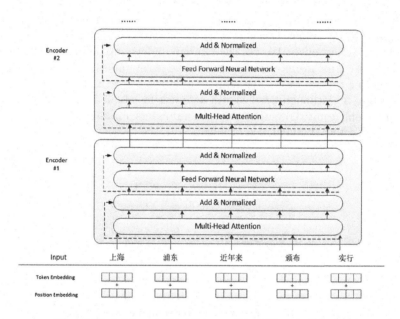

Fig. 4. Model based Transformer of two Encoder blocks.

Output Layer. In order to transform the vector dimension to be consistent with the number of label categories, we add a fully connected layer. The elu activation function is used to convert the output of the last Encoder block into a vector of a specified dimension. Finally, the probability of the output is obtained by using the softmax activation function. The function of softmax is defined as follows,

$$S_i = \frac{e^{V_i}}{\sum_i^C e^{V_i}} \tag{2}$$

Where V_i is the output of the fully connected layer, i represents the category index, and the total number of categories is C. S_i represents the ratio of the index of the current element to the exponential sum of all elements. A k-dimensional vector with any real number will be "compressed" into another k-dimensional real vector after passing through the softmax layer. Each element of the compressed vector is in the range $[0, 1]$, and the sum of all elements is 1.

3.4 Training and Prediction

This article actually solves a multi-classification problem. And the loss function adopted is cross-entropy loss function. The training objective of the model is to minimize the following loss function:

$$C = -\sum_i^n y_i ln a_i \tag{3}$$

Where y_i represents the distribution of the real label, a_i is the predicted label distribution of the model after training, and the cross entropy loss function can measure the similarity between y_i and a_i. In addition, cross-entropy as a loss function has the additional advantage of avoiding the problem of a reduced learning rate of the mean square error loss function, since the learning rate can be controlled by the error of the output.

The prediction process of the model is that for any input sequence, the Transformer Encoder outputs the conditional probability of annotation at each moment. In the prediction process, the model needs to further output the corresponding label according to the output value. In order to test the accuracy of the model, the label with the greatest probability is directly selected as the prediction result.

4 Experiment

4.1 Experimental Environment

The experimental environment is shown in Table 1:

The data set adopted is the Pennsylvania Chinese tree database (CTB)8.0 corpus in this paper, with a total number of about 1.3 million words. By combining automatic annotation with manual annotation, several kinds of punctuation (∘ ? ! ;) are regarded as the semantic complete mark in the dataset. And then the accuracy of the labeling is further improved through manual inspection. Finally, the data set was randomly divided into 90% training set and 10% test set.

The word vector data source is Baidu Encyclopedia, Wikipedia, news and novels. The vector dimension is 64-dimensional. In the process of obtaining the word vector, this paper replaces the unregistered words with special vectors.

Table 1. Experimental environment configuration.

Environment	Value
Server	DELL PowerEdge T640
Processor	Intel(R) Xeon(R) Bronze 3106 CPU @ 1 70 GHz
RAM	128 G
GPU	4*GeForce RTX 2080 Ti
OS	Ubuntu 16.04
JDE	Python3.6, TensorFlow, Keras, Pytorch

4.2   Evaluation Criteria

The model proposed belongs to the multi-classification problem in this paper. We use the accuracy rate (A), macro-P, macro-R and macro F1 as indicators to evaluate the effect of the model. A is the overall accuracy of the model. The other indicators are calculated as follows, where n is the number of categories, and P_i and R_i respectively represent the P value and the R value of the i-th category.

$$macro - P = \frac{1}{n} \sum_{i=0}^{n} P_i \tag{4}$$

$$macro - R = \frac{1}{n} \sum_{i=0}^{n} R_i \tag{5}$$

$$macro - F1 = \frac{2 X macro - P X macro - R}{macro - P + macro - R} \tag{6}$$

4.3   Model Parameter Setting

The main parameters affecting the semantic integrity analysis model are the layers of Encoder, the number of heads in the multi-head attention mechanism, the activation function and the choice of the model optimizer. In order to find a better solution for each parameter, the control variable method is used in this paper, and make the following experiment.

The Number of Encoder Block. Encoder is the core of the semantic integrity analysis model. In general, the more layers of Encoder, the more complex the model, and the longer the training time. Due to the limited amount of data in this paper, after comparative experiments, this paper selects a 2-layer Encoder for training and prediction.

The Number of Heads in the Multi-head Attention Mechanism. Transformer proposed a multi-head attention mechanism, which can improve the performance of the self-attention mechanism to a certain extent. On the one hand it can expand the ability of the model to focus on different positions. On the other hand, it gives multiple "representation subspace" of the attention layer. Experiments set the number of multi-head attentions to 2, 4, 8 and 16 respectively, and the results are shown in the following Fig. 5. In order to balance the effect of the model and the speed of training, the 4-head Attention selected in this paper.

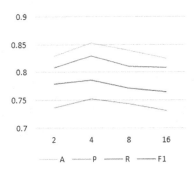

Fig. 5. Multi-head attention mechanism experiment comparison result.

Activation Function. The function of the activation function is to add nonlinear factors to the model, and increase the adaptability of the model to the data. It can make the classification more accurate. The activation functions commonly used in neural networks are sigmoid, tanh, elu, relu, etc. These four activation functions are selected for experiments. The experimental results are shown in Table 2. As can be seen from the figure, different activation functions have a great influence on the results. According to the experimental results, this paper selects elu as the activation function.

Table 2. Activation function experiment comparison result.

Activation function	macro-P	macro-R	macro-F1	A
elu	**0.7356**	**0.8114**	**0.7685**	**0.8318**
tanh	0.4795	0.5745	0.5167	0.6068
relu	0.7249	0.7943	0.7536	0.8126
Sigmoid	0.7234	0.7914	0.7505	0.8113

Model Optimizer. The model optimizer sets up a deep learning optimization algorithm. Its main purpose is to optimize the update strategy of the parameters. Improper optimization algorithms will cause the model to converge to a local optimal solution. This paper chooses the more common adam optimization algorithm, adadalta algorithm, RMSprop algorithm and AMSGrad algorithm for comparison. The experimental results are shown in Table 3. The parameters of the optimization algorithm use the default values or the recommended values in the paper. It can be seen from the table that the effect of the adadalt algorithm is relatively poor. AMSGrad and adam have similar effects, while the effect of the RMSprop algorithm is slightly better than the two. Therefore, the model optimization algorithm selected in this paper is RMSprop algorithm.

Table 3. Optimization algorithm comparison experiment results.

Optimization	macro-P	macro-R	macro-F1	A
adadelta	0.6118	0.6950	0.6502	0.7135
adam	0.7455	0.8156	0.7735	0.8303
RMSprop	**0.7499**	**0.8298**	**0.7846**	**0.8437**
AMSGrad	0.7453	0.8014	0.7648	0.8218

4.4   Model Comparison Experiment

In order to verify the effectiveness of the proposed method, the same data set is used to select the classic deep learning network for comparison experiments:

1. **RNN**, after the word vector passes RNN, connect the whole connection layer and SoftMax and output.
2. **LSTM**, which sends the feature vector directly to the LSTM extraction feature, and outputs the tag after the full connection layer and SoftMax.
3. **Bi-LSTM**, using the forward LSTM and the backward LSTM to obtain the context features in two directions and then splicing the vector, connecting the Dropout layer, the full connection layer and the SoftMax, then output.
4. **Double-layer LSTM**, the word vector of the word sequence mapping passes through two layers of LSTM, and finally prevents over-fitting via Dropout, and outputs through the fully connected layer.

The experimental parameters are set as follows: the number of LSTM neurons is 256, the Dropout layer setting ratio is 0.5 [7], the Transformer Encoder has 2 layers, the Multi-Head Attention is 4 heads, and the word sequence has a sliding window size of 9, each loop ends. The training data set is shuffle processed, the RMSprop optimization algorithm is used, the fully connected layer activation function is elu.

The experimental results are shown in Table 4:

Table 4. Model comparison experiment results.

Model	macro-P	macro-R	macro-F1	A
RNN	0.6837	0.6328	0.6573	0.7425
LSTM	0.7417	0.7165	0.7289	0.7909
Bi-LSTM	0.7906	0.8013	0.7985	0.8347
Double-layer LSTM	0.7955	0.7675	0.7764	0.8069
Transformer	**0.7529**	**0.8298**	**0.8555**	**0.8527**

It can be seen from the results that the accuracy of the Transformer-based semantic integrity analysis model proposed in this paper can reach 85.27%, which is better than other models. On the one hand, the loop window used in this paper can preserve the context features well in the undersampling process; on the other hand, Transformer can better learn the context features, and the Transformer model can obtain more accurate features, so it can achieve better results.

5   Conclusion

This paper proposes a semantic integrity analysis model based on Transformer. It can capture more context features by taking the advantages of using self-attention mechanism to process sequence data without distance limitation and multi-head attention to obtain features at various levels. Thus, automatic labeling of long text is realized. From the experimental results and project usage, this model can better solve the problem of marking semantic integrity. Subsequent models will be used in the production environment process, and can further improve the prediction result by combining the dependencies between tags and pos rules.

References

1. Mikolov, T., Chen, K., Corrado, G., et al.: Efficient estimation of word representations in vector space. arXiv preprint arXiv:1301.3781 (2013)
2. Graves, A.: Generating sequences with recurrent neural networks. arXiv preprint arXiv:1308.0850 (2013)
3. Tang, D., Qin, B., Liu, T.: Document modeling with gated recurrent neural network for sentiment classification. In: Proceedings of the 2015 Conference on Empirical Methods in Natural Language Processing, pp. 1422–1432 (2015)
4. Zheng, X., Chen, H., Xu, T.: Deep learning for Chinese word segmentation and POS tagging. In: 2013 Proceedings of the Conference on Empirical Methods in Natural Language Processing, pp. 647–657 (2013)
5. Chen, X., Qiu, X., Zhu, C., et al.: Long short-term memory neural networks for Chinese word segmentation. In: 2015 Proceedings of the Conference on Empirical Methods in Natural Language Processing, pp. 1197–1206 (2015)

6. Vaswani, A., Shazeer, N., Parmar, N., et al.: Attention is all you need. In: Advances in Neural Information Processing Systems, pp. 5998–6008 (2017)
7. Srivastava, N., Hinton, G., Krizhevsky, A., et al.: Dropout: a simple way to prevent neural networks from overfitting. J. Mach. Learn. Res. **15**(1), 1929–1958 (2014)

An Improvement of Coherent Semantic Attention for Image Inpainting

Weiqing Wang[1], Enming Gu[2], and Wei Fang[1,2,3(✉)]

[1] School of Computer & Software, Jiangsu Engineering Center of Network Monitoring,
Nanjing University of Information Science and Technology, Nanjing, China
Fangwei@nuist.edu.cn
[2] State Key Laboratory for Novel Software Technology, Nanjing University, Nanjing, China
[3] Jiangsu Key Laboratory of Computer Information Process Technology, SooChow University,
Suzhou, China

Abstract. In some image restoration algorithms of the past, they often do not consider the continuity between pixels, and the internal features of the hole region. The mapping to the image semantically does not take into account the continuity of the feature, resulting in the color of the fault. Or the deformation of the edge contour of the image. In some of the current popular algorithms and models, we can clearly see the color faults and artificial repair traces from their repair results. These discontinuities are mainly because these methods ignore the semantic relevance and feature continuity of the hole region. Therefore, if we want to get a better image repair effect. We have to improve on semantic relevance and feature continuity. We validated the effectiveness of our proposed method in image restoration tasks on the CelebA and Places2 datasets, and our results yielded a better visual experience in some images than existing methods.

Keywords: Image inpainting · Coherence · Semantic attention

1 Introduction

Image restoration problems have many applications in computer vision, including image editing, and image inpainting. In general, the image restoration process uses a portion of the image to fill the rest of its missing parts. The image restoration process is a subjective process. The quality of results is ultimately decided by people's judgment. Currently, manual image inpainting requires the following steps:

1) Imagine filling the semantic content according to the entire scene;
2) Ensure structural continuity between the missing area and the surrounding area.
3) Fill in the visually realistic content for the missing area.

In practice, each man who inpaint the image will give us different results completely different from each other in details. But the high-level semantics of these patching results

© Springer Nature Singapore Pte Ltd. 2020
X. Sun et al. (Eds.): ICAIS 2020, CCIS 1252, pp. 267–275, 2020.
https://doi.org/10.1007/978-981-15-8083-3_24

are consistent. For example, if a part of the face is missing, the corresponding part will be added to the final inpainting result.

Therefore, various image inpaint methods although having different effects, are basically similar in the inpaint results for specific images in recent years. The generative method of generating new samples through high-dimensional data distribution has been widely used in many problems. For example, image inpainting, speech synthesis, image transfer story, artistic style, etc. The most popular approaches are auto regressive models, variational auto encoders [4], and generative adversarial networks (GAN) [9].

But there are some problems with these methods, so they can't complete inpainting tasks perfectly. Our article focuses on solving image hole inpainting tasks and removing background content that should not be produced in the generated area. Because we found that in some models, such as PartialConv [1] and Gated-Conv [2], the experimental result was unable to infer the missing contour regions and gave false predictions. In addition, in the worst case, both will produce obvious artifact results. Sometimes these problems occur due to the complexity of the image structure. Sometimes because the wrong texture was generated during the inpainting process. We suspect that these failures may come from several problems with current learning-based inpainting systems, which typically approximate the foreground or background of the image randomly selected as part of the image to be repaired. In this case, if the area where the hole is close does not appear in the hole, then in the result of the inpainting, the content that should not appear in the hole may still appear, so the attention of the model is dispersed. Therefore, in order to obtain the accuracy of inpainting results, we must first detect the foreground content of the image, fill the contour of the damaged image, and then complete the contoured foreground object so that the entire module is completed.

In order to alleviate and solve these problems, we use image sampling as input to generate realistic images. In this process, we conduct a lot of research and some investigations on the repair methods. For example, in 2019 Chuanxia Zheng's [3] paper Pluralistic Image Completion, he proposed a fined deep generative model-based approach. They proposed the concept of novel coherent semantic attention (CSA) layer. [19] We improve the CSA layer and achieve a better result.

To summarize, our contributions are as follows:

1. We design a learning-based inpainting system to improve the Coherent Semantic Attention for Image Inpainting which can fill the hole of image.
2. To infer the structure of images, we adjust novel coherent semantic attention (CSA) layer so that the layer can better adapt to changes in semantics.
3. Our demonstrate that the system produces higher-quality inpainting results compared to existing methods.

2   Related Work

In this part of the article, we will make some concise and alienated work and research related to this article. The content will be divided into two parts, the first part is the introduction of non-learning methods, and the other part is the introduction of the current mainstream learning methods. Because in the past research, image restoration methods can be divided into the following two categories: traditional non-learning repair methods and learning repair methods [20].

2.1   Classic Non-learning Repair Method

Non-learning repair methods are based on diffusion or patch-based repair methods. Its repairing tasks are often simpler scenarios. The learning repair method is to complete the repair task by learning the semantics of the image, and then infer the content of the missing area through the neural network. Learning to fix often deals with complex semantic-based image restoration.

Non-learning methods mostly use similar information to copy adjacent regions or copy information from similar background pixel blocks, and then fill this information into the missing regions by algorithms. This technique was first introduced into image processing by Bertalmio, Sapiro et al. They used the edge information of the area to be repaired, and used a coarse-to-fine method to estimate the direction of the iso-illuminance line and used the propagation mechanism to transmit information. Spread to the repaired area to get better repair results. Essentially, it is an inpainting algorithm based on partial differential equation (PDE). [21] Although non-learning methods are very effective for surface texture synthesis, as we envision, the resulting images obtained by filling tend to have significant macroscopic discontinuities. They do not generate semantically meaningful content, nor are they suitable for handling large missing areas. In other words, the repair effect is not ideal.

2.2   Deep Learning Based Learning Repair Method

Different from non-learning methods, learning methods typically use deep learning and GAN strategies to generate pixels at breaks. The context encoder [10] first trains the deep neural network for image restoration tasks, brings the confrontational training into a novel encoder-decoder pipeline, and outputs the prediction of the missing regions. However, it does not perform well in generating fine detail textures. Phatak et al. used an encoder-decoder network (i.e., context encoder) and combined reconstruction and confrontational losses to better recover the semantic structure. Iizuka et al. [11] combine global and local specifiers to reproduce semantically plausible structures and local real-world details. Wang et al. [12] proposed a generated multi-column CNN combined with confidence-driven reconstruction loss and implicit diversification MRF (ID-MRF) terminology.

In addition, many previous Muti-stage methods have been proposed in previous studies. Zhang et al. [13] proposed a progressive generation network (PNG) for filling holes with multiple stages while deploying LSTM [17] to take advantage of cross-phase dependencies. Nazeri et al. [14] proposed a two-stage EdgeConnect model that first predicted significant edges and then generated edge-triggered patching results. Xiong et al. [15] proposed a foreground-aware repair method involving three phases, namely contour detection, contour completion and image completion, to eliminate structural inference and content illusion. Through the above estrangement and discussion, we can find that most existing CNN-based patching methods are generally not suitable for handling [18] irregular holes. To solve this problem, Liu et al. [16] a partial convolutional layer comprising three steps is proposed, namely a gated convolution provided by a mask that learns a channel-wise soft mask by considering corrupted images, masks and user sketches. However, PConv uses manual feature normalization and only considers forward mask updates, so it is still limited in handling color differences and ambiguity. To this end, we have done some work and improvement, and hope to improve the experimental results.

3   The Approach

Our model consists of two steps: rough inpainting and refinement inpainting. In this way, it helps us to stabilize the training speed and expand the acceptance field. The final framework of our inpainting system is shown in the Fig. 1.

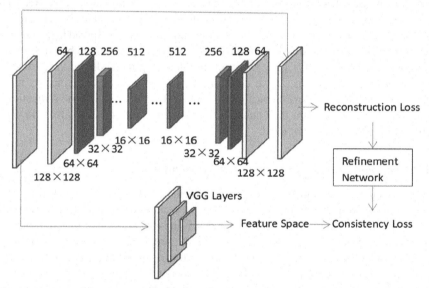

Fig. 1. The architecture of our model.

3.1   Rough Network

The input to the model contains a $3 \times 256 \times 256$ image. It also contains a mask as large as the image. The information of loss areas are in the mask. I_{out} is the output of the model. The structure of rough network is similar as the generative network in [5]. But we change the composition of convolutions. It trained with the L_1 reconstruction loss. All 16×16 convolutions are deconvolutions.

3.2   Refinement Network

The structure of refinement Network as Fig. 2. We will use the I_{in} as the input of the rough network to predict the final result I_{out}.

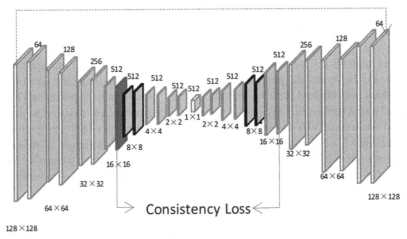

Fig. 2. The architecture of refinement Network. The orange part is CSA layer. (Color figure online)

Each layer of the encoder is connected to the corresponding decoder layer. For this type of reconstruction, the known area urges the network to restrict faster effectively, which is critical for rebuilding. The network consists of an encoder and a decoder, where the skip connection is also a network similar to coarse network. In the encoder, each layer is 3×3 convolution or 4×4 convolution. The result of the 3×3 convolution remains the same amount of space, while the number of channels doubles. The CSA layer is the fourth layer of the encoder. The CSA layer is not used in the decoder section, which uses deconvolution.

Coherent semantic attention is divided into two parts. The first part is called the search stage and the second part is called the generation stage. We use VGG to extract the feature space of the image, and use the patch discriminator to perform the loss calculation on this feature space, which can better help the generator to understand the image information and stabilize the discriminator training loss.

We use M and M′ represent missing regions and known regions in the feature map. We believe that it is not enough to consider only relatively. The relationship between M and M′ is reconstructed in the feature map. Sometimes this leads to the ductility and continuity of the final result. We first get a rough prediction of the inapinting result I_{out1}. Then, using a network with CSA layer to refine this result, the input of this network is M and M′. Finally, M and M′ get a higher resolution together.

Let's take the image with a hole in the center as an example: the CSA layer is divided into two phases: search and generation. For each patch generated in $m_i'(i = 1, ..., n)$, we search for patch m_i for initialization. To measure the correlation between these patches, the following cross-correlation metrics are used:

$$D_{max} = \frac{\langle m, m' \rangle}{||m|| \times ||m'||} \tag{1}$$

$$D' = \frac{\langle m, m_b \rangle}{||m|| \times ||m_b||} \tag{2}$$

D' represents two neighbor similarities. The m_b represent previous patch of m. With this relationship, we replace the original patch with the generated patch to get the new state.

Some methods [6] use perceptual loss [7] to improve the recognition capabilities of the network. However, the perceptual loss cannot directly optimize the convolutional layer, which may mislead the CSA training process. We adjusted the perceptual loss and eventually used the loss of consistency instead of the perceived loss to solve the problem. We used pre-trained VGG-16 to improve the layer feature space in the original image. Next, for any M, we set the feature space to the l_2 distance of the target CSA layer and the corresponding encoder in the CSA. In order to match the results, we use $4-3$ layers of VGG-16 to calculate the loss of consistency. The formula we used is as follows:

$$L_c = \sum_t \left\| CSA(I_{in})_t - \varphi_n(I_{gt}t) \right\|_2^2 + \left\| CSA_m(I_{in})_t - \varphi_n(I_{gt}t) \right\|_2^2 + KL(\varphi_n(I_{gt}t) \,\|\, \varphi_n(I_{gt}t)) \tag{3}$$

Where φ_n is the activated VGG-16 in the current layer and CSA indicates the content of the CSA layer. CSA_m is the corresponding function in the decoder.

3.3 Our Proposed Algorithm

Algorithm 1 Process of CSA layer
Reshape as a convolution filter and apply in M
Use Eq to get the and
Initialize with
for i = 1 to n do
Use Eq to calculate the
Use Eq to get the attention map for
end for
Combine from to to get a attention matrix
Reuse as a deconvolution to get
Return

4 Classification Model

We evaluated our approach on two datasets: Places2, CelebA. In order to conduct an assessment fairly, we experimented with regular and irregular holes. All masks and images used for training and testing are 256×256 in size. We trained on a single NVIDIA RTX 1080Ti (11 GB) with a batch size of 2. One week of training on Places2, and CelebA, respectively. Below are some examples of the results.

4.1 Qualitative Comparison

For a more regular mask, CA can achieve a satisfactory repair effect semantically. But its repairs will show a distorted structure and weird color changes. SH performs well due to shift operation and guidance loss, but the predicted image it obtains is somewhat ambiguous and lacks detail.

For irregular masks, PC and GC can produce smooth and reasonable results, but colors and lines still produce discrete results. These methods are mainly due to the fact that the correlation between the deep features of the pore regions is not taken into account as an influence parameter. Compared to these existing methods, our model can better handle these problems and produce better results visually. Our approach is superior in generating consistency of content and expanding the perceived domain of generated patches (Fig. 3).

Fig. 3. Some image inpainting examples generated by our network model has get good effect visually in practice.

4.2 Quantitative Comparisons

We randomly extracted 200 images from the datasets of CelebA and Places2, and generated corresponding rules or irregular masks for each image to train. We use TV loss PSNR and SSIM to quantify the performance of the model. It can be seen that our method improves the performance of the results to some extent (Table 1).

Table 1. Comparison of SSIM, PSNR, TV loss on ImageNet dataset

	SSIM+	PSNR+	TV loss
CA	0.872	23.25	19.55
SH	0.913	24.36	20.18
Our method	0.934	25.74	18.92

4.3 Ablation Study

Effect of Consistency Loss. We conducted further experiments in order to explore the impact of consistency. We trained the repair model by adding or reducing the loss of consistency Lc in the experiment. From the experimental results, we conclude that in the absence of loss of consistency, the center of the hole region generally appears distorted, and we speculate that this may be due to training instability and misinterpretation of the image semantics by the training model. Caused. The loss of consistency helps to solve these problems.

Effect of Feature Patch Discriminator. The experimental results show that when we only use the patch discriminator, the results will also show distorted results. So we added the traditional feature recognizer, but the result is still fuzzy. Finally, fine detail and reasonable structure can be obtained by executing the feature patch discriminator. In addition, our experimental results show that feature patch recognizers tend to process images faster than traditional image recognizers by 3 s.

5   Conclusion

We improved the original U-Net and VGG based image restoration algorithm model and designed a semantic focus layer to learn the relationship between the features of missing regions in the image restoration task. And our own training results show. Our approach has better results in producing clearer, more consistent and more detailed results. In the next work, we plan to apply it to other types of image restoration to improve the generalization performance of the model.

Acknowledgements. This work was supported in part by the Open Research Project of State Key Laboratory of Novel Software Technology under Grant KFKT2018B23, the Priority Academic Program Development of Jiangsu Higher Education Institutions, and the Open Project Program of the State Key Lab of CAD&CG (Grant No. A1916), Zhejiang University.

References

1. Liu, G., Reda, F.A., Shih, K.J., Wang, T.C., Tao, A., Catanzaro, B.: Image inpainting for irregular holes using partial convolutions. arXiv preprint arXiv:1804.07723 (2018)
2. Yu, J., Lin, Z., Yang, J., Shen, X., Lu, X., Huang, T.S.: Free-form image inpainting with gated convolution. arXiv preprint arXiv:1806.03589 (2018)
3. Liu, H., Jiang, B., Xiao, Y., Yang, C.: Coherent Semantic Attention for Image Inpainting. arXiv preprint arXiv:1905.12384 (2019)
4. Walker, J., Doersch, C., Gupta, A., Hebert, M.: An uncertain future: forecasting from static images using variational autoencoders. In: Leibe, B., Matas, J., Sebe, N., Welling, M. (eds.) ECCV 2016. LNCS, vol. 9911, pp. 835–851. Springer, Cham (2016). https://doi.org/10.1007/978-3-319-46478-7_51
5. Isola, P., Zhu, J.Y., Zhou, T., Efros, A.A.: Image-to-image translation with conditional adversarial networks. In: CVPR (2017)
6. Yeh, R.A., Chen, C., Lim, T.Y., Schwing, A.G., Hasegawa-Johnson, M., Do, M.N.: Semantic image inpainting with perceptual and contextual losses. arXiv preprint arXiv:1607.07539 (2016)

7. Johnson, J., Alahi, A., Fei-Fei, L.: Perceptual losses for real-time style transfer and super-resolution. In: Leibe, B., Matas, J., Sebe, N., Welling, M. (eds.) ECCV 2016. LNCS, vol. 9906, pp. 694–711. Springer, Cham (2016). https://doi.org/10.1007/978-3-319-46475-6_43

8. Yu, J., Lin, Z., Yang, J., Shen, X., Lu, X., Huang, T.S.: Generative image inpainting with contextual attention. In: Computer Vision and Pattern Recognition (cs.CV) (2018)

9. Goodfellow, I., et al.: Generative adversarial nets. In Advances in neural information processing systems, pp. 2672–2680 (2014)

10. Pathak, D., Krahenbuhl, P., Donahue, J., Darrell, T., Efros, A.A.: Context encoders: feature learning by inpainting. In: CVPR (2016)

11. Iizuka, S., Simo-Serra, E., Ishikawa, H.: Globally and locally consistent image completion. ACM Trans. Graph. **36**(4), 1–14 (2017)

12. Wang, Y., Tao, X., Qi, X., Shen, X., Jia, J.: Image inpainting via generative multi-column convolutional neural networks. In: Advances in Neural Information Processing Systems (NeurIPS), pp. 329–338 (2018)

13. Zhang, H., Hu, Z., Luo, C., Zuo, W., Wang, M.: Semantic image inpainting with progressive generative networks. In: ACM International Conference on Multimedia (ACMMM), pp. 1939–1947 (2018)

14. Nazeri, K., Ng, E., Joseph, T., Qureshi, F., Ebrahimi, M.: Generative image inpainting with adversarial edge learning. arXiv preprint arXiv:1901.00212 (2019)

15. Xiong, W., et al.: IEEE Conference on Computer Vision and Pattern Recognition (CVPR) (2019)

16. Liu, G., Reda, F.A., Shih, K.J., Wang, T.C., Tao, A., Catanzaro, B.: Image inpainting for irregular holes using partial convolutions. In: The European Conference on Computer Vision (ECCV), vol. 11215, pp. 89–105 (2018)

17. Fang, W., Zhang, F., Sheng, J., Ding, Y.: A new sequential image prediction method based on LSTM and DCGAN. CMC Comput. Mater. Continua **64**, 217–231 (2019)

18. Fang, W., Zhang, F., Sheng, V.S., Ding, Y.: A method for improving CNN-based image recognition using DCGAN. CMC Comput. Mater. Continua **57**(1), 167–178 (2018)

19. Pan, L., Qin, J., Chen, H., Xiang, X., Li, C., Chen, R.: Image augmentation-based food recognition with convolutional neural net works. Comput. Mater. Continua **59**(1), 297–313 (2019)

20. Tu, Y., Lin, Y., Wang, J., Kim, J.: Semi-supervised learning with generative adversarial networks on digital signal modulation classification. Comput. Mater. Continua **55**(2), 243–254 (2018)

21. Li, X., Liang, Y., Zhao, M., Wang, C., Jiang, Y.: Few-shot learning with generative adversarial networks based on WOA13 data. Comput. Mater. Continua **60**(3), 1073–1085 (2019)

Formal Verification of the Correctness of Operating System on Assembly Layer in Isabelle/HOL

Fei Yang Chen[1], Wen Tao Xu[1], Zhen Jiang Qian[1(✉)], Wei Yong Yang[2], and Wei Liu[2]

[1] School of Computer Science and Engineering, Changshu Institute of Technology, Suzhou, China
qianzj@cslg.edu.cn
[2] NARI Group Corporation, Nanjing, China

Abstract. Formal verification of the operating system refers to modeling the operating system in mathematical language, and proving the system fully implements the functions described in design. Isabelle/HOL is an interactive theorem prover that allows us to use formal expressions to describe mathematical formulas and provides a series of tools to prove these formulas. MINIX 3 is a microkernel-based open source operating system with high security. The context switching algorithm is used to switch the CPU from one process or thread to another, and saving the context is an important step. In this paper, we introduce the model of the related codes of operating system in Isabelle/HOL, and verify that the code performs expected results as an example of formal verification of operating system.

Keywords: Formal methods · Isabelle/HOL · Operating system · MINIX 3 · Save context · Interactive theorem prover

1 Introduction

Formal verification of operating system refers to modeling the operating system in mathematical language, and proving the system fully implements the functions described in design, indicating the system is safe.

MINIX 3 is a microkernel-based open source operating system with high security. In an operating system, the context switching algorithm is used to switch the CPU from one process or thread to another, and saving the context is an important step of which. This algorithm is usually implemented by C and assembly, and will be compiled into assembly code. In the source code of MINIX 3, the body of the algorithm is implemented by a series of assembly macros.

In this paper, we take the save context algorithm of MINIX 3 as an example. We model the relevant code in Isabelle/HOL to verify the execution of which can get the expected result, indicating the feasibility of verifying the correctness of operating system on assembly layer.

© Springer Nature Singapore Pte Ltd. 2020
X. Sun et al. (Eds.): ICAIS 2020, CCIS 1252, pp. 276–288, 2020.
https://doi.org/10.1007/978-981-15-8083-3_25

2   Related Work

Nowadays, we are more and more concerned about the security of programs. We tend to either to perform security inspection on existing programs or to propose verifiable protocols, interfaces, etc. For example, Chen et al. proposed a method to find functions that need to check parameters before calling [1]. Kou et al. use logical proof to verify the user authentication protocol they proposed is reliable [2]. Zhang et al. considered formal verification when designing the interface model for Cyber-Physical Systems [3].

Since the 1970s, there have been teams working on formal verification of operating systems, such as the LOCK project supported by the United States [4] and the VFiasco (Verified Fiasco) project by Hohmuth et al. [5,6] and so on.

Currently, the Flint project team [7] provides an extensible architecture named CertiKOS for building certified concurrent OS kernels [8], and based on this, they published a mechanized programming toolkit called CCAL [9]. The L4.verified project plans to use Isabelle/HOL to verify the seL4 kernel [10]. The members of the project have done a lot of work, such as YK Tan et al. introduced the verified CakeML compiler backend [11], Rob et al. introduced a process algebra for link layer protocols [12] and so on.

3   Save Context Algorithm in MINIX 3

In the source code of MINIX 3, save context algorithm is implemented by a series of assembly macros. Here we only consider the i386 architecture. The macro used to save context is named SAVE_PROCESS_CTX, which saves the process context. It consists of setting the direction register, saving the current process pointer, saving the general-purpose registers, saving the trap style, saving the stack pointer, saving the segment registers, and saving the trap context. Among them, saving the general-purpose registers is defined by the macro called SAVE_GP_REGS, saving the segment registers is defined by the macro called RESTORE_KERNEL_SEGS, and saving the trap context is defined by the macro called SAVE_TRAP_CTX.

4   Model of System State

4.1   Model of Registers

In i386, there are 32-bit general-purpose registers and 16-bit segment registers, which can be represented by the "word" datatype in Isabelle/HOL library as follows. Here "psw" refers to the program status word and "pc" refers to the program counter.

type_synonym $u16\_t$ = "16 word"
type_synonym $u32\_t$ = "32 word"

```
record register =
eax   ::  u32_t
pc    ::  u32_t
psw   ::  u32_t
ebp   ::  u32_t
esp   ::  u32_t
cs    ::  u16_t
...
```

Since we need to read and write registers frequently, a set of helper functions is defined as below. The "get_reg16" and "set_reg16" functions are 16-bit version functions used to read and write 16-bit registers while the "get_reg32" and "set_reg32" functions are 32-bit version functions. The implementation of 32-bit version functions is similar to the 16-bit version functions, so we will not list them here.

datatype *reg = EAX | PC | PSW | EBP | ESP | CS | ...*

definition *get_reg16::"sys_state ⇒ reg ⇒ u16_t"* **where**
"get_reg16 s r ≡ (case r of
  CS ⇒ cs (s_reg s)
| DS ⇒ ds (s_reg s)
| AX ⇒ ucast (eax (s_reg s))
...
)"

definition *set16::"sys_state ⇒ reg ⇒ u16_t ⇒*
sys_state" **where**
"set16 s r v ≡ set_reg32 s r ((get_reg32
s r AND 0xffff0000) + ucast v)"

definition *set_reg16::"sys_state ⇒ reg ⇒ u16_t ⇒*
sys_state" **where**
"set_reg16 s r v ≡ (case r of
  CS ⇒ s (| s_reg := (s_reg s) (| cs := v |) |)
| DS ⇒ s (| s_reg := (s_reg s) (| ds := v |) |)
...
)"

In particular, according to the manual provided by Intel, setting the direction register requires rewriting the 11th bit of the psw register. With the help of the "word" library, we can use "!!" operator to read as well as "setBit" function to write a bit in a word.

definition $get\_df::"sys\_state \Rightarrow bool"$ **where**
$"get\_df \ s \equiv (get\_reg32 \ s \ PSW) \ !! \ 10"$

definition $set\_df::"sys\_state \Rightarrow sys\_state"$ **where**
$"set\_df \ s \equiv set\_reg32$
$s \ PSW \ (setBit \ (get\_reg32 \ s \ PSW) \ 10)"$

4.2 Model of Memory

We define memory as a function from address to value and then we can simulate memory read and write operations.

type_synonym $mem = nat$
type_synonym $memory = "mem \Rightarrow u32\_t"$

Reading and writing memory is equivalent to modifying the value of the function at a certain point as follows.

definition $get\_mem::"sys\_state \Rightarrow mem \Rightarrow u32\_t"$ **where**
$"get\_mem \ s \ p \equiv (s\_mem \ s) \ p"$

definition $set\_mem::"sys\_state \Rightarrow mem \Rightarrow u32\_t \Rightarrow$
$sys\_state"$ **where**
$"set\_mem \ s \ p \ v \equiv s \ (\!| \ s\_mem := (s\_mem \ s) \ (p := v) \ |\!)"$

4.3 Model of Assembly Instructions

First, we include the registers and the memory in the system state.

record $sys\_state = s\_reg :: register$
$s\_mem :: memory$

Second, we want to describe the instructions to be used later in Isabelle/HOL. For example, we use "mov_r2r" to indicate transferring data from one register to another. The instructions used by save context algorithm are shown as bellow, where "mov_r2r' " and "mov_i2r' " are 16-bit version instructions.

datatype $instr =$
   $mov\_r2r \quad reg \quad reg$
| $mov\_r2r \ ' \quad reg \quad reg$
| $mov\_m2r \quad mem \quad reg$
| $push\_r \quad reg$
| $pop\_r \quad reg$
| cld
$\ldots$

Finally, the code is equivalent to the list of instructions, and the execution code is equivalent to executing the assembly instructions sequentially.

type_synonym $code = "instr \ list"$

4.4   Formalization of Execution Instructions

Now we are interested in describing the behavior of the previously defined assembly instructions. For example, "mov_r2r" involves reading and setting the register, and updating the pc register. We describe the behavior of all instructions by defining a function that steps through the assembly instructions.

primrec $step::"sys\_state \Rightarrow instr \Rightarrow sys\_state"$ **where**
$"step\ s\ (mov\_r2r\ r1\ r2)\ =\ update\_pc$
$(set\_reg32\ s\ r2\ (get\_reg32\ s\ r1))"\ |$
$"step\ s\ (mov\_r2r\ '\ r1\ r2)\ =\ update\_pc$
$(set\_reg16\ s\ r2\ (get\_reg16\ s\ r1))"\ |$
$"step\ s\ (mov\_m2r\ m\ r)\ =$
$update\_pc\ (set\_reg32\ s\ r\ (get\_mem\ s\ m))"\ |$
$...$

With the function above, we can define the process of executing code as a sequential execution of each instruction.

primrec $exec::"sys\_state \Rightarrow code \Rightarrow$
$sys\_state"$ **where**
$"exec\ s\ [\ ]\ =\ s"\ |$
$"exec\ s\ (i\ \#\ is)\ =\ exec\ (step\ s\ i)\ is"$

At this point, a system state model that can execute assembly code is established.

5   Model of Save Context Algorithm

5.1   Formalization of Constants

In addition to some of the constants defined directly by macros, MINIX 3 puts the relevant offsets in "procoffsets.cf" for the convenience of referencing the structure members. This file will generate a corresponding header file while compiling, part of the code of which is shown as follow.

include $"kernel/kernel.h"$

struct $proc$
member $DIREG\ p\_reg.di$
member $SIREG\ p\_reg.si$
member $BPREG\ p\_reg.bp$
$...$

Based on the premise that compiler and linker work correctly, the offsets of structure members is also defined as constants.

definition $DIREG::"int"$ **where**
$"DIREG \equiv 4\ *\ u16\_len"$

definition *SIREG*::*"int"* **where**
"SIREG ≡ DIREG + reg_len"
definition *BPREG*::*"int"* **where**
"BPREG ≡ SIREG + reg_len"
· · ·

5.2   Formalization of Save Context Macro

The save context macro and most of helper macros are defined in "sconst.h", as shown bellow is a macro that saves the general-purpose registers.

```
#define SAVE_GP_REGS( pptr )     \
mov %eax ,  AXREG( pptr )    ; \
mov %ecx ,  CXREG( pptr )    ; \
mov %edx ,  DXREG( pptr )    ; \
mov %ebx ,  BXREG( pptr )    ; \
mov %esi ,  SIREG( pptr )    ; \
mov %edi ,  DIREG( pptr )    ;
```

Macros are expanded during preprocessing, so we define macros as functions which unfold code, based on the premise that preprocessor works correctly. Taking the above code as an example, we defined the macro in Isabelle/HOL by the previously established model.

definition *SAVE_GP_REGS*::*"sys_state ⇒ reg ⇒ code"* **where**
"SAVE_GP_REGS s pptr ≡ [
(mov_r2m EAX (offset s pptr AXREG)),
(mov_r2m ECX (offset s pptr CXREG)),
(mov_r2m EDX (offset s pptr DXREG)),
· · ·
] "

After completing the definition of all helper macros, we define the macro that saves the context. The code for this macro in MINIX 3 is shown as below.

```
#define SAVE_PROCESS_CTX( displ ,  trapcode )  \
cld  ; \
push %ebp  ; \
movl  (CURR_PROC_PTR + 4 + displ )  \
(%esp) ,  %ebp  ; \
SAVE_GP_REGS(%ebp)  ; \
```
· · ·

The formalization of the save context macro is shown as follow. Note that the connection between macro and instruction should be a list splicing operation, since the helper macros will eventually expand into a list of instructions.

definition *SAVE_PROCESS_CTX::"sys_state $\Rightarrow$ int $\Rightarrow$ int $\Rightarrow$ code"* **where**
"SAVE_PROCESS_CTX s displ trapcode $\equiv$ [
(cld),
(push_r EBP),
(mov_m2r (offset s ESP (CURR_PROC_PTR + 4 + displ)) EBP)] @
(SAVE_GP_REGS s EBP) @
. . .
"

5.3 Formalization of Expanded Macros

Part of the switch context algorithm is implemented in "mpx.S", where "SAVE_PROCESS_CTX(0, KTS_INT_HARD)" is used to save the relevant context.

Now we manually expand this macro by previously defined assembly instructions. On one hand, we are interested in proving the correctness of the macro expansion result. On the other hand, we expand this macro to prepare for the subsequent verification of the state after execution of assembly instructions.

definition *save_process_ctx::"sys_state $\Rightarrow$ code"* **where**
"save_process_ctx s $\equiv$ [
cld,
push_r EBP,
mov_m2r (offset s ESP 24) EBP,
mov_r2m EAX (offset s EBP 256),
mov_r2m ECX (offset s EBP 224),
. . .
]"

6 Verify of Save Context Algorithm

6.1 Verify of Correctness of Expansion

To make sure that the expansion of the macro is correct, we can verify that the macro is expanded to the same content as the manually expanded instruction list. The process of simplifying the macro in Isabelle/HOL is shown as below.

lemma *unfold_code:"SAVE_PROCESS_CTX s 0 KTS_INT_HARD = save_process_ctx s"*
apply *(simp add: SAVE_PROCESS_CTX_def save_process_ctx_def)*
apply *(simp add: SAVE_GP_REGS_def RESTORE_KERNEL_SEGS_def SAVE_TRAP_CTX_def)*
apply *(simp add: CURR_PROC_PTR_def KTS_INT_HARD_def)*

```
apply (simp add: KERN_DS_SELECTOR_def
SEG_SELECTOR_def KERN_DS_INDEX_def)
unfolding AXREG_def CXREG_def DXREG_def
BXREG_def SIREG_def DIREG_def STYLE_def
BPREG_def PCREG_def CSREG_def PSWREG_def
PSWREG_def SPREG_def
apply (simp add: reg_len_def u32_len_def
u16_len_def ptr_len_def)
done
```

6.2 Verify of Single Steps

We define a helper function that takes part of the instruction list.

```
definition skip::"nat ⇒ nat ⇒ code ⇒ code" where
"skip m n c ≡ take n (drop m c)"
```

Then, taking the second sentence assembly instruction as an example, we take out the second instruction in the list.

```
definition ctx_step2::"sys_state ⇒ sys_state" where
"ctx_step2 s ≡ (exec s (skip 1 1
(save_process_ctx s)))"
```

The second instruction is "push_r". The behavior of this instruction consists of reducing the value of the stack pointer, storing the register value, and updating the pc register.

Reducing the value of the stack pointer corresponds to the reduction of the value of the esp register. Storing in memory corresponds to the value of the register stored in the memory pointed to by the stack pointer. Because the established model fetches instructions sequential, the behavior of updating the value of the program counter can be simply defined as the operation of adding one to the pc register.

```
lemma ctx_step2_be:" get_reg32
(ctx_step2 s) ESP = get_reg32 s ESP − 4"
apply (simp add: save_process_ctx_def
ctx_step2_def skip_def)
apply (simp add: update_pc_def)
apply (simp add: add_ri_def sub_ri_def
set_rm_def)
apply (simp add: get_reg32_def
set_reg32_def get_mem_def set_mem_def)
apply (simp add: u32_sub_def)
done
```

The above is part of the verification process of the second assembly instruction, the verification of the remaining code is similar, so we will not describe them here.

6.3   Model of State After Executing Instructions

We want to verify that the execution of save context algorithm can get the expected result, that is, the proposition — "the status of execution of corresponding code is consistent with the expected result" is true.

Since each assembly instruction only makes a small amount of modification to the system state, we can split the state into multiple unrelated substrates, and then we prove each substate is consistent with the expectation.

For each state, we give a proposition to indicate "the actual state of the system is consistent with the expected state after execution of relevant code." Thus, we can define the proposition as a conjunction, each clause of which corresponds to a substate being consistent with the expected result. Then the correctness of the proposition corresponds to the values of all clauses being true.

We have verified behaviors of all instructions. Obviously, the execution of other instructions does not involve changing the values of these memory regions, so other instructions have no effect on the value of this proposition.

The save general register proposition consists of six clauses as follow, each clause representing "the corresponding register is saved to the correct memory location".

definition $save\_gp\_regs::"sys\_state \Rightarrow bool"$ **where**
$"save\_gp\_regs \ s \equiv get\_mem \ (ctx\_step4 \ s)$
$(ax \ (ctx\_step4 \ s)) = get\_reg32 \ s \ EAX \ \wedge$
$get\_mem \ (ctx\_step5 \ s) \ (cx \ (ctx\_step5 \ s)) =$
$get\_reg32 \ s \ ECX \ \wedge$
$get\_mem \ (ctx\_step6 \ s) \ (dx \ (ctx\_step6 \ s)) =$
$get\_reg32 \ s \ EDX \ \wedge$
$get\_mem \ (ctx\_step7 \ s) \ (bx \ (ctx\_step7 \ s)) =$
$get\_reg32 \ s \ EBX \ \wedge$
$get\_mem \ (ctx\_step8 \ s) \ (si \ (ctx\_step8 \ s)) =$
$get\_reg32 \ s \ ESI \ \wedge$
$get\_mem \ (ctx\_step9 \ s) \ (di \ (ctx\_step9 \ s)) =$
$get\_reg32 \ s \ EDI"$

Thus we can split code into several segments, and we give each segment a proposition to assist the proof of the final state. The modeling of other states is similar and will not be listed here.

6.4   Verify of Correctness of Save Context Algorithm

We divide the verification process into three steps: verifying the single-step execution of all assembly instructions is same as the execution of the complete instruction list, verifying the corresponding code segment performs the excepted state, verifying the execution of save context algorithm can reach the excepted results.

First, we define a helper function to synthesize the assembly instructions.

primrec $steps::"nat \Rightarrow sys\_state \Rightarrow code \Rightarrow code"$ **where**
$"steps\ 0\ s\ c = c"\ |$
$"steps\ (Suc\ n)\ s\ c = steps\ n\ s\ (skip\ n\ 1$
$(save\_process\_ctx\ s)\ @\ c)"$

Second, we prove that the list synthesized by the 26 instructions is equivalent to the manually expanded instruction list above.

lemma $skip\_step:"steps\ 26\ s\ [\ ] =$
$skip\ 0\ 26\ (save\_process\_ctx\ s)"$
unfolding $save\_process\_ctx\_def$
$steps\_def\ skip\_def$
apply $(auto)$
done

Finally, we verify that the sequential execution of the list are the same as the execution of manually expanded instruction list.

theorem $"exec\ s\ (save\_process\_ctx\ s) =$
$exec\ s\ (steps\ 26\ s\ [\ ])"$
apply $(simp\ add:\ skip\_step)$
unfolding $save\_process\_ctx\_def\ skip\_def$
apply $(auto)$
done

At this point, the first step is completed.

We still use saving general-purpose register as an example to explain the second step. By introducing the behavior of single steps, we complete the proof as below. The verification of remaining auxiliary states is similar and we will not list here.

lemma $save\_gp\_regs:"save\_gp\_regs\ s"$
apply $(simp\ add:\ save\_gp\_regs\_def)$
apply $(simp\ add:\ ax\_def\ ctx\_step4\_be)$
apply $(simp\ add:\ cx\_def\ ctx\_step5\_be)$
apply $(simp\ add:\ dx\_def\ ctx\_step6\_be)$
apply $(simp\ add:\ bx\_def\ ctx\_step7\_be)$
apply $(simp\ add:\ si\_def\ ctx\_step8\_be)$
apply $(simp\ add:\ di\_def\ ctx\_step9\_be)$
done

The third step is to merge all the auxiliary states before, and prove that the conjunction of all the propositions is true, thus indicating that save context algorithm can reach the expected state. The proposition of the final state includes setting the direction register "set_direction", saving the current process pointer "save_ptr", saving the general-purpose register "save_gp_regs", saving the trap style "save_trapcode", saving the stack pointer "save_ebp", saving the segment register "restore_kernel_segs", and saving the trap context "save_trap_ctx".

theorem *save_process_ctx:" set_direction s*
∧ *save_ptr s* ∧ *save_gp_regs s*
∧ *save_trapcode s* ∧ *save_ebp s*
∧ *restore_kernel_segs s* ∧ *save_trap_ctx s"*
apply (*simp add: set_direction*)
apply (*simp add: save_ptr*)
apply (*simp add: save_gp_regs*)
apply (*simp add: save_trapcode*)
apply (*simp add: save_ebp*)
apply (*simp add: restore_kernel_segs*)
apply (*simp add: save_trap_ctx*)
done

At this point, we complete the proof, and Isabelle/HOL also shows that there are no sub-goals to prove, as shown in "Fig. 1".

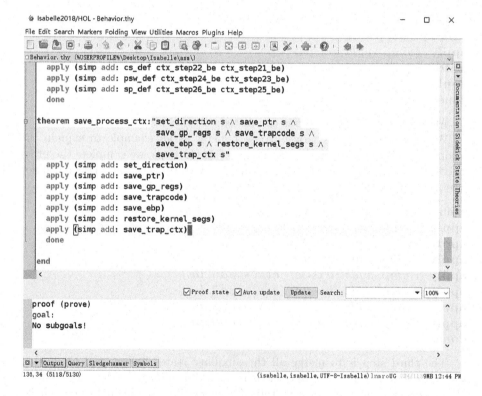

Fig. 1. Proof results.

7 Conclusion

In this paper, we use the formal method to model the operating system in Isabelle/HOL, describe the state of system from the assembly level, and describe the operation semantics of instructions. We take the context switching algorithm in MINIX 3 as an example, and verify the save context algorithm. However, the complete operating system source code is huge and requires a lot of work to complete the verification. We hope that the methods provided in this article can be used as a reference for formal verification of operating system.

Acknowledgment. This work is supported by the Natural Science Foundation of Jiangsu Province under grant No. BK20191475, the Qing Lan Project of Jiangsu Province in China under grant No. 2017 and 2019, 333 high-level personnel training project of Jiangsu Province in China under grant No. 2018, Key Areas Common Technology Tendering Project of Jiangsu Province in 2017 (Research on Information Security Common Technology of Industrial Control System), Science and Technology Project of State Grid Corporation in 2019 (Research on Lightweight Active Immune Technology for Power Monitoring System), "Tiancheng Huizhi" Innovation and Education Fund Project of Ministry of Education in China under grant No. 2018A03008, "Zhirong Xingjiao" Industry-University-Research Innovation Fund Project of Ministry of Education in China under grant No. 2018A01004, and "New generation information technology" Industry-University-Research Innovation Fund Project of Ministry of Education in China under grant No. 2018A01003.

References

1. Chen, L., Yang, C., Liu, F., Gong, D., Ding, S.: Automatic mining of security-sensitive functions from source code. Comput. Mater. Continua **56**, 199–210 (2018)
2. Kou, L., Shi, Y., Zhang, L., Liu, D., Yang, Q.: A lightweight three-factor user authentication protocol for the information perception of IoT. Comput. Mater. Continua **58**, 545–565 (2019)
3. Zhang, Y., Huang, M., Wang, H., Feng, W., Cheng, J., Zhou, H.: A co-verification interface design for high-assurance CPS. Comput. Mater. Continua **58**, 287–306 (2019)
4. Saydjari, O.S., Beckman, J.M., Leaman, J.R.: LOCK trek: navigating uncharted space. In: Proceedings of the 1989 IEEE Symposium on Security and Privacy (1989)
5. Hohmuth, M., Tews, H., Stephens, S.G.: Applying source-code verification to a microkernel: the VFiasco project. In: Proceedings of the 10th ACM SIGOPS European Workshop, pp. 165–169. ACM, New York, USA (2002)
6. Hohmuth, M., Tews, H., Stephens, S.G.: Applying source-code verification to a microkernel: the VFiasco project. TU Dresden Technical report (2002)
7. Yale flint project website (2019). http://flint.cs.yale.edu/
8. Gu, R., et al.: CertiKOS: an extensible architecture for building certified concurrent OS kernels. In: Proceedings of the 2016 USENIX Symposium on Operating Systems Design and Implementation, OSDI'16, pp. 653–669 (2016)
9. Gu, R., et al.: Certified concurrent abstraction layers. In: Proceedings of the 2018 ACM SIGPLAN Conference on Programming Language Design and Implementation, PLDI'18, pp. 646–661 (2018)

10. Klein, G., et al.: seL4: formal verification of an OS kernel. In: Proceedings of the ACM SIGOPS 22nd Symposium on Operating Systems Principles, SOSP2009, pp. 207–220 (2009)

11. Tan, Y.K., Myreen, M., Kumar, R., Fox, A., Owens, A., Norrish, M.: The verified CakeML compiler backend. J. Funct. Program. **29**, e2 (2009)

12. Hoefner, P., Glabbeek, R., Markl, M.: A process algebra for link layer protocols. In: 28th European Symposium on Programming (ESOP) (2019)

Nonlinear Correction Based on Depth Neural Network

Yanming Wang[1,2,3], Kebin Jia[1,2,3], Pengyu Liu[1,2,3(✉)], and Jiachun Yang[4]

[1] Beijing University of Technology, Beijing 100124, China
liupengyu@bjut.edu.cn
[2] Beijing Laboratory of Advanced Information Networks, Beijing 100124, China
[3] Beijing Key Laboratory of Computational Intelligence and Intelligent System, Beijing 100124, China
[4] Tianjin Huayun Tianyi Special Meteorological Detection Technology Co., Ltd., Tianjin 300392, China

Abstract. With the global climate change, the high-altitude detection is more and more important in the climate prediction. Due to the interference of the measured objects and the measured environment, the input and output characteristic curve of the pressure sensor will shift, resulting in nonlinear error. Aiming at the difficulty of nonlinear correction of pressure sensor and the low accuracy of correction results, depth neural network model was established based on wavelet function, and Levenberg-Marquardt algorithm is used to update network parameters to realize the nonlinear correction of pressure sensor. The experimental results show that compared with the traditional neural network model, the improved depth neural network not only accelerates the convergence rate, but also improves the correction accuracy, meets the error requirements of upper-air detection, and has a good generalization ability, which can be extended to the nonlinear correction of similar sensors.

Keywords: Depth neural network · Pressure sensor · Nonlinearity correction · Wavelet transform · LM algorithm

1 Introduction

The high-altitude weather detection is an important means to acquire the atmospheric change information. In the process of high altitude detection, the air pressure value is one of the important parameters, and the measurement accuracy of the pressure sensor directly affects the final detection result. In the process of meteorological measurement, the pressure sensor will show nonlinear characteristics affected by the external environment, for many reasons: (1) The nonlinear characteristics of the sensor can not be completely eliminated due to the limitations of its own material, design scheme, fabrication process and so on. (2) There is interference in the calibration environment of the sensor, so that the characteristic point of the sensor is drifting, and the measurement result is deviation, so that the non-linearity is caused [1].

© Springer Nature Singapore Pte Ltd. 2020
X. Sun et al. (Eds.): ICAIS 2020, CCIS 1252, pp. 289–301, 2020.
https://doi.org/10.1007/978-981-15-8083-3_26

For nonlinear correction, a large number of experiments have been carried out by relevant researchers. In reference [2], the nonlinear integrator is used for phase correction, which improves the stability of the control system. In reference [3], the series-parallel resistance network is used to correct the thermal sensor, so that the measurement accuracy of the temperature sensor is improved significantly. However, the correction by hardware circuit has the disadvantages of high cost, low precision and complex integration, which is not conducive to practical production and application [4]. With the development of computer technology, the error compensation of sensor is carried out by software algorithm, and the realization of nonlinear correction has become the main research method [5]. The main software compensation is look-up table method and curve fitting method. Reference [6] corrects the operational atmosphere of high score 2 image by looking up the table method, and reduces the error to 0.8%. In reference [7], the magnetic field sensor is corrected by the least square method, and the high accuracy is achieved. The table look-up method ignores the measurement error of calibration points, and the fitting method can only reflect the overall trend of the sensor. It is the approximation of several discrete measurement points to the global model of the sensor, and can not satisfy the nonlinear fitting in complex cases.

As a new information processing method, Neural Network has made some achievements in the field of sensor nonlinear correction. In reference [8], the BP neural network method is used to calibrate the angle sensor, which effectively reduces the measurement error and improves the accuracy of the measurement. In reference [9], the color sensor is calibrated by BP neural network, and the sensitivity of the sensor is improved. However, the traditional BP network has the disadvantages of slow convergence speed and poor non-linearity, and it still needs to be further optimized to suit the non-linear correction of the air pressure sensor.

In this paper, an pressure sensor is used as an example to carry out the data collection and calibration experiment on the standard calibration equipment under the influence of the external environment such as temperature and air pressure. The Depth Neural Network is optimized, the wavelet function is used as the activation function of the network hidden layer, and the Levenberg-Marquardt algorithm is introduced to update the parameters of each layer, and the model of the non-linear correction of the pressure sensor is obtained. The experimental results show that the proposed method is superior to the traditional network in the aspects of model accuracy and convergence speed, and can complete the nonlinear correction of the pressure sensor more quickly and accurately.

The structure of this paper is as follows: The first section introduces the principle of nonlinear correction of pressure sensor and the application method of correction model. In the second section, the Depth Neural Network model is analyzed, and the shortcomings of the network in sensor nonlinear correction and the corresponding solutions are pointed out. In the third section, according to the nonlinear correction principle of pressure sensor, the corresponding neural network model is established, and the network parameters are designed. In the fourth section, the correction experiment is carried out according to the data of air pressure sensor, and the experimental results are compared and analyzed to verify the effectiveness of the proposed method. Finally, the paper is summarized and the conclusion of nonlinear correction of pressure sensor is given.

2 Sensor Nonlinear Correction Principle

The nonlinear error of pressure sensor is composed of its physical characteristics and environmental influence [10]. The pressure sensor system model is shown in Fig. 1.

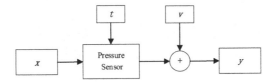

Fig. 1. Nonlinear model of pressure sensor system

The model of the pressure sensor is as follows:

$$y = f(x, t) + v \tag{1}$$

In the formula: y is the measured pressure value of the sensor output, x is the air pressure in the actual environment under measurement, t represents environmental variables, such as temperature, humidity etc. v is the interference noise of the sensor system. The function $f(x, t)$ is an unknown complex function, which is related to the characteristics of the pressure sensor and the external environmental factors. From the characteristics of the pressure sensor, for a specific environmental variable t, x and y are one-to-one correspondence, then there is a special function $X = g(y) = g(f(x, t)) = x$. That is, the search function g enables the output value of the sensor to accurately reflect the measured pressure after correction, and the correction schematic diagram is shown in Fig. 2.

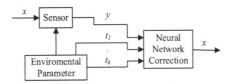

Fig. 2. Correction schematic diagram

3 Depth Neural Network Model and Improved Algorithm

3.1 Depth Neural Network Structure

The structure of the Depth Neural Network (DNN) model is shown in Fig. 3, which consists of an input layer, an output layer and at least one hidden layer. According to the general approximate theorem, a feedforward neural network with linear output layer and at least one hidden layer can approximate any function with any precision as long as a sufficient number of neurons are given.

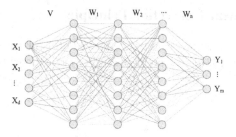

Fig. 3. DNN structure

The traditional neural network uses gradient descent method to update the parameters, and the parameters of the input layer and hidden layer network are updated as follows:

$$\triangle V_{ih} = \alpha e_h X_i = \alpha \left(\sum_{j=1}^{l} W_{hj} g_j \right) H_h (1 - H_h) X_i \tag{2}$$

$$\triangle \beta_h = -\alpha e_h \tag{3}$$

The hidden layer and output layer network parameters are updated as follows:

$$\triangle W_{hj} = \alpha g_j H_h = \alpha \left(Y_j - Y_j' \right) Y_j \left(1 - Y_j' \right) H_h \tag{4}$$

$$\triangle \beta_j = -\alpha g_j \tag{5}$$

Where α is the learning rate, g_j and e_h are error information, X_i is the i neuron input of the input layer, H_h is the h neuron output of the hidden layer, and Y_j' is the output of the j neuron in the output layer, and the Y_j is the corresponding real value.

3.2 Levenberg-Marquardt Algorithm

DNN has the ability to approximate arbitrary continuous function and nonlinear mapping, and can simulate nonlinear input-output relationship. However, it also has some shortcomings, such as poor modeling ability, slow learning convergence speed, easy to fall into local minima and so on. In this paper, the traditional DNN is improved by Levenberg Marquardt (LM) algorithm to improve the convergence rate of the network.

The LM algorithm is an improvement to the Gauss-Newton method. Its basic optimization idea is to use the Gauss-Newton method to generate an ideal search direction near the optimal value of the function, and to adjust the weight of the network through the adaptive algorithm, so as to overcome the shortcomings of the gradient drop method in one-way blind search and speed up the convergence speed of the network. The updated expression of the weight of each layer is as follows:

$$W_{n+1} = W_n - \left[J^T J^n + uI \right]^{-1} J_n^T E_n \tag{6}$$

Where I is the unit matrix, u is the proportional factor, E is the network prediction error, and J is the Jacob matrix, the matrix contains the first derivative of the prediction error to the parameters of each layer of the network, as follows:

$$J = \begin{bmatrix} \frac{\partial E_1}{\partial W_1} & \cdots & \frac{\partial E_1}{\partial W_n} \\ \vdots & \ddots & \vdots \\ \frac{\partial E_j}{\partial W_1} & \cdots & \frac{\partial E_j}{\partial W_n} \end{bmatrix} \tag{7}$$

3.3 Wavelet Analysis

In the traditional DNN, the hidden layer selects the Sigmoid function as the activation function for nonlinear transformation. However, for the nonlinear component of the pressure sensor, the Sigmoid function mapping ability is poor, and the correction can not be completed accurately. In this paper, the wavelet function is used to replace the original Sigmoid function as the activation function of the hidden layer node, and a series of wavelet generating functions are combined to approximate the measured values, so as to achieve the purpose of pressure sensor correction.

At present, the main wavelet functions are Harr wavelet, db wavelet, Morlet wavelet and Mexican Hat wavelet. Morlet wavelet has good nonlinear mapping ability, and has achieved remarkable results in precipitation analysis [13], atmospheric environment prediction [14], laser calibration [15] and so on. The expression of the Morlet wavelet function is:

$$h(x) = C * \cos(ux) * exp\left(-\frac{x^2}{2}\right) \tag{8}$$

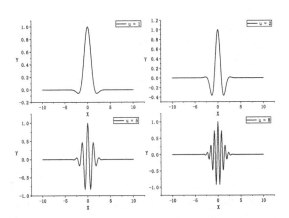

Fig. 4. The comparison of the u value and the Morlet function

In the formula, C is the normalization constant of reconstruction, and the value is 1. u controls the shape of the wavelet function. The shape comparison diagram of Morlet wavelet function corresponding to different values is shown in Fig. 4. The u value is determined by experiments, and the shape of Morlet wavelet function is determined in order to achieve the best correction effect.

4 Network Model Construction

4.1 Dataset

In order to test the nonlinear correction effect of the neural network on the pressure sensor, the training sample data should be obtained first. Therefore, it is necessary to use the standard equipment to carry out the calibration experiment on the pressure sensor, and the measured value of the pressure sensor is not only related to the atmospheric pressure but also related to the temperature, and the calibration can be carried out by using the control variable method.

The measurement error is less than 1 hPa at the range of 1100 hPa–500 hPa and the measurement error is less than 0.7 hPa in the range of 500 hPa–5 hPa according to the high-altitude weather detection specification. Therefore, the calibration pressure range is 5 hPa–1100 hPa. According to the needs of high altitude detection, the calibration temperature range is −30 °C–+40 °C. At 35 °C, some of the collected data are shown in Table 1.

Table 1. Data collected by pressure sensor

Measuring temperature/°C	Measurement pressure/hPa	Standard pressure/hPa	Measurement error/hPa
35	1103.2	1100	3.2
35	906.27	900	6.27
35	806.31	800	6.31
35	702.44	700	2.44
35	601.73	600	1.73
35	401.68	400	1.68
35	302.58	300	2.58
35	103.78	100	3.78
35	10.55	5	5.55

Figure 5 shows the measurement error distribution of pressure sensors at different temperatures. It can be seen from the diagram that the pressure sensor has a large temperature drift effect, and the temperature has a great influence on the measurement results of the sensor. After correction by neural network, the influence of temperature on the pressure sensor can be overcome, and the measured value can be more close to the real value.

4.2 Network Parameter Setting

According to the basic structure of DNN, a six-layer network is selected to construct the model, which includes one input layer, four hidden layers and one output layer. From

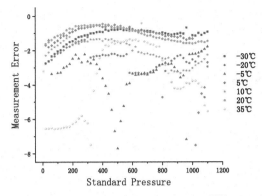

Fig. 5. Distribution of sensor measurement error at different temperatures

the data measured by the pressure sensor, it can be seen that the influencing factors are temperature and air pressure, so there are two neurons in the input layer. In order to prevent the occurrence of overfitting, the number of neurons in the hidden layer was 5–10–10–5. After the network calculation, it outputs the corresponding standard pressure, so there is a neuron in the output layer, that is, the network structure is 2–5–10–10–5–1. The measuring air pressure and temperature of the pressure sensor are input into the Depth Neural Network, and the corresponding standard pressure is output by the network calculation, so as to achieve the purpose of sensor correction.

For the different temperature ranges and different pressure ranges collected in Table 1, there are 800 pieces of data. In order to make the training results correctly reflect the inherent law of the sample, and in order to avoid overfitting, all the data are divided into training set and test set according to 8:2. The network is trained by the training set data, so that the network model parameters are optimized, and the final network is tested by the test set to detect the generalization ability of the model.

Table 2. Network training parameter setting

Learning rate	0.0001
Epochs	10000
Dropout	0.5
Loss function	Mean Square Error (MSE)
Optimization algorithm	Gradient descent
	LM algorithm
Activation function	Sigmoid
	Morlet wavelet

The initial weight value of each layer network in the range of [0–1] is generated by random function, the offset value is set to 0, and the other parameters are set as shown in Table 2.

5   Correction Results and Performance Comparison

5.1   Convergence Rate Comparison

In order to compare the influence of LM algorithm and gradient descent method on the convergence speed of the network, the hidden layer function adopts Sigmoid function to randomly generate 10 groups of initial weights. Two kinds of network parameter optimization algorithms are used to train, and the training period is recorded when the MSE is less than 0.7 in the training process. The experimental results are shown in Table 3.

Table 3. Convergence rate performance comparison

Number	Gradient descent	LM algorithm
1	3825	5
2	2022	5
3	2460	8
4	4041	5
5	7092	8
6	3034	10
7	5923	4
8	4423	4
9	1095	7
10	7431	4
Average	4135	6

In the training process, the change of the loss value of the gradient descent method is shown in Fig. 6, and the LM algorithm is shown in Fig. 7.

As can be obtained from Table 3, for random network weight initial values, the gradient descent method requires a large difference in the training period and is sensitive to the weight initial value. It can be seen from Fig. 6 that there is jitter phenomenon in the process of convergence by using gradient descent method to train the network, and the minimum value can not be approximated directly. In contrast, LM algorithm can overcome the shortcomings of gradient reduction method and complete convergence quickly and accurately. The average training period based on LM algorithm is about 6 times, which is much faster than that of gradient drop method. It can be seen that the LM algorithm can overcome the shortcomings of the gradient subtraction method, converge more quickly, and improve the stability of the network.

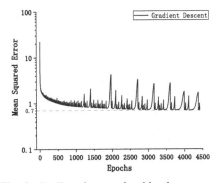 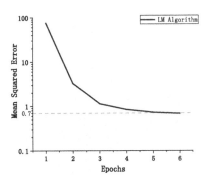

Fig. 6. Gradient descent algorithm loss diagram

Fig. 7. LM algorithm loss diagram

5.2 Wavelet Function Shape Comparison

It can be seen from Fig. 4 that for Morlet wavelet function, different n values correspond to different wavelet shapes, and the influence of different n values on the final calibration results is tested by experiments to determine the optimal activation function. The same test data are input into the network, and the network is trained to achieve the final convergence. The MSE between the corrected data and the standard measured value is calculated. The experimental results are shown in Table 4.

Table 4. n value and calibration error

n	MSE	n	MSE
1	0.413	6	0.432
2	**0.335**	7	0.509
3	0.431	8	0.401
4	0.506	9	0.522
5	0.430	10	0.513

As can be seen from the experimental results, in the vicinity of n = 2, the calibration error has a minimum value. For the accurate experiment of n = 2, it is found that when n = 1.5, the MSE of the data reaches the minimum value of 0.307. The best correction effect can be obtained by setting the n value of wavelet function to 1.5.

5.3 Comparison of Calibration Accuracy

The prediction accuracy of the network is an important index to evaluate the performance of the network. In order to compare the effect of the Simoid function and the wavelet function on the result of the final calibration, the network is trained by the gradient descent method, and the results of the partial calibration are shown in Table 5.

It can be seen from Table 5 that both network models can effectively correct the pressure sensor so that the average error is within the specified range. According to MSE, the prediction accuracy of using wavelet function as activation function is higher than that of Simoid function, and the whole MSE is reduced by 0.32, which makes the pressure sensor achieve higher measurement accuracy and is more conducive to high altitude meteorological detection.

Table 5. Comparison of calibration accuracy

Standard pressure	Pre-calibration pressure	Post-calibration pressure	
		Simoid	Morlet wavelet
1100	1103.2	1097.96	1097.42
1000	1006.54	1001.78	1000.61
900	906.27	902.05	900.63
800	806.23	802.37	801.14
700	702.44	698.44	699.63
600	601.61	599.41	599.66
500	501.35	498.46	500.01
400	401.48	399.39	400.05
300	302.58	299.84	300.13
200	204.23	200.91	200.64
100	103.78	101.15	99.45
5	10.55	6.74	5.87
MSE	2.10	0.63	0.31

In order to further analyze the effect of the Simoid function and the wavelet function on the calibration result of the pressure sensor, the measurement error curve of pressure sensor shown in Fig. 8 is drawn. It can be seen from Fig. 8 that compared with Simoid function, using wavelet function as activation function has better approximation ability, can compensate error more accurately, improve measurement accuracy and realize pressure sensor correction.

5.4 Prediction Capability Comparison

In order to test the generalization ability of the established model and whether the network is over-fitting, the different air pressure values are selected as test set data for model test at different temperatures. The partial test results are shown in Table 6.

According to Table 6, both the traditional Depth Neural Network and the Depth Neural Network based on wavelet function, the measurement accuracy of the sensor has been significantly improved. From the experimental results, it can be seen that the average error of the test set is close to that of the training set, and there is no over-fitting

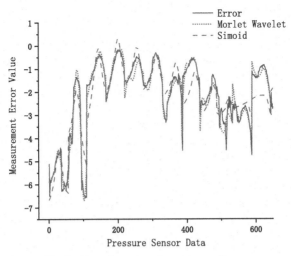

Fig. 8. Error compensation contrast diagram

phenomenon. The correction value error of neural network based on wavelet function is smaller, which is closer to the actual value, and can realize the nonlinear correction of pressure sensor more accurately, and has higher accuracy and generalization ability.

Table 6. Comparison of calibration accuracy of the test set

Standard pressure	Pre-calibration pressure	Post-calibration pressure	
		Simoid	Morlet wavelet
1100	1101.58	1099.67	1099.78
1000	1003.03	1000.92	1000.06
900	901.71	900.40	900.12
800	804.46	800.89	800.41
700	701.29	700.45	699.82
600	602.02	600.63	600.05
500	500.47	498.66	499.82
400	400.46	400.85	400.04
300	301.28	301.24	299.82
200	200.75	200.53	200.14
100	101.76	99.04	99.95
5	10.67	4.39	4.58
MSE	2.10	0.66	0.31

6 Conclusion

Aiming at the nonlinearity of the input and output of the pressure sensor, the error compensation is realized by introducing Depth Neural Network correction. In view of the shortcomings of the traditional neural network, LM algorithm is introduced to speed up the training speed of the network. By using the Morlet wavelet function, the measurement accuracy is further improved, and the nonlinear output error of the pressure sensor can be more accurately compensated. The experimental results show that, after the correction, the average error of the pressure sensor is 0.31 hPa, and the accuracy requirement of high altitude detection is fully satisfied. The method has good generalization ability and can be extended to nonlinear correction of similar sensors.

Acknowledgment. This paper is supported by the following funds: National Key R&D Program of China (2018YFF01010100), Basic Research Program of Qinghai Province under Grants No. 2020-ZJ-709, National natural science foundation of China (61672064), Beijing natural science foundation project (4172001) and Advanced information network Beijing laboratory (PXM2019_014204_500029).

References

1. Liu, X.D., Liu, Q.: A dual-spline approach to load error repair in a HEMS sensor network. Comput. Mater. Continua **57**(2), 179–194 (2018)
2. Zhao, X.H., Cao, L., Chen, M.L., et al.: Analysis of control system correction effect of nonlinear integrator. J. Beijing Univ. Technol. **17**(2), 138–141 (2002)
3. Zhou, S.H.: Hardware correction method for sensor non-linearity. Transducer Technol. **17**(2), 138–141 (2002)
4. Yao, Z., Wang, Z.: Empirical mode decomposition-adaptive least squares method for dynamic calibration of pressure sensors. Meas. Sci. Technol. **28**(4), 118–121 (2017)
5. Zhao, G.D., Zhang, Y.W., Zhang, Y.Q., et al.: The application of BP neural networks to analysis the national vulnerability. Comput. Mater. Continua **58**(2), 421–436 (2019)
6. Shu, M., Wen, D.B., Zhang, H., et al.: Design and implementation of operational atmospheric correction lookup table for high score no. 2 image. J. Beijing Univ. Technol. **43**(05), 683–690 (2017)
7. Zhang, Q., Pan, F.C., Chen, L.X., et al.: Calibration method of Triaxial magnetic field sensor based on linear parameter model. J. Sens. Technol. **25**(02), 215–219 (2012)
8. Xu, F., Zhang, X.F., Xin, Z.H., et al.: Investigation on the Chinese text sentiment analysis based on convolutional neural networks in deep learning. Comput. Mater. Continua **58**(03), 697–709 (2019)
9. Hu, W.J., Liu, X.H., Xin, Z.H., et al.: Study on BP neural network for colorimetric calibration of mini-color sensor. Opt. Tech. **18**(06), 97–109 (2006)
10. Jia, P., Meng, Q.X., Wang, H., et al.: The research on the static calibration of fingertip force sensor for underwater dexterous hand on RBF neural network. Appl. Mech. Mater. **48**(06), 10–12 (2007)
11. Svete, A., Bajsi, I., Kutin, J.: Investigation of polytrophic corrections for the piston-in-cylinder primary standard used in dynamic calibrations of pressure sensors. Sens. Actuators A Phys. **11**(02), 262–274 (2018)
12. Zhou, L., Ma, K., Wang, L.J., et al.: Binaural sound source localization based on convolutional neural network. Comput. Mater. Continua **60**(02), 545–557 (2019)

13. He, W.M., Song, X.Q., Gan, Y., et al.: Research on the method of the sensor-corrected optimization of the Grey neural network. J. Instrum. Instrum. **35**(03), 504–512 (2014)

14. Xia, T.C., Sun, Y., Zhao, X.B., et al.: Generating questions based on semi-automated and end-to-end neural network. Comput. Mater. Continua **61**(02), 617–628 (2019)

Spatial-Temporal Co-attention Network for Action Recognition

Shuren Zhou$^{(\boxtimes)}$ and Xiangli Zeng

School of Computer and Communication Engineering,
Changsha University of Science and Technology, Changsha 410114, China
zsr@csust.edu.cn

Abstract. In the traditional two-stream convolutional neural network, RGB image and optical flow image are trained separately and then simply fused, which results in the lack of fine-grained interaction between static image and dynamic clue, making the important clue of timing information unable to play its full role in the task of video action recognition. We propose a spatial-temporal co-attention network, which allows the attention of spatial features and temporal features to guide each other and collect basic information from the two features. The network utilizes the attention mechanism to estimate the commonality between static images and temporal information by focusing on their shared common semantics. Our experiments verify the effectiveness of the spatial-temporal co- attention network in combining spatial information and temporal information, and obtain better performance on three public standard datasets.

Keywords: Action recognition · Co-attention · Spatial-temporal features

1 Introduction

Understanding the content in the video is an important part of computer vision. Examples include video understanding and action recognition. Compared to image analysis tasks, it should not only focus on its static information, but also the temporal information of the frame sequence. Because CNN (Convolution Neural Networks) performs well in image analysis tasks, Karpathy [1] takes the advantages of convolution to directly extract the features of the video. The frame sequence of the superimposed video is directly input to the CNN for learning, but compared with some traditional methods [2, 3] and other methods of dense trajectory [4, 5]), this method does not show great advantages. The reason is that these CNN frameworks are not specifically designed for video task. Simonyan [6] and others proposed Two-Stream CNN signs that deep learning has taken a major step in action recognition. The Two-Stream CNN network is divided into two parts: spatial and temporal stream. The spatial stream processes the static frames of the video, and the temporal stream processes the optical stream of the video. Finally, the two networks unite to get the category of the action.

Although the original two-stream method has achieved good results in the action recognition task, most of the original two-stream derivative methods only use the

© Springer Nature Singapore Pte Ltd. 2020
X. Sun et al. (Eds.): ICAIS 2020, CCIS 1252, pp. 302–312, 2020.
https://doi.org/10.1007/978-981-15-8083-3_27

weighted average in the final classifier layer when fusing spatial and temporal streams. We carefully observe that there is usually one stream that fails, while the other stream is still correct in most misclassification cases of original methods, indicating that most of the original methods cannot distinguish the different contributions of spatial and temporal streams to the entire classification. We believe that temporal features and spatial features are the information that makes up the video, and are not independent of each other, but promote each other.

In order to solve these two limitations, in this paper, we propose a spatial-temporal co-attention network. Our model pays common attention to the spatial and temporal features of the video. The model can distinguish the different contributions of different regions of the image to the classification. Besides, we construct the spatial and temporal attention features and explore the subtle interactions between temporal and spatial cues. Then we optimize the temporal and spatial features, and finally obtain the feature representation of the video for classification.

In summary, our main contributions are as follows:

1) We propose a combined spatial and temporal co-attention framework that pays attention to key areas in both of video frames and optical flow images to improve recognition accuracy. A detailed visualization of the results of the attention mechanism validates that our model effectively pays attention to important parts of video frames and optical flow images for a given task.
2) We construct spatial-temporal features and capture the interactions between spatial features and temporal features. Besides, we optimize the temporal and spatial features, and obtain a better representation of video features for action recognition.

Our method has achieved outstanding results on 3 widely used datasets, UCF101 [7], HMDB51 [8], THUMOS14 [9], which illustrates the effectiveness of our work (Fig. 1).

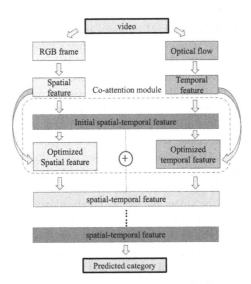

Fig. 1. The idea of the our method

2 Related Work

Action recognition has always been the focus of many scientific researchers, and good progress has been made in recent years [4, 11, 12]. Before deep learning applied the field of action recognition, early methods of human action recognition feature extraction include calculation methods based on human geometric features [14], motion information feature extraction methods [15]; Multi-scale feature extraction algorithms with prior knowledge such as HOG (Histogram of oriented gradient) [16] and SIFT (Scale-invariant feature transform) [17] has been proposed recently, thus, feature-based feature extraction methods such as HOG3D (Histogram of gradients 3D) combined with video sequence information have gained a lot developments [18, 19]. The above methods usually use common pattern recognition algorithms such as Support Vector Machine (SVM) for classification and recognition after feature extraction.

With the outstanding performance of CNN in tasks such as image classification, many researchers have also designed deep learning frameworks for video action recognition to capture static and motion information. Tranel [20] proposed a CNN model called C3D. This method directly performs 3D convolution on the video frame sequence. Its network structure is adapted from the 2D convolution of the VGGnet [21] network structure into 3D convolution. The purpose is to capture the features of the appearance information and motion information through 3D convolution of the video frame sequence. However, the sequence of stacked video frames does not capture the motion information of the video well. Simonyan [6] uses CNN to obtain the static information and motion information of the video. Therefore, a two-stream CNN is designed for spatial stream convolution. Spatial stream CNN captures spatial features containing video static information. Temporal stream CNN captures temporal features containing video motion information. Finally we fuses the two networks to achieve good performance, which illustrates that optical flow images have significant gains in performance for action recognition tasks. Some other motion recognition methods [22–29] also use video optical flow images to enhance the performance of the network.

The original two-stream method [6] achieves good results in the action recognition task, but it has some disadvantages. First, it only fuses temporal and spatial streams in a simple way, and it cannot capture the relationship between spatial and temporal features. For most misclassifications, we find that there is usually one stream failure and one stream success in the model. Second, the original method is to put all frames of the video and optical flow images into the network for training. The network cannot distinguish the contribution of different frames and different regions of the image to the final classification score. Recently, some methods of attention mechanism are applied in deep learning [12, 30, 31]. Its purpose is to focus on some important content of images (or other data) to infer the results. Neural networks have been successfully applied in the field of computer vision. We believe that temporal features and spatial features are the information that makes up the video, and are not independent of each other, but promote each other. Aiming at the limitations of the original two-stream method, we proposed a two-stream co-attention CNN. First, we designed the spatial-temporal feature to capture the subtle interaction of the spatial and temporal features of the video. Then we pay attention to the spatial and temporal features and optimize the spatial and temporal features. Finally we obtain the features of the video for classification.

3   Method

A very obvious problem in the traditional two stream method is that the spatial stream and the temporal stream are essentially independent of each other. They train independently and do not affect each other. The main cause of this problem is that the features of the two stream outputs each obtain a score after softmax, and we finally obtain the prediction result of the entire network after a simple fusion. We believe that spatial information and temporal information are components of video and should promote each other, not simply fusion.

The spatial-temporal co-attention network we proposed first constructs the spatial-temporal features by using spatial and temporal features to capture the interaction of static information and motion information. Then we use the temporal-spatial participation features and the original spatial feature sequence to pay attention to the original spatial features. We perform the same operation to temporal features so as to mine the spatial features that contain key information and the time point of action occurrence. We obtain the spatial and temporal features after attention and construct a new spatial-temporal feature again. Then we iterate this operation, and finally obtain the spatial-temporal feature, and use the spatial-temporal feature to identify actions.

In this section, we first describe the extraction of spatial and temporal features, and introduce the method of constructing spatial-temporal features. Then we explain the strategy of paying attention to spatial and temporal features, and finally obtain the optimized spatial-temporal features and introduce some recognition details.

3.1   Feature Extraction

Spatial Features. The static image features of a video contain a lot of semantic information, such as contours, textures, colors, etc. These apparent feature can be effectively utilized to classify images. Similar to the spatial feature extraction method in the traditional two stream network [6], we also use the VGG [] network for spatial feature extraction. The difference is that we use the output of the last pooling layer of VGG to obtain the feature vectors of different regions. In details, we divide the features output from the last pooling layer into the form of N feature vector sequences $\{v_1, \ldots v_N\}$, and then input the vector sequences into attention module. Each feature vector is a 512-dimensional vector representing the nth-region (Fig. 2).

Temporal Features. We represent the temporal change of a video action in the form of an optical flow image. We use the optical flow sequence images generated by the method based on TV-L1 [10] as the input of temporal stream, which is the same as the network that extracts spatial features. Subsequently, we input the optical flow feature sequence $\{o_1, \ldots o_T\}$ to the attention module.

3.2   Co-attention Module

Our method constructs a spatial-temporal feature representation of a video by collecting important information from spatial and temporal features. Then we optimize the original

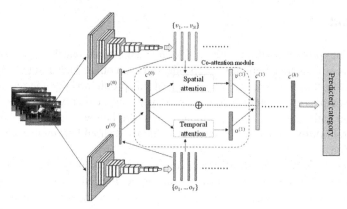

Fig. 2. The framework of our proposed method: the content in the dotted box represents the co-attention module, and the ellipsis after the network represents iterative co-attention operations.

features and obtain a better feature representation. This section mainly describes the co-attention module embedded in the learning process, which is an important module that composes the entire network.

First, we use the feature extraction method we introduced in the previous section to extract features. The spatial and temporal features are respectively represented as $\{v_1, \ldots v_N\}$ and $\{o_1, \ldots o_T\}$. We use Eq. 1 and Eq. 2 to merge the extracted spatial feature vectors and temporal feature vectors separately. The combined spatial feature is represented as $v^{(0)}$ and the temporal feature is represented as $o^{(0)}$. Then, the initialized spatial-temporal feature $c^{(0)}$ is obtained by Eq. 1.

$$v^{(0)} = tanh\left(\frac{1}{N}\sum_n v_n\right) \tag{1}$$

$$o^{(0)} = \frac{1}{T}\sum_t o_t \tag{2}$$

$$c^{(0)} = v^{(0)} \odot o^{(0)} \tag{3}$$

We generate feature vectors with specific spatial information by focusing on certain areas of the input image. Specifically, we use the initial spatial-temporal features and the feature sequence of the static image of this video to focus on the spatial features. The specific formula for spatial attention is as follows

$$v^{(1)} = v\_Att\left(\{v_n\}_{n=1}^N, c_v^0\right) \tag{4}$$

where c_v^0 is a memory vector that codes to initial spatial-temporal features. Finally, the spatial feature vector with attention information is obtained by weighted average of the input vector. Our spatial attention is calculated as follows:

$$v^{(1)} = tanh\left(\sum_n \alpha_{v,n}^{(1)} v_n\right) \tag{5}$$

where $\alpha_{v,n}^{(1)}$ is the visual attention weight, which is calculated by the double-layer feed-forward neural network (FNN) [13] and softmax function, where $W_v^{(k)}$, $W_{v,m}^{(k)}$, $W_{v,h}^{(k)}$ is the weight parameter in the network, $h_{v,n}^{(k)}$ is the state of the hidden layer, $\odot$ represents the product in element level. Calculation formula such as:

$$h_{v,n}^{(1)} = \tanh\left(W_v^{(1)} v_n\right) \odot \tanh\left(W_{v,m}^{(1)} c_v^0\right) \tag{6}$$

$$\alpha_{v,n}^{(1)} = softmax\left(W_{v,h}^{(1)} h_{v,n}^{(1)}\right) \tag{7}$$

We calculate a temporal feature vector with spatial information and context information by the temporal attention module, $o^{(1)}$.

$$o^{(k)} = V\_Att\left(\{o_t\}_{t=1}^T, m_o^{k-1}\right) \tag{8}$$

$$h_{o,t}^{(k)} = \tanh\left(W_o^{(k)} o_t\right) \odot \tanh\left(W_{o,m}^{(k)} m_o^{k-1}\right) \tag{9}$$

$$\alpha_{o,t}^{(k)} = softmax\left(W_{o,h}^{(k)} h_{o,t}^{(k)}\right) \tag{10}$$

$$o^{(k)} = \tanh\left(\sum_t \alpha_{o,t}^{(k)} o_t\right) \tag{11}$$

It is calculated in the same way as the spatial attention module.

How to integrate the static information of action and temporal changes of actions has not been well solved. In order to address this problem, we intuitively construct a joint memory vector consisting of spatial information and temporal information, which can better represent the spatial-temporal features of the entire video. It is calculated by the following formula,

$$c^{(1)} = c^{(0)} + v^{(1)} \odot o^{(1)} \tag{12}$$

where $o^{(k)}$ and $v^{(k)}$ are obtained from the spatial attention module and the temporal attention module mentioned above, respectively, and $m^{(0)}$ is the initial spatial-temporal feature containing the initial context.

Finally, we iterate the above operation and predict the category of video behavior by $c^{(k)}$. We use a single-layer softmax classifier with cross-entropy loss.

$$S_{class} = softmax\left(W_{class} c^{(k)}\right) \tag{13}$$

4 Experiments

4.1 Datasets

We conducted experiments on three widely used motion recognition datasets, UCF101 [7], HMDB51 [8] and THUMOS14 [9]. UCF101 by action video from YouTube. UCF101 contains 13,320 videos and 101 action classes. HMDB51 includes 766 video clips of 51 actions from various sources, such as online video and movies. THUMOS14 is a large video dataset for motion recognition and detection that includes long, untrimmed videos (Fig. 3).

Fig. 3. We have selected 3 different categories of examples from each of the three datasets UCF101, HMDB51 and THUMOS14. The three datasets have 101, 51 and 101 categories respectively.

4.2 Implementation Details

This section introduces the implementation details, including the network structure and training details in the experiments.

Feature Extraction
For feature extraction, we used the pre-trained VGG16 network on ImageNet to extract spatial and temporal features. The size of the image we input to the network is ($224 \times 224 \times 3$). The difference from the original VGG network is that the feature we obtain after the last pooling layer size is ($7 \times 7 \times 512$). The feature is divided into N 512-dimensional vectors as the input of the attention module, N is set as 49.

Co-attention Module
In the co-attention module, as mentioned in Sect. 3, the attention parameters are obtained by input features by double-layer feedforward neural network and softmax function, and then the attention memory vector is calculated. We set the number of iterations of the whole module k as 2, which is the setting that can get the best effect from our observation. Finally, we input the spatial and temporal features into the final full connection layer for evaluation, and set the hidden unit number in the final fully connected layer as the category number of the corresponding dataset.

Comparison with Existing Methods
Some original methods fuse the spatial feature and time feature in a simple way, but the two stream features do not influence each other essentially, so the effect has been curbed. Our method achieves better result than these methods, because we make the discriminating part of spatial and temporal features influence each other by attention mechanism. We form new spatial and temporal features by highlighting key part of the temporal features and spatial structure to conduct classification.

We evaluated our method on three widely used datasets and compared it with the state-of-the-art methods. The comparison results are shown in Table 1. Some of the earliest methods [4, 32, 33] are far less effective than ours because they use hand-crafted features as video representation. Reference [20, 34] perform 3D convolution to video, so as to obtain the spatial-temporal features and achieve good result. However, its computation cost is greatly increased. Our method uses 2D convolution method, the computation cost is much lower, and we achieve 0.9% improvement compared with [34] method. Some methods, such as [6], use two CNN to extract spatial features containing video static information and temporal features containing motion information. Then we classify the actions and results show better performance than original traditional recognition method [4, 32, 33].

However, [6] only fused the spatial features and temporal features in a simple manner in the later process and the improvement is limited. In addition, some methods [26] apply more complex fusion method to fuse the static and motion information, and achieve better results than [6]. However, they ignore the connection spatial and temporal features of video and the key information which is useful to classification of two kinds of features. Our method achieved best results among these state-of art methods. We achieve higher accuracy by 0.9% compared with 3DNet method.

Table 1. Our experimental results on three datasets of UCF101, HMDB51, and THUMOS14 are compared with the experimental results of some competitive action recognition methods. The evaluation metric of the HMDB51 and UCF101 datasets is the accuracy, and the evaluation metric of the THUMOS14 dataset is MAP.

Methods	UCF101	HMDB51	THUMOS14
(IDT) [4]	0.859	0.572	–
MV + FV [32]	0.785	0.467	–
EMV [35]	0.802	–	0.416
C3D (1 Net) [20]	0.823	0.497*	0.546
3DNet [37]	0.902	–	–
FSTCN (SCI fusion) [26]	0.881	0.591	–
Two-stream [6]	0.880	0.594	0.661
Ours	0.911	0.603	0.674

This result occurs because our method not only pays attention to key areas in video frames and optical flow images, but also constructs spatial-temporal features and captures the interaction between spatial features and temporal features. We optimize temporal and spatial features to obtain better representation of video features for action recognition.

Ablation Experiments

We designed the following ablation experiments to verify the effectiveness of each component of our co-attention network, and the experimental results are presented in Table 2.

Our method involves two features, spatial features and temporal features. First, we directly use the spatial features extracted from the RGB frames or the temporal features extracted from the optical flow images, and the results are shown in Table 2. Then we perform category prediction on the optimized features after a single feature input to our attention module. We observe that the frame + attention on the ucf101 dataset is 3% higher than the original frame. The classification result increased by 1.4%, which illustrates the effectiveness of our co-attention module and also shows that it is effective to focus on the key areas in the video RGB frames and optical flow images. At the same time, we observe that the result of fusion of spatial feature and temporal feature classification is improved compared to single stream.. Finally, the classification using the constructed temporal and spatial features compared to the original simple fusion, we improved 3.1% (k = 2), indicating that the spatial-temporal co-attention features we designed are helpful for action recognition tasks. Because we capture the results of the interaction between spatial features and temporal features and optimize the temporal features and spatial features, and obtain better representation of video features for action recognition.

Table 2. Comparison of experimental results of each part of the model

Method	UCF101	HMDB51	THUMOS14
Frame	0.809	0.514	0.554
Opticflow	0.841	0.545	0.596
Frame + attention	0.839	0.523	0.581
Opticflow + attention	0.855	0.563	0.631
Frame + opticflow	0.880		
Frame + opticflow + co-attention (k = 1)	0.905	0.594	0.672
Frame + opticflow + co-attention (k = 2)	0.911	0.603	0.681

5 Conclusions

This paper proposes a spatial-temporal co-attention network for video action recognition. Our method introduces a co-attention mechanism based on the two-stream network. Unlike the original two-stream simple fusion mechanism, our network guides the features of temporal and spatial streams to pay attention to each other and mines the key information of the two streams. We construct new spatial-temporal features to optimize the original spatial and temporal features, and improve the accuracy of recognition. Our experimental results on three public datasets demonstrate the effectiveness of our method.

Acknowledgments. This work was supported by the Scientific Research Fund of Hunan Provincial Education Department of China (Project No. 17A007); and the Teaching Reform and Research Project of Hunan Province of China (Project No. JG1615).

References

1. Karpathy, A., Toderici, G.: Large-scale video classification with convolutional neural networks. In: Proceedings of the IEEE Conference on Computer Vision and Pattern Recognition, CVPR, pp. 1725–1732 (2014)

2. Perronnin, F., Sánchez, J., Mensink, T.: Improving the fisher kernel for large-scale image classification. In: Daniilidis, K., Maragos, P., Paragios, N. (eds.) ECCV 2010. LNCS, vol. 6314, pp. 143–156. Springer, Heidelberg (2010). https://doi.org/10.1007/978-3-642-15561-1_11

3. Laptev, I., Marszalek, M.: Learning realistic human actions from movies. In: IEEE Conference on Computer Vision and Pattern Recognition, CVPR, pp. 1–8 (2008)

4. Wang, H., Schmid, C.: Action recognition with improved trajectories. In: Proceedings of the IEEE International Conference on Computer Vision, pp. 3551–3558 (2013)

5. Wang, L., Qiao, Y.: Action recognition with trajectory-pooled deep-convolutional descriptors. In: Proceedings of the IEEE Conference on Computer Vision and Pattern Recognition, pp. 4305–4314 (2015)

6. Simonyan K.: Two-stream convolutional networks for action recognition in videos. In: Advances in Neural Information Processing Systems, pp. 568–576 (2014)

7. Soomro, K., Zamir, A.R., Shah, M.: UCF101: a dataset of 101 human action classes from videos in the wild. CRCV-TR-12–01 (2012)

8. Kuehne, H., Jhuang, H.: A large video database for human motion recognition. In: International Conference on Computer Vision 2011, pp. 2556–2563. IEEE (2011)

9. Idrees, H., Zamir, A.R.: The THUMOS challenge on action recognition for videos "in the wild". Comput. Vis. Image Underst. **155**, 1–23 (2017)

10. Pérez, J.S.: TV-L1 optical flow estimation. Image Processing On Line **3**, 137–150 (2013)

11. Wu, Z., Wang, X.: Modeling spatialtemporal clues in a hybrid deep learning framework for video classification. In: ACM International Conference on Multimedia 2015, ACM MM, pp. 461–470 (2015)

12. Nam, H., Ha, J.W.: Dual attention networks for multimodal reasoning and matching. In: Proceedings of the IEEE Conference on Computer Vision and Pattern Recognition 2017, pp. 299–307 (2017)

13. Fine, T.L.: Feedforward Neural Network Methodology. Information Science and Statistics. Springer, New York (1999). https://doi.org/10.1007/b97705

14. Fujiyoshi, H., Lipton, A.J.: Real-time human motion analysis by image skeletonization. IEICE Trans. Inf. Syst. **87**, 113–120 (2004)

15. Chaudhry, R., Ravichandran, A.: Histograms of oriented optical flow and Binet-Cauchy kernels on nonlinear dynamical systems for the recognition of human actions. In: Proceedings of the IEEE Conference on Computer Vision and Pattern Recognition, pp. 1932–1939 (2009)

16. Dalal, N., Triggs, B.: Histograms of oriented gradients for human detection. In: Proceedings of the IEEE Conference on Computer Vision and Pattern Recognition 2005, USA, pp. 886–893. IEEE (2005)

17. Lowe, D.G.: Object recognition from local scale-invariant features. In: Proceedings of the 7th IEEE International Conference on Computer Vision, ICCV, Kerkyra, pp. 1150–1157 (1999)

18. Schuldt, C., Laptev, I.: Recognizing human actions: a local SVM approach. In: Proceedings of the 17th International Conference on Pattern Recognition, Cambridge, pp. 32–36. IEEE (2004)

19. Wang, H., Klaser, A.: Action recognition by dense trajectories. In: Proceedings of the 2011 IEEE Conference on Computer Vision and Pattern Recognition, CVPR, RI, pp. 3169–3176 (2011)

20. Tran, D., Bourdev, L.: Learning spatiotemporal features with 3D convolutional networks. In: IEEE International Conference on Computer Vision 2015, ICCV, pp. 4489–4497 (2015)

21. Simonyan, K., Zisserman, A.: Very deep convolutional networks for large-scale image recognition. In: Proceedings of the International Conference on Learning Representations, ICLR (2015)

22. Chéron, G., Laptev, I.: Pose-based cnn features for action recognition. In: Proceedings of the IEEE International Conference on Computer Vision, ICCV, pp. 3218–3226 (2015)

23. Donahue, J., Anne Hendricks, L.: Long-term recurrent convolutional networks for visual recognition and description. In: Proceedings of the IEEE Conference on Computer Vision and Pattern Recognition, CVPR, pp. 2625–2634 (2015)
24. Feichtenhofer, C., Pinz, A.: Convolutional two-stream network fusion for video action recognition. In: IEEE Conference on Computer Vision and Pattern Recognition, CVPR (2016)
25. Srivastava, N., Mansimov, E.: Unsupervised learning of video representations using LSTMs. In: International Conference on Machine Learning 2015, ICML, vol. 37, pp. 843–852 (2015)
26. Sun, L., Jia, K.: Human action recognition using factorized spatio-temporal convolutional networks. In: IEEE International Conference on Computer Vision 2015, ICCV, pp. 4597–4605 (2015)
27. Wang, X., Farhadi, A.: Actions transformations. In: IEEE Conference on Computer Vision and Pattern Recognition 2016, CVPR, pp. 2658–2667 (2016)
28. Weinzaepfel, P., Harchaoui, Z.: Learning to track for spatio-temporal action localization. In: IEEE International Conference on Computer Vision 2015, ICCV, pp. 3164–3172 (2016)
29. Ng, J.Y.H., Hausknecht, M.: Beyond short snippets: deep networks for video classification. In: IEEE Conference on Computer Vision and Pattern Recognition 2015, CVPR, pp. 4694–4702 (2015)
30. Xu, K., Ba, J.L.: Show, attend and tell: neural image caption generation with visual attention. In: 32nd International Conference on Machine Learning 2015, ICML, pp. 2048–2057 (2015)
31. Mnih, V., Heess, N.: Recurrent models of visual attention. In: Advances in Neural Information Processing Systems, NIPS (2014)
32. Kantorov, V., Laptev, I.: Efficient feature extraction, encoding and classification for action recognition. In: Proceedings of the IEEE Conference on Computer Vision and Pattern Recognition, CVPR, pp. 2593–2600 (2014)
33. Zhang, B., Wang, L.: Real-time action recognition with enhanced motion vector CNNs. In: Proceedings of the IEEE Conference on Computer Vision and Pattern Recognition, CVPR, pp. 2718–2726 (2016)
34. Diba, A., Pazandeh, A.M.: Efficient two-stream motion and appearance 3D CNNs for video classification. In: Proceedings of the IEEE Conference on Computer Vision and Pattern Recognition, CVPR (2016)
35. Long, M., Zeng, Y.: Detecting iris liveness with batch normalized convolutional neural network. Comput. Mater. Continua **58**(2), 493–504 (2019)
36. Zhang, J., Li, Y.: Improved fully convolutional network for digital image region forgery detection. Comput. Mater. Continua **60**(1), 287–303 (2019)
37. Xia, Z., Lu, L.: A privacy-preserving image retrieval based on AC-coefficients and color histograms in cloud environment. Comput. Mater. Continua **58**(1), 27–43 (2019)

Improved SSD for Object Detection

Shuren Zhou[(⊠)] and Jia Qiu

School of Computer and Communication Engineering,
Changsha University of Science and Technology, Changsha 410114, China
zsr@csust.edu.cn

Abstract. We proposal an improved Single-shot multi-boxes algorithm for ameliorating the detection on small object detection. As we know, single shot multi-boxes for detection (SSD) is a state-of-the-art algorithm of object detection in 2016 by balancing the contradictions between speed and accuracy of detection. But it did not perform well on smaller objects. So how to promote the performance is a meaningful thing. This way, we introduce receptive field and deep large dimensional features for small detection, and achieves 1.2% improved on PASCAL VOC dataset. "The lower the dimension" does not equals to "the higher the abstraction".

Keywords: Small object detection · Single shot multi-boxes for detection · Face detection · WIDER FACE dataset

1 Introduction

Object detection is one of the hot research fields in machine learning and computer vision. As one of the three basic tasks of computer vision, object detection is not only applied to target tracking, object segmentation, VQA tasks, but also has a wide range of applications in unmanned, automatic cruise, intelligent security, military and so on.

Early in 2001, Paul Viola and Michael Jones proposal a classical algorithm of face detection, which we called Viola-Jones (VJ) detector later. It's the first time to implement the real-time face detection on backward computing equipment. VJ detector combines three elements: fast calculation by integral figure for multi-scale Harr-features, effective feature selection algorithm for decreasing dimensions (Ada-boost classifier) and efficient multi-stage processing strategies (Cascade). VJ detector bring hope and guidance in object detection. Later, another classic algorithm came along – (Hog pedestrian detection). In 2005, Dalal N, Triggs B using the histogram of oriented gradient as the image description method for human object detection. HOG detector is the basis of object detector based on gradient feature. This way introduces two concepts: discrimination and invariance. Discrimination expresses the capacity of the features; and invariance contains translation invariance, rotation invariance, scale invariance, illumination invariance and so on.

In 2007 years, Deformable Part based Model (DPM) was introduced by P. Felzenszwalb and R. Girshick. DPM transforms the problem from the overall object detection

© Springer Nature Singapore Pte Ltd. 2020
X. Sun et al. (Eds.): ICAIS 2020, CCIS 1252, pp. 313–322, 2020.
https://doi.org/10.1007/978-981-15-8083-3_28

algorithm to the detection problem of each part of the target, and finally integrates the detection results of each part into the whole target, "As from whole to parts, and then from parts to whole". DPM is the peak of the development of detection algorithms based on classical manual features. It adopts two important methods for post-processing: Bounding boxes regression and context information integration. The former integrates the bounding boxes for exact coordinate regression. The last is helpful for readjust the detection results by global information.

Even the accuracy and speed of detectors have much improvement, however, the above methods all use artificial operators for feature extraction. Their robustness is conspicuously inadequate. Following the development of deep learning, the deep neuron network can learn very robust and expressive feature representations. In 2012 year's ImageNet classifier competition, Alex and Hinton provides Alex-Net and win the champion with huge advantages. And then, deep learning walking into researchers' eyes. Two years later, R. Girshick et al. firstly provide Regions with Convolutions Neural Network features, (R-CNN), and CNN for object detection begins with an unprecedented speed.

From 2014–2016, many object detectors are mentioned. Kaiming He and Shaoqing Ren provides algorithm of Faster Regions Convolutions Neural Network (Faster RCNN). Faster RCNN is the first truly end-to-end deep learning detection algorithm and first quasi-real-time (17 Frames per second, 640×480 pixels) deep learning object detection algorithm. This algorithm designed an region proposal network which combines the selective search or edge boxes into the object proposal detection network. Later in 2017, Tsung-Yi Lin using multiple detection ports are derived from different depths in the network to detect object of different scales. So feature pyramid networks has a natural advantage in detection for small targets and targets with large scale distribution.

In 2015, the algorithm You Only Look Once (YOLO) is proposed in 2015, faster is the best characteristics. Joseph, R. Girshick give up regions proposal completely and change to the whole image is directly taken as the input of the network, and the location of the object bounding-box with the category of the object are directly obtained through only one forward propagation. But the disadvantages are also obvious: poorly accuracy, especially the detection of small objects. Following then, Wei Liu provide single shot multi boxes for object detection (SSD). SSD's algorithm absorbs the advantages of fast speed of YOLO and accurate positioning of RPN, adopting multi-reference window technology in RPN, and further proposes to detect on multiple feature pyramid. Besides, in training term, the hard sample mining is also used to focus the hard sample in image. Nevertheless, the accuracy of SSD is still not as good as Faster RCNN, especially for small objects. Even in 2017, Retina-Net model based on unbalanced distributions of objects and background, and amend the cross entropy (CE) loss to Focal Loss (FL) which aims to learn the hard samples. This strategy like the hard sample mining in SSD. It performs not well on small objects.

For improve it, in this paper, we aim to provide a plan for improve the experience on tiny objects. In order to reduce the loss of information of small target images in the high layer as decreasing dimension, we try to change the convolution and pooling layer at the last three layers of the network. We adopt the original convolution method to carry out convolution, however, we don't use pooling operator to reduce its dimension, but followed by Re-LU layers to activate and filter the output of the convolutional layer. This can effectively reduce the loss of small target information, thus increasing the detection of small target. As shown in Fig. 1. One the one hand, it can effectively reduce the loss of small object information; on the other hand, we can increase the number of bounding boxes' prediction. We carry out the experiments on PASCAL VOC and shows 1.2% improvement.

2 Related Work

With the rapid development of deep learning, the algorithms of object detection based on deep learning emerge one after another. However, in general, the object detection algorithms based on deep learning can be divided into two mains according to the detection scene: one is the two-stage detection algorithm based on the bounding boxes, and another is a one-stage detection algorithm based on regression prediction, each with its own characteristics. The two-stage detection algorithm based on the proposal regions has relatively high accuracy but slower. The one-stage detection algorithm based on regression prediction is fast, but the detection accuracy is lower. The two-stage object detection method is represented with RCNN and so on, the one-stage is YOLO, SSD, Retina-Net and so on. Two-stage method is marked by the selection of proposal regions. From RCNN to Faster-RCNN, researchers constantly introduce traditional methods into neural networks. For example, extracting features from the original manual features to the features of CNN, input images from fixed-scale images to the adaptive multi-scale images' input of SPP; candidate regions from the prediction on the original images to the selected feature maps based on neural networks. In this way, not only in speeds but also in accuracy, the neural networks have a significant improvement.

This is the first time to achieve the transition from image-based processing to feature-based processing. But this still does not solve the problem of detection speed and training step by step. RGB et al. found that the selection of candidate regions seriously slow down the detection speed. In order to obtain a fast detector, therefore, they proposed a regression-based object detection method: abandoning the structure of selection for proposal regions, and directly realizing the regression prediction of bounding boxes on the neural network. YOLO is proposed, with the global retrieval for object detection. Although the idea is good, but the reality is very cruel. YOLO, lack of candidate box positioning, has a poor performance in accuracy (around VOC07 45%).

For this, SSD combines anchor positioning mechanism and multi-scale features for detection to adapt for targets of different scales and sizes. This balances detection accuracy and detection speed.

We understand the network in general to extract features from the senior managers to do the test, however, in the paper of residual neuron network has proved that the network is deeper, but its performance is not necessarily better. In addition, according to the theory of information transmission, small target image was smaller, stride and pooling operation will filter out part of the information. After the operation of convolution – pooling layer, the original image information may be throw up and did not transmit to the deep feature in deep network. Therefore, we try to carry out multi-scale detection and transmission in the information. In order to keep the information of small dimension, we choose to maintain the information dimension at deeper network, when the dimension drops to a certain degree in the detection process.

As shown in Fig. 1, in order to improve the information of small and medium-sized object in deep network, we improved the last three layers of SSD network, and we maintained the descending dimension of network at 10×10 (for example, input is 300×300). On the one hand, in terms of prediction, the increase in feature maps will increase the number of candidate boxes, On the other hand, keep the information of the small target as much as possible under the premise that the deep feature has the global perceptive field.

3 Model

In this section, we will describe the pre-training model and the SSD target detection network, and later focus on the improved SSD and sensor field calculation.

3.1 VGG (Visual Geometry Group)

VGG belongs to the department of science and engineering of Oxford University. It has published a series of convolutional network models starting with VGG, which can be applied in face recognition, image classification and other aspects, respectively from VGG16 to VGG19, which purpose to understand how the depth of convolutional network affects the accuracy of large-scale image classification and recognition. In order to avoid too many parameters, when VGG deepen the number of network layers, the small convolution kernel of 3×3 is used in all layers, and the step size of the convolutional layer is set to 1.

3.2 SSD (Single Shot Multi-box for Detection)

SSD uses the pre-trained VGG16 as the basic network for feature extraction. After removing the full connection layer of the network, the convolution kernel of 33×3 is used for classification and bounding box regression prediction on the multi-scale features. The size of input image is 3003×300 or 5123×512. SSD uses $33 \times 33 \times C$ dimensional small convolutional layer as detector, a kind of confidence evaluation classification, a regression for the precision of bounding boxes. Finally, Non-Maximum Suppression (NMS) processing the predictions.

3.3 Receptive Field

The region size of the pixel on the output feature map of each layer of the convolutional neural network is mapped on the input image. See Fig. 2. In the target detection of SSD, we calculated the perceptive field information of each layer as follow. We found that when the detected convolution features up to conv7 layer, it has cover the global image. So, let's start at this level and fixed the size of features.

$$RF_i = (RF_{i+1} - 1) \times stride_i + Ksize_i \tag{1}$$

3.4 Improved SSD (I-SSD)

On the basis of SSD, in order to ensure that the small target information will not be lost too much, we improved SSD in the enlightenment of feeling field. The dimension reduction of information is reduced by maintaining the size of the feature graph to increase the detection and recognition of small targets. See the Fig. 1. We show the difference between SSD and I-SSD.

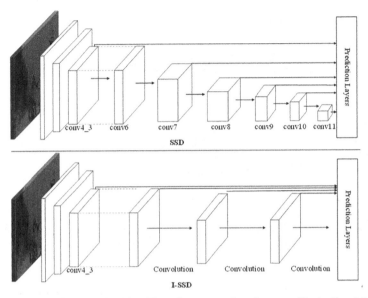

Fig. 1. The Model of SSD and I-SSD. There is a comparison between Single Shot Multi-boxes Detection (SSD) and Improved Single Shot Detection (I-SSD) models: The SSD network is cylindrical, on the other hand, shows like a pyramid of features, I-SSD keep the size of the feature unchanged, presenting a straight tube shape.

3.5 Optimization

Our optimization loss consists of two parts: classification loss and coordinate regression loss.

As Follow:

$$L_{loss} = \frac{1}{N}(L_{cls} + \alpha L_{loc}) \tag{2}$$

Among them: N: the number of matched boxes. N = 0; loss is 0; L_{cls}: classification loss; L_{loc}: coordinate regression loss; α: the weights between classification loss and coordinate regression loss.

At there, The function of Smooth L1 to measure the distances of boxes between predictions and ground truth. $b_{i,j}^k$ describes matched between i-th predicting default box and j-th bounding box of class k. p_i^l represent the i-th positive prediction distance replace directly predicting with the bounding box. g_j^l is the distance between the default boxes ($bound_i^l$, the i-th bounding box location) and ground truth boxes ($groud_j^l$, the j-th ground truth box location).

$$L_{loc}(b, p, t) = \sum_{i \in pos}^{N} \sum_{l \in \{x,y,w,h\}} b_{i,j}^k smooth_{L1}(p_i^l - g_j^l) \qquad (3)$$

Where:

$$g_j^x = (groud_j^x - bound_i^x)/bound_i^w \qquad (4)$$

$$g_j^y = (groud_j^y - bound_i^y)/bound_i^h \qquad (5)$$

$$g_j^w = \log(\frac{groud_j^w}{bound_i^w}) \qquad (6)$$

$$g_j^h = \log(\frac{groud_j^h}{bound_i^w}) \qquad (7)$$

Cross Entropy (CE) function to measure the loss of confidence score.

$$L_{conf}(x, conf) = -(\sum_{i \in Pos}^{N} x_{ij}^c \log(soft(conf_i^c)) + \sum_{i \in Neg} \log(soft(conf_i^0))) \qquad (8)$$

Where:

$$soft(conf_i^c) = \frac{\exp(c_i^c)}{\sum_{i \in N} \exp(c_i^c)}. \qquad (9)$$

On the above, the $soft(conf_i^c)$ represents a softmax loss among multi-classes.

3.6 Training

We training the model in pytorch-0.3 with a Graphics accelerator card–GTX Titan X (12 GB memory). In the experiment, we set the batch size = 32 for the I-SSD model with 300×30 inputs based on VGG-16, which is pre-trained on the ILSVRC CLS-LOC dataset. I-SSD begin with 10–3 as the initial learning rate then decreased it to 10–4 at 80 k, 10–5 at 100 k and iterated to 120 k, 0.9 momentum, 0.0005 weigh decay. We training our model in PASCAL VOC datasets, which contains VOC2007 datasets and VOC2012 datasets. We merge VOC2007 trainval and VOC2012 trainval as a total trainval dataset for I-SSD trainval.

4 Experiment

In this paragraph, We will compare ISSD and SSD results in detail and analyze the algorithm. Experiment on Pascal VOC datasets which contain VOC2007 datasets and VOC2012 datasets. For expanding training datasets, we unified VOC2007 trainval and VOC2012 trainval (16551 images). We test our model in PASCAL VOC 2007 test. The result in Table 1. Compared with SSD, ISSD has a certain improvement in accuracy (Table 2).

Table 1. The result between I-SSD and SSD

Methods	Model	mAP	Aero	Bicycle	Bird	Boat	Bottle	Bus	Car	Cat	Chai	Cow	Table	Dog	Horse	Motor	Person	Plant	Sheep	Sofa	Train	Tvmo
SSD	VGG	77.4	82.7	84.59	76.1	70.7	49.5	86.1	85.4	87.8	63.0	81.1	75.3	84.5	86.7	83.7	79.2	53.6	75.8	80.1	84.8	77.2
ISSD	VGG	78.6	82	84.9	80.5	68.4	53.9	85.6	86	88.9	61.1	83	78.9	86.7	88.2	86.5	79.2	52	78.0	80.5	87	79.4

Table 2. The result between I-SSD and other algorithm.

Methods	Model	mAP
Fast RCNN	–	70.0
Faster RCNN	VGG	73.2
ION	VGG	75.6
MR-CNN	VGG	78.2
SSD300	VGG	77.4
I-SSD	VGG16	78.6

Visualization. In Fig. 2 we show examples on VOC2007 between SSD and I-SSD models. Compare to SSD, I-SSD model have a better performance.

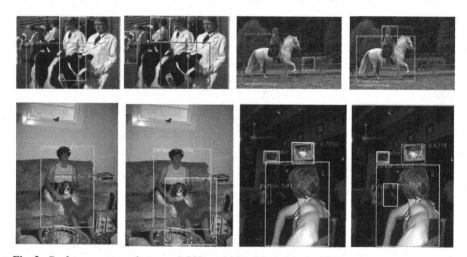

Fig. 2. Performance cases between I-SSD and SSD. The left is the I-SSD and the right is the SSD

5   Conclusion

At this paper, we proposal an improved Single-shot multi-boxes algorithm for ameliorating the detection on small object detection. We fixed the size of detected features of SSD to increase the network sensitivity to small objects. Our methods achieves 1.2% improved on PASCAL VOC dataset.

Acknowledgments. This work was supported by the Scientific Research Fund of Hunan Provincial Education Department of China (Project No. 17A007); and the Teaching Reform and Research Project of Hunan Province of China (Project No. JG1615).

References

1. Lecun, Y., Bengio, Y.: Deep learning. Nature **521**(7553), 436–444 (2015)
2. Liu, W., et al.: SSD: single shot multibox detector. In: Leibe, B., Matas, J., Sebe, N., Welling, M. (eds.) ECCV 2016. LNCS, vol. 9905, pp. 21–37. Springer, Cham (2016). https://doi.org/10.1007/978-3-319-46448-0_2
3. Sempau, J., Wilderman, S.J., Bielajew, A.F.: DPM, a fast, accurate Monte Carlo code optimized for photon and electron radiotherapy treatment planning dose calculations. Phys. Med. Biol. **45**(8), 2263–2291 (2000)
4. Buzcu, I., Alatan, A.A.: Fisher-selective search for object detection. In: Proceedings of the IEEE International Conference on Image Processing, ICIP, pp. 3633–3637 (2016)
5. Dalal, N., Triggs, B.: Histograms of oriented gradients for human detection In: Proceedings of the IEEE Computer Society Conference on Computer Vision & Pattern Recognition, CVPR, pp. 886–893 (2005)
6. He, K., Zhang, X., Ren, S., Sun, J.: Spatial pyramid pooling in deep convolutional networks for visual recognition. In: Fleet, D., Pajdla, T., Schiele, B., Tuytelaars, T. (eds.) ECCV 2014. LNCS, vol. 8691, pp. 346–361. Springer, Cham (2014). https://doi.org/10.1007/978-3-319-10578-9_23
7. Cai, Z., Fan, Q., Feris, R.S., Vasconcelos, N.: A unified multi-scale deep convolutional neural network for fast object detection. In: Leibe, B., Matas, J., Sebe, N., Welling, M. (eds.) ECCV 2016. LNCS, vol. 9908, pp. 354–370. Springer, Cham (2016). https://doi.org/10.1007/978-3-319-46493-0_22
8. Girshick, R., Donahue, J.: Rich feature hierarchies for accurate object detection and semantic segmentation. In: Proceedings of the IEEE Conference on Computer Vision and Pattern Recognition, CVPR, pp. 580–587 (2014)
9. Girshick, R.: Fast R-CNN. In: Proceedings of the International Conference on Computer Vision, CVPR (2015)
10. Ren, S., He, K.: Faster R-CNN: towards real-time object detection with region proposal networks. In: Proceedings of the International Conference on Neural Information Processing Systems, NIPS, pp. 91–99. MIT Press (2015)
11. Dai, J., Li, Y.: R-FCN: object detection via region-based fully convolutional networks (2016)
12. Redmon, J., Divvala, S.: You only look once: unified, real-time object detection. In: Proceedings of the IEEE Conference on Computer Vision and Pattern Recognition, CVPR, pp. 779–788 (2016)
13. Redmon, J., Farhadi, A.: YOLO9000: better, faster, stronger. In: Proceedings of the IEEE Conference on Computer Vision and Pattern Recognition, CVPR, pp. 6517–6525 (2017)
14. Redmon, J., Farhadi, A.: Yolov3: an incremental improvement. arXiv preprint arXiv:1804.02767 (2018)
15. Fu, C.Y., Liu, W.: DSSD: deconvolutional single shot detector. arXiv preprint arXiv:1701.06659 (2017)
16. He, K., Zhang, X.: Deep residual learning for image recognition. In: Proceedings of the IEEE Conference on Computer Vision and Pattern Recognition CVPR, pp. 770–778 (2016)
17. Simonyan, K., Zisserman, A.: Very deep convolutional networks for large-scale image recognition. arXiv preprint arXiv:1409.1556 (2014)
18. Krizhevsky, A., Sutskever, I.: ImageNet classification with deep convolutional neural networks. In: Proceedings of the International Conference on Neural Information Processing Systems, NIPS, pp. 1097–1105. Curran Associates Inc. (2012)
19. Huang, G., Liu, Z.: Densely connected convolutional networks. In: Proceedings of the IEEE Conference on Computer Vision and Pattern Recognition, CVPR, pp. 4700–4708 (2017)

20. Lin, T.Y., Goyal, P.: Focal loss for dense object detection. In: Proceedings of the IEEE International Conference on Computer Vision, CVPR, pp. 2980–2988 (2017)
21. Meng, R., Steven, G.: A fusion steganographic algorithm based on faster R-CNN. Comput. Mater. Contin. **55**(1), 1–16 (2018)
22. Deng, J., Dong, W.: ImageNet: a large-scale hierarchical image database. In: Proceedings of the IEEE Conference on Computer Vision and Pattern Recognition, CVPR, pp. 248–255 (2009)
23. Everingham, M., Van Gool, L.: The PASCAL Visual Object Classes Challenge 2007 (VOC2007) Results (2007)
24. Lin, T.Y., Dollar, P.: Feature pyramid networks for object detection. In: Proceedings of the IEEE Conference on Computer Vision and Pattern Recognition, CVPR, pp. 2117–2125 (2017)
25. Shrivastava, A., Gupta, A.: Training region-based object detectors with online hard example mining. In: Proceedings of the IEEE Conference on Computer Vision and Pattern Recognition, CVPR, pp. 761–769 (2016)
26. Lin, T.-Y., et al.: Microsoft COCO: common objects in context. In: Fleet, D., Pajdla, T., Schiele, B., Tuytelaars, T. (eds.) ECCV 2014. LNCS, vol. 8693, pp. 740–755. Springer, Cham (2014). https://doi.org/10.1007/978-3-319-10602-1_48
27. Zhang, J., Li, Y.: Improved fully convolutional network for digital image region forgery detection. Comput. Mater. Contin. **60**(1), 287–303 (2019)
28. Liu, Z., Wang, X.: Automatic arrhythmia detection based on convolutional neural networks. Comput. Mater. Contin. **60**(2), 497–509 (2019)
29. Wang, N., He, M.: Noise processing method for underwater target recognition convolutional neural network. Comput. Mater. Contin. **58**(1), 169–181 (2019)
30. Zhou, P., Ni, B.: Scale-transferrable object detection. In: Proceedings of the IEEE Conference on Computer Vision and Pattern Recognition, pp. 528–537 (2018)
31. Zhang, S., Wen, L.: Single-shot refinement neural network for object detection. In: Proceedings of the IEEE Conference on Computer Vision and Pattern Recognition, pp. 4203–4212 (2018)
32. Shen, Z., Liu, Z.: DSOD: learning deeply supervised object detectors from scratch. In: Proceedings of the IEEE International Conference on Computer Vision, pp. 1919–1927 (2017)
33. Chen, Y., Li, W.: Domain adaptive faster R-CNN for object detection in the wild. In: Proceedings of the IEEE Conference on Computer Vision and Pattern Recognition, pp. 3339–3348 (2018)

Sentiment Analysis on Weibo Platform for Stock Prediction

Wanting Zhao[✉], Fan Wu, Zhongqi Fu, Zesen Wang, and Xiaoqi Zhang

College of Computer Science and Technology, Jilin University, Changchun, China
zhaowt2117@mails.jlu.edu.cn

Abstract. Recent years has witnessed a growing trend on the stock prediction through sentiment analysis of social media. This paper proposes a stock-predicting method based on the sentiment analysis of Weibo, utilizing sentiment orientation exhibited in texts posted on Weibo and analysis on the historical data of stock market to forecast the price movements in stock market. To achieve the goal, three steps are strictly followed, corresponding to three parts of the paper: data pre-processing (DP), sentiment analysis (SA) and stock prediction (SP). In the data pre-processing phase, the construction of a financial dictionary is elaborated, and then, an improved LDA model is shown to classify Weibo text in accordance with Industrial Classification Benchmark (ICB) and to match them with corresponding topics. Then, the sentiment analysis part demonstrates that how the accuracy of sentiment analysis is enhanced through the newly designed method by incorporating the interaction between words to the rule set to quantify sentiment value. In the last part, the stock prediction is accomplished by using Multivariate SVM incorporating Weibo sentiment. The time range of collected Weibo data is 12 months.

Keywords: LDA · Weibo · Financial dictionaries · Sentiment analysis · Stock prediction

1 Introduction

With the development of the Internet and prevalence of the computer, internet-based stock prediction is gaining popularity. It used to be a prevailing view shared by most economists that stock market follows a random pattern. But as big data and the economic researches progress, it is believed that stock market, can be forecasted to some extent by using massive data.

Weibo is one of the biggest social media platforms through which users can exchange, disseminate and acquire information. Compared to the traditional network news and search engines, Weibo has a broader research spaces on sentiment analysis because of its timeliness, arbitrariness and numerous active users.

The existing domestic and international research have used Twitter as a corpus to conduct sentiment analysis [1, 2]. But relevant studies focusing on Chinese social media platform are still vacant. Also, most of the reviewed research pay more attention to

© Springer Nature Singapore Pte Ltd. 2020
X. Sun et al. (Eds.): ICAIS 2020, CCIS 1252, pp. 323–333, 2020.
https://doi.org/10.1007/978-981-15-8083-3_29

semantic and sentimental research approaches rather than to data filtering. Data filtering is necessary because the heterogeneous raw data in large quantities requires a large amount time to be fully analyzed. The current data mining technologies are VSM model, LSA model and LDA model. The text in the VSM model is represented as a high-dimensional vector, mining topics by constructing a word-text feature matrix. While the content of Weibo is short, resulting in a highly sparse result of the feature matrix [3]. The main idea of LSA model is to map documents and vocabulary to a low-dimensional vector space associated with semantics. LSA model performs singular value decomposition on the high-dimensional TF-IDF matrix, which is a linear algebra method with high algorithm complexity [4]. LDA model is a three-layer Bayesian production model of "Text-Theme-Words", which can achieve topic classification [5]. In the traditional LDA model, the theme distribution of the model is titled to the high-frequency words because the words in the text conform to the power law distribution, and most of the words that can represent the theme are submerged by a small number of high-frequency words. As a result, the subject expression ability is reduced. In this paper, the topic mining is implemented by an improved LDA model with weighted feature words, and then we obtained the distribution of the Weibo texts according to Industry Classification Benchmark (ICB) [6].

Another problem shown in these researches is that all users are treated as the same instead of being classified as they should be. The fact is that different users vary in their ability to cause influence. Some influencers with much more subscribers are able to make greater impact. Therefore, users are divided into 7 grades according to the number of their subscribers. Besides the factor of subscribers, the research model adopted by this paper takes more into account, such as what dissemination results have been achieved by the users, how many likes they have received and how many comments have been given by their followers. Finally, an effective model is designed to make prediction of stock market. By including all the information and weighting it, this model can also mitigate the bias of previous processing stages [7–9].

In this paper, a method is devised to forecast the trend of stock market on the basis of market sentiment expressed through Weibo and hierarchical decentralization method. And a data filtering technique based on LDA model are used. By utilizing these approaches, four achievements can be made: 1. The data is categorized in accordance to industries after being filtered. 2. A dictionary cataloguing financial terms for sentiment analysis on Weibo is created, which compensates for the lack of financial terms in other dictionaries. And emoticons are also included into the dictionary considering the function of emoticon in sentiment analysis. 3. Based on the financial dictionary and the improved rule set, we analyzed the Weibo text and specified different emotion index at different granularities, which increases the accuracy of sentiment analysis. 4. We proposed a hierarchical decentralization method, which can set weights for factors such as comment points and number of fans for the complex characteristics of Weibo users, so as to achieve the goal of grading to reduce the bias.

The second part of this paper aims to introduce adopted methods, which includes data pre-processing (DP), sentiment analysis (SA), stock prediction (SP). And the third part illustrate the testing process and the fourth part is the conclusion of the research conducted in this paper and the future research direction of the field.

2 Data and Method

The introduction of data and research methods is explained, consisting of data pre-processing (DP), sentiment analysis (SA), stock prediction (SP). The overall process is shown in Fig. 1.

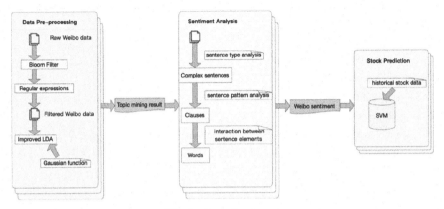

Fig. 1. Overall process.

2.1 Data Description

To conduct research, two types of data are required: text data and financial data. The text data is used for sentiment analysis, which refers to the text posted on Weibo and the relevant comments received. The financial data relating to stock data is collected to verify the prediction results.

The text is acquired from weibo.com, including text message, contents of the comments below, the forwarding volume, comments numbers and the timestamps. Despite of the fact that Weibo opens the APIs to make data accessible for researchers, the data amount and ranges are still restricted. To ensure the abundance and comprehensiveness of the information, the data is gleaned through two ways: Web Crawler and Weibo API, covering 12 months from June, 2018 to June, 2019. The data is used to train LDA model and to construct financial dictionary.

The stock data is obtained from open source Python financial data interface package, which completes several processes from data collecting, cleansing, processing to storing and classifies it based on Industry Classification benchmark (ICB). For each stock, we extract the times series of daily returns, T_d.

$$T_d = \frac{p_d - p_{d-1}}{p_{d-1}} \tag{1}$$

where p_d is the closing price of the stock at day d.

2.2 Data Pre-processing (DP)

Since the collected Weibo data is exceedingly huge and filled with repetition and disturbing information, Bloom Filter algorithm [10] and the regular expressions are employed to eliminate disturbing information.

Algorithm 1 is used to eliminate disturbing information

Algorithm 1.

Input: weiboSet, set of Weibo data

    stopWordSet, set of stop words

Output: dataSet, set of filtered data

1. S <- stopWordSet
2. for each weibo in weiboSet
3.   if not bloomfilter.contains(weibo) and contentLength(weibo)>0
4.   if not matchRegex(weibo)
5.   data <- depart(weibo)
6.   if data not in S
7.   dataSet <- dataSet {data}
8.   end if
9.   end if
10.   end if
11. end for
12. return dataSet

After the completion of data cleansing, topic mining is carried out by an improved LDA algorithm. The distribution of data is revealed as the algorithm classified the data in accordance with industrial Classification Benchmark (ICB). The traditional LDA model takes text as a package of equivalent words [11], which ignores the weights of each word. Therefore, the distribution result is disproportionately affected by high frequency words. To avoid such limitation, gaussian function is employed to modify LDA model [12], making justified decreases to the high frequency words and relative increase to the medium frequency words.

Algorithm 2 is an improved LDA algorithm based on GranphX.

Algorithm 2.

Input：α LDA parameters

β LDA parameters

V Number of Words in the disk matrix

prow A K-dimensional vector, set of professional words

Output：hfreqw set of frequency words

1. dv A K-dimensional vector, document vertex data

2. wv A K-dimensional vector, word vertex data

3. WV A K-dimensional vector，superposition of all word vertex vectors

4. srcld document vertex ID

5. dstld word vertex ID

6. msg A K-dimensional vector，message generated by edge triplet

7. edge(srcld,dv,freq,dstld,wv) dge triplet

8. while not reach the maximum number of iterations

9.   WV<- superposition of all word vertex vectors

10.   for all edge in EdgeRDD   //aggregateMasseges map

11.   for i<-0 until k

12.   msg[i]<-(wv[i]+ β)*(dv[i]+ α)/(WV[i]+V*β)

13.   end for

14.   msg=normalize(msg)*freq //normalize and use word frequency weighting

15.   sendToSrcld(msg) //send message to the source node

16.   SendTodstld(msg) // send message to the destination node

17.   end for

18.   The vertex superimposes the received message as vector //aggregateMasseges reduce

19.gauss_weight(hfreqw)

20.for j<-0 until k

21.   increase prow.weight //raise the weight of professional domain words in each topic

22.end for

The financial dictionary used in this paper is created as follows: Firstly, Hownet sentiment dictionary is combined with NTUSB as basic dictionary [13]. In the next step, frequent emotional words in stock industry are selected as candidate words, supplemented by frequent used emoticons in Weibo. These candidate words are sentimentally analyzed through SO-PMI algorithm [14] and then included into the basic sentiment dictionary. Finally, words are divided into six categories including words that express positive attitude, negative attitude, degree, negation, rhetorical question and transition.

Algorithm 3 aims to conduct sentiment analysis on words

Algorithm 3.

Input: distances, set of co-occurrence distance

alternative, set of candidate

p, positive emotion seed word

r, negative emotion seed word

negative, file of negative dictionary

neutral , file of neutral dictionary

positive , file of positive dictionary

Output: negative, file of negative dictionary

neutral , file of neutral dictionary

positive , file of positive dictionary

1. for each c in alternative

2.   num <- 0

3.   for each distance in distances

4.   num = num + 1

5.   d = d + distance

6.   end for

7.   d = d / num

8.   count0 <- count(c, p)

9.   count1 <- count(c, r)

10.   a = count(r) / count(p)

11.   result = getSO_PMI(d, count0, count1, a)

12.   if zoom(result) >= -1 and zoom(result) < -0.15

13.   negative <- negative {zoom(result)}

14.   else

15.   if zoom(result) >= -0.15 and zoom(result) < 0.15

16.   neutral <- neutral {zoom(result)}

17.   else

18.   if zoom(result) >= 0.15 and zoom(result) <= 1

19.   positive <- positive {zoom(result)}

20.end for

21.return negative, neutral, positive

2.3   Sentiment Analysis (SA)

Previous rule sets for sentiment analysis are semantic-oriented [15], which mainly focus on sentence patterns and the relationship between sentences but pay less attention to the function of emoticons. Such rule sets are undeniable to be useful for long text like press release. However, compared to long texts, Weibo texts and are relatively short, especially the comments below, mainly composed of one single sentence. Besides the length, the meaning of punctuation mark is partly different from large-content text. Under such background, the sentence-based analysis fails to maintain accuracy in Weibo data analysis. Consequently, as shown in Fig. 2, taking language characteristics exhibited in Weibo, this paper. This paper adds sentimental granularity analysis rules from a linguistic perspective. And the hierarchical decentralization method is adopted to form a multi-dimensional rule set for sentiment analysis, including sentence pattern, the relationship between sentences and the interaction between sentence elements. Further demonstration of these three dimensions is as below:

Rule 1. Rules for sentence type is used to proceed sentiment analysis in complex sentences. The possible influence of the complex sentences is defined by their markers and punctuations.

Rule 2. The relationship between clauses in a complex sentence is another factor to determine the influence of sentences, which is based on the level of clauses.

Rule 3. The interaction between sentence elements, which is identified by a lexical analysis system, can also give clues to the sentiment behind it through analysis focusing on the words level.

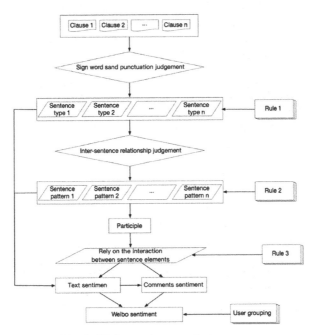

Fig. 2. Weibo sentiment analysis process.

2.4 Stock Prediction (SP)

After reviewing relevant domestic and international research, we found that the casual relationship between Weibo sentiment and stock price trend has been discussed in detail [16–18]. The next important question is how to combine Weibo sentiment to develop a more effective model to predict stock price trend.

In this paper, multivariate time-series SVM that introduce sentiment indicators is used to perform regression predictions [19] and compared with univariate SVM based on historical stock market data. While experimenting, the two are trained first. And we define seven trading days as one circle, using the closing price of the first six trading days to predict the closing price of the seventh trading day. After the training is completed, we start to use samples for prediction, and the results are used to evaluate the SVM performance after incorporating sentiment indicators. The accuracy of the rise and fall judgment and fitness are two important criteria for evaluating models.

3 Experiment

3.1 Data Pre-processing (DP)

90 topics consistent with 90 stock industries are identified on the basis of ICB and standard industries. The setting of parameters in this experiment is $\alpha = 50/T$, $\beta = 0.01$, T (topic) = 90, and the number of Gibbs sampling iterations is set to 1000.

Weibo topic mining is conducted through LDA model and LDA model with Gaussian weighting. 90 topics along with the key words within them arranged in a descending order are obtained. Experiment results are shown as Tables 1 and 2:

Table 1. Five topics and their high frequency words in LDA.

Topic	High frequency words
topic1	Gold, FED (the Federal Reserve), the rate of return
topic2	Housing price, housing, rise
topic3	Stable, market, metal
topic4	Medical care, industry, reform
topic5	Internet, technology, operate

It can be seen that compared with traditional LDA model, the improved LDA with Gaussian weighting filters out some common high-frequency words that do not affect the subject. Figure 3 further illustrates the experimental results.

3.2 Sentiment Analysis (SA)

This paper chooses new energy source topic as an example. 1000 Weibo posts relevant to the topic as well as the 50 most-favored comments below each post are selected to

Table 2. Five topics and their high frequency words in LDA with Gaussian weighting.

Topic	High frequency words
topic1	Gold, Gold futures, FED (the Federal Reserve)
topic2	Housing price, housing, Housing accumulation fund
topic3	Metal, colored, smelting
topic4	Medical care, Changsheng, vaccine
topic5	Internet, technology, Huawei

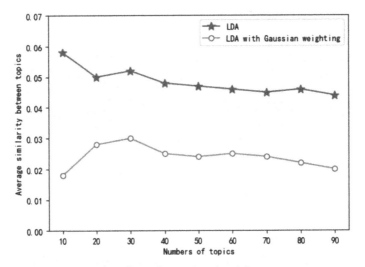

Fig. 3. Weibo LDA topic mining.

testify the effectiveness of the designed method. The data is tested by three distinct methods respectively afterwards, including dictionary statistics, traditional set of rules and hierarchical decentralization. And the test results will be checked by manually analyzed sentiment trend and corresponding sentiment value to assess these three methods from four aspects: accuracy, recall, F-Measure and variance. The results are shown in Table 3.

The training outcome shows that hierarchical decentralization method, which is the one proposed by this paper, is more reliable than the other two. Two reason accounts for the elevated reliability: 1. The analysis confirms the contribution of the newly created financial dictionary by showing that each evaluation indicator is advanced by more than 20 percent after the application of the dictionary. The achievement of the new dictionary is mainly result from the lack of sentiment words in traditional ones. 2. Interaction between words contributes a lot in a complex informal communicative setting, confirmed by statistics. From the perspective of variance, the deviation of the Dictionary statistics method is more serious, while the data set degree obtained by the Traditional set of rules is higher. Compared with Traditional set of rules, our Hierarchical decentralization still has a slight advantage.

Table 3. Results of Sentiment Analysis.

Method	New dictionary	Accuracy	Recall	F-measure	Variance
Dictionary statistics	N	0.533	0.471	0.500	–
	Y	0.564	0.488	0.523	0.4447
Traditional set of rules	N	0.622	0.593	0.607	–
	Y	0.661	0.637	0.649	0.3287
Hierarchical decentralization	N	0.686	0.664	0.675	–
	Y	0.712	0.682	0.697	0.3024

3.3 Stock Prediction (SP)

After completing the training of the univariate time series SVM model that is based on existing information and the training of the multivariate time series SVM that incorporates Weibo sentiment, the next 30dats opening price is used to testd. The results are shown as Table 4:

Table 4. Results of SVM model.

	Accuracy	Fitness
Univariate SVM	0.68965	0.979765659
Multivariate SVM	0.75862	0.979855272

It can be seen that the SVM model incorporating Weibo sentiment has higher accuracy in predicting stock price. The fitting effect is also improved to some extent. This shows that Weibo sentiment plays an important role in stock predicting.

4 Conclusion and Future Research Direction

This paper provides a data-based method to predict the stock market trend through sentiment analysis of Weibo texts. To achieve such objective, data pre-processing, sentiment analysis and the construction of the financial dictionary are conducted and fully demonstrated. Also, the improved LDA model modifies weights of diverse user groups. And the hierarchical decentralization approach elevates the accuracy of sentiment value calculated through Weibo data. In the end, the efficacy of the method is confirmed by the experimental results. In the future, the model will be further enhanced though more detailed granularity of sentiment analysis as well as a more extended time range.

References

1. Rao, T., Srivastava, S.: Analyzing stock market movements using twitter sentiment analysis. In: International Conference on Advances in Social Networks Analysis & Mining, pp. 119–123. IEEE Computer Society (2012)

2. Si, J., Mukherjee, A., Liu, B., Li, Q., Li, H., Deng, X.: Exploiting topic based twitter sentiment for stock prediction. In: Proceedings of the 51st Annual Meeting of the Association for Computational Linguistics, pp. 24–29 (2013)

3. Yao, Q.Y., Liu, G.S., Li, X.: VSM-based text clustering algorithm. Comput. Eng. **34**, 39–43 (2008)

4. Turney, Peter D.: Mining the web for synonyms: PMI-IR versus LSA on TOEFL. In: De Raedt, L., Flach, P. (eds.) ECML 2001. LNCS (LNAI), vol. 2167, pp. 491–502. Springer, Heidelberg (2001). https://doi.org/10.1007/3-540-44795-4_42

5. Wei, X., Croft, W.B.: LDA-based document models for ad-hoc retrieval. In: SIGIR 2006: Proceedings of the 29th Annual International ACM SIGIR Conference on Re-search and Development in Information Retrieval, Seattle, Washington, USA, pp. 178–185 (2006)

6. Zhang, C., Yang, M.: An improved collaborative filtering algorithm based on Bhattacharyya coefficient and LDA topic model. In: Zhou, Z.-H., Yang, Q., Gao, Y., Zheng, Yu. (eds.) ICAI 2018. CCIS, vol. 888, pp. 222–232. Springer, Singapore (2018). https://doi.org/10.1007/978-981-13-2122-1_17

7. He, L.L., Bai, H.T., Ouyang, D.T., Wang, C.S., Wang, C., Jiang, Y.: Satellite cloud-derived wind inversion algorithm using GPU. Comput. Mater. Continua **60**(2), 599–613 (2019)

8. Li, X., Liang, Y.C., Zhao, M.H., Wang, C., Jiang, Y.: Few-shot learning with generative adversarial networks based on WOA13 data. Comput. Mater. Continua **60**(3), 1073–1085 (2019)

9. He, L.L., Ouyang, D.T., Wang, M., Bai, H.T., Yang, Q.L., Liu, Y.Q., Jiang, Y.: A method of identifying thunderstorm clouds in satellite cloud image based on clustering. Comput. Mater. Continua **57**(3), 549–570 (2018)

10. Pagh, A., Pagh, R., Rao, S.S.: An optimal bloom filter replacement. In: Proceedings of the Sixteenth Annual ACM-SIAM Symposium on Discrete Algorithms, pp. 823–829 (2005)

11. Jing, Y.: Text Classification Based on LDA and Semantic Analysis. Southwest Petroleum University (2019)

12. Mcauliffe, J. D., Blei, D. M.: Supervised topic models. In: Advances in Neural Information Processing Systems, pp. 121–128 (2008)

13. Dong, Z., Dong, Q.: HowNet-a hybrid language and knowledge resource. In: International Conference on Natural Language Processing and Knowledge Engineering, pp. 820–824. IEEE (2003)

14. Yang, A.M., Lin, J.H., Zhou, Y.M., Chen, J.: Research on building a Chinese sentiment lexicon based on SO-PMI. In: Applied Mechanics and Materials, pp. 1688–1693. Trans Tech Publications Ltd (2013)

15. Li, G., Hoi, S.C., Chang, K., Jain, R.: Micro-blogging sentiment detection by collaborative online learning. In: 2010 IEEE International Conference on Data Mining, pp. 893–898. IEEE (2010)

16. Szabo, G., Huberman, B.A.: Predicting the popularity of online content. Commun. ACM **53**(8), 80–88 (2010)

17. Savage, N.: Twitter as medium and message. Commun. ACM **54**(3), 18–20 (2011)

18. Jonathan, P., Krzanowski, W.J., McCarthy, W.V.: On the use of cross-validation to assess performance in multivariate prediction. Stat. Comput. **10**(3), 209–229 (2000)

19. Jin, T., Yue, M., Mu, J.C.: On SVM-based multi-variable stock market time series prediction. Comput. Appl. Softw. **27**(6), 191–194 (2010)

Refinement Measurement and Evaluation of Streets in Shanghai Old City

Weiwei Liu[✉], Yuelin Zhang, Fulong Zhang, Dongqi Wan, Chenhao Li, and Hao Huang

Business School, University of Shanghai for Science and Technology, Shanghai 200093, China
Weiweiliu@usst.edu.cn

Abstract. The street is a basic urban linear open space, whose main functions are transportation, municipal administration, landscape and communication. In the past, people focused on streets as an urban space with transportation function. However, with the rapid development of the city, the streets of the past gradually failed to meet people's needs for streets. In this case, people began to apply the "people-oriented" concept to street design and transformation. Against this background, in this article, an old street in Shanghai is selected as an example, and it is compared with that in a new urban area. Using normalization and Pearson correlation analysis, a set of operable and quantifiable measures for evaluating streets are formed. By making the overall analysis and comparative analysis, the corresponding conclusions and optimization suggestions are obtained.

Keywords: Old town street · Street refinement · Pearson correlation analysis · Street evaluation

1 Introduction

Since the beginning of the 21st century, the construction of a city that is full of vitality, social harmony and sustainable development has become the common goal of major cities around the world, and has formed a wave of street reshaping. By following national policies, Shanghai's local policies, and the "vehicle-based" to "people-oriented" shift, Shanghai has also participated in the wave of street reshaping. Due to the rapid development of Shanghai, many streets in Shanghai's old city cannot keep up with the development of the times, and cannot satisfy people's needs.

For many years, scholars at home and abroad have conducted many studies on street walkability. Yang Junyan [1] took the downtown area of Nanjing as an example to study the spatial characteristics and optimization strategies of urban pedestrian walkability. Qi Shaohui [2] selected the typical pedestrian area in Jinshui District of Zhengzhou City, and adopted the evaluation system for quantitative analysis. The evaluation results are basically consistent with the actual walking conditions of the street, which proves that the quantitative analysis method of single street walking index is scientific and feasible. Yu Liping [3] and Wang Ze [4] conducted research on the normalization and standardization of indicators. Lu Yintao [5] discussed the progress and inspiration of

© Springer Nature Singapore Pte Ltd. 2020
X. Sun et al. (Eds.): ICAIS 2020, CCIS 1252, pp. 334–346, 2020.
https://doi.org/10.1007/978-981-15-8083-3_30

American walking measurement research. Liu Wei [6] further explored the main walking evaluation scope, indicators and standard settings in Europe and America, and finally, compared the characteristics and differences of various walking evaluation methods and tools.

However, most of these studies focus on street walkability, and this article is about the study of street refinement. The exquisiteness is not only walkable, but also reflects a cultural appeal [7]. Therefore, in this paper, the streets of the old city in Shanghai are selected as an example, and compared with a new urban street. Then, on-the-spot investigation is conducted to obtain the necessary data, and the street indicators and characteristics are analyzed to get the indicators that affect the street refinement and the street refinement score [8, 9]. In order to establish a standard for judging street refinement, in the end, a set of methods that can be adopted and quantifiable is measured, and the goal of evaluating refined streets is achieved. Through the overall analysis and comparative analysis, the corresponding conclusions and optimization suggestions are obtained.

2 Methodology

2.1 Research Street Segment Selection

In order to conduct a more dialectical research on the streets of Shanghai's old city, we selected two blocks for research and dialectical comparison. One is a typical Shanghai old city street, with Kailu Road as the core block, and the other is a commercial street that has been recently developed—University Road Block so as to have better fault tolerance and achieve a focused analysis of the problem. The location methods are all along the main road with the core road segment as the main body and directly contact with it.

Typical Old Town District - Kailu Road District. Kailu Road in Shanghai is named after the General Office of Shanghai Municipal People's Government on the name change of the city's place names and road names for the fourth time on April 16, 1984 (Shanghai Office [1984] No. 64). Although it has been continuously refurbished in the past seventy years, it still seems to be incapable in today's rapid development.

New Specialty Commercial Street - University Road Block. Since its renovation and reconstruction in 2009, the University Road has become a popular commercial street with a fresh academic style as its overall style, and brought a batch of traffic and economy. On the basis of maintaining its own characteristics, it has taken a long-term step towards refinement and sustainability.

Data Normalization. In order to perform more systematic and intuitive calculation and use the data, we have normalized the original data. There are mainly the following processing methods. After normalization, 1 is uniformly set to the optimal value.

(1) Ideal value ratio

$$x^* = \begin{cases} \frac{x_i}{x_a}, x_i < x_a \\ \frac{x_a - (x_i - x_b)}{x_a}, x_i > x_b \\ 1, x_a \leq x_i \leq x_b \end{cases}$$

x^*: The normalized value of an indicator before normalization
x_i: Raw data for item i of the indicator
x_a: The minimum value of the ideal interval of item i
x_b: The maximum value of the ideal interval of item i

(2) Range standardization

The expression for the range standardization is:

$$x^* = \frac{x_i - x_{min}}{x_{max} - x_{min}}$$

x^*: The normalized value of an indicator before normalization
x_i: The raw data for item i of the indicator
x_{min}: The minimum value of all data for this indicator
x_{max}: The maximum value of all data for this indicator

All normalized values range from 0–1.

2.2 Pearson Correlation Analysis

Software SPSS is adopted to make Pearson correlation analysis.

When both variables are normal continuous variables, and there is a linear relationship between them, the degree of correlation between the two variables is expressed by the correlation coefficient of the product difference, mainly Pearson simple correlation coefficient.

Its calculation formula is:

$$r = \frac{N \Sigma x_i y_i - \Sigma x_i \sum y_i}{\sqrt{N \Sigma x_i^2 - (\Sigma x_i)^2} \sqrt[2]{N \Sigma y_i^2 - \left(\sum y_i\right)^2}}$$

x_i, y_i: the value of two sets of variables
N: Sample size

Pearson correlation coefficient is used to measure whether two data sets are above a line, and the linear relationship between distance variables. The larger the absolute value of the correlation coefficient is, the stronger the correlation is; the closer the correlation coefficient is to 1 or –1, the stronger the correlation; the closer the correlation coefficient is to 0, the weaker the correlation is.

Import data and analyze the correlation of 38 pieces of data with normalized data using SPSS25 (Table 1).

The screenshot of running results (partial) (Table 2).

Table 1. Descriptive statistics

Descriptive statistics			
	Average value	Standard deviation	Number of cases
Motorway width	.795222	.1989621	9
Total	20.750011111111110	2.242092002708879	9

Table 2. Correlation

Correlation		Motorway width	Total
Motorway width	Pearson correlation	1	.459
	Sig. (two-tailed)		.214
	Number of cases	9	9
Total	Pearson correlation	.459	1
	Sig. (two-tailed)	.214	
	Number of cases	9	9

Finally, 38 sets of running results were obtained. Sort the results by relevance:

Extremely strong correlation: pre-construction area configuration, facility belts configuration and pedestrian rest facilities.

Strong correlation: drainage facilities, barrier-free facilities, pedestrian access area width and landscape lighting facilities.

Moderate correlation: motor vehicle width, isolation belts, non-motor vehicle parking facilities, road lighting facilities, transparency, flower gardens, green belts, tree pools, bus station design, space enclosure, store signboards, electronic bus stop sign quantity and bicycle parking spots.

Weak correlation: the number of lanes, buffer belt width and mixed utilization of noodle buildings.

Very weak correlation or no correlation: speed control, non-motor vehicle lane width, street crossing facilities, power distribution and substation facilities, the number of street entrances and exits, traffic sign facility problems, street trees, three-dimensional greening, the number of literary pieces, sanitation facilities, telephone booths, the ground floor line rate, the sunshade rate, wall ratio and cameras.

According to the results of the operation, strong correlation indicators, namely pre-construction area configuration, facility belt configuration, pedestrian rest facilities, drainage facilities, barrier-free facilities, pedestrian access area width and landscape lighting facilities are retained.

3 Correlation Data Analysis

(Fig. 1)

A: University Road   B: Zhixing Road   C: Kailu Road (West)
D: Kailu Road (Middle)   E: Kailu Road (East)   F: Zhongyuan Road (South)
G: Zhongyuan Road (North)   H: Baoyou Road (South) I: Baotou Road (North)

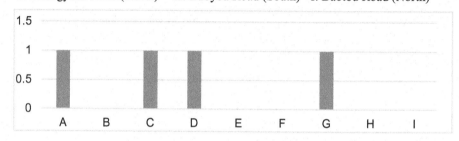

Fig. 1. Landscape lighting facilities

The table shows the 0–1 distribution. It can be seen from the map that there are landscape lighting facilities in University Road, Kailu Road (West), Kailu Road, and Zhongyuan Road (North) (Fig. 2).

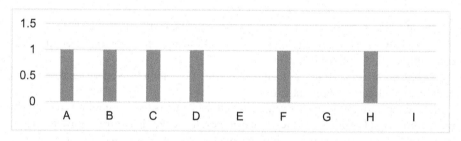

Fig. 2. Barrier-free facilities

The table displays the 0–1 distribution. It can be seen from the map that University Road, Zhixing Road, Kailu Road (West), Kailu Road (Middle), Zhongyuan Road (South) and Baotou Road (South) are equipped with barrier-free facilities (Fig. 3).

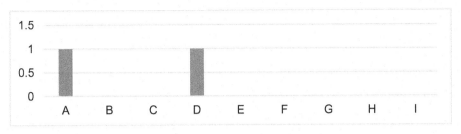

Fig. 3. Front area configuration

The table is the 0–1 distribution. It can be seen from the map that there is a pre-construction area in University Road and Kailu Road (Fig. 4).

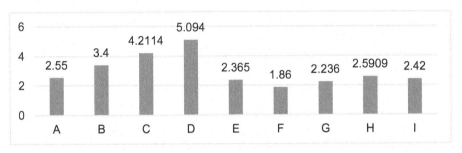

Fig. 4. Width of walking area

The figure above shows the width of the peer area of each road segment (Fig. 5).

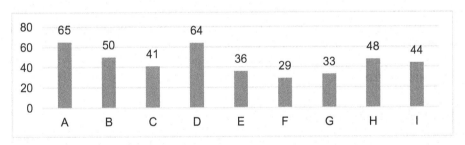

Fig. 5. Drainage facility

The above is the number of drainage facilities in each section. As you can see, the drainage facilities are an important indicator for the maintenance of the road sections (Fig. 6).

The above table shows the number of pedestrian leisure facilities in each section. There are fewer on Zhixing Roads, more on Kailu Roads, and the appropriate amount on University Road and Kailu Road (West), while no pedestrian facilities exist in other sections (Fig. 7).

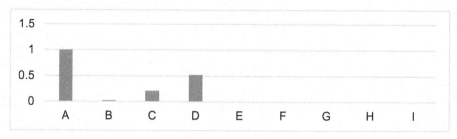

Fig. 6. Pedestrian facilities

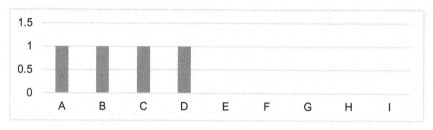

Fig. 7. Facilities belt configuration

The table is the 0–1 distribution. It can be seen from the map that there are facilities in University Road, Zhixing Road, Kailu Road West, and Kailu Road.

4 Street Refinement Analysis

Traffic streets: the south section of Zhongyuan Road and the north section of Zhongyuan Road (good).

Living streets: the east section of Kailu Road, the middle section (better), west end (the best), south end and north end of Baotou Road.

Commercial streets: University Road (Good) and Zhixing Road.

Comparison of traffic streets (Fig. 8).

4.1 Traffic Street Comparison

As shown in the above histogram, Zhongyuan Road is the main traffic road in the urban area. However, the northern part of Zhongyuan Road is more refined than the southern one. The north is featured with more drainage facilities than the south, so that the facilities in the north of Zhongyuan Road are more complete and safer. However, according to the data, in the northern part, there are landscape lighting facilities to bring a better night travel experience, and the evaluation of the two sections of roads is almost the same.

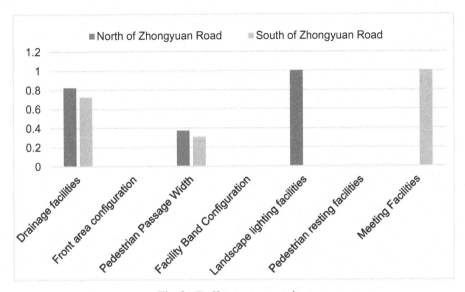

Fig. 8. Traffic street comparison

4.2 Comparison of Living Streets

Kailu Road is the main living street. Compared with the central part of Kailu Road, Kailu Road is equipped with more drainage systems, barrier-free facilities and landscape lighting facilities, which are convenient for people's travel. Moreover, wider pedestrian passages and more facilities provide more space for people's lives (Fig. 9).

Fig. 9. Comparison of living streets

4.3   Commercial Street Comparison

As shown in the relevant data of the table, although the configuration of the front area and facilities of Zhixing Road are similar to that of University Road, the latter is featured with a larger walking zone to bear more traffic and less street traffic. The entrance can reduce the loss of pedestrians (Table 3).

Table 3. Commercial street comparison

	University road	Zhixing road
Drainage facilities	0.375	0.75
Front area configuration	1	0
Pedestrian passage width	1	1
Facility band configuration	1	1
Landscape lighting facilities	1	0
Pedestrian resting facilities	1	0.0241
Meeting facilities	1	1
	5.5288	3.7537

At the same time, as University Road has a higher rate of shade and rain, pedestrians can have a better shopping experience. In this case, University Road has become the main commercial street in the city. Compared with Zhixing Road, University Road characterizes higher transparency, more cultural and artistic sketches, and landscape lighting facilities, so pedestrians on University Road can enjoy better views. Whether in shops or on the street, they will always have a better sense of security.

Therefore, it is a better place for shopping, and the mix of noodle and street buildings on University Road is lower. All are commercial buildings, and there are more shops for pedestrians to choose, thereby attracting more people (Fig. 10).

Fig. 10. Commercial street comparison

4.4 Traffic and Commercial Street Comparison

There are more pedestrian rest facilities on University Road, while Zhongyuan Road almost has no rest facilities, and the lighting facilities of Zhongyuan Road are poorly configured. Thus, the night travel experience is bad, and it has lower transparency, which cannot bring sufficient safety to pedestrians. For various reasons, there are fewer pedestrians and slower traffic on Zhongyuan Road (Fig. 11).

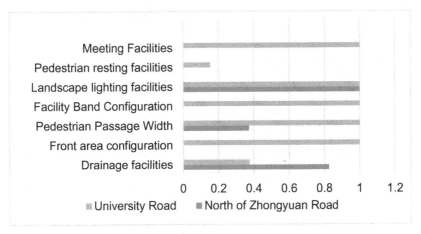

Fig. 11. Traffic and commercial street comparison

4.5 Comparison of Living and Traffic Streets

As Kailu Road (west) is equipped with barrier-free facilities and pedestrian rest facilities, there are better pedestrian traffic situations and services. The pedestrian zone on Kailu Road (west) is larger, so that people can enjoy more space without clogging. For the above reasons, the refinement of Kailu Road is higher than that of Zhongyuan Road (Fig. 12).

4.6 Comparison of Living and Commercial Streets

Compared with Kailu Road, the main gap between Kailu Road and University Road lies in the width of pedestrian recreation facilities and pedestrian traffic zones. As a commercial street, Kailu Road should have a larger pedestrian traffic zone to ensure more pedestrian shopping activities. More leisure facilities can meet more people's rest needs, and there are more drainage systems on Kailu Road (west) to ensure that there is little water accumulation on the road surface and people travel normally (Fig. 13).

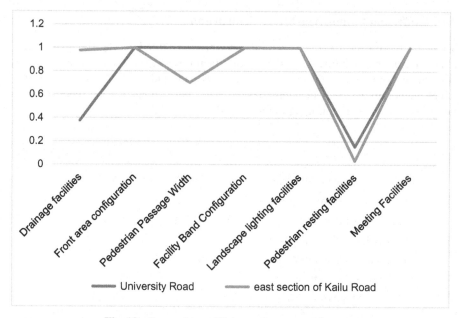

Fig. 12. Comparison of living and commercial streets

Fig. 13. Comparison of living and commercial streets

5 Street Refinement Measures and Recommendations

Firstly, improve the situation of the motorway, increase its proper transportation facilities and some configuration, determine its lane width according to its traffic flow and future development trend, and avoid too wide or too narrow roadways. Transportation facilities can upgrade the service level of roads and improve their capacity. The drainage facilities on the driveway can well avoid the accumulation of water, thus affecting the traffic capacity of the vehicle and the life of the road.

Secondly, from the analysis on pedestrians, increasing the appreciation of the road is not only conductive to pedestrians' fatigue relief and emotion regulation, but also adds a beautiful landscape to the city. Therefore, art pieces and their corresponding landscape lighting facilities are necessary. Three-dimensional greening and flowers are also a good choice. From the perspective of pedestrian safety, the facility belt and the buffer belt can enhance the safety of the sidewalk to a great extent, and reduce the impact of the vehicle on pedestrians, thus increasing the pedestrian comfort. From the perspective of humanity, the pedestrian rest facilities can help those who need to rest or some elderly people who walk, so that they can become both a popular street and a channel for watching.

Finally, for the buildings next to the road, the configuration of the front area of the building can largely reduce the interaction of the sidewalks, leave space for the front decoration of the building, increase its appreciation and attract more pedestrians.

Based on the above data analysis, the degree of refinement is shown be:

commercial street > living street > traffic street.

Increased refinement measures for commercial streets: increased drainage facilities, landscape lighting facilities and pedestrian rest facilities.

Enhance the refinement of living streets: increase drainage facilities, pedestrian facilities and pedestrian access areas.

Rehabilitation measures for traffic streets: mainly to increase the configuration of the front area of the building and that of the facility belt.

6   Conclusion

By taking a representative old urban street in Shanghai as an example, and comparing it with a new urban street, through normalization, the data is processed to obtain comprehensive indicators. Then, the Pearson test is conducted. With large amounts of data and recalculation, a comprehensive indicator is obtained. In this regard, from the perspective of street refinement, the street is elaborated, and several countermeasures are proposed. As only the data from the two urban streets is analyzed, the conclusions are incomplete, and more samples should be involved.

Acknowledgments. This work was supported by the Shanghai philosophy and social science planning project (2017ECK004), the research fund climbing program of humanistic and social science from University of Shanghai for Science and Technology (SK18PB05) and USST Innovation and Entrepreneurship Training Program (XJ2019132).

References

1. Yang, J.Y., Wu, H., Zhang, W.: Study on the characteristics and optimization strategies of urban pedestrian walkability based on multi-source big data–taking downtown area of Nanjing as an example. Int. Urban Plan. **34**(05), 3–42 (2019)
2. Yan, S.H., Xu, J.Q.: Quantitative research on Urban street pedestrian index–taking the old City of Zhengzhou as an example. Urban Archit. **16**(03), 7–9+20 (2019)
3. Yu, L.P., Song, X.Y., Wang, Z.G.: Research on the impact of standardization of evaluation indicators and evaluation methods on academic evaluation–taking TOPSIS evaluation method as an example. Inf. Theory Pract. 1–10 (2019)
4. Wang, Z.: Evaluation method and empirical research on the intensive use of cultivated land. Shandong Normal University (2019)
5. Lu, Y.T., Wang, D.: The progress of american walking measurement research and its enlightenment. Int. Urban Plan. **27**(01), 10–15 (2012)

6. Liu, W., Gou, W.: International experience in pedestrian evaluation methods and tools. Int. Urban Plan. **33**(04), 103–110 (2018)
7. Liu, W.W., Tang, Y., Yang, F., Dou, Y., Wang, J.: A multi-objective decision-making approach for the optimal location of electric vehicle charging facilities. Comput. Mater. Continua **60**(2), 813–834 (2019)
8. Zeng, D.J., Dai, Y., Li, F., Sherratt, R.S., Wang, J.: Adversarial learning for distant supervised relation extraction. Comput. Mater. Continua **55**(1), 121–136 (2018)
9. Tu, Y., Lin, Y., Wang, J., Kim, J.U.: Semi-supervised learning with generative adversarial networks on digital signal modulation classification. Comput. Mater. Continua **55**(2), 243–254 (2018)

A Traceability Architecture for the Fresh Food Supply Chain Based on Blockchain Technology in China

Yue Li[1], Xiaoquan Chu[1], Dong Tian[1], Jianying Feng[1], and Weisong Mu[1,2(✉)]

[1] College of Information and Electrical Engineering, China Agricultural University,
Beijing 100083, People's Republic of China
wsmu@cau.edu.cn
[2] Key Laboratory of Viticulture and Enology, Ministry of Agriculture,
Beijing, People's Republic of China

Abstract. Due to there are some issues such as information asymmetry and data tampering in the current traceability system in China, we propose a traceability architecture for the fresh food supply chain based on blockchain technology. Firstly, brief summaries of the traceability theory and blockchain principle are given. Business Process Reengineering (BPR) is applied to reorganize the original supply chain workflow. Then a blockchain-based traceability framework is designed for the fresh food supply chain in the BPR project. We explore the basic architecture, product identification, data recording and storage of critical information in the fresh food supply chain. Finally, the architecture innovations and conclusions are summarized. BPR and blockchain are integrated in the supply chain traceability architecture, which provides a basic theoretical support for the further implementation of practical application and paves the way for the supply chain research of other foods.

Keywords: Business Process Reengineering · Blockchain technology · Supply chain · Traceability architecture · Fresh food

1 Introduction

With the continuous development of national economy, people's living standards have improved significantly. More and more attention is paid to the food quality and safety [1]. However, food-related accidents or scandals have occurred frequently in the past few years. Especially for fresh food, once the safety issues happen, it will seriously affect people's health [2, 3]. Thus, looking into the fresh food supply chain traceability is becoming more and more urgent [4, 5].

In the key technologies of fresh food traceability, research suggests that most traceability systems in China are supported by Internet of Things (IoT) [6, 7]. At present, it has a great breakthrough in the food traceability [8]. In the 2008 Beijing Olympic Games, RFID technology was used to track and monitor the Olympic food. Liu et al. [9] presented a RFID-based "from farm to fork" solution to ensure food safety. Feng

© Springer Nature Singapore Pte Ltd. 2020
X. Sun et al. (Eds.): ICAIS 2020, CCIS 1252, pp. 347–358, 2020.
https://doi.org/10.1007/978-981-15-8083-3_31

et al. [10] developed and evaluated a cattle traceability system that integrated RFID technology with PDA and barcode printer. The results showed that the major benefits of RFID-enabled traceability system included the accurate data acquisition and transmission, the high efficiency of information tracking and tracing across the cattle supply chain. These studies have well satisfied the traceability quality and safety of the fresh food supply chain. However, several issues are still not addressed in current solutions, including the centralized system, low data security, and information asymmetry.

Blockchain technology is a huge innovation, which has risen to the level of national science and technology strategy. Many scholars have begun to focus on the field of food quality and safety traceability based on blockchain [11, 12]. In China, many companies have achieved the practical applications by using the blockchain technology, such as anti-counterfeiting, tracking, and traceability of food supply chain [13, 14]. In 2016, Tsinghua University cooperated with Wal-Mart and IBM to track food supply chain by using blockchain technology [15]. Sun et al. [16] believed that the introduction of blockchain could solve the trust problem, yet the improvement of information quality also depended on the IoT. With the increasing demand of agricultural product supply chain, Yu et al. [17] analyzed the blockchain concept, technical characteristics and structure. He put forward the logic structure of agricultural product supply chain based on blockchain, which provided useful reference value for the research of agricultural product supply chain. These findings clearly demonstrate that blockchain technology is introduced into the traceability system of the fresh food supply chain is reasonable, the problems in traditional traceability can be solved.

In this paper, we propose a traceability architecture for the fresh food supply chain based on blockchain technology in China. The rest of paper is organized as follows: In Sect. 2, we begin with a brief introduction to the traceability theory and explain what the blockchain is. BPR is used to restructure the fresh food supply chain process. Then the blockchain-based traceability framework is illustrated in Sect. 3, including system analysis, basic architecture and operation mechanism. Section 4 explores the blockchain innovations in the traceability system for the fresh food supply chain. Finally, the conclusions are given in Sect. 5.

2   Preliminaries

2.1   Traceability Theory of the Fresh Food Supply Chain

Codex Alimentarius Commission (CAC) considers the traceability can be defined as the ability to trace the product information at any link of the production, processing and transportation, etc. International Organization for Standardization (ISO) defines it as the ability to track or trace the history, location, and distribution of products with traceability code. It can be seen that the traceability of the fresh food supply chain is divided into the tracking and tracing. In other words, traceability not only from farm to table, but also from table to farmland [18]. The quality and safety traceability of fresh food in China is the supervision of the whole supply chain process from production to consumption [19]. The supply chain consists of the logistics, capital flow and information flow. It is a complex structure that connects the producers, suppliers, manufacturers, distributors, retailers and consumers (see Fig. 1).

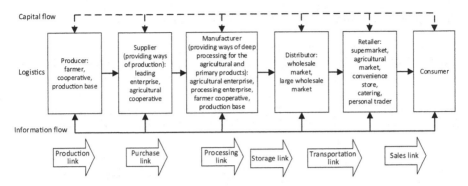

Fig. 1. Logical structure of the fresh food supply chain.

2.2 Blockchain Technology

Blockchain is a data structure generated by the cryptographic algorithms. The verified block is time-stamped with a cryptographic hash, and all blocks are connected to each other in chronological order [20]. Blockchain is a distributed database that is multi-participated and co-maintained [21]. The problems existing in the current traceability system can be well solved by using blockchain technology due to its advantages [22], including the decentralization, openness, encryption security, and traceability.

Key Technologies. Blockchain technology mainly includes the Peer to Peer (P2P) network, distributed storage, encryption algorithms, consensus mechanisms, and smart contracts [23, 24]. P2P network is a peer-to-peer transaction without the intermediary, in which the rights and obligations among all nodes are equal. All nodes in distributed storage have uniform information, and the transactions cannot be tampered with. Encryption algorithms mainly include the hash function and asymmetric cryptography, which ensure the information security of user privacy and transaction record. Consensus mechanisms solve the problem of data inconsistency in distributed scenarios. Smart contracts are the basis for blockchain programmability, which can be automatically executed on behalf of the signing parties without any central agency [25].

Basic Architecture. Blockchain system consists of six layers, including the data, network, consensus, incentive, contract, and application layers [26]. Data layer encapsulates the underlying data and basic algorithms to ensure the block data cannot be tampered with. Network layer is the structural basis of decentralized storage, which mainly includes the propagation protocols and data verification mechanisms so that each node can verify and record the block data. Consensus layer is the guarantee for normal operation in the distributed network, it mainly enables all nodes to reach an efficient consensus for the validity of block data. Incentive layer integrates the economic factors into the blockchain system, which encourages each node to verify the data. Contract layer is the basis for implementing the data programmability and operability, and it mainly encapsulates various script algorithms and smart contracts. Application layer contains the application scenarios and cases [27].

2.3   Optimization and Design of the Fresh Food Supply Chain

BPR supply chain is a complex project involving the reorganization of businesses (supply chain links), resources (capital, information), and information technologies (blockchain, RFID, Barcode, GPS). It takes advantage of the modern management and blockchain, which optimizes the whole supply chain and eliminates the information asymmetry among the entities. In this paper, the original fresh food supply chain process is redesigned by using the BPR (see Fig. 2), and blockchain is one of the technical tools used in the BPR project (see Fig. 3).

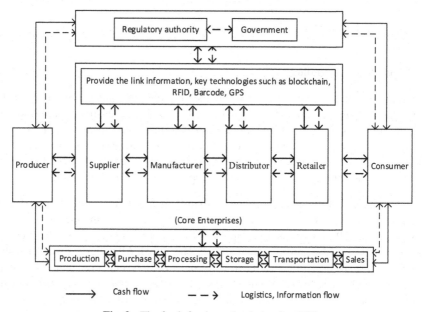

Fig. 2. The fresh food supply chain after BPR.

The businesses and resources in the fresh food supply chain are integrated by using the BPR, and the information technologies play a good catalytic role in the BPR project. The supply chain process is redesigned through the BPR to achieve the most profit, the management process is shown in Fig. 4. The application of information technologies ensures timely data collection and transmission, and realizes the accurate information interaction in the whole supply chain.

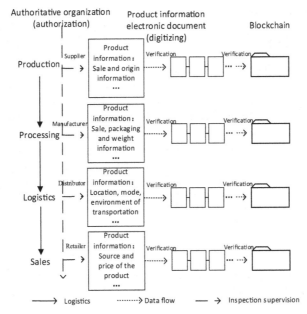

Fig. 3. The restructured traceability process of the fresh food supply chain.

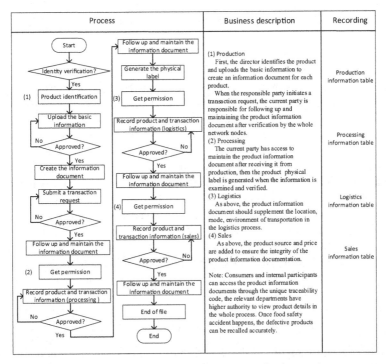

Fig. 4. Supply chain management process after integration.

3 System Conceptual Framework

3.1 System Analysis

User Requirement. The main participants in the whole supply chain include the producers, suppliers, manufacturers, distributors, and retailers. They are responsible for uploading link data and viewing critical indicators that affect product quality. Consumers can query and trace the product quality information of key links, and they can make complaints about the defective products. The regulatory authorities manage user permissions, and they are also responsible for reviewing data and establishing regulations. The governments can view the statistical analysis results of quality monitoring and provide decisions for real-time tracking products. The system use case diagram is shown in Fig. 5.

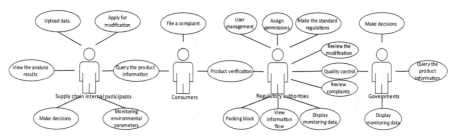

Fig. 5. System use case diagram.

Functional Requirement. (1) Registration and login. First, users register their identities. The regulators then generate a pair of public and private keys for each user and assign them permissions after approval. All data on blockchain can be accurately located to an actual individual by mapping the users and nodes. (2) Upload data. Data information mainly includes the link data related to the product quality and transaction information between parties. Identification technologies such as the sensor, RFID, GPS, barcode are used to obtain data. The start and end of each link will be recorded with smart contracts. (3) Transfer and share data. The data is encapsulated and broadcast in the whole network to ensure the authenticity and integrity of data information. (4) Verify and store data. The uploaded data is verified with consensus mechanisms, then a certain amount of data will be packaged into a block and broadcast over the whole network. The verified blocks are time-stamped and stored in each node. (5) Management information. If the supply chain internal participants modify the product information, they need to submit the modification application. Similarly, the modified data is broadcast to the whole network. (6) Query information. Consumers can view product quality information of key supply chain links. By comparing the calculated hash result and digital abstract stored on blockchain, they can verify the integrity of product information.

Performance Requirement. In the architecture of this study, there is no consensus mechanisms. The regulators authorize the designated nodes to pack blocks, which overcomes the waste of resources. Moreover, there is no reward mechanisms because the internal and external participating nodes in the supply chain are jointly responsible for maintaining the data information. Therefore, the alliance chain is chosen as the organizational form for the fresh food supply chain. Ethereum platform Geth is used as the underlying architecture of blockchain [28]. The traceability architecture is based on Java development. JSP technology is used to realize the business logic and data presentation. MySQL is used to store the traceability data. The combination of blockchain technology and Java development makes data information more transparent and traceable.

3.2 System Basic Architecture

Architecture (see Fig. 6). (1) Data collection layer mainly includes the operation and IoT levels. Operation level is the data source for the traceability system, and the aim of IoT level is to acquire and transmit the key data of operation level, which can improve the effectiveness of data circulation and management. (2) Blockchain layer mainly includes the data, consensus and contract levels. Data level is composed of Geth and MySQL. All time-stamped blocks are linked in a chain, so that the data cannot be tampered with. Network consensus level mainly implements the data verification and consensus, which guarantees the data transmission and circulation. Contract level is mainly responsible for the contract deployment and invocation. The safety regulations and health management standards of fresh food are embedded in the smart contracts, which can effectively reduce the contradiction of human supervision and realize the standardized management [29]. (3) Physical layer mainly includes application, interface and user levels. Application and interface levels mainly display the key data information according to user's needs, and provide the corresponding permissions or interfaces for different users. User level represents individuals and organizations in real life, including the supply chain internal participants, consumers, regulatory authorities, and governments.

Overall Network Architecture (see Fig. 7). The blockchain-based overall traceability architecture for the fresh food supply chain is based on the product quality data of key links and transaction information between parties. The data information is stored in both blockchain system and traceability database. The blockchain system is jointly maintained through consensus mechanisms among the supply chain internal participants, consumers, regulatory authorities and governments. Using blockchain to automatically store data on each computer in blockchain network, which ensures the data authenticity and immutability for the fresh food supply chain. The traceability database is managed by the regulatory authorities. The aim of establishing traceability database is to compare with the original digital abstract on blockchain, and to ensure the integrity of data information.

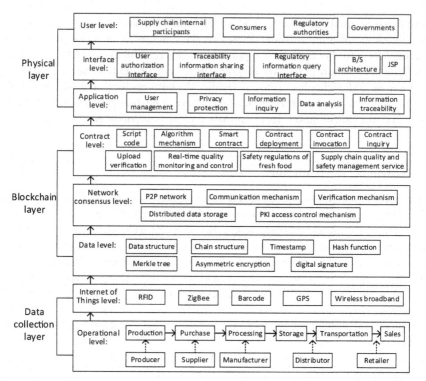

Fig. 6. Traceability system architecture of the fresh food supply chain based on blockchain.

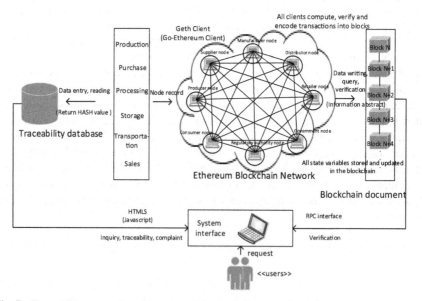

Fig. 7. Traceability network architecture of the fresh food supply chain based on blockchain.

3.3   System Operation Mechanism

Product Identification. The basic operation of fresh food traceability is product identification and coding. The effective tracking and tracing can be achieved when the product is correctly identified. EAN UCC system (Global Open Logistics Information Identification and Barcode Representation System) includes the data carriers (barcode, RFID) and data exchange. GS1 (Global Traceability Standard System) provides the coding standards that can be used to assign the unique identification [30]. In this paper, UCC/EAN-128 barcode and RFID are used to identify information such as the traceable objects, participants and locations. The quality-controlled data is written to the blockchain system for verification by other nodes. The data collection and coding carriers for each link in the fresh food supply chain is shown in Table 1.

Table 1. Data collection and coding carriers.

Link	Collected data	Coding carriers
Production	Operator, planting enterprise, variety, medication, quantity, production base, implementation time, inspector, inspection date, certificate number, environment, etc.	RFID
Purchase	Purchaser, purchasing unit, purchase quantity, variety, environment, etc.	RFID, sensor
Processing	Operator, processing enterprise, batch quantity, processing process, material, ingredient, date, etc.	RFID, barcode, sensor
Storage	Operator, shelf life, specification quantity, quality grade, storage environment, etc.	Barcode, sensor
Transportation	Distribution enterprise, transporter, receiving enterprise, consignee, transport vehicle, arrival time, quantity, weight, GPS information, environment, etc.	Barcode, sensor, GPS
Sales	Salesperson, sales method, purchase time, shelf time, sales status, environment, etc.	Barcode, sensor

Data Recording and Storage (see Fig. 8). (1) When we submit the link data, it is necessary to examine the data format and food quality and safety standards through the automated smart contracts. The checked data is calculated as the digital abstract and broadcast over the P2P network. The data information is put into the trading pool after verification to wait for being packaged by the regulators. Additionally, the product ownership is transferred when we submit the transaction information. The transaction information is signed by using the sender's private key, and both parties need to reach a consensus. Subsequently, the transaction information is verified by all nodes in blockchain network. Finally, it is put into the trading pool. (2) After the detailed data information is packaged into a block, the block still needs to be verified by all nodes. The verified block is connected in chronological order on blockchain. What's more, the data information successfully entered into the blockchain will return the corresponding hash value. The value is a query index to verify whether the data has been tampered with. Finally, the complete data information and the index are stored in the traceability database, ensuring that the information cannot be tampered with.

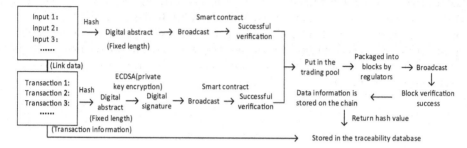

Fig. 8. Data recording and storage processes.

4 Innovations

Compared with the traditional traceability, the main innovations of blockchain-based traceability are as follows: 1) Efficient supply chain. To maximize the benefits of supply chain management, the original supply chain process is reorganized through the BPR and blockchain is used as a technology tool. The traceability architecture reduces a large number of human errors and costs, and significantly improves the efficiency of data transmission. 2) Perfect traceability system. By setting different user permissions, the interfaces are opened to the supply chain internal participants, consumers, regulatory organizations and governments. The data information is completely recorded on the blockchain by building an alliance chain, which reduces the trust cost among the supply chain objectives. The regulatory authorities and governments create an atmosphere of mutual supervision and self-discipline. 3) Safe traceability information. The secure access and one-way hash are established to address the data privacy [31]. The data information is jointly maintained by all nodes in the whole blockchain network, each node records and verifies the data information. In this paper, data layer consists of the blockchain system and traceability database, ensuring the data security and integrity.

5 Conclusions

There are some issues such as the improper supply chain management, centralized structure, information asymmetry, and data tampering in the traditional traceability. BPR contributes to improve the benefits of supply chain management. Blockchain technology takes advantages of decentralization, non-tampering and distributed storage, which provides a solution to overcome the problems existing in the current traceability field. We focus on the blockchain-based network architecture. The management model has been changed from traditional centralization to jointly maintenance by all nodes in the whole supply chain, which reduces the traceability centralization and trust. Moreover, the data integrity verification can be realized by mapping the unique relationship between the traceability code and returned hash value. The combination of BPR and blockchain not only improves the supply chain management process, but also ensures the safety and reliability of traceability information for fresh food.

References

1. Xinqing, X., Xiang, W., Xiaoshuan, Z., Enxiu, C., Jun, L.: Effect of the quality property of table grapes in cold chain logistics-integrated WSN and AOW. Appl. Sci. **5**(4), 747–760 (2015)
2. Jing, W., Huili, Y., Zenan, Z.: An improved traceability system for food quality assurance and evaluation based on fuzzy classification and neural network. Food Control **79**, 363–370 (2017)
3. Weisong, M., Chengcheng, L., Dong, T., Jianying, F.: Chinese consumers' behavior and preference to table grapes. Br. Food J. **118**(1), 231–246 (2016)
4. Shaosheng, J., Yan, Z., Yining, X.: Amount of information and the willingness of consumers to pay for food traceability in China. Food Control **77**, 163–170 (2017)
5. Maitri, T., Charles, R.H.: Framework for implementing traceability system in the bulk grain supply chain. J. Food Eng. **95**(4), 617–626 (2009)
6. Ihsuan, H., et al.: An RFID application in the food supply chain: a case study of convenience stores in Taiwan. J. Food Eng. **106**(2), 119–126 (2011)
7. Jianping, Q., Xinting, Y., Xiaoming, W., Li, Z., Beilei, F., Bin, X.: A traceability system incorporating 2D barcode and RFID technology for wheat flour mills. Comput. Electron. Agric. **89**(3), 76–85 (2012)
8. Zetian, F., Shaohua, X., Xiaoshuan, Z.: Development trend of food quality safety traceability technology. Transactions of the Chinese Society for Agricultural Machinery **44**(7), 144–153, 210 (2013)
9. Yu, L., Junfang, Z., Limei, T.: RFID based solution for food safety. Computer Engineering and Applications **42**(24), 201–203, 210 (2006)
10. Jianying, F., Zetian, F., Zaiqiong, W., Mark, X., Xiaoshuan, Z.: Development and evaluation on a RFID-based traceability system for cattle/beef quality safety in China. Food Control **31**(2), 314–325 (2013)
11. Rita, A., RimaKilany, C., Maria, S.: Food quality traceability prototype for restaurants using blockchain and food quality data index. Comput. Ind. Eng. **135**, 582–592 (2019)
12. Andreas, K., Agusti, F., FrancescX, P.: The rise of blockchain technology in agriculture and food supply chains. Trends Food Sci. Technol. **91**, 640–652 (2019)
13. Xiwei, X., Qinghua, L., Yue, L., Liming, Z., Haonan, Y., AthanasiosV, V.: Designing blockchain-based applications a case study for imported product traceability. Future Generation Computer System **92**, 399–406 (2019)
14. Guoqing, Z., et al.: Blockchain technology in agri-food value chain management: a synthesis of applications, challenges and future research directions. Comput. Ind. **109**, 83–99 (2019)
15. Blockchain + supply chain! Wal-Mart pilot food traceable. http://www.sohu.com/a/198873844_170950. Accessed 18 Oct 2017
16. Zhiguo, S., Xiufeng, L., Wensheng, W., Zhiqiang, J.: Application prospect of block chain technology in food safety. Agriculture network information **12**, 30–31 (2016)

17. Lina, Y., Guofeng, Z., Jingdun, J., Wanlin, G., Ganghong, Z., Sha, T.: Modern agricultural product supply chain based on block chain technology. Transactions of the Chinese Society for Agricultural Machinery **s1**, 387–393 (2017)
18. Aihwa, C., Chunghui, T., Minyeh, C.: Value creation from a food traceability system based on a hierarchical model of consumer personality traits. British Food Journal **115**(9), 1361–1380 (2013)
19. Xiang, W., Qile, H., Maja, M., Tomislav, J., Xiaoshuan, Z.: Development and evaluation on a wireless multi-gas-sensors system for improving traceability and transparency of table grape cold chain. Comput. Electron. Agric. **135**, 195–207 (2017)
20. Jingzhong, W., et al.: A blockchain based privacy-preserving incentive mechanism in crowdsensing applications. IEEE Access **6**, 17545–17556 (2018)
21. Florian, T., Bjorn, S.: Bitcoin and beyond: a technical survey on decentralized digital currencies. IEEE Communications Surveys and Tutorials **18**(3), 2084–2123 (2016)
22. Jegaanish, D.: Bitcoin mining acceleration and performance quantification. In: IEEE 27th Canadian Conference on Electrical and Computer Engineering (CCECE), Toronto, Canada, pp. 1–6 (2014)
23. Konstantinos, C., Michael, D.: Blockchains and smart contracts for the internet of things. IEEE Access **4**, 2292–2303 (2016)
24. Don, J., Alfred, M., Scott, V.: The elliptic curve digital signature algorithm (ECDSA). Int. J. Inf. Secur. **1**(1), 36–63 (2001)
25. Rui, S., Yubo, S., Ziming, L., Min, T., Kan, Z.: GaiaWorld: a novel blockchain system based on competitive PoS consensus mechanism. Computers, Materials & Continua **60**(3), 973–987 (2019)
26. Javed, B., Timo, H.: Goldstrike 1: Cointerra's first-generation cryptocurrency mining processor for Bitcoin. IEEE Micro **35**(2), 68–76 (2015)
27. Xin, J., Mingzhe, L., Chen, Y., Yanhua, L., Ruili, W.: A blockchain-based authentication protocol for WLAN mesh security access. Computers, Materials & Continua **58**(1), 45–59 (2019)
28. Xiwei, X., et al.: The blockchain as a software connector. In: IEEE 13th Working IEEE/IFIP Conference on Software Architecture (WICSA), Venice, Italy, pp. 182–191 (2016)
29. Chaoyang, L., Gang, X., Yuling, C., Haseeb, A., Jian, L.: A new anti-quantum proxy blind signature for blockchain-enabled Internet of Things. Computers, Materials & Continua **61**(2), 711–726 (2019)
30. Myomin, A., Yoonseok, C.: Traceability in a food supply chain: safety and quality perspectives. Food Control **39**, 172–184 (2014)
31. Jiye, W., Lingchao, G., Aiqiang, D., Shaoyong, G., Hui, C., Xin, W.: Block chain based data security sharing network architecture research. Journal of Computer Research and Development **54**(4), 742–749 (2017)

Research Progress in Blind Forensics of Digital Image Smooth Filtering

Jian Wu[✉], XinHua Tang, Kai Feng, and TongFeng Yang

School of Cyberspace Security, Shandong University of Political Science and Law,
Jinan 250014, China
jinanwujian@163.com

Abstract. Digital image blind forensics technology is a hot research direction in the field of information security. It can realize the authenticity and integrity verification of digital images without embedding the authentication information in the image in advance. In recent years, it has been widely researched and quickly developed. In this paper, a post-processing method-smoothing filter commonly used in digital image processing is summarized. The traditional forensic methods and representative work proposed in the early stage are summarized and discussed. Combined with deep learning technology, the main deep learning based smooth filtering is introduced in detail. Combined with deep learning technology, the main detection method based on smooth filtering is introduced in detail. Finally, we discussed the problems that still needed to be solved by blind learning technology based on deep learning and future research trends.

Keywords: Digital image forensics · Deep learning · Smooth filtering

1 Introduction

In today's highly developed digital technology, with the increasing popularity of image editing software, digital images can be easily forged and falsified, making it difficult or even impossible for human eyes to recognize. Especially when such images are used in scientific research, legal forensics, news reports, insurance claims, etc. will have irreversible negative impacts. Therefore, image forensics techniques for identifying the accuracy, integrity and originality of digital images have emerged as the times require, and have become a concern in the field of computer forensics [1]. In the existing digital image forensics technology, image blind forensics belongs to a passive authentication technology, which does not need to embed authentication information in the image in advance, so it has higher authentication and higher application value than active authentication technologies such as digital watermarking.

The blind forensic analysis methods currently involved mainly include the following three categories: First, the detection method based on imaging device consistency [2]. This method is similar to the image source forensics method and is based on the imaging consistency feature of digital cameras to identify whether the image is from different imaging devices, the current research methods include CFA interpolation detection, CCD

© Springer Nature Singapore Pte Ltd. 2020
X. Sun et al. (Eds.): ICAIS 2020, CCIS 1252, pp. 359–370, 2020.
https://doi.org/10.1007/978-981-15-8083-3_32

mode noise detection, color difference detection, camera response function detection, etc. Second, based on the natural image statistical characteristics detection method [3]. The tamper image and the natural image are regarded as two classification problems, and the high-order statistical characteristics of the image are extracted as features, and the training classifier completes the detection. Third, the detection method for the post-splicing processing operation is used for the tampering after the image splicing, such as JPEG compression [4], resampling [5], filtering [9] and other operations to erase the traces left by tampering to the image, this method determines the tampering area by analyzing the characteristics of a tampering operation.

Since the smooth filtering operation is a very common post-processing method, it can be used to hide the tampering target edge. Therefore, many scholars have realized the forensic analysis of tampering images by detecting the smooth filtering operation traces, which are proposed to include SPAM [9], MFF [12] and MFR [14] and other series of results. In recent years, the rise of deep learning has injected new vitality into the forensic method. Many scholars have improved the deep learning network structure according to the smoothing filter tampering operation characteristics. Combining deep learning technology with image tamper detection has achieved a lot of creative results [25, 31–40]. This paper will introduce the development of traditional detection methods and deep learning techniques in the field of image smoothing blind forensics in recent years. The situation is summarized, and its technical characteristics, existing problems, and future research trends are discussed.

2   Traditional Detection Method

The smooth filtering operation is mainly divided into two categories: one is linear filtering, such as average filtering, Gaussian filtering, etc. The second type is nonlinear filtering, such as median filtering. Smooth filtering is a common post-processing technique for image denoising and smoothing, and is often used by counterfeiters to destroy the statistical properties and tampering artifacts that occur during tampering. Median filtering can even reduce the reliability of forensic tools, such as eliminating linear correlation between adjacent pixels to hide evidence of resampling [6], or to remove blockiness statistics introduced by JPEG compression to achieve the anti-forensics for JPEG compression detection [7], therefore, the existing research work mainly focuses on the detection and analysis of median filtering, including the detection method based on streaking characteristics, the detection method based on adjacent pixel correlation, and the residual-based on median filtering detection method and detection method based on frequency domain residual.

2.1   Detection Method Based on Streaking Characteristics

As early as 1987, Bovik and other scholars [8] found that the median filtered image not only has good edge retention characteristics, but also usually contains many constant image blocks. This feature is called the streaking artifact characteristic of median filtered image. In 2010, Kirchner et al. proposed the median filtering detection method based on the first-order difference image histogram ratio based on the characteristics of streaking artifact [9], which performed well on uncompressed images. For JPEG compressed images, the scholars used the subtractive pixel adjacency model (SPAM) [10] in the field of image steganalysis to detect the median filtering operation. The SPAM feature is to model the first-order difference values of the horizontal, vertical and diagonal directions of the image into n-order Markov chains, and combine their transition probability matrices into a set of feature vectors, when the JPEG quality factor is greater than 70, the detection algorithm performs better, but it decreases rapidly as the quality factor decreases. And because the SPAM feature dimension is very high, when the number of pixels of the image to be tested decreases, the detection performance will also be significantly deteriorated. Also based on the streaking property, Cao et al. [11] calculated the first-order differential zero-value probability f of the image texture region as the median-filtered statistical fingerprint feature, and designed another median filter detection method, which can also preliminarily distinguish median filter from other operations such as image scaling bilinear scaling (BS), Gaussian filter (GF) and mean filter (AF). However, the detection performance of JPEG compressed images has not changed significantly.

2.2 Detection Method Based on Adjacent Pixel Correlation

The median filtering detection method based on streaking characteristics does not perform well for image post-processing such as JPEG compression. The main reason is that SPAM and other features after various filtering operations are often masked by JPEG compression effects, so other filtering traces need to be considered. From 2011 to 2012, a series of detection methods based on adjacent pixel correlations were produced. In 2011, Yuan [12] observed that there are some common pixels in the overlapping filter window, and the median filtering of these overlapping windows introduces special features (local dependent effects) into the image. The author defines 44 features based on sequential statistics and gray values contained in the filter window, named median filtering forensics features (MFF) and based on MFF combined with SVM to achieve median filtering detection (recorded as MFF method). The test results show that the algorithm can effectively distinguish other smoothing filters such as median filtering and mean filtering. In terms of JPEG compression and low resolution images, although the detection performance is weakened with the reduction of JPEG compression factor and image resolution, however, the proposed algorithm is superior to the median filtering detection method based on streaking characteristics, and the localization of the local median filtering region in uncompressed images is realized for the first time. In 2012, Chen et al. [13] found that the median filtering and other filtering operations differed in the first-order differential cumulative distribution function of the image. At the same time, the correlation between local image differences was also studied, and the global directions were extracted for these two directions. The global probability feature (GPF) and the local correlation feature (LCF) form a 56-dimensional global and local feature GLF. Experimental results show that the feature vector can be well distinguished from the median value after training with SVM. The filtered image and the original image are less affected by JPEG compression and image resolution.

2.3 Detection Method Based on Median Filtering Residual

In 2013, Kang et al. [14] defined the difference image obtained by filtering the median value and calculating the difference from the original image as the median filter residual (MFR). Based on the characteristics that the MFR is reduced after the image is again median filtered, the median value of the image to be detected at the input is calculated by MFR, which is modeled as a linear autoregressive (AR) model, using 10-dimensional autoregressive coefficients as a detection feature (denoted as AR method). Compared with SPAM, MFF and GLF methods, AR method is not easily affected by image content and JPEG compression, and the detection result of median filtering is better, but the method extracts too few features. Robustness needs to be improved. In 2016, the research team [15] further proposed a median filtering residual difference (MFRD) based median filtering forensics technique (denoted as MFRD method). First, the multi-directional MFRD is grouped according to the directivity and symmetry, then the autoregressive model is established and its model parameters and histogram features are extracted respectively. Finally, all the grouped features are combined into 48-dimensional median filter detection features, which are trained and tested in the hybrid image database composed of five image databases of UCID [27], BR [28], DID [29], NRCS [30] and BOWS2 [43] by SVM. Compared with the above SPAM, MFF, GLF and AR detection results, MFRD method reduces the interference from image content and JPEG compression block effect trace, greatly improves the detection accuracy for JPEG compressed image and low-resolution image, and can better distinguish median filter and image scaling, low-pass Gaussian filter and mean filter and other operations.

2.4 Detection Method Based on Frequency Domain Residual

Xu et al. [16] observed that after the second filtering, the frequency domain residuals of both the original image and the filtered image will show as band-pass signals, but the bandwidth and other parameters are different, and different filtering operations correspond to different bandpass filters of different bandwidth. Therefore, the image is filtered again by a frequency domain low-pass filter at the detection end to obtain the frequency domain residual and convert it to the normalized Radon domain. Finally, the Radon transform curve is fitted to an 8-order Fourier series. The 18 parameters of the Fourier series are used as the classification feature VF for filtering detection, and the filtering is performed by SVM. The experimental results show that the proposed algorithm has a good detection effect on Gaussian filtering, mean filtering and median filtering, and can judge the size of the filter, and has good robustness for JPEG compression, but the method does not test the low-resolution image.

2.5 Summary of Traditional Detection Methods

Table 1 lists representative research results of traditional detection methods, not only lists feature dimensions, classification algorithms, and image sets, but also specifically points out the detection performance and detection image resolution when jpeg compression. The reason is that JPEG is the most widely used image format in image transmission and storage applications. Image compression will cover up the traces of smooth filtering.

Therefore, the detection algorithm needs to consider the robustness of JPEG compression with a small quality factor. The performance of low-resolution image detection is based on small images. The detection period of the block is beneficial to the classification algorithm for the localization analysis of the tamper region. Therefore, some studies compare the low resolution image and JPEG compression to show the advanced nature of the algorithm. In general, the traditional smooth filtering detection the feature design and extraction of the method mainly rely on manual experience manual extraction, and combined with traditional machine learning techniques such as SVM for training. Because feature extraction and classifier training are performed separately, they cannot be optimized simultaneously. With the rise of deep learning technology, the traditional smooth filtering detection method is gradually transitioning to the detection method based on deep learning.

Table 1. Traditional detection methods.

Paper, Year	Type of forgery	Features (dimension)	Classifier	Dataset	Performance and limitations
[9] 2010	MF	SPAM(686)	SVM	6500 images	Performance is acceptable while JPEG qualities >70, but deteriorates with decreasing image resolution
[11] 2010	MF, GF AF, BS	f	–	UCID	Performance degrades significantly in JPEG compressed images
[12] 2011	MF, GF, AF	MFF(44)	SVM	BOWS2, BR, NRCS, UCID	Robust to the low image quality(i.e., low resolution and JPEG); Local median filtering area can be localized
[13] 2012	MF	GLF(56)	SVM	9000 images from BOWS2, NRCS, DID	Significant performance improvement in the case of low resolution and strong JPEG post-compression
[14] 2013	MF, GF, AF, Scaling	MFR(10)	SVM	6690 images From UCID, BR,BOWS2, DID, NRCS	Performance is acceptable while JPEG qualities as low as 30; The method can identify median filtering in small image block
[15] 2016	MF, GF, AF, Scaling	MFRD(48)	SVM	6690 images From UCID, BR, BOWS2, DID, NRCS	The proposed detector performs better than SPAM, MFF, GLF, AR methods, especially in the detection of median filtering under heavy JPEG compression

(continued)

Table 1. (*continued*)

Paper, Year	Type of forgery	Features (dimension)	Classifier	Dataset	Performance and limitations
[16] 2013	MF, GF, AF	VF(18)	SVM	BOWS2	The method can predict parameters of MF, GF and AF filters

3 Smooth Filtering Detection Method Based on Deep Learning

3.1 Introduction to Convolutional Neural Networks

Deep learning is an emerging direction in the field of machine learning. By simulating the human brain to automatically learn the abstract features of each level of data, it is more convenient and realistic to extract the essential features of data [17]. Since 2006, Hinton [18] proposed a multi-layer Restricted Boltzmann Machine (RBM) based on probability map model. Deep learning has become a leading tool in image processing and computer vision. In particular, Convolutional Neural Network (CNN) [19], Deep Belief Network (DBN) [20], Stacked Auto-Encoder (SAE) [21], long and short time memory deep models such as Long-Short Term Memory (LSTM) [22] and Generative Adversarial Network (GAN) [23] have produced a large number of breakthroughs in various fields [24]. Among them, CNN directly processes 2D images through weight sharing and convolution operations, which avoids the complex feature extraction and data reconstruction process in traditional pattern recognition algorithms, which is deeply concerned by researchers. Especially with the generation of large-scale image data and the rapid development of computer hardware performance, convolutional neural network and its improved method have achieved breakthrough results in image segmentation, image recognition and image classification. In the field of digital image smoothing and filtering forensics, CNN has gradually replaced SVM and become the mainstream feature extraction and classification tools.

3.2 Smooth Filtering Detection Based on Deep Learning

Chen et al. [25] proposed the CNN-based median filtering forensics method for the first time, and designed a network structure consisting of one preprocessing layer, five convolutional layers and three fully connected layers. The pre-processing layer filters the input image median value and calculates the difference (MFR) from the original image as the input of the subsequent convolution layer, the principle is that MFR can suppress the original content pair classification such as image edge and texture. The effect, and the MFR of the image after filtering, is significantly reduced relative to the MFR of the untampered image. The network selects the ReLU activation function and the maximum pooling operation after the convolutional layer, and sets the dropout mechanism at the full connection layer to prevent the network from overfitting. Training and testing by image set extracted in BOSSbase 1.01 [26], UCID [27], BOSS RAW [28], DID [29] and NRCS [30], the detection rate of this method (defined as MFR method) is significantly improved compared with AR, MFF and GLF algorithms, but it is only suitable for detection of MF tampering.

In order to realize the preprocessing of training and test images, and extract the weak residual information left after image tampering, Bayar et al. [31] designed a new convolution structure with constraints on the first layer of traditional CNN, adding constraints on the convolution kernel property, as shown in

$$\begin{cases} w_k^{(1)}(0, 0) = -1 \\ \sum_{l,m \neq 0} w_k^{(1)}(l, m) = 1 \end{cases} \tag{1}$$

Where w is the new convolution kernel and $w(0,0)$ is the value of the center of the convolution kernel. The convolutional layer constrained by this constraint can learn the pixel and the relationship features around the pixel, not just the image content itself. By using the network structure established by the constrained convolution layer and the following two convolution layers, two maximum pooling layers and three full connection layers, we can realize the classification and forensics of four tampering modes, such as median filter, Gaussian blurring, additive white Gaussian noise and resampling. This shows that the constrained convolutional network structure can suppress the influence of image content and capture the operating characteristics, and realize the automatic learning of image pre-processing convolution kernel. In 2017, the team transformed the image tampering manipulation parameter estimation problem into a classification problem [32], and divided the parameter spaces of the four tampering methods, such as resizing, JPEG compression, median filtering, and Gaussian blurring, into disjoint subsets. Each subset of parameters is assigned to a different class. The scaling factor, the JPEG compression factor, the median filter kernel size, the Gaussian blur kernel size, and the fuzzy parameters are separately estimated based on a constrained convolution network similar to the literature [31].

Some scholars have not preprocessed the image, but use a more complex network structure and training method than the literature [31, 32] for detection. In 2018, Boroumand et al. [40] considered four basic image processing-low-pass filtering, high-pass filtering (sharpening), denoising and tone adjustment (including contrast and gamma adjustment), designed to accommodate resolution changes and JPEG compressed image manipulation detection method. This method increases the network depth, width (increased number of convolution kernels), and the amount of training data than the above studies. The network structure uses 8 convolutional layers and 3 fully connected layers. Considering that the average pooling operation will eliminate valuable noise, no pooling operation is used after the first two layers, and the average pooling operation is used after each of the last six convolution layers. The network training adopts the method of training the small image and the image of any size in stages and parts to ensure that the network can adapt to the detection of the size change of the detected image. One of the highlights is that the detection accuracy of the MF operation without the training set can also be more than 94%.

In order to achieve more tamper-type detection including smooth filtering, in 2019, Wu et al. [33] defined compression, blurring, morphology, contrast manipulation, additive noise, resampling and quantization as level0, and then these types of tampering are subdivided, such as subdividing blurring into Gaussian blur, box blurring, median blur, etc., increasing in turn, up to a total of 385 tamper types at level 5, including even in painting based on deep learning. The network structure of the design is divided into two sub-networks. The first sub-network mainly adopts the VGG network structure, which is responsible for tampering the trace feature extraction. In the first layer of image preprocessing, not only the tape proposed in the literature [2] is utilized, but also the SRM (spatial rich models) [34], which performs well in the field of steganalysis, is introduced. A total of 16 convolution kernels were designed for image preprocessing. The detection accuracy of the sub-network for 25 types of tampering operations in the level 1 can reach more than 85%, but even with a deeper and wider network structure, the recognition rate of 385 tamper types can only reach 51.8%. The second sub-network is responsible for locating the tampered area. The innovation is to use the tampering location problem as a local anomaly detection problem. The tamper-resistant regional features are taken as the main features, and the local features that differ from the main features are mapped to a specific tampering type. It can be seen from the research that in the image detection based on image space domain, by adding more types of filtering kernels to preprocess the image, it is possible to learn richer tampering features, and can realize the detection and analysis of more tampering modes including median filtering and Gaussian filtering.

Since the filtering operation is equivalent to removing certain frequency components in the frequency domain, the variation of the image in the frequency domain can also reflect the corresponding filtering operation. For example, in [35], a conversion layer is added before CNN, and the original image is converted into a frequency domain image by discrete Fourier transform and logarithmic transformation, and then input to the convolutional layer of CNN, and the image frequency is filtered by CNN. The possibility of domain feature learning realizes the detection of mean filtering, Gaussian filtering and median filtering under different parameter settings. The detection accuracy of low resolution image and JPEG compressed image is higher than that of MFF, AR, MFR and AAP mentioned in [35]. In [36], the CNN-based filtering image frequency domain feature learning method is also designed for the above three common filtering operations. The main difference is that the conversion layer adopts the filtering residual in frequency (FRF) of the input image block, and improves the recognition of the network model for the primary and secondary filtering operations based on the frequency domain features of the image.

In addition to traditional CNN, some scholars have customized the CNN, or introduced a new deep learning model (GAN) into the smoothing filter detection. In view of the weak nonlinear learning ability of traditional CNN networks, Tang et al. [37] introduced the multi-layer perceptron layer (mlpconv) contained in the NIN network [41] into the convolutional layer of the CNN network in 2018, and used MLP's nonlinear learning ability to learn the nonlinear characteristics of median filtering operation. Compared with the literature [25], the method solves the problem of median filtering detection of low resolution images and low quality compression factor JPEG images better. Higher detection accuracy can also be obtained without increasing the filter residual calculation. The study also performs the nearest neighbor interpolation and amplification on the original image, which expands the difference between the traced traces of the median filter between the falsified image and its original version, which is beneficial to improve the detection performance. In 2019, Shan et al. [38] further analyzed the influence of the block effect generated by JPEG compression on the median filtering feature, deblocking the JPEG image by the maximum a posteriori (MAP) framework to eliminate the block effect, and using the image deblocking method effectively suppressing the interference of JPEG compression, and then deblocking the image into the fused filtered residual (FFR) layer composed of MFR, average filtered residual (AFR), and Gaussian filtered residual (GFR) for the second step of preprocessing. The difference is blended to highlight the fingerprint left by the MF. Finally, the output of the FFR layer becomes the subsequent network input to further classify multiple features using a tailored parallel two-way CNN. Its detection performance is superior to the MFF, AR and MFR methods. In 2018, Jin et al. [39] applied the GAN to the median filter detection of low-resolution image and JPEG image for the first time. It does not analyze grayscale images like the above research methods, but directly to RGB images. The dark channel residual (DCR) set 3×3, 5×5, 7×7 three kinds of filter kernel analysis and detection, not only make full use of the rich information contained in the color image, but also improve the indicators of AUC, recall and F1 detection. Moreover, it is possible to directly perform detection and analysis on color images widely used in a real environment.

3.3 Summary of Deep Learning Smoothing Filter Detection Methods

Digital image smoothing detection is a category of pattern recognition. The successful application of deep learning in the field of pattern recognition has also led to the development of smooth filtering detection technology. Since 2015, a series of achievements including CNN, GAN, NIN, LSTM and other deep learning technologies have emerged. The main innovations of these studies are: 1) design or introduce MFR, SRM and other filters to achieve effective calculation of residual signals; 2) comprehensively use a variety of filters to extract features from the detected images, and use new network structure guarantees the diversity of the residual signal; 3) reduces the residual signal loss by reducing the pooling operation (such as canceling the pooling layer at the network front) or using the average pooling instead of the maximum pooling in the network training process. Compared with the traditional detection method, the training data is expanded in various ways, the feature learning is more autonomous, and the various detection performances are significantly improved, which also shows the great potential of deep learning technology in the field of digital image blind forensics.

4   Conclusion and Outlook

Based on the various traces left in the digital image by the tampering operation, the forensic personnel can discover digital image tampering without prior knowledge. Among various image blind evidence methods, image smoothing detection technology based on machine learning plays an important role. From the technical point of view, the image smoothing filter detection can be summarized as a two-category problem. The key is to extract the features of extracting specific tamper traces through machine learning. The difficulty and challenge lies in how to extract all kinds of features from the weak traces left by tamper operation, which take into account the distinguishing ability and generalization ability. At present, there is no perfect solution.

With the advent of the artificial intelligence era, deep learning technology has brought effective solutions for a series of digital image forensics problems such as smooth filtering detection. However, to date, deep learning based methods have not exhibited superior performance in the image recognition field. The main reasons are as follows: 1) Most of the current network structures adopt the network structure framework of image recognition. The detection method is susceptible to interference from image content, which is not conducive to extracting weak tampering operation features such as smooth filtering, and cannot guarantee end-to-end learning. Feature learning still requires some manual intervention; 2) Compared with image recognition mature datasets such as ImageNet, image tampering deep learning training sample sets are not enough to train more complex network structures, and the existing training data are mostly generated based on the simplified tampering mode, lacking the data set close to the real tampering scene. With the advent of image forgery based on deep learning [44], the detection of image tampering becomes more and more difficult. Although deep learning technology has broad prospects in the field of forensics, it still needs to carry out in-depth research in combination with new technologies and new theories, in order to solve the problems of end-to-end learning and feature learning as soon as possible.

Acknowledgment. This material is based upon work supported by Program for Young Innovative Research Team and Big Data and Artificial Intelligence Legal Research Collaborative Innovation Center in Shandong University of Political Science and Law; Key Laboratory of Evidence-Identifying in Universities of Shandong (SDUPSL); Projects of Shandong Province Higher Educational Science and Technology Program under Grant No. J16LN19, J18KA357, J18KA383.

References

1. Zhang, J., Li, Y., Niu, S., Cao, Z., Wang, X.: Improved fully convolutional network for digital image region forgery detection. Comput. Mater. Continua **60**(1), 287–303 (2019)
2. Gao, S., Xu, G., Hu, R.-M.: Camera model identification based on the characteristic of CFA and interpolation. In: Shi, Y.Q., Kim, H.-J., Perez-Gonzalez, F. (eds.) IWDW 2011. LNCS, vol. 7128, pp. 268–280. Springer, Heidelberg (2012). https://doi.org/10.1007/978-3-642-32205-1_22
3. Ye, S., Sun, Q., Chang, E.C.: Detecting digital image forgeries by measuring inconsistencies of blocking artifact. In: Proceedings of 2007 IEEE International Conference on Multimedia and Expo, Beijing, China (2007)
4. Bianchi, T., Piva, A.: Detection of nonaligned double JPEG compression based on integer periodicity maps. IEEE Trans. Inf. Forensics Secur. **7**(2), 842–848 (2012)
5. Bappy, J.H., Mohammed, T.M., et al.: Detection and localization of image forgeries using resampling features and deep learning. In: CVPRW, pp. 1181–1189 (2017)
6. Kirchner, M., Bohme, R.: Hiding traces of resampling in digital images. IEEE Trans. Inf. Forensics Secur. **3**(4), 582–592 (2008)
7. Stamm, M.C., Liu, K.J.R.: Anti-forensics of digital image compression. IEEE Trans. Inf. Forensics Secur. **6**(3), 1050–1065 (2011)
8. Bovik, A.C.: Streaking in median filtered images. IEEE Trans. Acoust. Speech Signal Process. **35**(4), 493–503 (1987)

9. Kirchner, M., Fridrich, J.: On detection of median filtering in digital images. In: Proceedings of SPIE-Electronic Imaging 2010: Media Forensics and Security II, San Jose, CA, USA, 17–21 January 2010. International Society for Optics and Photonics, Bellingham, 7541101–7541112 (2010)

10. Pevny, T., Bas, P., Fridrich, J.: Steganalysis by subtractive pixel adjacency matrix. IEEE Trans. Inf. Forensics Secur. 5(2), 215–224 (2010)

11. Cao, G., Zhao, Y., Ni, R., Yu, L., Tian, H.: Forensic detection of median filtering in digital images. In: Proceedings of 2010 IEEE International Conference on Multimedia and Expo, Singapore, Singapore, 19–23 July 2010, pp. 89–94. IEEE, Piscataway (2010)

12. Yuan, H.: Blind forensics of median filtering in digital images. IEEE Trans. Inf. Forensics Secur. 6(4), 1335–1345 (2011)

13. Chen, C., Ni, J., Huang, R., Huang, J.: Blind median filtering detection using statistics in difference domain. In: Proceedings of Information Hiding, Berkeley, CA, USA, May 2012

14. Kang, X., Stamm, M.C., Peng, A., Ray Liu, K.J.: Robust median filtering forensics using an autoregressive model. IEEE Trans. Inf. Forensics Secur. 8(9), 1456–1468 (2013)

15. Peng, A.J., Kang, X.G.: Median filtering forensics based on multi-directional difference of filtering residuals. Chin. J. Comput. 39(3), 503–515 (2016)

16. Xu, F.-Y., Su, Y.-T.: Smoothing filtering detection for digital image forensics. J. Electron. Inf. Technol. 35(10), 2287–2293 (2013)

17. Schmidhuber, J.: Deep learning in neural networks: an overview. Neural Netw. 61, 85–117 (2015)

18. Salakhutdinov, R., Mnih, A., Hinton, G.: Restricted Boltzmann machines for collaborative filtering. In: Proceedings of the 24th International Conference on Machine learning, pp. 791–798. ACM (2007)

19. Sahiner, B., Chan, H.P., Petrick, N., et al.: Classification of mass and normal breast tissue: a convolution neural network classifier with spatial domain and texture images. IEEE Trans. Med. Imaging 15(5), 598–610 (1996)

20. Hinton, G.E., Salakhutdinov, R.R.: Reducing the dimensionality of data with neural networks. Science 313(5786), 504–507 (2006)

21. Poultney, C., Chopra, S., Cun, Y.L.: Efficient learning of sparse representations with an energy-based model. In: Advances in Neural Information Processing Systems, pp. 1137–1144 (2007)

22. Hochreiter, S., Schmidhuber, J.: Long short-term memory. Neural Comput. 9(8), 1735–1780 (1997)

23. Fang, W., Zhang, F., Sheng, V.S., Ding, Y.: A method for improving CNN-based image recognition using DCGAN. Comput. Mater. Continua 57(1), 167–178 (2018)

24. Oquab, M., Bottou, L., Laptev, I., et al.: Learning and transferring mid-level image representations using convolutional neural networks. In: Proceedings of the IEEE Conference on Computer Vision and Pattern Recognition, 1717–1724 (2014)

25. Chen, J., Kang, X., Liu, Y., Wang, Z.J.: Median filtering forensics based on convolutional neural networks. IEEE Signal Process. Lett. 22(11), 1849–1853 (2015)

26. Bas, P., Filler, T., Pevny, T.: Break our steganographic system: the ins and outs of organizing BOSS. In: International Conference on Information Hiding, pp. 59–70 (2011)

27. Schaefer, G., Stich, M.: UCID - an uncompressed colour image database. In: Proceedings of SPIE, Storage and Retrieval Methods and Applications for Multimedia, San Jose (2004)

28. http://boss.gipsa-lab.grenoble-inp.fr/BOSSRank/index.php?mode=VIEW&tmpl=materials

29. Gloe, T., Böhme, R.: Dresden image database (DID), the 'Dresden image database' for benchmarking digital image forensics. In: Proceedings of ACM Symposium Applied Computing, March 2010, vol. 2, pp. 1584–1590 (2010)

30. NRCS United States Department of Agriculture, Natural Resources Conservation Service Photo Gallery (2002). http://photogallery.nrcs.usda.gov

31. Bayar, B., Stamm, M.C.: A deep learning approach to universal image manipulation detection using a new convolutional layer. In: ACM Workshop on Information Hiding and Multimedia Security, pp. 5–10 (2016)

32. Bayar, B., Stamm, M.C.: A generic approach towards image manipulation parameter estimation using convolutional neural networks. In: The 5th ACM Workshop, pp. 147–157. ACM (2017)

33. Wu, Y., AbdAlmageed, W., Natarajan, P.: ManTra-Net: manipulation tracing network for detection and localization of image forgeries with anomalous features. In: CVPR, pp. 9543–9552 (2019)

34. Fridrich, J., Kodovsky, J.: Rich models for steganalysis of digital images. IEEE Trans. Inf. Forensics Secur. **7**(3), 868–882 (2012)

35. Liu, A., Zhao, Z., Zhang, C., Su, Y.: Smooth filtering identification based on convolutional neural networks. Multimedia Tools Appl. **78**(19), 26851–26865 (2016). https://doi.org/10.1007/s11042-016-4251-z

36. Yang, B., Zhang, T., Chen, X.-Y.: Local blur detection of digital images based on deep learning. J. Appl. Sci. Electron. Inf. Eng. **36**(2), 321–330 (2018)

37. Tang, H., Ni, R., Zhao, Y., Li, X.: Median filtering detection of small size image based on CNN. J. Vis. Commun. Image Represent. **51**, 162–168 (2018)

38. Shan, W., Yi, Y., Qiu, J., Yin, A., et al.: Robust median filtering forensics using image deblocking and filtered residual fusion. IEEE Access **7**, 17174–17183 (2019)

39. Jin, X., Jing, P., Su, Y.: AMFNet: an adversarial network for median filtering detection. IEEE Access **6**, 50459–50567 (2018)

40. Boroumand, M., Fridrich, J.: Deep learning for detecting processing history of images media. Watermarking Secur. Forensics. **9**, 213-1–213-9 (2018)

41. Lin, M., Chen, Q., Yan, S.: Network in network. In: Proceedings of ICLR (2014)

42. IEEE's signal processing society-camera model identification (2018). https://www.kaggle.com/c/sp-society-camera-model-identification

43. Bas, P., Furon, T.: Break our watermarking system. http://bows2.ec-lille.fr/2nd

44. Li, C., Jiang, Y., Cheslyar, M.: Embedding image through generated intermediate medium using deep convolutional generative adversarial network. Comput. Mater. Continua **56**(2), 313–324 (2018)

Research on Video Violence Detection Technology of UAV on Cloud Platform

Chen Zhi[1,2(✉)] and Weidong Bao[1]

[1] College of Systems Engineering, National University of Defense Technology,
Changsha 410073, China
672016260@qq.com, milanchenko@126.com, 25429688@qq.com
[2] Hu Nan Vocasional Institute of Science and Technology, Changsha 410018, China

Abstract. Violence is the main cause of crime, affecting people's security and social stability directly. Video surveillance, as an important means of security, plays an increasingly important role in the fight against crime. The traditional video monitoring system records and stores the video only, and the monitoring range is affected by the location, and it can only rely on human analysis to monitor the video information and find the criminals after the violence. UAV (Unmanned Aerial Vehicle) is regarded as a camera that can move freely. UAV cameras are used to monitor public places, shoot videos and send them to the cloud platform to detect the violence in the videos, which can discover the violence in public places in time and give early warning to prevent criminal incidents.

Keywords: Detection technology · Violence · OpenStack

1 Introduction

With the rapid development of human society, the events occurring in today's society have become more and more complicated, and there are more and more sudden abnormal events that may occur. In August 2019, the shooting incident in Dayton, United States, a man was shot in the Oregon area of Dayton until the man was killed by the police, killing 10 people, also in August 2019, In Hong Kong, China, violent incidents happened: strikes, obstruction of traffic, burning of police stations, disrupting public security and other serious violent incidents have caused serious adverse effects on the regional economy and society. In order to cope with various emergencies, local governments and all walks of life in China have invested heavily in building a safe city. China has built the world's largest video surveillance network. Video surveillance cameras have spread all over the city to achieve security control. But there are still dead spots. With the development of UAV and 5g technology, UAV cruise is used to monitor the security status of public areas, and the cruise video can be transmitted to the cloud

The original version of this chapter was revised: The name of one of the authors has been changed to Chen Zhi. The correction to this chapter is available at
https://doi.org/10.1007/978-981-15-8083-3_63

platform in real time. However, most of the video surveillance now only plays the role of real-time preview and storage of surveillance video. The current video surveillance still were used by manual viewing to conduct video review. This way will inevitably lead to the omission and negligence of important information. It not only makes the sudden anomalies that endanger the public safety of the city, such as terrorist incidents and gathering stampede events, cannot be discovered and controlled in time, but also causes a certain waste of human and financial resources. In addition, in the process of criminal investigation, police officers have to spend a lot of time to check the data in the massive video recorded by a large number of cameras. It is impossible for video surveillance and video information retrieval only through manpower. . Therefore, how to intelligently identify individual emergencies such as violent behaviors from monitoring video massive data and timely issue early warning information has become an increasingly acute scientific problem in the field of video surveillance. In view of the above problems, studying the violence in the video under the cloud platform can effectively make up for the shortcomings of current security monitoring.

2 Materials and Methods

With the maturity of cloud computing technology, it provides scientific solutions and ideas for the construction of video surveillance information. By using the cloud computing solution, the problems of video storage and sharing, video intelligent analysis and the like can be better solved. With its high-capacity storage, high computing performance, and convenient centralized management, the cloud computing platform has become an efficient platform for massive surveillance video processing. Human behavior video detection processing system based on the cloud platform, and use a distributed method to identify video faces and video behavior by using effective algorithms in different cloud hosts, which can not only satisfy the storage of massive video data but also process video frames with high efficiency. Face and behavior, especially as violence action detection, feature extraction and recognition in massive video, the monitoring system "automatically" determines the specific person information in the video, and gradually realizes the transition from "human eye judgment" to "smart recognition". Therefore, the automatic recognition of video face and behavior based on cloud platform can better realize the intelligent urban management and the more precise social management. Design a cloud-based video capture and human behavior recognition processing system, and use a distributed method to identify violent scenes in video using effective algorithms in different cloud hosts, not only to satisfy the storage of massive video data but also to efficiently video. The frame is processed to complete the feature extraction, detection and recognition of the violent scene in the massive video, and the monitoring system "automatically" determines the specific human information in the video, and gradually realizes the transition from "human eye judgment" to "smart recognition".

2.1 Designation of Video Surveillance Platform on OpenStack

OpenStack is a free software and open source project licensed and developed by NASA and Rackspace under the Apache license [1]. OpenStack covers all aspects of networking, virtualization, operating systems, servers, and more. Its purpose is to manage and automate computer resources for broader use of virtualization technologies, as well as configuration work for bare metal and high-performance computing. OpenStack is used to construct a cloud platform with a certain scale, and a certain number of cloud hosts are released on the cloud platform. The video capture and violence identification program is deployed on the cloud host to call the webcam to obtain the face video stream and extract key frames. The webcam collects Monitor the data and store it on the cloud disk, test whether the human violence detection program can call the camera normally and collect the video data stream, analyze whether the deployed experimental environment can effectively collect and store the monitoring data captured by the camera.

In this paper, an intelligent monitoring system based on OpenStack cloud platform is designed. Firstly, OpenStack service is installed on CentOS Linux operating system to build Iaas cloud platform. Using virtualization technology, Ubuntu Linux image is made into qcow2 format and published as a virtual machine. IP on the virtual machine is connected with the IP of the monitoring webcam. The virtual machine can connect the monitoring camera in the public area through the wired network The image head can also obtain video data through wireless networks such as WiFi, 5G and other on-board cameras connected to the UAV; secondly, video behavior recognition program is deployed on the virtual machine, and in-depth learning algorithm is used to detect and identify the characters in the video. Once the detection program detects the violence in the video characters, it will send an alarm signal to the police officers and the police officers The UAV controller can send a remote call to the video shooting site or inform the nearby police to take countermeasures. The monitoring platform is shown in Fig. 1.

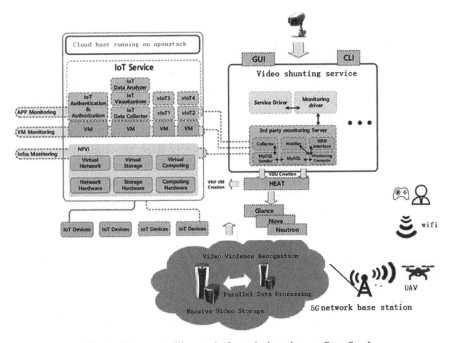

Fig. 1. Video surveillance platform designation on OpenStack

Intelligent video surveillance system based on OpenStack platform needs to be deployed on the OpenStack cluster, release cloud hosts through OpenStack platform, and then deploy intelligent surveillance programs to cloud hosts. The monitoring data processing flow is as follows:

(1) OpenStack: Open source cloud computing project, deployed on physical clusters, docking multiple virtualization technologies at the lower level.
(2) Ceilometer: It is a sub project of OpenStack. Monitoring can obtain monitoring information of CPU, network, disk, etc. by deploying compute service in the computing node, polling the instance on the computing node, and sending it to collector service is responsible for receiving information for persistent storage. The collected data is provided for monitoring, billing, panel and other projects.
(3) Esper: CEP (complex event process) analysis and processing engine, real-time analysis of data flow, storage is the analysis rules.
(4) Pycharm; OpenStack is written in python. Pycharm is the development environment of Python language. Because of the huge amount of code in OpenStack project, it is convenient to use the development environment recommended by the government for source code analysis and secondary development of Ceilometer plug-ins.

2.2   Violence Behavior Recognition Method in Video

In this work, we will regard aggressive human behavior as violence, which often contains a large number of human movement characteristics. Human motion recognition in video is an important branch in the field of computer vision and pattern recognition. Human Motion Recognition in Video, Especially Violence Recognition has broad application prospects in many fields such as intelligent video surveillance, human-computer interaction, motion analysis, video retrieval, etc., and has attracted extensive attention from scholars at home and abroad. With the generation of massive visual data such as images and videos, it poses a daunting challenge for how to deal with these massive video data. Taking video surveillance systems widely used in airports, plazas, and traffic intersections as an example, manual monitoring is used to heck whether surveillance videos in the past period contain abnormal events. Usually, a monitor can only record limited video images, and cannot accurately and timely detect abnormal events. In practical applications, video surveillance systems usually install a large number of cameras to generate massive amounts of video data. Take a living community as an example. The number of cameras is usually in the dozens or even hundreds. For a city, the number of cameras installed will be more. Take a high-definition camera as an example, it can generate as much as 40 GB of massive video data in one day. Therefore, there is an urgent need for computer simulation of human brain to analyze and process massive video, freeing humans from heavy and impossible visual information processing and analysis, and automatically and effectively managing these huge amounts of video data. The basic task of human behavior recognition is to use the computer to automatically judge the human behavior in the input video. These human behaviors include simple actions such as walking, running, jumping, waving, clapping, and the interaction between people and things such as kicking, answering the phone, getting on the bus, and even groups between people and people. behavior. The human body model representation is modeled by the postures exhibited by various parts of the human body (such as the head, limbs, torso, etc.) [2]. The construction of the human body model is based on the fact that the human body is composed of multiple limbs, and each limb is connected by joints. In 1973, psychologist Johansson revealed the mechanism of motion perception in the human brain in the MLD (moving light display) experiment. Johansson's MLD experiments and subsequent studies [3] show changes in posture and spatial position of the body during exercise, such as the movement of human joints in space, and temporal changes in joint angles and other information can be used to describe and distinguish different human movements. This provides theoretical support for the use of human body models for human motion representation. After effectively displaying the observation frame or the observation sequence in the human motion video, the human motion recognition problem converts the adult body motion classification problem. At present, human motion classification algorithms generally include three methods: template matching method, space-time state method, and direct classification method [4]. Template matching is to compare the sample to be processed with the template in the static template library to find the optimal matching result as the classification result. Skyspace features such as silhouette, gradient, and optical flow, and time domain features such as motion trajectory can be used for template matching. The similarity between templates is generally measured by the Euclidean distance or the Mahalanobis distance between the feature vectors.

2.2.1 Space-Time State Method

When the human body conducts aggressive actions (such as boxing and kicking), the actions are a process of time and space changes, and can look at a sequence of changes in human posture at different times. The graph model is a very effective sequence change modeling tool. Its main elements include states and edges, where the state corresponds to a node in the graph model, and the edge represents the transition probability between the state (node) and the state (node). By entering observations, it can be predicted and judged the category of a change sequence. The human body hole classification method based on the spatiotemporal state method is to model and classify human body motion based on the graph model. It takes the static pose of the human body in the video as a state (node) in the graph model, then the edge in the graph model represents the probability of the human body's posture change.

2.2.2 Direct Classification

The basic feature of the direct classification method is that all the human motion information in the observation sequence is described as a whole by a certain method, that is, the video representation vector, and then the video representation vector is classified by the classifier, and the obtained video classification result is the human motion recognition result. The most representative is the human motion recognition method based on the BoF model [5]. Because of this method, the time series of the observation sequence is not considered, and the dynamic sequence does not need to be modeled, and the template matching method and the space-time state method are more flexible and easy to use. In summary, the main method of human motion recognition is to extract human motion related features from human motion video, represent human motion based on these features, and then use pattern recognition methods to classify human motion.

2.3 Human Behavior Video Database

Human behavior video database plays an important role in judging the merits of human behavior recognition algorithm. In the research and development process of human behavior recognition, some researchers put forward different databases according to different purposes, which are mainly divided into the following databases:

1) UCF101
   Content:
   1) a total of 13320 video 101 categories, real scenes collected from YouTube.
   2) it can be divided into five categories: human and object interaction, baby action, human interaction, musical instrument performance and movement.
   3) specification: 320 × 240, 25FPS, the minimum video is 28 frames.

(2) HMDB51
   Content:
   1) there are totally 51 categories and 6849 videos. Each category contains at least 101 videos.
   2) collect from movie and video websites.
   3) it includes five categories: facial movements (smile, laugh, chew, speak); facial and object interaction (eating, drinking, smoking); body movement (somersault, clapping, climbing, etc.); body and object interaction (combing hair, drawing sword, etc.); everyone interaction (fencing, hugging, kissing, etc.)

3) MSR action 3D (based on skeleton information)
   Content:
   There are 20 action types and 10 categories. Each category performs each action 2 or 3 times. There are 567 depth map sequences. The resolution is 640 × 240. Use a depth sensor similar to Kinect device to record data.

2.4 Detection of Violent Behavior

Violent behavior is generally accompanied by the rapid movement and large amplitude of the human trunk. Bermejo et al. [8] use STIP to deal with violence force behavior is classified. Tai [9] and others calculate the flow of light, and then detection of violence. Martin et al. [10] use multiscale local biphasic modes Violence detection using histogram. Wang [11] uses trajectory-based analysis Violence identification method. Therefore, the Shi-Tomasi corner detection is first performed to obtain the properties of the feature points suitable for tracking, and then the Lucas-Kanade optical flow calculation method is used for detection. Violent frames are generated when more than 10 squares of optical flow exceed a certain threshold. In order to eliminate the noise caused by misdetection and the like, a first-order integrator with clipping is used to filter the violent frame response output, and when the system filter value reaches a certain threshold, it is considered that violent behavior occurs. Common violence in public places is passenger violence. Passenger violence is one of the most common anomalies in elevator cars, including inter-passenger violence, such as fighting and looting of property, as well as violent acts that disrupt public facilities. For the detection of violent behavior, Ankur Datta et al. [12] first used the adaptive background difference method to obtain the foreground region in the video, and then used the statistical information of the foreground pixels to obtain the motion trajectory of the person and its parts, thinking that when the person's hand or foot lifted A violent frame appears when it is as high as parallel to the ground or a larger slope. Many scholars have introduced machine learning into the detection of violent behaviors; Fillipe et al. [13] extracted the local spatiotemporal features of BoVM representation, and used the support vector machine to conduct supervised learning to determine whether the video was violent; the literature [14] first video The sequence is detected by the corner point, then the Lucas-Kanade optical flow is calculated, and the angular kinetic energy is used as the basis of feature vector detection. Finally, the SVM classifier is established to identify the violent behavior. Qi Haiyan et al. [15] proceed from the kinematics of violent behavior. When the violent behavior occurs, the speed is faster, and the human body has greater kinetic energy. Therefore, the kinetic energy of human body can also reflect whether there is violence.

2.4.1 Shi-Tomasi Corner Detection

Image point of interest features are the most commonly used image local features. It detects localized regions of image content by detecting local saliency regions such as corners and spots in the image. The most commonly used feature detection algorithms include: Harris [16] corner detection, SIFT [17], FAST [18], SURF [19], and so on. Scholars such as Shi and Tomasi [15] also clearly pointed out that corner points are the best choice for local feature tracking. Corner Detection is a method used to obtain image features in computer vision systems. It is widely used in motion detection, image matching, video tracking, 3D modeling and target recognition. Also known as feature point detection. A corner point is usually defined as the intersection of two sides. More strictly speaking, the local neighborhood of a corner point should have a boundary of two different areas in different directions. In practical applications, most of the so-called corner detection methods detect image points with specific features, not just "corner points." These feature points have specific coordinates in the image and have certain mathematical features such as local maximum or minimum gray levels, certain gradient features, and the like. Jianbo Shi and Carlo Tomasi proposed a feature point suitable for tracking [20], which is called Shi-Tomasi corner point. In image tracking, no matter what tracking algorithm is used, not all parts of the image contain complete motion information. In order to solve this problem, the researchers propose to track only corners or windows that change dramatically in space. The Shi-Tomasi algorithm gives a criterion for judging whether a feature point in an image is suitable for tracking. The Shi and Tomasi [21] algorithm uses the minimum eigenvalue of the image block autocorrelation matrix as the corner feature metric to detect local features using tracking. The point of interest detection algorithm based on the image block autocorrelation matrix eigenvalues was first proposed in Harris corner detection. The basic idea is to use the first derivative of the image to estimate the local gradient autocorrelation matrix:

$$H = \sum_{x,y} g(x, y) \begin{bmatrix} I_x^2 & I_x I_x \\ I_x I_y & I_y^2 \end{bmatrix} \tag{1}$$

Where Ix Iy is the first derivative of the x, y direction, and g(x, y) is the window function, usually taking the 0 g(σ), mean Gaussian function, σ which is the scale parameter of the Gaussian function. The eigenvalues of the autocorrelation matrix H are obtained, and are respectively the curvatures of the local autocorrelation function. If the two eigenvalues are small, the change of the local autocorrelation in any direction is small, representing the flat area of the image; if the two eigenvalues are large or small, the local autocorrelation changes greatly in a certain direction, satisfying The characteristics of the edge represent the edge region of the image; if both values are large, the local autocorrelation varies greatly in all directions, representing the image corner point [22]. Shi and Tomasi use the minimum eigenvalue as the corner response function: If the response value R is greater than the threshold, there is a corner feature that is easy to track at that location. Usually set to:

$$T_r = \alpha \times \max_{ij \in I}(R_{ij}) \tag{2}$$

Among them, α is an empirical parameter less than 1, in this paper α take 0.01

2.4.2 Lucas-Kanade Optical Flow

The optical flow is the distribution of the velocity vector of the luminance mode motion in an image, which can be generated by the relative motion of the observer and the object. Therefore, the optical flow can give important information about the spatial variation of the observed object and its rate. The Lucas-Kanade algorithm can effectively track corner features. However, the Lucas-Kanade algorithm is prone to the problem of corner tracking loss, and it is easy to generate track fragments. For the video in the experiment, the length of the track segment is fixed to 10 frames. Tested on a desktop PC with an Intel(R) Xeon X3450 2.67 GHz and 8 GB RAM. All algorithms are implemented on the OpenCV 2.4.7 platform. Lucas-Kanade feature point tracking and dense optical flow are implemented by OpenCV functions. Lucas-Kanade local feature trajectory extraction algorithm. Due to the data set, the camera displacement is very large in the first two frames. Therefore, the feature search matching window could be increased to 51 $\times$ 51. It can be seen from the results that the method can effectively acquire the local feature motion trajectory.

2.5 Experiments

2.5.1 Video Violence Frame Detection

The information about the location is also present in the ViF algorithm proposed by Hassner et al. The network architecture is based on the architecture presented in the paper [24], In Fig. 2 we describe the architecture build upon four type of layers, the first is the input layer that receive a sequence of 10 frames that are a computed difference of two adjacent frames from the original video. The second type of layers belongs to a Resnet50 CNN network that aim to classify images, the initial weights of the layers are taken form a pre-trained model on image-net, the CNN process each frame separately and during training the weights of the network are shared. The third layer is the Convolution LSTM (ConvLSTM) where each frame from the CNN enters into a ConvLSTM cell

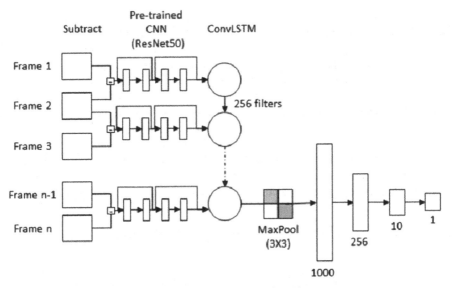

Fig. 2. Violence detection model architecture

with an hidden state of 256 convolution filters of size 3. The forth type of layers process the ConvLSTM and output the binary prediction, a Max polling layer of size 2 reduces the data and chooses the most informational pixels, then the data is batch normalized and connected to a series of fully connected layer of sizes 1000, 256, 10 and finally a binary output perception with a sigmoid activation function. Between each of the fully connected layers we use RELU activation. We use binary cross entropy as our loss function and RMSprop as an optimizer, 20% of the data is select for validation and rest 80% is selected to train. The learning rate of the network starts with value of 0.0001 and is reduced by half after 5 epochs of no improvement in the validation loss. We train the model with 50 epochs but also use early stopping in case where the network validation loss haven't improve for 15 epochs.

In actual monitoring scenarios, violent behavior may occur in any area. From a holistic perspective, statistics on different areas of a frame of images do not accurately predict violent and non-violent behavior. For a set of input frame sequences, the two consecutive frames are first grayed out, and then the frame difference calculation is performed to obtain different parts in the two frames of images. In the actual situation, slight jitter or illumination changes will be applied to the frame. The image after the difference causes a relatively large influence. In order to mitigate the influence of the noise, and also to obtain the motion agglomerate, it is binarized and the noise formed by the influence of jitter or illumination is mitigated by adjusting the appropriate threshold [23]. Under this basic assumption, this paper analyzes the characteristics of the motion information contained in the video to determine whether the current frame is a violent frame.

In this work we have made some changes from original architecture, We evaluate different CNN architectures instead of using only AlexNet. Furthermore, we use dynamic learning rate adjustments, reduced the sequence length and use one perceptron with sigmoid instead of two perceptron with softmax activation. We use the following procedure to determine the violence frame in the video: Firstly, initialize the parameters, read the video frame image and establish the Gaussian background image; secondly, segment the moving blocks through the difference between the current video frame and the background image frame; then detect the optical flow in each moving block and remove the optical flow vector whose optical flow amplitude is less than the preset threshold A1; then process the moving blocks in the continuous K frame image and count the amplitude of the optical flow vector of the moving block Finally, the violence alarm information is given by judging whether the sum value of the optical flow amplitude of the continuous k-frame image is greater than the preset threshold A2 and whether the optical flow angle distribution meets the uniform condition.

Table 1. Modification from the original paper

Parameter	Original paper	This project	Reason
CNN architecture	AlexNet	VGGNET	Improvement
Learning rate reducing	Fix	Dynamic	Improvement
Cross-entropy (loss)	Categorical	Binary	Improvement
Evaluation	K - Fold	Simple split	GPU
Batch size	16	2	GPU
Sequence length	20 or average	20 or 10	Both

We train the networks on a NVIDIA GTX1080Ti GPU, the original paper GPU was NVIDIA K40 GPU which is significantly stronger and allow them to train larger sequences with 16 samples per batch while we could use only fit 2 samples per batch with up to 20 frames per sequence. In Table 1 we summarize the modifications we made in our implementation, some of the changes are due to lack of GPU power, an algorithmic improvement we suggest or both. As suggested in the original paper we evaluated the different hyper-parameters of the network based on the "Hockey" dataset and then apply them for each dataset. We use only 20 epochs and early stopping of 5 instead of 15 as we apply in the final optimal network training. the original paper use 10 fold cross validation but because we are limited in training resources we used a simple split as follows: 80% for training and 20% for testing (where 20% of the training is used for validation). Our tunning starts with baseline hyper-parameters which most of them presented in the original paper. We evaluate each hyper parameter separately and choose the best value for the next evaluations. We determined the order of the hyper-parameters to execute in a descending order of importance as follows: CNN architecture type, Learning rate, sequence length, augmentation usage, dropout rate and CNN network training type (retrain or static).

2.5.2   Violent Behavior Alert

The violent incident generally lasts for a period of time. The output of the violent frame detection is considered as the input of the alarm system. The violent frame detection may have some false detections, which brings noise to the system. Therefore, a suitable filtering algorithm should be set to detect the violent frame. The time series is filtered to obtain a continuous, reliable alarm signal.

Among them, the detection of violent frame occupancy rate refers to the ratio of the number of violent frames to the total number of frames detected in a continuous violent incident. Since the alarm of the algorithm is based on violent frames, this indicator indicates The stability of the algorithm. The detection rate of violent incidents refers to the proportion of the number of algorithmic alarms to the total number of events for a violent incident as a whole. The violent incident false alarm rate refers to the ratio of the number of false detections to the total number of violent incidents for non-violent incidents. The video violence detection method used in this paper can effectively analyze the occurrence of violence from the video based on the "hockey" dataset, and the specific effect is shown in Fig. 3. The method is robust to some extent, and has strong pertinence and low false alarm rate for multi-person violence in public places.

Original video frame in hockey dataset   This method detects the effect of violence in video

Fig. 3. The effect of violence detection in hockey video in this paper

3   Results Analysis

In this paper, vggnet and flow netare are used to initialize network parameters in space flow and time flow respectively by using flow net pre training model and fine tune the network by using the target task database. The target task network model is composed of RGB image for spatial interference CNN, while vggnet model is composed of IM RGB image training in the agenet database. In order to improve the efficiency of network operation, we initialize the time flow model of ucf101 database. In addition, we need to reduce the scale of the model to train the initial learning rate according to the number of iterations of training In order to increase the number of iterations, this paper modifies vggnet in two aspects: first, the value of num_out put of the original vggnet network is adjusted from the original 64, 128, 256, 512, 1024, 2048, 4096 to 32, 64, 128, 256, 512, 1024, 2048, which reduces the width of the network; second, to some network layers in CNN, we remove the net.conv3-2 of the convolutional network of the third layer, layer net.conv4-2 of convolution network in the fourth layer and layer net.conv5-2 of convolution network in the fifth layer, and the FC layer is removed to reduce the network scale of vggnet. When testing different data sets, different test methods are used due to different data sets. First, for the Hockey data set, the test methods of other algorithms in the world generally use 10-fold cross-validation. Therefore, a 10-fold cross-validation is used when testing 9 pairs of parameters for the Hockey data set. We used different verification methods for each data set. The Hockey data set uses 10-fold cross-validation. Among them, 900 videos are training sets, and the remaining 100 videos are test sets. 900 videos. It contains 450 positive samples and 450 negative samples. There are 50 positive samples and 50 negative samples in the 100 test set.

The optimized model classifying the "Violent-Flow" dataset has reached the lowest score out of all the 3 datasets settling at 86% accuracy. the original paper has reached 94% accuracy and was the most difficult dataset to classify for the original paper model out of all the 3 datasets, reviewing the videos and the misclassification outputs this dataset contains high variance of video's length with the highest average length of 90 frames per video and shortest length videos, with the lowest resolution camera. Furthermore, the videos contain large crowd where even in the "violent" videos most of the crowd is a spectator and doesn't intervene in the violent act. one suggestion brought up is to split the videos into smaller chunks and to agree on a bagging method to produce the final classification. Because the Violent Flow dataset is first and foremost varied, various backgrounds, various scales, and its video has both grayscale and color maps, video capture is not clear, etc. The requirement, in addition, the data set collects a small number of videos, only 246 videos, which will affect the training of the classifier. It is very likely that the classifier will not reach the optimal state because the training video is too small. Test. The lowest accuracy is obtained at h = 0.2 and K = 9, which is 86.80 ± 0.57%. The highest accuracy is obtained at h = 0.15, K = 8. It is 90.02 ± 2.12%. The difference between the highest value and the lowest value is only 3.22%. And when the segmentation threshold h is fixed, the number of clusters K changes or K is fixed, and the change of h has little effect on the accuracy of the algorithm. Therefore, it can also be proved that the accuracy rate of the minority situation in the monitoring scenario has found the optimal parameter pair in the parameter adjustment, and the rest of the impact on the accuracy rate is on the extraction and processing of the feature. The date of algorithm accuracy as shown in Table 2:

Table 2. Algorithm accuracy

Algorithm	Accuracy ± standard deviation
MoSIFT + HIK [2]	90.90%
ViF [15]	82.9 ± 0.14%
STIP	HOG + HIK [2] 91.70% Proposed method 92.23 ± 0.96%

4   Discussion

In this work we implemented deep learning model to predict violence in video data, We found our implementation to deal well with this task. The potential of deep learning models is high and can be used easily by law enforcements officers to identifying violence in the streets. To eliminate noise caused by false detections, etc., a first-order integrator with clipping is used to filter the violent frame response output. When the system filter value reaches a certain threshold, a violent event is considered. At the same time, this paper provides a reference algorithm for the reasonable selection of various parameters. This paper proposes a brute force recognition algorithm with high recognition rate in multiple cases. The algorithm proposes a new feature. The new feature extracts the properties of the moving mass and the optical flow histogram as features, and also adds time information to the new feature to reduce the false alarm rate and false positive rate. Testing on the public datasets Hockey and Violent Flow has yielded significant results. At the same time, the violent behavior monitoring video data set in the self-made monitoring scene has also achieved significant results, indicating that the proposed algorithm has good detection results in the violent behavior under the monitoring scene. This shows that the proposed algorithm has quite good versatility, whether it is a minority in a sports background, a crowd situation, or a minority or crowd situation in a static background. This also provides some new ideas for the video feature extraction algorithm. At the same time, there is good real-time performance. This article is tested in the 2019 Hong Kong riot video. The video violence test results are shown in Fig. 4.

Original video   Use the method in this article to detect violence

Fig. 4. The video violence test results

5   Conclusions

In this paper, the advantages of MoSIFT algorithm and ViF algorithm are combined into a new feature, which combines the advantages of MoSIFT algorithm for a few people's violent behavior description and the description of ViF algorithm for violent behavior in crowded situations. Advantages, and from the test results, the combined features have a great improvement in accuracy compared to the original features. The standard deviation obtained from the ViolentFlow data set is relatively large, which indicates that the video segment in the data set is too small, which has a certain impact on the generation of the model. Comparing with other algorithms on the same data set illustrates the objectivity of the experimental test data. The proposed algorithm can have a good recognition rate in a few people and in the crowd, and has versatility in other scenarios. Tests on the monitoring dataset also yielded good results. In a few cases, the test results were similar to the Hockey dataset, either in terms of accuracy, standard deviation, or variation of the polyline, but in crowd scenarios. The accuracy rate is lower than that of a few people, which shows that in the crowd situation, the algorithm also has an improved direction in feature extraction or feature processing.

Acknowledgements. This paper is funded by the National Natural Science Foundation of China, "Research on Human Behavior Recognition Technology Based on Deep Learning in Video Surveillance", project number 61862015. General support for the 13th five year plan of Education Science in Hunan Province, China, project approval No.: XJK19bzy037.

References

1. Liu, H., Wu, X., Yang, L., Ding, Y.: Safe zones for miniscrews in maxillary dentition distalization assessed with cone-beam computed tomography. Am. J. Orthod. Dentofac. Orthop. **151**(3), 500–506 (2017)
2. Taskin, Y., Hacioglu, Y., Ortes, F., Karabulut, D., Arslan, Y.Z.: Experimental investigation of biodynamic human body models subjected to whole-body vibration during a vehicle ride. Int. J. Occup. Saf. Ergon. JOSE (4) (2019)
3. Wang, H., Kläser, A., Schmid, C., Liu, C.-L.: Dense trajectories and motion boundary descriptors for action recognition. Int. J. Comput. Vis. **103**(1), 60–77 (2013). https://doi.org/10.1007/s11263-012-0594-8
4. Ellis, C., Masood, S.Z., Tappen, M.F., LaViola, J.J., Sukthankar, R.: Exploring the trade-off between accuracy and observational latency in action recognition. Int. J. Comput. Vis. **101**(3), 420–436 (2013). https://doi.org/10.1007/s11263-012-0550-7
5. Wang, L., Wang, Z., Liu, S.: An effective multivariate time series classification approach using echo state network and adaptive differential evolution algorithm. Expert Syst. Appl. **43**, 237–249 (2016)
6. Zhang, J., Gong, S.: Action categorization by structural probabilistic latent semantic analysis. Comput. Vis. Image Underst. **114**(8), 857–867 (2010)
7. Lin, L., Gong, H., Li, L., Wang, L.: Semantic event representation and recognition using syntactic attribute graph grammar. Pattern Recogn. Lett. **30**(2), 180–186 (2008)
8. Nievas, E.B., Suarez, O.D., García, G.B., et al.: Violence detection in video using computer vision techniques. In: Proceedings of the 14th International Conference on Computer Analysis of Images and Patterns. Seville, Spain, pp. 331–340 (2011)
9. Martin, V., Glotin, H., Paris, S., et al.: Violence detection in video by large scale multi-scale local binary patterns dynamics. In: MediaEval 2012 Workshop, Pisa, Italy (2012)
10. Hassner, T., Itcher, Y., Kliper-Gross, O.: Violent flows: realtime detection of violent crowd behavior. In: Proceedings of 2012 IEEE Computer Society Conference on Computer Vision and Pattern Recognition Workshops. Providence, RI, USA, pp. 1–6 (2012)
11. Patrona, F., Chatzitofis, A., Zarpalas, D., Daras, P.: Motion analysis: action detection, recognition and evaluation based on motion capture data. Pattern Recogn. **76**, 612–622 (2018)
12. Gadaleta, M., Rossi, M.: IDNet: smartphone-based gait recognition with convolutional neural networks. Pattern Recogn. **74**, 25–37 (2018)
13. Rawat, W., Wang, Z.: Deep convolutional neural networks for image classification: a comprehensive review. Neural Comput. **29**(9), 2352–2449 (2017)

14. Mehta, D.: VNect. ACM Trans. Graph. (TOG) **36**(4), 1–14 (2017)
15. Tang, Z., Li, C., Sun, S.: Single-trial EEG classification of motor imagery using deep convolutional neural networks. Optik Int. J. Light Elect. **130**, 1–18 (2017)
16. Zhang, J., Li, W., Ogunbona, P.O., Wang, P., Tang, C.: RGB-D-based action recognition datasets: a survey. Pattern Recogn. **60**, 86–105 (2016)
17. Luo, J., Tang, J., Tjahjadi, T., Xiao, X.: Robust arbitrary view gait recognition based on parametric 3D human body reconstruction and virtual posture synthesis. Pattern Recogn. **26**(1), 7–22 (2016)
18. Kastaniotis, D., Theodorakopoulos, I., Fotopoulos, S.: Pose-based gait recognition with local gradient descriptors and hierarchically aggregated residuals. J. Electron. Imaging **25**(6), 063019 (2016)
19. Loper, M., Mahmood, N., Romero, J., Pons-Moll, G., Black, M.J.: SMPL. ACM Trans. Graph. (TOG) **34**(6), 1–16 (2015)
20. Martín-Félez, R., Xiang, T.: Uncooperative gait recognition by learning to rank. Pattern Recogn. **47**(12), 3793–3806 (2014)
21. Rourke, L.L., Leduc, D.G., Rourke, J.T.: Rourke baby record 2000. Collaboration in action. Can. Fam. Physician **47**(2), 333 (2001)
22. Amaury Lélis, D.-F.: Adherence to long term therapies: evidence for action. Cadernos de Saúde Pública (4) (2005)
23. Jaimes Ocazionez, S.N.: Reemerging illnesses in Colombia: prevention is action. MedUNAB (19) (2004)
24. Li, S., Zhang, F., Ma, L., Ngan, K.N.: Image quality assessment by separately evaluating detail losses and additive impairments. IEEE Trans. Multimedia **13**(5), 935–949 (2011)
25. Goga, Y., Lioura, T., Gouzaris, A., Konstandinidis, L.: Konstandinidis LefterisPersonality factors associated with dropping out of cognitive behavioural treatment. Ann. Gen. Psychiatry (Suppl+1) (2006)
26. Bolwig, N.: Further observations on the physiological and behavioural characteristics of small animals in the Southern Kalahari. Koedoe Afr. Protected Area Conserv. Sci. **2**(1), 70–76 (1959)
27. Landman, K., Mcguinness, M.: Mean action time for diffusive processes. Journal of Applied Mathematics and Decision Sciences **4**(2), 125–141 (2000)
28. Akbarzadeh, M., Akbarzadeh, R., Akbarzadeh, R.: The behavioural neurogenetics of Fragile X syndrome: a model of gene-brain behaviour relationships. Annals of General Psychiatry **5**(Suppl+1), S266 (2006). https://doi.org/10.1186/1744-859X-5-S1-S266
29. Yun, K., Kwon, Y., Oh, S., Moon, J., Park, J.: Vision-based garbage dumping action detection for real-world surveillance platform. ETRI J. **41**(4), 494–505 (2019)
30. McKinley, E., Grant, B., Middleton, S., Irwin, K., Williams, L.: He Rautaki mo te Akoranga Kairangi 2. Reasons for doing a doctorate. Supervision Project Student Resources. MAI Rev. (3) (2009)

A Generative Steganography Method Based on WGAN-GP

Jun Li[1(✉)], Ke Niu[1], Liwei Liao[2], Lijie Wang[2], Jia Liu[1], Yu Lei[1],
and Minqing Zhang[1]

[1] College of Cryptographic Engineering, Engineering University of PAP, Xi'an 710086, China
lijun92501j@163.com
[2] Engineering University of PAP, Xi'an 710086, China

Abstract. With the development of Generative Adversarial Networks (GAN), GAN-based steganography and steganalysis techniques have attracted much attention from researchers. In this paper, we propose a novel image steganography method without modification based on Wasserstein GAN Gradient Penalty (WGAN-GP). The proposed architecture has a generative network, a discriminative network, and an extractor network. The Generator is used to generate the cover image (also is the stego image), and the Extractor is used to extract secret information. During the process of stego image generation, no modification operations are required. To make full use of the learning ability of convolutional neural networks and GAN, we synchronized the training of Generator and Extractor. Experiment results show that the proposed method has the advantages of higher recovery accuracy and higher training efficiency.

Keywords: Steganography without modification · Convolutional neural networks · Generative adversarial networks

1 Introduction

Steganography is the art of hiding the secret message by embedding it into inconspicuous cover data, such as images. In this communication system, there are two important roles to participate in, named defender and attacker, which correspond to steganography and steganalysis. The defender wants to hide a message in a cover object, but the attacker wants to distinguish plain covers from those with a hidden message.

In the past few years, steganographic algorithms with higher statistical security are Content-based adaptive minimization of embedding distortion. The main idea of this method is to embed the secret information in texture regions that were hard to model, such as HUGO [1], UNIWARD [2], HILL [3], MG [4], MiPOD [5], J-MSUNIWARD [6]. As a counter measure, steganalysts usually extracting high-dimensional features [7] of the image and classifying them with classifiers.

With the development of deep learning, especially the advent of GAN [8], more and more studies combine deep learning with information hiding. Steganography with GAN can be divided into three categories [9]. The first one is to generate a cover image by GAN

© Springer Nature Singapore Pte Ltd. 2020
X. Sun et al. (Eds.): ICAIS 2020, CCIS 1252, pp. 386–397, 2020.
https://doi.org/10.1007/978-981-15-8083-3_34

and then to embed the message by the traditional distortion minimization method. An example is SGAN [10] (Steganographic GAN) proposed by Volkhonskiy et al., which consists of three parts: Generator(G), Discriminator(D), and Steganalyzer(S). As these three parts are trained together in the training process, the stego images can ensure not only visual indistinguishability but also resist certain steganalysis attacks. The second kind is to generate distortion function by GAN. This kind of method does not directly generate a cover image but obtains distortion function represents the suitability for the embedding of image elements. Steganography method with minimizing embedding distortion will be used to execute the embedding process. This kind of method essentially changes the design method of distortion function from manual design to automatic learning by a neural network. For example, Tang et al. [11] proposed an automatic steganographic distortion learning framework with GAN (ASDL-GAN). The probability of data embedding is learned via the adversarial training between the Generator and the discriminator. Based on ASDL-GAN, UT-SCA-GAN (U-net Tanh-simulator, selection-channel awareness, GAN) [12] achieves better performance in statistical security and training time, according to incorporate the U-net based Generator, the Tanh-simulator function, and the selection-channel awareness based discriminator. The third kind is to generate the stego image directly by GAN. This kind of method belongs to the category of steganography without modification [13]. Two methods can achieve it before GAN: the cover-selection-based approach [14] and the cover-synthesis-based approach [15]. With the help of GAN, Hayes et al. proposed HayesGAN [16], whose network structure includes three parts, Generator(G), Discriminator(D), and Steganalyzer(S), just like SGAN. The difference is that there is no embedding operation in HayesGAN. The stego images are generated automatically by the network structure. The defect of HayesGAN is the existence of errors, which can not guarantee the correct extraction of secret information. Zhu et al. [17] proposed a robust steganography method based on HayesGAN. Hu et al. [18] proposed a novel method based on Deep Convolutional GAN (DCGAN) [19], they map the secret information into a noise vector and use the trained Generator neural network to generate the carrier image based on the noise vector. No modification or embedding operations are required during the process of image generation, and the information contained in the image can be extracted successfully by another neural network, called the Extractor, after training. The Generator and Extractor are trained separately in this method. That is to say, extracting secret information is independent of GAN. We think that the training of these two networks can be carried out simultaneously so that the learning ability of GAN can be fully utilized to improve the extraction rate and training efficiency of the model.

In this work, we propose a new Generative Steganography method without modification based on WGAN-GP (Wasserstein GAN Gradient Penalty) [20]. Compared with the previous method [18], the main contributions of this paper are as follows.

- In this paper, we use WGAN-GP instead of DCGAN to generate cover images to achieve generative images with higher visual quality and ensure a faster training process. WGAN-GP is an improved version of WGAN (Wasserstein GAN) [21] with an alternative to clipping weights: penalize the norm of the gradient of the critic concerning its input.

- We construct a message Extractor using a convolutional neural network with a similar structure of Discriminator in WGAN-GP. However, the last layer is replaced by a fully connected layer so that we can recover secret information from stego images.
- To make full use of the learning ability of convolutional neural networks and WGAN-GP, we synchronized the training of Generator and Extractor. Experiment results show that the proposed steganography method has the advantages of higher accurate recovery accuracy and higher training efficiency.

The rest of this paper is arranged as follows. Section 2 introduces the overall framework of the proposed method. The experimental results and analysis are shown in Sect. 3. The conclusion and future works are presented in Sect. 4.

2 Proposed Method

In this section, firstly, we introduce the basic knowledge of GAN. Secondly, we present the overall framework of the proposed method based on WGAN-GP, which synchronizing the training of Generator G and Extractor E. Then, the detailed structure of Generator G, Discriminator D, and Extractor E are described.

2.1 GAN

Generative adversarial networks (GAN) have become a new research hot spot in artificial intelligence, the main idea of which is to train a Generator and a discriminator network through playing a minimax game:

$$\min_{G} \max_{D} \leftarrow J(D, G) =$$
$$E_{x \sim p_{data}(x)} \log(D(x)) + E_{z \sim p_{noise}(z)} \log(1 - D(G(z))) \tag{1}$$

In the image domain, for a data set generated by some density $p_{data}(x)$, a Generator G attempts to approximate the image generating distribution and to synthesize as a realistic image as possible. In contrast, a discriminator D strives to distinguish real images from fake ones. To solve the minimax problem, in each iteration of the mini-batch stochastic gradient optimization, we can first perform the gradient ascent step on D and then perform the gradient descent step on G. Let w_N represents the neural network N, we can get the optimization steps:

- Let the G fixed to update the model D by $w_D \leftarrow w_D + \gamma_D \nabla_D J$, where

$$\nabla_D J = \frac{\partial}{\partial w_D} \{ E_{x \sim p_{data}} \log(D(x, w_D))$$
$$+ E_{z \sim p_{noise(z)}} \log(1 - D(G(z, w_G), w_D)) \} \tag{2}$$

- Let the D fixed to update the model G by $w_G \leftarrow w_G - \gamma_G \nabla_G J$, where

$$\nabla_G J = \frac{\partial}{\partial_{w_G}} \left\{ E_{z \sim p_{noise(z)}} \log(1 - D(G(z, w_G), w_D)) \right\} \tag{3}$$

Figure 1 shows the main idea of GAN:

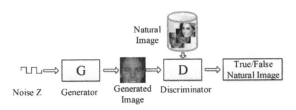

Fig. 1. Generative adversarial network.

2.2 Overall Framework

The proposed overall framework is shown in Fig. 2. Since we want the Generator to generate stego images directory, we force Generator(G) to compete against the Discriminator(D) and Extractor(E) at the same time, which construct the proposed minimax game:

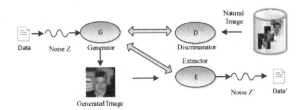

Fig. 2. Steganographic framework of the proposed method

$$\min_{G} \max_{D} \min_{E} \leftarrow J(D, G, E) = \left\{ E_{x \sim p_{data}(x)}[D(x)] - E_{z \sim p_{noise}(z)}[D(G(z))] + \right.$$

$$\left. \lambda E_{\hat{x} \sim p_{data}(\hat{x})} \left[\left(\|\nabla_{\hat{x}} D(\hat{x})\|_2 - 1 \right)^2 \right] \right\} + \beta \left\{ E_{z \sim p_{noise}(z)} \log(z - E(G(z))) \right\} \tag{4}$$

Where β is a positive number which controls the trade-off between the importance of realism of generated images and correct extraction rate of noise z, we will determine the value of β by experiment in Sect. 3. $E_{x \sim p_{data}(x)}[D(x)] - E_{z \sim p_{noise}(z)}[D(G(z))] +) \left(\lambda E_{\hat{x} \sim p_{data}(\hat{x})} \left[\left(\|\nabla_{\hat{x}} D(\hat{x})\|_2 - 1 \right)^2 \right] \right)$ is the objective function of WGAN-GP [20], in which we define $p_{data}(\hat{x})$ sampling uniformly along straight lines between pairs of points sampled from the data distribution

$p_{data}(x)$ and the Generator distribution $p_z(G(z))$, λ is the gradient penalty coefficient. $E_{z \sim p_{noise}(z)} \log(z - E(G(z)))$ is the objective function of Extractor, whose goal is to minimize the distance between the Generator noise z and the Extractor noise $z' = E(G(z))$. Stochastic mini-batch Gradient descent update rules for components of this game are listed below:

- Let the G and E fixed to update the model D by $w_D \leftarrow w_D + \gamma_D \nabla_D J$, where

$$\nabla_D J = \frac{\partial}{\partial w_D} \Big\{ E_{x \sim p_{data}(x)}[D(x, w_D)] - E_{z \sim p_{noise}(z)}[D(G(z, w_G), w_D)] + \lambda E_{\hat{x} \sim p_{data}(\hat{x})} \Big[\big(\|\nabla_{\hat{x}} D(\hat{x}, w_D)\|_2 - 1 \big)^2 \Big] \Big\}$$

(5)

- Let the D and G fixed to update the model E by $w_E \leftarrow w_E - \gamma_E \nabla_E J$, where

$$\nabla_E J = \frac{\partial}{\partial w_E} \Big\{ E_{z \sim p_{noise}(z)} \log(z - E(G(z, w_G), w_E)) \Big\}$$

(6)

- Let the D and E fixed to update the model G by $w_G \leftarrow w_G - \gamma_G \nabla_G J$, where

$$\nabla_G J = \frac{\partial}{\partial w_G} \Big\{ -E_{z \sim p_{noise}(z)}[D(G(z, w_G), w_D)] \Big\} + \frac{\partial}{\partial w_G} \beta \Big\{ E_{z \sim p_{noise}(z)} \log(z - E(G(z, w_G), w_E)) \Big\}$$

(7)

The training steps are described as Algorithm 1.

Algorithm 1: The proposed method

Require: The gradient penalty coefficient λ, the number of critic iterations per Generator iteration n_{critic}, the batch size m, Adam hyperparameters α, β_1, β_2. We use default vaules of $\lambda = 10$,

$n_{critic} = 5, \alpha = 0.001, \beta_1 = 0, \beta_2 = 0.9, m = 64$.

Initialize: initial discriminator parameters w_{D_0}, initial Generator parameters w_{G_0},

initial Extractor parameters w_{E_0}.

Steps:

1: while w_G, w_D and w_E has not converged do

2:   for $t=1,...,n_{critic}$ do

3:    for $i = 1, \dots , m$ do

4:      Sample real data $x \sim P_{data}(x)$, latent variable $z \sim P_{noise}(z)$, a random number $\gamma \sim U[0,1]$.

5:      $\tilde{x} \leftarrow G_{w_G}(z)$

6:      $\tilde{x} \leftarrow \gamma x + (1-\gamma)\tilde{x}$

7:      $L^{(i)} \leftarrow D_{w_D}(\tilde{x}) - D_{w_D}(x) + \lambda(\| \nabla_{\hat{x}} D_{w_D}(\hat{x}) \|_2 - 1)^2$

8:    end for

9:    $w_D \leftarrow Adam(\nabla_{w_D} \frac{1}{m} \sum_{i=1}^{m} L^{(i)}, w_D, \alpha, \beta_1, \beta_2)$

10:   end for

11:   Sample a batch of latent variables $\{z^{(i)}\}_{i=1}^{m} \sim p_{noise}(z)$

12:   $w_G \leftarrow Adam(\nabla_{w_G} \frac{1}{m} \sum_{i=1}^{m} (-\beta D_{w_D}(G_{w_G}(z)) + (1-\beta)\log(z - E_{w_E}(G_{w_G}(z)))), w_G, \alpha, \beta_1, \beta_2)$

13:   $w_E \leftarrow Adam(\nabla_{w_E} \frac{1}{m}(1-\beta)\log(z - E_{w_E}(G_{w_G}(z))), w_E, \alpha, \beta_1, \beta_2)$

14: end while

2.3 The Structure of Neural Networks

The structures of the Generator G and discriminator D are the same with WGAN-GP. G and D are both CNN (Convolutional Neural Networks). G consists of a fully connected layer and four fractional-stride convolutions layers and is used to fit the data distribution of the real images in training set to produce an artificial image. The input of G is a noise vector with dimensions of 1 * 100, and the output is an image with dimensions of 64 * 64 * 3.

D has a similar structure, which consists of four convolutional layers, and then a fully connected layer, the last layer is a two-class softmax that outputs the probability of the image is from G or the training image set.

E has the same structure of D, but the last layer is replaced by a fully connected layer, which we can get the Extractor noise z'. The input of Extractor E is an image of dimensions 64 * 64 * 3, and the output is a noise vector with the dimensions of 1 * 100.

2.4 Message Communication

As introduced in Sect. 2.2, according to the proposed model, we can generate a cover image (which is also a stego image) from a noise vector and recover the original noise vector from the model. The rest is to establish the relationship between message and noise, and we use the method proposed in paper [18]. We divide the secret information

S into segments s_i and then map each segment s_i to noise vector z_i, several bits (2 or three) of the segment are mapped to a noise value with a given interval according to the following equation:

$$r = random\left(\frac{m}{2^{\sigma-1}} - 1 + \delta, \frac{m}{2^{\sigma-1}} - 1 - \delta\right) \tag{8}$$

where the function $random(a, b)$ denotes a random noise value produced between a and b, r is the mapped noise within the interval $\left(\frac{m}{2^{\sigma-1}} - 1 + \delta, \frac{m+1}{2^{\sigma-1}} - 1 - \delta\right)$, m is the decimal value of the secret data bits to be mapped, and σ represents the number of secret data bits carried by one random noise. δ is the gap between the divided intervals, which allows a deviation tolerance when extracting data from a stego image and ensures the extraction accuracy of the secret data during the secret communication phase.

3 Experiment

3.1 Set up

All experiments in this paper are based on CelebA database [22] with a number of 202,599 color face images with size 178 * 218 pixels. We pre-process the image so that all images are cropped to 64 * 64 pixels. All experiments are performed in TensorFlow [23] on a workstation with an NVIDIA TITAN Xp GPU whose memory is 12 GB. The models are trained with mini-batch stochastic gradient descent (SGD) with a mini-batch size of 64.

Our experiments consist of the following three parts.

- We train the model to determine the value of parameter β proposed in Sect. 2.2, which controls the trade-off between the importance of realism of generated images and the secret information recovery accuracy.
- We train the model on the real image sets to obtain the Generator G and the Extractor E to create cover images (stego images) and extract messages, respectively. Moreover, we will also observe whether the trained model can converge steadily through experiments.
- We compare the proposed method with the previous method [18] to show that the synchronized training of G and E is effective.

3.2 Determination of Parameter β

As mentioned in formula (4), the parameter β trade-off between the importance of realism of generated images and the secret information recovery accuracy. The recovery accuracy is defined as the ratio of the number of binary bits recovered correctly from the stego image to the length of the original secret information. In order to get a more suitable value for β, we train the model on the CelebA database with 70,000 images, and the iteration epochs were 300. The capacity parameter σ is 1, and the gap parameter δ is 0.01. There is tens of times difference between the values of loss of G and the loss of E, so we let β varied from 1, 5,10, and 60.

In Fig. 3, the abscissa is the training steps, and the ordinate is the recovery accuracy of secret information. We can see that under the same training steps, with the increase of β, the recovery accuracy also increases, which is because the bigger the β is, the bigger the proportion of training for Extractor in the proposed model. However, In Fig. 4, we list the training loss of Generator under different β. Obviously, when β is greater than 10, the training for the Generator becomes very unstable. In order to reach a compromise, in the remains experiment, we set the parameter β to 5, so that we can get not only a higher recovery accuracy for secret information but also to produce better visual effect images.

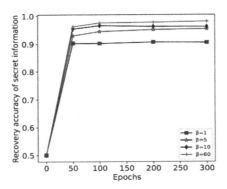

Fig. 3. Recovery accuracy of secret information extracted from stego images with different β

3.3 Model Training and Recovery Accuracy of Secret Information

In this section, the training of the proposed model is carried out on the CelebA dataset with 202,599 images, we set the value of β to 5 and δ to 0.1, the capacity parameter σ is varied from 1 to 3, and the training epoch is set to 400. The loss curves for Generator and Extractor with steps of training are shown in Fig. 5. The Generator can converge smoothly. With the training, the Extractor can converge quickly in about 50000 steps (about 80 epochs, every epoch has 633 steps).

After training with the help of WGAN-GP, the sample images of Generator G shown in Fig. 6, which fit the data distribution of the images in the corresponding training set.

Figure 7 shows the curves of secret message recovery accuracy under different σ values. Recovery accuracy increases as the number of training steps increases. After about ten epochs, the recovery accuracy rapidly increased to a higher level. When σ is 1, the final recovery accuracy is 0.9842. It can be seen that with the increase of σ, the recovery accuracy decreases, which shows that the larger the capacity of the embedded secret information, the lower the recovery accuracy of secret information.

3.4 Comparison with the Previous Algorithm [18]

We experimented with the algorithm of paper [18] under the same conditions as the proposed algorithm in this section. As the training of G and E in paper [18] is separated, we set the training steps of every epoch to 2000 in E.

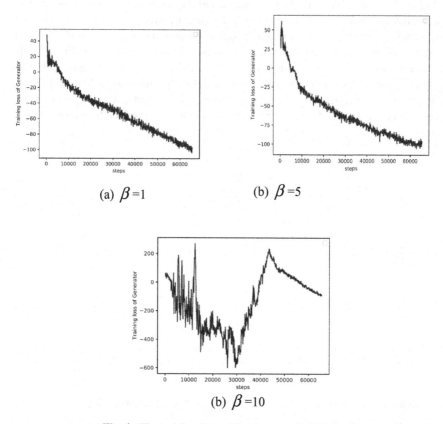

(a) β=1   (b) β=5

(b) β=10

Fig. 4. The training loss of Generator with different β

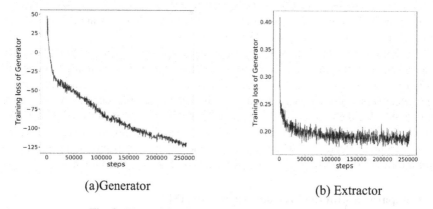

(a)Generator   (b) Extractor

Fig. 5. The training loss of Generator(a) and Extractor(b)

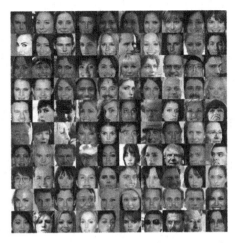

Fig. 6. Generated images output from G trained on CelebA images set

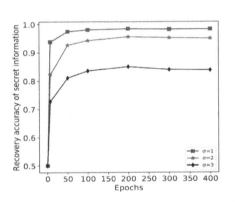

Fig. 7. Recovery accuracy.

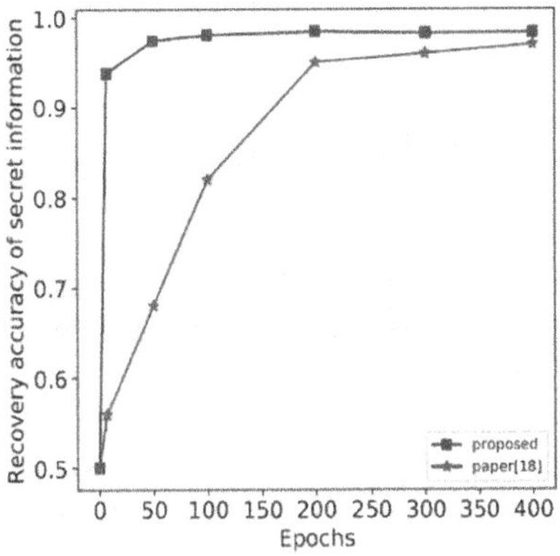

Fig. 8. Recovery accuracy contrast with paper [18]

It is worth mentioning that the embedding capacity of the algorithm proposed in this paper is the same as that of paper [18]. That is, the embedding capacity is only related to the length of the original noise Z and the number of secret data bits that every random noise can carry. Therefore, if we want to improve the embedding capacity of the algorithm, we can increase the length of the original noise Z or the number of secret data bits carried by every random noise. We will complete these experiments in the future research.

Figure 8 shows the contrast of recovery accuracy between the proposed method and the algorithm of paper [18] when $\sigma = 1$. Results from the figure show that the correct extraction rate of the proposed algorithm has been increased by 20% on average, which shows that the synchronized training of G and E is effective. Also, the convergence speed of the proposed algorithm is faster. When the training epoch is just 50, the correct extraction rate has reached a high level.

3.5 The Model's Training Efficiency

Table 1 shows the comparison of the training time between the proposed algorithm and the method in paper [18]. In paper [18], the training of G and E are separated, and the training time is 88 h and 11 h, respectively. On the other hand, the training of G and E in this paper is carried out at the same time, the total time is 36 h, so the efficiency is relatively high. It can be seen that the training time required by the proposed algorithm is about one-third of that of the paper [18].

Table 1. The efficiency contrast with training for 400 epochs.

Method	G	E	Total
Proposed	36 h	Synchronized with G	36 h
Paper [18]	88 h	11 h	99 h

4   Conclusions

In this paper, we propose a novel image steganography method without modification based on WGAN-GP. The proposed architecture has a generative network G, a discriminative network D, and an extractor network E. The main contribution of this paper is to synchronize the training of G and E in the process of training the neural network. So we can save training time and improve the efficiency of the proposed model. Besides, through the experimental result, we can see that this scheme also improves the accuracy of information recovery due to WGAN-GP. However, the problem of the method is that the image size is still small, and we cannot extract secret data bits correct Absolutely. We believe that these problems will be solved with the development of GAN or deep learning.

Acknowledgment. This paper was supported by the National Natural Science Foundation of China (Grant No. 61872384), and Basic research foundation for Engineering University of PAP(Grant No. WJY201918).

References

1. Pevný, T., Filler, T., Bas, P.: Using high-dimensional image models to perform highly undetectable steganography. In: Böhme, R., Fong, Philip W.L., Safavi-Naini, R. (eds.) IH 2010. LNCS, vol. 6387, pp. 161–177. Springer, Heidelberg (2010). https://doi.org/10.1007/978-3-642-16435-4_13
2. Holub, V., Fridrich, J., Denemark, T.: Universal distortion function for steganography in an arbitrary domain. EURASIP J. Inf. Secur. 1(1), 1–14 (2014)

3. Li, B., Tan, S., Wang, M., et al.: Investigation on cost assignment in spatial image steganography. IEEE Trans. Inf. Forensics Secur. **9**(8), 1264–1277 (2014)
4. Fridrich, J., Kodovský, J.: Multivariate Gaussian model for designing additive distortion for steganography. In: Presented at the Proceedings of IEEE ICASSP, Vancou-ver, BC, 26–31 May 2013
5. Sedighi, V., Cogranne, R., Fridrich, J.: Content-adaptive steganography by minimizing statistical detectability. IEEE Trans. Inf. Forensics Secur. **11**(2), 221–234 (2016)
6. Chen, K., Zhou, H., Zhou, W., Zhang, W., Yu, N.: Defining cost functions for adaptive JPEG steganography at the microscale. IEEE Trans. Inf. Forensics Secur. **14**(4), 1052–1066 (2019)
7. Fridrich, J., Kodovský, J.: Rich models for steganalysis of digital images. IEEE Trans. Inf. Forensics Secur. **7**(3), 868–882 (2012)
8. Goodfellow, I., Pouget-Abadie, J., Mirza, M., Xu, B., Warde-Farley, D., Ozair, S., Courville, A., Bengio, Y.: Generative adversarial nets. In: Presented at the International Conference on Neural Information Processing Systems (2014)
9. Liming, Z.H.A.I., Ju, J.I.A., Weixiang, R.E.N., Yibo, X.U., Lina, W.A.N.G.: Recent advances in deep learning for image steganography and steganalysis. J. Cyber Secur. **3**(6), 2–12 (2018)
10. Volkhonskiy, D., Nazarov, I., Borisenko, B., et al.: Steganographic generative adversarial networks (2017). arXiv preprint arXiv:1703.05502
11. Tang, W., Tan, S., Li, B., et al.: Automatic steganographic distortion learning using a generative adversarial network. IEEE Signal Process. Lett. **24**(10), 1547–1551 (2017)
12. Yang, J., Liu, K., Kang, X., et al.: Spatial image steganography based on generative adversarial network (2018). arXiv preprint arXiv:1804.07939
13. Fridrich, J.: Steganography in Digital Media: Principles, Algorithms, and Applications. Cambridge University Press (2009)
14. Zhou, Z., Sun, H., Harit, R., Chen, X., Sun, X.: Coverless image steganography without embedding. In: Huang, Z., Sun, X., Luo, J., Wang, J. (eds.) ICCCS 2015. LNCS, vol. 9483, pp. 123–132. Springer, Cham (2015). https://doi.org/10.1007/978-3-319-27051-7_11
15. Otori, H., Kuriyama, S.: Data-embeddable texture synthesis. In: Butz, A., Fisher, B., Krüger, A., Olivier, P., Owada, S. (eds.) SG 2007. LNCS, vol. 4569, pp. 146–157. Springer, Heidelberg (2007). https://doi.org/10.1007/978-3-540-73214-3_13
16. Hayes, J., Danezis, G.: Generating steganographic images via adversarial training. In: Presented at NIPS 2017: Neural Information Processing Systems, Long Beach, California, USA, December 2017
17. Zhu, J., Kaplan, R., Johnson, J., et al.: HiDDeN: Hiding Data With Deep Networks (2018). arXiv preprint arXiv:1807.09937
18. Donghui, H., Liang, W., Wenjie, J., et al.: A novel image steganography method via deep convolutional generative adversarial networks. IEEE Access **6**, 38303–38314 (2018)
19. Radford, A., Metz, L., Chintala, S.: Unsupervised Representation Learning with Deep Convolutional Generative Adversarial Networks (2016). arXiv preprint arXiv:1511.06434
20. Gulrajani, I., Ahmed, F., Arjovsky, M., et al.: Improved training of wasserstein GANs. In: Advances in Neural Information Processing Systems 30 - Proceedings of the 2017 Conference, pp. 5768–5778 (2017)
21. Arjovsky, M., Chintala, S., Bottou, L.: Wasserstein GAN (2017). arXiv preprint arXiv:1701.07875
22. Liu, Z., Luo, P., Wang, X., Tang, X.: Large-scale CelebFaces Attributes (CelebA) Dataset. http://mmlab.ie.cuhk.edu.hk/projects/CelebA.html
23. Abadi, M., Agarwal, A., et al.: Tensorflow: Large-scale machine learning on heterogeneous distributed systems (2016). arXiv preprint arXiv:1603.04467

A Deep Learning Network for Coarse-to-Fine Deformable Medical Image Registration

Lintao Zhang[1,2(✉)], Shunbo Hu[1,2(✉)], Guoqiang Li[1,2(✉)], Mingtao Liu[1,2], Yongfang Wang[1,2], Deqian Fu[1,2], and Wenyin Zhang[1,2]

[1] School of Information Science and Engineering, Linyi University, Linyi, Shandong, China
{zhanglintao,hushunbo,liguoqiang}@lyu.edu.cn
[2] Linda Institute, Shandong Provincial Key Laboratory of Network Based Intelligent Computing, Linyi University, Linyi, Shandong, China

Abstract. Deformable image registration was a fundamental task in medical image analysis. Recently published registration methods based on deep learning have shown promising results. However, these algorithms brought limited precision improvement due to the similar learning framework. In order to address this shortcoming, we proposed a novel two-stage framework for deep learning based image registration. The new network computed deformation fields on different scales, similar to methods using auto-context strategy. Thereby, a coarse-scale alignment was obtained by the first half part of our network, which was subsequently improved on finer scale by the second half part. The new model could directly estimate the final deformation field in an end to end way. We demonstrated our method on the task of brain magnetic resonance (MR) image registration and showed that the new model could reach significantly better registration results.

Keywords: Auto-context · Deformable medical image registration · MR · Coarse-to-fine registration

1 Introduction

Deformable image registration was a fundamental task in medical image analysis to find voxel correspondences in a pair of images, which has been an active field of research for decades. Since recently, more and deep learning based approaches have been proposed for image registration, image segmentation and shown promising results in a wide range of tasks [1–14]. However, these deep learning based registration approaches showed limited precision improvement compared to conventional methods. In common iterative medical image segmentation and synthesis approaches, an auto-context strategy was often used and has shown significant gain in accuracy [1, 2]. The strategy was also applied to multi-scale coarse-to-fine registration by training multi-models iteratively [5–10]. The first model computed a coarse deformation field that typically captured the large motion components. The subsequent models improved the coarse deformation on finer scales for the alignment of more local details. In [4] a patch based approach was proposed, where multiple CNN networks were combined to perform coarse-to-fine

© Springer Nature Singapore Pte Ltd. 2020
X. Sun et al. (Eds.): ICAIS 2020, CCIS 1252, pp. 398–407, 2020.
https://doi.org/10.1007/978-981-15-8083-3_35

image registration of patches. The results from the patches were then combined into a deformation field warping the whole image. In [5] the authors proposed an architecture which was divided into a global and a local network, which were optimized together. In [6] a multilevel strategy was used to train the registration network, which was similar to coarse-to-fine image registration.

Inspired by those works, we presented a deep learning network for coarse-to-fine image registration to advance state-of-the-art approaches. The contribution of this paper included:

- We presented deep learning based coarse-to-fine registration network that was able to compute deformation fields on different scales and significantly improve the accuracy.
- Most deep learning methods realized auto-context strategy by cascaded networks. Thus multiple models needed to be trained and the deformation field was inferenced iteratively. Our method was a theoretically sound and a direct integration of coarse-to-fine registration strategy to the architecture of deep learning networks. Thus the model could be trained as a whole and inferenced the deformation in an end to end way.
- The network could take 3D image pairs as inputs and take the whole image information into account.

2 Method

In deformable registration of medical images a deformation field ϕ was estimated which could warp a moving image $M \in \Re^3$ to the fixed image $F \in \Re^3$ and make the warped image $W(M, \phi) \in \Re^3$ similar to F. For each voxel $p \in F$, $\phi(p)$ was a location such that $T(p)$ and $M(\phi(p))$ defined similar anatomical locations. The warping operation could be described as $W(M, \phi) = M(\phi(p))$. Then the deformation field ϕ could be estimated by minimize the energy function as:

$$\hat{\phi} = \arg\min_{\phi} \mathcal{L}(F, M, \phi) = \arg\min_{\phi}[-\mathcal{L}_{sim}(F, W(M, \phi)) + \lambda \mathcal{R}(\phi)], \qquad (1)$$

where function $\mathcal{L}_{sim}$ quantified the images similarity between the fixed image F and the warped moving image $W(M, \phi)$. The similarity function $\mathcal{L}_{sim}$ could use metrics of SSD (sum of squared difference), CC (cross-correlation) or MI (mutual information). $\mathcal{R}(\phi)$ was the regularization to preserve the spatially smoothness of the deformation field, ϕ and λ was the regularization parameter.

As for registration based on deep learning network in our paper, the network model could be described by a function $\mathcal{F}_\theta(F, M) = \phi$, where the θ were learnable parameters of model $\mathcal{F}$. And the energy function (1) could be rewrite as a loss function for the deep learning network:

$$\hat{\theta} = \arg\min_{\theta} \mathcal{L}(F, M, \mathcal{F}_\theta(F, M)) \qquad (2)$$

By minimizing loss function (2) and updating θ iteratively with enough training data, the deep learning network $\mathcal{F}_\theta$ could find optimal parameters $\hat{\theta}$, which could be used to estimate the deformation field ϕ directly. Figure 1 presented an overview of our method.

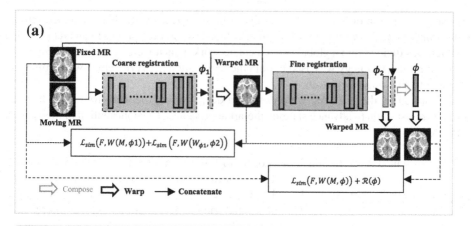

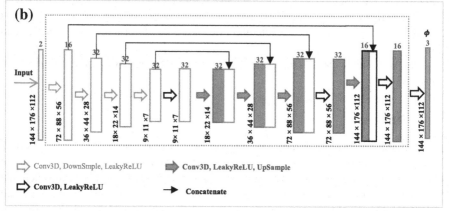

Fig. 1. (a) The coarse-to-fine registration deep learning framework. (b) The CNN network of coarse and fine registration module

2.1 Coarse-to-Fine Network Architecture

The proposed auto-context deep learning network for coarse-to-fine registration was shown in Fig. 1 (a). The network had two registration modules with U-Net-like architecture. The first module was trained to estimate a coarse deformation field ϕ_1 and warp the moving MR image M to fixed MR image F. The second module took MR image warped by ϕ_1 (W_{ϕ_1}) and the fixed MR image F as inputs and estimated a finer deformation field ϕ_2 with which W_{ϕ_1} could be warped to W_{ϕ_2}. The warped MR image W_{ϕ_2} was more similar to fixed MR image F than W_{ϕ_1}. Then the final deformation field ϕ was composed by ϕ_1 and ϕ_1:

$$\phi = \phi_1 \circ \phi_2 \tag{3}$$

The final warped image W_ϕ was got by warping moving MR image M with ϕ. The similarity of W_{ϕ_1} and F was used to train the coarse registration module. The similarity of W_{ϕ_2} and F was used to train the fine registration module. The final similarity of W_ϕ and

F was used to train the whole networks. It's quite similar to the auto-context strategy but did not need to train multi models one by one. It has been proved that the second stage of the auto-context algorithm usually gave the biggest improvement while iterating more did not bring more accuracy gain [1]. Thus we only integrated two modules. The two modules shared the same architecture for simple realization which was not necessary. The architecture was shown in Fig. 1 (b) that was the same as VoxelMorph [3].

2.2 Multi-stage and Multi-scale Loss Function

The proposed framework realized two stage coarse-to-fine registration, so the loss function could be different for similarity function $\mathcal{L}_{sim}$ in (1) at different stage.

$$\mathcal{L}_{sim}(F, W) = \alpha\left[\mathcal{L}_{coarse}(F, W_{\varnothing 1}) + \mathcal{L}_{fine}(F, W_{\varnothing 2})\right] + \beta\mathcal{L}_{final}(F, W_{\varnothing}), \qquad (4)$$

where α and β denoted weighted coefficients. $W_{\varnothing 1} = W(M, \phi 1)$. $W_{\varnothing 2} = W(W_{\varnothing 1}, \phi 2)$. $W_{\varnothing} = W(M, \phi)$. $W(*)$ stood for the warping operation.

As for the MR images, the local cross-correlation of warped MR (W) and fixed MR (F) were often used because of the robustness to intensity variations that defined as:

$$CC_n(F, W) = \sum_{p \in T} \frac{\left(\sum_{p_i}\left(F(p_i) - \hat{F}(p)\right)\left(W(p_i) - \hat{W}(p)\right)\right)^2}{\left(\sum_{p_i}\left(F(p_i) - \hat{F}(p)\right)\right)\left(\sum_{p_i}\left(W(p_i) - \hat{W}(p)\right)\right)}, \qquad (5)$$

where p_i denoted all locations over an n^3 volume centered at p. $\hat{F}(p)$ and $\hat{W}(p)$ denoted local mean intensities of the n^3 volume. Other evaluate metrics like SSIM could also be used. We set $n = 9$ for $\mathcal{L}_{coarse}$, $n = 5$ for $\mathcal{L}_{fine}$ and $\mathcal{L}_{final}$ to realize the Multi-scale coarse-to-fine registration Then for the coarse-to-fine registration network, the $\mathcal{L}_{sim}$ could be defined as:

$$\mathcal{L}_{sim}(F, W) = \alpha[CC_9(F, W_{\varnothing 1}) + CC_5(F, W_{\varnothing 2})] + \beta CC_5(F, W_{\varnothing}) \qquad (6)$$

A higher $\mathcal{L}_{sim}$ indicated more similarity for the input image pairs and better alignment but may generate a discontinuous ϕ, so the regularizer $\mathcal{R}(\phi)$ was often defined on its spatial gradients:

$$\mathcal{R}(\phi) = \sum_p \|\nabla\phi(p)\|^2 \qquad (7)$$

The complete loss was:

$$\mathcal{L}(F, M, \phi) = -\{\alpha[CC_9(F, W_{\varnothing 1}) + CC_5(F, W_{\varnothing 2})] + \beta CC_5(F, W_{\varnothing})\} + \lambda\sum_p \|\nabla\phi(p)\|^2, \qquad (8)$$

where α, β and λ denoted weighted coefficients that weight the tradeoff between the registration performance and smoothness of the deformation. So $2\alpha + \beta = 1$ was required to make setting λ convenient. In our experiments, we simply set $\alpha = 0.2$, $\beta = 0.6$ and $\lambda = 1.5$ in order to make comparison with VoxelMorph [3].

3   Experimental Results

3.1   Dataset

In this section, we trained and compared performance of the proposed method with Demons in SimpleITK [15, 16] and VoxelMorph [3, 17] based on two brain MR Datasets.

The first dataset consisted of totally 24 infant subjects at 0 (2 weeks old), 3, 6, 9 and 12 months old. Each subject had T1-weighted and T2-weighted MR images and corresponding segmentation labels. All images were linearly aligned and resampled to the same size of $256 \times 256 \times 198$ with the same resolution of $1 \times 1 \times 1$ mm^3. The image data preprocessing included skull stripping, bias correction, histogram equalization, segmentation, etc. All images were cropped to the same size of $144 \times 176 \times 112$ to reduce computing burden. During training, one subject was selected as the fixed image and 13 subjects were selected to train the model with data augmentation. The remaining 10 subjects were used as testing data. The data augmentation was implemented for every training image by applying a random affine transformation with open source code in NiftyNet [18, 19]. All experimental results on this dataset in terms of Dice Similarity Coefficient (DSC) were shown in Tables 1, 2, 3, 4, 5, 6, 7 and 8 separately.

The second dataset was public adult brain MR dataset OASIS1 [11]. The OASIS1 dataset consists of a cross-sectional collection of 416 subjects aged 18 to 96. For each subject, 3 or 4 individual T1-weighted MRI scans obtained in single scan sessions were included. In the dataset we selected preprocessed brain MR images and corresponding segmentation images. All images have the same size of $176 \times 208 \times 176$ with the same resolution. During training, one subject was selected as the fixed image and 316 subjects were selected to train the model with data augmentation. The remaining 100 subjects were used as testing data. Experimental results in terms of DSC were shown in Table 9.

In addition to compare the Demons and pre-trained VoxelMorph model downloaded from GitHub, the VoxelMorph was retrained in the same way as ours for overfitting evaluation.

The network was trained on a 12 GB NVidia Titan X GPU with 10000 iterations. In each iteration, a pair of randomly augmented MR images were produced.

3.2   Registration Results

The average DSC values of Cerebro Spinal Fluid (CSF), Gray Matter (GM) and White Matter (WM) with different registration models on infant MR Dataset were shown in Tables 1, 2, 3, 4, 5, 6, 7 and 8.

For infant brain, the T1 MR clearly delineated GM and WM, whereas T2 MR delineated CSF from cortical tissue. Moreover, for images obtained before 6 months, the tissue contrast of T2 images was higher than that of T1 images. So for the 0-, 3- and 6-month old dataset, the registration results based on both T1 and T2 MR images were shown in Tables 1, 2, 3, 4, 5 and 6,. Registration results of Demons in Tables 1, 2, 3 and 4 showed that DSC values were much higher on T2 MR images than T1 MR images for 0- and 3-month old dataset. The smallest DSC difference of T1 and T2 MR was at 6-month-old as shown in Tables 5 and 6. The registration results of VoxelMorph in the 3rd and 4th row followed the same rules. Due to the low tissue contrast of infant brain, the proposed method did not gain the highest DSC of all tissue than other models. But obvious improvement still were got compared with pre-trained and re-trained VoxelMorph in Tables 2 and 4. In Tables 1 and 3, the improvements were not so obvious. The most probable reason was that the low contrast of MR images would limit the performance of the proposed model.

As for the 9- and 12-month old T1 MR images, the performance of the proposed model was closer to that of the adult dataset as shown in Tables 7, 8 and 9. Thus only the registration results based on T1 MR were shown. From Table 7 and 8, the DSC showed that the proposed model could gain much better registration accuracy than Demons and VoxelMorph, when the infant brain reached near adulthood. It could be inferred that the proposed registration models would performed better with a higher tissue contrast of MR images.

The average DSC values of CSF, GM and WM with different registration models on adult MR Dataset OASIS1 were shown in Table 9. The proposed algorithm achieved the best performance using coarse-to-fine registration framework, compared with other registration algorithms.

The performance of Demons and pre-trained VoxelMorph was comparable as shown in Tables 1, 2, 3, 4, 5, 6, 7, 8 and 9, which meant the deep-learning based model brought limited registration accuracy improvement on infant and adult brain MR images. The results showed that deep learning based image registration approaches performed no much better than conventional methods on DSC by comparing the performance of Demons and VoxelMorph. Even the retrained VoxelMorph gained limited improvement. While the last row in Tables 2, 4, 6, 7, 8 and 9 showed the DSC values were much improved with our new coarse-to-fine registration model. Compared the improvements of DSC values between CSF, GM and WM in Tables 2, 4, 6, 7, 8 and 9, it was showed that the proposed coarse-to-fine registration algorithm promoted the DSC values much more when the original values was poor. By and large, the proposed algorithm achieved better performance compared with other registration algorithms.

In order to evaluate the overfitting problem, VoxelMorph was retrained the same way as our model. By comparing the performance of pre-trained and re-trained VoxelMorph in Tables 1, 2, 3, 4, 5, 6, 7, 8 and 9, they showed comparable performance in most cases. That meant the overfitting problem was not serious to some extent due to the data augmentation operation when training.

Table 1. DSC (%) of CSF, GM and WM on 0-old-month infant Brain T1 MR images

Method	DSC (%)		
	CSF	GM	WM
Affine only	55.4 ± 4.2	60.5 ± 0.8	60.9 ± 1.5
Demons	59.2 ± 6.0	66.2 ± 2.8	66.3 ± 3.0
VoxelMorph(pre-trained)	57.5 ± 6.4	$\mathbf{68.7 \pm 3.8}$	67.1 ± 3.6
VoxelMorph(re-trained)	58.9 ± 5.8	68.3 ± 3.5	$\mathbf{68.5 \pm 3.9}$
Ours	$\mathbf{59.5 \pm 6.2}$	68.1 ± 3.7	$\mathbf{68.5 \pm 4.1}$

Table 2. DSC (%) of CSF, GM and WM on 0-old-month infant Brain T2 MR images

Method	DSC (%)		
	CSF	GM	WM
Affine only	55.4 ± 4.2	60.5 ± 0.8	60.9 ± 1.5
Demons	**72.4 ± 3.1**	71.3 ± 1.0	72.6 ± 1.2
VoxelMorph(pre-trained)	68.8 ± 3.8	70.0 ± 1.1	73.1 ± 0.7
VoxelMorph(re-trained)	70.9 ± 3.7	72.8 ± 0.7	73.1 ± 0.9
Ours	71.3 ± 3.6	**72.9 ± 0.8**	**74.1 ± 0.7**

Table 3. DSC (%) of CSF, GM and WM on 3-old-month infant Brain T1 MR images

Method	DSC (%)		
	CSF	GM	WM
Affine only	56.0 ± 8.1	59.7 ± 1.8	56.2 ± 2.3
Demons	61.2 ± 10.1	64.6 ± 3.3	60.1 ± 3.7
VoxelMorph(pre-trained)	60.6 ± 10.4	**65.4 ± 3.8**	60.8 ± 3.4
VoxelMorph(re-trained)	61.2 ± 10.1	64.5 ± 3.7	60.8 ± 3.5
Ours	**62.0 ± 10.5**	65.3 ± 4.0	**61.4 ± 3.7**

Table 4. DSC (%) of CSF, GM and WM on 3-old-month infant Brain T2 MR images

Method	DSC (%)		
	CSF	GM	WM
Affine only	56.0 ± 8.1	59.7 ± 1.8	56.2 ± 2.3
Demons	**75.1 ± 0.9**	69.7 ± 0.8	66.4 ± 1.5
VoxelMorph(pre-trained)	72.9 ± 2.4	69.5 ± 1.1	65.4 ± 1.3
VoxelMorph(re-trained)	74.0 ± 0.9	69.7 ± 0.7	63.6 ± 1.1
Ours	74.5 ± 1.2	**71.2 ± 1.0**	**66.9 ± 1.1**

Table 5. DSC (%) of CSF, GM and WM on 6-old-month infant Brain T1 MR images

Method	DSC (%)		
	CSF	GM	WM
Affine only	43.3 ± 1.6	67.0 ± 0.9	58.7 ± 1.0
Demons	59.1 ± 1.1	**73.8 ± 1.5**	67.9 ± 1.4
VoxelMorph(pre-trained)	56.8 ± 1.2	73.1 ± 1.4	67.9 ± 1.4
VoxelMorph(re-trained)	57.6 ± 1.0	73.7 ± 1.2	68.2 ± 1.2
Ours	**59.1 ± 1.0**	73.7 ± 1.4	**68.4 ± 1.5**

Table 6. DSC (%) of CSF, GM and WM on 6-old-month infant Brain T2 MR images

Method	DSC (%)		
	CSF	GM	WM
Affine only	43.3 ± 1.6	67.0 ± 0.9	58.7 ± 1.0
Demons	55.6 ± 2.3	70.3 ± 1.3	**62.2 ± 1.2**
VoxelMorph(pre-trained)	53.7 ± 2.5	69.5 ± 1.2	60.7 ± 1.0
VoxelMorph(re-trained)	54.0 ± 2.4	69.4 ± 0.8	60.1 ± 1.0
Ours	**56.1 ± 2.3**	**70.7 ± 0.8**	61.2 ± 0.7

Table 7. DSC (%) of CSF, GM and WM on 9-old-month infant Brain T1 MR images

Method	DSC (%)		
	CSF	GM	WM
Affine only	41.3 ± 0.9	68.5 ± 0.7	57.3 ± 0.7
Demons	58.7 ± 0.8	77.4 ± 0.7	69.9 ± 0.8
VoxelMorph(pre-trained)	56.8 ± 0.7	77.0 ± 0.6	70.5 ± 0.4
VoxelMorph(re-trained)	57.1 ± 0.7	77.4 ± 0.5	71.2 ± 0.6
Ours	**59.9 ± 0.5**	**78.4 ± 0.5**	**72.6 ± 0.6**

Table 8. DSC (%) of CSF, GM and WM on 12-old-month infant Brain T1 MR images

Method	DSC (%)		
	CSF	GM	WM
Affine only	42.0 ± 1.5	68.1 ± 0.6	57.9 ± 0.7
Demons	60.6 ± 1.7	78.2 ± 0.7	72.6 ± 0.8
VoxelMorph(pre-trained)	57.8 ± 1.6	77.0 ± 0.8	74.0 ± 0.5
VoxelMorph(re-trained)	58.4 ± 1.5	77.9 ± 1.0	75.5 ± 0.5
Ours	$\mathbf{60.9 \pm 1.4}$	$\mathbf{79.6 \pm 1.5}$	$\mathbf{80.3 \pm 0.6}$

Table 9. DSC (%) of CSF, GM and WM on adult OASIS1 Dataset

Method	DSC (%)		
	CSF	GM	WM
Affine only	45.2 ± 6.3	58.4 ± 1.9	60.1 ± 1.9
Demons	67.1 ± 5.4	75.8 ± 1.2	81.9 ± 1.1
VoxelMorph(pre-trained)	70.1 ± 5.7	75.9 ± 1.4	83.8 ± 0.9
VoxelMorph(re-trained)	72.2 ± 4.0	76.5 ± 1.3	84.7 ± 0.8
Ours	$\mathbf{74.9 \pm 3.9}$	$\mathbf{79.7 \pm 1.1}$	$\mathbf{86.4 \pm 0.8}$

4   Discussion and Conclusion

In this paper, we proposed a deep learning based coarse-to-fine registration network to significantly improve the registration accuracy. The auto-context strategy was integrated into the framework. Thus network was able to compute deformation field on different scales in an end-to-end way. The model could be trained as a whole with multi-stage and multi-scales loss functions which was much more flexible. The experimental results on both infant and adult barin MR images registration indicated that the model could significantly improve accuracy compared to other state-of-art deep learning based methods. The model had great potential to be used for a wide range of tasks for medical image registration.

Acknowledgment. This work was supported in part by NSFC 61771230, 61773244, Shandong Provincial Natural Science Foundation ZR2016FM40, ZR2019PF005, and Shandong Key R&D Program Project 2019GGX101006, 2019GNC106027. We also thank for the open source code of VoxelMorph published by Balakrishnan et al.

References

1. Tu, Z., Bai, X.: Auto-context and its application to high-level vision tasks and 3d brain image segmentation. IEEE Trans. Pattern Anal. Mach. Intell. **32**(10), 1744–1757 (2010)

2. Huynh, T., et al.: Estimating CT image from MRI data using structured random forest and auto-context model. IEEE Trans. Med. Imaging **35**(1), 174–183 (2015)
3. Balakrishnan, G., Zhao, A., Sabuncu, M.R., Guttag, J., Dalca, A.V.: VoxelMorph: a learning framework for deformable medical image registration. IEEE TMI **38**(8), 1788–1800 (2019)
4. de Vos, B.D., Berendsen, F.F., Viergever, M.A., Sokooti, H., Staring, M., Išgum, I.: A deep learning framework for unsupervised affine and deformable image registration. Med. Image Anal. **52**, 128–143 (2019)
5. Hu, Y., et al.: Label-driven weakly-supervised learning for multimodal deformableimage registration. In: Proceedings of ISBI 2018, pp. 1070–1074. IEEE (2018)
6. Eppenhof, K.A., Lafarge, M.W., Pluim, J.P.: Progressively growing convolutional networks for end-to-end deformable image registration. In: Medical Imaging 2019: Image Processing, vol. 10949, p. 109491C. International Society for Optics and Photonics (2019)
7. Hering, A., Heldmann, S.: Unsupervised learning for large motion thoracic CT follow-up registration. In: SPIE Medical Imaging: Image Processing, vol. 10949, p. 109491B (2019)
8. Hering, A., Kuckertz, S., Heldmann, S., Heinrich, Mattias P.: Enhancing label-driven deep deformable image registration with local distance metrics for state-of-the-art cardiac motion tracking. Bildverarbeitung für die Medizin 2019. I, pp. 309–314. Springer, Wiesbaden (2019). https://doi.org/10.1007/978-3-658-25326-4_69
9. Rohé, M.-M., Datar, M., Heimann, T., Sermesant, M., Pennec, X.: SVF-Net: learning deformable image registration using shape matching. In: Descoteaux, M., Maier-Hein, L., Franz, A., Jannin, P., Collins, D.L., Duchesne, S. (eds.) MICCAI 2017. LNCS, vol. 10433, pp. 266–274. Springer, Cham (2017). https://doi.org/10.1007/978-3-319-66182-7_31
10. Rühaak, J., et al.: Estimation of large motion in lung CT by integrating regularized keypoint correspondences into dense deformable registration. IEEE TMI **36**(8), 1746–1757 (2017)
11. Marcus, D.S., Wang, T.H., Parker, J., Csernansky, J.G., Morris, J.C., Buckner, R.L.: Open access series of imaging studies (oasis): cross sectional mri data in young, middle aged, nondemented, and demented older adults. J. Cogn. Neurosci. **19**(9), 1498–1507 (2007)
12. Zou, M., Jinrong, H., Zhang, H., Xi, W., He, J., Zhijie, X., Zhong, Y.: Rigid medical image registration using learning-based interest points and features. Comput. Mater. Continua **60**(2), 511–525 (2019)
13. Liu, Z., Xiang, B., Yuqing Song, H., Liu, Q.: An improved unsupervised image segmentation method based on multi-objective particle, swarm optimization clustering algorithm. Comput. Mater. Continua **58**(2), 451–461 (2019)
14. Hao, W., Liu, Q., Liu, X.: A review on deep learning approaches to image classification and object segmentation. Comput. Mater. Continua **60**(2), 575–597 (2019)
15. Vercauteren, T., Pennec, X., Perchant, A., Ayache, N.: Diffeomorphic demons: efficient non-parametric image registration. Neuroimage **45**, S61–S72 (2009)
16. https://itk.org/SimpleITKDoxygen/html/DemonsRegistration1_2DemonsRegistrtion1_8py-example.html
17. https://github.com/voxelmorph/voxelmorph
18. Gibson, E., et al.: NiftyNet: a deep-learning platform for medical imaging. Comput. Meth. Prog. Bio. **158**, 113–122 (2018)
19. https://github.com/NifTK/NiftyNet

Research on Cross-lingual Machine Reading Comprehension Technology Based on Non-parallel Corpus

Zhao Yi, Wang Jin, and Xuejie Zhang[✉]

School of Information Science and Engineering, Yunnan University,
Kunming 650504, Yunnan, People's Republic of China
xjzhang@ynu.edu.cn

Abstract. Machine reading comprehension (MRC) has attracted considerable attention in NLP. However, due to the singularity of the word vector space, MRC models cannot be used for multiple languages. Developing a separate training model for each language would be time consuming. In addition, a supervised machine reading comprehension model for multiple languages would require many training samples and expensive parallel corpora. Therefore, this paper adopts cross-lingual word embedding for cross-lingual MRC for multiple languages. The bilingual word-embedding model discards the dependence on the parallel corpus to train the shared word vector using adversarial learning. In addition, the Procrustes method and cross-domain similarity local scaling are introduced in confrontation training to fine-tune the transition matrix so that the representations of the bilingual word vectors in the shared word vector space overlap as much as possible to achieve better performance. The final experimental results show that the orthogonal Procrustes method and local scaling of cross-domain similarity enhance the training effect of cross-lingual word vectors. Compared with monolingual MRC models, the proposed machine reading comprehension model, which uses cross-lingual word vectors, works effectively.

Keywords: Cross-lingual MRC · Cross-lingual word embedding · Adversarial learning · Procrustes analysis · Cross-domain similarity local scaling

1 Introduction

As a key technology for constructing artificial intelligence, machine reading comprehension has become a frontier topic in natural language processing. The purpose of this technology is to enable computers to extract knowledge from text and answer relevant questions. However, because of economic globalization, this

This work was supported by the National Natural Science Foundation of China (NSFC) under Grant No. 61702443, No. 61762091 and No. 61966038.

technology will inevitably have users from all over the world. In every country, each language has its own rules and usage. One cannot directly apply one language's reading comprehension technology to another language. Moreover, building a separate machine reading comprehension system for each language would take considerable time and effort. It would take much time and effort to build a separate machine reading comprehension system for each language. At the same time, depending on the number of language users and the generality of the language, languages are divided into large and small languages. Unlike large languages (such as English), which have widely used groups, corpus resources and data for small languages are insufficient.

Therefore, developing a machine reading comprehension model for small languages, which have relatively scarce resources, by training a resource-rich large-language corpus and achieving cross-lingual machine reading comprehension is a difficult problem in natural language processing and is still at the exploratory stage.

In recent years, due to the rapid development of deep learning and the availability of large-scale corpora, research on machine reading comprehension technology has achieved good results. The main work of this thesis is to develop a cross-lingual word-embedding model, which maps words from different languages into a shared embedding space to achieve model migration between different languages, and finally develop a multilingual machine reading comprehension model. Implementing a cross-lingual model mainly involves creating a relationship mapping over multiple languages by using parallel corpora to construct a multilingual corpus and then understand the word embedding of the cross-lingual model. In fact, all these embedded models rely on large-scale parallel corpora.

In this study, we find a way to create a relationship mapping without the parallel corpora. We build a cross-lingual machine reading comprehension system. That is, we train the model using an adversarial method in English text, then migrate the model to the Chinese text for inference, and measure the effect of cross-lingual models by using the relevant evaluation indicators of machine reading comprehension. Experimental results show that it is feasible to use adversarial learning to generate the shared word vector, and the accuracy of the word vector when using the Procrustes and cross-domain similarity methods are obviously improved. Therefore, it is feasible to train the cross-lingual word-embedding model by using adversarial learning.

The rest of the paper is organized as follows: Sect. 2 presents a brief review of the previously proposed methods. Section 3 describes the monolingual machine reading comprehension model. Section 4 shows the comparative experiment results. Conclusions are drawn in Sect. 5.

2 Related Work

The long-term goal of natural language processing is to enable computers to read, process, and understand the intrinsic meaning of texts. Therefore, research on machine reading comprehension has been ongoing, and there are many models for different reading comprehension tasks. For example, the Attentive Reader [1], used in the cloze machine reading comprehension task, proposes an attention-based neural network for reading comprehension; the Attention Sum Reader proposes the pointer network [2]; the CAS Reader is proposed for Chinese understanding; and the AS Reader (Attention Sum Reader) is extended with a neural network structure based on consensus attention [3].

In recent years, models based on span-extraction machine reading comprehension have become a topic of intense interest. The current mainstream machine reading comprehension model is based on End2End, which is used mainly for the Encode-Interaction-Pointer framework, such as that used by R-Net of Microsoft Research Asia. Compared to traditional models, the self-matching and gated attention mechanism became the first deep-learning model to approach humans according to some indicators in the SQuAD (The Stanford Question Answering Dataset) [4], as well as the SLQA (Semantic Learning for Question Answering) system. While focusing on capturing problems and specific areas of relevance in the article, the model has achieved good results in gradually focusing on the use of stratification strategies to incorporate global information into the attention mechanism. The more classic reading comprehension model is BiDAF (Bidirectional Attention Flow) [5]. The most significant feature of this model is the introduction of a two-way attention mechanism in the interaction layer and the calculation of Query2Context and Context2Query, as well as Match-LSTM [6], which improved the aforementioned two methods of answer extraction.

Current mainstream span-extraction machine reading comprehension models mostly use the attention mechanism [7]. There are also many variations of the attention mechanism in machine reading comprehension [8]. Co-Attention is a variant of the attention mechanism that simulates a technique in which people are doing reading comprehension. By combining the information of both the question and the text paragraph, a focused weight is generated on each part of the text paragraph. Weight the text information. The AOA (Attention-over-Attention) Reader model proposed by HKUST and the Harbin Institute of Technology at the 2017 ACL meeting is a two-dimensional matching model [3]; this model combines the column-based and row-based attention calculations and uses secondary verification to reverify the answers calculated by the AOA Reader model; this model also improved and applied the attention mechanism.

To complete the migration of cross-lingual models [9], we need to rely on cross-lingual word-embedding models [10]. In recent years, many models have been able to obtain accurate representations of words due to the success of word embedding. Most of the methods currently used are based on supervised learning monolingual mapping, which maps the independent words of two languages into the space of the same shared word vector by a linear transformation; an example of such a method is the regression method originally proposed by Mikolov [11]. By maximizing the similarity between the source language and the target language, the source language word vector is mapped into the space of the target language. In addition, the typical correlation analysis, CCA [12] (canonical correlation analysis), proposed by Faruqui and Dyer, embeds the words of the two languages into a third-party shared space and uses bilingual word embedding to improve the quality of the monolingual model. Later, some orthogonal transformations were proposed, but this method needs to be normalized by length normalization under orthogonal constraints.

3   Mono-Lingual Machine Reading Comprehension Model

For a given passage D and its corresponding textual form of the questions set Q = $q1$, $q2$, ... qn, the reading comprehension system is required to automatically analyze the passage and the questions and then to output a, which satisfies the question.

Therefore, the monolingual MRC model is divided mainly into four layers, as shown in Fig. 1:

1. Embed Layer: this layer consists of word and char embedding and encodes articles and questions separately.
2. Attention Flow Layer: The two-way attention mechanism integrates passage and questions so that they each have three layers of information: word, char and sentence.
3. Modeling Layer: this layer capture the relationship between contexwords in a given question through a Bi-LSTM.
4. Output Layer: This layer determines the positions of start and end in the text and then uses the pointer network for answer extraction.

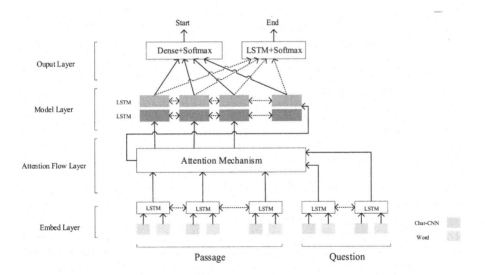

Fig. 1. Model of span-extraction MRC

4   Adversarial Learning for Cross-lingual Machine Reading Comprehension

In current studies of cross-lingual word embedding models, most methods learn the transfer matrix from the source language to the target language by using a single-word vector representation of different languages, and this operation requires a word-aligned dictionary or sentences to align parallel corpora as a training sample. Because of the high cost of parallel corpora and the limitation of data volume, we introduce the Procrustes analysis method and cross-domain similarity scaling to improve the effect of the cross-lingual word vector on the unsupervised training of cross-lingual word embedding [13].

4.1   Procrustes Analysis

In face recognition training, the face images in the training samples differ mostly in shape, and it is often necessary to perform feature point detection and then normalize the processing to make faces of different shapes overlap as much as possible. The Procrustes analysis method mainly translates, rotates and scales the first vector so that its shape matches the second image as close as possible; the method then uses the least squares method to find the affine transformation with the smallest sum of the distances between the changed points and the target point [14].

Since the trained word vector has certain characteristics in the distribution of the embedded space, the similar word vector representation is relatively concentrated, and a vector of the same type as that of the original vector can be obtained by adding or subtracting the vector distance. If the source language word vector is mapped in the target language word vector space, and if it is assumed that the two-language word vector distributions of the target vector space are consistent or slightly offset by the same distance, then all the vector operations of the original language word-embedding space can be performed. A moving operation causes the two-language word vectors to coincide in shape within the vector space. From this, it can be inferred that the original word meanings corresponding to the two-word vectors that coincide are identical.

4.2   Cross-domain Similarity Local Scaling

In fine-tuning the vector, the first step is to find the vector pairs that need to be fine-tuned. The most common method used to find vector pairs is the nearest neighbor algorithm. A vector y may be among the top-K nearest neighbor vector of vector x, but the top-K neighbors of x may not include y. In high-dimensional spaces, this results in some vectors having a high probability of nearest neighbor vectors, while some vectors are not nearest neighbor vectors of any other point. This is very disturbing for vector matching. From the matching of visual image features to the translation of words in text comprehension, a series of solutions have been proposed in different fields to alleviate this problem, but most studies solve this problem in single-feature distributions. The literature [15] proposes using the two-neighbor neighborhood $\Omega_T(Wx_{src})$, $\Omega_S(y_{tgt})$ to connect each word of a given dictionary to the top-K nearest neighbor of another language. In the domain diagram of the two sides, $\Omega_T(Wx_{src})$ represents the K vector field of the mapped word vector Wx_{src}, and the K vectors of the vector domain are the target language word vectors. Similarly, $\Omega_S(y_{tgt})$ refers to the top-K target language word vector field of the target language word vector y_{tgt}. Therefore, the average approximation of the source language word vector Wx_{src} and its top-K word vector is:

$$\Gamma_T(Wx_{src}) = \frac{1}{K} \sum_{y_{tgt} \in \Omega_T(Wx_{src})} \cos(Wx_{src}, y_{tgt}) \tag{1}$$

The average approximation of the target language word vector and its top-K word vector is:

$$\Gamma_S(y_{tgt}) = \frac{1}{K} \sum_{y_{tgt}^* \in \Omega_S(y_{tgt})} \cos(y_{tgt}^*, y_{tgt}) \tag{2}$$

Integration optimization:

$$\text{CSLS}(Wx_{src}, y_{tgt}) = 2\cos(Wx_{src}) - \Gamma_T(Wx_{src}) - \Gamma_S(y_{tgt}) \tag{3}$$

4.3   Fine-Tuning the Adversarial Model

In the case technology that is not based on parallel corpora, which uses the source language word vector and the target language word vector as parallel sample data, there is a significant error in statistical word frequency or random sampling. To solve this problem, the Facebook AI team introduced the classic algorithm Procrustes analysis in image face recognition tasks. Xing also proposed in 2015 that in bilingual translation tasks, applying orthogonal constraints to the transfer matrix can effectively improve the experimental results. This paper also uses the Procrustes analysis and orthogonal constraint methods in the cross-lingual text classification model, thereby making the matrix W obtained by training more reliable.

Adversarial Learning: In adversarial learning, the structure of the encoder-decoder is used [16]. The source language vector is mapped to the target language vector space, and the similarity between the source vector and its reconstructed vector is calculated to adjust the training to obtain the transition matrix W, and a discriminator is trained to continue adjusting the transition matrix W [17]. The detailed learning procedure is described as follow,

1. The two language corpus training words into the model, and the vector space is recorded as X, Y respectively.

$$X = \{x_1, x_2, ..., x_n\}, Y = \{y_1, y_2, ..., y_n\} \tag{4}$$

2. The discriminator is used to classify the mapped original vector WX and the target vector: in addition, the mapped original vector is used as a positive sample, and the target vector sample is used as a negative sample to perform iterative training.

$$L_D(\theta_D|W) = -\frac{1}{n} \sum_{i=1}^{n} \log P_D(source = 1|Wx_i)$$
$$-\frac{1}{m} \sum_{i=1}^{m} \log P_D(source = 0|y_i) \tag{5}$$

3. In mapping the original and target vectors, the classification method is also used to classify and predict the mapped original vector and target vector. Contrary to discriminator training, this method takes the mapped original vector as a negative sample and the target vector sample as a positive sample. To avoid the single vector after mapping, the mapped vector is inversely mapped back to the original space; (that is, the reconstructed vector of the original vector, and the similarity value between the original vector), and the reconstructed vector is calculated. This not only solves the case where the mapping vector is often a fixed value, but also makes the vector preserve the original vector information as much as possible. The mapping loss function is:

$$L_W(W|\theta_D) = -\frac{1}{n} \sum_{i=1}^{n} \log P_D(source = 0|Wx_i)$$
$$-\frac{1}{m} \sum_{i=1}^{m} \log P_D(source = 1|y_i)$$
$$-\lambda_{\cos} \cos(x, W^T Wx) \tag{6}$$

4.4 Vector Fine-Tuning

After the completion of the anti-learning training, a transfer matrix W with a good effect can be initially obtained, but there is still a large gap in the results, compared with the results based on the parallel corpus supervised method. In addition, combating learning involves training all the word vectors of different languages to be aligned regardless of their respective word frequency factors. This will result in too few iterations of word iterations with low word frequency or inconsistent word frequency in both languages, thereby resulting in the mapping vector not matching the target word vector.

To solve this problem, this paper uses the Procrustes algorithm to fine-tune the map vector to achieve the same possible overlap with the target vector. Assuming that the word vector space conversion methods used are linear mapping, it is more efficient and reliable to use only words with high word frequency to align the reference points. Moreover, after the completion of the antilearning training, words with higher word frequency are also significantly more accurate than words with lower word frequency.

In fine-tuning the map vector, only words with high word frequency and their nearest words are considered to ensure the accuracy of the final bilingual word vector space. Calculating the affine transformation matrix by using the Procrustes algorithm introduces the orthogonal Procrustes problem [18], which is the matrix approximation problem in linear algebra: for a given matrix A and B, an orthogonal matrix of the minimum distance from A to B is to be found. The fine-tuning alignment can be converted into a solution to the orthogonal Procrustes problem. The solution formula is as follows:

$$M = YX^T \tag{7}$$

$$U \sum V^T = M \tag{8}$$

$$W^* = \operatorname{argmin} \|WX - Y\| = UV^T \tag{9}$$

Assuming that the word vector space conversion methods used are linear mapping, comparing the use of all global mapping word vectors, it is more reliable and efficient to use only words with high word frequency as the alignment reference point. In addition, after the completion of the anti-learning training, words with higher word frequency are also significantly more accurate than words with lower word frequency. In fine-tuning the map vector, only words with high word frequency and their nearest words are considered to ensure the accuracy of the final bilingual word vector space.

4.5   Experiments

Dataset: In this experiment, nonparallel corpora are used to train cross-lingual word-embedding models. Therefore, for the dataset, only the single language corpus of English and Chinese is needed. The classification model training sample only needs the English training set, and the cross-lingual model will directly predict the Chinese test sample [13].

The Chinese dataset used in the experiment was from the Chinese dataset [19] provided by The Second Evaluation Workshop on Chinese Machine Reading Comprehension (CMRC2018) [20]. The English dataset was SQuAD1.1.

Evaluation Metrics: Evaluation using EM and F1 as evaluation indicators and EM as the main evaluation index.

Mono-Lingual Comparative Results: For the monolingual language, this experiment uses English and Chinese as examples, using BiDAF, QANet and Match-LSTM. The experimental results are as follows:

As seen in Table 1, span-extraction MRC models using the attention mechanism integrate chapters and problems better than the traditional model. In particular, BiDAF uses self-attention to improve the results significantly by approximately 4%–7%.

Table 1. Mono-lingual comparative results on SQuAD1.1

Models	SQuAD1.1		CMRC2018	
	EM	F1	EM	F1
BiDAF	62.31	73.12	45.33	65.41
Match-LSTM	61.35	74.36	44.92	64.41
BiDAF+self attention	68.15	77.91	49.12	71.91
QANet	64.32	74.21	47.14	69.56

Cross-lingual Comparative Results: The predictive output is obtained by training the machine reading comprehension model using a shared word vector generated against the learning. The English-Chinese experimental results are as follows: The Table 2 shows a comparison between the results of only adversarial learning and the results after adversarial learning and fine-tuning the vector.

Table 2. Adversarial learning experiment results

BiDAF	Methods	EM	F1
EnZh-Zh	Adversarial learning	17.11	25.58
(CMRC2018)	Vector fine-tuning	21.25	28.21
EnZh-En	Adversarial learning	64.54	77.15
(SQuAD1.1)	Vector fine-tuning	68.37	79.53

Since, in this experiment, adversarial learning uses English as the source target and maps to the target Chinese vector space, and since the machine reading comprehension model directly uses the English training samples for training, the direct prediction results obtained from using the Chinese data set are not as good as the results obtained from using single model training. The lesser quality of the results obtained from using the Chinese dataset also indicates that current unsupervised models and methods still have some limitations. However, the results show the feasibility of the cross-language model in machine reading comprehension: after adding the fine-tuning model, the result obtained from using direct confrontation learning improved by approximately 3%–4%.

5   Conclusion

This paper abandons the practice of developing multiple single-language machine reading comprehension systems based on large-scale parallel corpora and proposes an exploratory cross-lingual machine reading comprehension system based on a nonparallel corpus. The proposed cross-lingual machine reading comprehension system can be applied to multiple languages using only a single language training corpus. This paper mainly proposes an unsupervised cross-lingual word-embedding model based on adversarial learning. The model adds orthogonal constraints to the mainstream adversarial learning method that currently processes nonparallel samples so that learning the word vector mapping is possible through the encoder-decoder model, and the source language word vector and the target language word vector are determined by the discriminator. Make a judgment. This not only makes the word vector after training include the implicit information of the source language word vector but also maps the word vector to the target space. Finally, the mapping matrix is iteratively updated by using orthogonal Procrustes analysis so that the potential word pairs are as close as possible. In this paper, relevant experiments and corresponding comparative experiments illustrate the possibility of obtaining shared word vectors through adversarial learning; however, in future work, we will consider extending our model to incorporate the joint optimization method, which is conducive to the next step of vector fine-tuning. Moreover, we will consider further exploring how the words are paired. We will try to use nonlinear transformation to map from the source language to the target language.

References

1. Hermann, K.M., et al.: Teaching machines to read and comprehend. In: Advances in Neural Information Processing Systems, pp. 1693–1701 (2015)
2. Kadlec, R., Schmid, M., Bajgar, O., Kleindienst, J.: Text understanding with the attention sum reader network. arXiv preprint arXiv:1603.01547 (2016)
3. Cui, Y., Liu, T., Chen, Z., Wang, S., Hu, G.: Consensus attention-based neural networks for Chinese reading comprehension. arXiv preprint arXiv:1607.02250 (2016)
4. Rajpurkar, P., Zhang, J., Lopyrev, K., Liang, P.: Squad: 100,000+ questions for machine comprehension of text. arXiv preprint arXiv:1606.05250 (2016)
5. Seo, M., Kembhavi, A., Farhadi, A., Hajishirzi, H.: Bidirectional attention flow for machine comprehension. arXiv preprint arXiv:1611.01603 (2016)
6. Wang, S., Jiang, J.: Machine comprehension using match-LSTM and answer pointer. arXiv preprint arXiv:1608.07905 (2016)
7. Qu, Z., Cao, B., Wang, X., Li, F., Xu, P., Zhang, L.: Feedback LSTM network based on attention for image description generator. CMC-Comput. Mater. Con. **59**(2), 575–589 (2019)
8. Qiu, J., et al.: Dependency-based local attention approach to neural machine translation. Comput. Mater. Con. **58**(2), 547–562 (2019)
9. Hong, X., Zheng, X., Xia, J., Wei, L., Xue, W.: Cross-lingual non-ferrous metals related news recognition method based on CNN with a limited bi-lingual dictionary. Comput. Mater. Con. **58**(2), 379–389 (2019)
10. Joulin, A., Bojanowski, P., Mikolov, T., Jégou, H., Grave, E.: Loss in translation: learning bilingual word mapping with a retrieval criterion. arXiv preprint arXiv:1804.07745 (2018)
11. Mikolov, T., Le, Q.V., Sutskever, I.: Exploiting similarities among languages for machine translation. arXiv preprint arXiv:1309.4168 (2013)
12. Hardoon, D.R., Szedmak, S., Shawe-Taylor, J.: Canonical correlation analysis: an overview with application to learning methods. Neural Comput. **16**(12), 2639–2664 (2004)

13. Lample, G., Conneau, A., Denoyer, L., Ranzato, M.: Unsupervised machine translation using monolingual corpora only. arXiv preprint arXiv:1711.00043 (2017)
14. Zhang, J.: Sparse orthogonal procrustes problem based regression for face recognition with pose variations. Comput. Sci. **44**(2), 302–305 (2017)
15. Lample, G., Conneau, A., Denoyer, L., Jégou, H., et al.: Word translation without parallel data (2018)
16. Zhang, M., Liu, Y., Luan, H., Sun, M.: Adversarial training for unsupervised bilingual lexicon induction. In: Proceedings of the 55th Annual Meeting of the Association for Computational Linguistics (Volume 1: Long Papers), pp. 1959–1970 (2017)
17. Cho, K., Van Merriënboer, B., Bahdanau, D., Bengio, Y.: On the properties of neural machine translation: encoder-decoder approaches. arXiv preprint arXiv:1409.1259 (2014)
18. Schönemann, P.H.: A generalized solution of the orthogonal procrustes problem. Psychometrika **31**(1), 1–10 (1966). https://doi.org/10.1007/BF02289451
19. Cui, Y., et al.: A span-extraction dataset for Chinese machine reading comprehension, pp. 5886–5891, November 2019. https://www.aclweb.org/anthology/D19-1600
20. Cui, Y., Che, W., Liu, T., Qin, B., Wang, S., Hu, G.: Cross-lingual machine reading comprehension, pp. 1586–1595, November 2019. https://www.aclweb.org/anthology/D19-1169

Research on the Data Reference Model of NMIS

Yi Yang[(⊠)]

School of Management Science and Engineering and China Institute of Manufacturing, No. 219,
Ningliu Road, Nanjing, Jiangsu, China
yiyang0803@163.com

Abstract. This paper analyzed the conception and characters of net-centric military information system (NMIS), and proposed a data reference model for NMIS to support data sharing, business interoperability and flexible system reconstructing. Furthermore, the paper give the analysis of the data application modes of NMIS, which describe how the data reference model performed in data sharing, business interoperability and flexible system reconstructing.

Keywords: Net-centric · Military information system · Data classification · Data reference model

1 Introduction

With development of information technology and military theroy, it is demonstrated that the network-centric warfare [1] has appeared to be the prime modality of the future warfare.

The network-centric warfare, which is not limited to the function of separate weapon platform, is committed to the optimized utilization of battlefield reource to support information sharing and cooperation, and then achieve the superiority in warfare [2]. With the coming of net-centric warfare, more problems are bring front for the data using, which call for data sharing and business interoperability [3–13].

Aimed to solve the problem appeared in net-centric construction, we proposed a data reference model to organize the data of net-centric military information system(NMIS) . Furthermore, the paper give the analysis of the data application modes of NMIS, which describe how the proposed data reference model performed in data sharing, business interoperability and system reconstructing.

2 The Analysis of NMIS

2.1 Characteristics of Data in the Network Centric Environment

Since the second half of the 20th century, high-tech with information technology as the core has led to profound changes in military theory, weapons and equipment, military organization, command system and combat style, which is the so-called new military change in the world.

© Springer Nature Singapore Pte Ltd. 2020
X. Sun et al. (Eds.): ICAIS 2020, CCIS 1252, pp. 419–426, 2020.
https://doi.org/10.1007/978-981-15-8083-3_37

From the Gulf War, Kosovo war, Afghanistan war to the recent Iraq war, the modern war has the new characteristics of weapon equipment systematization, integration of attack and defense patterns, combination of combat forces and multidimensional battlefield space. Data demand and military demand are inseparable.

Combined with the development trend and characteristics of military demand, the characteristics of data in the network centric environment are mainly reflected in the following aspects:

The Amount and Types of Data Have Increased Dramatically. Sensors embedded in reconnaissance satellites, early warning aircraft, individual systems and other platforms generate a large number of real-time data; the diversification of operational materials has led to the multiple increase of logistics support data; geographic information (especially 3D terrain information) has also introduced a large number of data, which are too numerous to enumerate.

Cross System and Cross Platform Data Sharing. The systematization of weapon equipment requires that the weapons in the system share the operational data, and the coordination and synchronization between the systems are also required through the operational data.

With the combination of combat forces and multidimensional battlefield space, command and control information is no longer limited to vertical flow, but must be able to flow horizontally or even cross.

With the integration of battlefield attack and defense and the blurring of front and rear boundaries, commanders and staff officers must be able to take a panoramic view of the overall situation. They should not only master the overall operation plan, operation process, strength comparison between the enemy and us, the status of friendly forces, terrain and landform, but also understand the logistics support, weather forecast, and even the physical and mental status of soldiers.

These data often come from different systems, so the high-speed sharing of battlefield data between information systems is very important to win the modern war.

Data Security and Confidentiality. Data and information are the key to victory. The belligerents, who can not only effectively break the data of the other party, but also ensure the security of their own data, will have the initiative in the battlefield. Therefore, the security and confidentiality of operational data can not be ignored.

2.2 Characteristics of Data in NMIS

NMIS is certain military system constructed on the base of information infrastructure to share data and computation with each other, and provide the capability to support the integrated joint operation, such as cooperation of application layer, cohesive capability of various network resources, flexible system reconstruction for missions, and service on-demand [14].

From the application need of NMIS, the data characteristics are summarized as follows, which should be taken into consideration in the construction of NMIS.

Support Rapid Increase of Data Size and Variety. With the development of military informationization, the data size and variety is increased rapidly, which almost cover all the business domain and organization, such as business domain of command, control, communicating, computer, intelligence, reconnaissance, navigation and location, management of common information as well as information campaign and so on.

Support Inter-organization Data Sharing. Owing to the bond of combat force and multi-dimension of battlefield space, information should be shared between different organization and system, so that the commander can grip the comprehensive survey for battlefield to make correct combat plan, and the soldiers can get the information need for action. While information are generally collected from different organizations and sectors, it is an essential issue that data can be shared with high speed between organization and platform.

Support Business Interoperability. Based on the resource sharing, NMIS should have the ability to support business interoperability referring to the requirements of the combat mission. By transforming the business data, the inheritable business can be performed in various systems and platforms to realize the business interoperability between the existing and in-developing system.

Support System Reconstruction. NMIS should sustain not only the specific combat missions, but also the uncertain missions, which mean NMIS can utilize the resource provided by the network environment and construct the combat system dynamically to ensure the accomplishment of the mission.

3 Data Reference Model of NMIS

3.1 Classification of Data

NMIS have the capability to integrate various combat forces and information systems. It is reflected that NMIS is not only the simple improvement of the traditional system, but also the system qualitative change resulting from the innovative intersection and integration of information system technologies.

Synthetically considering the NMIS requirements of data sharing and professional application, it is illustrated that the NMIS data is classified and organized with the view of business region, organization and data modality and a corresponding data variety framework of NMIS is proposed in the paper, as shown in Fig. 1.

The **business dimension** gives a detail by classifying the data application region according to the military business activity, including command and control, detecting and early-warning, intelligence and reconnaissance, climate and hydraulic, electromagnetism environment, weapon control, logistical support as well as device support and so on.

The **organization dimension** illustrates that the organizations, where the data is applied, are classified by the entire army, theater and sector. The behavior ensures not only the sharing of common data, but also the proprietary of the private data in sectors.

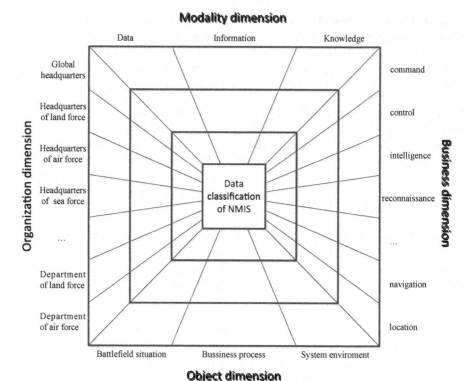

Fig. 1. Data classification of NMIS

In the **modality dimension**, according to the essential described objects, the data modalities are mainly divided into data, information and knowledge. Therein, as the lowest level, the data is almost composed of text, graphic, image, cartoon, video and audio. The information constructed based on the combination and association of the above six modalities, gives a detail description of system operation, system environment configuration and system physical environment. Knowledge is abstracted from amount of information from operation experience and rule of physical environment. The modality specification boosts the efficient application of data, with helping the users explore for the required data in real time.

The **object dimension** give the classification according to the objective of the data use, which mainly include supporting battlefield situation, supporting business process, supporting system enviroment.

3.2 Data Reference Model

NMIS should support rapid increase of data size and variety, inter-organization data sharing, business interoperability. So we introduce the data reference model of NMIS, with the consideration of data sharing, business interoperability and flexible system reconstruction (Fig. 2).

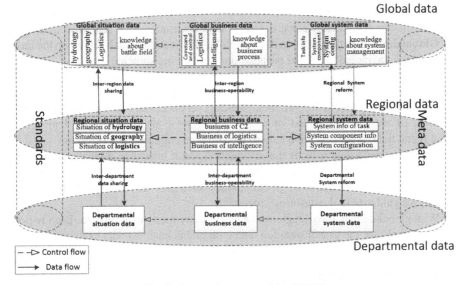

Fig. 2. Data reference model of NMIS

Departmental data is the minimal data-organization of NMIS, which provide the private data for each department, including department-business data, departmental situation data and departmental system data.

Department-business data records the information about business management processes of each department, such as command and control process, logistics management process, etc.

Departmental situation data records the monitoring and analysis information that each department collect about battle filed, such as logistics, hydrology and soon.

Departmental system data records the information about the system used by each department, such as system function and configuration information.

Regional data store the common data for region application, which is built on the base of department-level dataset, including regional business data, regional situation data and regional system data.

Regional situation data records all the monitoring and analysis information produced by the department belongs to the region, which is extracted from departmental situation data and integrated into a complete dataset about the regional situation.

Regional business data records all the information about business management processes inter and inner the departments belongs to the region, which is extracted from departmental business data and integrated into a complete dataset about the regional business management.

Regional system data records the information about the system function and configuration which can help to construct the system environment to support business tasks of the region.

Using Tactical-level data Tactical-level data, the departments of same region can easily share their situation data, which can be controlled with business data exchanging

In the same way, each department or system user is able to apply for the Regional system data, which can dynamically construct the system environment for task execution.

Global data store the common data for global application, which is built on the base of regional data, including global business data and global situation data.

Global situation data records all the monitoring and analysis information which is extracted from regional situation data. With global situation data, we can get a global view showing every part of the battlefield, which is very necessary for the strategic-policy decision. In addition, the global situation data Strategic also provides the knowledge about battle field, which can give help to the situation cognition and reaction.

Global business data records the information about inter-region business management processes, which is extracted from regional business data and used to support the inter-region process. In addition, global business data provide the business knowledge which give guidance to the business procession.

With global data, deferent regions can easily share their situation data. Each region is able to apply for the global situation data with global business data exchanging.

4 Data Application Modes of NMIS

4.1 Data-Sharing Mode

In the proposed data reference model, the data exchanges between neighboring layers provide the base of data sharing.

When a department needs the situation data produced by another department in the same region, it can apply for the situation data through business data exchange with regional data center, which will control the situation data delivery.

Similarly, when a department needs the situation data belongs to another region, it can apply for the situation data through business data exchange with global data center. In this way, inter-department and inter-region data-sharing are supported.

4.2 Business-Interoperability Mode

The business-interoperability is realized based on the exchange of business data between neighboring layers.

The departments in the same region share the business data with the business data exchanges between departmental data and regional data, which support the realization of inter-department business interoperability.

Similarly, through the business data exchange between regional data and global data, inter-region business interoperability is supported.

4.3 System-Reconstructing Mode

System-reconstructing is the characteristic application mode Of NMIS, which is supported by the system-data exchange between layers of the proposed data reference model.

In this application mode, the information of system environment, which provides the system component and configuration for each mission, is stored in the regional data center and global data center.

The users of NMIS can get the system data for specific mission remotely through business data exchange, and constructing the system for the mission dynamically. When the mission changes, the user can get the system data for the new mission and reconstruct system.

5 Conclusion

This paper analyzed the conception and characters of net-centric military information system, and proposed a data framework of NMIS, which give the data classification and data reference model for NMIS to support data sharing, business interoperability and flexible system reconstructing.

Furthermore, the paper give the analysis of the data application modes of NMIS, which describe how the proposed data framework performed in data sharing, business interoperability and flexible system reconstructing.

Our paper gives a possible data organization of NMIS, which might have reference value on data planning of NMIS.

References

1. Albert, D.S., Garstka, J.J., Stein, F.P.: Network Centric Warfare: Developing and Leveraging Information Superiority. CCRP Library of Congress Cataloging in Publication Data, Washington, DC (2000)
2. Tao, Y.: Development trends and analysis of the network centric warfare. Ship Electron. Eng. **8**, 17–20 (2012)
3. Ling, P., Liu, Y.: Problem analysis of military data engineering. Military Oper. Res. Syst. Eng. **26**, 14–17 (2012)
4. Chong, F., Carraro, G., Wolter, R.: Multi-tenant data architecture. http://msdn.microsoft.com/en-us/library/aa479086.aspx
5. Dong, X., Zheng, B.: Research on Military logistics information standard system and military material classification an coding. Logist. Technol. **10**, 29–31 (2008)
6. Mietzner, R., Metzger, A., Leymann, F., et al.: Variability modeling to support customization and deployment of multi-tenant-aware software as a service applications
7. Proceeding of the 2009 ICSE Workshop on Principles of Engineering Service Oriented Systems (2009)
8. Wei, J., Zifeng, C.: Net-centric environment of information service and its development in military field. Comm. Inf. Syst. Technol. **4**, 10–16 (2011)
9. Gong, J., Wu, Z.: Thinking of data resource development and management. Office Inf. **2**, 7–9 (2012)
10. Wu, C., Zapevalova, E., Chen, Y., Li, F.: Time optimization of multiple knowledge transfers in the big data environment. Comput. Mater. Cont. **54**(3), 269–285 (2018)
11. Wang, G., Liu, M.: Dynamic trust model based on service recommendation in big data. Comput. Mater. Cont. **58**(3), 845–857 (2019)
12. Zhang, Z., Chen, J., Chen, L., Liu, Q., Yang, L., Wang, P., Zheng, Y.: A scalable method of maintaining order statistics for big data stream. Comput. Mater. Cont. **60**(1), 117–132 (2019)

13. Wu, C., Lee, V., McMurtrey, M.E.: Knowledge composition and its influence on new product development performance in the big data environment. Comput. Mater. Cont. **60**(1), 365–378 (2019)

14. Lan, Y., Deng, K., Mao, S.: Capability evaluation of net-centric military information system. Comm. Inf. Syst. Technol. **1**, 1–7 (2012)

A Real-Time Recommender System Design
Based on Spark Streaming

Qihang Zhang[1,2], Xue Yu[1,2], Keke Ling[1,2], Tianhao Wang[1,2], and Baili Zhang[1,2(✉)]

[1] School of Computer Science and Engineering, Southeast University, Nanjing 211189, China
zhangbl@seu.edu.cn
[2] Research Center for Judicial Big Data, Supreme Count of China, Nanjing 211189, China

Abstract. In the big data environment, the personalized recommender system based on offline batch processing has the advantages of accurate calculation and high fault tolerance. However, due to its large amount of calculation, it cannot satisfy the real-time requirement. At present, the real-time recommender system architecture based on the combination of offline layer and online layer also has some disadvantages in summarizing results and maintaining updates, and the recommended result depends on the offline layer. If the user behavior changes in a short time and the result update of the offline layer is lagging, the final recommendation will not reflect the user's interest change very well. Aiming at these problems, this paper makes use of the Spark Streaming micro-batch data stream processing function to implement a real-time recommendation system. The system realized a real-time recommendation composed entirely of online stream computing based on the consistency of the user positive and negative evaluation of the item .Considering the problem of unstable data flow in the actual application scenario, the message queue Kafka is introduced to ensure the smooth and stable real-time data inflow speed. Finally, the performance of the entire system and the effectiveness of the recommendation are verified by Movielens data set.

Keywords: Real-time recommendation · Spark streaming · Collaborative filtering

With the rapid development of the Internet, the data information carried by the network is exploding. In the face of such massive information, it is often difficult for people to find what they want and what they are interested in. In order to solve this problem, a search engine is born. Those users with clear goals can quickly and accurately find keywords based on keyword search, but in actual daily life, the needs of many users are vague and potential, in order to tap the potential interest of these users, the recommender system is introduced. The recommender system is a tool for solving information overload and helps users discover information that they may be interest in. In this era of information explosion, the recommender system can help users greatly reduce the time to find interesting content, thereby improving the user experience and increasing the user's stickiness of the website.

Hadoop, Which is the traditional platform where recommender system based on the offline batch processing, although it can calculate relatively accurate recommended

© Springer Nature Singapore Pte Ltd. 2020
X. Sun et al. (Eds.): ICAIS 2020, CCIS 1252, pp. 427–438, 2020.
https://doi.org/10.1007/978-981-15-8083-3_38

content from the massive data, but its computational complexity is very high, can not meet the real-time requirements of recommendation, can not respond quickly to changes in user hobbies, and it's hard to capture the user's instant interests.

The real-time recommendation system of Lambda big data processing architecture based on offline layer and online layer has the problems of high system complexity, difficulty in maintenance, and poor timeliness caused by relying on the offline layer.

To handle these problems, this paper uses Spark Streaming's micro-batch data stream processing capability, based on the user evaluation of the positive and negative consistency of the similarity of the item similarity update method, realizing a real-time recommendation system, its recommended calculation entirely consists of online flow calculation. Considering the problem of unstable data flow in the actual application scenario, the message queue Kafka was introduced, utilizing Kafka's high throughput and high speed in data caching ensures smooth and stable real-time data inflow speed. Finally, the performance of the whole system and the recommended timeliness were verified by experiments.

1 System Design

The real-time recommender system architecture diagram designed and implemented based on Spark and Kafka is shown in Fig. 1. There are three main modules: data cache, online stream computing and data storage.

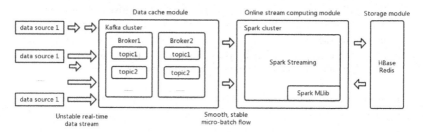

Fig. 1. System architecture diagram

1.1 Data Cache Module

Consisting of a Kafka cluster, Kafka is a distributed message queuing system that acts as a data cache throughout the system. The role of the data caching module is to smooth unstable data streams coming in real time. In the actual industrial application environment, due to the uncertainty of the number of data sources and the fluctuation of the data generation rate, the data flow has great instability. If the data is directly input to the online stream computing platform, the calculation overload and the system jam may occur due to sudden increase in data input. Therefore, the real-time data stream needs to be uniformly cached before being calculated, and then the data is imported into the online stream computing module at a steady speed, and the real-time inflow of data is controlled according to the actual processing capability of the stream computing module. Kafka can cache data according to topic. With this feature, data streams can be classified into Kafka clusters according to data categories. As a message consumer, the stream computing platform can execute multiple stream computing instances, and specifically acquire data in the specified topic to customize the data processing task. In addition, Kafka can support a variety of data sources, such as flume, files, sockets, etc., using the Promoter API provided by Kafka can also import the recommended data set as streaming data to facilitate testing of the system.

1.2   Online Stream Computing Module

The online stream computing module utilizes Spark's stream processing component Spark Streaming and the machine learning component Spark MLlib; the recommended algorithm module updates the recommendation results in real time according to the data stream. Spark is a distributed computing framework for big data processing, it integrates large data processing components such as batch computing and stream processing to provide a stack of support for big data processing tasks in different scenarios. Spark Streaming can convert continuous data streams into continuous micro-batch data for continuous batch processing, which has seconds delay but greatly improves data throughput. As a consumer, Spark Streaming will process certain data from Kafka in the way of Direct Approach integration from Kafka according to the set batch time interval, and perform recommendation calculation to update the recommendation result. Each pull amount needs to be balanced according to the actual computing power. If the pull amount is too high, the calculation load will cause Spark Streaming to not process the current batch data in time, resulting in data accumulation. If the pull amount is too small, it will cause Spark Steaming to do nothing after completing the calculation task ahead of time, resulting in wasted computing resources. The amount of each pull can be fixed by setting the spark.streaming.kafka.maxRatePerPartition parameter, but this parameter is difficult to select due to the actual situation. A better solution is to set the back-pressure mechanism provided by Spark Streaming by setting the spark.streaming.backpressure.enabled parameter to true. Spark Streaming introduces a back-pressure mechanism from v1.5. According to dynamically controlling data reception to adapt cluster data processing capabilities.

Spark Streaming encapsulates successive batches of data into a contiguous DStream, each DStream being an ordered RDD collection. RDD (Elastic Dataset) is a basic abstraction of Spark data. Spark provides some column transformation operations and Output operations for these RDDs. The Transformation operation converts an RDD to another RDD, including map, reduce, join, etc. The Output operation can output the processed RDD to a file or distributed storage platform such as Hadoop or HBase. Spark Streaming needs to use the Transformation and Output operations to implement the recommendation algorithm in the data flow environment, and update the recommendation results in real time according to the data flow. Different from the offline environment, the data in the data flow environment is constantly coming, and continuous recommendation calculation is needed. The core issue to be solved by the online stream computing module is how to reduce the time required for recommendation calculation to meet the requirement of real-time recommendation.

1.3 Data Storage Module

The data storage module is responsible for storing information such as intermediate results of online stream calculations and recommendation results, such as user rating information, item similarity, etc. The choice of storage tools can greatly affect the performance of the entire system. In order to recommend calculations, the storage module needs to provide massive data storage capacity for the entire recommender system while ensuring fast reading and writing of some data. Otherwise, the recommended real-time performance of the entire system cannot be guaranteed, so the column-oriented distributed storage database HBase is selected, which provides random read and write capabilities for stored large amounts of data, and uses WAL, first log and then write data to ensure that no data will be lost.

Due to the slow reading and write speed nature of HBase, in order to improve the performance of the recommended system in the recommended calculation, the data storage module uses Redis to cache some data. Spark Streaming will storage some data that needs to be frequently operated in the calculation process in Redis. This part of the data reading and writing can increase the efficiency of the reading operation by increasing the number of writing, that is, writing data to Redis and HBase simultaneously. Read from Redis first, if Redis has data loss, read from HBase and recover this part of the data in Redis, which ensures the reliability of the data and improves the efficiency of data reading. In general, the data reading speed is much slower than the data writing, so the Redis cache can greatly improve the performance of the recommender system, and for those Spark Streaming calculations that do not need to be read again, such as item similarity matrix, scoring matrix and other information can be written directly to HBase.

2 Data Stream-Oriented Recommendation Algorithm

Although the traditional recommendation algorithm can achieve better recommendation effects in an offline environment, it is often difficult to directly use in the streaming data environment. In addition to can not meeting the recommended real-time requirements, other problems may occur. How to apply the recommendation algorithm in the data flow environment is an important issue that the real-time recommender system must solve. Since the collaborative filtering recommendation algorithm has no special requirements for the recommended objects, it can handle unstructured complex objects such as music, movies, etc., and the data set used in this article for the system testing is the Movielens movie data set, so the main research is how to apply a collaborative filtering recommendation algorithm in the data flow environment.

2.1 Item Similarity Incremental Update Strategy

The collaborative filtering algorithm is the most widely used and most successful recommendation algorithm currently. It is divided into user-based user-cf and item-based item-cf. Since the number of users in a general movie website is much larger than the number of items (movies), it is more appropriate to select item-cf.

Item-cf first needs to calculate the similarity between items according to cosine, Pearson, Jaccard coefficient, etc. from the user-item scoring matrix. In the data flow environment, since the new score (user, item, rating) will continue to arrive, the change of the score matrix will change very frequently. To apply item-cf in a data flow environment, it is necessary to make the item similarity update an incremental update process, avoid getting it out of the entire user scoring matrix each time. In order to achieve this goal, the calculation of item similarity is based on two basic ideas:

(1) If the item has a significant proportion of personal hobbies (such as music, movies, books, etc., rather than the goods on the shopping site), then the similarity between the items can be expressed as: the user's preference and dislike of the item(positive and negative evaluation) is more consistent.
(2) For scores that do not significantly represent user's preferences or dislike, it can be considered to have less impact on item similarity (such as 3 points in a 5-point scoring system), which can be ignored in real-time updates.

A method for calculating the similarity of items based on the user's consistency of positive and negative evaluation. The formula is shown in (1).

$$sim(x, y) = \alpha_{xy} * correlation(x, y) \tag{1}$$

Correlation(x, y) is the user's consistency of positive and negative evaluation of the item x and the item y, and the calculation formula is as shown in (2).

$$Correlation(x, y) = \frac{|R(x) \cap R(y)|}{\sqrt{|R(x)| * |R(y)|}} \tag{2}$$

|R(x)| is the number of users who tend to positively and negatively evaluate item x (take a 5-point movie score as an example. 1 to 2 points can be considered as a user's dislike, a negative evaluation, and 4 to 5 points are user-like.), |R(y)| is the number of users who tend to positively and negatively evaluate the item y, and $|R(x) \cap R(y)|$ is the number of users who agree on the positive and negative evaluation of the items x and y. And α_{xy} is the confidence level according to the user's calculation result of the consistency of positive and negative evaluation of the items. The reason for adding this is that for the correlation (x, y) calculation, the more the two items have the common score of the users, the more credible it is, so the calculation formula is (3).

$$\alpha_{xy} = \sqrt{\frac{num(x,y)}{num_{cur}}} \tag{3}$$

Where num(x, y) is the number of users who have a common evaluation of $item_x$ and $item_y$ in the current system, and num_{cur} is the number of users in the current system. Figure 2 shows an example of similarity calculations in this way.

	Item1	Item2	Item3	Item4	Item5
User1	2	3	3	5	4
User2		5	4	4	3
User3	4	3	4		3
User4	2	4	2	4	2
User5	3	2	4	3	4

$$sim(item2, item4) = \sqrt{4/5} * (2/\sqrt{3 * 3}) = 0.596$$

Fig. 2. An example of calculating the similarity of articles according to the consistency of positive and negative evaluations

In the data flow environment, the user's feedback ($user_i, item_x, rating$) on the item will continue to arrive. According to the basic idea 2, if it does not reflect the positive and negative evaluation tendency of the $user_i$ to $item_x$, ignore the influence of this record on the correlation (x, y). It is only necessary to update the correlation (x, y) when it reflects the positive and negative evaluation tendency of the user, The update formula is shown in (4).

$$correlation'(x, y) = \frac{|R'(x) \cap R(y)|}{\sqrt{|R'(x)| * |R(y)|}} \tag{4}$$

$|R'(x)|$ is $|R(x) + 1|$, which means that it can be directly incremented based on the last result, and $|R'(x) \cap R(y)|$ is:

(1) $|R(x) \cap R(y)| + 1$, if the new scoring data($user_i, item_x, rating$) can reflect the positive and negative evaluation of $user_i$ on $item_x$ and the positive and negative tendency is consistent with $user_i$ for $item_x$.

(2) $|R(x) \cap R(y)|$, if the positive and negative tendency is inconsistent, the original value can be maintained.

The update of α_{xy} is very simple, maintaining a common user count for item x and item y, if the new ($user_i$, $item_x$, rating) comes, $user_i$ has scored on $item_y$, then directly increments num(x, y) and divides by num_{cur}(the current number of users in the system).

Because it is a real-time recommendation system, you only need to make recommendations for users in the current batch of data. After the item similarity is updated, the user u's rating of the unevaluated item i is predicted according to the item similarity matrix, the method is to use the user u to rate the first k most similar items of the item i that have not been evaluated, and calculate the weighted average, the formula is shown in (5).

$$\hat{r}_{ui} = \frac{\sum\limits_{j \in N_k(i)} \omega_{ij} \cdot r_{uj}}{\sum\limits_{j \in N_k(i)} |\omega_{ij}|} \tag{5}$$

$N_k(i)$ represents the set of K most similar items with the item i, ω_{ij} is items similarity between the items i and j, and r_{ui} is the score of the item j by the user u.

2.2 Data Stream Real-Time Filtering Strategy

When the recommendation result is incrementally updated according to the item similarity calculation formula based on the user's consistency of positive and negative evaluation in Sect. 2.1, it is found that when the item dimension is too large, the similarity calculation with other items caused by the change of the item score is still bring huge calculations, although this problem can be solved by adding hardware computing resources, this is not always the best solution.

When using the formula (5) to predict the user $user_i$'s rating of the $item_x$, the first k items that are most similar to the $item_x$ are used, so what is useful for the prediction result is actually the similarity between the item and the itemx of the k items. However, when the item similarity is updated in real time in the data stream environment, the similarity between itemx and all other items is updated, and the similarity of many items is useless. Therefore, if you can ignore this part when updating the similarity of items, you can greatly reduce the amount of calculation.

The proposed algorithm in this paper introduces Hoeffding's Boundary Theory to implement a strategy for real-time filtering of data streams. The Hoeffding Boundary Theory is used to help establish a fast decision tree in data flow analysis. It can be expressed like this: Let x be a random variable whose range is R (The range is 0 to 1 for item similarity), suppose we have n independent observations for this variable, and the average of these n independent observations is $\hat{x}$, then according to the Hoeffding bound theory, under the probability of 1-δ, the true mean of the random variable x is at most $\hat{x} + \epsilon$, Where ϵ is:

$$\epsilon = \sqrt{\frac{R^2 \ln(1/\delta)}{2n}} \tag{6}$$

You can think of the similarity between items as a random variable from 0 to 1, so that t is the threshold of the list of similar items for item x. For example, take the minimum value of the similarity in Nk $(item_x)$, for any δ, If there is already an update of n similarities at a time and $\epsilon < t - \hat{x}$, according to Hoeffding's Boundary Theory, there is a fact that the probability that the mean value of the actual similarity between the item and the item will not be greater than t is 1-δ. That is to say, after updating the similarity of the item x with other items several times in the streaming data environment, it is possible to filter out dissimilar items, that is, items that are unlikely to appear in Nk $(item_x)$. The minimum similarity in the similar item list $N_k(item_x)$ of the item x can be filtered as t. For item y, only sim(x, y) may appear in Nk $(item_x)$ when it is larger than t. Incremental update of items combined with real-time filtering is shown in Table 1, n_{xy} records the number of similarity updates for items x and y, L_x represents the filtered item set for item x, and interestCount(x) indicates the number of users who have a positive or negative tendency to evaluate item x. In order to improve the filtering efficiency, the minimum value of similarity in $N_k(item_x)$ and $N_k(item_y)$is taken as the threshold, and the L_x and L_y sets are expanded.

Table 1. Algorithm 1

Algorithm 1: Incremental update of item similarity combined with real-time filtering of data streams

---

Input: User's rating behavior data, user u, item x and rating r

1   Get L_x
2   **for** each item y rated by user u **do**
3   **if** y in L_x **then**
4   Continue
5   **end**
6   Update
7   Update sameInterestCount(x,y)
8   Get interestCount(X) and interestCount(Y)
9   Compute sim(x,y) use Equation(4-4)
10   Increment n_{xy}
11   Get threshold t_1 of x's similar-items list
12   Get threshold t_2 of y's similar-items list
13   t = min (t_1, t_2)
14   Compute ϵ using Equation (4-6)
15   **if** $\epsilon <$ t-sim(x,y) **then**
16   Add y to L_x
17   Add x to L_y
18   **end**
19 **end**

---

3   Experimental Results

This article builds a real-time recommendation system based on Kafka and Spark in a stand-alone environment. The hardware configuration of a single machine is 16 GB memory, 500 GB solid state hard disk, the CPU model is Intel Core i5-6300, and the software configuration is JDK1.8, Hadoop2.6, HBase1. .2, Kafka 2.11, Spark 2.2.0. The data set used in the experiment is the Movielens data set, including 943 users' 100000 scoring records for 1682 movies, the scoring values are 1 to 5 integer values, as well as user information and movie information. What the real-time recommendation system needs to do is to be able to recommend the movies that users may be interested in for the current active users in real time when the new user rating data is constantly coming.

Firstly, Kafka's producer API is used to continuously read records from the movie scoring data. The advantage of this is that the reading speed of data can be controlled by reading the number of threads and setting the reading time interval, so as to simulate the situation that the amount of streaming data in the actual scene is unstable. After the data is cached in the Kafka message queue, spark streaming pulls data from the Kafka message queue according to the set time batch and the pulled batch processing amount to get new recommended results. The recommendation results also need to be displayed to users to improve the usability of the system. This paper constructs a recommendation result visualization module based on SpringBoot. For the current active users, select the top 8 items that the system has not evaluated for users, and generate a recommendation list to show to users on the page. The final recommendation effect is shown in Fig. 3.

Fig. 3. Recommended effect display

For real-time recommendation, the recommendation results need to be updated in seconds. Therefore, the batch processing time of spark streaming is set to 5 s, 10 s, 15 s and 20 s at the interval of 5 s. The pull amount of spark streaming is adjusted by configuring spark.streaming.kafka.maxrateperpartition parameter, so that the data in each batch can be completed in each batch processing time. Finally, the relationship between the recommended real-time performance and data throughput of the system is shown in Table 2.

Table 2. Data real-time inflow speed of Spark Streaming

Batch time (s)	Processing capacity per batch (items)	Average time required for batch processing (s)
5	300	5.06
10	500	11.64
15	700	17.72
20	900	23.02

It can be seen from the experiment that the more data processing capacity of each batch, the lower the calculation efficiency. Increasing the batch processing time does not significantly improve the data throughput. Moreover, for the real-time recommendation system, if the batch time is set too large, the recommendation result will be more lagged, so for the real-time recommendation system in this paper, it is more appropriate to set the batch processing time to 5 s.

In terms of recommendation accuracy, the evaluation index used in the experiment is root mean square error (RMSE), and its calculation formula is shown in (7). It uses the actual score of the user for the movie and the prediction score of the recommendation system for the item.

$$\sigma_{RMSE} = \sqrt{\frac{\sum_i^n p_i - r_i^2}{n}} \tag{7}$$

p_i is the prediction score of item I, while r_i is the actual score of user for item i, the smaller RMSE is, the higher the accuracy of recommendation is. Because the real-time recommendation system is designed and implemented in this paper, the starting point at the beginning is not to rely on the offline recommendation layer, so that the real-time recommendation system can reduce the complexity, make it easier to maintain and improve the real-time recommendation results, so the accuracy is certainly not as high as the results based on offline batch computing, but in terms of accuracy, we hope to achieve at least two goals: First, the accuracy cannot be much worse than the results of off-line batch calculation. Second, it is hoped that with the passage of time, the user behavior data in the system will continue to increase, and the accuracy of system recommendation will continue to improve. The test accuracy of this paper is mainly compared with the user-based collaborative filtering user-cf, item-based collaborative filtering item-cf and ALS collaborative filtering in the three offline environments. These three types of recommendation algorithms and the real-time recommendation system of this paper (Spark Streaming's batch time is set to 5 s) were tested by using Movielens ml-100 k data set. The results are shown in Fig. 4.

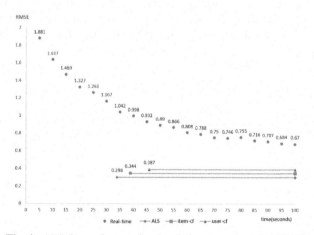

Fig. 4. ALS, item-cf, user-cf and real-time recommended RMSE

The recommendation algorithm based on offline is less error, but the recommended calculation time is more than 30 s, and can not be directly applied to the data flow environment. For real-time recommendation, because the recommendation calculation is not based on the full amount of data, the amount of data needs to accumulate over time, so the RMSE recommended at the beginning is large, but as time increases, the RMSE is gradually decreasing. Finally, the error gap between the recommended algorithm and the offline recommendation algorithm is kept within 2 times, but the trend of reduction is more stable. The reason is that the recommendation algorithm that relies only on the online layer is not as complicated and fine-grained as the recommendation algorithm in the offline environment because of the consideration of the recommendation delay, and the recommendation accuracy is sacrificed to ensure the real-time recommendation.

4 Conclusions

At present, the recommendation system based on offline batch calculation can not meet the requirement of real-time recommendation very well, and the real-time recommendation system based on offline layer and online layer Lambda big data processing architecture has problems such as high system complexity, is difficult to maintain and poor timeliness caused by relying on the offline layer. Aiming at these problems, this paper designs and implements a real-time recommendation system based on Kafka and Spark. Based on the micro-batch processing capability of Spark Streaming component Spark Streaming, an incrementally incremental collaborative filtering algorithm is implemented, and removed the dependence on the offline layer during the recommended calculation process, reducing the complexity of the system. Which makes the system easier to maintain and expand, Meanwhile, Kafka was introduced to ensure the stability of real-time data inflow. Finally, the experiment proved the availability of the whole system. I hope this work can provide new ideas for real-time recommendations under big data The next work will design more processing methods for multiple types of user behavior data and improve the incrementally updateable recommendation algorithm to improve the real-time and accuracy of the recommendation system.

References

Garg, N.: Apache Kafka. Packt Publishing Ltd., Birmingham (2013)

Goldberg, D., Nichols, D., Oki, B.M., Terry, D.: Using collaborative filtering to weave an information tapestry. Commun. ACM **35**(12), 61–71 (1992)

Liu, G., Meng, K., Ding, J., Nees, J.P., Guo, H., Zhang, X.: An entity-association-based matrix factorization recommendation algorithm. Comput. Mater. Cont. **58**(1), 101–120 (2019)

Wang, G., Liu, M.: Dynamic trust model based on service recommendation in big data. Comput. Mater. Cont. **58**(3), 845–857 (2019)

Kreps, J., Narkhede, N., Rao, J.: Kafka: a distributed messaging sys-tem for log processing. In: Proceedings of the NetDB, pp. 1–7 (2011)

Li, Y., Xu, Z.: A survey of internet personalized information services. Comput. Eng. Appl. **38**(19), 183–188 (2002)

Zaharia, M., Das, T., Li, H., Shenker, S., Stoica, I.:Discretized streams: an efficient and fault-tolerant model for stream processing on large clusters. HotCloud (2012)

Bin, S., et al.: Collaborative filtering recommendation algorithm based on multi-relationship social network. Comput. Mater. Cont. **60**(2), 659–674 (2019)

Wang, H., Wu, B., Liu, W.: Spark-based parallel graph data analysis system. Comput. Sci. Explor. **9**(9), 1066–1074 (2015)

Yan, Y., Dong, Y., He, X., Wang, W.: FSMBUS: aspark-based large-scale frequent subgraph mining algorithm. Comput. Res. Dev. **52**(8), 1768–1783 (2015)

Zaharia, M., et al.: Apache spark: a unified engine for big data processing. Commun. ACM **59**(11), 56–65 (2016a)

Zaharia, M., et al.: Apache spark: a unified engine for big data processing. Commun. ACM **59**(11), 56–65 (2016b)

Zaharia, M., et al.: Resilient distributed datasets: a fault-tolerant abstraction for in-memory cluster computing. In: Proceedings of the 9th USENIX Conference on Networked Systems Design and Implementation, p. 2. USENIX Association, April 2012

Zaharia, M., Das, T., Li, H., Hunter, T., Shenker, S., Stoica, I.: Dis-cretized streams: fault-tolerant streaming computation at scale. In: Proceedings of the Twenty-Fourth ACM Symposium on Operating Systems Principles, pp. 423–438. ACM, November 2013

A Novel Clone Detection Scheme Based on Generative Adversarial Networks

Zhuohua Liu[1], Hui Suo[1], and Bin Yang[2(✉)]

[1] School of Computer and Design, Guangdong Jidian Polytechnic, Guangzhou, China
[2] School of Design, Jiangnan University, Wuxi, China
yangbin@jiangnan.edu.cn

Abstract. Copy-move is one of the simple and effective operations to create digital image forgeries due to the gradually evolved image processing tools. In recent years, many studies were proposed by the literature to help restore some trust to digital images. In this paper, for the first time, we introduce a new end-to-end Generative Adversarial Networks (GAN) to the image copy-move forgery detection problem. Unlike classic solutions requiring carefully extracted features, the proposed solution only needs authentic and forge samples. Our experimental results demonstrate that the proposed method achieves better forgery detection performance than classic approaches relying on different features and/or Convolutional Neural Network (CNN).

Keywords: Image forensic · Generative Adversarial Networks · Convolutional Neural Network · Tempering detection · System design

1 Introduction

With the rapid development of science and technology and economy, digital image has been widely used in various fields and industries. With the development of image processing technology and the popularization of image editing software, people can easily tamper with a digital image. The tampered image obtained is natural and lifelike, and it is difficult for human eyes to distinguish the true from the false [1]. The authenticity and integrity of digital images have been destroyed after being tampered. When they are used in some special occasions such as news reports, reliable intelligence, judicial proof, etc., the problems such as misjudgment, misleading and fraud will bring great impact and damage to the country and society. Figure 1(a), for example, was released by Sepah News, the media arm of Iran's Revolutionary Guard, on July 9, 2008. This image firstly appeared on the front pages of The Los Angeles Times, The Financial Times, The Chicago Tribune and several other newspapers as well as on BBC News, MSNBC and many other major news Web sites. However, The Associated Press received another image, Fig. 1(b), from the same source one day later. This image appeared to be taken from the same vantage point at almost the same time. Finally, Fig. 1(a) was proved to be tempered [1]. Digital images are being more and more undependable as a definitive record of an event. It's necessary to develop a set of tools to authenticate digital images.

© Springer Nature Singapore Pte Ltd. 2020
X. Sun et al. (Eds.): ICAIS 2020, CCIS 1252, pp. 439–448, 2020.
https://doi.org/10.1007/978-981-15-8083-3_39

(a)   (b)

Fig. 1. An example of copy-move forgery: (a) the forged image with four missiles and (b) the original image with three missiles

Passive or blind forgery detection technique uses the received image only for assessing its authenticity or integrity, without any signature or watermark of the original image from the sender. It assumes that although digital forgeries may leave no visual clues of having been tampered with, they may highly likely disturb the underlying statistics property or image consistency of a natural scene image which introduces new artifacts resulting in various forms of inconsistencies. These inconsistencies can be used to detect the forgery. As such, passive forensics is, in theory, applicable to a broader range of operating scenarios [2]. Existing techniques identify various traces of tampering and detect them separately with localization of tampered region [3]. This paper focus on the detection of splicing forgery. Inspired by game theory, a scheme of training neural network to detect tamper model by generating confrontation is proposed.

Copy-move would be the most common image forgery, usually to hide certain details or to copy some aspect of the image [4–7]. Copy-move detection methods often use texture regional inconsistencies, because the texture regions with similar colors and noise variability. Most Copy-move detection methods validate each pair of blocks that are subdivided from the image. In order to reduce the processing time of block matching and improve the robustness of block matching, some technologies adopt the DCT, DWT and PCA and other down-dimensional methods [5].

In computer vision applications, deep learning performs well in different visual recognition tasks such as image classification and semantic segmentation. Recently, a unique network using convolution layers and LSTM networks has been proposed in [8]. The boundaries between the manipulated area and the adjacent non-manipulate area are different. Then use the LSTM network to learn the tempering feature. When the tempering boundary is clear, they achieve significant performance [9]. However, when the JPEG compressed image is detected, the detection accuracy drop machine should be able to effectively identify the forging traces. To achieve this, we used convolutional neural networks as a tool for in-depth forensic learning. Related Research [10, 11] shows that in digital forensics, the original image cannot directly enter the traditional CNN. Counterfeit Drugs are often overshadowed by the manipulation of the traces left behind, not only visually, but also in the statistics. Therefore, there is a need to reveal the identity of the track. Recently, [12] used convolutional neural networks to extract block like features from images and calculate the autocorrelation between different blocks. Then, the point by point feature extractor was used to locate the match point {[Yang, 2015 #377]}. The reconstruction of forgery mask by deconvolution network was different from the traditional solution which needs multi-stage training and parameter adjustment from feature extraction to post-processing. Therefore, the solution they proposed was fully trainable and can be jointly optimized.

2   Review of Generative Adversarial Network

In 2014, Christian Szegedy and others added synthetic noise to the sample data and proposed the concept of confrontation samples [13]. Many depth models, including CNN, made false judgments in experiments, that is, for the confrontation samples, CNN's robustness performance is extremely poor. Inspired by the zero-sum game, Goodfellow proposed the confrontation generation network Gan [14], which includes two phases: generator and discriminator. The network model of mutual confrontation. The generator generates images by inputting data of arbitrary distribution. Generally, the input data is Gaussian noise, that is, the data distribution adopts Gaussian distribution, which has randomness and universality; the discriminator can judge whether the input is the real image or the forged image generated by the generator. In the whole training process of Gan, the generator is oriented to enable the discriminator to give In fact, the result of Gan optimization is to let the generator produce a kind of probability distribution PG of data, that is, the generator will form a special mapping relationship from the internal complex layer structure [6]. This paper hopes that PG will gradually approach the probability distribution PDA of real data in the optimization process, when the gap between the two is the smallest. At that time, the model converges.

The standard structure of Gan is shown in Fig. 2, where Z represents noise. There is no label in the whole structure. Therefore, Gan is designed as unsupervised learning network. Other generalized models will change on this basis, and finally form a training mode that conforms to the characteristics of supervised learning.

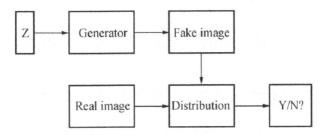

Fig. 2. An example of copy-move forgery: (a) the forged image with four missiles and (b) the original image with three missiles

With the network structure, we need the corresponding loss function as the optimization basis. For the discriminator, its loss J(D) comes from two sources: one is to distinguish the false graph as the true graph, the other is to distinguish the true graph as the false graph, and the specific formula is:

$$\begin{cases} J(D) = -\frac{1}{2}E_{x \sim P_{\text{data}}(x)} \log D(x) \\ \qquad - \frac{1}{2}E_{z \sim P_z(z)}[\log(1 - D(G(Z)))], \\ J(G) = -J(D). \end{cases} \tag{1}$$

where $E_{x \sim P_{\text{data}}(x)}$ refers to the expectation that the sample comes from the real data; and $E_{x \sim P_z(z)}$ is the sample from the expectation of the generator. Formula (1) is a process of finding cross entropy. For the generator, since it is a zero-sum game, its loss $J(G)$ is a negative value of the discriminator loss, so as to keep the sum as 0. According to formula (1), the loss function of Gan can be defined as:

$$\min_G \min_D V(D, G) = E_{x \sim P_{\text{data}}(x)} \log D(x) + E_{z \sim P_z(z)}[\log G(Z)]. \tag{2}$$

The function wants to maximize the difference value of the discriminator in identifying the false data, and minimize the difference value of the discriminator in identifying the true when the generator generates the false graph. Since it is difficult for the generator to generate false graphs with high similarity to the real data in the early stage, the discriminator will quickly complete the convergence. At this time, when the false graph generated by the generator is sent to the discriminator for judgment, the discriminator will accurately determine that it is a false graph, the loss value obtained by feedback will be very small, and the generator will also generate a minimum gradient in the back propagation due to the too small loss value. If there is not enough gradient, the generator's parameter optimization will decline or even stop. At this time, it can be considered that the generator stops learning [15]. In short, the generator will stop learning as the discriminator first converges. Therefore, when the generator was trained, the lost $log(1 - D(G(Z))$ was replaced by log $G(Z)$, which can solve the model divergence problem caused by the generator's weak gradient [16].

In the above zero-sum game, the sum of loss of both sides is strictly 0, which is also called saturated zero-sum game. Obviously, there is also a kind of zero-sum game called unsaturated zero-sum game. It can also solve the problem that the model is difficult to converge due to the weak gradient problem of generator. Its corresponding loss function is defined as:

$$\begin{cases} J(D) = -\frac{1}{2}E_{x \sim P_{\text{data}}(x)} \log D(x) \\ \qquad - \frac{1}{2}E_{z \sim P_z(z)}[\log(1 - D(G(Z)))], \\ J(G) = -\frac{1}{2}E_{z \sim P_z(z)} \log D(G(Z)). \end{cases} \tag{3}$$

Formula (2) is all around the discriminator, so once the discriminator converges, it is difficult to optimize the generator. Therefore, Eq. (3) redefines the loss of the generator, so that the loss of the generator is no longer the negative number of the loss of the discriminator. At this time, their sum is no longer 0. Even if the discriminator converges first, it will not seriously restrict the training of the generator [17].

Based on GANs, a study [18] develop a common framework suitable for different problems, the generator in [18] is an encoder-decoder network which tries to synthesize fake image conditioned on a given image to fool discriminator, while the discriminator tries to identify the fake image by comparing with the corresponding target image. However, this work is supervised learning, therefore, it needs intensive input of labeled data for training, which is not always applicable in real cases.

In [19], Odena and Augustus proposed a novel extension to GANs which was called the Semi-Supervised GAN, or SGAN. A generative model and a classifier can be learned simultaneously by using SGAN. The training of SGAN is similar to GAN. Only the higher granularity tags for half of the small batches are needed to extracted features from the data generation distribution. D/C is trained to minimize the negative log likelihood relative to a given label, and G is trained to maximize it.

Recently, [20] discovered that the pre-trained convolution neural network retrieval of the middle-level characteristics of these specific areas where it has been surprisingly effective description. However, the Select Similarity Measure to the sample will be matched to the query image for good performance is crucial in order to match the characteristics of the multi-channel depth, they made the use of multi-channel normalization of inter-related and an analysis of their effectiveness. The performance in matching crime scene shoeprints to laboratory test impressions was greatly improved. Although many GAN-based algorithms were proposed in various fields, few researches made used of GAN in forensic researches. In this paper, a novel copy-move detection scheme based on GAN was proposed, which was called as CD-GAN.

3 Method

CD-GAN is a generalized model of Deep Convolution GAN (DCGAN) [21]. Its standard structure is consistent with the standard structure of GAN theory. And the internal structure of generator is replaced by convolution network in DCGAN as shown in Fig. 3. There is no change in the input of the generator, the noise is still used, and then the feature points are expanded through the linear layer, and then the shape is reshaped into a $4 \times 4 \times 1024$ feature map, and then the real convolution operation is started. Conv in the figure represents a layer structure, including convolution, bias, batch normalization, activation and other four parts. Among them, deconvolution is used for up-sampling, and Relu is used for activation.

In the construction of discriminator, DCGAN uses CNN network to complete, but different from general CNN, it uses the step-by-step convolution to replace the pooling layer to complete the de sampling operation and convolution operation at the same time [22]. The advantage of step convolution is that it can train the network's own down-sampling method, rather than the simple way of extracting pixel points like pooling; when activating, leaky Relu is used to activate instead of general Relu, in order to reduce network sparsity and make network convergence easier. The formulas of leaky Relu and Relu are shown in formula (4) and formula (5), respectively. Leaky Relu is composed of two linear segments [23]. The positive half axis is a positive proportion map, and the

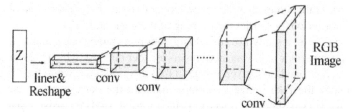

Fig. 3. The internal structure of generator of DCGAN

negative half axis has the parameter leak as the slope adjustment negative value. Relu is equivalent to the mapping part of the positive half axis of leaky Relu, and the negative half axis is always 0, that is to say, the negative value is filtered.

$$LeakyRelu(x) = \begin{cases} x, x > 0 \\ -leak \cdot x, else \end{cases} \tag{4}$$

$$Relu(x) = \begin{cases} x, x > 0 \\ 0, else \end{cases} \tag{5}$$

Inspired by DCGAN, we proposed an improved standard structure in CD-GAN as shown in Fig. 4.

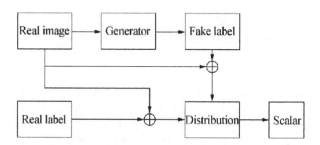

Fig. 4. The improved standard structure of proposed CD-GAN

The generator of traditional GAN cannot meet the requirements. Therefore, the generator needs to be improved. Its structure is shown in Fig. 5.

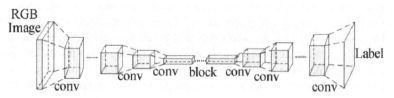

Fig. 5. The internal structure of generator of CD-GAN

Compared with other computer vision applications, the tampered image is more difficult to detect, and it is difficult to obtain enough and rigorous feature images only through step convolution down sampling [24]. Therefore, the block structure in ResNet is added, as shown in Fig. 5. It is composed of three convolution layers, three batch normalization layers, three Relu activation layers and one accumulator. The output of block is the superposition of the feature map after three convolutions and the input of block, so as to maintain the continuity of the feature, alleviate the network degradation caused by the network too deep and the feature loss caused by the continuous convolution operation (Fig. 6).

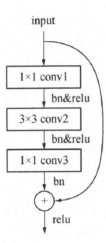

Fig. 6. Flowchart of block structure in ResNet

Corresponding to the network structure, the loss function also needs to be adjusted, especially for the generator, it needs not only the discrimination feedback of the discriminator, but also the difference between the generated segmentation results and the real tags, forming a supervised learning mode.

$$
\begin{cases}
J(D) = -\frac{1}{2}\left(E_{x \sim P_{data}(x), y \sim P_{lab}(y)} \log D(x,y) + E_{x \sim P_{data}(x), z \sim P_z(z)}[\log(1-D(G(Z),y))]\right) \\
J(G) = -\frac{1}{2}E_{x \sim P_{data}(x), z \sim P_z(z)} \log D(x, G(Z)) - E_{y \sim P_{lab}(y)} \log D(G(Z))
\end{cases}
\tag{6}
$$

Corresponding formula (6), the discriminator needs to judge whether there is a high correlation between the image and the label, that is, to make the correlation between the real label and the real image the highest, and to make the correlation between the false label and the real image the lowest. In addition to the high correlation between the generated false label and the real image, the generator also needs to minimize the difference between the false label and the real label. In addition, the network can also use unsupervised learning, and its loss function is

$$
\begin{cases}
J'(D) = -\frac{1}{2}E_{x \sim P_{data}(x), z \sim P_z(z)}[\log(1-D(G(Z),y))] \\
J'(G) = -\frac{1}{2}E_{x \sim P_{data}(x), z \sim P_z(z)} \log D(x, G(Z))
\end{cases}
\tag{7}
$$

The combination of formula (6) and formula (7) can form a semi supervised learning mode, that is, the training in a certain period of time has a corresponding label to match with it, and the rest of the time uses the data set without label matching to participate in the training, and the training cycle between the supervision and the unsupervised is in accordance with the set time proportion to achieve the semi-supervised training mode.

4   Experimental Results

All experiments were performed on a personal computer equipped with one GPU (Nvidia GeForce GTX 2080Ti with 11 GB RAM). To evaluate the performance of the proposed model and compare its performance with other schemes, we tested on a composite image database containing 12120 images. These images are from three image databases: the BOSSbase 1.01 [25], CASIA v2.0 [26], and laboratory database. BOSSbase database contributes 10000 uncompressed images with the size of 512×512. The rest of 3 databases contributes 2120 images with the resolution of 348×256 to 4032×3024.

We used True Positive Rate (TPR) and False Positive Rate (FPR) to present the performance of forensic. Where TP and TN denote as the number of the true detection of forged images and original images, respectively. Denote the FP and FN as the number of the wrong detection of original images and forged images, respectively. Then, the TPR is the fraction of tampered images correctly identified as such, while FPR is the fraction of identifying an original image as a tampered one. They can be represented as:

$$TPR = TP/(TP + FN) \tag{8}$$

$$FPR = FP/(FP + FN) \tag{9}$$

Our proposed method is compared with some classical methods [7, 27–32]. All methods were tested on same dataset. Comparison results are presented in Table 1, and the first and second rows of each are the TPR and FPR, respectively.

Table 1. The TPR (%) and FPR (%) of different methods.

Methods	TPR	FPR
Kakar and N. Sudha [27]	90.21	8.65
Pan et al. [28]	88.66	10.31
Neamtu et al. [29]	87.37	10.17
Popescu [30]	75.49	14.81
Yang et al. [31]	91.47	8.65
Liu et al. [7]	80.14	12.21
Silva et al. [32]	85.63	9.88
Proposed	96.77	9.54

The results indicate that our copy-move forgery detection method have considerably higher performance. Thanks to GAN, the forensic approach was able to learn the characteristics of tampering in self-confrontation.

5 Conclusion

We have proposed a novel network model to detect copy-move forgery, which is based on GAN. An improvement based on generic network DCGAN was developed, which can use semi supervised learning mode to complete model training when there are few labeled data sets. We also provided an effective training method for GAN that is generally considered as a challenge in GAN training. Experiment results demonstrate that the proposed method based on CD-GAN is able to detect copy-move forgery efficiently. In the future, we will improve the neural network model to recognize more types of tampering.

Acknowledgments. This paper is supported by the 2016 Guangdong Provincial Higher Vocational Education Leading Talent Project (Hui Suo); the National Natural Science Foundation of China (NO. 51505191); the Humanities and Social Sciences Projects of the Ministry of Education (NO. 18YJC760112); the Social Science Fund of Jiangsu Province (NO. 18YSD002) and the Philosophy and Social Science Fund of Education Department of Jiangsu Province (NO. 2015SJD344).

References

1. Yang, B., et al.: An efficient forensic method for copy-move forgery detection based on DWT-FWHT. Radioengineering **22**(4), 1098–1105 (2013)
2. Feng, X., Cox, I.J., Doerr, G.: Normalized energy density-based forensic detection of resampled images. IEEE Trans. Multimedia **14**(3), 536–545 (2012)
3. Birajdar, G.K., Mankar, V.H.: Digital image forgery detection using passive techniques: a survey. Digit. Invest. **10**(3), 226–245 (2013)
4. Yang, B., Li, Z., Zhang, T.: A real-time image forensics scheme based on multi-domain learning. J. Real-Time Image Proc. **17**(1), 29–40 (2019). https://doi.org/10.1007/s11554-019-00893-8
5. Yang, B., Sun, X., Guo, H., Xia, Z., Chen, X.: A copy-move forgery detection method based on CMFD-SIFT. Multimed. Tools Appl. **77**(1), 837–855 (2017). https://doi.org/10.1007/s11042-016-4289-y
6. Yang, B., et al.: Convolutional neural network for smooth filtering detection. IET Image Proc. **12**(8), 1432–1438 (2018)
7. Liu, Y., Guan, Q., Zhao, X.: Copy-move forgery detection based on convolutional kernel network. Multimed. Tools Appl. **77**(14), 18269–18293 (2017). https://doi.org/10.1007/s11042-017-5374-6
8. Bappy, M.J.H., et al.: Exploiting spatial structure for localizing manipulated image regions. In: International Conference on Computer Vision (2017)
9. Cao, Y., et al.: Coverless information hiding based on the molecular structure images of material. Comput. Mater. Con. **54**(2), 197–207 (2018)
10. Chen, J., et al.: Median filtering forensics based on convolutional neural networks. IEEE Signal Process. Lett. **22**(11), 1849–1853 (2015)

11. Bayar, B., Stamm, M.C.: A deep learning approach to universal image manipulation detection using a new convolutional layer. In: ACM Workshop on Information Hiding and Multimedia Security (2016)
12. Yue, W., Abd-Almageed, W., Natarajan, P.: Image copy-move forgery detection via an end-to-end deep neural network. In: 2018 IEEE Winter Conference on Applications of Computer Vision (WACV) (2018)
13. Ledig, C., et al.: Photo-realistic single image super-resolution using a generative adversarial network. In: 2017 IEEE Conference on Computer Vision and Pattern Recognition (CVPR) (2017)
14. Goodfellow, I.: NIPS 2016 Tutorial: Generative Adversarial Networks (2016)
15. Li, J., et al.: Perceptual Generative Adversarial Networks for Small Object Detection
16. Guérin, É., et al.: Interactive example-based terrain authoring with conditional generative adversarial networks. ACM Trans. Graph. **36**(6), 1–13 (2017)
17. Wolterink, J.M., et al.: Generative adversarial networks for noise reduction in low-dose CT. IEEE Trans. Med. Imaging **36**(12), 2536–2545 (2017)
18. Isola, P., et al.: Image-to-image translation with conditional adversarial networks. In: 2017 IEEE Conference on Computer Vision and Pattern Recognition (CVPR), Honolulu, pp. 5967–5976 (2017)
19. Odena, A.: Semi-Supervised Learning with Generative Adversarial Networks (2016)
20. Kong, B., Supančič, J., Ramanan, D., Fowlkes, C.C.: Cross-domain image matching with deep feature maps. Int. J. Comput. Vision **127**(11), 1738–1750 (2019). https://doi.org/10.1007/s11263-018-01143-3
21. Radford, A., Metz, L., Chintala, S.: Unsupervised representation learning with deep convolutional generative adversarial networks. Comput. Sci. (2015)
22. Yang, B., et al.: Exposing photographic splicing by detecting the inconsistencies in shadows. Comput. J. **58**(4), 588–600 (2014)
23. Chen, X., Zhong, H., Bao, Z.: A GLCM-feature-based approach for reversible image transformation. Comput. Mater. Con. **59**, 239–255 (2019)
24. Wang, B., et al.: A dual-chaining watermark scheme for data integrity protection in Internet of Things. Comput. Mater. Con. **58**(3), 679–695 (2019)
25. Bas, P., Filler, T., Pevný, T.: "Break our steganographic system": the ins and outs of organizing BOSS. In: Filler, T., Pevný, T., Craver, S., Ker, A. (eds.) IH 2011. LNCS, vol. 6958, pp. 59–70. Springer, Heidelberg (2011). https://doi.org/10.1007/978-3-642-24178-9_5
26. Dong, J., Wang, W., Tan, T.: CASIA image tampering detection evaluation database. In: IEEE China Summit & International Conference on Signal and Information Processing (2013)
27. Kakar, P., Sudha, N.: Exposing postprocessed copy-paste forgeries through transform-invariant features. IEEE Trans. Inf. Forensics Secur. **7**(3), 1018–1028 (2012)
28. Pan, X., Lyu, S.: Region duplication detection using image feature matching. IEEE Trans. Inf. Forensics Secur. **5**(4), 857–867 (2010)
29. Neamtu, C., et al.: Exposing copy-move image tampering using forensic method based on SURF. In: 2013 International Conference on Electronics, Computers and Artificial Intelligence (ECAI) (2013)
30. Popescu, A.C., Farid, H.: Exposing digital forgeries by detecting traces of resampling. IEEE Trans. Signal Process. **53**(2), 758–767 (2005)
31. Yang, B., et al.: Exposing copy-move forgery based on improved SIFT descriptor. J. Internet Technol. **18**(2), 417–425 (2017)
32. Silva, E., et al.: Going deeper into copy-move forgery detection: exploring image telltales via multi-scale analysis and voting processes. J. Vis. Commun. Image Represent. **29**, 16–32 (2015)

Design of Vehicle Remote Monitoring System Based on LoRa Technology and QT Platform

Haiming Du$^{(\boxtimes)}$

School of Electrical and Information Engineering, Zhengzhou University of Light Industry, Zhengzhou 450002, China

Abstract. Due to the rapid growth in the number of urban vehicles especially electrical bikes and electrical cars, the dispatch management and safety issues of electrical bikes have become increasingly critical and prominent. With the development of IoT communication technology, traditional wireless technologies such as Bluetooth, ZigBee, WiFi and GPRS have some shortcomings for examples short communication distances and large power consumption. However, LoRa wireless communication technology has the advantages of long communication distance and low power consumption. Therefore, this paper proposes the remote monitoring vehicle system for electrical bikes based on LoRa wireless communication technology. The system consists of electrical bikes terminal and a remote monitoring center. The electrical bikes terminal adopts the architecture association of ARM, GPS and LoRa to complete the acquisition and wireless transmission of electrical bikes position information. The GPS module provide the position information, and the ARM transmit the location information to the monitoring center by LoRa wireless communication. The remote monitoring center is based on QT and GIS technology to complete the real-time display of the electrical bikes. The actual test results show that the system can meet the monitoring requirements, the communication quality is reliable, the communication distance is long, and it can be displayed in real time, dynamic and real scene.

Keywords: GPS · Lora · QT · Remote vehicle monitoring system · ARM

1 Introduction

Owing to the air pollution and energy consumption produced by gasoline motor car, the Chinese government encourages strongly energy conservation and emission reduction and green travel. More and more urban population adopted electrical bikes as the transportation facility. The rapid growth of urban vehicles especially the electrical bikes and the electrical cars is obvious and sharp in China. How to manage and dispatch effectively electrical bikes to improve vehicle utilization efficiency and ensure vehicle safety has become one of the hot issues of concern to all sectors of society [1].

In order to solve these problems well, vehicle monitoring systems, as an important part of intelligent transportation systems, have received more and more attention from scholars at home and abroad. Most of the existing vehicle monitoring systems use GPS

© Springer Nature Singapore Pte Ltd. 2020
X. Sun et al. (Eds.): ICAIS 2020, CCIS 1252, pp. 449–460, 2020.
https://doi.org/10.1007/978-981-15-8083-3_40

satellite positioning information combined with the GPRS technology. The GPRS network communication mode uses the FDMA/TDMA(frequency/time division multiple access) technology, which the wireless communication technology has the disadvantage on the high power consumption and the positioning terminal consumes more power [2], the life of batteries will be short, and the GPRS network has been in operation since 2005 and has been in operation for more than a decade. The mobile communication technology has experienced multiple generations of updates from 2G to 4G. Recently, China's telecommunications operators will gradually shut down the 2G communication network. Therefore, the remote vehicle monitoring system using the GPRS technology station needs to face the risk of the communication operator gradually shutting down the GPRS network and exiting the operation [3].

With the rapid growth of wireless communication technology, the wireless sensor network will be widely used in several areas such as smart city, intelligent transportation system and intelligent instrumentation and meter system. The short distance communication technology such as Zigbee, Bluetooth and WiFi would not satisfy the fields application for wireless meter reading and long distance etc. The new challenge and requirement are flexible networking, wider coverage distance, better safety performance and lower cost and lower power consumption, etc.

In recent years, IoT (Internet of Things) technology has developed rapidly. How to design the wireless communication terminal needing the requirement lower power consumption and high performance of anti-interference is the hot issue. As one of the emerging Internet of Things technologies, LoRa has received extensive attention from academic and business circles due to its low power consumption and wide-area coverage [4–6]. LoRa spread spectrum communication technology benefits from the advantages of free frequency band self-organizing network. Users can set up signal blind spots such as bad and remote environments to achieve regional wireless private network coverage. Because of the adoption of advanced spread spectrum communication technology, the communication distance has been greatly improved [7, 8]. All over the world, more than two hundred long-distance wireless communication networkings has been built and tested based on the LoRa technology.

With the popularity of smart telephones, position service applications based on mobile intelligent terminals are rapidly expanding. At present, GPS and GLONASS are used widely and more mature global navigation and positioning system (GNSS), and the BDS (BeiDou system) that is the china's satellite navigation and positioning system is used widely in the Asia-pacific region. The real-time dynamic relative positioning and navigation with GPS/BDS is becoming a popular research topic. The usage of wide area differential augmentation technology to improve the accuracy of indoor and outdoor location services, has been used in many areas. Now the location module such as ATGM322 can develop the BDS + GPS wide area differential positioning algorithm and can process the data of the original BeiDou mobile terminal, analyzes the difference data flow correct real-time orbit and clock, to achieve augmentation positioning through the serial port, which has important application value in GNSS satellite technology in low cost mobile terminal location service.

Therefore, we use GPS/BDS satellite positioning technology and LoRa communication technology to develop electrical bikes monitoring system through embedded control technology and electronic map technology to realize electrical bikes position data collection, electrical bikes information management, remote monitoring and other functions. This paper introduces in detail the key parts of the hardware design and software design of the electrical bikes positioning terminal, as well as the development key of the monitoring center PC system, and tests the overall communication quality and PC function of the system. Provides a reliable solution for electrical bikes safety management.

An outline of this paper is as follows. Section 2 describes the general scheme of remote monitoring system. Section 3 addresses the hardware design about the monitoring system. Section 4 gives the software design and programming. And Sect. 5 shows the test results of Monitoring System followed by conclusions in Sect. 6.

2 The General Scheme of Remote Monitoring System

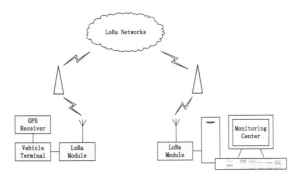

Fig. 1. Overall structure of the system

The overall structure of the remote monitoring system designed in this paper is shown in Fig. 1. It consists of three parts: the electrical bikes terminal, the LoRa wireless network and the remote monitoring center. The electrical bikes terminal generally includes three parts: a GPS positioning module, an MCU central control module, and a LoRa wireless communication module. The central processing unit of the electrical bikes terminal collects the GPS data through the serial port, and completes the data transmission between the monitoring center and the monitoring center through the LoRa network. After receiving the positioning information, the monitoring center performs the position tracking of the moving electrical bikes through the Baidu map in the upper computer software.

The electrical bikes terminal is a hardware component of the whole system. It mainly receives signals and navigation messages by GPS satellites through the GPS module, then performs carrier phase measurement to obtain measurement pseudoranges, and establishes a positioning equation group to solve the pseudorange equations. Finally, the clock error and the correction of the atmospheric refraction error are performed to obtain more accurate positioning information [9]. The data is then passed to the MCU control unit for processing, packaging, and ready to send.

In order to realize real-time monitoring of the electrical bikes, the location information of the electrical bikes must be transmitted to the monitoring center in time. The electrical bikes terminal accesses the LoRa network established by the user through the LoRa wireless module, and then completes the data transmission through the wireless network and the monitoring center LoRa receiving end.

The upper computer of the monitoring center is developed by QT platform, and the upper computer software is written in object-oriented C++ language. Through the call based on the Baidu map API, the display of the remote electrical bikes location and the drawing of the driving trajectory in the Baidu map street background are realized.

3   Hardware Design

3.1   Power Supply Unit

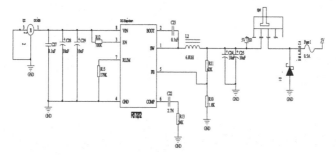

Fig. 2. 9 V to 5 V step-down circuit

In order to meet the practical application of the electrical bikes terminal in the field of Internet of Things using the LoRa technology, the long-distance electrical bikes terminal module designed in this paper should content the portable requirements and be convenient to install and use in daily life. Therefore, this paper uses a carbon dry battery to the power management circuit design. Since the power supply voltage of various types of chips included in the terminal mainly includes 5 V and 3.3 V. In order to ensure the stable use of each module, this paper adopts the common 9 V dry battery as the power supply. By designing the 9 V to 5 V, 5 V to 3.3 V power conversion circuit, the required power supply voltage is finally obtained. The RT7272 is a highly efficient synchronous DC step-down converter that can achieve a maximum output current of 3A with an input voltage of 4.5 V to 36 V [10]. By designing a DC/DC current synchronous buck converter circuit based on RT7272, the 9 V voltage is converted to 5 V voltage, and the conversion circuit is shown in Fig. 2. The 5 V to 3.3 V circuit uses the AMS1117-3.3 V linear regulator chip is shown in Fig. 3.

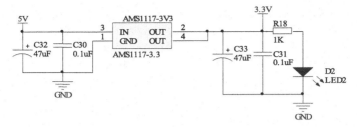

Fig. 3. 5 V to 3.3 V circuit

3.2 Microprocessor Unit

The processor unit is an indispensable bridge support for the normal operation of the entire hardware system. It is mainly responsible for controlling the extraction and transmission of location data. In this paper, from the perspective of system function requirements, development convenience and cost, the STM32F103ZET6 chip with the Cortex-M3 core produced by ST is used as the microprocessor unit. The processor has high performance and operates at up to 72 MHz [11]. It has a variety of control peripherals, rich interrupt resources, 112 general-purpose input/output ports, and low price. In addition, the library functions based on STM32F1 are rich and convenient for program development. In the development process, the system clock of the main control chip, different pins such as serial port, GPIO port, timing, etc. need to be functionally configured to meet the needs of different development functions.

3.3 GPS/DBS Positioning Unit

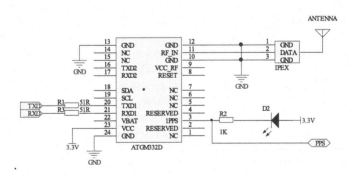

Fig. 4. GPS/BDS module circuit

In order to minimize the volume to ensure the positioning accuracy, this paper selects Zhongke Microelectronics ATGM332D-5 N as the GPS positioning unit. The positioning module includes 32 tracking channels, which can receive all GPS and BDS visible satellites at the same time. It supports single system positioning and dual system joint positioning of GPS and BDS. The positioning accuracy is up to 5 m and the size is only 16 mm × 12.2 mm × 2.4 mm. The module has high sensitivity, low power consumption and low cost, and is suitable for ship navigation, car navigation, wearable devices, etc. [12]. After the ATGM332D is powered on, it outputs a positioning data packet of the NMEA-0183 protocol format through the serial port every second. The circuit connection principle is shown in Fig. 4. The RF_IN pin is the antenna signal input, TXD1 is the positioning data output, and RXD1 is the configuration command input.

3.4   LoRa Communication Unit

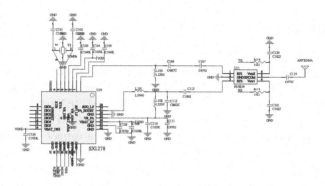

Fig. 5. SX1278 circuit diagram

The communication between the positioning terminal and the monitoring station is the key to the positioning data transmission process, and its communication performance determines the quality of the positioning quality. The LoRa communication module used this time is E32-TTL-100, which uses 433 MHz as the working frequency band [13, 14], and the working voltage is compatible with 3.3 V and 5 V. The core of the module uses the SX1278 RF chip from Semtech. The SX1278 uses a LoRa remote modem with a bandwidth of 7.8–37.5 kHz and a communication transmission rate of 180 bps to 37.5 kbps. It uses spread spectrum modulation and forward error correction. Compared with traditional modulation techniques such as FSK, it not only expands the link range of wireless communication, but also improves the robustness of the link. At the same time, researchers can rationally use data rate, bandwidth size, link budget, and anti-jamming by adjusting the three design variables of spreading factor (SF), spread spectrum modulation bandwidth (BW), and error correction rate (CR). The design circuit of the SX1278 module is shown in Fig. 5.

4   Software and Programming

4.1   Terminal Program Software Design

ATGM332 positioning module after power started to search for the visible satellite broadcast and receive satellite navigation message, obtain the measurement pseudor-ange according to the carrier phase measurement and establish the positioning equations to solve the pseudorange equations, and through the fixed clock error, the ionosphere effect, in order to get more precise geographic coordinate information. Finally, the positioning data is output through fixed frame format. The navigation message output by the positioning module adopts the NMEA-0183 protocol, which has now become a unified standard protocol for navigation equipment. The output format of this protocol includes GGA (Global Positioning Data), RMC (Transport Positioning Data), and VTG (Ground Speed Information).), GLL (geodetic coordinate information), ZDA (UTC time and date), GSA (satellite PRN data), GSV (satellite status information) [15, 16]. This article mainly uses the GGA sentence to extract the current longitude, latitude and other information. Before the extraction, the data format judgment and data validity judgment are first performed. Figure 6 shows the process of obtaining and processing the location information.

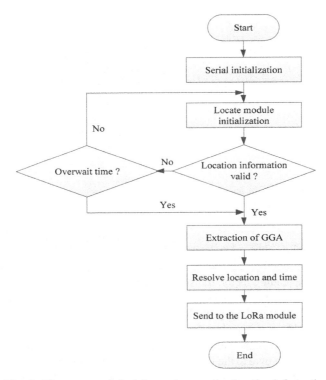

Fig. 6. The process of obtaining and processing location information

The DIO0 ~ DIO5 ports of SX1278 are used to indicate the current status to the STM32 processor. Among them, DIO0 provides status prompts of RxDone and TxDone. STM32 can use DIO0 port to judge the status of data reception and transmission completion. Although SX1278 is a half-duplex transceiver, it can only receive or transmit at the same time. However, in the vehicle monitoring system designed in this paper, the LoRa communication of the vehicle terminal part mainly transmits positioning data, and the LoRa communication part of the monitoring center mainly performs Reception of positioning data. Therefore, through the register configuration of SX1278, the LoRa communication module of the vehicle terminal always maintains the data sending state, and the LoRa communication module of the monitoring center always maintains the data receiving state. The subroutine flow of the vehicle terminal transmission is shown in Fig. 7.

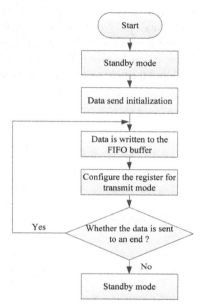

Fig. 7. SX1278 data sending procedure flow

First, the LoRa chip completes some initialization operations through the SX1278Tx_Init () function in standby mode, including the operating frequency band, used bandwidth, spreading factor, transmit power, etc., and then sets the first address of the FIFO data buffer as the data to be sent to the buffer. The start address of the developer can be configured through the register RegFifoTxBaseAddr. Subsequently, the value of RegFifoTxBaseAddr is assigned to the pointer RegFifoAddrPtr, which is used to read the pending data stored in the buffer area, and then set the read byte length by writing the RegPayloadLength byte to the FIFO (RegFifo). Finally, under the TX mode request, the data transmission is started. When the transmission is completed, TxDone responds to the interrupt. At this time, the chip repeatedly writes the data to the buffer operation if there is data to be transmitted. If there is no data to transmit, the chip enters the standby mode.

4.2 Monitoring Center PC Software Design

The host computer interface mainly includes two parts: the first part is mainly the upper part of the positioning data display area, which includes the specific longitude, latitude, and time values of the remote vehicle analysis, and other navigation data from the vehicle terminal device the second part is the map display area in the lower part of the interface. The browser function needs to be integrated to display the target vehicle position on the map by loading the electronic map. In addition, this article uses the QlineEdit class to design two open and close buttons, so that monitoring personnel can easily complete the software start and stop.

Monitoring System Testing the LoRa communication part of the monitoring center is connected to the host computer through a USB serial port. Therefore, the program of the host computer needs to have the serial port communication function. This design uses the QtSerialPort module provided by the Qt development framework. This module provides two C ++ classes, QSerialPort and QSerialPortInfo [18], which provide developers with an interface to operate the serial port and information on the existence of the serial port. When developing, you first need to scan the serial port resources currently connected to the PC, view the current serial port resources, create a QSerialPort object, and set the serial port parameters. The serial port parameters set the baud rate to 9600, 8 data bits, no parity bit, and no stop bit. After the setting is successful, the click event is connected to the corresponding slot function, and the open () and close () functions are called by reading and writing to make the UI button have the start and stop functions.

The position information we obtain is only the data value such as latitude and longitude. It cannot express the information contained in the data visually and intuitively. It has little meaning for monitoring and management. Therefore, it is necessary to convert the data information into position coordinates and display it on the map. The functions of vehicle positioning and path playback in the monitoring center are realized by calling the Baidu map Java Script API. Baidu Maps JavaScript API is a set of application interfaces written in JavaScript language to help users build feature-rich and interactive map applications on the website, and support map applications for PC, mobile and server devices. It also has a map development function with HTML5 features [19]. Before using the Baidu Map Java Script API interface, you need to apply for a key before you can use it [20]. After the key is created, the electronic map is generated by creating an html file, and the API interface required for monitoring the system function is added to the html file.

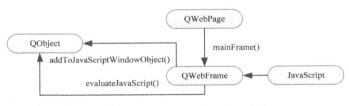

Fig. 8. Calling process

After the map is created, QT needs to interact with javascript. The mutual call between QT and Java Script is implemented by two functions in QwebFrame, addToJavaScriptWindowObject() and evaluateJavaScript().addToJavaScriptWindowObject() passes the QObject object to JS so that JS can call QObject's public slots function. QT directly calls the function in JS through evaluateJavaScript(). The calling process is shown in Fig. 8.

5   System Communication Test

We use the Dongfeng Campus of Zhengzhou Light Industry College as the test area to carry out systematic road test of the communication function of the monitoring system. The Dongfeng Campus covers an area of more than 400 mu, and the height of the building is generally 5–10 layers. This area can approximate most of the city's application scenarios. We installed the monitoring station on the roof of the school's electrical information engineering school, installed the vehicle terminal on a bicycle in the school, working in the 433 MHz frequency band, transmitting power 20 dBM, air speed 2.4 kbps. After the terminal is ready to be powered on, the system is powered on, and the positioning is performed to send the data packet containing the location information to the monitoring station, and the monitoring station receives the data packet for storage. In order to test the effective transmission distance of LoRa communication, driving bicycle is gradually moved away from the monitoring station with the monitoring station as the center point, and 10 groups of communication tests are performed, and 1000 data packets are transmitted each time. The test results are shown in Table 1, and draw the change trend of packet loss rate and communication distance, as shown in Fig. 10. The communication distance is much larger than ZigBee, WiFi and Bluetooth, which meets the requirements for monitoring communication.

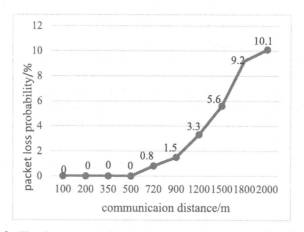

Fig. 9. The change trend of packet loss rate and communication distance

Analysis of experimental results, it can be seen from Fig. 9 that as the communication distance increases, the number of data packets received by the system gradually decreases, and the packet loss rate gradually increases. In general, the system has a good communication quality within a communication range of less than 2 km, and the packet loss rate is basically less than 10%. When the communication distance exceeds 2 km, the communication quality gradually decreases, and the packet loss rate will exceed 10%, exceeding the design goal. Therefore, the system can better complete the vehicle monitoring work within the 2 km communication range.

5.1 PC Software Function Verification

In order to verify the function of the monitoring upper computer system, the host computer was tested with the vehicle terminal. According to the 4.1 communication test results, the bicycle with the terminal is driven in the range of the communication quality of Zhengzhou University of Light Industry campus to ensure that the functional test of the host computer will not be affected by the quality of LoRa communication. Here we select the autumn section of the campus. After the vehicle terminal is powered on, the positioning transmission function is turned on, the monitoring station starts the PC end software, and the serial port function is set to enable real-time monitoring. When the monitoring station receives the vehicle location information, it will transmit the real-time data to the top computer QT monitoring terminal, which can obtain the longitude and latitude of the current vehicle, as well as the current time and other data information. QT terminal can realize the online call to baidu map and display the current position coordinates of the bicycle in the upper computer interface. The real-time interface display of the monitoring system is shown in Fig. 10.

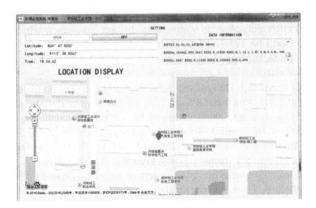

Fig. 10. Host computer monitoring interface

During the test, the software system runs normally, realizing data transmission, data display, vehicle map location display and route drawing with the on-board terminal. The test results show that the monitoring system can monitor the driving position of the vehicle terminal in real time. The monitoring system has strong data processing and real-time display functions, the interface operation is simple and convenient, to meet the requirements of the remote vehicle monitoring system.

6   Conclusion

Based on QT platform and LoRa communication technology, this paper designs a vehicle remote monitoring system combining STM32 single-chip technology and GPS satellite positioning technology, and introduces the realization of key technologies of the system in detail. The test results show that the system can obtain farther data transmission distance and reliable communication quality. It can realize dynamic, real-time and real-time positioning display, and can accurately complete the positioning and tracking of mobile vehicles, which has certain significance for the safety management and dispatching of urban vehicles.

References

1. Yiming, G.: Vehicle monitoring management system based on GPS/GPRS. Dissertation, Yanshan University (2013)
2. Zhongxiang, Y., Jiefeng, Z., Peiqiang, Z.: Design of IOT gas meter reading system based on LORA. Electron. Technol. Softw. Eng. (15), 172–174 (2018)
3. Jiwen, H.: "Smart water" meter reading system based on NB-IoT mobile communication network. Guangxi Water Resour. Hydropower (04), 90–93 (2018)
4. Yang, W., Xiangming, W., Zhaoming, L., Gang, C., Qi, P.: Emerging internet of things technology——LoRa[J]. Inf. Commun. Technol. 11(01), 55–59 + 72 (2017)
5. Jing, Z., Guangtian, S.: Analysis of LoRa wireless network technology. Mob. Commun. 40(21), 50–57 (2016)
6. Hao, Z.: Implementation and application of LoRa technology in low power wide area network. Inf. Commun. Technol. 11(01), 19–26 (2017)
7. Tianping, G.: LORA technology to achieve long-distance, low-power wireless data transmission Electron. World 10, 115 +117 (2016)
8. Huakai, Z.: LoRa technology brings a new starting point for future IoT products. Electron, World, (15), 146 (2016)
9. Kexin, L., Hongsen, X.: Design and implementation of autonomous positioning and orientation system based on dual GPS receiver. Sci. Surv. Map. 35(03), 180–182 (2010)
10. Zhenyao, W.: Design and implementation of battery remote monitoring system based on network technology. Dissertation, Southwest Jiaotong University (2016)
11. Wenchao, L., Yaosheng, Z., Hongyu, Z., Jinzhe, L., Xiaoxu, P.: Design of blackboard cleaner with embedded system. Sci. Technol. Innov. Prod. (08) 86–89 (2018)
12. Yongle, L.: Research on the positioning system of the elderly based on Beidou navigation and Android platform. Dissertation, Donghua University (2017)
13. Yuyu, X.: Particle concentration monitoring system based on LoRa wireless communication technology. Dissertation, Beijing University of Technology (2017)
14. Guangming, L., Haixia, L.: Application of LoRa communication technology in natural gas well data monitoring system. Comput. Knowl. Technol. 14(27), 237–240 (2018)
15. Dejun, Q., Zhe, Z., Chen, H.: Analysis of NMEA0183 protocol. Electron. Devices (02), 698–701 (2007)
16. Xing, Z., Yanyan, Y., Wentao, W.: Electric vehicle anti-theft system based on GPS and GSM network. Technol. Dev. Appl. (31), 32-34 (2018)
17. Wuming, Z., Xinxin, Z., Ma Songsong, P., Kaixuan, G., Qindong, S.: QT-based automatic chemiluminescence immunoassay analyzer PC system. Comput. Digit. Eng. 46(10), 2011–2015 (2018)
18. Pengjun, L., Dianxing, L., Wenbin, N., Pan, Y., Junwei, S.: Realization of serial communication between Qt and pulse generator based on windows. Comput. Meas. Control 24(04), 206–209 (2016)
19. Baidu map open platform. JavaScript development document [DB/OL]. http://lbsyun.baidu.com/index.php?title=jspopular.2018-10
20. Zhiliang, J.: Design and implementation of location monitoring system based on embedded and Baidu map. Dissertation, Inner Mongolia University (2014)

Unifying Domain Adaptation into Simultaneous Discriminant Analysis: A Method for Low-Resolution Face Recognition with Single Sample Per Person

Yongjie Chu[1][(✉)], Cheng Su[2], and Lindu Zhao[2]

[1] School of Management, Nanjing University of Posts and Telecommunications, Nanjing, China
yongjiechu@yeah.net
[2] Institute of Systems Engineering, Southeast University, Nanjing, China

Abstract. In some real-world applications, such as law enforcement, it is required to find out the true identity of an LR face image by using only the high-resolution (HR) profile face image. This leads to LR face recognition with single sample per person (SSPP). As it is intractable to find a match between LR and HR images directly and difficult to explore variations from SSPP, LR face recognition with SSPP is quite a challenging problem. To address the problem, based on simultaneously discriminative analysis (SDA), we propose to introduce an auxiliary dataset (source domain) containing multiple samples per person and integrate domain adaptation into the learning of coupled mappings. In the proposed method, the discriminative analysis of source domain and target domain, together with the domain adaptation between the source domain and target domain are unified into one framework, which produces Enhanced SDA. In this framework, the distribution mismatch is reduced, and the information in both the source domain and target domain are used to learn the coupled mappings. Enhanced SDA is extensively evaluated on LFW and SC face databases, the promising results of Enhanced SDA show its effectiveness in LR face recognition with single sample per person.

Keywords: Low-resolution face recognition · Domain adaptation · Single sample per person

1 Introduction

With the increasing security demands, more and more surveillance cameras are installed in public places nowadays. There is obvious distance between the pedestrians' faces and these surveillance cameras. As a result, the face images captured by the cameras in public are usually of small sizes or low-resolution. How to successfully recognize LR face images becomes a hot issue. The typical LR face recognition problem is to recognize the identity of an LR face image according to available high-resolution (HR) face images. Compared with high resolution (HR) face recognition, LR face recognition is more difficult. One reason is that the LR images contain less information, the other reason is that

© Springer Nature Singapore Pte Ltd. 2020
X. Sun et al. (Eds.): ICAIS 2020, CCIS 1252, pp. 461–471, 2020.
https://doi.org/10.1007/978-981-15-8083-3_41

the feature dimensions of HR and LR images are different. To address these problems, many LR face recognition algorithms have been proposed, which can be categorized into two classes: super-resolution (SR) based methods, and coupled mappings (CM) based methods.

Super-resolution based methods employ SR techniques to recover the HR counterparts from LR face images [1], and further use the recovered images to identify an unknown person. In order to use SR techniques to boost LR face recognition, researchers propose recognition-oriented SR techniques, which take face recognition into account while performing super-resolution. It is proposed in [2] to perform SR on coherent feature domain by establishing a nonlinear mapping between HR and LR features. A discriminative approach which simultaneously combines recognition with HR reconstruction is developed in a regularization framework [3]. Similarly, a new data constraint and a discriminative constraint are developed for good visual quality of image reconstruction and discriminative feature extraction [4]. Because those SR based methods integrate SR into LR face recognition, they improve the performance of LR face recognition to an extent. Nevertheless, for images of quite low-resolution, it is difficult to recover much meaningful information from such limited pixels by super-resolution.

Coupled mappings (CM) based methods learn two mappings, one for HR images and the other for LR images, and project HR and LR images into a common subspace. Coupled locality preserving mappings (CLPM) is first proposed to address LR face recognition [5], which is an unsupervised method. To boost the discriminative ability of CM models, the sample label information is incorporated into coupled mappings based models. For example, coupled marginal fisher analysis (CMFA) [6], which is inspired by marginal fisher analysis; simultaneous discriminant analysis (SDA) [7], coupled marginal discriminant mappings (CMDM) [8] and large margin coupled mapping (LMCM) [9]. [10] combine CM with canonical correlation analysis and propose discriminant correlation analysis (DCA) for LR face recognition. Different from above CM models, DCA aims to find projections that maximize the pair-wise correlations. To make full use of the local structure information of samples, a semi-coupled locality-constrained representation approach is developed to simultaneously learn the discriminative representations and the mapping relationship [11]. Differently, coupled discriminant manifold analysis considers the local information by manifold learning in a supervised manner [12, 13]. Most recently, deep network and CM are integrated to deal with LR face recognition. For example, the deep coupled ResNet model [14], which involves two branch networks as the coupled mappings and a trunk network for discriminative feature extraction.

Although the methods mentioned above are able to address LR face recognition, they are designed relying on multiple images of each subject in the training/gallery set. In some real-world applications, it is difficult to collect multiple samples for each person, and even single sample per person (SSPP) may occur, resulting in LR face recognition with SSPP. Though many approaches have been developed to deal with face recognition with SSPP, less attention has been paid on LR face recognition with SSPP. To solve the challenging problem, cluster-based regularized simultaneous discriminant analysis (C-RSDA) [15] is proposed. The variations used to enrich the intra-class and inter-class variation in C-RSDA are constrained by the limited samples in the gallery set, making it less effective in recognizing LR faces involving more variations. To capture more variations, Boosted CMFA [16] is designed by introducing an auxiliary database, it first reduces the distribution difference between the gallery and auxiliary dataset, then applies CMFA to learn discriminative subspace.

To further improve the recognition performance of LR face recognition with SSPP, we make some contribution in this paper. We propose Enhanced SDA from the perspective of domain adaptation. The auxiliary database contains abundant variations is introduced as the source domain, while the gallery set and probe set are seen as the target domain. Enhance SDA learns two mappings, one is for HR images and the other is for LR images. Meanwhile, it considers two aims, one is domain adaptation and the other is discriminative learning. The significance of Enhanced SDA is that it includes the knowledge exploited from two different domains by unifying domain adaptation and SDA into one scheme, producing more discriminative features.

The rest of this paper is organized as follows. Section 2 describes the proposed Enhanced SDA model. In Sect. 3, we evaluate the proposed method on two widely used databased for LR face recognition with SSPP. Finally, we make our conclusion in Sect. 4.

2 Proposed Approach

In this paper, we utilize coupled mappings to address the mismatch problem between HR images and LR images. Assume that there is a set of HR face images $\mathbf{H} = [\mathbf{h}_1, \mathbf{h}_2, \cdots, \mathbf{h}_N]$, in which $\mathbf{h}_i \in \mathfrak{R}^M$, N is the number of samples in $\mathbf{H}$, M is the feature dimension of HR images. Meanwhile, there is a set of LR face images $\mathbf{L} = [\mathbf{l}_1, \mathbf{l}_2, \cdots, \mathbf{l}_N]$, in which $\mathbf{l}_i \in \mathfrak{R}^m$, m is the feature dimension of LR images, and $m << M$. To solve the mismatch of feature dimensions between HR and LR images, coupled mappings based methods learn two mappings, i.e., $\mathbf{P}_H \in \mathfrak{R}^{M \times d}$ for HR images, and $\mathbf{P}_L \in \mathfrak{R}^{m \times d}$ for LR images. These two mappings are able to project HR and LR images into a common subspace, thus the similarity among HR gallery projections and probe LR projections can be calculated. The projections of HR and LR samples in the common subspace can be expressed by $\tilde{\mathbf{h}}_j = \mathbf{P}_H^T \mathbf{h}_j$ and $\tilde{\mathbf{l}}_j = \mathbf{P}_L^T \mathbf{l}_j$, where $j = 1, 2, \cdots, N$; $\tilde{\mathbf{h}}_j$ and $\tilde{\mathbf{l}}_j$ denotes the projections of HR and LR images, respectively. Assume that samples in $\mathbf{H}$ and $\mathbf{L}$ are from K classes. Let $\mathbf{H}_i$ denote a set contains HR samples from i-th class, $c(\mathbf{h}_j)$ denote the class label of $\mathbf{h}_j$, and $c(\mathbf{h}_j) \in (1, 2, \cdots, K)$.

In the following of the section, we first briefly review two techniques which are quite related to our proposed Enhanced SDA, then elaborate on the Enhanced SDA model, which addresses LR face recognition with SSPP by using auxiliary HR and LR face datasets.

2.1 Related Work

Simultaneous Discriminant Analysis (SDA). SDA is a coupled mappings based method to address LR face recognition. SDA follows the idea of linear discriminant analysis (LDA), and explores the discriminative knowledge by maximizing the distances between the class means meanwhile minimizing the distance between each sample and its corresponding class mean in the common projection subspace. Before the mapping, the class means of LR and HR face images, the total means of all LR face images and all HR face images are computed by the following four formulations, respectively:

$$\mu_{L_i} = \frac{1}{N_i} \sum_{c(l_j)=i} l_j, \mu_{H_i} = \frac{1}{N_i} \sum_{c(h_j)=i} h_j; \ \mu_L = \frac{1}{N} \sum_{i=1}^{K} \sum_{c(l_j)=i} l_j, \mu_H = \frac{1}{N} \sum_{i=1}^{K} \sum_{c(h_j)=i} h_j.$$
(1)

where N_i is the sample number in the i-**th** class. After the mapping, regardless of the original identity (HR or LR) of all projections and consider only their class labels, the class means and the total mean of projections in the common subspace are calculated as follows:

$$\mu_i = \frac{1}{2N_i} \left(\sum_{c(h_j)=i} \tilde{h}_j + \sum_{c(l_j)=i} \tilde{l}_j \right) = \frac{1}{2} \left(\mathbf{P}_H^T \mu_{H_i} + \mathbf{P}_L^T \mu_{L_i} \right),$$
(2)

$$\mu = \frac{1}{2N} \left(\sum_{i=1}^{K} \sum_{c(h_j)=i} \tilde{h}_j + \sum_{i=1}^{K} \sum_{c(l_j)=i} \tilde{l}_j \right) = \frac{1}{2} \left(\mathbf{P}_H^T \mu_H + \mathbf{P}_L^T \mu_L \right).$$
(3)

Note that in the projection subspace, $\tilde{h}_j = \mathbf{P}_H^T h_j, \tilde{l}_j = \mathbf{P}_L^T l_j$, then the between-class scatter value $tr(J_b)$ and within-class scatter value $tr(J_w)$ can be derived, in which J_b and J_w are obtained by

$$J_b = \left[\mathbf{P}_H^T \ \mathbf{P}_L^T \right] \sum_i^K \begin{bmatrix} \frac{1}{2} \sum_{i=1}^{K} N_i \mathbf{B}_H \mathbf{B}_H^T & \frac{1}{2} \sum_{i=1}^{K} N_i \mathbf{B}_H \mathbf{B}_L^T \\ \frac{1}{2} \sum_{i=1}^{K} N_i \mathbf{B}_L \mathbf{B}_H^T & \frac{1}{2} \sum_{i=1}^{K} N_i \mathbf{B}_L \mathbf{B}_L^T \end{bmatrix} \begin{bmatrix} \mathbf{P}_H \\ \mathbf{P}_L \end{bmatrix} = \mathbf{P}^T \mathbf{S}_b \mathbf{P},$$
(4)

$$J_w = \left[\mathbf{P}_H^T \ \mathbf{P}_L^T \right] \sum_i^K \begin{bmatrix} \sum_{c(h_j)=i} \Psi(h_j, \mu_{H_i}) & -\frac{1}{2} N_i \mu_{H_i} \mu_{L_i}^T \\ -\frac{1}{2} N_i \mu_{L_i} \mu_{H_i}^T & \sum_{c(l_j)=i} \Psi(l_j, \mu_{L_i}) \end{bmatrix} \begin{bmatrix} \mathbf{P}_H \\ \mathbf{P}_L \end{bmatrix} = \mathbf{P}^T \mathbf{S}_w \mathbf{P},$$
(5)

where $\mathbf{B}_H = \mu_{H_i} - \mu_H$, $\mathbf{B}_L = \mu_{L_i} - \mu_L$; Ψ is a function defined as $\Psi(\mathbf{x}, \mathbf{y}) = (\mathbf{x} - 1/2\mathbf{y})(\mathbf{x} - 1/2\mathbf{y})^T + 1/4 \mathbf{y}\mathbf{y}^T$, $\mathbf{P} = \left[\mathbf{P}_H^T \ \mathbf{P}_L^T \right]^T$ is the concatenation of $\mathbf{P}_H$ and $\mathbf{P}_L$; $\mathbf{S}_b$ and $\mathbf{S}_w$ are the between-class and within-class scatter matrix of all images in the common subspace, respectively. To find out the optimal $\mathbf{P}_H$ and $\mathbf{P}_L$, SDA formulates its objective function using the Fisher discriminant criterion as follow:

$$\left[\mathbf{P}_H \ \mathbf{P}_L \right]_{opt} = \arg \max_{\mathbf{P}_H, \mathbf{P}_L} J_{Fisher}(\mathbf{P}) = \arg \max_{\mathbf{P}_H, \mathbf{P}_L} \frac{tr(J_b)}{tr(J_w)} = \arg \max_{\mathbf{P}_H, \mathbf{P}_L} \frac{tr(\mathbf{P}^T \mathbf{S}_b \mathbf{P})}{tr(\mathbf{P}^T \mathbf{S}_w \mathbf{P})}.$$
(6)

Transfer Component Analysis (TCA). The key idea of this work is to utilize an auxiliary database to enhance the performance of SDA on recognizing LR faces with SSPP. The auxiliary face dataset and the unknown LR face images are from two different domains, named as source domain and target domain, respectively. But these two domains may have a large discrepancy. Therefore, eliminating or reducing the discrepancy between the source and target domain is essential before transferring the knowledge of the source domain to the target domain. This idea is widely used in sentiment analysis [17] and multi-label learning [18]. TCA [19] is a popular and effective way to reduce the discrepancy between the two domains, it is also known as domain adaptation. TCA aims to find a transfer subspace, in which the difference in data distribution of the source domain and target domain is dramatically reduced, while the data properties of each domain are best preserved.

Assume that $\mathbf{X}^s \in \Re^{d \times n_s}$ and $\mathbf{X}^t \in \Re^{d \times n_t}$ ar dataset from the source domain and target domain, respectively; where d is the dimension of samples, n_s and n_t are the total number of samples in the above datasets, respectively. We use the symbols s and t in the superscript to denote the source domain and target domain, respectively. TCA learns a transfer subspace to achieve domain adaptation by the following model, which reduces the difference of data distributions between $\mathbf{X}^s$ and $\mathbf{X}^t$:

$$
\begin{aligned}
\mathbf{W}^* &= \arg \min_{\mathbf{W}} \left\| \frac{1}{n_s} \mathbf{W}^T \mathbf{X}^s \mathbf{1}^s - \frac{1}{n_t} \mathbf{W}^T \mathbf{X}^t \mathbf{1}^t \right\|_F^2 + \lambda \|\mathbf{W}\|_F^2 \\
&= \arg \min_{\mathbf{W}} \ tr\left(\mathbf{W}^T [\mathbf{X}^s \ \mathbf{X}^t] \mathbf{K} [\mathbf{X}^s \ \mathbf{X}^t]^T \mathbf{W} \right) + \lambda \ tr\left(\mathbf{W}^T \mathbf{W} \right), \\
&= \arg \min_{\mathbf{W}} \ tr\left(\mathbf{W}^T \mathbf{X} \mathbf{K} \mathbf{X}^T \mathbf{W} \right) + \lambda \ tr\left(\mathbf{W}^T \mathbf{W} \right)
\end{aligned}
\tag{7}
$$

$$
\text{s.t.} \ \mathbf{W}^T \mathbf{X} \mathbf{R} \mathbf{X}^T \mathbf{W} = \mathbf{I}_m,
\tag{8}
$$

where $\mathbf{X} = [\mathbf{X}^s, \mathbf{X}^t] \in \Re^{d \times (n_s + n_t)}$, $\|\cdot\|_F$ denotes the Frobenius norm of a matrix, and $\mathbf{W} \in \Re^{d \times m} (m < d)$ is the transform matrix of domain adaptation; $\mathbf{1}^s \in \Re^{n_s \times 1}$ and $\mathbf{1}^t \in \Re^{n_t \times 1}$ are the column vectors with all 1's; $\mathbf{K}$ is an indicator matrix, $\mathbf{K}_{ij} = 1/(n_s)^2$ if $i \leq n_s$ and $j \leq n_s$, else $\mathbf{K}_{ij} = 1/(n_t)^2$ if $i > n_t$ and $j > n_t$; otherwise, $\mathbf{K}_{ij} = -1/(n_s n_t)$; $\mathbf{R} \in \Re^{n \times n}$, $\mathbf{R} = \mathbf{I}_n - \frac{1}{n} \mathbf{1} \mathbf{1}^T$ is a centering matrix, $n = n_s + n_t$; $\mathbf{I}$ denotes the identity matrix, λ is a scalar and $\lambda \|\mathbf{W}\|_F^2$ is a regularization term to control the complexity of $\mathbf{W}$. Note that Eq. (7) is used to reduce the distance between different distributions across domains in the latent transfer subspace, while Eq. (8) is used to preserve the variance of the data as much as possible.

2.2 Enhanced SDA

Different from the traditional domain adaptation problem, in LR face recognition, both the target domain and source domain contains two different sub-domains, i.e., HR sub-domain and LR sub-domain. Let $T = \{ \{\mathbf{X}_H^t\} ; \{\mathbf{X}_L^t\} \}$ be the target domain, in which $\{\mathbf{X}_H^t\}$ and $\{\mathbf{X}_L^t\}$ are HR sub-domain and LR sub-domain, respectively. For the purpose of clarity in description, we name dataset $\mathbf{X}_H^t$ and $\mathbf{X}_L^t$ as HR target dataset and LR target dataset, respectively. For LR face recognition with SSPP, $\mathbf{X}_H^t$ contains single HR face image per person, and $\mathbf{X}_L^t$ contains single LR face images per person. Let $S = \{ \{\mathbf{X}_H^s\} ; \{\mathbf{X}_L^s\} \}$ be the source domain, in which $\{\mathbf{X}_H^s\}$ and $\{\mathbf{X}_L^s\}$ are HR sub-domain and LR sub-domain, respectively; $\mathbf{X}_H^s$ and $\mathbf{X}_L^s$ are named as HR source dataset and LR source dataset, respectively. Both HR source dataset and LR source dataset include multiple samples per person. We assume in this paper that there is an equal number of samples for each person in HR source dataset and LR source dataset.

The fundamental idea of the proposed approach is to learn a common subspace, where the source domain and the target domain are sufficiently interlaced, meanwhile, samples are clustered according to their class labels. Although both the source domain and target domain contains HR sub-domain and LR sub-domain, both the HR sub-domains between two domain and LR sub-domains between two domains have large discrepancies. To reduce the discrepancies, we propose to learn a coupled projections, denoted as $\mathbf{P}_H$ and $\mathbf{P}_L$, to respectively project the HR images in two sub-domains and LR images in two sub-domains into a common subspace. In order to well transfer the knowledge embedded into the source domain to the target domain, and enhance the performance of SDA on recognizing LR face images in the target domain with SSPP, the common subspace should be able to achieve domain adaptation and discriminative learning at the same time.

For low-resolution face recognition problem, according to TCA, the data distribution mismatch between $\left\{\mathbf{X}_H^t\right\}$ and $\left\{\mathbf{X}_H^s\right\}$, $\left\{\mathbf{X}_L^t\right\}$ and $\left\{\mathbf{X}_L^s\right\}$ should be minimized simultaneously; meanwhile variance of the data is best preserved in the transferred subspace. Let $\mathbf{X}_H = \left[\mathbf{X}_H^s, \mathbf{X}_H^t\right]$, which includes all HR face images from both source domain and target domain; similarly, $\mathbf{X}_L = \left[\mathbf{X}_L^s, \mathbf{X}_L^t\right]$ contains all LR face images from both domains. According to TCA, we get

$$
\begin{aligned}
\left[\mathbf{P}_H^*, \mathbf{P}_L^*\right] &= \arg\min_{\mathbf{P}_H,\mathbf{P}_L} \; tr\left(\mathbf{P}_H^T \mathbf{X}_H \tilde{\mathbf{K}}_H \mathbf{X}_H^T \mathbf{P}_H\right) + tr\left(\mathbf{P}_L^T \mathbf{X}_L \tilde{\mathbf{K}}_L \mathbf{X}_L^T \mathbf{P}_L\right) \\
&= \arg\min_{\mathbf{P}_H,\mathbf{P}_L} \; tr\left(\left[\,\mathbf{P}_H^T\ \mathbf{P}_L^T\,\right]\begin{bmatrix}\mathbf{X}_H \tilde{\mathbf{K}}_H \mathbf{X}_H^T & \mathbf{0} \\ \mathbf{0} & \mathbf{X}_L \tilde{\mathbf{K}}_L \mathbf{X}_L^T\end{bmatrix}\begin{bmatrix}\mathbf{P}_H \\ \mathbf{P}_L\end{bmatrix}\right), \\
&= \arg\min_{\mathbf{P}_H,\mathbf{P}_L} \; tr\left(\mathbf{P}^T \mathbf{K}_{HL}\mathbf{P}\right)
\end{aligned} \tag{9}
$$

$$
\begin{aligned}
\left[\mathbf{P}_H^*, \mathbf{P}_L^*\right] &= \arg\max_{\mathbf{P}_H,\mathbf{P}_L} \; tr\left(\mathbf{P}_H^T \mathbf{X}_H \tilde{\mathbf{R}}_H \mathbf{X}_H^T \mathbf{P}_H\right) + tr\left(\mathbf{P}_L^T \mathbf{X}_L \tilde{\mathbf{R}}_L \mathbf{X}_L^T \mathbf{P}_L\right) \\
&= \arg\max_{\mathbf{P}_H,\mathbf{P}_L} \; tr\left(\left[\,\mathbf{P}_H^T\ \mathbf{P}_L^T\,\right]\begin{bmatrix}\mathbf{X}_H \tilde{\mathbf{R}}_H \mathbf{X}_H^T & \mathbf{0} \\ \mathbf{0} & \mathbf{X}_L \tilde{\mathbf{R}}_L \mathbf{X}_L^T\end{bmatrix}\begin{bmatrix}\mathbf{P}_H \\ \mathbf{P}_L\end{bmatrix}\right). \\
&= \arg\max_{\mathbf{P}_H,\mathbf{P}_L} \; tr\left(\mathbf{P}^T \mathbf{R}_{HL}\mathbf{P}\right)
\end{aligned} \tag{10}
$$

The ultimate purpose of the proposed method is classification, so discriminant analysis is essential. In the source domain $S = \left\{\left\{\mathbf{X}_H^s\right\}; \left\{\mathbf{X}_L^s\right\}\right\}$, when using the coupled mappings $\mathbf{P}_H$ and $\mathbf{P}_L$ to respectively project the HR and LR samples into the common subspace, the distance between the projections with the same class label should be minimized, meanwhile the distance between the projections with different class labels should be maximized. It is the same for the target domain $T = \left\{\left\{\mathbf{X}_H^t\right\}; \left\{\mathbf{X}_L^t\right\}\right\}$. According to Eq. (4, 5), we obtain

$$
\left[\mathbf{P}_H^*, \mathbf{P}_L^*\right] = \arg\max_{\mathbf{P}_H,\mathbf{P}_L} \; tr\left(\mathbf{P}^T \mathbf{S}_b^s \mathbf{P}\right) + tr\left(\mathbf{P}^T \mathbf{S}_b^t \mathbf{P}\right), \tag{11}
$$

$$[\mathbf{P}_H^*, \mathbf{P}_L^*] = \arg \min_{\mathbf{P}_H, \mathbf{P}_L} \quad tr\left(\mathbf{P}^T \mathbf{S}_w^s \mathbf{P}\right) + tr\left(\mathbf{P}^T \mathbf{S}_w^t \mathbf{P}\right), \tag{12}$$

where $\mathbf{S}_b^s$ and $\mathbf{S}_w^s$ are calculated by using face images in the source domain $S = \left\{ \{\mathbf{X}_H^s\} ; \{\mathbf{X}_L^s\} \right\}$, while $\mathbf{S}_b^t$ and $\mathbf{S}_w^t$ are calculated by using face images in the target domain $T = \left\{ \{\mathbf{X}_H^t\} ; \{\mathbf{X}_L^t\} \right\}$.

Our goal is to find a common subspace, in which both domain adaptation and reduction of dimension mismatch are realized. For this purpose, we integrate the domain adaptation and SDA for LR face recognition into a unified framework as below:

$$
\begin{aligned}
[\mathbf{P}_H^*, \mathbf{P}_L^*] &= \arg \max_{\mathbf{P}_H, \mathbf{P}_L} \frac{tr\left(\mathbf{P}^T \mathbf{S}_b^s \mathbf{P}\right) + tr\left(\mathbf{P}^T \mathbf{S}_b^t \mathbf{P}\right) + \tau\, tr\left(\mathbf{P}^T \mathbf{R}_{HL} \mathbf{P}\right)}{tr\left(\mathbf{P}^T \mathbf{S}_w^s \mathbf{P}\right) + tr\left(\mathbf{P}^T \mathbf{S}_w^t \mathbf{P}\right) + \gamma\, tr\left(\mathbf{P}^T \mathbf{K}_{HL} \mathbf{P}\right)} \\
&= \arg \max_{\mathbf{P}_H, \mathbf{P}_L} \frac{tr\left(\mathbf{P}^T \left(\mathbf{S}_b^s + \mathbf{S}_b^t + \tau \mathbf{R}_{HL}\right)\mathbf{P}\right)}{tr\left(\mathbf{P}^T \left(\mathbf{S}_w^s + \mathbf{S}_w^t + \gamma \mathbf{K}_{HL}\right)\mathbf{P}\right)}, \\
&= \arg \max_{\mathbf{P}_H, \mathbf{P}_L} \frac{tr\left(\mathbf{P}^T \Theta \mathbf{P}\right)}{tr\left(\mathbf{P}^T \Omega \mathbf{P}\right)}
\end{aligned}
\tag{13}
$$

in which we add two parameters τ and γ to control the contribution between data variance preservation and distribution mismatch reduction, respectively. From this formulation, it is clear that we jointly optimize domain adaptation and discriminative learning. This model utilizes an auxiliary dataset to enhance the performance of SDA, hence we call it Enhanced SDA. The optimal $\mathbf{P} = \left[\mathbf{P}_H^T \ \mathbf{P}_L^T\right]^T$ consists of the eigenvectors of $\Omega^{-1}\Theta$ corresponding to its first largest d eigenvalues, in which $\Theta = \mathbf{S}_b^s + \mathbf{S}_b^t + \tau \mathbf{R}_{HL}$ and $\Omega = \mathbf{S}_w^s + \mathbf{S}_w^t + \gamma \mathbf{K}_{HL}$.

3 Experimental Analysis

3.1 Dataset Description

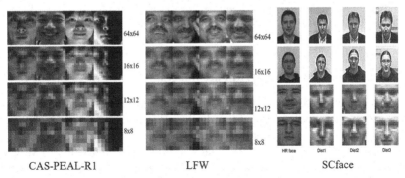

Fig. 1. Sample face images from three databases: (a) CAS database, (b) LFW database and (c) SCface database.

CAS-PEAL-R1 Dataset [20]. In this work, the CAS dataset is used as the source data only, and we select a training set to represent the source domain, which consists of 1200 images of 300 subjects, four images for each individual. Figure 1(a) shows some HR sample images and their corresponding LR counterparts in this dataset.

LFW Dataset [21]. Following the work of [15], we choose a subset of 158 subjects from LFW-a database, and further choose one most frontal face image for each subject to construct the HR gallery set, then select the first 5 face images from the remaining ones for every person to construct HR probe set. The HR probe set is also used as source data when LFW database is seen as the source domain. Figure 1(b) displays some HR sample images and their LR counterparts (16 × 16, 12 × 12 and 8 × 8).

SCface Dataset [22]. SCface database contains images of 130 subjects, which are taken in a simulating real-world unconstrained environment. Therefore, recognizing LR faces in this dataset is much more challenging. In the experiments, a subset containing five sections of images is selected: the first section, which consists of HR faces, includes images captured by a high-quality photo camera; the other four sections, which consist of LR faces, include images captured by camera 1–4 at 2 different distances. Figure 1 displays the samples face images used in the experiments of three databases.

3.2 Experimental Setting

In the experiments, all HR face images are aligned and cropped to 64 × 64 pixels. For images in LFW database, the LR face images are obtained by down-sampling from the HR ones, and our task is to recognize LR face images of three resolutions, i.e., 8 × 8, 12 × 12, 16 × 16 pixels. For the SCface dataset, all LR images are 16 × 16 pixels. For training, both HR and LR images of each person are required, please note that the training set in target domain contains only one HR sample and one LR sample. PCA is firstly applied to reduce the dimensionality of input raw features and 99% and 99.99% energy is maintained for HR and LR face images, respectively; then the first 3 principal components of PCA are eliminated as they usually involve more information about variations. The two parameters in Enhanced SDA is set to be $(\tau, \gamma) = (1e^{-3}, 1e^{-3})$, and the nearest neighbor classifier with cosine distance is employed for classification, and the rank-1 recognition rate is reported for each experiment.

3.3 Evaluation on Recognizing LR Face Images

To evaluate the effectiveness of the proposed Enhanced SDA on recognizing LR face images, we conduct experiments on LFW database and SCface database. In these experiments, four coupled mappings based methods which are designed to address LR face recognition, i.e., CLPM, CMFA, SDA and C-RSDA, are compared. CLPM, CMFA, SDA and C-RSDA use the single sample training set only in the target domain for training, thus they are not domain adaptation (Non-DA) based method, but C-RSDA is specifically designed for LR face recognition with SSPP. Additionally, we also evaluate another domain adaptation based method, denoted by "SDA + DA", which means employing domain adaptation to reduce the distribution difference between source and target domain before conducting SDA for discriminative learning. SDA + DA is quite different from Enhanced SDA as our proposed method unifies domain adaptation and SDA into one framework.

Evaluation on LFW Dataset. Let LFW dataset be the target domain, we use CAS database as the source domain. Table 1 lists the accuracy of various methods on recognizing LR faces with 8×8, 12×12 and 16×16 pixels. As can be seen, domain adaptation based methods perform significantly better than CLPM, CMFA and SDA after introducing auxiliary datasets. Because the latter three methods explore the little within-class variations from limited samples in the gallery set, while domain adaptation based methods employ more variations explored from the auxiliary set. C-RSDA explores additional variations from the clusters of gallery set, and its performance is better than SDA + DA, but still worse than Enhanced SDA. Enhanced SDA outperforms SDA + DA, which implies that learning a set of coupled mappings to realize domain adaptation and discriminative analysis simultaneously is more helpful for LR face recognition with SSPP.

Table 1. Recognition accuracy of the various method on LFW database

		8×8	12×12	16×16	Ave.
Non-DA	CLPM	4.10	6.58	7.47	6.05
	CMFA	9.49	10.38	10.89	10.25
	SDA	4.94	6.96	7.85	6.58
	C-RSDA	12.28	14.43	15.06	13.92
CAS → LFW	SDA + DA	8.61	12.41	15.57	12.19
	Enhanced SDA	12.53	15.44	18.86	15.61

Evaluation on SCface Dataset. In SCface dataset, the LR face images are real and captured by the surveillance cameras. On this dataset, the gallery set in target domain includes HR and LR images of the first 65 persons. The prose set in target domain contains the LR images of the remaining 65 subjects. We apply CAS and LFW database as the source domain respectively to evaluate Enhanced SDA. When the LR images are taken at the distance of 1 m, 2.6 m, the recognition accuracy of various approaches is shown in Table 2 and Table 3, respectively. According to these tables, whatever database is used as the source data, Enhanced SDA obviously outperforms other compared methods. Compared with C-RSDA. We also observe that using the LFW database as source domain produces better recognition results than using the CAS database.

Table 2. Recognition accuracy of the various method on SCface database (Distance 3 = 1 m)

		Cam1	Cam2	Cam3	Cam4	Ave.
Non-DA	CLPM	6.15	1.54	1.54	3.08	3.08
	CMFA	10.00	4.62	7.69	8.46	7.69
	SDA	16.92	12.31	20.00	16.92	16.54
	C-RSDA	20.00	10.77	23.08	20.00	18.46
CAS → SCface	Enhanced SDA	21.54	18.46	20.00	24.62	21.15
LFW → SCface	Enhanced SDA	18.46	27.69	21.54	26.15	23.46

Table 3. Recognition accuracy of the various method on SCface database (Distance 2 = 2.6 m)

		Cam1	Cam2	Cam3	Cam4	Ave.
Non-DA	CLPM	3.08	6.15	4.62	3.08	4.23
	CMFA	5.38	5.38	7.69	5.38	5.96
	SDA	15.38	18.64	10.77	23.08	16.97
	C-RSDA	16.92	20.00	10.77	24.62	18.08
CAS → SCface	Enhanced SDA	21.54	20.00	16.92	23.08	20.38
LFW → SCface	Enhanced SDA	23.08	21.54	15.38	24.62	21.16

4 Conclusions

In this paper, we propose an Enhanced SDA approach to address LR face recognition with SSPP, which applies an auxiliary set, which unifies domain adaptation and discriminative analysis when learning coupled mappings. Enhanced SDA aims to enrich the variations in target domain by using variations explored from the source domain, so the learned coupled mappings cover knowledge not only from the target domain but also from the source domain, making them more discriminative. The proposed approach is assessed on three widely used face databases, and the promising results on recognizing LR face images captured in unconstrained environments show its effectiveness.

Not that in Enhanced SDA, we only use one database as source data, multiple databases would be used as the source data to improve the performance, as multiple databases contain more samples and more variations. Thus, integrating multiple domains adaptation with coupled mappings to address LR face recognition with SSPP will be a new research interest.

Acknowledgment. This work was partially supported by the Humanities and Social Science Research on Youth Fund Project of Ministry of Education of China (19YJC870003), the Special Fund for Basic Research in Central University, i.e., Fund for Graduate Research Project of Jiangsu Province (KYZZ15_0072), and sponsored by NUPTSF (Grant No. NY219038).

References

1. Zou, J., et al.: Super-resolution reconstruction of images based on microarray camera. Comput. Mater. Continua **60**(1), 163–177 (2019)
2. Huang, H., He, H.: Super-resolution method for face recognition using nonlinear mappings on coherent features. IEEE Trans. Neural Netw. **22**(1), 121–130 (2011)
3. Hennings-Yeomans, P.H., Baker, S., Kumar, B.: Simultaneous super-resolution and feature extraction for recognition of low-resolution faces. In: IEEE Conference on Computer Vision and Pattern Recognition. IEEE (2008)
4. Zou, W.W., Yuen, P.C.: Very low resolution face recognition problem. IEEE Trans. Image Process. **21**(1), 327–340 (2012)
5. Li, B., et al.: Low-resolution face recognition via coupled locality preserving mappings. IEEE Sig. Process. Lett. **17**(1), 20–23 (2010)
6. Siena, S., Boddeti, V.N., Vijaya Kumar, B.V.K.: Coupled marginal fisher analysis for low-resolution face recognition. In: Fusiello, A., Murino, V., Cucchiara, R. (eds.) ECCV 2012. LNCS, vol. 7584, pp. 240–249. Springer, Heidelberg (2012). https://doi.org/10.1007/978-3-642-33868-7_24
7. Zhou, C., et al.: Low-resolution face recognition via simultaneous discriminant analysis. In: International Joint Conference on Biometrics. IEEE (2011)
8. Zhang, P., et al.: Coupled marginal discriminant mappings for low-resolution face recognition. Optik-Int. J. Light Electron Optics **126**(23), 4352–4357 (2015)
9. Zhang, J., Guo, Z., Li, X., Chen, Y.: Large margin coupled mapping for low resolution face recognition. In: Booth, R., Zhang, M.-L. (eds.) PRICAI 2016. LNCS (LNAI), vol. 9810, pp. 661–672. Springer, Cham (2016). https://doi.org/10.1007/978-3-319-42911-3_55
10. Haghighat, M., Abdel-Mottaleb, M.: Low resolution face recognition in surveillance systems using discriminant correlation analysis. In: IEEE International Conference on Automatic Face & Gesture Recognition (2017)
11. Lu, T., et al.: Very low-resolution face recognition via semi-coupled locality-constrained representation. In: IEEE International Conference on Parallel and Distributed Systems (2017)
12. Jiang, J., et al.: CDMMA: coupled discriminant multi-manifold analysis for matching low-resolution face images. Sig. Process. **124**, 162–172 (2016)
13. Xing, X., Wang, K.: Couple manifold discriminant analysis with bipartite graph embedding for low-resolution face recognition. Sig. Process. **125**, 329–335 (2016)
14. Lu, Z., Jiang, X., Kot, A.: Deep coupled ResNet for low-resolution face recognition. IEEE Sig. Process. Lett. **25**(4), 526–530 (2018)
15. Chu, Y., et al.: Low-resolution face recognition with single sample per person. Sig. Process. **141**, 144–157 (2017)
16. Chu, Y., et al.: Low-resolution face recognition with single sample per person via domain adaptation. Int. J. Pattern Recognit. Artif. Intell. **33**(05), 1956005 (2019)
17. Wu, S., et al.: Sentiment analysis method based on Kmeans and online transfer learning. Comput. Mater. Continua **60**(3), 1207–1222 (2019)
18. Yang, K., et al.: Multi-label learning based on transfer learning and label correlation. Comput. Mater. Continua **61**(1), 155–169 (2019)
19. Pan, S.J., et al.: Domain adaptation via transfer component analysis. IEEE Trans. Neural Netw. **22**(2), 199–210 (2011)
20. Gao, W., et al.: The CAS-PEAL large-scale chinese face database and baseline evaluations. IEEE Trans. Syst. Man Cybern. - Part A: Syst. Hum. **38**(1), 149–161 (2008)
21. Huang, G.B., et al.: Labeled faces in the wild: a database forstudying face recognition in unconstrained environments (2007)
22. Grgic, M., Delac, K., Grgic, S.: SCface–surveillance cameras face database. Multimed. Tools Appl. **51**(3), 863–879 (2011). https://doi.org/10.1007/s11042-009-0417-2

An Exploratory Study of Blending Smart Classroom in Database Course

Chuanhui Huang[✉]

School of Education, South-Central University for Nationalities, Wuhan, China

Abstract. Research takes the basic compulsory course "Database" of educational technology major as an example. Based on the current problems in Database classroom teaching: the teaching objectives are not clear, the teaching methods are single, the practical teaching needs to be improved, and the teaching content needs to be optimized. We propose exploratory research on database courses that integrate into the smart classroom, with the aim of achieving fundamental changes in the classroom teaching structure. The research of the paper will reposition the curriculum training objectives, optimize the curriculum content, reform the teaching model, change the traditional classroom teaching structure, and change the traditional "teacher-centered" teaching structure to new teaching structure of "dominant-subject combination" of status. The purpose of the research is to improve the quality of teaching and the level of teaching, and to achieve the goal of practical talent training for the society.

Keywords: Teaching approaches · Course design · Educational reform · Educational theory · Experiments

1 Introduction

The current construction of educational informatization has entered the stage of educational application innovation. Seeking the overall reform of the education system has become a new goal for the development of educational informatization.

This paper takes the basic compulsory course "Database" of the education technology major as an example, and takes the smart growth and cultivation of students as the value orientation. Adhering to the educational philosophy of teaching, educating, and people-oriented, we analyze the problems in the teaching process of the Database. Then the paper repositions the curriculum training objectives, optimizes the curriculum content, reforms the teaching model, and promotes the transformation of classroom teaching structure based on the smart classroom to promote the deep integration of information technology and classroom teaching.

2 The Concept of Smart Classroom and Application Analysis

2.1 The Concept of Smart Classroom

To understand the connotation of the concept of smart classroom, we must first analyze the basic connotation of smart education. Smart education is the education of developing

© Springer Nature Singapore Pte Ltd. 2020
X. Sun et al. (Eds.): ICAIS 2020, CCIS 1252, pp. 472–483, 2020.
https://doi.org/10.1007/978-981-15-8083-3_42

students' intellectual ability under the support of information technology. Smart Education Through the construction of a smart learning environment, the teacher uses the smart teaching method to promote learners to learn smart and cultivate intelligent talents with high intelligence and creativity. Smart education is a new stage in the development of education informatization. It is necessary to use the smart learning environment as a technical support to enable students to learn smart in a technology-rich environment and achieve student intelligence generation. Smart education needs to build a smart classroom to complete the two-way integration of technology and education to cultivate students' intellectual ability. Therefore, the smart classroom can be defined as: with the support of information technology, by transforming teaching methods and integrating technology into classroom teaching, build A personalized, intelligent, and digital classroom learning environment that effectively promotes a new classroom for the development of intellectual skills. Smart classrooms are the core of smart education.

2.2 Analysis of the Application of Smart Classroom

The application analysis of smart classrooms focuses on building a smart teaching environment through various information technologies and applying them to specific teaching subjects. Researchers built a junior high school mathematics wisdom classroom based on micro-courses, and carried out case design and analysis; For example, based on the network learning space, the primary school mathematics wisdom classroom teaching strategy research is guided by the wisdom education concept, supported by information technology, and analyzes the construction methods and application cases of the smart classroom. It can be seen that the deep integration of information technology and classroom teaching based on smart classrooms is effective for the reform of classroom teaching in the context of smart education. Therefore, this paper proposes the use of database classroom as a case to analyze the application of smart classroom in teaching.

3 The Problems in the Traditional Database Course

In the context of educational informatization, the database is the backbone of various educational information systems. As a subject-based basic course for educational technology, the database course plays a role in laying the foundation of the discipline. The database plays an irreplaceable role in helping students to find employment and social orientation. Colleges and universities attach great importance to the teaching process, but because the content of this course is complex and complicated, it is not easy to be understood and mastered by students. In the traditional teaching mode, There are some problems with the Database course, as shown in Fig. 1:

3.1 The Teaching Objectives Are Not Clear

The goal of the course is to train professionals. Even if the same course faces different majors, the teaching objectives should be targeted and flexible. At present, there are many problems in the classrooms of colleges and universities where the teaching objectives are not clear. The different professional teaching objectives are the same, resulting in

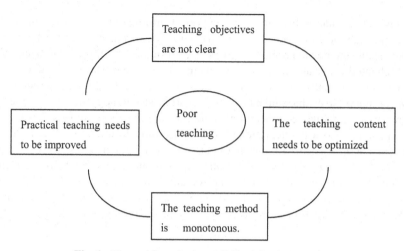

Fig. 1. The problems in the traditional database course

poor students' ability to work and social adaptability. In the face of the application of professional talent training, the database course objectives should pay special attention to practice, stimulate students' interest in learning, improve students' self-learning ability, and cultivate practical talents combining theory and practice.

3.2 The Teaching Content Needs to Be Optimized

The traditional database course content generally includes basic theory, database management system, system design and so on. The theoretical content of the course is too strong and practical. The students generally feel too difficult in the learning process, the interest in learning is not great, and the initiative in learning is not strong. And lack of close ties with professional links, the system is less systematic and scientific, lacking flexibility and pertinence.

3.3 The Teaching Method Is Relatively Monotonous

As a core course of education technology, the Database course has the characteristics of difficult and practical practice. The teaching method of over-reliance on teaching materials may not be suitable. The traditional teacher-centered and crammed teaching mode in the teaching process. Relatively boring and monotonous, students' interest is not great, and the desire to explore is difficult to be stimulated. It is difficult for students to truly understand the use of theoretical knowledge. Although the exam passed, it lacks the ability to solve practical problems.

3.4 Practical Teaching Needs to Be Improved

The traditional "database" teaching method is relatively simple, and the training of students' practical ability and professional ability is not enough. The theory is taught too much in the teaching process, and it is too far out of the actual demand. The students' practical ability needs to be improved.

These problems will lead to less satisfactory teaching results in the "Database" course. The students' fears are more serious, the learning enthusiasm is not high, and the curriculum reform is not waiting.

4   The Smart Classroom Construction Idea of Database Course

Under the background of the new form of education informatization–intelligence education, how to fully allow students to identify the teaching content and how to make the implementation of the teaching process move towards the smart of students has become the focus of the database teaching.

Based on the existing problems in the actual teaching of Database, this paper proposes the deep integration of information technology and classroom teaching based on smart classroom to realize the transformation of classroom teaching structure. The essence of smart education is to build a learning environment that integrates technology, teachers use effective teaching methods, and cultivate intelligent talents with active practical ability. The essence and foothold of deep integration is to change the traditional classroom teaching structure, and to change the traditional "teacher-centered" teaching structure into a "dominant-subject combination" that can fully exert the leading role of teachers and reflect the main position of teachers. "The new teaching structure." Smart classroom refers to the new classroom that effectively promotes the cultivation of intellectual ability by transforming teaching methods, integrating technology into classroom teaching, and constructing a personalized, intelligent and digital classroom learning environment with the support of information technology. The purpose of smart education is to cultivate students' intellectual ability. It is necessary to realize the deep integration of information technology and classroom teaching through the construction of smart classroom.

For students majoring in education technology, the work related to database knowledge after graduation is a creative intellectual work, which needs to test the students' intellectual ability. Therefore, the Database course is very suitable for teaching in a smart classroom. In the smart classroom, information technology has become a tool for students to conceive and verify. Through effective self-management, students abandon the current situation of passively accepting knowledge in traditional teaching, and turn passive classroom into active constructive classroom. The teacher guides students through the organization of their learning styles and the choice of learning strategies. Through the emotional learning in the process of student learning. The teacher stimulates students' interest, cultivates creative thinking, and helps students complete the internalization of knowledge.

5   The Smart Classroom Construction Strategy of Database Course

The construction of the Database smart classroom includes both macro and micro aspects, as shown in Fig. 2: Macroscopically, the training objectives should be repositioned, the teaching content should be optimized, and the teaching model should be reformed. Microscopically, we should create a situational teaching environment and individualized guidance in the classroom to promote the cultivation of students' innovative thinking ability.

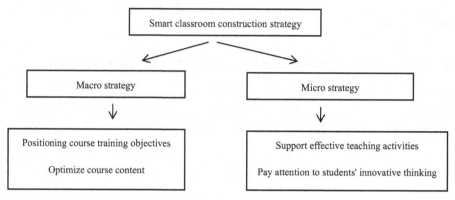

Fig. 2. The smart classroom construction strategy

5.1 Macro Strategy

In view of the confusion in the teaching of the Database course, the educational reform action plan to be implemented on the macro level is as follows:

5.1.1 Repositioning the Course Development Goal

The t development goal is the concrete manifestation of the curriculum value. It is the core content of the talent training model. According to the characteristics of the education technology major of our university, the goal of the database curriculum is repositioned, and the curriculum development goal is refined. We consider that most graduates are engaged in teaching design and digital media development in relevant enterprises and institutions. The development goal will be to realize the transformation of curriculum objectives from knowledge-cultivation to innovative practice, and to develop practical talents. Graduates will be more satisfied with the needs of enterprises and institutions. We will help students find jobs, increase the employment rate of graduates, and improve the quality of employment.

5.1.2 Optimizing Course Content

The re-positioning of the curriculum development goal will be decomposed into specific class hours. In the education technology professional training program of our university, the database course hours are 56, of which the theoretical time is 32, and the actual practice time is 24. In the course of teaching, the Database course uses the relational database management system Microsoft SQL Server. The database management system SQL Server can well meet the development goal of practical talents for educational technology students. This course requires the use of SQL Server for database design and programming. To this end, after scheduling the course content for 2 h of theoretical time, immediately arrange 2 h of practical lessons, and carry out the experiment on the theoretical content of the class to strengthen the students' hands-on programming ability.

5.1.3 Reforming Teaching Mode

After optimizing the teaching content of the Database course, we also need to reform the teaching mode around the teaching objectives. In the process of teaching, The teacher finds that students often have a great fear when they study the course. If they have not started studying, they think that the course is too difficult to learn. Therefore, the teacher must first encourage students to build confidence and cultivate students' interest in learning. The teacher can use the actual development projects in combination with the enterprise, and use teaching modes such as teaching observation, expert lectures, and case teaching to stimulate students' initiative. In order to cultivate students' habit of independent thinking, The teacher can also use the teaching mode of flipping classrooms and micro-curriculum to improve students' innovative ability. Based on a specific problem, we can use interactive lectures and group discussions to form an interactive teaching model that allows students to think positively. In short, adopting a flexible and versatile teaching model to maximize students' willingness to learn, take the initiative to learn, improve their practical ability, and become an excellent practical professional.

5.2 Micro Strategy

5.2.1 Building Perspective

The construction of the smart classroom at the micro level is the key to the realization of smart education. By combing the literature and combining the existing research, this paper believes that the micro-level should be based on the dual perspective of technology-learning to build a smart classroom. First, how to use technology to better complete teaching and learning. Focus on the level of technical support, and second, study how to make students' smart develop. In order to help students become practical talents that meet the needs of society, better and faster to adapt to social development, while learning professional knowledge, cultivate students' diverse smart. Therefore, we must make full use of information technology to build high-quality and efficient smart classrooms. One is to effectively support the implementation of education and teaching activities, and the second is to pay more attention to the cultivation of students' innovative thinking and students' smart.

5.2.2 Building Path

The traditional teaching mode of the Database course is often that students are highly dependent on teachers and learn first. Students only begin to flip through books after entering the classroom. Students do not have pre-study, no thinking before class, no homework after class, no group discussion, and more. There is no smart and innovative thinking. The database smart classroom for practical talent training must break the traditional classroom teaching mode. The basic process is divided into three parts: pre-class, in-class and after-class. The process includes teachers and students relying on information technology to complete online and offline. Teaching and learning activities are shown in Fig. 3. In the smart classroom process, before the class, the teacher releases the preparatory tasks through micro-courses, WeChat or Weibo, and constantly updates the teaching resources, including micro-videos, text materials, and so on. Before the class, students should complete the preparatory tasks and upload the completed work materials such as audio and text. When they encounter problems, they will discuss each other, form a discussion group, and enter the class with questions. The teacher uses heuristic teaching in the class to create and guide students through the creation of situational tasks. Students form cooperative groups, and the group explores and discusses specific issues and inspires each other. After class, students share the results of innovative thinking, the teacher timely tutors students, scientifically evaluate students' learning outcomes, expand learning tasks, broaden students' horizons, tap student smart, and consolidate and grow knowledge.

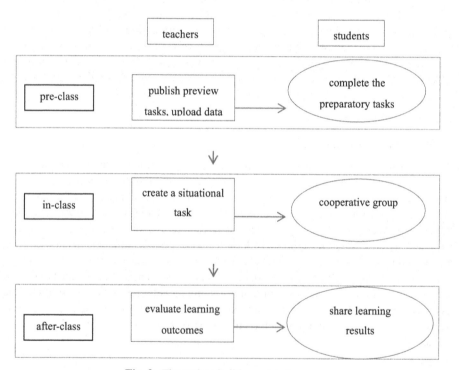

Fig. 3. The path to build a smart classroom

6   Realization of Database Smart Classroom

In this paper, the "Creation of Tables" in the database course is used as a case to realize the smart classroom. The "Database System Principles and Applications (SQL Server

2005)" published by Liu Zhicheng and Ning Yunzhi and the Mechanical Industry Press are used as teaching materials. 45 pages, using T-SQL to create a database as a research case, before the classroom implementation, the teacher first established the "database" course on the network platform, as shown in Fig. 4. In the database teaching for many years, the content of this section has always been a difficult point for students to learn, and it is also the focus. The content of this section is very representative as a smart classroom implementation case.

Fig. 4. Establishing a database course on the web-based learning platform

6.1 The Teacher Arranges Tasks Before Class, and Students Learn Independently

The teacher logs in and publishes the learning task through the network teaching platform of the South-Central University for Nationalities, as shown in Fig. 5:

Fig. 5. Network teaching platform of South-Central University for nationalities

On the network teaching platform, the teacher arranges the learning tasks that the students need to preview in advance according to the content of the teaching, and publishes before the class.

6.1.1 Learn the Basic Format of CREATE DATABASE

CREATE DATABASE <database file name>

[ON <data file>]

([NAME=<logical file name>]

FILENAME='<physical file name>'

[,SIZE=<size>]

[, MAXSIZE=<maximum size that can grow>]

[, FILEGROWTH=<growth ratio>])

[LOG ON <log file>]

([NAME=<logical file name>,]

FILENAME='<physical file name>'

[,SIZE=<size>]

[, MAXSIZE=<maximum size that can grow>]

[, FILEGROWTH=<growth ratio>])

6.1.2 Pre-class Tasks

Students upload pre-study materials and questions during study, and seek guidance from teachers and help from classmates in the classroom as shown in Fig. 6:

Fig. 6. Pre-class students preparation tasks and question release

One of the questions submitted by one of the classmates is: In the basic format of the statement, why are some statements angle brackets? And some statements are square brackets? Why do some statements have a comma before them? What is the difference between the various symbols? What conditions apply to each?

At the same time, the teachers are grouped according to the students' interests, hobbies and achievements. The group conducts pre-study preparations and prepares for the group discussion in the class.

6.2   In the Class, the Teacher Explained the Guidance, the Students Thought, the Group Discussion

6.2.1   Teachers Explain Knowledge Points and Answer Questions from Students

The teacher's explanation mainly includes: 1 When creating the database, you must determine the name, owner, size of the database and the files and file groups in which the database is stored. The name of the database must follow the rules of the SQL Server identifier. 2 For students' pre-class questions, emphasize that the content in the angle brackets in the basic format of the statement is mandatory, and the square brackets are optional; the comma in the 3 statement indicates that the statement has not been written, and the parameters need to continue to be written; 4 Reminder The specific meaning of the student parameters can be referred to as "SQL Server Books Online" as an after-school knowledge extension.

6.2.2   Teachers Create Scenarios and Guide Students to Learn

After the statement format is explained, the teacher creates situations to guide students and inspire the smart of the students. For undergraduate students, choose a book management system that they are familiar with: If you need to create a book management system, how to create a database? Should I include several data files? How many log files are there? What rules should I follow during the process of writing code? Have the student write the code first, then the teacher explains the correct code:

```
CREATE DATABASE Library
ON
( NAME = Library_dat,
    FILENAME = 'd:\data\Library_dat.mdf',
    SIZE =20,
    MAXSIZE = 60,
    FILEGROWTH = 5 )
LOG ON
( NAME = 'Library_log',
    FILENAME = 'd:\data\Library_log.ldf',
    SIZE = 5MB,
    MAXSIZE = 25MB,
    FILEGROWTH = 5MB )
```

In the process of explaining the code, the teacher reminds the students to refer to the statement format in the process of writing the code, answer the questions raised in the previous question one by one, and then guide the students to think about the following questions: Why do some attributes in the code have a unit MB followed by some attributes? No unit MB? Does it conform to the statement format? Can the path 'd:\data\' after the FILENAME attribute be changed? Students take these questions and the students conduct group discussions and inspire each other.

6.2.3 Group Discussion, Mutual Inspiration

The teacher organizes students according to prior groups to guide students to inspire each other. Students use Keynote, online teaching platform and other APPs to conduct collaborative research and complete learning. After the student group discussion, use the iPad to submit group assignments.

6.3 After Class, Teachers Guide Students to Learn and Expand

6.3.1 Teachers Evaluate the Learning Outcomes, Personalize Guidance, and Teach Students in Accordance with Their Aptitude

After the class, the teacher evaluates the assignments submitted by the students, and through the exchange of WeChat and Weibo, it is found that some minority students have to overcome the language barriers in addition to the professional knowledge. Due to the English grammar, the content of this section is more difficult than other students. Teachers immediately apply personalized counseling to minority students, teach students in accordance with their aptitude, first explain the sentence format in Chinese, and slow down the speed of speech, and then explain the content in the class with the easy-to-understand terms as far as possible, until the students fully understand.

6.3.2 Students Learn to Expand and Promote Innovation

Group students expand in after-school learning. For example, a group of students ask questions during the after-school study: If there are two or more data files, how do you build the code? This content has already exceeded the content of the textbook. There are no ready-made examples for reference in the textbook, and it is not within the scope of the teacher's preparation. Therefore, the students first searched through the Internet and found that the answers were not clear enough. Therefore, they are ready to be brought to the classroom to ask the professional teachers as the next class, and the teachers need to demonstrate on the machine.

7 Conclusion

This course promotes the deep integration of information technology and curriculum through smart classrooms. Students deeply feel that this study has expanded the learning space, increased smart, and has no end to learning. By establishing a course on the online platform, the teacher feels that the teacher is always around, which stimulates the students' interest in learning. The teacher evaluates the student's homework in a timely manner after class, and improves the student's participation and the students' participation. The distance from the students has improved the teaching effect and provided reference for future teaching. In the future teaching, teachers and students must change their concepts, advance with the times, make up for the shortcomings in current teaching, and constantly explore the teaching model based on smart classrooms to achieve the goal of common progress for teachers and students.

References

1. Connolly, T.M., Boyle, E.A., MacArthur, E., Hainey, T., Boyle, J.M.: A systematic literature review of empirical evidence on computer games and serious games. Comput. Educ. **59**, 661–686 (2012)
2. Liu, Z.C., Ning, Y.Z.: Principles and Applications of Database Systems (SQL Server 2005), pp. 45–46. Mechanical Industry Press, Beijing (2010)
3. Mohammadi, F., Abrizah, A., Nazari, M., Attaran, M.: What motivates high school teachers to use web-based learning resources for classroom instruction? An exploratory case study in an Iranian smart school. Comput. Hum. Behav. **51**, 373–381 (2015)
4. Hodges, G.W., Wang, L., Lee, J., Cohen, A., Jang, Y.: An exploratory study of blending the virtual world and the laboratory experience in secondary chemistry classrooms. Comput. Educ. **122**, 179–193 (2018)
5. Lin, Y., Liu, H., Chen, Z., Zhang, K., Ma, K.: Stream-based data sampling mechanism for process object. Comput. Mater. Continua **60**(1), 245–257 (2019)
6. Zhong, S.: Heterogeneous memristive models design and its application in information security. Comput. Mater. Continua **60**(2), 465–479 (2019)

Optimization and Simulation of Pre-warehouse Multi-objective Stock Levels Based on the Weibull Distribution Function

yang Yang[1]([✉]), jianmin Zhang[1], Yi Wang[1], and Guiyan Hu[2]

[1] School of Management, China University of Mining
and Technology (Beijing), Beijing 100083, China
bwu_yangyang@126.com
[2] School of Logistics, Beijing Wuzi University, Beijing 100049, China

Abstract. Fresh agricultural products are essential products characterized by production value-added, perishability and short sales cycles. By setting up of front positions, retailers can effectively use their own characteristics, reduce spoilage of products, expand the sales cycle, provide goods as soon as possible and offer better delivery to consumers. Therefore, this paper studies the Multi-Target optimization and simulation of the front position based on the Weibull distribution function under a model with demand uncertainty. This paper uses AnyLogic simulation modeling to find the optimal pre-warehouse stock ratio to reduce inventory costs, improve customer satisfaction rates, improve overall profit and obtain a perfect three-level model. The results of the study have strong practical significance and can provide a reference for e-commerce enterprises similar to that in this study

Keywords: Fresh agricultural products · Weibull distribution function · Multi-objective

1 Introduction

To improve service capacity and meet the demand for faster logistics, "pre-warehouse" was born. The "pre-warehouse" is a small warehouse that is set up closer to consumers in order to meet the timeliness of delivery. Many e-commerce companies, such as MISSFRESH, Fruit Day, and so on, have adopted this model.

Many scholars have further analyzed the pre-warehouse model from the perspective of the logistics system. Based on the EOQ model, Su Xueling calculated the optimal inventory decision by using modeling and sensitivity analysis [1]. By constructing two comparative judgment matrices, Hao Shi Mian obtained a series of indicators for multitarget fresh inventory management evaluation and provided countermeasures for inventory management [2].

Fund Project: Funded by the YueQi Young Scholars of the Chinese University of Mining and Technology (Beijing); the funding for the basic business of the Central University (No. 2014QG01).

© Springer Nature Singapore Pte Ltd. 2020
X. Sun et al. (Eds.): ICAIS 2020, CCIS 1252, pp. 484–495, 2020.
https://doi.org/10.1007/978-981-15-8083-3_43

All fresh product e-suppliers in the process of actual operation front positions have different problems. Xia Manlu and others combined the MISSFRESH platform operation mode to analyze the main problems encountered in the use of the front warehouse in SKU quantity shortages, the coexistence of high inventory and high out-of-stock rates, and higher operating costs. Suggestions have been made from the perspectives of big data analysis, procurement and inventory management, and advanced warehouse resources [3]. The optimization of the delivery system should be made from a multitiered integration perspective. Based on this, the overall framework of site selection—inventory—path integration optimization for fresh electricity e-commerce distribution systems is constructed [4].

Multilevel inventory optimization goals are basically focused on ensuring the accuracy of the optimal inventory quantity, the accuracy of time, a minimum cost, a high customer service level, and high management efficiency. For multilevel inventory optimization, the research objects are mostly secondary supply chains, with the literature less focused on the tertiary cold chain inventory system and more concentrated on the cold chain and large equipment and other special product areas [5–10]. Most of the research related to pre-warehouses storage optimization is based on single-level inventory research, and it is not common to assess multilevel inventory as a system for overall optimization.

Based on the Weibull distribution function, a Multi-Target three-level inventory optimization system for fresh produce under demand uncertainty is established in this paper. In determining the market demand for fresh agricultural products and the deterioration rate of fresh products, the optimization objectives are to reduce inventory costs, improve customer satisfaction, and increase overall profit. In addition, AnyLogic is used to construct and carry out the simulation to find the optimal front warehouse inventory ratio. Further optimization is done on the fresh product front warehouse inventory system.

2 Analysis of the Business Model and Inventory Optimization Problem of Pre-warehouses

The pre-warehouses model was born to enhance service capacity and to meet the needs of faster logistics. To a large extent, this new model solves difficult problems of traditional online or offline channels, such as the difficulty of disposing of the remaining inventory, high losses caused by multiple flows, and high cold storage costs and losses caused by long-term storage.

The features and problems of the front warehouse are very distinct, as follows:

1. The front warehouse is closer to consumers, allowing more convenient and faster delivery of products.
2. It avoids large inventory backlogs and forecast replenishments are made based on orders.
3. Supply chains are integrated, but unlike in traditional industries, e-commerce is often made up of multiple fixed producers, a central warehouse, multiple pre-warehouses, and multiple consumers.

4. Fresh product demand is low, but the variety requirements are very high, the quality requirements are high, and the profit is low.
5. Shortage situations rarely occur.

In general, a front warehouse shop is small, high-cost and multigoal, making it difficult to ensure optimal operation.

2.1 Problem Description

The "A" e-commerce firm considered here is a fresh product O2O e-commerce platform that supplies common consumers' tables. It covers all kinds of fruits and vegetables, seafood, meat, poultry, milk, snacks, etc. At present, the company's scale is Series C, and it is in the leading position in the e-commerce fresh products industry. Many enterprises have established the "urban distribution center + community distribution center (central warehouse + pre-warehouses)" model in major cities to provide users with a fast cold chain logistics system, including 2-h delivery services for the global fresh products chain.

This paper will study how the inventory of the pre-warehouses and central warehouse can be configured within a certain period of time to minimize the overall cost and maximize profit and the consumer satisfaction rate. In a certain area of Beijing, three pre-warehouses are evenly distributed, and there is a certain stock of fresh products in the pre-warehouses. A central warehouse is set up in the regional center for forward replenishment. In the suburban area, three fixed cooperative manufacturers supply the central warehouse. Based on the uncertainty of the independent variables and waiting time, the best possible service level is achieved.

The basic structure of the supply chain network is shown in Fig. 1.

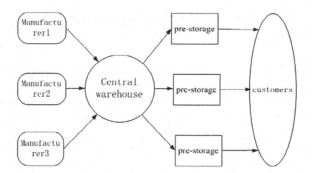

Fig. 1. Front warehouse mode supply chain network diagram

2.2 Cost Analysis and Construction Model

The problem studied in this article is the tertiary inventory of suppliers, central warehouses and pre-warehouses. Replenishment only occurs when the existing inventory is insufficient. Each node in the inventory system has its own fixed ordering cycle; that is, the replenishment cycle of the pre-warehouse j is constant at T_{1j}, and the central warehouse is also replenished according to the order status. The capacity of each node of the system is sufficient, but it cannot be replenished instantaneously, and each node considers a safe inventory. The actual situation should consider the supplier's inventory problem, namely, that the supplier's supply is sufficient and that the cost is determined by the number of replenishment orders. Each order of each node enterprise of the system will not exceed its maximum inventory capacity at the next level. The unit storage cost of fresh products in each node in the inventory system is nonfixed, the holding cost is calculated according to the number and the daily storage rate of the cold bank, and the unit storage cost of different nodes is different. Assume that the unit storage cost rate of the pre-warehouse is the highest.

3 Optimization Model of Preposition Inventory Based on the Weibull Distribution Function

Consumers have higher requirements for the freshness of fresh agricultural products. Therefore, the cold chain has been added to the supply chain system by most fresh product electronic business enterprises. For the research on cold chain inventories, the deterioration rate is one of the important factors that must be considered [11–13]. Therefore, this paper introduces the three-parameter Weibull function, which is different from the two-parameter Weibull function, to describe the characteristics of the spoilage rate of fresh products. The three-parameter Weibull function can fully fit the spoilage rate under different conditions. This distribution function can be more consistent with the characteristics of fresh agricultural products.

3.1 Cost Analysis

3.1.1 Cost of Forward Warehouse Inventory

The inventory cost of each front warehouse node in the community includes the ordering cost, cold chain inventory storage cost, out-of-stock cost, deterioration cost, and cold chain transportation cost. Therefore, in the cycle $[0, T_j]$, the various inventory-related costs for pre-warehouse j are as follows:

1. C_R: Ordering cost. This refers to the related costs incurred when the node enterprise engages in ordering activities. The inventory replenishment strategy selected by each node at the front warehouse is (Q, R), and the economic volume of its order is Q_{ij}. The order cost C_R consists of two parts: a fixed order cost and an order variable cost. The fixed order cost depends on the number of orders, and the variable cost depends on the quantity and unit price.

2. C_H: Storage cost. The cost of cold storage is considered in the front warehouse storage center warehouse within one cycle. Considering the complexity of the model studied in this paper, when calculating the storage cost, we do not consider the part of the inventory level affected by the deterioration factor; that is, only the approximate value of the storage cost is taken. Because the inventory is stored in the cold chain, a fixed parameter is used to represent the daily cost coefficient of the cold chain. The strategy adopted by the forward warehouse is (Q, R), and the average inventory level of the forward position is $ES_j = \frac{1}{2}Q_{ij}$.

3. C_S: Out-of-stock cost. This is the out-of-stock cost of n nodes within an order period.
4. C_B: Cost of deterioration. This is the total deterioration cost of n front warehouses in one order cycle.
5. C_T: Transportation cost. This is the transportation cost incurred by pre-warehouse j in a cycle. This article assumes that the unit price of a product during an order cycle is y_{ij}. In addition, the transportation distance is not considered.

Based on the analysis, the total inventory costs incurred by n pre-warehouses in an order cycle C'_{TR} are as follows:

$$C'_{TR} = C_R + C_H + C_B + C_T \tag{1}$$

Therefore, the total inventory cost generated by n pre-warehouses per unit of time is C'_R, as follows:

$$C'_R = \sum_{i=1}^{m} \sum_{j=1}^{n} \frac{d_j}{Q_{ij}} \{ (K_{ij} + a_{ij}A_{ij}Q_{ij}) + \tfrac{1}{2}b_{ij}Q_{ij}t_{1j} + (T_j - t_{1j})f_{ij}d_j \\ + A_{ij}[\int_{\gamma_0}^{t_{1j}} \alpha\beta(t - \gamma_0)^{\beta-1} e^{-\alpha(t-\gamma_0)^\beta} (\int_{t}^{t_{1j}} d_j e^{\alpha(t-\gamma_0)^\beta} dt)dt] + y_{ij}a_{ij}Q_{ij} \} \tag{2}$$

3.1.2 Cost of Central Warehouse Inventory

Due to the assumptions in this article, we do not consider the temporary out-of-stock cost at the central warehouse. Therefore, the cost of the central warehouse system consists of four parts: ordering cost, storage cost, deterioration cost, and transportation cost.

Therefore, in $[0, T_i]$, the costs associated with various inventories of central warehouse j are as follows:

1. C'_R: Ordering cost. The order cost of the central warehouse includes fixed costs and variable replenishment costs. Since a central warehouse can order goods from multiple manufacturers and the cost of ordering from different enterprises is different, e_{ki} represents the proportion of orders when a central warehouse orders from multiple manufacturers. The inventory replenishment strategy selected by each node company in the central warehouse system is (s, S, T). Since the inventory system in this article runs continuously, s can be regarded as the base point, so the expected batch of one order is $Q_k = S_k(i, j) - s_k(i, j), k = 1, 2, 3 \cdots$. Because the central warehouse system in this paper is instant replenishment and there is no order lead time, $s_k(i, j) = 0$.
2. C'_H: Storage cost. The cost to a central warehouse of storing a manufacturer's products within an order cycle is the same as that of the front storage system. For the time being, the effect of the deterioration factor on the storage cost is not considered, and the storage cost is multiplied by the refrigeration coefficient.
3. C'_B: Cost of deterioration. This is the deterioration cost of the distribution system in an order cycle.
4. C'_T: Transportation cost. This is the transportation cost of ordering from a central warehouse within an order cycle. This article assumes that the unit price of a product during an order cycle is y_{ki}.

Based on the analysis, the total inventory cost C'_{TD} incurred by the central warehouse system in one order cycle is as follows:

$$C'_{TD} = C'_R + C'_H + C'_B + C'_T \tag{3}$$

The total inventory cost C'_D incurred by the central warehouse system in a unit of time is as follows:

$$C'_D = \sum_{k=1}^{q} \sum_{i=1}^{m} \frac{1}{T_i} \{K_{ki} + (S_i - s_i)e_{ki}A_{ki}] + \frac{1}{2}b_{ki}(S_i - s_i + d_i + \frac{\sigma_i}{d_i})T_i$$
$$+ A_{ki}[\int_{\gamma_0}^{T_i} \alpha\beta(t - \gamma)^{\beta-1}e^{-\alpha(T_i-\gamma_0)^{\beta}}(\int_{t}^{T_i} d_i e^{\alpha(t-\gamma_0)^{\beta}}dt)dt] + (S_i - s_i)y_{ki}e_{ki}\}$$
$$\tag{4}$$

The cost of the manufacturer's inventory C'_F is the same as the total inventory cost C'_D and is not further described.

$$C'_F = C'_D \tag{5}$$

In summary, it can be concluded that the total cost, TC, of the fresh agricultural product supply chain inventory system in a unit of time is as follows:

$$TC = C'_R + C'_D + C'_F \tag{6}$$

3.2 Average Customer Demand Satisfaction Rate

To measure the customer service level, this article uses the average customer waiting time for the prestock when there is no way to guarantee the delivery within the time required by the customer. The service level decreases rapidly in line with the growth in the average waiting time. According to the assumption that the stock shortage in the inventory system studied in this paper only considers the stock shortage in the prewarehouse, the consumer's consumption principle is to receive fresh products in a short period of time. It is necessary for fresh product electronic business enterprises to meet these needs of consumers. Therefore, this article assumes that fresh product electronic business enterprises can ensure that the products are delivered to customers within a specified time but that increasing the average customer demand satisfaction rate is one of multiple goals. This goal is to make delivery optimal; that is, the shorter the average customer waiting time within the specified time is, the better.

3.3 Total Profit Function of the System

As a fresh food e-commerce company, profit is a relatively important indicator. The higher the profit, the more optimistic the company's operating conditions are. Therefore, maximizing the total profit of the system is one of the goals of this experiment. According to the total sales volume in the statistical period, the total profit function of the entire supply chain can be obtained:

$$max\, f_2 = TR - minTC = \sum_1^{n=20} Q * P - \sum_1^{n=20} TC \qquad (7)$$

Among them: P-total profit; R-total revenue; C-total cost (level 3 inventory); Q-total sales volume; p-unit price.

3.4 Establish a Multigoal Model

According to the above analysis, the overall objective function of the three-level supply chain inventory model established in this paper consists of three objective functions: the total inventory cost function, the total profit function, and the average customer demand satisfaction function. Therefore, the multiobjective model of this supply chain inventory system is as follows:

$$min\, f_1 = min\, TC = min(C'_R + C'_D + C'_F)$$
$$max\, f_2 = TR - min\, TC = TR - min(C'_R + C'_D + C'_F)$$
$$min\, f_3 = min(T_{M_j}) \qquad (8)$$

3.5 Establish a Judgment Matrix

Using the judgment matrix method to determine the weight of each goal, the multiobjective problem is transformed into a single-objective problem that can be quantified and compared [14]. Afterwards, the data are normalized and substituted into the equation to obtain the optimal solution of the multiobjective function.

$$w_i = \sqrt[n]{\prod B_{ij}} \qquad (9)$$

$$w_o = \frac{w_i}{\sum_{i=1} w_i} \qquad (10)$$

$$\Upsilon_{max} = \frac{1}{n} * \left(\sum_{i=1}^n AW_i\right) \Big/ W_i \qquad (11)$$

$$C.I = (\Upsilon_{max} - n)\big/(n - 1) \qquad (12)$$

R.I is an average and immediately consistent indicator. The data is not difficult to obtain through search.

$$C.R = C.I\big/R.I(C.R < 0) \qquad (13)$$

The three objective functions constructed in this paper are the optimal solutions of the array based on the highest weights of profit, cost, and customer satisfaction. Finally, the conclusion is drawn. The following are the constructed matrices and modeling processes:

Table 1. Score of judgment matrix

$$
\begin{pmatrix}
B_1 & B_2 & B_3 & W_i & W_0 & C.I & C.R & \gamma_{max} \\
1 & 2 & 3 & 1.81 & 0.54 & 0 & 0 & 3 \\
1/2 & 1 & 2 & 1 & 0.3 \\
1/3 & 1/2 & 1 & 0.55 & 0.16
\end{pmatrix}
$$

A pairwise comparison method is used to establish a judgment matrix. The target A: select the appropriate three-tier inventory ratio; the criterion layer C (with 3 criterion factors): C_1 cost, C_2 profit, and C_3 product freshness. Since in this case the three goals are relatively important, there is no situation where the degree of importance is much higher. The rank scores are given 3, 2, and 1 for obvious satisfaction, relative satisfaction, and slight satisfaction, respectively. The elements on the diagonal of the square matrix are equally important relative to each other. Conversely, those off the diagonal are given weights of 1/3, 1/2, and 1.

A	C_1	C_2	C_3
C_1	1	2	3
C_2	1/2	1	2
C_3	1/3	1/2	1

The root mean square method is used to calculate the geometric mean value $\overline{\omega}_i$ of all the elements in each row of the judgment matrix, which is normalized, and $\overline{\omega}=(0.54, 0.3, 0.16)^T$ is calculated by calculation, which is the approximate value of the required feature vector, that is, the relative weight of each element, see Table 1. At this time, the maximum eigenvalue[1] $\lambda_{max} = 3$ of the judgment matrix can be used to obtain the consistency index[2] $CI = 0$ of the judgment matrix. For complete consistency, the consistency of the judgment matrix is considered acceptable. After getting the data, substitute it into Formula $x^* = \frac{x-min}{max-min}$. And normalize all data to make the schemes comparable.

Table 2. Sorting of target weights

Number	Target	Weights
1	Cost	0.54
2	Profit	0.3
3	Product freshness	0.16

---

[1] Calculation formula of maximum eigenvalue of judgment matrix: $\lambda_{max} = \sum\limits_{i=1}^{n} \frac{(A\overline{\omega})_i}{n\overline{\omega}_i}$.

[2] Calculation formula for consistency index of judgment matrix: $CI = \frac{\lambda_{max}-n}{n-1} = \frac{\sum\limits_{i\neq max} \lambda_i}{n-1}$.

The calculation results are observed, and the explicit model is a multiobjective optimization with cost as the highest weight. Therefore, when selecting this data model, the optimal cost should be solved under multiobjective conditions. The single objective function that is ultimately used to measure data is as follows:

$$f = -0.54f_1 + 0.3f_2 - 0.16f_3 \qquad (14)$$

4 Research on Analogic Simulation

4.1 Simulation Model Construction

The nodes of the prewarehouse distribution mode system of fresh product e-merchants include manufacturers, central warehouses, prewarehouses, e-commerce enterprises, and customers. In this paper, we only simulate the process of distribution and replenishment after receiving the order information from the forward warehouse. Further modeling ideas are as follows: Under uncertain demand, the manufacturer determines the amount of replenishment based on expectations and current inventory, etc. The central warehouse determines how many goods are ordered from the supplier based on inventory and expectations, and the prewarehouse orders goods from the central warehouse based on inventory and expectations.

The specific steps of the simulation modeling process are as follows. The model is shown in Fig. 2.

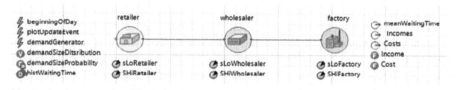

Fig. 2. Simulation model

Step 1: Set up the urban service area and simulate the operation of the fresh products supply chain in the urban area.

Step 2: Establish three agents, namely, the prewarehouse, central warehouse, and supplier.

Step 3: Draw connectors that connect the three agents and make them a whole.

Step 4: Set the parameters for each agent, as shown in Table 3.

Step 5: Add the output module. Add all functions that require statistical output in the top area of the figure, including demand generation, profit, cost statistics, maximum/minimum inventory setting, etc.

Step 6: Add statistics. Statistical indicators include cold storage inventory, cold chain transportation, out-of-stock costs, ordering costs, profit, and average customer waiting time. In addition, set up the corresponding chart (in this example a stacked chart and a line chart).

Step 7: Run the model, adjust the parameters, observe the changes in the data and perform a record analysis.

Table 3. Model parameter table

Parameter	Supplier	Central warehouse	Pre-warehouse
Transportation cost	3	1.5	0.5
Unit cost	7	17	17
Unit price	15	17	33
Storage costs	2.4	1.8	3.6
Order cost	–	3000	500
Shortage cost	1	2	3

4.2   Analysis of Simulation Model Results

According to the above parameters, the simulation is carried out, first controlling the number of prewarehouses and central warehouses, adjusting and fixing the number of suppliers, adjusting the number of central warehouses, and finally fixing the central warehouse inventory and adjusting the number of prewarehouses, so that the simulation is divided into three steps. It is hoped that the overall optimal number of prewarehouses in the supply chain is obtained. The ellipse box shows the maximum value (max) in each group of data, and the rectangle box shows the minimum value (min) in each group of data. In this study, more than 60 model experiments were performed. The following 16 representative stable experimental data are displayed (Fig. 3 and Table 4).

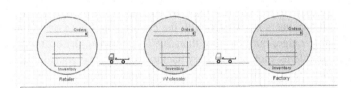

Fig. 3. Simulation result chart

Obviously, the 14th group scored the same as the 15th group, and both scored an optimal score of 0.20. However, since this study is a cost-oriented multiobjective optimization, the 15th group was selected as the final solution. By observing the statistical results map and the average daily income map and using the multiobjective evaluation method described above, the 15th group is the optimized alternative among the 16 randomly selected schemes; that is, the cost is 470,000, the profit is ¥2,000, and the average waiting time is 0.3 days. The prewarehouse stock level is 5 pieces, the central warehouse level is 100 pieces, and the supplier level is 60 pieces. According to the analysis of the experimental results, we can obtain the following:

5. The prewarehouse. Although the prewarehouse has high costs, it is necessary to maintain a certain level of safety stock due to the proximity to the consumer group,

Table 4. Statistical result simulation data

Group	Cost(yuan)	Profit(yuan)	Mean-waiting time(day)	Standardized multi-objective score
1	0.6225	0	1	-0.50
2	1	0.8119	0.0101	-0.30
3	0.2035	0.8869	0.0107	0.15
4	0.3190	0.9309	0.0032	0.11
5	0.4484	0.9521	0	0.04
6	0	0.3989	0.3625	0.06
7	0.4144	1	0.0021	0.08
8	0.3984	0.9367	0.0021	0.07
9	0.3349	0.9872	0.0027	0.11
10	0.3349	0.9872	0.0027	0.11
11	0.3349	0.9872	0.0027	0.11
12	0.3593	0.9628	0	0.09
13	0.3813	0.9202	0.0085	0.07
14	0.1766	0.9727	0.0037	**0.20**
15	0.0287	0.8069	0.1356	**0.20**
16	0.3915	0.9331	0.0027	0.07

the low cost of distribution to consumers, and the high cost of shortages. According to the solution of this model, considering that the area of the prewarehouse is much smaller than that of the central warehouse and the rent is high, it is optimal that each front warehouse has a stock ratio with the central warehouse of 5%, and 5–20% is an acceptable range, but not more than 20%. Otherwise, the cost will rise linearly and cause problems such as inventory backlog and insufficient front warehouse area to ensure high returns, low costs, and high customer satisfaction.

6. The central warehouse. Since the central warehouse has high mainline transportation costs, high costs for single orders, and the shortage cost is higher than the cost of holding more inventory, according to the model data, when there is only one central warehouse, it is recommended to maintain a high stock level in the central warehouse, that is, a safety stock (higher than that of the manufacturer) to ensure the supply of goods.

7. The manufacturer. Manufacturers are suggested to reduce their inventory. In the simulation of this model, the manufacturer's inventory level affects the central warehouse more, which in turn affects the front-end shortage level. The low inventory level does not have much effect. It is recommended that manufacturers not hold too much inventory, with the central warehouse inventory serving as a reference: not less than 10% but not higher than 50% of the central warehouse stock level, which can effectively avoid the problems that cause product backlogs and cost rises.

5 Conclusion

This article mainly studies the tertiary inventory optimization problem in the front warehouse distribution model. The research object is a retailer of fresh products with a deterioration rate that conforms to the Weibull distribution. Through AnyLogic, multiple groups of different inventory ratios are simulated, and the order quantity is finally found. Under normal circumstances, the optimal ratio of three-tier inventory (not suitable for large-scale order quantities) is the scale of 1 manufacturer, 1 central warehouse, and 10 front warehouses. With the central warehouse inventory as the reference, the front warehouse inventory level should be controlled at 5–20% of the central warehouse inventory, and the manufacturer's inventory level should be controlled at 10–50% of the central warehouse inventory. This inventory ratio achieves a multiobjective optimization: a reduction in total cost, an increase in total profit, and a maximum customer satisfaction rate. It is hoped that the research in this article can provide a reference for the operation of fresh e-commerce enterprises.

References

1. Su, X., Ma, Z.: Consideration of the pricing and inventory decision-making of fresh products in stock under the conditions of advance payment. Chin. Manage. Sci. **24**(S 1), 617–625 (2016)
2. Hao, S., Hu, Y., Zhong, D.: Study on the joint stock of fresh food based on multi-goal optimization. Contemp. Econ. Manage. **39**(01), 24–29 (2017)
3. Xia, M., Xu, H., Yi, C.: Study on dilemma and strategy of daily preposition mode. Introd. Sci. Technol. Econ. **27**(24), 196+194 (2019)
4. Yiyi, C.: Study on the optimization of commodity distribution system based on the "preposition" model. Wuhan University of Technology (2018)
5. Weekly Cambridge: Multi-level inventory control model and solution for multi-constrained single-target supply chain. Control Works **24**(03), 511–517 (2017)
6. Wang, A.: Multi-level inventory cost optimization model based on random requirements. J. Henan Inst. Mech. Electr. Sci. **25**(05), 56–59 (2017)
7. Song, Z., Xu, Q., Kong, P., Liu, Z.: Research on multi-level inventory cost optimization model in supply chain environment. Logist. Technol. **41**(06), 126–132 (2018)
8. Hu, X., Liu, X.: Optimization of three-level inventory model of spare parts for large equipment repairable service. Logist. Eng. Manage. **38**(01), 121–124+118 (2016)
9. Wang, S., Jiang, Y., Wang, X.: Research on the three-level stock integration strategy of agricultural products cold chain. Chin. Manage. Sci. **24**(02), 108–114 (2016)
10. Tianjin: Application of multi-objective optimization in supply chain inventory management. Bus. Econ. Study (16), 34–35 (2016)
11. http://www.zgjtb.com/youzheng/2018
12. Wu, C., Zapevalova, E., Chen, Y., Li, F.: Time optimization of multiple knowledge transfers in the big data environment. Comput. Mater. Continua **54**(3), 269–285 (2018)
13. Chen, W., et al.: Development and application of big data platform for garlic industry chain. Comput. Mater. Continua **58**(1), 229–248 (2019)
14. Xi, X., Sheng, V.S., Sun, B., Wang, L., Fuyuan, H.: An empirical comparison on multi-target regression learning. Comput. Mater. Continua **56**(2), 185–198 (2018)

Research and Analysis of Fine Management
of Engineering Cost Based on BIM

Liu Yi[✉]

Nanjing Technical Vocational College, Nanjing 210019, China
123274850@qq.com

Abstract. With the continuous improvement of economic development level, the construction engineering industry is developing rapidly. As an important technology in project cost management, BIM is of great significance for saving construction cost and improving the management level of engineering cost. In the construction project cost management, the application of BIM technology can make up for the shortage of traditional engineering cost management, and adopt an intuitive cost management mode to standardize the whole process of construction and promote the construction cost management of China to better. Direction development [1].

Keywords: BIM technology · Engineering cost · Refined management

The cost of building construction management is a very important link and plays a very important role in the cost management of the entire project. The project cost runs through every link of the project construction, including the cost of all aspects of the enterprise from decision-making to completion. Therefore, it is of non-daily importance to do a good job in project cost control to ensure the construction quality of the project and promote the smooth development of the project. The BIM-based project cost management, attention to detail, can strictly control the cost of each link, which will be of great significance to improve the quality of project cost.

1 Overview of BIM Technology and Refined Management of Engineering Cost

1.1 BIM Technology

The Chinese translation of BIM is a building information model. It uses advanced digital information technology to establish a digital model for the engineering information involved in the whole process of construction. Professionals can use this model to design, construct and later operate and maintain the building. Efficient management as shown in Fig. 1.

The application of BIM technology is mainly based on computer and network technology, which can integrate multiple models and transform information in specific application process, so as to facilitate the planning, implementation and maintenance of engineering personnel. The transmission and sharing of information enables staff to better understand and apply information. As shown in Fig. 2.

© Springer Nature Singapore Pte Ltd. 2020
X. Sun et al. (Eds.): ICAIS 2020, CCIS 1252, pp. 496–502, 2020.
https://doi.org/10.1007/978-981-15-8083-3_44

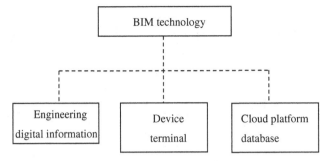

Fig. 1. System composition of BIM technology

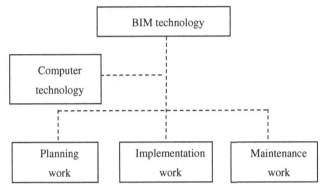

Fig. 2. Application principle of BIM technology

1.2 Main Contents of Refined Management of Project Cost

The fine management of engineering cost means that in the process of construction engineering construction, it is necessary to adhere to the principle of strict management and detail management, and carry out detailed management and control of each link and content in the construction process to ensure project cost management. The work went smoothly. The refined management of project cost has a phased feature, which can optimize the allocation of resources according to the actual conditions of the project and the contract, avoiding the phenomenon of over-cost in the construction process and reducing the cost in the construction. Specifically, it includes the following aspects: project investment estimation, engineering design budget, contract price, construction and completion stage. In the construction process of an engineering project, the participants are multi-faceted, so the content of the project cost in each construction phase is different, but there are roughly the above aspects. Therefore, by adopting the method of fine management of engineering cost, the project cost can be determined and controlled in real time, and the whole process of project construction can be effectively controlled and standardized from the decision-making stage in the early stage of the project [2].

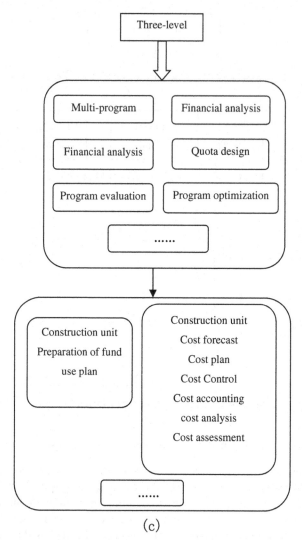

Fig. 3. BIM technology cost management process

1.3   Process of Managing Project Cost by Using BIM Technology

When using BIM technology to manage project cost, it is mainly based on the following process. First of all, the first-level process - the consulting management in the decision-making stage of the project, the tracking management in the design phase, and the project management in the construction phase. Second, the secondary process - different management at different stages. In the project decision-making and design phase of the cost management process, from the technical point of view, the project function and positioning analysis, design comparison and optimization, to economic efficiency evaluation, target cost determination. When the cost management is carried out during the construction phase, the construction unit will timely measure and settle, prevent and handle the changes and claims; the construction unit will arrange the supply of construction resources through a reasonable cost plan, and dynamically monitor the cost changes and timely correction during the implementation process. Effectively control construction costs. Finally, the three-level process - mainly in the above three stages to develop a specific implementation plan, also known as detailed work. The process is shown in Fig. 3.

2 BIM-Based Engineering Cost Management Strategy

2.1 Strengthen the Education and Guidance of Employees and Improve the Level of Refined Management

In recent years, the construction industry has developed rapidly, and the market competition pressure between industries has continuously increased. The most important competition in enterprise competition is the competition of talents. Therefore, the development of BIM-based engineering cost management must pay attention to the cultivation of talents. Increase the management and training of talents, and promote the improvement of the competitiveness of enterprises on the basis of improving the quality of talents. In the specific management process, enterprises should strengthen the education and guidance of employees, so that employees are consciously aware of the importance and significance of refined management of project cost, strengthen the development of training management, and improve the cost accounting level of employees. At the same time, it is necessary to carry out various courses on cost learning and management for employees to improve their professional level of engineering cost. This is the key and prerequisite for ensuring the smooth implementation of the fine management of enterprise engineering cost. In addition, to enhance employees' awareness of cost management and control, each employee recognizes the importance of cost control for production, thereby controlling the cost of engineering projects and improving the economic efficiency of the company.

2.2 Improve the Stratified Assessment System to Ensure the Efficient Implementation of Refined Management

At present, the development of the construction industry is very rapid, and competition among industries is intensifying. Therefore, enterprises must constantly improve their management systems and enhance their management capabilities so as to provide higher quality construction services to the society. In the process of fine management of project cost, enterprises must improve the assessment mechanism, ensure that the capabilities and requirements of all employees in the enterprise are consistent, and ensure the efficient use of enterprise resources, so as to avoid waste of resources and increase the cost of enterprises. Therefore, in the specific management process, it is necessary to establish a sound and stratified assessment system. On the basis of ensuring that employees complete their duties, strengthen the cooperation between various departments, and give full play to the enthusiasm of employees to ensure the project cost. Fine management can be implemented efficiently.

2.3 Strengthening the Application of BIM Information Sharing and Promoting the Function of BIM Technology

In the past construction project cost management process, the design software and methods used were not very informative, and the data resources could not be effectively shared. Therefore, only the drawings can be transmitted during the construction process, but such information, the delivery method requires a lot of time and labor costs, and the accuracy is low, which is not conducive to effective communication between enterprises. However, the application of BIM technology in engineering cost management can effectively improve the drawbacks of traditional technology methods, effectively realize the efficient sharing of data information, and improve the efficiency of information transmission and communication between departments and enterprises. At the same time, the application of BIM technology can be updated and improved according to the actual construction conditions of the project, thereby promoting the overall construction efficiency of the project and ensuring the smooth implementation of the project cost management. In addition, the application of BIM technology in the fine management of engineering cost requires the construction of model and the application of sharing technology, which can effectively solve various problems in engineering construction cost management, simplify the difficulty of enterprise cost management, and improve the engineering cost. The efficiency of management.

3 Improve the Application Efficiency of BIM Technology in Various Construction Stages of the Project

For the engineering cost consulting industry, BIM technology will be a subversive revolution that will completely change the behavioral model of the engineering cost industry. The use of BIM technology to fine-tune the cost control of the entire project can eliminate extra-budgetary changes, shorten the estimated time, reduce the contract price, and shorten the construction period [3].

First, the application in the decision-making stage. The decision-making phase is the most critical phase in each phase of project construction. At this stage, economic and technical arguments are made for different investment options, and the best solution is finally selected. Statistics show that the impact of the decision-making stage on project cost is as high as 80% to 90%. It can be seen that investment estimates play an important role in the decision-making of program selection. In the decision-making stage of the project, it is necessary to comprehensively consider all aspects of the content, and then carry out research from both technical and economic aspects, not only to ensure the quality of construction, but also to save construction costs. The application of BIM technology in the fine management of engineering cost can help the cost personnel to calculate the various information in the project, and then collect, analyze and organize the corresponding engineering database to provide a scientific basis for the decision-making of the cost personnel. Improve the accuracy of decision making.

Second, the application in the design phase. In the design stage, the BIM technology is used to construct and apply the model, which can realize the collision of data resources, visually display the problems that may occur in the architectural design, and improve the efficiency of manual review and the progress of the entire building construction. At the same time, the application of BIM technology can promote the coordination between the design phase and the cost control phase. As long as the data is processed for the second time, the staff can quickly obtain the corresponding data content and improve the efficiency of building personnel data acquisition, to enhance the accuracy of the data.

Third, the application in the bidding stage

(1) Determination of the base

Using BIM technology to carry out refined cost management, the construction unit can directly extract the total project quantity information of the project through the BIM model provided by the designer, and can directly obtain the closest price to avoid the project shortage, and can directly calculate the budget result of the construction drawing. Used as a part of the base to complete the preparation of the base.

(2) Generation of bid documents

When the construction unit conducts the bidding, it can issue the bill of quantities and drawings to the bidding unit, and the BIM model can be issued to the bidding unit together. The bidder can quickly approve the bill of quantities according to the BIM model and make the list bid according to the requirements of the bidding documents, saving time for quotation.

Fourth, the application in the construction phase. The application of BIM technology in the construction phase can collect and integrate the situation during the construction process, predict the problems that may occur during the construction, assist the staff to establish emergency plans, and reduce the risk of construction accidents. At the same time, the application of BIM technology can update the cost of the construction process in real time to ensure the accuracy of the cost information. At the same time, it is also possible to simulate and summarize the engineering quantity in the construction process, and accurately calculate and evaluate the engineering cost, so as to improve the efficiency of cost accounting.

In the project construction process, the BIM technology is used to carry out refined management of the project, which makes the project settlement simple and easy, not only can realize settlement on time, but also can accurately purchase and receive materials according to the progress of the project, and prepare capital plans and materials. Procurement plans and workforce plans, etc. The BIM technology is used to finely manage the project, and the cost model is established according to the requirements of the construction unit. The modification of the original design can minimize the probability of occurrence of engineering changes, or even completely eliminate it.

Fifth, the application in the completion phase. The application of BIM technology in the construction project management can store the data information of the whole project, which provides great convenience for the auditors after the completion of the project, and the accuracy of the stored information is extremely high, which improves the efficiency and accuracy of the calculation.

4 Conclusion and Suggestion

In summary, construction engineering is a large-scale and cost-intensive industry. It is very important to carry out rigorous, comprehensive and detailed management of project cost in engineering, which is of great significance for saving engineering cost and improving construction quality of engineering projects. BIM is a great driving force for the cost profession, and it can deliver a large amount of repetitive and mechanical calculations to the machine. Whether it will be eliminated by the industry does not depend on the popularity of BIM, but on how we use it to save time. In addition, BIM has a great effect on promoting the upgrade of cost management. From the perspective of future trends, basically all engineering projects will use BIM technology to control cost. Therefore, in the construction cost management of engineering projects, it is necessary to strengthen the training of relevant personnel, improve their professional quality, make good use of BIM technology, fully utilize the application and advantages of BIM technology in the fine management of engineering cost, and promote the project cost management. Efficient work.

References

1. Qi, H., et al.: A weighted threshold secret sharing scheme for remote sensing images based on Chinese remainder theorem. Comput. Mater. Continua **58**(2), 349–361 (2019)
2. Feng, G., et al.: Research on the law of garlic price based on big data. Comput. Mater. Continua **58**(3), 795–808 (2019)
3. Hao, W., Qi, L., Xiao, D.L.: A review on deep learning approaches to image classification and object segmentation. Comput. Mater. Continua **60**(2), 575–597 (2019)

Survey of Software-Defined Network Security Issues

Chao Guo[1(✉)], Dingbang Xie[1], Yanyan Han[1], Juan Guo[2], and Zhanzhen Wei[1]

[1] Department of Electronics and Communication Engineering,
Beijing Electronics Science and Technology Institute, Beijing 100070, China
guo99chao@163.com
[2] Vocational and Technical College, Guilin University of Electronic Technology,
Beihai 536000, Guangxi, China

Abstract. The Software-Defined Network is a new network architecture, which changes the traditional network management mode, decouples the traditional network control layer and data layer, and realizes more convenient network management by building a common interface between each layer, with the advantages of openness and centralized management. However, the existing research usually focuses on the development of software defined network technology, but ignores many security problems. Software defined network contains many security problems of traditional network, but also produces some special security problems. According to the network architecture defined by software, this paper analyzes the unique security problems faced by the network defined by software, and classifies the security problems. From the aspects of improving controller security, denial of service attack defense, flow rule consistency and improving application security, some existing security solutions and development directions are listed. Finally, the current and future security challenges of Software-Defined Network are summarized, and the future research direction of Software-Defined Network security is prospected.

Keywords: Software-Defined Network · Network security · OpenFlow

1 Introduction

In traditional networks, due to differences in equipment vendors and the diversity of network elements, network configuration and installation require skilled technicians with many network element configurations [1]. With the rapid growth of connected devices and the development of technologies such as cloud services, the difficulty and complexity of network management will increase. Therefore, traditional network architectures are in urgent need of innovation to simplify management and enhance flexibility.

The Stanford University Clean Slate Research Group proposed a new network architecture-Software-Defined Network (SDN) [2]. Its emergence makes it possible to break through the bottlenecks faced by traditional networks in terms of management, maintenance, and expansion. SDN simplifies the network structure by separating the control layer and the data layer. Complex control logic capabilities such as packet forwarding

© Springer Nature Singapore Pte Ltd. 2020
X. Sun et al. (Eds.): ICAIS 2020, CCIS 1252, pp. 503–514, 2020.
https://doi.org/10.1007/978-981-15-8083-3_45

decisions are stripped from devices such as switches/routers. The SDN controller delivers the forwarding rules to the underlying switching device through the unified interface protocol OpenFlow [3]. The data layer switch only needs to be forwarded according to the flow table rules. Moreover, the control layer is characterized by logic concentration and programmability. The control layer provides a global abstract view of the network to the upper layer. Users can customize the writing logic policy to deploy to the device.

SDN is considered to be one of the key technologies for implementing 5G networks, promoting the development of communication networks [4], and being listed by MIT as "One of the Top Ten Innovative Technologies to Change the world" [5]. As an innovative network architecture, SDN is effective in terms of openness, management concentration, and programmable, but SDN also has its own challenges and limitations. For example, a logically centralized controller can grasp the entire network situation, but it is more likely to cause a single point of failure, being hijacked or unable to work, causing the entire network to collapse. Despite the deployment of multiple controllers in the actual environment, the data is maliciously tampered with It is still an inevitable problem. SDN, as a new development direction of cloud service and cloud control platform network model, still faces malicious data tampering and deletion by cloud service providers [6]. SDN should not only solve its own security problems, but also face security problems in different application scenarios.

Section 1 introduces the concept of software-defined networking. Section 2 introduces the basic architecture of a software-defined network and analyzes the unique threats it faces. Section 3 describes the security issues faced by each layer and interface. Section 4 lists current major security problem solutions based on four aspects. Section 5 summarizes and explores the future direction of software-defined cybersecurity research.

2 Architecture and Threat Vector Analysis

2.1 Architecture of SDN

The SDN architecture was first proposed by the Open Network Foundation (ONF) in 2012 [7]. It is divided into application layer, control layer, data layer, northbound interface and southbound interface (see Fig. 1). The data layer consists of routers, switches, and other basic equipment of traditional networks. The data packet will be processed and forwarded according to the flow rules issued by the controller. The control layer includes a set of logically centralized SDN controllers. Each controller independently controls one or more network infrastructure devices in the data plane, maintains a global view of the network, and uniformly manages the network through NOS to achieve network optimization and troubleshooting functions. The application layer includes various applications written by developers, each of which has exclusive control over a set of resources exposed by one or more SDN controllers, such as network management, policy enforcement, and security services. The northbound interface is used for communication between the application layer and the control layer. The control layer provides abstraction of network resources for application developers through this interface, and then developers develop applications according to their needs. The southbound interface is used to control the communication between the control and data layers. It is responsible for passing the forwarding rules to the data layer, and the status and requests of the data layer to the control layer.

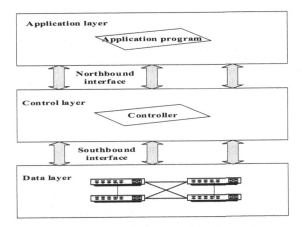

Fig. 1. Architecture of SDN.

The Open Day Light (ODL) architecture was proposed by Linux foundation in 2015 [8]. Its goal is to promote its implementation and deployment in the industry through open source SDN development. Its main object-oriented is also the equipment supplier, which is restricted by the equipment supplier on a large scale. ONF is for service providers and enterprise backbone. ODL architecture is divided into application service layer, control plane layer, service abstraction layer and data plane layer. The control layer of ODL is directly implemented by the built-in Java virtual machine. On request, the controller provides a range of pluggable modules that are compatible with third-party modules for maximum flexibility. Unlike ONF, ODL introduces a service abstraction layer between the control layer and the data layer. This is used to transform various underlying protocols into request services supported by the control layer. Therefore, the architecture can handle different standard protocols and has strong scalability. ODL's work on the South interface shows that in some cases, the South interface does not completely abstract the underlying device, and then hand it over to the control plane for processing, which may also be the performance of ODL on behalf of the device manufacturer. The SDN architecture comparison is shown in Table 1.

Table 1. Comparison of SDN architecture.

SDN architecture	Interface standard	Propose organization	Characteristics
ONF-SDN	OpenFlow	ONF	Data and control analysis
ODL	Multiple agreements	Linux	Service abstraction

3 Security Issues Faced by SDN Layers/Interfaces

3.1 Application Layer Security

The application layer directly interacts with the control layer through the northbound interface. Since the northbound interface does not have specific standards and specifications, the application may pose a serious security threat to network resources, services, and functions. Although the application layer can also develop security applications to defend against threats, inconsistencies in the development environment and network programming patterns may lead to irresistible issues such as policy deployment conflicts and interoperability. The security threats facing the application layer are as follows:

- Authentication and authorization. Most of the functions implemented by the controller are done by the application running on it, the application has the privilege of accessing network resources and manipulating network behavior, and it is difficult to establish a trusted relationship between the application and the controller. Without proper security authentication mechanisms, malicious applications will arbitrarily disrupt the network, so a large number of application authentications in programmable networks are currently a major security challenge.
- Malicious stream injection. Malicious or corrupted applications may generate incorrect flow rules that use legitimate user credentials to inject into the network and are difficult to detect for such malicious flow injections. Lee et al. [9] describe three application scenarios for well-known controllers (Open Networking Operating System (ONOS) [10], ODL [8], and Floodlight [11]). These attack cases may be critical to the SDN environment.
- Access control and accountability. Access control or firewalls, as well as content inspection or intrusion detection services, can be exploited by malicious applications to bypass access control. In addition, access control and accountability for nested applications is also an important aspect.

3.2 Control Layer Security

The control layer security is the backbone of the SDN network. The control layer logic is centralized and is the key entity for issuing decisions. Therefore, the controller becomes the main target of the attacker, and the attacker often obtains the maximum benefit through the attack control layer. The security threats facing the control layer are as follows:

- DoS/DDoS attacks. DOS/DDoS attacks have become a common attack method for attackers [12]. Although there are many solutions to mitigate DDoS attacks, threats still exist [13]. A common method is to use the Packet_in request to cause the control plane to saturate, thereby disabling the controller and affecting the network.
- Controller illegal control and malicious damage. The control layer lacks effective application access control, which can lead to attackers hijacking the controller. The hijacked controller poses many security risks [14]. The controller may also be physically or logically damaged. Applications with different security must provide different

authorizations, and malicious applications may illegally access and modify network resources.

- Multi-controller deployment. Multi-controller cooperative clusters can manage more and more switches in the network and avoid single-controller failures. The traditional solution is to use redundant controllers for redundancy, but there is a lack of re-examination of safety issues caused by multiple controllers [15]. The maintenance status of the controller must be consistent, otherwise, security problems may occur, such as firewall policy conflicts [16].

3.3 Data Layer Security

The data layer only forwards the data packet and performs unconditional execution on the upper layer policy. Therefore, there is a problem with spoofing. The security threats facing the date layer are as follows:

- Legality and consistency of flow rules. An attacker can generate a large amount of spurious traffic through a malicious switch or host, tamper with the flow table information, or cause the switch flow table to overflow and fail to work properly. The control of the application server is obtained in an abnormal way, so the data layer needs to recognize normal traffic and spurious traffic.
- Switch denial of service and hijacking. The switch flow table space is limited. The attacker can initiate flooding attacks on the switch, which in turn makes the switch flow table space saturated, causing a denial of service. Attackers can even hijack control switches, steal data, generate malicious traffic, and launch DoS attacks on controllers.

3.4 Southbound Interface Security

Currently, the Southbound interface generally uses the OpenFlow protocol. The Open-Flow secure channel uses the SSL/TLS protocol to encrypt data. After Open-Flow 1.3.0, SSL/TLS becomes optional, and the SSL/TLS protocol itself is not secure [17]. Implementing the lightweight PRESENT encryption algorithm in a reconfigurable platform (FPGA) can provide secure communication services and flexibility. Liu et al. completed this work and used it for secure video streaming in SDN test platforms. This provides a new idea for SDN secure stream transmission [18]. The southbound interface faces security issues such as middleman and data leakage.

3.5 Southbound Interface Security

The application is oriented to developers, and the variety is very fast, so the northbound interface is difficult to standardize, which is one of the problems faced by SDN [19]. The northbound interface does not improve the authentication method and authentication granularity of the application. The attacker can utilize the openness and programmability of the northbound interface to illegally access the controller resources. The security issues facing the northbound interface mainly include data leakage, message tampering, identity spoofing, the vulnerability of the application itself, and new vulnerabilities introduced by different applications when they cooperate.

4 SDN Security Issues Existing Solutions

4.1 Improve SDN Controller Security

The controller is the core device of the SDN control plane. It runs the operating system of the management network. The SDN network is characterized by the rapid deployment of services, and the controller is an important device for delivering business policies. Improving the security of the controller is the key to the entire SDN network. Currently, it is the application layer. The problem of illegal access or data layer identity fraud is always the imperfection of the SDN authorization authentication mechanism.

Abdulqadder et al. proposed a secure cloud architecture-SecSDNcloud, which includes user authentication, routing, attack defense, and third-party monitoring [20]. The goal is to design an SDN-cloud environment that combines security mechanisms to defend against flow tables. Overload attacks, control plane saturation attacks, and Byzantine attacks; use digital signatures to complete user authentication, use particle swarm multi-class routing protocols to improve service quality, and combine genetic algorithms with improved cuckoo search algorithms to complete controller assignment; Analysis of the quintuple information extracted in the packet to identify the malicious stream. According to the packet loss rate of the simulated SecSDNcloud, the end-to-end delay, throughput, and bandwidth performance show better performance than the previous SDN. However, exceeding the limit will still cause normal packet loss.

Abdou et al. analyzed the security risks of the control plane brought about by the structure of SDN and analyzed the typical network attributes and the conversion, security threats and protection measures between these attributes between the SDN control plane and the traditional network [21]. If the two network structures provide the same network attributes, although the structure is different, the security risks of the control plane are similar; the protection measures are different, SDN cannot rely on the boundary device to protect the control plane; the distributed SDN architecture means fault tolerance and Consistency detection is critical to the security of the SDN control plane. The analysis method of the paper can be used as an independent research hotspot for future SDN and traditional network security analysis.

Xu et al. proposed a model with fine-grained access control and ciphertext search function [22], which combines traditional attribute-based searchable ciphertext encryption with SDN structure to achieve intra-domain information sharing. The introduced attribute encryption algorithm consists of a five-term polynomial random algorithm: Setup, KeyGen, IndexGen, Trapdoor, and Test. Fine-grained access control and ciphertext retrieval; The proposed model can securely store ciphertext in the data center, preventing unauthorized access to information or using network resources, and reducing network bandwidth and resource consumption. This model can resist certain attacks and improve performance.

Porras et al. designed the security kernel FortNox based on the open-source controller NOX [23], added role-based data source authentication on the NOX controller and solved the authorization authentication problem from the kernel. In addition, FortNox has added modules such as state table management, flow rule conflict analysis detection and flow conflict timeout, which also improves the SDN flow rule conflict detection capability. These security modules work together to greatly improve the conflict detection and maintenance consistency of SDN flow rules. Fortnox's use of role-based authorization schemes has limitations in determining the appropriate level of security authorization, and FortNox cannot address application deployment and priority enforcement issues.

Scott-Hayward et al. proposed an application deployment strategy to improve controller security [24]. The Operational Check Point was designed and deployed based on the Floodlight controller. The difference from SE-Floodlight is the granularity of the method. In the case of SE-Floodlight signing and verifying the complete application, the permission-based method allows a set of operations to be granted to the application. This set of permissions can be enhanced or reduced based on monitoring application activity throughout the lifecycle of the application. In addition, this solution is extensible and can apply intrusion detection methods based on monitoring operational logs. This solution is suitable for both internal and external applications and can be further audited through subsequent related weblogs. However, Operation Check Point stores the program ID and access rights in the management table. Once the form is leaked or tampered with, the authorization will be invalid.

4.2 DoS/DDoS Attack Defense

DoS/DDoS attacks are currently a major issue in SDN security. The attacker is divided into an internal attacker and an external attacker. The external attacker is a legitimate device of the intruder, and the internal attacker is an internal damaged legal device. The attack mode is mainly for the OpenFlow protocol, forging fake traffic packets, requesting response flow forwarding rules from the controller, and other common types of attacks, such as ICMP, SYN flooding, HTTP flooding, Ping of Death, and Smurf attacks. The DoS/DDoS attack is effective and direct. It consumes SDN controller resources and occupies control link bandwidth and flow table space. As a result, services cannot be performed normally. Current research on DoS/DDoS attacks is divided into detection and defense, and timely response is the best way to deal with such attacks.

De Assis et al. proposed to quickly defend against DDoS attacks and port scans [25]. The attack scenario runs directly on the controller, using game theory to mitigate the attack. For the detection, the paper compares three different methods: particle swarm optimization, multilayer perceptron neural network and discrete wavelet transform. The IP flow data generated by the Mininet network simulator and the method of the Floodlight controller are tested. The proposed defense system has achieved good results in the detection and mitigation process.

Wu et al. proposed Prio Guard [26], a DoS mitigation framework based on the non-cooperative game model. The DoS is detected based on information entropy, rate packet and response rate packets. In addition, the penalty incentives of repeated games are used to punish these attackers and postpone their requests by lowering their priority. Requests from the attacker will be migrated to the data plane cache, which eases the interface cache of the control plane and enables the controller to effectively process normal requests. The average response time, packet loss rate and controller load can be significantly reduced.

Kalkan et al. proposed a joint entry-based security scheme (JESS) to defend against DDoS attacks and enhance the security of SDN, especially using statistical methods to detect and mitigate these security threats [27]. JESS is the first. Using joint entropy to detect and mitigate DDoS attacks in SDN, because it is based on statistical models, it not only mitigates known attacks but also works against some less common attacks.

4.3 Flow Rule Consistency Protection

Because the data layer only carries the task of data forwarding and does not distinguish between normal and malicious flows, when the attacker performs operations such as controlling the switch, implementing man-in-the-middle attacks, and changing the flow forwarding path, the flow table rules are falsified, information is stolen, and Tampering and other security issues. Therefore, the detection of the validity and consistency of flow rules in the network is critical to the stability and reliability of the SDN network.

Since the flow rules of SDN are often generated by different applications, these rules may conflict in the data plane and cause a violation of the security policy, which is similar to the firewall rule conflict of the IP network; eliminating rule conflicts should generate a small processing delay [28]. So that all rules of the data plane ca n be safely and correctly processed in real-time. SDN allows users to specify flow rules using 35 fields, so preventing SDN rules from conflicting with security policies is much more complicated than preventing firewall conflicts, especially when performing field conversion rules; this is resolved in real-time before the rules are distributed to the data plane. Rule conflicts are more difficult. The thesis deeply studies the rule conflict problem of SDN and identifies the hidden channel attack caused by the rule conflict. The hidden channel defense mechanism CCD is proposed to identify and resolve the hidden channel attack caused by the rule conflict. All the rules insertion on the CCD tracking controller and modifying the message, analyzing the correlation between the rules according to the multiple header fields, and solving the identified rule conflicts in real-time before the rules are loaded. The paper implements CCD on the Floodlight controller and simulates the performance using real Stanford topology data. CCD can effectively identify and resolve rule conflicts that may lead to hidden channel attacks within a few hundred microseconds with little overhead. Based on SDN technology, Wan et al. introduced a software-defined security function model through a separate architecture of logical control and data forwarding. An event-based anomaly detection method for non-public industrial communication protocols is proposed in a SDN-based control system [29].

Communication between the data plane and the control plane in SDN may pose security risks, such as controller saturation attacks and switch buffer overflow attacks. These attacks can be initiated by flooding TCP SYN packets to the control plane through the data plane, Kumar et al. proposed a solution SAFETY that can detect and be below the TCP SYN flood attack [30]. he entropy method is used securely to detect the data stream. The entropy information includes the destination IP and some TCP flag bits. When the entropy drops suddenly, it will cause an alarm. Whether the entropy is continuously increased or decreased over the selected time range.

$$E(X)|_{t=t_0} - E(X)|_{t=t_0+\Delta t} \geq \Delta \tag{1}$$

Where t is time and $\Delta (\Delta \geq 0)$ is the threshold entropy at that point in time, which can be judged according to the entropy derivative:

$$E'(X) = \lim_{\Delta t \to 0} \frac{E(X)|_{t=t_0+\Delta t} - E(X)|_{t=t_0}}{\Delta t} \tag{2}$$

The paper uses SAFETY as the Floodlight controller. The control module verifies its flexibility and effectiveness in different situations. The results show that SAFETY increases latency by 13% compared to the latest technology, while also increasing CPU utilization and attack detection time. There have also been improvements in terminology.

4.4 Improve Application Security

In addition to architecture security, protocol security, and resource security, SDN security is most important for the security of various applications deployed in actual scenarios. The application layer directly configures the controller through the north-bound interface. If the application is maliciously controlled or implanted with malicious programs, it will pose a threat to the entire SDN network. Mutual interference or operational errors between common applications can also pose a threat.

Varadharajan et al. proposed a security policy-based SDN service and communication protection model that describes how to use the security policy language to control the flow of information between different SDN domains, enabling fine-grained security based on various attributes [31]. Policies such as user or device parameters, location and routing information, security attributes of switches and controllers between different domains. The biggest feature of the proposed structure is the ability to implement path-based and flow-based security policies to protect end-to-end services in SDN and apply the proposed model to intra-domain communication and multi-controller-controlled inter-domain communication, security analysis. And simulation results show that the model can resist various common attacks.

At present, the solutions for the application layer of FortNOX, SE-Floodlight, etc. are mainly in the access control and authority management of the controller. Beckett proposes an assertion language that supports the verification and debugging of SDN applications through dynamically changing validation conditions [31]. An incremental data structure and an underlying validation engine are proposed to quickly revalidate the entire data plane as these validation conditions change. It can be easily integrated into existing control systems with very few changes. Kissel proposes an XSP framework [32], which controls the access of SDN applications through authentication and authorization mechanisms. Applications that pass authentication can dynamically invoke SDN resources and can exchange information across SDN. For malicious applications, malicious applications can be mitigated by malicious code detection and application auditing. The number and complexity of applications are increasing, and the increase in the size of the code increases the concealment of attacks. Code detection and auditing mechanisms can effectively alleviate this danger.

In addition, for the security problem of the northbound interface, the focus of various northbound interface designs is different, some design from the user's point of view, some from the operational point of view, etc., the SDN platform does not form a unified northbound interface specification, and may be difficult in the future. A unified standard is formed, but interfaces such as RESTful API and Net-conf are widely used open interfaces in SDN networks. It is helpful to fully understand the main security challenges and countermeasures they face to improve the security of SDN networks.

5 Conclusion

This paper discusses the security problems and solutions of SDN from the perspective of SDN architecture. The control layer is the backbone of SDN network. Improving the security of control layer is an important research direction in the future. The open API also propagates security threats from the application layer to the control layer, and from the control layer to the data layer. New agreements between layers need long-term security assessment. Application layer applications need a complete application audit mechanism to ensure access to secure applications and reduce the security caused by malicious applications. Finally, give full play to the advantages of SDN global view to reduce the security risks brought by SDN centralized control and open interface.

Acknowledgment. We gratefully acknowledge anonymous reviewers who read drafts and made many helpful suggestions. This work is supported by Fundamental Research Funds for the Central Universities of China (328201911), Higher Education Department of the Ministry of Education Industry-university Cooperative Education Project and Education and Teaching Reform Project of Beijing Electronic and Technology Institute.

References

1. Sezer, S., et al.: Are we ready for SDN? Implementation challenges for software-defined networks. IEEE Commun. Mag. **51**, 36–43 (2013)
2. Feldmann, A.: Internet clean-slate design: what and why? ACM SIGCOMM Comput. Commun. Rev. **37**, 59–64 (2007)
3. McKeown, N., et al.: OpenFlow: enabling innovation in campus networks. ACM SIGCOMM Comput. Commun. Rev. **38**, 69–74 (2008)
4. Yousaf, F.Z., Bredel, M., Schaller, S., Schneider, F.: NFV and SDN—key technology enablers for 5G networks. IEEE J. Sel. Areas Commun. **35**, 2468–2478 (2017)
5. Simonite, T.: MIT Technology Review Announces 10 Breakthrough Technologies. Sensors (2015)
6. Li, C., Wang, P., Sun, C., Zhou, K., Huang, P.: WiBPA: an efficient data integrity auditing scheme without bilinear pairings. Comput. Mater. Continua **58**, 319–333 (2019)
7. Shin, M.-K., Nam, K.-H., Kim, H.-J.: Software-defined networking (SDN): a reference architecture and open APIs. In: 2012 International Conference on ICT Convergence (ICTC), Jeju Island, South Korea, pp. 360–361. IEEE (2012)
8. Medved, J., Varga, R., Tkacik, A., Gray, K.: OpenDaylight: towards a model-driven SDN controller architecture. In: Proceeding of IEEE International Symposium on a World of Wireless, Mobile and Multimedia Networks, Sydney, NSW, Australia, pp. 1–6. IEEE (2014)
9. Lee, S., Yoon, C., Shin, S.: The smaller, the shrewder: a simple malicious application can kill an entire SDN environment. In: Proceedings of the 2016 ACM International Workshop on Security in Software Defined Networks & Network Function Virtualization, New Orleans, Louisiana, USA, pp. 23–28. ACM (2016)
10. Berde, P., et al.: ONOS: towards an open, distributed SDN OS. In: Proceedings of the Third Workshop on Hot Topics in Software Defined Networking, Chicago, Illinois, USA, pp. 1–6. ACM (2014)
11. Mar. http://www.openflowhub.org/display/floodlightcontroller/Architecture. Accessed 24 Feb 2015

12. An, X., Su, J., Lü, X., Lin, F.: Hypergraph clustering model-based association analysis of DDOS attacks in fog computing intrusion detection system. EURASIP J. Wirel. Commun. Netw. **2018**(1), 1–9 (2018). https://doi.org/10.1186/s13638-018-1267-2
13. Raghunath, K., Krishnan, P.: Towards a secure SDN architecture. In: 2018 9th International Conference on Computing, Communication and Networking Technologies (ICCCNT), pp. 1–7 (2018)
14. Zhou, H., et al.: SDN-RDCD: a real-time and reliable method for detecting compromised SDN devices. IEEE/ACM Trans. Netw. (TON) **26**, 2048–2061 (2018)
15. Maziku, H., Shetty, S., Jin, D., Kamhoua, C., Njilla, L., Kwiat, K.: Diversity modeling to evaluate security of multiple SDN controllers. In: 2018 International Conference on Computing, Networking and Communications (ICNC), Maui, HI, USA, pp. 344–348. IEEE (2018)
16. Shin, S., Yegneswaran, V., Porras, P., Gu, G.: AVANT-GUARD: scalable and vigilant switch flow management in software-defined networks. In: Proceedings of the 2013 ACM SIGSAC Conference on Computer & Communications Security, Berlin, Germany, pp. 413–424. ACM (2013)
17. Fossati, T., Tschofenig, H.: Transport layer security (TLS)/datagram transport layer security (DTLS) profiles for the internet of things. Transport (2016)
18. Liu, P., Wang, X., Chaudhry, S., Javeed, K., Ma, Y., Collier, M.: Secure video streaming with lightweight cipher PRESENT in an SDN testbed. Comput. Mater. Continua **57**, 353–363 (2018)
19. Vasconcelos, C.R., Gomes, R.C.M., Costa, A.F., da Silva, D.D.C.: Enabling high-level network programming: a northbound API for software-defined networks. In: 2017 International Conference on Information Networking (ICOIN), Da Nang, Vietnam, pp. 662–667. IEEE (2017)
20. Abdulqadder, I.H., Zou, D., Aziz, I.T., Yuan, B., Li, W.: SecSDN-cloud: defeating vulnerable attacks through secure software-defined networks. IEEE Access **6**, 8292–8301 (2018)
21. Abdou, A., Van Oorschot, P.C., Wan, T.: Comparative analysis of control plane security of SDN and conventional networks. IEEE Commun. Surv. Tutorials **20**, 3542–3559 (2018)
22. Xu, J., Hong, H., Lin, G., Sun, Z.: A new inter-domain information sharing smart system based on ABSES in SDN. IEEE Access **6**, 12790–12799 (2018)
23. Porras, P., Shin, S., Yegneswaran, V., Fong, M., Tyson, M., Gu, G.: A security enforcement kernel for OpenFlow networks. In: Proceedings of the First Workshop on Hot Topics in Software Defined Networks, Helsinki, Finland, pp. 121–126. ACM (2012)
24. Scott-Hayward, S., Kane, C., Sezer, S.: OperationCheckpoint: SDN application control. In: 2014 IEEE 22nd International Conference on Network Protocols, Raleigh, NC, USA, pp. 618–623. IEEE (2014)
25. De Assis, M.V., Novaes, M.P., Zerbini, C.B., Carvalho, L.F., Abrãao, T., Proença, M.L.: Fast defense system against attacks in software defined networks. IEEE Access **6**, 69620–69639 (2018)
26. Wu, G., Li, Z., Yao, L.: DoS mitigation mechanism based on non-cooperative repeated game for SDN. In: 2018 IEEE 24th International Conference on Parallel and Distributed Systems (ICPADS), Singapore, pp. 612–619. IEEE (2018)
27. Kalkan, K., Altay, L., Gür, G., Alagöz, F.: JESS: joint entropy-based DDoS defense scheme in SDN. IEEE J. Sel. Areas Commun. **36**, 2358–2372 (2018)
28. Li, Q., Chen, Y., Lee, P.P., Xu, M., Ren, K.: Security policy violations in SDN data plane. IEEE/ACM Trans. Netw. (TON) **26**, 1715–1727 (2018)
29. Wan, M., Yao, J., Jing, Y., Jin, X.: Event-based anomaly detection for non-public industrial communication protocols in SDN-based control systems. Comput. Mater. Continua **55**, 447–463 (2018)

30. Kumar, P., Tripathi, M., Nehra, A., Conti, M., Lal, C.: SAFETY: Early detection and mitigation of TCP SYN flood utilizing entropy in SDN. IEEE Trans. Netw. Serv. Manage. **15**, 1545–1559 (2018)
31. Varadharajan, V., Karmakar, K., Tupakula, U., Hitchens, M.: A policy-based security architecture for software-defined networks. IEEE Trans. Inf. Forensics Secur. **14**, 897–912 (2018)
32. Kissel, E., Fernandes, G., Jaffee, M., Swany, M., Zhang, M.: Driving software defined networks with XSP. In: 2012 IEEE International Conference on Communications (ICC), Ottawa, ON, Canada, pp. 6616–6621. IEEE (2012)

A Fall Detection Algorithm Based on a Support Vector Machine

Juan Guo[1], Yilin Tang[2], Siyuan Fu[2], Chao Guo[2(✉)], and Chanjuan Yu[2]

[1] Vocational and Technical College, Guilin University of Electronic Technology, Beihai,
Guangxi 536000, People's Republic of China
[2] Department of Electronics and Communication Engineering, Beijing Electronic Science and
Technology Institute, Beijing 100070, People's Republic of China
guo99chao@163.com

Abstract. As the world's population aging degree increasing. The quantity and size of public services for the elderly existed can no longer meet the requirements, the quality of service for the elderly cannot be guaranteed. The size of the special group of "empty nesters" is getting larger and larger. This makes it more difficult to care for the elderly. Due to a decline in bodily functions. Older people are more likely to fall, Falls become one of the most important factors affecting the physical and mental health of the elderly. Wearable sensors are called one of the basic components of smart medical systems in the new era. A series of data such as heart rate and blood pressure changes can be obtained through induction, and send the data back for later study and research. By analyzing the sensor data at the time of falling, design an algorithm to find falls in time, and care for the health of the elderly.

Keywords: Wearable sensor · Fall-detect · GLS · Support vector machine · Body area networks

1 Introduction

With the increasing aging of the population, the number and scale of existing public service facilities for the elderly can no longer meet the demand, and the quality of services for the elderly cannot be guaranteed. In addition, due to various family reasons, the trend of the elderly living alone is more and more obvious, and this group of elderly people has become a special social group, known as "empty-nesters" [1, 2].

The problem of fall detection is a hot research direction of domestic and foreign scholars because the health of the elderly has always been a hot social issue, fall is an important factor affecting the health of the elderly [3]. This topic is of great practical significance and challenge. With the development of the economy in recent years, the health of the elderly has drawn more and more attention from Chinese people. Technology related to fall detection and protection for the elderly is also being developed.

At present, the automatic fall detection system at home and abroad can be divided into three types: the fall detection system based on video image processing, the environmental fall detection system and the fall detection system based on wearable devices.

© Springer Nature Singapore Pte Ltd. 2020
X. Sun et al. (Eds.): ICAIS 2020, CCIS 1252, pp. 515–526, 2020.
https://doi.org/10.1007/978-981-15-8083-3_46

The fall detection system based on video image processing is to install one or more cameras in the room to capture images of human movement, and then analyze them through visual processing or image processing to extract image features to judge human posture and further judge whether or not people fall [4].

The environmental fall detection system is to arrange different types of sensors in the activity area of the monitor, obtain kinematics data of human body activity, and then determine whether the human body falls after a series of detection algorithm analyses [5]. There are three kinds of environmental detection systems that have been realized. There is an environmental detection system based on the pressure sensor, which can obtain the pressure change data of the human body to the ground through the sensor to predict the change of human body posture, so as to judge whether the human body falls or not.

The fall detection system based on wearable devices is to wear sensors collecting kinematic data on the user's body and judge whether a fall occurs through data processing and analysis. The sensor types used by the system mainly includes a gyro-scope, triaxial acceleration sensor, pressure sensor, etc. According to the data collected by the sensor, such as triaxial attitude Angle, instantaneous acceleration, pressure, etc., it can identify whether a fall occurs by combining with the corresponding support vector machine learning algorithm.

2 Related Work

With flow chart in detail, description supervise the whole process of learning, to assume that the input variables x and output variables to y, function is obtained by monitoring study h (x) (x, y) is a set of training sample, through the supervision of learning machine learning method, can use a pair of input and output values (x, y) to "paint" out of the system function h (x), "paint" is to supervise the process of learning process, namely the learning analysis given training sample shows the mapping relationship between input variable and output variable, the producing process of model function [6] (Fig. 1).

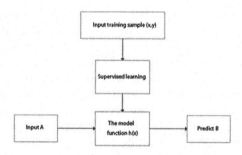

Fig. 1. Supervised the learning process

Supervised learning algorithm includes two types: when the variables that need to be predicted are continuous, the supervised learning algorithm solves a regression prediction problem. When variables are discrete, the problem of pattern classification is solved.

Unsupervised learning, also known as inductive learning, is another machine learning algorithm. The core idea is to build the center by learning the algorithm, and then reduce the error by a repeated decrease. Content-based image retrieval (CBIR) techniques have been widely deployed in many applications for seeking the abundant information existed in images. Due to large amounts of storage and computational requirements of CBIR, outsourcing image search work to the cloud provider becomes a very attractive option for many owners with small devices. However, owing to the private content contained in images, directly out-sourcing retrieval work to the cloud provider apparently bring about privacy problem, so the images should be protected carefully before outsourcing. With this scheme, the discrete cosine transform (DCT) is performed on the Y component. When receiving a query trapdoor form on query user, the server extracts AC-coefficients histogram from the encrypted Y component and extracts two-color histograms from the other two color components. The similarity between query trapdoor and database image is measured by calculating the Manhattan distance of their respective histograms. Finally, the encrypted images closest to the query image are returned to the querying user [7].

Reinforcement learning, also known as reinforcement learning and reinforcement learning, is an important machine learning algorithm, which has many applications in intelligent robot control and analysis and prediction [8].

Support Vector Machine (SVM) is an important classification and pattern recognition technology [9]. The main idea is to establish a classification hyperplane to maximize the isolated edge between two types of data, so as to achieve the best classification effect.

SVM algorithm belongs to a supervised learning algorithm. In the algorithm, it is assumed that there is a hyperplane, which can divide a given training data set into two categories when confronted with a dichotomy problem [10]. When the hyper-plane is the most separated from the two types of data, the hyperplane classification has the highest accuracy and the best classification effect (Fig. 2).

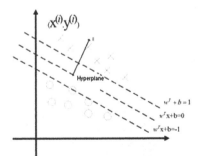 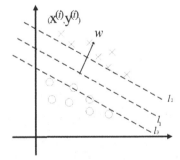

Fig. 2. Schematic diagram of support vector machine

Fig. 3. Schematic diagram of support vector classification

Firstly, the classification problem in two-dimensional space is considered. Suppose that the direction of the dividing line has been given, as shown in Fig. 3. In conclusion, when the normal direction of the line is determined, the corresponding line and the middle line are the optimal dividing line [11, 12].

The next question is how to determine the most appropriate method of direction, for each is suitable for the normal vector, there are two support lines and, the distance between the two straight lines called "interval", our direction is to find such a method, make the corresponding "interval" maximum, and then find the best line [13].

According to the above theory, we transform the problem of finding the optimal partition line into the problem of solving the optimal solution of, set the appropriate, and two expressions supporting the line can be equivalent to and, calculate the corresponding "interval" is, and finally, the expression of maximizing the interval is [14, 15].

In order to reduce the memory use of the computer and improve the operation efficiency, the concept of kernel function is introduced. Kernel functions are divided into linear kernel functions, radial basis kernel functions, Gaussian kernel functions, etc. [16].

In the training data set, there are often some "outliers", that is, some data with large errors. The existence of these points may seriously affect the solution accuracy of the partitioning hyperplane [17–19]. The introduction of the soft intervals can solve this problem to a certain extent. In the process of classification, if some data with large errors make the interpretation of experimental results poor, the soft interval can allow the occurrence of errors and ensure the correctness of most data.

To fulfill the requirements of data security in environments with nonequivalent resources, a high capacity data hiding scheme in the encrypted image based on compressive sensing (CS) is proposed by fully utilizing the adaptability of CS to nonequivalent resources. For data security management, the encrypted non-image data is then embedded into the encrypted image, and the scrambling operation is used to further improve security. Finally, the original image and non-image data can be separably recovered and extracted according to the request from the valid users with different access rights. Experimental results demonstrate that the proposed scheme outperforms other data hiding methods based on CS, and is more suitable for nonequivalent resources [20].

3   Design and Implementation of Fall System

This part introduces the design and implementation of the fall detection system, including the introduction of input data, data processing methods and the application of the SVM algorithm as shown in Fig. 4.

3.1   Description of Input Data

The original Data Set used in this project comes from the UCI machine learning database of the University of California, whose name is Location Data for Person Activity Data Set. The data were collected by four wearable sensors located at the chest, waist, left ankle and right ankle. The 3d coordinate value of the sensor can be obtained at a certain time as shown in Fig. 5.

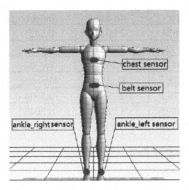

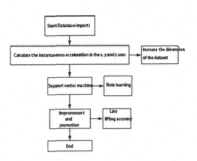

Fig. 4. Overall structure of the system   **Fig. 5.** Distribution of wearable sensors

The data set consists of eight dimensions. Is A human action, the data set is made up of five kinds of people in five different scenarios for five consecutive moves to collect, such as A, in A scene for five consecutive times the same action with A01 - A05 annotation, 2 it is used for the difference between sensors identity, 3 it is used to ensure data security timestamps, four is the time when the collected data, accurate to milliseconds, and the three-dimensional coordinate values and action.

When the data set was downloaded, it was in the TXT text format. For better use in the future, the database in text format was first imported into excel as shown in Fig. 6.

A01	010-000-0:	6.3379E+17	27.05.200!	1.977785945	2.026065111	0.136417091	lying down
A01	010-000-0:	6.3379E+17	27.05.200!	1.737197638	2.182474852	0.178937942	lying down
A01	010-000-0:	6.3379E+17	27.05.200!	1.81145978	2.220902205	-0.009763938	lying down
A01	010-000-0:	6.3379E+17	27.05.200!	1.612939	1.971904516	0.16817449	lying down
A01	010-000-0:	6.3379E+17	27.05.200!	1.729831934	2.088561773	-0.04558384	lying down
A01	010-000-0:	6.3379E+17	27.05.200!	1.669772387	2.455868006	-0.135364503	lying down
A01	010-000-0:	6.3379E+17	27.05.200!	1.616240263	2.344589233	-0.056503426	lying down
A01	010-000-0:	6.3379E+17	27.05.200!	1.655242562	2.442194462	-0.073911294	lying down
A01	010-000-0:	6.3379E+17	27.05.200!	1.663643479	2.448137045	-0.18168886	lying down

Fig. 6. Sensor database imported into excel

The format of the database is shown in Table 1 as follows:

Table 1. Table captions should be placed above the tables.

User ID	Sensor ID	Time-stamp	Time	x	y	z	States

First, the data of each sensor was analyzed separately, and the results of the maximum, minimum, median and variance of the data were shown in Fig. 7, 8 and 9.

Matlab data of the four sensors were used to draw the figure as shown in Fig. 10.

Left ankle sensor	Max	Min	Median	Variance
x	5.5328	0.2034	2.9032	0.5021
y	3.8935	-0.1324	1.7204	0.2024
z	2.5543	-1.4523	0.2532	0.0702
Right ankle sensor	Max	Min	Median	Variance
x	5.4532	0.1705	2.7968	0.5034
y	3.9525	-0.4805	1.7034	0.2043
z	2.1986	-2.5328	0.2553	0.0726

Fig. 7. Right ankle sensor data

Chest sensor	Max	Min	Median	Variance
x	5.6986	-0.2695	2.7013	1.3956
y	3.9545	-0.5034	1.6931	0.2705
z	2.6105	-2.0253	0.6895	0.1786

Fig. 8. Chest sensor data

Waist sensor	Max	Min	Median	Variance
x	5.4034	0.0203	2.8038	0.9798
y	3.9543	-0.4786	1.6795	0.2543
z	2.5986	-1.9560	0.5315	0.1334

Fig. 9. Data of waist sensor

Through the above simple analysis of the data, it can be found that the data variance is relatively small, which reflects that the midpoint of the graph is relatively concentrated and the data availability is relatively good. It is also easy to find that there are some "scatter" points in the data obtained by each sensor. In the use of later data, some processing is needed to reduce the impact of these data on the classification results.

3.2 Establishment of Attribute Acceleration

The data collected by the four sensors in the human activity positioning database is the three-dimensional coordinate value data of the human body when the corresponding movement occurs, while in the real algorithm application, we use the instantaneous acceleration in the three-dimensional coordinate direction. Instantaneous acceleration can better describe the trajectory of human beings, and the classification accuracy of the algorithm can be improved when the instantaneous acceleration in the three-dimensional coordinate direction is input into the learning algorithm as a one-dimensional attribute of the data. For this, we need to process the 3d coordinate data in the human activity location database to obtain the 3d acceleration data needed by the algorithm.

First, extract the time recorded by the sensor when the action occurs from the database. See Fig. 11.

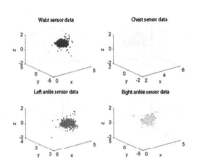

Fig. 10. Sensor data

27.05.2009 14:03:25:127
27.05.2009 14:03:25:237
27.05.2009 14:03:25:343
27.05.2009 14:03:25:453
27.05.2009 14:03:25:560
27.05.2009 14:03:25:670
27.05.2009 14:03:25:777
27.05.2009 14:03:25:883
27.05.2009 14:03:25:993
27.05.2009 14:03:26:100

Fig. 11. Sensor time

The instantaneous acceleration of x, y, and z coordinate axes is obtained by using the basic physical formula. As shown in Fig. 11, four columns are added to the database, respectively representing the time difference between two adjacent times collected by the sensor and the instantaneous acceleration of the x, y and z three-dimensional axes at this time (Fig. 12).

3.156413	1.658062	0.03169	falling	0.107	0.741890209	1.26519696	5.350848633
3.164907	1.672547	0.092952	falling	0.11	0.853637025	1.831222149	-2.104640579
3.175236	1.694705	0.067486	falling	0.107	0.848698489	0.449338545	8.862784173
3.184952	1.699849	0.168956	falling	0.106	-1.331014774	-3.503348434	5.128299039
3.169997	1.660486	0.226578	falling	0.11	11.32974942	-0.502570579	-23.57270041
3.307087	1.654404	-0.05865	falling	0.107	-1.703540222	-11.0777281	8.691184907
3.287583	1.527575	0.040853	falling	0.11	-8.633806694	4.51817	31.85192752
3.183114	1.582245	0.426262	falling	0.107	5.323570967	12.21754136	-42.42191659

Fig. 12. Processed time difference and instantaneous acceleration in the direction of three-dimensional coordinate.

The use of LIBSVM is divided into three main steps, SVM training, SVM size, and SVM prediction. The scale of support vector machines is mainly used to standardize data sets. SVM size and SVM prediction are shown in Table 2.

Table 2. Related description of svm-train (-s)

Options	Description
0	C-SVC
1	nu-SVC
2	one-class SVM
3	epsilon-SVR
4	nu-SVR

C-svc and nu-svc in the table are usually used for multi-level classification problems, one-class SVM is usually used for distribution estimation, epsilon-SVR and nuSVR are mainly used for regression analysis, and c-svc method is mainly adopted in this topic.

Table 2 shows the five types of LIBSVM kernel functions. According to the difference of training data set, the classification accuracy of different kernel functions is different when different kernel functions are used. After several attempts in this subject, it is found that a Radial basis function, that is a Radial basis function, performs best in this subject.

3.3 SVM Algorithm Simulation Results

In the human activity location database, we randomly selected 200 pieces of data, among which 100 pieces were randomly selected data collected by the sensor in falling state and 100 pieces were randomly selected data in other states of action. Among these data, 180 data were randomly selected as the training set and 20 data were left as the test set. The simulation results of the algorithm are shown in Fig. 13.

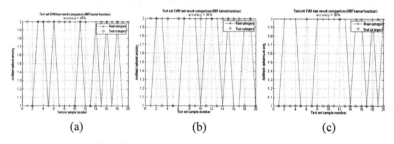

| (a) | (b) | (c) |

Fig. 13. The results of algorithm simulation

The training set and test set used by the algorithm are all random, and the final classification accuracy also fluctuates up and down. It is found from the experimental results that the classification accuracy is between 30%–50%, and the classification effect is poor, which cannot meet the requirements of algorithm classification accuracy in the application scenario of the algorithm, and it needs to seek for improvement and improvement in the later stage.

4   Algorithm Improvement and Promotion

4.1 Database Preprocessing

From the original data of the database analysis, although data comparison, to the situation in response to human activities, but there are also some "dirty data", the presence of these data can cause great influence to the final results, so before using these data, the data preprocessing, we want to reduce or eliminate the adverse impact of these data, improve the classification accuracy of the algorithm.

Normalization is to limit the data to a certain range after the data needs to be processed by some algorithm, which facilitates the application and processing of later data and reduces the impact of "dirty data" on the results. The training set and test set are normalized and preprocessed, and the normalized mapping is as follows: The effect of normalization is to make the original data be normalized to the range of [0,1]. When the "scatter" data is large, the value of different features of the feature vector in the support vector will be greatly different.

In MATLAB, map min-max function can be used to achieve the normalization of data processing. The simulation results of the algorithm after normalization processing are shown in Fig. 14.

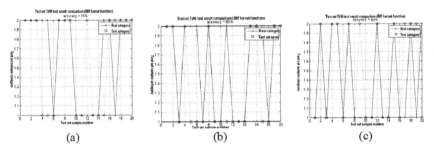

(a)   (b)   (c)

Fig. 14. Simulation results after normalization

After data normalization and preprocessing, the performance of the SVM classifier has been greatly improved. It can be found that the existence of "dirty data" has a serious impact on the performance of the classifier.

4.2 Parameter Optimization

In strain during SVM training, there are penalty parameters C and kernel function parameters G. The default values of the two parameters should be based on the test experience. Consider whether the values of the two parameters can be adjusted to achieve better experimental results.

Validation CV (Cross) is a kind of analysis method based on statistical principle, the principle and the principle of supervised learning, according to certain rules will be given the original data into training set and testing set two groups, with training set of training data, system learning model system function, then validation set of data import, system test model function classification accuracy, and performance of the system under the condition. Let c and g take discrete values within a certain range of mo, compare the classification accuracy of the model functions obtained by the system under different parameter groups, and finally make the group of parameters with the highest classification accuracy of the system namely the optimal parameters c and g of the system under this condition.

The improved simulation results are shown in Fig. 15.

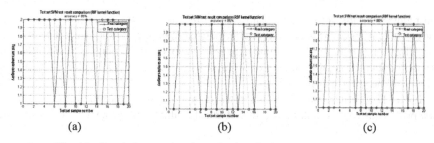

Fig. 15. Simulation results after selecting the best parameters c and g.

After selecting the best parameters c and g, the classification accuracy of the classifier was slightly improved by 5%–10%.

4.3 Select More Appropriate Training and Test Sets

For machine learning, more data is more likely to improve the accuracy of the model. For this reason, during the later improvement and promotion, 4600 data were randomly selected from the database, and 4500 data were randomly selected from the 4600 data as the training set and the remaining 100 as the test set.

After changing the training set and data set, the algorithm simulation results are shown in Fig. 16.

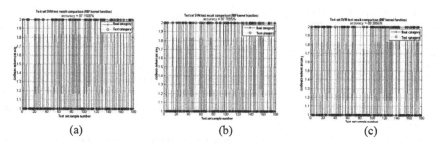

Fig. 16. Simulation results after selecting a larger data set

The simulation shows that the performance of the SVM classifier is improved slightly after selecting a larger training set and test set. Due to the limitation of computer memory, it is believed that the performance of the classifier will continue to be improved by increasing the capacity of the training set. An explicit extraction of the retinal vessel is a standout amongst the most significant errands in the field of medical imaging to analyze both the ophthalmological infections, for example, Glaucoma, Diabetic Retinopathy (DR), Retinopathy of Prematurity (ROP), Age-Related Macular Degeneration (AMD) as well as non-retinal sickness such as stroke, hypertension and cardiovascular diseases. Firstly, the fundus image pre-processing is done for contrast enhancement and in-homogeneity correction. Then, a set of core features is extracted, and the best features are selected using "minimal Redundancy-maximum Relevance (mRmR)." Later, using MAD-ELM method vessels and non-vessels are classified. DRIVE and DR-HAGIS datasets are used for the evaluation of the proposed method. The algorithm's performance is assessed based on accuracy, sensitivity and specificity. The proposed technique attains the accuracy of 0.9619 on the DRIVE database and 0.9519 on the DR-HAGIS database, which contains pathological images. Our results show that, in addition to healthy retinal images, the proposed method performs well in extracting blood vessels from pathological images and is therefore comparable with state of the art methods [21].

5 Conclusion

This paper briefly introduces the background of social research on the fall detection system and the research status at home and abroad. This paper introduces the basic concept and structure of machine learning, analyzes the characteristics and application scope of supervised learning, unsupervised learning, and reinforcement learning, and finally chooses the implementation method of support vector machine based on supervised learning. This paper introduces the theoretical basis and algorithm principle of the support vector machine (SVM). The algorithm of the designed fall detection system was realized. In the case that the early experiment was not successful, the system structure optimization and improvement in the later period were emphasized. Finally, the system function was well-realized and the high-precision fall detection algorithm was simulated.

Acknowledgment. We gratefully acknowledge anonymous reviewers who read drafts and made many helpful suggestions. This work is supported by Guangxi Vocational Education Teaching Reform Research Project (GXGZJG2018A040), Fundamental Research Funds for the Central Universities of China (328201911), Higher Education Department of the Ministry of Education Industry-university Cooperative Education Project and Education and Teaching Reform Project of Beijing Electronic and Technology Institute.

References

1. An, X., Lü, X., Yang, L., Zhou, X., Lin, F.: Node state monitoring scheme in fog radio access networks for intrusion detection. IEEE Access **7**, 21879–21888 (2019)
2. Lin, F., Zhou, Y., An, X., You, I., Choo, K.-K.R.: Fair resource allocation in an intrusion-detection system for edge computing: ensuring the security of Internet of Things devices. IEEE Consum. Electron. Mag. **7**(6), 45–50 (2018)
3. An, X., Su, J., Lü, X., Lin, F.: Hypergraph clustering model-based association analysis of DDOS attacks in fog computing intrusion detection system. EURASIP J. Wirel. Commun. Network. **2018**(1), 1–9 (2018). https://doi.org/10.1186/s13638-018-1267-2
4. Qing, G., Hongbo, C., Tao, F., et al.: Research status and development trend of the elderly fall detection system. Med. Health Equip. **36**(12), 102–105 (2015)
5. BU Nations: department of economic and social affairs: population ageing 2009. Popul. Dev. Rev. **37**(2), 403 (2011)
6. Wanni, L., Huan, W., Xi, L., et al.: Intervention effect of Alighieri fall risk assessment method in preventing falls in elderly hospitalized patients. Chin. J. Gerontol. **34**(14), 4027–4029 (2014)

7. Xia, Z., Lu, L., Qiu, T., Shim, H.J., Chen, X., Jeon, B.: A privacy-preserving image retrieval based on AC-coefficients and color histograms in cloud environment. Comput. Mater. Continua **58**(1), 27–43 (2019)
8. Suya, Z., Keyan, W., Yanzi, H., et al.: Elderly fall detection algorithm based on SVM_KNN. Comput. Mod. **12**, 49–55 (2017)
9. Xiangxin, Z.: Research on fall monitoring based on a three-dimensional acceleration sensor. Master's thesis of Zhejiang University (2008)
10. Lixin, C.: Research on the wearable fall detection system based on MEMS inertial sensor. Xi'an Jiaotong University (2018)
11. Kwan, M.M., Close, J.C., Wong, A.K., Lord, S.R.: Falls incidence, risk factors, and consequences in Chinese older people: systematic review. J. Am. Geriatr. Soc. **59**(3), 536–543 (2011)
12. Xin, S., Tao, Z.: Design of a wearable fall detection device. Chin. J. Instrum. **33**(3), 575–580 (2012)
13. Fan, Y., Jing, X., Yu, Z., et al.: Fall detection system based on head movement trajectory and 3D vision. Mod. Electron. Technol. **35**(2), 54–57 (2012)
14. Friedman, S.M., Munoz, B., West, S.K., Rubin, G.S., Fried, L.P.: Falls and fear of falling: which comes first? A longitudinal prediction model suggests strategies for primary and secondary prevention. J. Am. Geriatr. Soc. **50**(8), 1329–1335 (2002)
15. Xiaowen, S., Ziwen, S., Fang, Q.: Study on human fall detection based on threshold and PSO-SVM. Comput. Eng. **42**(5), 318–321 (2016)
16. Tong line: study on the identification method of human fall process based on mechanical quantity information acquisition system. University of Science and Technology of China, Hefei (2011)
17. Hadjistavropoulos, T., Delbaere, K., Fitzgerald Ltd.: Reconceptualizing the role of fear of falling and balance confidence in fall risk. J. Aging Health **23**(1), 3–23 (2011)
18. Su, J., Lin, F., Zhou, X., Lu, X.: Steiner tree based optimal resource caching scheme in fog computing. China Commun. **12**(8), 161–168 (2015)
19. Di, X., Jia, L., Qingqing, M., Yanping, X., Yushu, Z.: High capacity data hiding in encrypted image based on compressive sensing for nonequivalent resources. Comput. Mater. Continua **58**(1), 1–13 (2019)
20. Santhosh Krishna, B.V., Gnanasekaran, T.: Retinal vessel extraction framework using modified Adaboost extreme learning machine. Comput. Mater. Continua **60**(3), 855–869 (2019)

A Multi-AGV Optimal Scheduling Algorithm Based on Particle Swarm Optimization

Pingping Xia[1], Aihua Xu[2], and Ying Zhang[3](✉)

[1] Department of Information Engineering, Jiangsu Maritime Institute, Nanjing 211170, China
[2] Nanjing Institute of Science and Technology Information, Nanjing 210018, China
[3] Nanjing University of Information Science and Technology, Nanjing 210044, Jiangsu, China
1175666021@qq.com

Abstract. With the increasing use of AGV in industrial automation system, it is necessary to study reasonable task allocation plan and optimized scheduling of AGV to ensure efficient transportation. This paper proposes a multi-AGV optimal scheduling algorithm based on particle swarm optimization in intelligent warehousing system. Based on the analysis of the operating mechanism of the AGV equipment and the scheduling requirements of the warehouse environment, a mathematical model is established to optimize the scheduling strategy. The minimum value of the objective function of the optimization problem is obtained by using the particle swarm optimization algorithm, that is, the time for the multi-AGV to complete the transportation task in the fixed cycle is the shortest. Combining the characteristics of this problem, the particle swarm optimization algorithm is able to enhance the ability of global search and increase the possibility of finding the optimal scheduling strategy. The simulation results show that the proposed algorithm can shorten the AGV waiting time and improve the system operation efficiency, which provides an optimized and practical way for multi-AGV scheduling in warehouse system.

Keywords: Automatic guided vehicle · Optimal scheduling · Particle swarm optimization · Intelligent warehousing

1 Introduction

The Automatic Guided Vehicle (AGV) is an automatic load transport device that transports objects from one location to another, and is a new alternative to fixed-route conveyors and high-altitude material handling equipment. The AGV is currently controlled by a flexible, online microcomputer that uses intelligent terminals and radio frequency controllers for navigation.

In the process of warehousing and logistics, the time spent in loading, unloading, transportation and other parts accounts for the majority of the entire logistics process

Supported by the Natural Science Foundation of the Jiangsu Higher Education Institutions of China (19KJB520028), and the Shipping Big Data Collaborative Innovation Center of Jiangsu Maritime Institute.

© Springer Nature Singapore Pte Ltd. 2020
X. Sun et al. (Eds.): ICAIS 2020, CCIS 1252, pp. 527–538, 2020.
https://doi.org/10.1007/978-981-15-8083-3_47

time, which results in higher material transportation costs in total cost, and the space utilization rate of logistics warehouses will also decrease. AGV has been widely recognized as a good solution for material handling due to its flexibility, efficiency and flexibility. If the multi-AGV optimization scheduling can be effectively carried out, the logistics transportation system structure can be further improved, the logistics transportation cost can be reduced, and the system operation efficiency can be improved, which has great application value in intelligent warehousing logistics [1, 2].

But the design and control of the AGV system is not an easy task, because it takes into account multiple factors such as scheduling, routing and layout. In the actual warehouse, due to the dynamic changes of AGV, shelf storage and map environment information, complex road conditions can cause blockage and collision problems. Choosing the best set of tasks and the best path for the AGV is a scheduling task. The traditional method uses mathematical programming to seek the optimal solution of the scheduling problem. It regards the scheduling problem as the optimization under the condition of limited resources. The disadvantage of this type of method is that the time consumption increases exponentially as the size of the problem increases. Therefore, in practical applications, it is inclined to replace the purely theoretical optimal scheduling with an approaching optimization schedule.

In recent years, domestic and foreign scholars have conducted in-depth research on AGV path planning and scheduling from different levels and perspectives. For the path planning problem of a single AGV, the global optimal solution is usually solved spatially by genetic algorithm [3], ant colony algorithm [4], particle swarm optimization algorithm [3], etc. Time window can also be added to solve the optimal solution in time and space [5]. Chen Tianjian used the improved Dijkstar shortest path algorithm for multi-AGV path planning [6]. This method reduces the difficulty of multi-AGV path planning and scheduling, but it is computationally intensive and time consuming. Dorigo et al. first proposed the ant colony algorithm [7]. On the basis of this, Yee et al. presented an improved ant colony algorithm [8], which converges quickly when seeking the shortest path, but It is easy to cause local optimum. Kim et al. studied the use of conservative myopic to explore collision-free AGV paths [9], but only for off-line task scheduling and path planning in a few AGV environments. Because neural network algorithm has parallelism, distribution storage, adaptability and other advantages, using it to solve scheduling problems is a promising direction.

This paper considers the scheduling mechanism [10, 11] of AGV in the intelligent warehousing system, and uses the optimized particle swarm optimization algorithm to solve the scheduling problem of AGV. Based on the analysis of the problem, the mathematical model is established and the method of improving the particle swarm optimization algorithm is given. The algorithm is verified by simulation and the rationality of the algorithm is proved. The algorithm can avoid collisions, deadlocks and partial or even large-area congestion problems, and finally achieve stable and efficient operation of the system in complex environments, which provides an effective method and practical approach for AGV scheduling in the warehouse system.

The paper is organized as follows. In Sect. 2, we analyzes the main problems of multi-AGV scheduling and the conflicts that may be encountered in scheduling. The mathematical model of the problem is established on the premise of making reasonable assumptions. The Sect. 3 briefly describes the process of solving multi-AGV scheduling optimization problem based on particle swarm optimization algorithm [12], and analyzes the effectiveness of the algorithm with the simulation results. A brief conclusion follows in Sect. 4.

2 Modeling of Multi-AGV Scheduling Problem in Intelligent Warehousing System

2.1 Analysis of Multi-AGV Scheduling Problem

This paper studies the optimization of AGV scheduling in the context of warehousing logistics. The basic mode of an AGV job is that when the AGV receives a task from the system, it runs from the unloading point of the previous task to the loading point of the current task, and then runs to the unloading point of the current task at full-load, which is regarded as the task completion. Finally, the system will pre-allocate the next task for the AGV. The workflow of the AGV in the actual warehousing system is shown in Fig. 1.

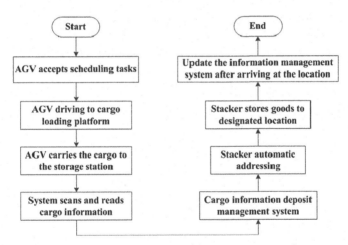

Fig. 1. The flow chart of the intelligent warehousing system automated transportation (taking inbound task as an example)

According to the system operating environment and operation mode of the AGV in actual industrial applications, the following assumptions are made:

- The number of AGVs in the system is known, and each AGV has a constant speed during straight and corner travel under no-load and full-load conditions. Each AGV takes the same time to load and unload cargo, and the time of braking and starting process is negligible.
- The inbound and outbound buffers operate according to the principle of first-come, first-served basis.
- After the current task is completed, each AGV stops next to the unloading position and does not return to its original position.

- The AGV can run to the charging station when the battery is low, and the charging time is constant.
- During the operation of each AGV, the probability of occurrence of all faults is negligible, and manual processing is required after the fault occurs.

The scheduling goal of the AGV in the warehouse system is to find a scheduling scheme that makes the AGV system the most efficient to carry out the handling task, while satisfying the above constraints. Therefore, the scheduling optimization of multi-AGV mainly includes three aspects:

- Determining the allocation relationship between the inbound task and the AGV.
- Determining whether there is a feasible path from the starting point to the target point.
- Planning and scheduling should avoid the occurrence of blocking, conflict and deadlock.

2.2   Overview of Multi-AGV Conflicts

Conflicts, deadlocks, etc. only occur when multi-AGV path planning. Collision conflicts of multi-AGV can be included as node conflicts, opposite conflicts, and chasing conflicts [13]. Since the driving speed of the AGV is assumed to constant, the chasing conflicts of multi-AGV with different speeds in driving are not considered in this paper.

Node Conflict. As shown in Fig. 2(a), the traveling directions of AGV_1 and AGV_2 at the cross node are different, but the two AGVs arrive at the same node at the same time, and finally a node conflict occurs.

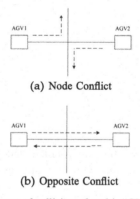

(a) Node Conflict

(b) Opposite Conflict

Fig. 2. Schematic diagram of collision of multi-AGV scheduling warehouse

Opposite Conflict. As shown in Fig. 2(b), the two AGVs travel in opposite directions. Since the two AGVs cannot pass through the path at the same time, a opposite conflict will occur, that is, a deadlock.

The AGV obstacle ultrasonic detector is generally placed directly in front of the direction of travel. When the AGV coming across is detected, it is assumed that the AGV_1 has a lower priority than AGV_2, and AGV_1 is just on the route that AGV_2 needs to travel. At this time, if AGV_1 pauses to avoid, AGV_2 cannot continue to move forward. If the system re-plans the path for AGV_1, because the information is complex and variable, it may cause a chain reaction, and the surrounding AGV needs to be re-planned. This will result in a large amount of computation and temporary local congestion, and sometimes there may be no solution in multi-AGV planning resulting in a final deadlock.

2.3 Multi-AGV Scheduling Model in Intelligent Warehousing System

Considering the impact of the time node of the task on the assignment selection of the AGV task and the effect of the AGV travel path on the total time of the AGV system operation. The following mathematical model was established with the goal of optimizing the total time of operation of the AGV system. The objective function:

$$f = \min\left(\sum_{i=1}^{M}\sum_{j=1}^{Z} t_{ij}X_{ij} + \sum_{i=1}^{M}\sum_{j=1}^{Z} t_{i(j-1)}X_{ij} + \sum_{i=1}^{M}\sum_{j=1}^{Z} L_{ij}X_{ij} + \sum_{i=1}^{M}\sum_{j=1}^{Z} U_{ij}X_{ij}\right), \quad (1)$$

with the restrictions:

$$\sum_{i=1}^{M} X_{ij} = 1 \tag{2}$$

$$\sum_{i=1}^{M}\sum_{j=1}^{Z} X_{ij} = N \tag{3}$$

$$\sum_{j=1}^{Z} t_{ij}X_{ij} \leq T \tag{4}$$

$$t_{ij} = \frac{S_{sj}}{V_s} + \frac{S_{cj}}{V_c} \tag{5}$$

$$t_{i(j-1,j)} = \frac{S_{s(j-1,j)}}{V_s} + \frac{S_{c(j-1,j)}}{V_c} \tag{6}$$

$$T_{ij} = T_i + t_{ij} + t_{i(j-1,j)} \tag{7}$$

Where the Eq. 1 indicates that the total time for the AGV system to complete all tasks is the shortest; the Eq. 2 indicates that each task is completed with only one AGV; the Eq. 3 indicates that the tasks completed in one operation cycle T of the AGV system are all tasks issued by the system, and all the walking processes are controlled by the system; the Eq. 4 indicates that the AGV system must complete all tasks in one cycle T; the Eq. 5 indicates the calculation of the travel time of the AGV from the start position to the end position of the current mission; the Eq. 6 indicates the calculation of the travel time of the AGV from the end position of the previous task to the start position of the current task; the Eq. 7 indicates that the estimated completion time of the tasks is the sum of the completion time of the last task and the estimated operation time of the current task.

Assuming that the number of AGVs in the intelligent Warehousing system is M, and there are N task points that can be loaded and unloaded. A total of Z tasks need to be performed in one cycle T. t_{ij} indicates the time for the ith AGV to do the jth task, and $t_{i(j-1,j)}$ represents the time taken by the ith AGV to reach the start position of the jth task after completing the $(j-1)$th task. T_i represents the travel time required for the ith AGV to complete a task, and L_{ij} and U_{ij} respectively indicate the loading and unloading time of the jth task by the ith AGV. V_s and V_c respectively indicate the speed of the AGV in straight and corner path. $S_{s(j-1,j)}$ and $S_{c(j-1,j)}$ respectively represent the distance of the straight path and the turning path from the unloading position of the $(j-1)$th task to loading position of the jth task and S_{sj} and S_{cj} respectively represent the straight path and the turning path between the loading position and the unloading position of the jth task. T_j indicates the specified time to complete the jth task, T_j indicates the time when the ith AGV completed the most recent work task, and T_{ij} indicates the expected time of the ith AGV completed the jth task. X_{ij} indicates whether the jth task is operated by the ith AGV.

3   Multi-AGV Optimal Scheduling Algorithm Based on Particle Swarm Optimization

The intelligent warehousing system needs to make path planning and scheduling for each AGV in real time. The accuracy and speed of the algorithm directly affect the timeliness and accuracy of the distribution of the warehouse system, so an accurate algorithm is crucial for the warehouse system to solve. The particle swarm optimization algorithm has the advantages of fast convergence and fewer setting parameters, which can reduce the calculation time and improve the logistics transportation efficiency [14–16]. As the particle swarm algorithm has the problems of premature and local optimization, so this paper improves the particle swarm optimization algorithm.

3.1   The Process of Particle Swarm Optimization Algorithm

Encoding and Decoding of Particles. The scheduling of AGV includes the work order of tasks assignment problems, so this paper uses three-dimensional vector groups to represent particles in the particle coding process, as shown in Table 1.

Table 1. Representation of the ith particle

Task number	1	2	3	4	5	...	Z
Task order	d_{i1}	d_{i2}	d_{i3}	d_{i4}	d_{i5}		d_{iN}
Task assignment	z_{i1}	z_{i2}	z_{i3}	z_{i4}	z_{i5}		z_{iN}

Where: Z is the total number of scheduling tasks, M is the total number of AGVs, D is the population of particles; the first dimension represents the number of the AGV task; the second dimension represents the order of tasks. When decoding, the tasks belonging to the same resource are sorted by the particle vector by the size of the $D_{i(1-z)}$ value; the third dimension represents the assignment of the AGV task, giving the upper and lower limits when initializing the particle: $z_{i(1-N)} \in [1, M + 1)$, obtain a natural number between 1 and M by rounding $INT(z_{ij})$, which corresponds to the number of the AGV. Then, when the algorithm is initialized, the range of values of each dimension vector has been given, which is equivalent to the value range of the feasible solution of the particle swarm optimization algorithm.

Objective Function and Constraint Settings. The objective function of the paper is that the total time of the AGV system operation is the shortest, and the uniformity of the AGV assignment task should be considered, each AGV has a certain time for picking and unloading, and only two parts of each task can be changed, Therefore, the time of the AGVs tasks depend only on the time from the current position to the start position of the task and the time from the start position of the task to the end position.

In each queue that will perform the task, first calculate the velocity-displacement based on the encoding of the particles, and then decode the calculated new position of the particle. The first dimension is the task number of the application AGV; the second dimension decoding obtains its order of delivery tasks; the third-dimensional codec obtains the task assignment, that is, the number of the AGV corresponding to the task number. After decoding, determine the departure and destination of each task according to the task order corresponding to each AGV number, the total running time of each AGV is the total running time of the AGV system. Then compare the total running time of all AGVs, find the maximum total time and the maximum running time uniformity of each AGV as the objective function of this iteration.

According to the improved particle swarm algorithm described above, the encoding, decoding, objective function calculation method and pre-allocation strategy of the AGV task. When a task assignment is completed, the system will use the focus of this task as the starting point to pre-allocate the remaining tasks. The implementation of the improved particle swarm optimization algorithm is shown in Fig. 3:

3.2 The Improvement of Particle Swarm Optimization Algorithm

In the basic particle swarm algorithm, $P_i = (p_{i1}, p_{i2},..., p_{iD})$, $i = 1, 2,..., n$ is used to represent the best position that the ith particle has searched so far, also known as the individual extreme value p_{best}. The $P_g = (p_{g1}, p_{g2},..., p_{gD})$ is used to represent the optimal position that the entire particle swarm has searched so far. The global extremum g_{best}, each particle updates its speed and position based on P_g and P_i. All particles update their speed and position according to Eq. 8 and Eq. 9.

$$v_{id}(k + 1) = wv_{id}(k) + c_1 r_1 (p_{id}(k) - x_{id}(k)) + c_2 r_2 (p_{gd}(k) - x_{id}(k)) \quad (8)$$

$$x_{id}(k + 1) = x_{id}(k) + v_{id}(k + 1) \quad i = 1, 2, \cdots, n; d = 1, 2, \cdots, D. \quad (9)$$

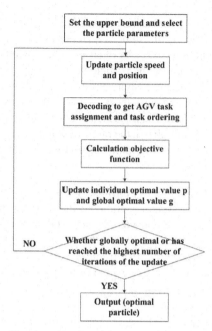

Fig. 3. The flow chart of improved particle swarm algorithm implementation in multi-AGV

Here, the learning factors c_1 and c_2 are non-negative constants, and r_1 and r_2 are random numbers between [0, 1]. $w \geq 0$ is called the inertia weight. If P_g is a local optimal value, the entire particle swarm will quickly converge to near P_g, it is difficult to find the global optimal solution, and the ability to find global optimality is lost.

The specific improvements to the basic particle swarm algorithm in this paper are as follows:

(1) v_{id} improvement

First, the improvement of the individual extremum p_{id} in the particle swarm is as follows

$$P_r = (p_{r1}, p_{r2}, \cdots, p_{rD})r = 1, 2, \cdots, n, \tag{10}$$

where

$$p_{rj} = (p_{1j} + p_{2j} + \cdots + p_{nj})/nj = 1, 2, \cdots, D. \tag{11}$$

The speed of the updated particle is

$$v_{id}(k+1) = wv_{id}(k) + c_1 r_1(p_{rd}(k) - x_{id}(k)) + c_2 r_2(p_{gd}(k) - x_{id}(k)). \tag{12}$$

(2) p_{id} improvement

In the process of evolution, particles learn from other individuals or learn from the best individuals with a certain probability, generally in the early stages of evolution, particles learn from the history of other particles with greater probability, in the later stage, the particles learn from the current global optimal individual with a large probability, this learning method can enhance the search for the overall space. Thereby increasing the probability of finding the global optimal solution.

During the evolution of the tth generation, a random number r between 0 and 1 is randomly generated, and R_i is obtained according to the formula $R_i = t/G_{max}$. If $r > R_i$, randomly select a particle, and use the optimal position of the particle as P_{rnd} instead of p_{gd} in Eq. 12 to update the particle velocity according to Eq. 13; otherwise, according to Eq. 12.

$$v_{id}(k+1) = wv_{id}(k) + c_1 r_1 (p_{rnd}(k) - x_{id}(k)) + c_2 r_2 (p_{gd}(k) - x_{id}(k)),   (13)$$

where t is the current evolutionary algebra, G_{max} is the largest evolutionary algebra, and P_{rnd} is randomly selected from the P_i of other particles and is not equal to p_g.

3.3 Simulation Analysis

By modeling the actual scheduling environment, thus computer simulation of the implementation of a scheduling scheme. Users and researchers can use simulation methods to test, compare, and monitor certain scheduling scenarios to change and select scheduling strategies [17]. Although the study of simulation and the simulation of the scheduling scheme are time consuming, however, in terms of the foresight level of scheduling problem research, simulation has become a method often used by researchers. Taking the actual data of a smart storage system as an example, the AGV scheduling strategy proposed in this chapter is used for analysis and calculation, and the scheduling strategy proposed in this paper is described in detail.

According to the actual working environment of a intelligent warehousing AGV system, a topology simulation method is used to design a map for simulation experiments [18]. To better test the performance of the algorithm, assume that the intelligent warehousing AGV system has a total number of 8 AGVs of the same model, at some point in its mission cycle, the system has 22 tasks, of which the number of outbound tasks is 11 and the number of inbound tasks is 11. According to the data table construction method proposed above, the tasks of the intelligent storage AGV system are analyzed, and the tasks and statuses number table of the the AGVs system is constructed (see Table 2).

In the process of task assignment, this paper aims to solve the model by establishing the mathematical model constructed above and taking the total time of the operation as the goal, and using the improved particle swarm optimization algorithm using Matlab software. Thus, the task assignment results and allocation order of each AGV can be obtained.

Setting the initial conditions of the particle swarm: particle coding uses a three-dimensional vector group, the learning factor c_1 and c_2 are set as 2, the inertia weight w is set as 0.6, maximum number of iterations G_{max} is set as 200, the total number of task schedules z is set as 22, total number of AGVs M is set as 8, the population of particles D is set as 40, the operation precision is set as 0.5.

In each AGV operation, the system completes the assigned tasks without interruption, and at the same time has new tasks to reach the AGV system. After each task is released, the AGV system will again aim at the shortest working time, and under the premise of ensuring the time node, the improved particle swarm algorithm will be used to calculate

Table 2. Assignment table of AGV system tasks and statuses

Number of AGV	Assigned task number	Pre-allocated task task 1 task 2 task 3 task x			AGV status
AGV 1	1	2	16		Occupation
AGV 2	4	3			Occupation
AGV 3	5	6	17		Occupation
AGV 4	7	8	18		Occupation
AGV 5	9	11	22		Occupation
AGV 6	10	13	21		Occupation
AGV 7	12	15	18		Occupation
AGV 8	14	19	20		Occupation

all tasks to be reassigned to each AGV through Matlab software. After the task assignment is updated, the pre-allocated tasks may be completed by other AGVs. The task assignment of the AGV after 15 min is calculated using the data of the current system operation. The updated task assignment table is shown in Table 3.

Table 3. The updated assignment table of AGV system tasks and statuses

Number of AGV	Assigned task number	Pre-allocated task task 1 task 2 task 3 task x			AGV status
AGV 1	32	31	43		Occupation
AGV 2	24	44	33	38	Occupation
AGV 3	27	26	35		Occupation
AGV 4	30	34	36	46	Occupation
AGV 5	29	28	41		Occupation
AGV 6	23	32	42		Occupation
AGV 7	39	34	37		Occupation
AGV 8	25	45	40		Occupation

In order to verify the superiority of the proposed algorithm, a new task for the simulation system to randomly release a cycle is used to compare the results of the scheduling algorithm with the random scheduling. The simulation results show that if the AGV system is continuously iterated according to the schedule of Table 3, the AGV no-load waiting time will be reduced, and the time required to complete the fixed task optimized. In the case of the same path planning, the utilization efficiency of the

AGV is significantly improved. In that the simulation results verify the effectiveness and efficiency of the proposed method.

4 Conclusion

This paper conducts an in-depth study on the optimal scheduling of AGV in automated warehousing logistics. Combined with the on-the-spot investigation of the AGV intelligent warehousing project environment, a mathematical model that meets the practical application value is established. The priority queue of the task is established according to the urgency of the storage task, and the priority of the storage task is dynamically allocated. This step can effectively avoid task hunger and deadlock, so as to find the conflict-free scheduling scheme with the lowest transportation time cost. The particle swarm optimization algorithm heuristically calculates a reasonable solution for the scheduling of multi-AGV by improving the particle update speed v_{id} and the individual extremum p_{id}. The particle swarm optimization algorithm makes the particles learn to the current global optimal individual with a large probability in the calculation. This learning method strengthens the search for the overall space, thereby increasing the probability of finding the global optimal solution. In addition, the algorithm formulates a task pre-allocation mechanism for solving the problem, so that the AGV can invest in the next task as soon as possible after completing the current task, thereby improving the overall operating efficiency of the system. Finally, the reliability of the algorithm is verified by simulation. It is concluded that the algorithm can minimize the time cost of AGV task and improve the efficiency of task scheduling while ensuring that there is no conflict in multi-AGVs. It has certain reference significance for enterprise research AGV intelligent optimization scheduling and planning path.

References

1. Draganjac, I., Miklic, D., Kovacic, Z., et al.: Decentralized control of multi-AGV systems in autonomous warehousing applications. IEEE Trans. Autom. Sci. Eng. **13**(4), 1433–1447 (2016)
2. Zhang, P.: The design of AGV control system and its application in printing center. Adv. Mater. Res. **605–607**, 1696–1699 (2012)
3. Maryam, M.: Multi-objective AGV scheduling in an FMS using a hybrid of genetic algorithm and particle swarm optimization. PLoS ONE **12**(3), 1–24 (2017)
4. Huang, J.Z., Cen, Y.W.: A path-planning algorithm for AGV based on the combination between ant colony algorithm and immune regulation. Adv. Mater. Res. **422**, 3–9 (2011)
5. Smolic-Rocak, N., Bogdan, S., Kovacic, Z., Petrovic, T.: Time windows based dynamic routing in multi-AGV systems. IEEE Trans. Automat. Sci. Eng. **7**, 151–155 (2010)
6. Chen, T.J., Sun, Y., Dai, W., et al.: On the shortest and conflict-free path planning of multi-AGV system based on dijkstra algorithm and the dynamic time-window method. Adv. Mater. Res. **645**, 267–271 (2013)
7. Dorigo, M., Gambardella, L.M.: Ant colony system: a cooperative learning approach to the traveling salesman problem. IEEE Trans. Evolut. Comput. **1**(1), 53–66 (1997)
8. Yee, Z.C., Ponnam, S.G.: Mobile robot path planning using ant colony optimization. In: IEEE/ASME International Conference on Advanced International Mechatronics, pp. 851–856 Singapore (2009)

9. Kim, C.W., Tanchoco, J.M.A.: Operational control of a bi-directional automated guided vehicle systems. Int. J. Prod. Res. **31**(9), 2123–2138 (1993)
10. Lu, T.B., Yan, R., Li, C., Yin, L.H., Chen, H., Zou, X.Y.: SWRR: the link scheduling algorithm based on weighted round-robin. Comput. Mater. Continua **59**(3), 965–982 (2019)
11. Zhang, X.W., Li, Z.H., Liu, G.S., Xu, J.J., Xie, T.K., Nees, J.P.: A spark scheduling strategy for heterogeneous cluster. Comput. Mater. Continua **55**(3), 405–417 (2018)
12. Liu, Z., Xiang, B., Song, Y.Q., Lu, H., Liu, Q.F.: An improved unsupervised image segmentation method based on multi-objective particle, swarm optimization clustering algorithm. Comput. Mater. Continua **58**(2), 451–461 (2019)
13. Miyamoto, T., Inoue, K.: Local and random searches for dispatch and conflict-free routing problem of capacitated AGV systems. Comput. Ind. Eng. **91**, 1–9 (2016)
14. Cao, Y., Wang, L.: Globol path planning for automated guided vehicles based on improved particle swarm optimization. Comput. Eng. Appl. **45**(27), 224–227 (2009)
15. Hu, W.: A simpler and more effective particle swarm optimization algorithm. J. Softw. **18**(4), 861–868 (2007)
16. Hou, Y.B., Yuan, Y.Q., Li, B.P.: Path optimization for automatic guided vehicle based on fusion algorithm of particle swarm and ant colony. Appl. Mech. Mater. **182–183**, 1452–1457 (2012)
17. Lin, J.J., Sun, Y., Zheng, X.J.: Optimal AGV configuration by simulation of flow shop scheduling in an assembly plant. Adv. Mater. Res. **926–930**, 3132–3136 (2014)
18. Beinschob, P., Meyer, M., Reinke, C., et al.: Semi-automated map creation for fast deployment of AGV fleets in modern logistics. Robot. Autonom. Syst. **87**, 281–295 (2016)

An Efficient Quantum Private Comparison Protocol Based on Conjugate Coding

Shimin Liu$^{(\boxtimes)}$

Information and Telecommunication Company, State Grid East Inner Mongolia Electric Power Supply Co., Ltd., Hohhot 010010, China
make163@sina.com

Abstract. Quantum private comparison (QPC) allows at least two participants who do not trust each other to compare whether their secret data are the same while maintaining data privacy. In order to improve the qubit efficiency and avoid using entangled state, we propose an efficient quantum private comparison based on conjugate coding. Our protocol only uses a set of qubits which are X-basis or Z-basis, as the information carrier. Participants use conjugate coding rules to encode their information into these qubits, which is to make the qubit efficiency of the protocol reach 100%. And these qubits transmitted through a circular path, which can effectively reduce resource consumption. Moreover, decoy photon technology and quantum key distribution (QKD) are used to ensure the security of information, making both external and internal attacks invalid.

Keywords: Quantum private comparison · Conjugate coding · Decoy photon · Quantum key distribution

1 Introduction

With the continuous development of science and technology, in today's big data era, safe multi-party computing has attracted the attention of the public, which has sparked a research boom. It has an invaluable research significance for the fields of anonymous authentication, database security query, transmission, and probabilistic verification. Secure multi-party computation (SMC) is the theoretical basis of distributed cryptography [1, 2]. Its main function is that in a multi-user network that is not trusted, each user can collaboratively calculate the result of a function without revealing their private input information. Secure multi-party computing has extremely broad application prospects in the fields of medical, financial, and political.

Unfortunately, the security of SMC schemes based on computational complexity assumptions has been severely challenged with the rapid development of quantum computing [3, 4]. Against such a background, it is of great significance to study the solutions with unconditional security. Quantum secure multi-party computation (QSMC) is a combination of quantum information technology and secure multi-party computing, forming a new interdisciplinary discipline. Due to the introduction of the excellent characteristics of quantum information technology, the QSMC protocol has greatly improved the

© Springer Nature Singapore Pte Ltd. 2020
X. Sun et al. (Eds.): ICAIS 2020, CCIS 1252, pp. 539–548, 2020.
https://doi.org/10.1007/978-981-15-8083-3_48

security, robustness and communication efficiency compared with the classical SMC protocol. Nowadays, there are a lot of research branches in the field of QSMC, among which including the hot topics such as quantum private query [5, 6], quantum oblivious set-member decision [7], and quantum private set intersection cardinality [8, 9] etc.

As an important branch of QSMC, quantum private comparison (QPC) proposed in 2009 [10, 20], aims to solve "Tierce problem" [1, 2, 11, 12] by using some quantum mechanics principles, where "Tierce problem" can be described as follows: Participants Alice and Bob have wealth of x and y respectively, and they are richer by calculating the function f(x, y) without revealing their private wealth. Among them, QPC is divided into two types: quantum private comparison of equality (QPCE) and quantum private comparison in size (SQPC). QPCE has more research results than SQPC. The two-party QPCE can be divided into three categories according to its implementation: based on quantum super-density coding, quantum encryption or quantum entanglement switching. In 2009, the first two-party QPCE protocol was proposed by Yang and Wen [10]. The protocol uses the EPR pair as the information carrier, and uses the Hash function to calculate the hash value of the private information, and encodes the hash value into the quantum state. The unidirectional nature of the Hash function guarantees the security of private information, while using ultra-compact coding schemes to improve quantum utilization. Subsequently, Liu et al. [14] analyzed the protocol, pointing out that the protocol is not secure, because the loyal third party (TP) can perform the "same coincidence attack", thereby increasing the random unitary operation of Liu et al. [13] to resist the "same initial state attack".

In order to improve the efficiency of quantum use, Yang et al. [15] and Liu et al. [17] proposed a novel single-photon QPCE protocol based on quantum super-density coding. In Yang et al., the use of partial decoy photons for channel security detection improves quantum utilization; while in protocols such as Liu, the security of private information is guaranteed by using Hash functions and QKD techniques [15]. In addition, based on the non-maximally entangled state ultra-compact coded QPCE, there are certain research results. In 2011, Liu et al. [18] proposed a QPCE protocol based on a three-particle symmetric W-state. In 2012, in order to further improve the efficiency and security of the protocol, Jia et al. [19] proposed a QPCE protocol based on the four-particle χ-type state, in which $N + N'$ four-particle χ-type states need to be prepared. After that, in order to avoid the possible security risks, three ways are usually adopted in QPC protocols: additional entangled states, decoy photon technology and quantum key distribution (QKD). However, qubit efficiency is not ideal in most quantum private comparison protocols, which is one of the key indicators used to evaluate the efficiency of a QPC protocol. However, only the protocol of Jia et al. [19] currently achieves 100% quantum bit efficiency, while other protocols have a bit efficiency of only 50%. Indeed, there is a trade-off between qubit efficiency and resource consumption, so designing a secure protocol with high qubit efficiency and low resource consumption is often challenging.

To improve the qubit efficiency and guarantee the security, i.e., preventing TP and each party from knowing each party's information, we propose a two-party quantum private comparison protocol based on conjugate coding. In the protocol, we use $\{|0\rangle, |1\rangle, |+\rangle, |-\rangle\}$ as information carrier. The third party firstly generates a sequence qubits from $\{|0\rangle, |1\rangle, |+\rangle, |-\rangle\}$ according to the shared key with Alice, and send these qubits to Alice. Alice gets these qubits and makes unitary transforms on these qubits based on her information and the shared key with Bob. Then, she sends these qubits to Bob. Bob still makes unitary transforms on these qubits as the same way. Finally, Bob sends encoded qubits back to TP. TP also makes unitary transforms on these qubits and determine whether the obtained state is equal to the original state. If it is equal, then Alice's information is as same as Bob's. Note that, they should insert decoy qubits into the sequence to check channel when they transmit these qubits.

The structure of this paper is as follows: Sect. 2 presents some preliminary knowledge about quantum computation and conjugate coding in detail. In Sect. 3, we present the two-party QPC protocol using conjugate coding and bell state and verify the correctness of our protocol. Section 4 analyzes the security of our protocols. Section 5 is devoted to compare our protocols with some existing ones. We summarize this paper in Sect. 6.

2 Preliminaries

2.1 Quantum Computation

As we all know, bits are the basic concept of classical information, and its state is 0 or 1. Similar to the classical position, the quantum bit (called qubit) [21] is the basic unit of quantum information has two possible states $|0\rangle$ and $|1\rangle$, usually called quantum superposition state,

$$|\varphi\rangle = \alpha|0\rangle + \beta|1\rangle \tag{1}$$

where α, β are complex numbers, and $|\alpha|^2 + |\beta|^2 = 1$. $|0\rangle$ and $|1\rangle$ can be represented by vectors,

$$|0\rangle = \begin{bmatrix} 1 \\ 0 \end{bmatrix}, |1\rangle = \begin{bmatrix} 0 \\ 1 \end{bmatrix}. \tag{2}$$

Then, $|\varphi\rangle$ can be expressed in vector form $|\varphi\rangle = \begin{pmatrix} \alpha \\ \beta \end{pmatrix}$.

Similar to the way a classic computer is built from a circuit containing wires and logic gates, a quantum computer is constructed from quantum circuits containing wires and basic quantum gates to carry and manipulate quantum information. Single-qubit gates, such as *Pauli-X*, *Pauli-Z*, and *H (Hadamard)*, are the simplest form of quantum gates, and they can be described as 2×2 unitary matrices as below,

$$X = \begin{bmatrix} 0 & 1 \\ 1 & 0 \end{bmatrix}, Z = \begin{bmatrix} 1 & 0 \\ 0 & -1 \end{bmatrix}, H = \frac{1}{\sqrt{2}} \begin{bmatrix} 1 & 1 \\ 1 & -1 \end{bmatrix}. \tag{3}$$

Multi-qubit gates are also the important units in a quantum circuit. The prototypical multi-qubit quantum logic gate is *controlled-NOT* (i.e., *CNOT*) gate (shown in Fig. 1), which has two input qubits, known as the control qubit and the target qubit, respectively. If the control qubit is set to 0, then the target qubit is left alone. If the control qubit is set to 1, then the target qubit is flipped.

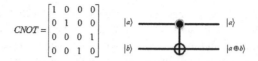

Fig. 1. Matrix representation and quantum circuit of *CNOT* gate.

Besides *CNOT* gate, *Toffoli* gate is another frequently used multi-qubit gate. As illustrated in Fig. 2, *Toffoli* gate has three input bits and three output bits: two of the bits are control bits that are unaffected by the action of the *Toffoli* gate; the third bit is a target bit that is flipped if both control bits are set to 1, and otherwise is left alone.

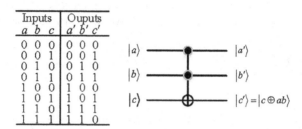

Fig. 2. Truth table and quantum circuit of *Toffoli* gate.

2.2   Conjugate Coding

Then, we introduce the quantum cash scheme based on conjugate coding proposed by Wiesner [22], The bank chooses

$$K = (a_1, b_1, a_2, b_2, \cdots , a_m, b_m), \tag{4}$$

for each banknote with L_K, where L_K is a kind of serial number (used as a label for K) and $a_i, b_i \in \{0, 1\}$. A quantum banknote is $(L_K, |\phi\rangle)$, in which

$$|\phi\rangle = |\psi_{a_1,b_1}\rangle \otimes |\psi_{a_2,b_2}\rangle \otimes \cdots \otimes |\psi_{a_m,b_m}\rangle \tag{5}$$

where $|\psi_{a_i,b_i}\rangle$ is one of four states as below:

$$|\psi_{0,0}\rangle = |0\rangle, |\psi_{1,0}\rangle = |1\rangle, |\psi_{0,1}\rangle = (|0\rangle + |1\rangle)/\sqrt{2}, |\psi_{1,1}\rangle = (|0\rangle - |1\rangle)/\sqrt{2}. \tag{6}$$

The value of b_i determines the basis. If b_i is 0 then a_i is encoded in the Z basis $\{|0\rangle, |1\rangle\}$; otherwise, a_i is encoded in the X basis $\{|+\rangle, |-\rangle\}$. The bank keeps L_K and K in a database and issues a quantum banknote $(L_K, |\phi\rangle)$. A user withdraws a quantum banknote from the bank, pays with the banknote at a shop, and the shop transmits the banknote to the bank for the validity check. The bank measures each qubit $|\psi_{a_i,b_i}\rangle$ in the basis Z (or X) if the b_i in the database is 0 (or 1) and checks whether the result is a_i. Even if just one result does not pass the verification, the bank rejects the banknote. The impossibility of counterfeiting in Wiesner's scheme was shown using the quantum key distribution approach [23].

3 Quantum Private Comparison Based on Conjugate Coding

3.1 Preparation

1. Suppose that Alice and Bob have the secret data X and Y, respectively. X and Y can be converted to binary form, $(x_1, x_2, \cdots, x_M)$ and $(y_1, y_2, \cdots, y_M)$, respectively, where $x_i, y_i \in \{0, 1\}, i \in \{1, 2, \cdots, M\}, X = \sum_{i=1}^{M} x_i 2^{i-1}$ and $Y = \sum_{i=1}^{M} y_i 2^{i-1}$.

2. Alice and Bob divide the $(x_1, x_2, \cdots, x_M)$ and $(y_1, y_2, \cdots, y_M)$ into $\lceil M/2 \rceil$ groups, i.e.,

$$K_A = (G_A^1, G_A^2, \cdots G_A^{\lceil M/2 \rceil}), K_B = (G_B^1, G_B^2, \cdots G_B^{\lceil M/2 \rceil}), \qquad (7)$$

where each group (G_A^j or G_B^j) has two qubits, $j \in \{1, 2, \cdots, \lceil M/2 \rceil\}$ and $i = 2j - 1$. If $M\%2 = 1$, then Alice and Bob must insert a 0 after the last group ($G_A^{\lceil M/2 \rceil}$ and $G_B^{\lceil M/2 \rceil}$) of strings.

3. TP firstly generates an authenticated key sequence $K_{TA} = (G_{TA}^1, G_{TA}^2, \cdots G_{TA}^{\lceil M/2 \rceil})$ with Alice through QKD, where $G_{TA}^j \in \{00, 01, 10, 11\}$. Then, similarly, Alice also generates an authenticated key sequence $K_{AB} = (G_{AB}^1, G_{AB}^2, \cdots G_{AB}^{\lceil M/2 \rceil})$ with Bob. Finally, Bob also needs to generates an authenticated key sequence $K_{BT} = (G_{BT}^1, G_{BT}^2, \cdots G_{BT}^{\lceil M/2 \rceil})$ with TP. Note that, the key generated by QKD is confidential and is always assumed to be secure in QPC.

4. Alice computes $K_A \oplus K_{AB}$ and get the result R_A, where $R_A = (R_A^1, R_A^2, \cdots R_A^{\lceil M/2 \rceil})$ and $R_A^j = G_A^j \oplus G_{AB}^j$. Similarly, Bob also computes $K_{AB} \oplus K_B \oplus K_{BT}$ and get the result R_B, where $R_B = (R_B^1, R_B^2, \cdots R_B^{\lceil M/2 \rceil})$ and $R_B^j = G_{AB}^j \oplus G_B^j \oplus G_{BT}^j$.

3.2 Process of the Proposed Protocol

1. TP prepares a quantum state

$$|\phi_T\rangle = \left|\psi_{G_{TA}^1}\right\rangle \otimes \left|\psi_{G_{TA}^2}\right\rangle \otimes \cdots \otimes \left|\psi_{G_{TA}^{\lceil M/2 \rceil}}\right\rangle \qquad (8)$$

where $\left|\psi_{G_{TA}^1}\right\rangle$ is defined in the same form as Eq. 6, the value of two bits in G_{TA}^j are corresponding to a_j, b_j.

2. TP prepares a set of decoy photons, each of which is randomly selected from four single particle states $\{|0\rangle, |1\rangle, |+\rangle, |-\rangle\}$ ($|\pm\rangle = \frac{1}{\sqrt{2}}(|0\rangle \pm |1\rangle)$). And he inserts these decoy qubits into $|\phi_T\rangle$ at random positions to get $|\phi_T\rangle'$ and records the insertion positions. Then, he sends $|\phi_T\rangle'$ to Alice.

3. When Alice gets $|\phi_T\rangle'$ from TP, TP announces the positions and the state of inserted decoy qubits. Alice verifies that the channel is being eavesdropped by measuring these bait qubits. If the measurement results are not corresponding to the announcement from TP, Alice rejects all of the qubits and lets the TP re-operate Step 1 and 2; otherwise, the protocol will proceed to the next step.

4. Alice removes all decoy photons and applies the following transformation W_A to $|\phi_T\rangle$ according to the value of R_A^j:

$$W_A = U_{R_A^1} \otimes U_{R_A^2} \otimes \cdots \otimes U_{R_A^{\lceil M/2 \rceil}}, \tag{9}$$

where

$$U_{00} = I = \begin{bmatrix} 1 & 0 \\ 0 & 1 \end{bmatrix}, U_{01} = H = \frac{1}{\sqrt{2}} \begin{bmatrix} 1 & 1 \\ 1 & -1 \end{bmatrix},$$

$$U_{10} = XZ = \begin{bmatrix} 0 & -1 \\ 1 & 0 \end{bmatrix}, U_{11} = XZH = \frac{1}{\sqrt{2}} \begin{bmatrix} -1 & 1 \\ 1 & 1 \end{bmatrix}. \tag{10}$$

Alice then obtains $|\phi_A\rangle$ by the unitary transformation

$$W_A : |\phi_T\rangle \rightarrow |\phi_A\rangle. \tag{11}$$

5. Alice prepares a set of decoy photons and inserts them into $|\phi_A\rangle$ to get $|\phi_A\rangle'$ at random. Similarly, she needs to record the positions and the state of these decoy qubits. Then, she sends the $|\phi_A\rangle'$ to Bob.

6. When Bob gets $|\phi_T\rangle'$ from Alice, Alice announces the positions and the state of inserted decoy qubits. After eavesdropping checking (see Step 3), similar to Step 4, Bob performs the corresponding unitary transforms W_B on the $|\phi_A\rangle$ according to the values of R_B^j and gets $|\phi_B\rangle$.

$$W_B = U_{R_B^1} \otimes U_{R_B^2} \otimes \cdots \otimes U_{R_B^{\lceil M/2 \rceil}} \tag{12}$$

7. Similar to Step 5, Bob sends $|\phi_B\rangle'$ which is inserted decoy qubits, to TP.

8. After checking eavesdropper (see Step 3), TP performs the corresponding unitary transforms W_C on the $|\phi_B\rangle$ to get $|\phi_C\rangle$. Then, TP performs the measurement on $|\phi_C\rangle$ according to the process of preparing $|\phi_T\rangle$ in Step 1, and get the result K_C. If $K_C = K_{TA}$, then $X = Y$; otherwise, $X \neq Y$.

$$W_C = U_{R_{BT}^1} \otimes U_{R_{BT}^2} \otimes \cdots \otimes U_{R_{BT}^{\lceil M/2 \rceil}} \tag{13}$$

3.3 Correctness of the Protocol

TP encodes the string bits K_{TA} into the state $|\phi_T\rangle$ based on conjugate coding. Alice performs the unitary transform W_A on the state $|\phi_T\rangle$, i.e., get the string bits $K_{TA} \oplus R_A = K_{TA} \oplus K_A \oplus K_{AB}$ (Hereafter, we ignore the global phase introduced by the operator XZ because the global phase factor does not affect the statistics of a measurement.). Similarly,

Bob performs W_B to get the string bits $K_{TA} \oplus R_A \oplus R_B = K_{TA} \oplus K_A \oplus K_B \oplus K_{BT}$. Similarly, TP performs W_C to get the string bits $K_C = K_{TA} \oplus K_A \oplus K_B$. So, if $K_A = K_B$, then $K_C = K_{TA}$, i.e., $X = Y$; otherwise, $X \neq Y$.

Now let us give an example to verify the correctness. Suppose that $K_{TA} = 01$, $K_A = 10$, $K_B = 10$, $K_B T = 10$, $K_A B = 11$. TP firstly prepares the state $|\phi_T\rangle = |+\rangle$. Then, Alice performs the unitary transform $W_A = H$ on $|\phi_T\rangle$ to get $|\phi_A\rangle = |0\rangle$. Then, Bob performs $W_B = XZH$ on $|\phi_A\rangle$ to get the state $|\phi_B\rangle = -|-\rangle$. Finally, TP performs $W_C = XZ$ on the state $|\phi_B\rangle$ to get the state $|\phi_C\rangle = |+\rangle$. We can see that $|\phi_C\rangle = |\phi_{TA}\rangle$, i.e. $K_C = K_{TA}$. So, $K_A = K_B$. Therefore, we can correctly determine whether X and Y are equal.

4 Security Analysis

We will analyze the security of our protocol in two ways: external attacks and internal attacks. The previous attack refers to the attack of the eavesdropper outside, while the later refers to the attack of the participants and the TP inside.

4.1 External Attacks

In the protocol, when the two parties want to communicate or share the same secret key, we use the QKD method to check whether the channel is security, where QKD has been proved to be perfect security. Besides, we use decoy qubits to prevent the eavesdropper eavesdropping the information, which include the intercept-resend attack, entanglement-measurement attack and so on.

4.2 Internal Attacks

In Step 2, if Bob wants to eavesdrop the information K_{TA} when TP sends $|\phi_{TA}\rangle'$ to Alice, he will be detected as the eavesdropper by decoy qubits. TP and Alice will give up this communication, they will restart communication. Likewise, if Alice wants to eavesdrop the information $K_{TA} \oplus R_A \oplus R_B$ when Bob sends $|\phi_B\rangle'$ to TP in Step 7, she will also detected as the eavesdropper by decoy qubits.

In Step 6, Bob may attempt to measure each qubit in $|\phi_A\rangle$. But Bob cannot know what basis to measure each qubit, which the state of each qubit is composed of different basis (X basis or Z basis). If Bob wants to measure $|\phi_B\rangle$ in Step 7, she cannot know $K_A \oplus K_B$. Because she can only get $K_{TA} \oplus K_A \oplus K_B \oplus K_{BT}$, and cannot get the information of K_{TA}. So, she cannot know the result of $K_A \oplus K_B$.

TP is assumed to be semi-honest and is responsible for preparing the quantum states as the information carriers. So, he will take all possible attack means to steal the participants' data. Especially in Step 5, he may eavesdrop the state $|\phi_A\rangle'$ and resend fake qubits to Bob. When Alice announce the position of decoy qubits, TP may get $K_{TA} \oplus K_A \oplus K_{AB}$ from $|\phi_A\rangle$. But he cannot know K_{AB}, so he can get nothing from this eavesdropping.

5 Performance of the Protocol

We make a comparison between our protocols and several existing protocols in Table 1. We can see that these protocols basically use QKD technology. Although QKD consumes qubit resources, it can guarantee unconditional security. Compared with most existing QPC protocols, our protocols have the following advantages: Firstly, all the qubits are transmitted in a circular path, which makes our protocols have advantages over existing ones in resource consumption. Secondly, Secondly, the qubit efficiency of our protocols is 100%, which is much higher than that of all existing protocols except Jia et al.'s protocol [19]. In Jia et al's protocol, four-particle χ-type states are used as information carriers, dense coding technology and entanglement swapping technology are used to make the qubit efficiency reach 100%. However, the entanglement swapping technology requires additional quantum devices. Finally, all the qubits are not entangled in our protocol, which is easy to implement and compute.

Table 1. Comparison between our protocols and several existing ones.

Ref.	[10]	[24]	[25]	[18]	[19]	[26]	[27]	[28]	Our protocol
QKD	√	√	√	√	×	√	√	√	√
Hash function	√	×	×	×	×	×	×	×	×
Dense coding	√	×	×	×	√	√	√	×	√
Entanglement	×	√	√	√	√	×	√	√	×
Qubit efficiency	25%	33.3%	33.3%	50%	100%	25%	50%	50%	100%
Decoy photons for Eavesdropping checking	√	√	×	√	×	√	√	√	√

6 Conclusion

We have proposed a QPC protocol based on conjugate coding. The qubit efficiency of our protocol is much higher than that of most existing protocols due to the use of conjugate coding technology. Besides, all the qubits are transmitted in a circular path, which makes our protocols have advantages over existing ones in resource consumption. And these qubits are not in entanglement, which is easy to implement and compute. What is more, TP cannot steal the participants' data, and one dishonest participant cannot steal the others' data except in the case where all of the participant's data are the same.

References

1. Boudot, F., Schoenmakers, B., Traore, J.: A fair and efficient solution to the socialist millionaires' problem. Discrete Appl. Math. **111**, 23–36 (2001)

2. Yao, A.C.: Protocols for secure computations. In: Proceedings 23rd Annual Symposium on Foundations of Computer Science, vol. 82, pp. 160164 (1982)
3. Zhang, H.G., Han, W.B., Lai, X.J., Lin, D.D., Ma, J.F., Li, J.H.: Survey on cyberspace security. Sci. China Inf. Sci. **58**(11), 1–43 (2015)
4. Wu, W.Q., Zhang, H.G.: Quantum algorithm to solve function inversion with time–space trade-off. Quantum Inf. Process. **16**(7), 1–10 (2017)
5. Gao, F., Qin, S.J., Huang, W., Wen, Q.Y.: Quantum private query: a new kind of practical quantum cryptographic protocol. Sci. China Phys. Mech. Astron. **62**(7), 1–12 (2019)
6. Wei, C.Y., Cai, X.Q., Liu, B., Wang, T.Y., Gao, F.: A generic construction of quantum oblivious-key-transfer-based private query with ideal database security and zero failure. IEEE Trans. Comput. **67**, 2–8 (2017)
7. Shi, R.H., Mu, Y., Zhong, H., Zhang, S.: Quantum oblivious set-member decision protocol. Phys. Rev. A **92**, 022309 (2015)
8. Shi, R.H., Mu, Y., Zhong, H., Zhang, S., Cui, J.: Quantum private set intersection cardinality and its application to anonymous authentication. Inf. Sci. **370**, 147–158 (2016)
9. Liu, W.J., Xu, Y., Yang, C.N., Yu, W.B., Chi, L.H.: Privacy-preserving quantum two-party geometric intersection. Comput. Mater. Continua **60**(3), 1237–1250 (2019)
10. Yang, Y.G., Wen, Q.Y.: An efficient two-party quantum private comparison protocol with decoy photons and two-photon entanglement. J. Phys. A Math. Theor. **42**, 055305 (2009)
11. Li, S.D., Wang, D.S., Dai, Y.Q., Luo, P.: Symmetric cryptographic solution to Yao's millionaires problem and an evaluation of secure multiparty computations. Inf. Sci. **178**, 244–255 (2008)
12. Yan, L.L., Chang, Y., Zhang, S.B., Wang, Q.R., Sheng, Z.W., Sun, Y.H.: Measure-resend semi-quantum private comparison Scheme using GHZ class states. Comput. Mater. Continua **61**(2), 877–887 (2019)
13. Liu, W.J., Liu, C., Chen, H.W., Li, Z.Q., Liu, Z.H.: Cryptanalysis and improvement of quantum private comparison protocol based on bell entangled states. Commun. Theor. Phys. **62**(2), 210–214 (2014)
14. Liu, W.J., Liu, C., Liu, Z.H., Liu, J.F., Geng, H.T.: Same initial states attack in Yang et al.'s quantum private comparison protocol and the improvement. Int. J. Theor. Phys. **53**(1), 271–276 (2014)
15. Yang, Y.G., Cao, W.F., Wen, Q.Y.: Secure quantum private comparison. Phys. Scr. **80**(6), 065002 (2009)
16. Xiao, H., Zhang, J., Huang, W.H., Zhou, M., Hu, W.C.: An efficient quantum key distribution protocol with dense coding on single photons. Comput. Mater. Continua **61**(2), 759–775 (2019)
17. Liu, B., Gao, F., Jia, H., Huang, W., Zhang, W., Wen, Q.: Efficient quantum private comparison employing single photons and collective detection. Quantum Inf. Process. **12**(2), 887–897 (2013)
18. Liu, W., Wang, Y.B., Jiang, Z.T.: An efficient protocol for the quantum private comparison of equality with W state. Opt. Commun. **284**(12), 3160–3163 (2011)
19. Jia, H.Y., Wen, Q.Y., Li, Y.B., Gao, F.: Quantum private comparison using genuine four-particle entangled states. Int. J. Theor. Phys. **51**(4), 1187–1194 (2012)
20. Liu, W., Liu, C., Wang, H., Jia, T.: Quantum private comparison: a review. Iete Tech. Rev. **30**(5), 439–445 (2013)
21. Nielsen, M.A., Chuang, I.: Quantum Computation and Quantum Information. Cambridge University Press, New York, pp. 1–120 (2002)
22. Wiesner, S.: Conjugate Coding. SIGACT News **15**(1), 78–88 (1983)
23. Lo, H.K., Chau, H.F.: Unconditional security of quantum key distribution over arbitrarily long distances. Science **283**(5410), 2050–2056 (1999)

24. Liu, W., Wang, Y.B.: Quantum private comparison based on GHZ entangled states. Int. J. Theor. Phys. **51**(11), 3596–3604 (2012)
25. Li, J., Zhou, H.F., Jia, L., Zhang, T.T.: An efficient protocol for the private comparison of equal information based on four-particle entangled w state and bell entangled states swapping. Int. J. Theor. Phys. **53**(7), 2167–2176 (2014)
26. Liu, W., Wang, Y. B., Jiang, Z. T., Cao, Y. Z. Cui, W.: New quantum private comparison protocol using χ-Type state. Int. J. Theor. Phys. **51**(6), 1953–1960 (2012)
27. Wang, F., Luo, M., Li, H., Qu, Z., Wang, X.: Quantum private comparison based on quantum dense coding. Sci. China Inf. Sci. **59**, 112501 (2016)
28. Li, C., Chen, X., Li, H., Yang, Y., Li, J.: Efficient quantum private comparison protocol based on the entanglement swapping between four-qubit cluster state and extended Bell state. Quantum Inf. Process. **18**(5), 1–12 (2019)

Deliberated Vulnerable Environment Generating Based on Container and Structured Vulnerability Intelligence

Hailiang Feng and Yugang Li[✉]

Academy of Broadcasting Science, Beijing 100866, China
{fenghailiang,liyugang}@abc.ac.cn

Abstract. The number of vulnerabilities in modern IT systems is explosive growing. Security researchers spend a lot of time on the work of vulnerability reproduce. In this process, an important work is building the vulnerable environment. Traditional technologies have two problems: different vulnerability report format from different sources and lack of network devices simulation. We propose an automatic deliberated vulnerable environment generating framework with network devices simulation based on structured vulnerability intelligence. And we implemented a prototype system to demonstrate the framework.

Keywords: Threat intelligence · Vulnerability intelligence · Deliberated Vulnerable Environment

1 Introduction

The complexity and scale of IT systems have increased dramatically. Meanwhile the number of vulnerabilities in modern IT systems is explosive growing. According to NVD [1], the number of vulnerabilities reported in 2017 has doubled in 2016, and is still increasing in 2018 and 2019. These vulnerabilities make companies, organizations suffer security attacks. To solve this problem, companies and organizations have set up Security Response Center (SRC) [2], use crowdsourcing to detect vulnerabilities and prevent attacks. Security researchers can detect vulnerabilities and report them to SRC.

There are so many vulnerabilities reported, they need to be verified and evaluated. It costs lots of manual workload. For example, it takes 5 h to verify the existence of a vulnerability on average based on vulnerability reports for vulnerabilities on CVE. At the same time, security researchers in these companies and organizations try to build a Deliberated Vulnerable Environment (DVE). With DVE, they can simulate the penetration attack and prevent it.

As we known, most security researchers subscribe some threat intelligence resources [3–5] and build Deliberated Vulnerable Environment manually. Threat intelligence can be found from different resources with different format. Threat intelligence contains information of attack environment, vulnerabilities and others information about security

© Springer Nature Singapore Pte Ltd. 2020
X. Sun et al. (Eds.): ICAIS 2020, CCIS 1252, pp. 549–557, 2020.
https://doi.org/10.1007/978-981-15-8083-3_49

threat. In past years, some researchers focus on create unified format of threat intelligence for communication and automatic analysis. The MITRE Corporation developed Structured Threat Information eXpression (STIX) [6–10]. It is based on standard XML.

The first problem of automatic construction of DVE is inaccurate detail description in vulnerability reports. These inaccurate details may lead to wrong Deliberated Vulnerable Environment and failure of vulnerability reproduce. For automatic building Deliberated Vulnerable Environment, vulnerability intelligence is more specific than threat intelligence. But vulnerability intelligence or vulnerability reports also exists some problem. There are some researchers try to compare format of vulnerability reports [11]. They found there are lots of inaccurate or inconsistencies details in the vulnerability reports. Construct DVE with these reports will get wrong environment.

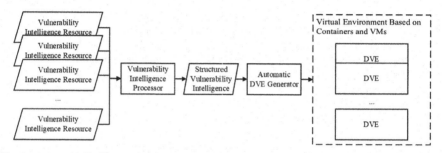

Fig. 1. Automatic Deliberated Vulnerable Environment generating framework based on container and structured vulnerability intelligence.

The second problem is some vulnerability reports can only be found in complex network with different services and devices like routers [12]. Some vulnerability reports of standalone software are easily to be construct. Based on container technology like docker, we can just pull an image of specific version of the software as DVE. But most vulnerabilities are found in real-world business systems. These vulnerable environments consist of different software and complex network devices.

In this paper, we propose an automatic Deliberated Vulnerable Environment generating framework based on container and structured vulnerability intelligence (see Fig. 1). Our contributions are listed as follow: 1. Design an accurate, structured, machine-oriented vulnerability intelligence specification, 2. Use container and network simulator to construct DVE which contain complex network devices, 3. Implement a prototype system to automatic generate DVEs.

2 Related Work

Threat intelligence is hotspot of some security companies and organizations. They proposed different strategy for threat intelligence exchange. Some researchers focus on classifying threat intelligence [13–15]. They also provided an anonymous threat intelligence exchange strategy based on trust. Threat intelligence sharing has an important principle. Organizations or security companies should share threat intelligence based on trust. If the threat intelligence is public and some key information of vulnerabilities is expose to public, may lead to security threat to the affected companies. The exchange strategy is: vulnerability reports only be sharing with the vendors affected by vulnerabilities.

Meanwhile, STIX project creates and refines sharing and structuring threat information. STIX project developed a language to describe cyber threat information. Jessica Steinberger and her partner provided a structured overview of existing exchange formats and protocols [16]. But there is no detail about vulnerabilities in these threat intelligence specifications or languages.

Other researchers focus on cyber range [17, 18]. CyRIS build a cyber range instantiation system [19]. CyRIS define a cyber range with a description file based on YAML. The system can read a description file and construct a cyber range with KVM. But they did not simulate network devices.

3 Vulnerability Intelligence and Deliberated Vulnerable Environment

There are two main parts in the framework:

- **Vulnerability intelligence processor.** The processer will get and parse vulnerability intelligence in different formats from different resources. Then it will generate a standardized, structured, machine-oriented DVE description file.
- **Automatic DVE generator.** The generator is based on virtual machine, docker and simulator. It takes DVE description file as input and create DVE automatically.

To achieve these goals, we need to solve a few problems. First, we need to compare and analysis existing threat intelligence specifications and formats. And find information that can be used for DVE generation. Second, the information in the existing vulnerability reports may not contain key details to reproduce vulnerabilities. We should refine and standardize the details of these vulnerability reports based on the experience and make a specification of vulnerability intelligence. At last, we need build a framework which can simulate network devices.

Vulnerabilities reproduce relies on the experience and skills of security researchers. In order to avoid abuse of vulnerability intelligence, vulnerability reports may hide some key information of vulnerabilities. The lack of key information leads to errors during the automatic DVE generate process. Users will not be able to reproduce the vulnerability in DVE. Therefore, we should analyze which information in the vulnerability reports is important for the automatic DVE generate process.

In this case, we have to make trade-offs in the process of designing vulnerability information specifications. First, we need to filter the source of vulnerability intelligence, select some sources of vulnerability intelligence that can provide vulnerability details as much as possible. At the same time, we compare and analyze the vulnerability reports with different formats and related details of many national vulnerability intelligence sources including CVE, NVD, and CNNVD. According to the manual building process of the vulnerability environment and the virtual environment configuration APIs, we design a vulnerability intelligence specification. The specification of vulnerability intelligence is based on the YAML language and contains the software name, version, operating system and network topology information that may be involved in the process of vulnerability reproduce. Key fields of vulnerability intelligence specification are shown in Table 1.

Table 1. Key information of vulnerability intelligence specification.

Sections	Fields	Description
Basic	Vulnerability-os	Software operating system
	Exploit-os	Exploit operating system
Software	Name	Software name
	Version	Software version
	Dependencies	Software dependencies
	Configuration	Software configuration
	Script	Software startup script
Exploit	Dependencies	Exploit dependencies
	Configuration	Exploit configuration
	Script	Exploit startup script
Vulnerability	Flag	Vulnerability verification flag
	Database	Vulnerability database
	Id	Vulnerability identification
	Type	Vulnerability type
	Effect	Vulnerability effect
	Description	Vulnerability description

Basic Section. All basic elements is in this section.

The vulnerability operating system is the operating system which vulnerable software is running with. The vulnerability may be related with operating system. So the operating system is one of the key information used to reproduce the vulnerability environment.

Exploit Operating system refers to the operating system on which the Proof of Vulnerability (PoV) is based. Exploit and software dependencies may be only be running on specified operating system, so we should indicate the operating system on which the exploit depends on.

Software Section. This section contains information about software in the environment.

The name of software is a basic information of vulnerability. This field used to declare the name of the software affected by the vulnerability. Automatic DVE generator will fetch the software or find related container to build the environment.

The version is another basic information of vulnerability. Most vulnerabilities affect only a few specific versions of the software. We need indicate the specific software versions affected by the vulnerability.

Dependencies of software refers to a list of dependencies package required by the software. Most of modern software cannot run standalone. For reducing development works, developers use some third-party function modules and tools in software development.

Configuration refers to the software configuration used to install and configure the software. And some vulnerabilities can only be triggered in specific configuration. Automatic DVE generator will read this field and make sure the vulnerability will be triggered. Software configuration is also a very important part of the vulnerability, but it is often ignored by researchers. More than 87% of vulnerability reports do not include information such as configuration and options in software installation [20, 21].

Some software should be run with specific arguments and permissions. Security researcher should compose some start-up script. There are many development languages for software configuration scripts, like ansible playbook or YAML file in CI/CD.

Exploit Section. This section contains information of exploit environment.

Exploit dependencies refers to a list of dependencies package required by the software. Exploiting scripts may be rely on some third-party tools like Metasploit. Without these third-party modules or tools, an exploit may fail and it cannot verify that the vulnerability.

Exploit configuration refers to the PoV related configuration that exploits the vulnerability to trigger a specific vulnerability. An important step in automatic DVE generator is to verify that the existing environment does have a target vulnerability, so we should configure the exploit automatically.

Exploit script is programmed by researchers. It can be a single bash command or some script file written by Python, Perl, and etc.

Vulnerability Section. This section contains information of vulnerability.

The vulnerability flag is used to indicate whether the verification exploit script successfully triggered the vulnerability. In the exploit stage, although there are exploit scripts to help us trigger the vulnerability, the trigger may be failed, so we should check whether the vulnerability is already triggered or not. For example, if you want to achieve remote arbitrary code execution, the exploit script can create a flag file in the specified directory after successfully triggering the vulnerability. Then we can judge the status of the vulnerability reproducing by monitor the read and write status of the file in the specified directory.

Vulnerability database defines the source of the vulnerability. This field can be combined with vulnerability identifier to locate the source of the vulnerability intelligence resource. Researchers can find further information there.

Vulnerability identifier is an identifier that uniquely represents the vulnerability. Typical identifier defined by the CVE official is CVE serial number.

Vulnerability type is very important field in this specification. The architecture of vulnerability reproduce environment is completely different for different types of vulnerability. Local file vulnerabilities can only be reproduced by a virtual machine with a specific version of software. But some Web service vulnerabilities may require a set of service software like web server, database server, and etc. We need to indicate the type of vulnerability in this specification.

Vulnerability effect refers to the effect that can be achieved by the exploit. For example, some exploit can achieve remote arbitrary code execution and take the ownership of the target host.

Vulnerability description is some extra information of this vulnerability.

4 Experiments

4.1 Prototype Design

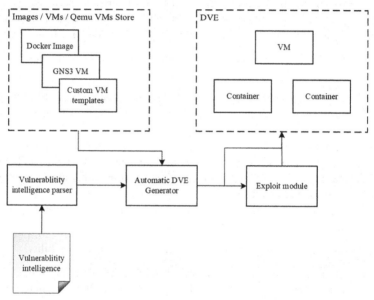

Fig. 2. Flowchart of Automatic Deliberated Vulnerable Environment generating prototype system

We develop a prototype system to verify our ideas. The flowchart of this system is shown in Fig. 2. Vulnerability intelligence parser will parse the vulnerability intelligence file with YAML format. Extract the fields and send to automatic DVE generator. The host module of automatic DVE generator will build the host according to *vulnerability-os, exploit-os, software name, software version*. The configuration module will install all *dependencies* of software, and then run it with *software configuration* and *software script*. When DVE is set up, DVE generator will send exploit information to Exploit module. And Exploit module will install *dependencies* of exploit, configure them and run exploit script according to exploit *configuration* and *script*.

The interface of different module is designed like pipeline operations. After receiving the information send by the vulnerability intelligence parser, the DVE generator will search for specific image or template from the store. Then DVE generator run the host and connect to it for software installation and configuration. After these works, the environment is set up and the vulnerability can be triggered now. In the next stage, the DVE generator configures the host environment to which the exploit belongs. The main steps include installing and configuring dependencies that the exploit depends on, and configuring these dependencies to ensure that the exploit script can execute. The last stage is the vulnerability triggering check phase. The exploit module will attack the automatically built DVE and trigger the vulnerability. The exploit module will continuously monitor the status of the DVE to confirm whether the vulnerability is triggered successfully. We reproduced CVE-2018-7600 to verify the above design (see Fig. 3).

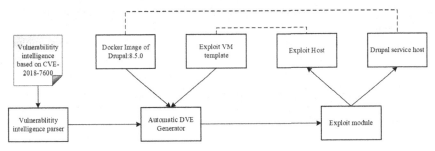

Fig. 3. Vulnerability reproduce process of Drupal

After writing the DVE description file of CVE-2018-7600 vulnerability intelligence, the vulnerability intelligence parser will parse the details. The vulnerability identifier is CVE-2018-7600 and the software name is Drupal and the version of Drupal is 8.5.0. According to the design of the parsing process, the DVE generator can find the corresponding image in the Docker Hub or the self-built docker registry. Take Docker Hub as an example. First DVE generator will search for the software name "drupal", and then look for the TAG which contains version 8.5.0 image in the TAGS list, for example, drupal:8.5.0 image. After finding the available image, the DVE generator calls the Docker API to pull the image file from the Docker Hub, and then configure and launch the container according to the official container configuration commands and parameters.

In this example, the docker image already contains all the dependencies, so we don't have to further configure the dependencies. However, in order to reproduce the runtime environment of this vulnerability, we still need to further configure the software itself in the container of drupal:8.5.0 image. We need to connect to the container and provide configuration files and configuration scripts for targeted settings. After completing the relevant configuration, the DVE can be successfully built.

After the software configuration phase is complete, we can configure the exploit host. Many exploits are based on the same host environment, so we built a series of exploit virtual machine templates. The DVE generator can automatically initialize and configure an attack environment based on these exploit virtual machine templates. In the configuration stage, the DVE generator installs and configures the dependencies of exploit. The type of vulnerability is a remote arbitrary code execution vulnerability, and we can create a file in a specific directory to verify the vulnerability.

Finally, both the DVE and the attack environment have completed the initialization work. We use the Exploit module to drive exploit host attack the DVE. The ideal target for the CVE-2018-7600 vulnerability is remote arbitrary code execution. Therefore, the exploit module monitors the creation of a specific name file in the specified directory, if exploit module finds a file with a specific name, it proves that our vulnerability has been successfully reproduced.

4.2 Implementation

This section will introduce our specific implementation of the above prototype design. We refer to the current virtual environment management configuration tool, such as as Kubernetes, and use YAML language as the basic language of vulnerability information specification.

In terms of virtual environment, we used three virtual environments, including Docker, KVM and Qemu to create various virtual environments to support the simulation of network devices. Corresponding to these three different virtual environments, we built the corresponding docker registry and template library locally. In terms of configuring and running scripts, we mainly wrote a series of software configurations, running scripts based on Python, and combined with bash scripts to complete the specific configuration process of exploit and DVE. In terms of exploits, we mainly use Metasploit as the main exploit framework, and combine some of the exploit scripts with Kali.

5 Conclusion

In this paper, we summarize the problems in the process of recurring vulnerabilities in the automated building system of traditional cyber range types. The study analyzes the impact of some network or software details in the existing vulnerability report on the recurrence of the vulnerability, and proposes a structured and standardized vulnerability intelligence specification for DVE automatic construction. Based on this specification, we designed an automated vulnerability re-creation environment build framework and implemented a prototype system.

References

1. NVD - CVSS Severity Distribution Over Time. https://nvd.nist.gov/general/visualizations/vulnerability-visualizations/cvss-severity-distribution-over-time. Accessed 06 Nov 2019
2. Ruefle, R., Dorofee, A., Mundie, D., Householder, A.D., Murray, M., Perl, S.J.: Computer security incident response team development and evolution. IEEE Secur. Priv. **12**, 16–26 (2014)
3. Magee, J.C., et al.: Collective threat intelligence gathering system (2014)
4. Wang, J., Min-Yi, S., Palkar, P., Ramachandran, S.: Collaborative and adaptive threat intelligence for computer security (2015)
5. Nunes, E., et al.: Darknet and deepnet mining for proactive cybersecurity threat intelligence. In: 2016 IEEE Conference on Intelligence and Security Informatics (ISI), pp. 7–12. IEEE (2016)

6. Barnum, S.: Standardizing cyber threat intelligence information with the structured threat information expression (STIX). Mitre Corporation **11**, 1–22 (2012)

7. Burger, E.W., Goodman, M.D., Kampanakis, P., Zhu, K.A.: Taxonomy model for cyber threat intelligence information exchange technologies. In: Proceedings of the 2014 ACM Workshop on Information Sharing & Collaborative Security, pp. 51–60. ACM (2014)

8. Qamar, S., Anwar, Z., Rahman, M.A., Al-Shaer, E., Chu, B.-T.: Data-driven analytics for cyber-threat intelligence and information sharing. Comput. Secur. **67**, 35–58 (2017)

9. Asgarli, E., Burger, E.: Semantic ontologies for cyber threat sharing standards. In: 2016 IEEE Symposium on Technologies for Homeland Security (HST), pp. 1–6. IEEE (2016)

10. Kampanakis, P.: Security automation and threat information-sharing options. IEEE Secur. Priv. **12**, 42–51 (2014)

11. Menges, F., Pernul, G.: A comparative analysis of incident reporting formats. Comput. Secur. **73**, 87–101 (2018)

12. Chou, T.-S., Jones, J.: Developing and evaluating an experimental learning environment for cyber security education. In: Proceedings of the 19th Annual SIG Conference on Information Technology Education, pp. 92–97. International World Wide Web Conferences Steering Committee (2018)

13. Tounsi, W., Rais, H.: A survey on technical threat intelligence in the age of sophisticated cyber attacks. Comput. Secur. **72**, 212–233 (2018)

14. Mavroeidis, V., Bromander, S.: Cyber threat intelligence model: an evaluation of taxonomies, sharing standards, and ontologies within cyber threat intelligence. In: 2017 European Intelligence and Security Informatics Conference (EISIC), pp. 91–98. IEEE (2017)

15. Syed, Z., Padia, A., Finin, T., Mathews, L., Joshi, A.: UCO: a unified cybersecurity ontology. In: Workshops at the Thirtieth AAAI Conference on Artificial Intelligence (2016)

16. Steinberger, J., Sperotto, A., Golling, M., Baier, H.: How to exchange security events? Overview and evaluation of formats and protocols. In: 2015 IFIP/IEEE International Symposium on Integrated Network Management (IM), pp. 261–269. IEEE (2015)

17. Ferguson, B., Tall, A., Olsen, D.: National cyber range overview. In: 2014 IEEE Military Communications Conference, pp. 123–128. IEEE (2014)

18. Han, W., Tian, Z., Huang, Z., Zhong, L., Jia, Y.: System architecture and key technologies of network security situation awareness system YHSAS. Comput. Mater. Contin. **59**, 167–180 (2019)

19. Pham, C., Tang, D., Chinen, K., Beuran, R.: CyRIS: a cyber range instantiation system for facilitating security training. In: Proceedings of the Seventh Symposium on Information and Communication Technology - SoICT 2016, Ho Chi Minh City, Vietnam, pp. 251–258. ACM Press (2016). https://doi.org/10.1145/3011077.3011087

20. Centonze, P.: Security and privacy frameworks for access control big data systems. Comput. Mater. Contin. **59**, 361–374 (2019)

21. Park, Y., Choi, H., Cho, S., Kim, Y.-G.: Security analysis of smart speaker: security attacks and mitigation. Comput. Mater. Contin. **61**, 1075–1090 (2019)

Deep Neural Network Watermarking Based on Texture Analysis

Kuangshi Wang[1](✉), Li Li[1](✉), Ting Luo[2](✉), and Chin-Chen Chang[3](✉)

[1] School of Computer Science, Hangzhou Dianzi University, Hangzhou 310018, China
1583121815@qq.com, lili2008@hdu.edu.cn
[2] College of Science and Technology, Ningbo University, Ningbo 315212, China
53873308@qq.com
[3] Department of Information Engineering and Computer Science, Feng Chia University,
Taichung 40724, Taiwan
alan3c@gmail.com

Abstract. In recent years, deep neural network is active in the field of computer image vision. The existing digital watermarking technology based on deep neural network can resist image attacks, but image quality is not satisfied. In order to improve the quality of the watermarked images, a neural network watermarking method based on image texture analysis is proposed. Firstly, image texture features are analyzed by gray co-occurrence matrix, and the image is divided into texture complex region and flat region. Secondly, in order to reduce the degree of image modification for better quality, StegaStamp network is adopted to embed the watermark into the flat texture area. Finally, from the perspective of traditional multiplicative watermarking embedding, the watermark embedding process of deep neural network is improved to enhance the watermarked image quality. Experimental results show that the proposed method can effectively improve the quality of the watermarked images without degrading the robustness.

Keywords: Digital watermarking technology · Deep neural network · Image texture analysis · Multiplicative watermarking

1 Introduction

The rapid development of mobile Internet is changing People's Daily life. There are more and more ways for people to get multimedia information, such as digital images, music, short video and so on. The diversity and complexity of multimedia information bring great challenges to humane life and work [1, 2]. Digital image is the most commonly used way of multimedia information interaction in the Internet, and it is easy to be stolen and tampered [3]. In the large-scale e-commerce platform, the updated commodity images reach tens of millions of pieces every day, and piracy emerges in endlessly. In the current digital image network, privacy disclosure and copyright theft have caused huge economic losses to the society. With the improvement of various demands in work and life, people are more and more dependent on sharing digital images in mobile Internet, and image

© Springer Nature Singapore Pte Ltd. 2020
X. Sun et al. (Eds.): ICAIS 2020, CCIS 1252, pp. 558–569, 2020.
https://doi.org/10.1007/978-981-15-8083-3_50

security has become particularly important. Digital watermarking is an effective way to provide image security.

Digital watermarking technology can be classified into fragile watermarking and robust watermarking [4, 5]. Fragile watermarking methods are mainly used for integrity protection and authentication, which embed invisible watermarks in the image content to detect the tamper. When the content is modified, the corresponding watermark is changed to some extent so that the tampered region can be detected. Least significant bit (LSB) replacement is a classic fragile watermarking method that hides secret information by modifying the LSB of each image pixel [6, 7], but it cannot resist image attacks. In the actual scene of digital network, the image will be attacked by different image processing, such as screen shooting, physical print, blur and so on. Robust watermarking methods can resist various attacks for copyright protection and anti-counterfeiting traceability. Robust watermarking technology can be divided into watermarking based on spatial domain and watermarking based on transform domain [4, 5]. For watermarking based on spatial domain, Shi et al. proposed a reversible watermarking method based on image histogram [9, 10], which can resist geometric attacks. However, compared with watermarking based on spatial domain, transform domain watermarking methods can obtain more robustness. Barni et al. embedded watermark into coefficients of DCT transformation, which could resist JPEG compression [8]. Moreover, various transformations are combined to improve the robustness of watermarking. Fazli et al. proposed a robust watermarking method based on DWT, DCT and SVD, which can resist a certain degree of geometric attacks and JPEG compression [11]. However, traditional robust watermarking methods are difficult to resist the joint attacks in real world, such as screen shooting and physical print. Recent research shows that watermarking based on deep neural network has great performance for resist above attacks.

Shi et al. proposed a watermarking method based on deep learning, which has the capability of information hiding but it cannot resist image attacks [12]. Mun et al. used convolutional neural network to embed watermark, which has certain robustness, but it is difficult to resist a higher degree of JPEG compression [13]. Jiren et al. proposed an end-to-end HiDDeN network [14] and introduced various types of noise in the network training process to enhance the robustness of watermarking. HiDDeN is robust to JPEG compression and cropping, but it is difficult to resist the distortion caused by shooting and printing. Compared with HiDDeN network, the StegaStamp network is more robust [15]. The watermarking method based on StegaStamp can resist camera out-of-focus, blur, printer printing distortion, JPEG compression and other attacks. However, the quality of watermarked images generated by StegaStamp network is unstable, and some watermarked images are degraded to poor visualization.

In view of the disadvantages of StegaStamp network, this paper proposes a neural network watermarking method based on image texture analysis to improve the quality of watermarked images. First, by analyzing the texture features of the image, the image is divided into complex texture region and flat texture region, and StegaStamp network is used to embed the watermark into the flat region. In addition, from the perspective of multiplicative watermark embedding, the deep neural network based embedding process is improved, and the watermarked image quality is enhanced. Experimental results show that the proposed method can effectively improve the quality of watermarked images and resist image attacks.

Fig. 1. Framework of watermark embedding and extraction based on StegaStamp network.

2 Related Work

2.1 StegaStamp

Figure 1 presents an overview of StegaStamp network, in the context of a typical usage flow. Encoder and Decoder correspond to the embedding process and extraction process of watermarking, respectively. StegaStamp network differs from existing technologies, because it assumes that the watermarked image is attacked by a variety of perturbations between Encoder and Decoder. The watermarked image is physically printed (or shown on an electronic display) and presented in the real world. The camera then captures the watermarked image printed physically or on the electronic display screen. This kind of process causes the destruction and distortion of the watermarked image to a large extent. After the basic positioning and correction of the obtained watermark image, the watermark can be detected by using Decoder. Encoder uses a U-Net [16] style architecture and the embedding processes of watermark are listed as follows:

Step 1. The watermark is firstly replicated in space to form a watermark volume of the same size and channel as the input image.

Step 2. The extended watermark volume is concatenated to the image to form an intermediary representation and then sent into the Encoder. This ensures that each convolutional filter in the next layer has access to the entire message as it convolves across each spatial location.

Step 3. After more convolutional layers, the image and watermark are fully integrated, and the Encoder produces the watermarked image.

The Decoder is a network trained to recover watermarks from the watermarked image. It uses spatial transformation network [17] that can resist the attack of perspective change. The watermarked image passes through a series of convolution and, dense layers and a sigmoid to obtain the final output with the same length as extract the watermarks.

2.2 Additive and Multiplicative Watermarking

Digital watermarking technology mainly includes two key links of watermark embedding and extraction. For identification or verification watermarking channel [18, 19], a watermark is embedded at the transmission end. In the literature, the embedding makes use of either an additive watermark embedding rule or a multiplicative one. The commonly used additive embedding criterion is defined as

$$y_i = x_i + \gamma w_i \quad i = 1, \ldots, N \tag{1}$$

$X = \{x_1, \ldots, x_N\}$ is a sequence of data from the cover (transformed) image, $W = \{w_1, \ldots, w_N\}$ is a sequence of watermark, γ is a gain factor (also known as weight factor), and $Y = \{y_1, \ldots, y_N\}$ is a sequence of watermarked image. The common multiplication embedding rule is defined as

$$y_i = x_i(1 + \gamma w_i) \quad i = 1, \ldots, N \tag{2}$$

The above watermarking embedding criteria are called additive and multiplicative watermarking, respectively.

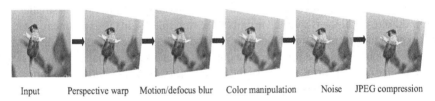

| Input | Perspective warp | Motion/defocus blur | Color manipulation | Noise | JPEG compression |

Fig. 2. Image perturbation pipeline.

3 Proposed Watermarking Method

In the following, network training, image texture analysis and watermark embedding are described in detail.

3.1 Network Training

During the training, images from large data sets are used in combination with random binary watermarks. At the same time, a set of differentiable image disturbances, as shown in Fig. 2, are applied between the encoder and decoder to approximate the distortion. A network of critic is used to predict whether a watermark is embedded in an image and is used as the perceived loss of the Encoder/Decoder pipeline. The network consists of a series of convolutional layers and max pooling. The critic training process is to first classify the input and watermarked images, and then Wasserstein loss [20] is used as the supervisory signal. The critic and encoder/decoder are trained together. In order to minimize the perceptual distortion of watermarked images, the system uses the weighted sum of three image loss terms (residual regularization, perceptual loss, critic loss) and the cross entropy message loss.

3.2 Image Texture Analysis

The proposed texture analysis method based on StegeStamp network improves the quality of watermarked images. Experimental data show that the qualities of StegaStamp network-generated watermarked images are related to the contrast of the cover image. The lower the contrast value, the higher the quality of watermarked images generated by StegaStamp network. Contrast statistics comes from the gray co-occurrence matrix [21, 22] in the cover image. The formula of contrast is defined as

$$Con = \sum_i \sum_j i - j^2 P(i,j) \tag{3}$$

$i - j$ represents the difference between a pixel and its neighboring pixel, and $P(i, j)$ represents the probability that the pair of pixels will appear as neighboring pixels.

At first, when entering a cover image, make a reasonable partition. Then the gray co-occurrence matrix of each block and the contrast of each block are calculated. Finally, compared the contrast of each block with the threshold set, if the value is smaller than the threshold, the block is selected to embed the watermarks. In the experiment, Sect. 4.1 will explain the setting of threshold. This method improves the operation of the network greatly. On the one hand, it improves the quality of watermarked images by the network. On the other hand, it further analyzes the applicability of the network and improves the utilization rate of the network.

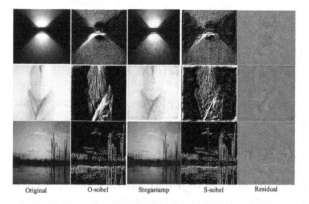

Original   O-sobel   Stegastamp   S-sobel   Residual

Fig. 3. Sobel operator edge detection images.

3.3 Watermark Embedding

Firstly, it is proved from two perspectives that the embedding watermarks generated by StegaStamp network are multiplicative watermark. Secondly, according to the viewpoint of multiplicative watermarking, a new watermarking embedding process based on StegaStamp network is proposed.

From an intuitive point of view, additive watermark is evenly distributed linearly on the image. Additive watermarking images have searchable visual distribution patterns, such as similar changes in adjacent pixels. Multiplicative watermarking image is the opposite, because multiplicative factors will lead to the complexity and irregularity of the data. The contour and edge of the watermarking image with multiplicative feature are protruding, and the modification of adjacent pixels is quite different. As illustrated in Fig. 3, the Sobel operator [23, 24] is used to detect the edges of the cover image and the watermarked image, respectively. It retains the important structural attributes of the image, presents the contour and edge of the whole image, and also shows the obvious difference between the images. The sharp change of watermarked image and residual image is in the edge contour, which is not the effect that additive watermarking can be achieved. Therefore, it is judged that the watermark embedding mode is multiplicative watermarking.

From the perspective of the counter-evidence method, the StegaStamp network embedding watermark method is similar to the multiplicative watermark. Firstly, on the basis of the cover image, subtract the residual image (the amount of change between the watermarked image and the cover image) to obtain a difference image. Then, the StegaStamp network is used to embed the same watermark in the difference image to generate a new watermarked image. Finally, the Decoder network is used to extract watermark from the watermarked image. If the embedding watermark generated by StegaStamp network is additive watermarks, the above process is equivalent to the image not being altered, or causes only minor changes. It contradicts the definition of additive watermarking. The conclusion is that watermark embedding by using StegaStamp network are multiplicative watermark.

In the following, it is explained that watermark embedding based on StegaStamp is the multiplicative watermarking. The traditional multiplicative watermarking embedding process is to simulate the proposed embedding process based on StegaStamp network.

$$y_i = x_i(1 + \gamma w_i) \quad i = 1, \ldots, N \tag{4}$$

$$z_i = y_i - x_i = x_i \gamma w_i \quad i = 1, \ldots, N \tag{5}$$

$$c_i = x_i - z_i = x_i(1 - \gamma w_i) \quad i = 1, \ldots, N \tag{6}$$

$$g_i = c_i(1 + \gamma w_i) = x_i \left[1 - (\gamma w_i)^2 \right] \quad i = 1, \ldots, N \tag{7}$$

where $X = \{x_1, \ldots, x_n\}$ is a sequence of data from the (transformed) cover image. $W = \{w_1, \ldots, w_n\}$ is a sequence of watermark signals. γ is a gain factor (also known as weight factor. In the deep neural network, it can be understood as the sum of encoded bits, anti-interference ability and the weight of image texture features during training. $Y = \{y_1, \ldots, y_n\}$ is a sequence of the cover watermarked image data, and $Z = \{z_1, \ldots, z_n\}$ is a sequence of the residual image data. $C = \{c_1, \ldots, c_n\}$ is a sequence of data from the difference image after processing, and $G = \{g_1, \ldots, g_n\}$ is a sequence of the new watermarked image data. The formula (4) represents the original network embedding watermarking process. Formula (4), (5), (6) and (7) are combined to form a new embedding process. By comparing Y and G from the formula, when $\gamma w_i < 1$, the change in G is less than the change in Y, therefore the quality of the watermarked image will be improved.

Figure 4 shows the overall flow chart of the proposed method. Firstly, the cover image was segmented and texture analyzed. Second, select the block less than the threshold value and embed the watermarks by using the new embedding process based on StegaStamp network. Finally, the obtained watermarked image block will replace the original block.

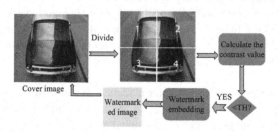

Fig. 4. Flow chart of the proposed method.

4 Experimental Results and Discussion

During the StegaStamp network training, using images from the MIRFLICKR dataset [25], we resampled the images to 400 × 400 pixels. The trained network determines the watermark length to be 100 bits because it provides a good tradeoff between image quality and information transmission. At least 56 correction bits are encoded using BCH code [26] with an estimated recovery accuracy of at least 95%. 100 images from the MIRFLICKR dataset [25] were randomly selected for the experiment. The method proposed in this paper is compared with Matthew's method [15] in terms of visual quality and robustness.

4.1 Visual Quality

Peak signal-to-noise ratio (PSNR) is used to evaluate watermarked image quality [27].

$$PSNR = 10 \times \log_{10}\left(\frac{(2^n - 1)^2}{MSE}\right) \tag{8}$$

$$MSE = \frac{1}{H \times W} \sum_{i=1}^{H} \sum_{j=1}^{W} \left(Y(i,j) - Y'(i,j)\right)^2 \tag{9}$$

where Y and Y' represent the luminance component of the cover image and the watermarked image, respectively, for YcbCr [28], H and W are the height and width of the image, respectively, and n is the number of bits per pixel. MSE represents the Mean Square Error of the watermark image Y and the cover image Y'.

In order to show why we choose contrast as the important factor for texture analysis, the mean values of four statistics of homogeneity, energy, correlation and contrast in the gray co-occurrence matrix of 10 cover images in four directions were calculated

Table 1. Texture analysis statistics table.

Index	PSNR	Contrast	Homogeneity	Energy	Correlation
0	26.59	6.07	0.60	0.04	0.85
1	26.92	4.26	0.62	0.02	0.88
2	28.59	3.18	0.63	0.04	0.71
3	28.84	2.01	0.77	0.05	0.87
4	28.81	1.26	0.83	0.07	0.91
5	29.91	1.22	0.84	0.08	0.94
6	31.40	1.14	0.88	0.06	0.96
7	31.01	0.87	0.95	0.36	0.99
8	32.03	0.37	0.89	0.11	0.99
9	33.02	0.12	0.96	0.09	0.99

as shown in Table 1. Homogeneity, energy and correlation are not directly related to the change of PSNR. Contrast is particularly prominent, and the lower the contrast, the higher the watermarked image quality. Empirically, the contrast threshold of image texture analysis is set as 1.2.

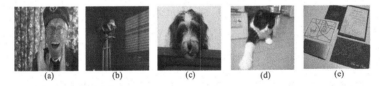

(a)   (b)   (c)   (d)   (e)

Fig. 5. Test images. (a) Old man, (b) Red house, (c) Dog, (d) Cat, and (e) Painting.

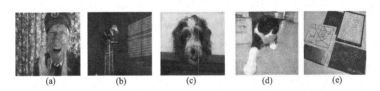

(a)   (b)   (c)   (d)   (e)

Fig. 6. Watermarked images.

As shown in Fig. 5, 5 cover images were selected as tested images. Figure 6 shows the watermarked images by using the proposed method, and it is obvious that the watermarked images are imperceptive.

In order to show the objective quality of the proposed method, PSNRs are compared with those of Matthew's method as shown in Table 2. PSNRs of the proposed method are higher than those of Matthew's method. Especially for images (a) and (c), it is 1 dB higher than those of Matthew's method. It is easily concluded that the proposed embedding method is beneficial to the generation of high qualities watermarked images by StegaStamp network.

Table 2. PSNR comparison of different methods.

Images	Matthew's method [15]	The proposed method
(a)	29.14	30.39
(b)	31.50	33.16
(c)	30.78	31.90
(d)	32.03	32.35
(e)	29.90	30.43

4.2 Robustness

In order to prove the robustness of the proposed embedding method while guaranteeing high quality watermarked images, a series of attack tests are also conducted in this section. In order to obtain the numerical results of robustness, an attack set is used. This attack set consists of 10 attacks, which are listed as in Table 3. Table 4 shows the extraction rates of watermarks under different attacks by the two methods. The data in the table indicate that the proposed method and Matthew's method [15] have a similar extraction rate. Therefore, it is proved that the proposed method can not only obtain great quality watermarked images, but also ensure the robustness of watermarking.

Table 3. Different attacks.

Index	Attacks
0	No attack
1	Perspective warp: up to ± 40 pixels from their original coordinates
2	Motion/defocus blur: straight line blur kernel with a width between 3 and 7 pixels
3	Color Manipulation: Hue shift, Desaturation, Brightness and contrast
4	Gaussian noise: sampling the standard deviation $\sigma \sim U[0, 0.2]$
5	JPEG compression (QF = 20%)
6	Positive Shoot: The distance is set to 30 cm
7	Lateral Shoot: 45° angle
8	Post print shooting
9	Salt and pepper noise (0.05)
10	Gamma Correction (0.2)

Table 4. Accuracy of watermark extraction accuracy.

Attacks	Matthew's method [15]	The proposed method
0	100%	100%
1	100%	100%
2	100%	100%
3	98%	98%
4	100%	100%
5	100%	100%
6	98%	98%
7	96%	96%
8	96%	96%
9	100%	100%
10	100%	100%

5 Conclusion

Based on StegaStamp network, this paper proposes a neural network watermarking method based on image texture analysis. The method improves the shortcomings of the original network and ensures the quality of watermarked images generated by the network. In addition, from the perspective of traditional multiplicative watermarking, a new embedding method based on StegaStamp network is proposed. The proposed embedding method not only guarantees the watermarking robustness, but also improves the qualities of watermarked images greatly. In the experiments, it is proved that the proposed method can effectively improve the quality of watermarked images and resist some attacks.

Acknowledgments. This work was partially supported by National Natural Science Foundation of China (No. 61971247, No. 61370218), and Public Welfare Technology and Industry Project of Zhejiang Provincial Science Technology Department (No. LGG19F020016).

References

1. Wason, R., Jain, V., Narula, G.S., Balyan, A.: Deep understanding of 3-D multimedia information retrieval on social media: implications and challenges. Iran J. Comput. Sci. **2**(2), 101–111 (2019)
2. Zhang, H., Wei, Z.: Risk management of commodity trade business based on deep learning and parallel processing of visual multimedia big data. Multimedia Tools Appl. **79**(13), 9331–9349 (2019). https://doi.org/10.1007/s11042-019-7508-5
3. Dou, K., Guo, B., Kuang, L.: A privacy-preserving multimedia recommendation in the context of social network based on weighted noise injection. Multimedia Tools Appl. **78**(19), 26907–26926 (2017). https://doi.org/10.1007/s11042-017-4352-3

4. Cox, I.: Digital watermarking. J. Electron. Imaging **11**(3), 414 (2002)

5. Podilchuk, C.I., Delp, E.J.: Digital watermarking: algorithms and applications. IEEE Signal Process. Mag. **18**(4), 33–46 (2001)

6. Xia, Z., Wang, X., Sun, X., Liu, Q., Xiong, N.: Steganalysis of LSB matching using differences between nonadjacent pixels. Multimedia Tools Appl. **75**(4), 1947–1962 (2014). https://doi.org/10.1007/s11042-014-2381-8

7. Luo, W., Huang, F., Huang, J.: Edge adaptive image steganography based on LSB matching revisited. IEEE Trans. Inf. Forensics Secur. **5**(2), 201–214 (2010)

8. Barni, M., Bartolini, F., Cappellini, V.: A DCT-domain system for robust image watermarking. Sig. Process. **66**(3), 357–372 (1998)

9. Shi, Y.Q.: Reversible data hiding. In: Cox, I.J., Kalker, T., Lee, H.-K. (eds.) IWDW 2004. LNCS, vol. 3304, pp. 1–12. Springer, Heidelberg (2005). https://doi.org/10.1007/978-3-540-31805-7_1

10. Shi, Y.Q., Ansari, N., Su, W., Ni, Z.: Reversible data hiding. IEEE Trans. Circuits Syst. Video Technol. **16**(3), 354–362 (2006)

11. Fazli, S., Moeini, M.: A robust image watermarking method based on DWT, DCT, and SVD using a new technique for correction of main geometric attacks. Optik-Int. J. Light Electron Opt. **127**(2), 964–972 (2016)

12. Shi, H., Dong, J., Wang, W., Qian, Y., Zhang, X.: SSGAN: secure steganography based on generative adversarial networks. In: Zeng, B., Huang, Q., El Saddik, A., Li, H., Jiang, S., Fan, X. (eds.) PCM 2017. LNCS, vol. 10735, pp. 534–544. Springer, Cham (2018). https://doi.org/10.1007/978-3-319-77380-3_51

13. Mun, S.M., Nam, S.H., Jang, H.U., Kim, D., Lee, H.K.: A robust blind watermarking using convolutional neural network. arXiv:1704.03248 [cs.MM] (2017)

14. Zhu, J., Kaplan, R., Johnson, J., Fei-Fei, L.: HiDDeN: hiding data with deep networks. In: Ferrari, V., Hebert, M., Sminchisescu, C., Weiss, Y. (eds.) ECCV 2018. LNCS, vol. 11219, pp. 682–697. Springer, Cham (2018). https://doi.org/10.1007/978-3-030-01267-0_40

15. Matthew, T., Ben, M., Ng, R.: StegaStamp: invisible hyperlinks in physical photographs. arXiv preprint arXiv:1904.05343 (2019)

16. Ronneberger, O., Fischer, P., Brox, T.: U-Net: convolutional networks for biomedical image segmentation. In: Navab, N., Hornegger, J., Wells, W.M., Frangi, A.F. (eds.) MICCAI 2015. LNCS, vol. 9351, pp. 234–241. Springer, Cham (2015). https://doi.org/10.1007/978-3-319-24574-4_28

17. Jaderberg, M., Simonyan, K., Zisserman, A., Kavukcuoglu, K.: Spatial transformer networks. In: Neural Information Processing Systems (2015)

18. Cheng, Q., Huang, T.S.: Robust optimum detection of transform domain multiplicative watermarks. IEEE Trans. Signal Process. **51**(4), 906–924 (2003)

19. Sadreazami, H., Ahmad, M.O., Swamy, M.N.S.: Multiplicative watermark decoder in contourlet domain using the normal inverse gaussian distribution. IEEE Trans. Multimedia **18**(2), 196–207 (2015)

20. Arjovsky, M., Chintala, S., Bottou, L.: Wasserstein generative adversarial networks. In: International Conference on Machine Learning (2017)

21. Huang, Z.K., Li, P.W., Hou, L.Y.: Segmentation of textures using PCA fusion based Gray-Level Co-occurrence Matrix features. In: International Conference on Test and Measurement, Hong Kong, pp. 103–105 (2009)

22. Baraldi, A., Parmiggiani, F.: An investigation of the textural characteristics associated with gray level cooccurrence matrix statistical parameters. IEEE Trans. Geosci. Remote Sens. **33**(2), 293–304 (1995)

23. Kanopoulos, N., Vasanthavada, N., Baker, R.L.: Design of an image edge detection filter using the sobel operator. IEEE J. Solid-State Circuits **23**(2), 358–367 (1988)

24. Kuppili, S.K., Prasad, P.M.K.: Design of area optimized sobel edge detection. In: Jain, L.C., Behera, H.S., Mandal, J.K., Mohapatra, D.P. (eds.) Computational Intelligence in Data Mining - Volume 2. SIST, vol. 32, pp. 647–655. Springer, New Delhi (2015). https://doi.org/10.1007/978-81-322-2208-8_59

25. Huiskes, M.J., Lew, M.S.: The MIR flickr retrieval evaluation. In: ACM International Conference on Multimedia Information Retrieval (MIR 2008), Vancouver, Canada (2008)

26. Bose, R.C., Raychaudhuri, D.K.: On a class of error correcting binary group codes. Inf. Control **3**(1), 68–79 (1960)

27. Huynh-Thu, Q., Ghanbari, M.: Scope of validity of PSNR in image/video quality assessment. Electron. Lett. **44**(13), 800–801 (2008)

28. Soleimanizadeh, S., Mohamad, D., Saba, T., Rehman, A.: Recognition of partially occluded objects based on the three different color spaces (RGB, YCbCr, HSV). 3D Res. **6**(3), 22 (2015). https://doi.org/10.1007/s13319-015-0052-9

A Robust Reversible Image Watermarking Scheme Based on Singular Value Decomposition and Quantization Technique

Zhihao Chen[✉]

Shanghai University, Shanghai 200444, People's Republic of China
charlieczh@shu.edu.cn

Abstract. In this paper, we present a robust reversible watermarking scheme, which is capable of embedding both robust and fragile data in one image at the same time. If the image with watermarking is unaltered during transmission, the intended receiver can restore the original copy of the cover image. Otherwise, if the watermarked copy is processed in some way, although we may loss the fragile data, the robust information is still supposed to be recovered. The robustness is achieved by modulating the maximum SVD (Singular Value Decomposition) coefficients of image blocks by QIM (Quantization Index Modulation), and the fragile message for reversibility is embedded using histogram shifting. Compared with the other state-of-the-art schemes, our method has more advantages on robustness and visual quality. The experimental results show that the proposed scheme is robust to a series of attacks.

Keywords: Robust reversible watermarking · SVD · Histogram shifting · QIM · Copyright protection

1 Introduction

With the rapid development of internet and big data technology, digital images are being transmitted all the time via social apps, and networks which allows it to be easily intercepted, copied and spread by criminals. Then it breeds out the particular importance of protecting information transmission security. Digital watermarking technology appeared as a new method of ensuring information security. By embedding digital information into various digital media as a carrier, people cannot visually observe the existence of hidden watermark, and basically does not affect the related use, preventing tampering, attack and counterfeiting of digital products effectively.

Reversible watermarking is a special type of image watermarking, which helps to restore the exact original cover image after data extraction. Based on this, robust reversible image watermarking offers robustness other than reversibility. Its main feature is that it can withstand a certain degree of attacks. Of course, when the watermarked image is not attacked, and the original copy of the cover image can be perfectly restored.

In 2003, De Vleeschouwe proposed a method of mapping transformation [1, 2]. This method can resist certain JPEG compression, but does not deal with the salt and pepper noise generated after the watermark is embedded, resulting in a decrease in robustness. Ni uses a method of dividing an image into several sub-blocks and using differences of the pixels as a statistic [3, 4]. Li then improved the use of histogram bin, and increased the information embedding capacity, but the high algorithm cost caused the high-overflow problem [5]. Kim also proposed a watermark algorithm based on the block of gravity center [6]. Using frequency-domain methods, the statistical characteristics of the original image can be reused. In 2007, Coltuc proposed a two-stage approach to the implementation of robustness and reversibility [7]. To achieve robustness, the image is transformed from the spatial domain to the frequency domain by DCT transform and the information is hidden in DCT coefficients. The information in the frequency domain can still be extracted after being attacked. To achieve reversibility, the fragile information is processed and embedded in side information, the difference of the watermarked image and the original image. Such information cannot be restored after being attacked, but it can be exactly extracted in a non-destructive environment. However, the amount of side information data is too large, which has a great influence on the image quality after embedding the watermark. Subsequently, An L *et al.* [8] designed a robust reversible watermarking scheme with histogram translation, wavelet transform and clustering as key points. It effectively improves the robustness and reduces the degree of calculation, thus improving the image quality.

Singular value decomposition (SVD) [9] becomes popular recently, because it can resist attacks and provide good robustness. Liu *et al.* proposed a scheme that the water-mark image is embedded into the singular value matrix of its host [10]. The SVD is repeated in the embedding matrix to find a modification singular value matrix and then saves twice the size of the information of host protected image during watermark embed-ding. Bao and Ma [11] embed the watermark to the SVs of all block-based wavelet coef-ficients in certain sub-bands. The scheme of Mohammad *et al.* divides the host image into several blocks, and each block utilizes SVD to embed a watermark bit [12]. First, the host protected image is used DWT to generate four reference sub-images. Then, any reference sub-images are chosen for SVD utilization during watermark embedding [13]. The major drawback if it is that they need to use extra information, such as part information of host protected image or watermark image in watermark extraction.

In this paper, SVD value modulation and histogram shifting techniques are used to achieve both robustness and reversibility of our proposed watermarking scheme. First, the image is divided into non-overlapping pixel blocks and then each block is fed to SVD. The robust message is embedded by modifying the maximum SVD value of each block by Quantization Index Modulation (QIM) [14, 15]. Secondly, the information of how the SVD values are modified is encoded and embedded in the pixels of the corresponding image block by histogram shifting. If the watermarked image is unaltered, the receiver can read the information for restoration first, and then recover the original SVD values and the original image cover. Otherwise If the image is compressed, it is not likely to completely restore the image, but the robust message is expected to be read since the robustness is ensured by SVD and QIM.

The rest of the paper is organized as follows. In Sect. 2, we briefly introduce the SVD and QIM techniques. In Sect. 3, the details of the embedding and extraction processes of the proposed scheme are described. In Sect. 4, comparative experiments are conducted and experimental results are provided and analyzed. Finally, the conclusions are given in Sect. 5.

2   Backgrounds

There are two techniques that are related to the proposed image watermarking scheme, i.e., SVD and QIM. The proposed scheme uses the SVD technique and QIM technique for robust embedding. These techniques are described in this section.

2.1   Singular Value Decomposition (SVD)

The singular value decomposition (SVD) technique is a very powerful tool for matrix decomposition, and it can be used in many in many tasks, such as image recovery, signal processing and numerical analysis, etc.

The SVD of a square pixel matrix A of size $N \times N$ can be represented by

$$A = USV^T = [u_1, u_2, \ldots, u_n] \begin{bmatrix} \sigma_1 & 0 & & 0 \\ 0 & \sigma_2 & \cdots & 0 \\ \vdots & & \ddots & \vdots \\ 0\,0 & & & \\ 0\,0 & & \cdots\,\sigma_n & \end{bmatrix} [v_1, v_{2,\ldots,}v_n]^T \tag{1}$$

In the equation above, both U and V are $N \times N$ orthogonal matrices, which means that $U \times U^T = 1$ and $V \times V^T = 1$. The vectors of u_n are called left singular vectors, the vectors of v_n are called right vectors and S is called a diagonal matrix of singular values. Its special property is that when the rank of the picture A (matrix A) is m, the matrix S ($S = diag(\sigma_1, \sigma_2, \ldots, \sigma_m, \ldots, \sigma_N)$) satisfies $\sigma_1 \geq \sigma_2 \geq \cdots \geq \sigma_m \geq \sigma_{m+1} = \ldots = 0$. Then several attractive properties for applications of image processing can be drawn from the special property mentioned above. The attractive properties of the singular values are explained as following three:

1) Property for rotation: The image matrix of A^r is transformed from the A image matrix by rotating. Then A's singular values and the A^r's are the same.
2) Property for transpose: The image matrix of A^t is transposed from the matrix of the image A. Then the singular values of A and the singular values of A^t are the same.
3) Property for translation: The matrix is of A^T is translated from the matrix of image A by adding rows and columns of black pixels. Then the singular values of A and the singular values of A^T are the same.

Thanks to these properties, the watermark can still be extracted with few losses from the attacked watermarked image, even if the watermarked image is corrupted by attacks.

2.2 Quantization Index Modulation (QIM)

Quantization index modulation is a class of provably good methods for digital watermarking and information embedding [14], and its operation can be either scalar or vector. Because the operation of vector QIM on each dimension is similar to that of scalar QIM, our proposed scheme implements one-dimensional QIM algorithm.

As what Fig. 1 is depicted, The QIM applies different quantization methods to embed the bits of hidden information in the original signal. In this figure, every point is marked as either ● or ○, both of them represent the reconstruction points of two quantitative methods respectively. When the bit of the hidden information m equals to 1, the point is quantified to the nearest ●; when the bit of the hidden information m equals to 0, the point is quantified to the nearest ○.

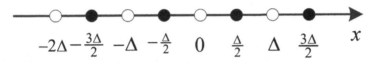

Fig. 1. Schematic diagram of reconstruction points hidden by QIM information

Let x ($x = (x_1, x_2, \ldots, x_n)$) be the original carrier signal and m ($m = (m_1, m_2, \ldots, m_n)$) the message bit vector. Here, Δ stands for the quantifying step size, s ($s = (s_1, s_2, \ldots, s_n)$) stands for steganographic signal, $round(\bullet)$ denotes the function to get the nearest integer.

Then the embedded process of QIM technique can be presented as the following:

$$s_i = round\left(\frac{x_i}{\Delta}\right) \cdot \Delta + m_i \cdot \frac{\Delta}{2} \tag{2}$$

And the extraction process can be presented as the following:

$$m_i = \begin{cases} 0, |s_i| mod \Delta \in [0, 0.25\Delta) \cup [0.75\Delta, \Delta) \\ 1, |s_i| mod \Delta \in [0.25\Delta, 0.75\Delta) \end{cases} \tag{3}$$

The Eq. (3) means that when s_i is closer to $(k + 0.5) \cdot \Delta$ (near the ● in the Fig. 1), the decode is 1; when s_i is closer to $k \cdot \Delta$ (near the ○ in the Fig. 1), the decode is 0.

QIM can be carried out on pixels, sample points or transform domain coefficients in space-time domain. The advantages of the QIM algorithm is high embedding rate and good robustness.

3 Proposed Scheme

In our proposed scheme, the watermark is embedded into the cover image by a series of actions including SVD, QIM and histogram shifting. The details of the watermark embedding and extraction procedures are described as follows.

3.1 Watermarking Embedding

During the embedding process, the SVD technique, the QIM technique and the histogram shifting technique are used subsequently.

The overall embedding process is depicted in Fig. 2. After image partition, each pixel block is fed to SVD, then the largest singular value is altered by QIM to carry robust information. After that, the information about how the value is altered is encoded and embedded in the pixel block by histogram shifting.

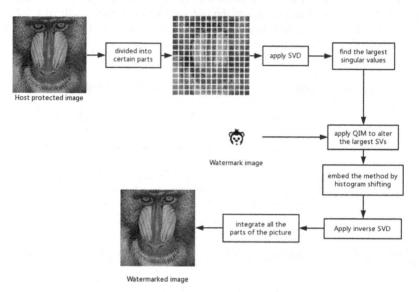

Fig. 2. The watermarking embedding procedure.

The detailed embedding steps are described as follows:

Step 1: Divide the cover image I into pixel blocks ($N \times N$).

Step 2: Apply SVD to each pixel block I, and get the largest singular value denoted as σ_{max}.

Step 3: Using QIM to embed 1 bit of the watermark into σ_{max}.

Step 4: Embed the information of how we alter the σ_{max} by histogram shifting. For example, if σ_{max} is added by 31, the embedded bit sequence is "111111". Note that, the first bit indicates whether it is added or subtracted. So, if σ_{max} is subtracted by 31, the corresponding bit sequence should be "011111".

Step 5: Obtain the watermarked image I_w by inverse SVD.

3.2 Watermarking Extraction

The extraction process does not require either the original cover image or the original watermark image. As shown in Fig. 3, the main extraction steps are introduced as follows:

Step 1: Divide the watermarked image I_w into $N \times N$ pixel blocks

Step 2: Block by blocks, obtain the histogram and extract the bits indicating how σ_{max} was altered.

Step 3: Apply SVD to each block and recover the largest singular values σ_{max} according to the information acquired in Step 2.

Step 4: Recover the original cover image block by inverse SVD.

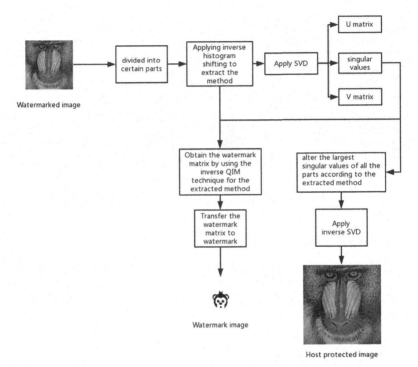

Fig. 3. The watermarking extraction procedure

The original cover image can be fully recovered provided that the watermarked image is not attacked. However, if the watermarked image has to go through certain processing, it is still possible to exact the robust watermarking information with a low error rate, which will be demonstrated in the next experiment section.

4 Experiments

In this section, experiments are carried out to demonstrate the effectiveness of our proposed method. We embed a 32×32 binary watermark image (see Fig. 4) into several 512×512 images (see Fig. 5) using our proposed scheme, and different quantization step values are tested. The robustness is evaluated by testing the achieved bit error rate under various attacks including JEPG compression of different quality factors (QFs), adding Gaussian, Salt and Pepper noises, rotation, cropping and resizing.

Fig. 4. Binary watermark image

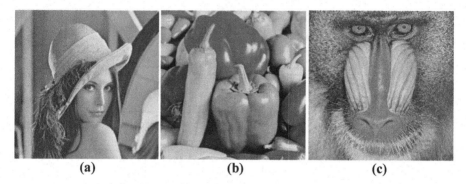

(a)   (b)   (c)

Fig. 5. Used cover images: (a) Lena (b) Pepper (c) Baboon

4.1 Experimental Setups

The original covers are 512×512 grayscale (8-bit) bmp images. The image is partitioned into 16×16 pixel blocks. For QIM, the considered quantization step values are 20, 24, 28 and 32 cover image. To perform JPEG compression attacks are set to 60, 65, 70, 75, 80, 85, 90 and 95.

4.2 Results and Discussions

Performance of Different Quantization Step Values. This part shows the impact of the quantization step choices and symbol error rate (SER) under JPEG compression attacks with different QFs, the used original cover image is Lena.bmp (Fig. 5(a)).

When the quantization step is set to 20, the peak signal-to-noise ratio (PSNR) between the cover image and the image with watermark is 47.0129. When the quantization step is 24, the PSNR between the cover image and the image with watermark is 46.7310. When the quantization step is 28, the PSNR between the cover image and the image with watermark is 45.6508. When the quantization step is 32, the PSNR between the cover image and the image with watermark is 45.0476.

$$SER = symbol\ error / the\ amount\ of\ all\ the\ symbols \qquad (4)$$

The following table (see Table 1) shows the achieved SERs using different quantization step values and different QFs.

Performance Under Different Attacks. In this part, more attacks are leveraged to test the achieved visual quality and robustness of our proposed method.

Table 1. Achieved SERs of different quantization step values and different QFs.

QF	Quantization step			
	20	24	28	32
95	0	0	0	0
90	0	0	0	0
85	0	0	0	0
80	0.0020	0	0	0
75	0.0244	0.0020	0	0
70	0.0684	0.0303	0.0088	0
65	0.0938	0.0420	0.0156	0.0068
60	0.1689	0.0977	0.0518	0.0225

The PSNR measures the visual quality of watermarked images and the normalized correlation coefficient (NC) measures the robustness.
The NC is defined as:

$$NC = \frac{\sum_{i=0}^{size-1} \sum_{j=0}^{size-1} W(i,j) W'(i,j)}{\sum_{i=0}^{size-1} \sum_{j=0}^{size-1} \bar{W}(i,j)^2} \tag{5}$$

$$\bar{W} = \begin{cases} W, & if\ W \geq W' \\ W', & if\ W < W' \end{cases} \tag{6}$$

Here W denotes the original watermark image, W' represents the extracted watermark image and $\bar{W}$ is used to preserve the values lies between 0 and 1.

To test the robustness of the proposed watermarking algorithm, the watermarked images are processed by a set of attacks including JPEG compression, adding Salt and Pepper noises, Rotation, Cropping and Resizing. For further analysis, the Pepper and the Baboon image are attacked and the results are shown in Table 2 and Table 3. The first row is JPEG compression with QF set to 65. The second row is Salt and Pepper noise whose density is set to 0.001. The third row is Rotation by 90°. The fourth row is Cropping with 25% and the fifth row is Resize from 512×512 to 256×256 and then back to 512×512 again.

Comparisons with Existing Techniques. For comparison, A. A. Mohammad *et al.'s* method [12] is also implemented. In this part, five types of attack, i.e., JPEG compression, Salt and Pepper noises, Rotation, Cropping and Resizing are leveraged to show the performances of the two methods.

The JPEG compression uses a QF of 70. The image is cropped by 25%. The Salt and pepper noise density is set to 0.05. The rotation for the image is 90°. For the resize,

Table 2. Extraction results under different attacks (Pepper)

Attack type	Attacked image	Extracted watermark image	NC	SER	PSNR (dB)
JPEG compression QF = 65			1	0	32.0366
Salt and pepper value = 0.001			1	0	32.4944
Rotation (90°)			0.6672	0.4141	10.4491
Cropping (25%)			0.7922	0.1309	11.3678
Resize (512 → 256 → 512)			0.9953	0.0029	31.3157

Table 3. Extraction results under different attacks (Baboon)

Attack type	Attacked image	Extracted watermark image	NC	SER	PSNR (dB)
JPEG compression QF = 65			1	0	32.5734
Salt and pepper value = 0.001			1	0	32.3707
Rotation (90°)			0.6672	0.4141	13.3565
Cropping (25%)			0.7922	0.1309	10.5404
Resize (512 → 256 → 512)			0.9984	0.0010	28.4463

the image will be resized to the shape of 256 × 256 and then resized to the shape of 512 × 512.

The results are recorded in Table 4, which shows that our proposed scheme has an equivalent performance in achieved visual quality, but outperforms its competitor in robustness by a large margin.

Table 4. Comparisons with Mohammad's method

Attacks	Mohammad's method		Our method	
	PSNR (dB)	NC	PSNR (dB)	NC
JPEG compression (QF = 70)	37	0.3563	36.5701	0.9984
Salt and pepper (value = 0.05)	18	0.1791	18.4727	0.5093
Rotation (90°)	11	0.4682	11.1518	1
Cropping (25%)	12	0.7797	11.6744	0.7922
Resize (512 → 256 → 512)	34	0.2479	33.7937	0.9721

5 Conclusions

This paper presents a robust reversible watermarking scheme, which is capable of embedding both robust and fragile data in one image at the same time. The robust information is embedded using a combination of the SVD and QIM techniques, and the fragile information used for reversibility is embedded by histogram shifting. Experimental results indicate that, compared with other similar watermarking schemes, our method has more advantages on robustness and visual quality. It is robust to image processing attacks including JPEG compression, Gaussian filtering, noise adding, cropping, rotation and resizing.

References

1. De Vleeschouwer, C., Macq, B.: Circular interpretation of bijective transformations in lossless watermarking for media asset management. IEEE Trans. Multimedia 5(1), 97–105 (2003)
2. De Vleeschouwer, C., Delaigle, J.F., Macq, B.: Circular interpretation of histogram for reversible watermarking. In: Proceedings of the IEEE Workshop Multimedia Signal Process, October 2001, pp. 345–350 (2001)
3. Ni, Z., Shi, Y.Q., Ansari, N., et al.: Robust lossless image data hiding designed for semi-fragile image authentication. IEEE Trans. Circuits Syst. Video Technol. 18(4), 497–509 (2008)

4. Ni, Z., Shi, Y.Q., Ansari, N., Su, W., Sun, Q., Lin, X.: Robust lossless image data hiding. In: Proceedings of the IEEE International Conference on Multimedia Expo, June 2004, pp. 2199–2202 (2004)

5. Li, X., Zhou, Q.: Robust lossless image data hiding with statistical quantity shifting. J. Image Graph. **17**(11), 1359–1366 (2012)

6. Kim, K.S., Lee, M.J., Suh, Y.H., et al.: Robust lossless data hiding based on block gravity center for selective authentication. In: IEEE International Conference on Multimedia and Expo 2009, ICME 2009, pp. 1022–1025. IEEE (2009)

7. Coltuc, D.: Towards distortion-free robust image authentication. J. Phys. Conf. Ser. **77**(1), 012005 (2007)

8. An, L., Gao, X., Li, X., et al.: Robust reversible watermarking via clustering and enhanced pixel-wise masking. IEEE Trans. Image Process. **21**(8), 3598–3611 (2012)

9. Ganic, E., Eskicioglu, A.M.: Robust DWT-SVD domain image watermarking: embedding data in all frequencies. In: Proceedings of International Workshop on Multimedia and Security, pp. 166–174 (2004)

10. Liu, R., Tan, T.: An SVD-based watermarking scheme for protecting rightful ownership. IEEE Trans. Multimedia **4**(1), 121–128 (2002)

11. Bao, P., Ma, X.: Image adaptive watermarking using wavelet domain singular value decomposition. IEEE Trans. CSVT **15**(1), 96–102 (2005)

12. Mohammad, A.A., Alhaj, A., Shaltaf, S.: An improved SVD based watermarking scheme for protecting rightful ownership. Signal Process. **88**(9), 2158–2180 (2008)

13. Bhatnagar, G., Raman, B.: A new robust reference watermarking scheme based on DWT-SVD. Comput. Stand. Interfaces **31**(5), 1002–1013 (2009)

14. Chen, B., Wornell, G.W.: Quantization index modulation: a class of provably good methods for digital watermarking and information embedding. IEEE Trans. Inf. Theory **47**(4), 1423–1443 (2001)

15. Oostveen, J., Walker, T., Staring, M.: Adaptive quantization watermarking. In: Proceedings of SPIE – IS&T Electronic Imaging, vol. 5306, pp. 296–303 (2004)

16. Jayashree, N., Bhuvaneswaran, R.S.: A robust image watermarking scheme using Z-transform, discrete wavelet transform and bidiagonal singular value decomposition. Comput. Mater. Contin. **58**(1), 263–285 (2019)

17. Zhang, Y., Ye, D., Gan, J., Li, Z., Cheng, Q.: An image steganography algorithm based on quantization index modulation resisting scaling attacks and statistical detection. Comput. Mater. Contin. **56**(1), 151–167 (2018)

18. Chen, Y., Yin, B., He, H., Yan, S., Chen, F., Tai, H.: Reversible data hiding in classification-scrambling encrypted-image based on iterative recovery. Comput. Mater. Contin. **56**(2), 299–312 (2018)

Boolean Function Decomposition Based on Grover Algorithm and Its Simulation Using Quantum Language Quipper

Dong Wang[1], Yiwei Li[2], Edison Tsai[2], Xiaoyu Song[2], Marek Perkowski[2], and Han Li[1(✉)]

[1] Henan University, Kaifeng 475001, HA, China
4837068@qq.com
[2] Portland State University, Portland, OR 97201, USA

Abstract. Decomposition of functions is a general method frequently used in binary logic circuit synthesis, Data Mining and Machine Learning. Ashenhurst-Curtis (AC) decomposition belongs to one of the best known decomposition methods. However, it is really challenging to find the exact minimum AC decomposition for large functions because it requires many exhaust searches. In the hope that large scale quantum computers will be build in the future, we propose an quantum approach based on Grover algorithm to find the optimal AC decomposition in terms of partition theory. The detailed quantum circuit design was created and simulated using Quipper language. According to the experimental results, it is learnt that the quantum algorithm presented in this paper can decompose Boolean function successfully with almost 100% probability and $o\left(\sqrt{N}\right)$ iterations.

Keywords: Grover algorithm · Boolean function decomposition · Partition · Quipper · Ashenhurst-Curtis

1 Introduction

Function decomposition converts a large function into a structured network of small simple functions and eliminates redundant functions, so as to reduce the complexity and cost of function implementation. Ashenhurst-Curtis (AC) decomposition is one of the most famous Boolean function decomposition methods [1]. In 2010, Scholl used function decomposition as a key technology to describe the logic synthesis of Field Programmable Gate Array (FPGA) [2]. In 2016, Alexander proposed the algebraic model design for digital system debugging based on function decomposition [3]. In 2014, Bouyer used the theory of function decomposition to conduct data mining in cloud computing to improve the online education system and achieved good results [4]. With the rapid growth of various applications, the theory of functional decomposition itself is also being perfected.

This work was supported by Henan Natural Science Foundation under Grant 192102210271, Henan University Graduate Education Innovation and Quality improvement project-Graduate Education Innovation Training Base under Grant syl18020105.

X. Sun et al. (Eds.): ICAIS 2020, CCIS 1252, pp. 582–592, 2020.
https://doi.org/10.1007/978-981-15-8083-3_52

In 1995, Luba first proposed the universal method of Boolean function decomposition [5]. In 2006, Lee summarized the related methods of function decomposition of logic circuit [6]. In 2015, Afshord proposed to optimize the function decomposition process by partitioning input variables using the Trivariate matrix covering method [7].

However, decomposition of complex functions is a difficult problem. The space-time complexity of the algorithm is quite high. In order to accelerate solving problem, we design and implement a quantum framework for decomposition of functions, embed it into Grover's quantum algorithm [8], based on which quadratic speedup of function decomposition is obtained. The simulation experiment results show that the quantum function decomposition algorithm we designed effectively reduces the space-time complexity of function decompostion.

2 Preparatory Knowledge

Definition 1. The minterm of n variables in the truth table is sequence number of n input variables, which is expressed by m. As shown in Table 1. Input variable $X = \{a, b, c, d, e\}$, output variable is f. There are 8 minterms: m_1–m_8, where $m_1 = \{00000\}$, $m_4 = \{01010\}$ and so on. Let $A = \{a, b, c\}$, $B = \{d, e\}$, then $A \subseteq X$, $B \subseteq X$. m_A means that in the minimum item the value of the variable that belongs to the set A is reserved, so $m_{4A} = \{010\}$, $m_{4B} = \{10\}$. The minterm is often expressed directly in numbers.

Table 1. Sample of boolean function

Minterm	A			B		
	a	b	c	d	E	f
1	0	0	0	0	0	0
2	0	0	0	0	1	1
3	0	0	0	1	0	0
4	0	1	0	1	0	0
5	1	0	1	0	0	1
6	1	0	1	0	1	0
7	1	1	0	1	0	0
8	1	1	0	1	1	1

Definition 2. Unidentifiable relationship between two minterms is represented by IND. $m_1, m_2 \in IND(B)$ iff $m_{1B} = m_{2B}$. As shown in Table 1, $m_{1B} = \{00\}$, $m_{5B} = \{00\}$, then $m_1, m_5 \in IND(B)$. likewise, $m_2, m_6 \in IND(B)$, $m_3, m_4, m_7 \in IND(B)$.

Definition 3. The partition of set S is nonempty set and represented by π_s, which satisfies the condition $B \neq \phi$ for all $B \in \pi_s$, $B_i \cap B_j = \phi$ and $\bigcup_{B \in \pi_s} = S$. B is called partition block. The every element in S must belong to one of these partition blocks.

For example. $\pi_{S1} = \{\{1, 2\}, \{3, 5\}, \{4\}\}$ is a partition of $S = \{1, 2, 3, 4, 5\}$, $\pi_{S2} = \{\{1, 2\}, \{1, 3, 5\}, \{4\}\}$ is not a partition of S because the intersection between the first element and the second elements is not empty. $\pi_{S3} = \{\{1, 2\}, \{3, 5\}\}$ is not a partition of S because that the union set of all elements in π_{S3} is not S.

Definition 4. Y is the set of input or output variables, $B \subseteq Y$, $P(B)$ represents a partition which obtained by dividing minterm set M into equivalence classes according to $IND(B)$. In Table 1, $B = \{d, e\}$, $P(B) = \{\{1, 5\}, \{2, 6\}, \{3, 4, 7\}, \{8\}\}$.

Definition 5. Given two partitions of S: π_1, π_2. $\pi_1 \geq \pi_2$ *iff* $B \in \pi_2$, $\exists B' \in \pi_1$ and $B \subseteq B'$. Of course, there may not be any size relation between two different partitions of one set.

Definition 6. $\pi_1 \cdot \pi_2 = \{B_1 \cap B_2 | B_1 \in \pi_1, B_2 \in \pi_2, B_1 \cap B_2 \neq \phi\}$. The product of two partitions is a new partition of a set, $\pi_1 \cdot \pi_2 \leq \pi_1$ and $\pi_1 \cdot \pi_2 \leq \pi_2$. Such as if $\pi_1 = \{\{1, 3, 4\}, \{2, 5, 6\}\}$, $\pi_2 = \{\{1, 3, 5\}, \{2, 4, 6\}\}$ then $\pi_1 \cdot \pi_2 = \{\{1, 3\}, \{4\}, \{5\}, \{2, 6\}\}$.

3 Decomposition of Boolean Function

3.1 Serial Decomposition

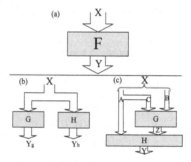

Fig. 1. Schematic diagram of function decomposition, (a) Function F with input X and output Y (b) Parallel decomposition (c) Serial decomposition

Theorem 1 [5]. The serial decomposition as shown in Fig. 1(c) exists if and only if there is a partition $\prod_G$ satisfying the following two conditions simultaneously. Theorem 1 is used to calculate G and H.

$$\prod_G \geq P(B \cup C) \tag{1}$$

$$P(A) \cdot \prod_G \leq P_F \tag{2}$$

Definition 7. m' and m'' are two minterms of original function F, and they belong to the same block in partition $\prod_G$, if and only if $G(m'_{B \cup C}) = G(m''_{B \cup C})$, so if G is determinted then $\prod_G$ is uniquely determinted. $\prod_G$ is a partition of minterms of F corresponding to the outputs of G whose inputs are $B \cup C$. The number of blocks in $\prod_G$, $NB(\prod_G)$, just is the number of outputs of G and determine the number of output variables N_G, $N_G = \lceil \log_2 NB(\prod_G) \rceil$. In the same way, P_F is a partition of minterms of F corresponding to the outputs of F whose inputs are X.

Once the set of input variables, A, B, C is determined and $\prod_G$ is found, the truth table of G and H can be easily derived from $P(A)$, $\prod_G$, P_F. So, The problem of serial decomposition is transformed into the problem of finding $\prod_G$. From theorem 1, it is known that we need to found out $P(A)$, $P(B \cup C)$, P_F in order to find out $\prod_G$.

Calculating $P(A)$, $P(B \cup C)$ and P_F. Because at the beginning of the algorithm running it is not known how to divide X into A, B, C to get $\prod_G$, we must keep trying to divide the input variables into different A, B, C, and thus $P(A)$ and $P(B \cup C)$ are constantly changing. In order to ensure the efficiency and speediness of the algorithm, we design a quantum circuit to calculate $P(A)$ and $P(B \cup C)$, as shown in Fig. 2.

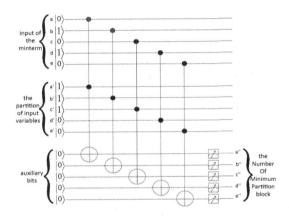

Fig. 2. The quantum circuit to generate partition of minterms

According to definition 5, in order to compare the size relations of two partitions P_1, P_2, it is necessary to verify whether any two minterms belong to the same partition block in P_2, if so, then verify whether these two minterms belong to the same partition block in P_1. For all of the minterms, if these two verifications are valid then there is $P_1 \geq P_2$. To complete the verification, we need to numbered each partition block. The length of block number is $\lceil \log n \rceil$.

Quantum circuit to verify whether two minterms belong to the same block is shown in Fig. 3. If the partition numbers of two minterms are the same, they are in the same partition block (equivalence relation).

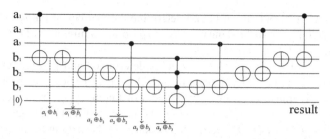

Fig. 3. The quantum circuit to calculate whether two minterms belong to the same block

If any two minterms in P_2 belong to the same partition block, these two minterms also belong to the same partition block in P_1, which is a typical implication relation, $x \rightarrow y \Leftrightarrow \overline{x} + y = \overline{x \cdot \overline{y}}$, its quantum circuit is shown in Fig. 4.

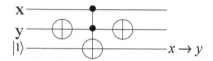

Fig. 4. The quantum circuit of implication relation

The quantum circuit comparing the size relation between two partitions is shown in Fig. 5, where "=" represents the circuit shown in Fig. 3 and "imply" represents the implication circuit shown in Fig. 4. This figure determines whether any two minimum terms belonging to one partition block in P_2 belong to one partition block in P_1. If all implication relations are valid then there is $P_1 \geq P_2$.

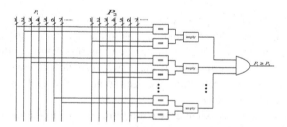

Fig. 5. Schematic diagram comparing the size of two partitions

Figure 6 shows a quantum circuit with three minterms to calculate $P_1 \geq P_2$. To ensure the reuse of quantum bits and the reversibility of quantum circuits, the quantum circuit always maintains symmetrical structure.

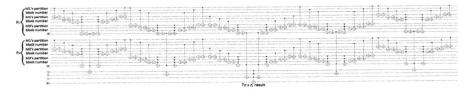

Fig. 6. Sample quantum circuit to calculate $P_1 \geq P_2$ (three minterms in function)

To verify theorem 1, it is needed to compute the product of two partitions. According to definition 6, the minterms belonging to the same partition block in P_1 and P_2 still belong to the same partition block in $P_1 \cdot P_2$. The minterms not belonging to the same partition block in P_1 and P_2 will generate new partition block in $P_1 \cdot P_2$. Therefore, each minterm will have a new partition block number which easier generated by cascading method. It is assumed that the partition block numbers in $P(A)$ and $\prod_G$ are shown in Table 2. $p(A) = \left\{ \frac{00}{1,2,3}; \frac{01}{4}; \frac{10}{5,6}; \frac{11}{7,8} \right\}$, $\prod_G = \left\{ \frac{0}{1;2;3;4}; \frac{1}{5,6,7,8} \right\}$, $p(A) \cdot \prod_G = \left\{ \frac{000}{1,2,3}; \frac{010}{4}; \frac{101}{5,6}; \frac{111}{7,8} \right\}$.

Table 2. Sample of partition block number

Minter	$P(A)$	$\prod_G$	$P(A) \cdot \prod_G$
1	00	0	000
2	00	0	000
3	00	0	000
4	01	0	010
5	10	1	101
6	10	1	101
7	11	1	111
8	11	1	111

The circuit shown in Fig. 7 is to verify theorem 1. The circuit in box is shown in Fig. 5. If the two conditions of theorem 1 are satisfied, the auxiliary bits connected to these two boxes on the left will be flipped to 1 respectively, which means $\prod_G$ satisfies Theorem 1, and $\prod_G$ is found.

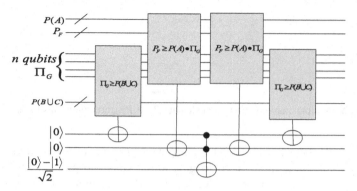

Fig. 7. The quantum circuit to find $\prod_G$

3.2   Boolean Function Decomposition Based on Grove Algorithm

Each minterm belongs to a numbered partition block. Every partition can be represented by cascading all partition block number of all minterms in partition. Take Table 2 as example, $p(A) = \{0000000110101111\}$, $\prod_G = \{00001111\}$. Because $\prod_G$ is unknown, the length of partition block number can be determined according to $\lceil \log n \rceil$. $\prod_G$ is generated by cascading all partition block number, whose length is $n \cdot \lceil \log n \rceil$. For example, in function with 8 minterms, according to the minimum partition, the length of the block number is 3, and the length of $\prod_G$ is $3 \times 8 = 24$ bit. $\prod_G$ is hidden in these tremendous states space from {000000000000000000000000} to {111111111111111111111111}. Because of huge search space, it is very difficult to find $\prod_G$ using classical algorithm.

Grover algorithm is a quantum search algorithm framework for searching in disordered state space. Quantum circuits to solve specific search problems can be embedded into Grover framework to speed up searching. In n states space, the Grover algorithm can search the exact state by $o(\sqrt{n})$ searching with the probability close to 100% [9, 10]. The framework of the Grover algorithm is shown in Fig. 8, where the module G is the iterative main body in the algorithm which is shown in Fig. 9.

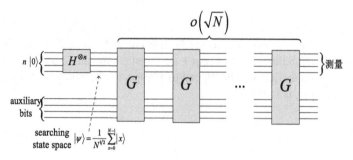

Fig. 8.   The framework of Grove

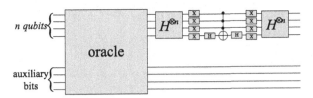

Fig. 9. The circuit of G in Grove algorithm

In order to speed up searching $\prod_G$ in the process of function decomposition, the circuit to find $\prod_G$ is embedded into the framework of Grover as Oracle, as shown in Fig. 10. The input of Grover algorithm is n qubits. State spaces which $\prod_G$ is hidden in are generated after evolution of Hadmard gates. Initializing auxiliary qubit to $|1\rangle$ not $|0\rangle$ is helped to realize phase transformation because $|1\rangle$ transform to $\frac{|0\rangle - |1\rangle}{\sqrt{2}}$ through Hadmard gate. If the state of candidate $\prod_G$ is $|x\rangle$, which is the exact one we search, the auxiliary qubit will be flipped to make $|x\rangle \left(\frac{|0\rangle - |1\rangle}{\sqrt{2}}\right) \xrightarrow{oracle} |x\rangle \left[-\left(\frac{|0\rangle - |1\rangle}{\sqrt{2}}\right)\right] = (-|x\rangle)\left(\frac{|0\rangle - |1\rangle}{\sqrt{2}}\right)$. So phase of the state of $\prod_G$ is inverted, thus $\prod_G$ is identified. Afterwards Boolean function decomposition is run according to $\prod_G$.

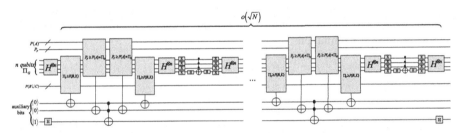

Fig. 10. The quantum circuit to identify $\prod_G$

4 Experimental Simulation Results

Quipper is the latest quantum programming language. It has perfect grammar and semantic system, abundant data types, self-correction and symbol system and is easy to expand and use. Quipper is considered to be the quantum programming language which is most likely to run on a real quantum computer [11, 12]. Quipper is also the most effective and large-scale quantum algorithm and quantum circuit simulation tool [13–16]. We use Quipper to generate and run the quantum circuit which realize the proposed algorithm in this paper. The type of machine we used is lenovo Thinkpad laptop, CPU Intel Core i-4700HQ@2, 4 Ghz, 16 GB memory. Operation System is Linux distro, Mint18.1 Quipper 0.8. Because of too much size-scale of the circuit, Fig. 11 just show the quantum circuit to identify $\prod_G$ with 3 minterms, where include 4320 quantum gates and 40 qubits.

Fig. 11. The quantum circuit to identify $\prod_G$ with 3 minterms generated in quipper

We simulate the Boolean functions with 3, 4, 5, 6 minterms and 5 input variables respectively, and use Qipper's own functions to automatically count the experimental results as shown in Table 3.

From Table 3, we know that the Boolean function decomposition based on Grover framework is very successful for the Boolean functions with three and four minterms respectively. It not only generates quantum circuit but also finds $\prod_G$ with a probability of nearly 100% in the shortest time. Finally the Boolean function decomposition is completed. This quantum circuit is the largest one so far, which include 53 classical bits and qubits and 17418 quantum gates. When the minterms of Boolean function is increased to 5 and 6, circuits still can be generated but not be realized because of too many Grover iterations in the circuit. This also illustrates the authenticity and reality of our experimental results because the authors of references 11 and 12 had proved that the traditional computer analog quantum computation with up to 50 qubits. Our experiment is close to the upper limitation.

Table 3. Comparison of experimental results for different Boolean functions

Funtions with Different numbers of minterm	Boolean function			Π_G qubits Π_G	Qubits required by circuit	Statistics of different quantum gate in the circuit						Number of iterations in Grove	Probability to find Π_G	Simulation time (minute)
	Input qubits A	B	Output qubits F			Not gates	CNOT gates	Toffli gates	Hadmard gates	X gate	Total number of gates			
3	2	3	2	2	40	1820	1540	770	106	84	4320	7	100%	2
4	2	3	2	2	53	7488	6336	3040	298	256	17418	16	98%	22
5	2	2	1	2	62	26752	24320	10048	716	640	62476	32	–	–
6	2	2	1	2	79	66304	58880	26496	1678	1536	154894	64	–	–

5 Conclusion

The design idea of the complex Boolean function decomposition algorithm based on Grove framework is proposed and realized for the first time on Quipper. From the simulation results, it is known that if the limitations of qubits and quantum gates in current quantum simulation platform are removed, this algorithm can always realize Boolean function decomposition with probability close to 100% and $o\left(\sqrt{N}\right)$ searches. The implementation of this quantum algorithm is of great significance for expanding the practical application of Grover algorithm and accelerating the classical algorithm.

References

1. Ashenhurst, R.L.: The decomposition of switching functions of a proceedings paper. In: 1959 International Symposium on the Theory of Switching, vol. 29, pp. 74–116 (1959)
2. Scholl, C.: Functional Decomposition with Application to FPGA Synthesis. Kluwer Academic Publishers, Holland (2010)
3. Ivannikov, A., Kulagin, V., Romanov A., et al.: Algebraic models of digital system design debugging decomposition. In: East-West Design & Test Symposium (EWDTS) (2016)
4. Bouyer, A., Arasteh, B.: The necessity of using cloud computing in educational system. Procedia Soc. Behav. Sci. 143(214), 581–585 (2014)
5. Luba, T., Selvaraj, H.: A general approach to boolean function decomposition and its application in FPGA based synthesis. VLSI Des. 3(3–4), 289–300 (1995)
6. Lee, T., Ye, T.: A relational approach to functional decomposition of logic circuits. ACM Trans. Database Syst. 36(2), 1–30 (2006)
7. Afshord, S.T., Pottosin, Y., Arasteh, B.: An input variable partitioning algorithm for functional decomposition of a system of Boolean functions based on the tabular method. Discrete Appl. Math. 85(20), 208–219 (2015)
8. Nielsen, M.A., Chuang, I.L.: Quantum Computation and Quantum Information. Cambridge University Press, England (2000)
9. Holweck, F., Jaffali, H., Nounouh, I.: Grover's algorithm and the secant varieties. Quantum Inf. Process. 15(11), 4391–4413 (2016). https://doi.org/10.1007/s11128-016-1445-2
10. Grover, L.K.: Quantum mechanics helps in searching for a needle in a haystack. Phys. Rev. Lett. 79(2), 325–328 (1997)
11. Green, A.S., Lumsdaine, P.L., Ross, N.J., et al.: Quipper: a scalable quantum programming language of a proceedings paper. In: The 34th ACM Conference on Programming Language Design and Implementation (PLDI), Acm Sigplan Notices, vol. 48(6), pp. 333–342 (2013)
12. Häner, T., Steiger, D.S.: 0.5 Petabyte Simulation of a 45-Qubit Quantum Circuit. arXiv:1704. 01127v2[quant-ph] (2017)
13. Siddiqui, S., Islam, M.J., Shehab, O.: Five Quantum Algorithms Using Quipper. arXiv:1406. 4481v2[quant-ph] (2014)
14. Perkowski, M., Mareksadowska, M., Jozwiak, L., et al.: Decomposition of multiple-valued relations. In: International Symposium on Multiple-valued Logic on proceedings, pp. 13–18, Antigonish, NS, Canada (1997)
15. Liu, W.J., Xu, Y., Yang, C.N., et al.: Privacy-preserving quantum two-party geometric intersection. Comput. Mater. Continua 60(3), 1237–1250 (2019)
16. Liu, W.J., Chen, Z.Y., Liu, J.S., et al.: Full-blind delegating private quantum computation. Comput. Mater. Continua 56(2), 211–223 (2018)

Research on Emotional Recognition of EEG Signals in Experimental Paradigm

Huiping Jiang$^{(\boxtimes)}$ ⓘ, Zequn Wang ⓘ, and Rui Jiao ⓘ

Brain Cognitive Computing Lab, School of Information Engineering,
Minzu University of China, Beijing 100081, China
jianghp@muc.edu.cn

Abstract. To study the effect of the design of the experimental paradigm on the accuracy of emotion recognition based on picture-stimulated EEG signals. Using the comparison of three innovative models (random presentation, sequential presentation and independent presentation), we identified the experimental paradigm that had the highest impact on the accuracy of emotional recognition. We used by principal component analysis (PCA) and support vector machine (SVM) to extract and classify emotions separately. The results show that in the three experimental paradigms highest accuracy rate is when positive and negative emotion pictures are presented in sequence. The innovative model presented in the series has the highest accuracy and is more consistent with the dynamic process of emotion generation, ensuring that the evoked EEG signals imply complete emotional information. This research on the experimental paradigm is mostly convenient for follow-up scholars to continue to explore EEG signals.

Keywords: Electroencephalogram · Emotional recognition · Support vector machine

1 Introduction

Emotion is a mental and physiological state that is accompanied by the process of cognition and consciousness, and is the external expression of the human inner world, including limbs, sounds, actions, etc. It plays a very important role in daily human communication. At the same time, emotion recognition is also a key technology in the field of artificial intelligence. Therefore, more and more researchers have developed a strong research interest in emotion recognition, so that emotion recognition has been more widely used in actual life [1]. The related research on emotion has become one of the critical research contents of current psychology. In recent years, with the development of computers in various research fields, people are expecting to have more intelligent and humanized compute. This requires us to use research methods of information science and technology. To change the course of human emotions for practical experiments, modelling, identifying and understanding. So that the computer can recognize the different social, emotional state, to achieve human-computer interaction more convenient purposes.

© Springer Nature Singapore Pte Ltd. 2020
X. Sun et al. (Eds.): ICAIS 2020, CCIS 1252, pp. 593–604, 2020.
https://doi.org/10.1007/978-981-15-8083-3_53

With the advancement of technology, our understanding of emotions has deepened, and the opportunities for automatic emotion recognition systems have also increased. The use of text, speech, facial expressions or gestures as stimuli has become a research breakthrough in the field of emotion recognition. However, in the actual application environment, the emotions shown by humans through external behaviors and expressions do not necessarily represent the true and objective emotional state in human hearts. This is because both voice signals and facial expression signals have a certain camouflage, and the generation of emotions does not necessarily change people's external behavior. The human physiological signal is controlled by the central nervous system; it is not affected by other irrelevant factors, and can truly and objectively reflect the human state [2]. EEG signals in physiological signals are directly generated by the human central nervous system, which is closely related to the production of emotions. EEG signals can more directly and objectively reflect the physiological state of the human body, because it exists objectively. Moreover, EEG-based emotion recognition technology is an exciting new direction for emotion research, because it is becoming less invasive and the price is getting cheaper, so it is used in many fields such as medical applications, emotion testing, etc. [3].

Research on EEG-based emotion recognition, the primary problem is to make the subject in a specific emotional state, which is also a prerequisite for emotional recognition research. At present, there are three main ways to generate emotions: spontaneous emotions, powerful emotions and induced emotions. Among them, induced emotions are considered to be the most effective way of generating emotions, and they are the most commonly used emotion generation methods in the laboratory. Evoked emotions refer to the fact that different emotion-inducing materials allow subjects to be in a specific emotional state for as long as possible, thus effectively recording various information. The commonly used emotion recognition methods can be mainly divided into three categories: video-based emotion recognition, speech-based emotion recognition, and picture-based emotion recognition. After selecting a certain way for emotion recognition, it is necessary to determine the presentation mode of the selected stimulation materials, which are mainly divided into three types: random presentation, sequential presentation, and independent presentation. In the paper [4], based on image-stimulated emotion recognition research, the pictures are presented separately. Using WT and SVM for classification, the average accuracy is 78.57%. The paper [5] is also used in the semi-random presentation method based on image stimulus. They are using CSP and SVM methods for classification, with a preparation rate of 85%. The paper [6] used EEG-based emotion recognition in a random presentation manner. They are using CSP and SVM methods for classification, with an average accuracy of 74.56%. Paper [7] in the study of EEG-based emotional information features and classification methods, using a random presentation method and CSP for emotion recognition, the average accuracy rate is 65.59%. In the Paper [8], based on EEG emotion recognition research, the pictures are presented separately. Using SVD and SVM for classification, the average accuracy rate is about 75%. The paper [9–11] mainly improves the accuracy by researching algorithms. We consider improving the accuracy of experiments from the perspective of experimental paradigms.

When inducing emotions at home and abroad, the methods of collection are random presentation, sequential presentation, and independent presentation. However, there is no specific comparison of these three different experimental paradigms. In the research of image-based emotion recognition process, this paper makes a simple comparison of these three experiments and hopes to provide some reference for future research.

2 Related Works

Emotion, a general term for a series of subjective cognitive experiences, is a psychological and physiological state produced by a variety of feelings, thoughts and behaviors. Researchers believe that the hypothalamus determines the generation of emotions. When external stimulation is transmitted to the cerebral cortex, the cerebral cortex will activate the thalamus, and thus generate different emotions.

There are many kinds of emotion classification methods, including cognitive emotion and non-cognitive emotion, instinctive emotion (produced in the amygdala) and cognitive emotion (built in the cerebral cortex), primary emotion and complex emotion. In the research, researchers usually divide emotions into three categories: positive emotions (including pride, joy, gratitude, etc.), neutral emotions, negative emotions (including sadness, anger, tension, pain, etc.).

2.1 EEG Signal

To design a suitable experimental paradigm, you first need to know how EEG data is generated. EEG signals are thought to originate from the post-synaptic potentials of the vertebral neurons in the upper cortex. The reason is mainly the morphological and agglomeration effects of these cells. It has an elongated shape and gathers approximately perpendicular to the surface of the cortex. These effects can be conveniently modelled with current dipoles distributed along with the cortical shell, as shown in Fig. 1.

Brain electrical activity is the sum of postsynaptic potentials of pyramidal cells and their vertical dendrites in the cerebral cortex, which is regulated by nonspecific nuclei in the midline of the thalamus. The possibility of neurons is the basis of physiological activities of the central nervous system so that it can reflect the changes of its function and pathology. Electroencephalogram (EEG), the most sensitive method to monitor brain function, is a method to amplify and record the changes of brain potential from the scalp by precise electronic instruments.

According to the frequency, EEG can be divided into five frequency bands: δ wave (1–3 Hz), θ wave (4–7 Hz), α wave (8–13 Hz), β wave (14–30 Hz), γ wave (31–50 Hz).

δ wave (1–3 Hz): the brain wave often appears in the frontal area, and only looks when people are asleep.

θ wave (4–7 Hz): when people's mental state is deeply relaxed, the brain wave will appear. At this time, people are highly focused and creative.

α wave (8–13 Hz): it mainly appears in the second half of the cerebral hemisphere, most of which occurs when people are quiet and close their eyes. When it comes to mental activity, thinking about the problem is that the wave can inhibit or disappear.

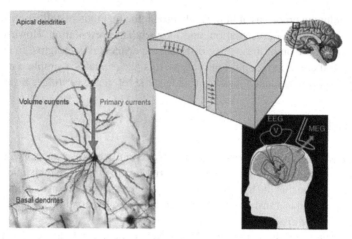

Fig. 1. EEG generation mechanism diagram [12]

β wave (14–30 Hz): when people are emotional, conscious, excited or engaged in mental activities, the wave will be more visible.

γ wave (31–50 Hz): it frequently occurs in frontal and central areas. It has a lot to do with attention, excitement, object recognition and perception binding under some conditions.

2.2 Emotion Recognition Based on EEG

In the research of emotion recognition using EEG signal, it mainly includes the following steps: emotion induction, EEG signal acquisition, signal preprocessing, EEG feature extraction, feature selection and dimensionality reduction, emotion pattern learning and classification.

Emotional Induction. Emotion elicitation mainly relies on emotion pictures, audio materials and emotion-related video clips as stimulation files to induce different emotions of subjects. For example, Frantzidis [13] and others selected pictures from the international emotional picture system (IAPS) as stimulus materials. Because the images in IAPs are marked by two-dimensional measurement of value and arousal, four quadrants in two-dimensional space represent four emotion types, respectively. They took 40 pictures from each of the four quadrants as stimulus pictures to induce emotion. Hadjidimitriou [14] and others used music as stimulus materials to study the different EEG characteristics of the subjects for the music they like and dislike. Besides, the international emotional digital sound system established by Lang [15] and others is often used as emotional inducing materials. Soleymani et al. [16]. Selected 20 emotion-related video clips from movies and the Internet, and measured their validity and arousal using an online questionnaire. They were divided into three categories in these two dimensions: unhappy, neutral and happy, calm, moderate and awake. Then 24 subjects were collected to watch the EEG signals and eye gaze data. The classification accuracy of validity can reach 68.5%, while that of arousal can reach 76.4%.

Classic EEG Feature Extraction and Classification. In the standard EEG classification and emotion recognition cases, researchers mainly use the classical feature extraction, clustering and classification algorithms such as Fourier transform, wavelet transform, K-means, KNN, and SVM to extract and classify EEG features. Abdulhamit subasi et al. [17] used wavelet transform to extract the sub-band features of EEG signals, PCA, ICA and LDA Algorithm to reduce the dimension of features, and took the results of dimension reduction as the input of SVM classifier to carry out the diagnosis of epilepsy patients. Xiao Wei Wang et al. [18]. Extracted three EEG features for comparison: power spectrum calculated by Fourier transform, different frequency band energy obtained by wavelet transform, and nonlinear dynamic emotion features. The SVM classifier is used for pattern learning and classification, and the average accuracy is 87.53% after training the power spectrum characteristics of five sub-bands with a linear kernel function. Murugappan et al. [19] studied four emotions: fear, pleasure, surprise and disgust. They mixed the EEG samples of the four passions of the subjects. They used the fuzzy c-means method to cluster the samples, to find the inherent characteristics of each emotion, to find the examples with similar features, to divide the four categories of emotion. Frantzidis [13] and others used the C4.5 decision tree algorithm and Mahalanobis distance classifier to train and learn four emotional states, with an average accuracy of 77.68%.

In the classical EEG classification research, most of them use the universal time domain, frequency domain or frequency domain EEG features to classify. Still, there are relatively few researches to find the specific brain region and specific frequency band most related to emotion. Therefore, how to combine the mechanism of emotion and EEG to extract the EEG features that can best reflect the emotional attributes needs further study.

New Achievements of EEG Signal Classification. With the development of neural networks, deep learning, sparse representation and other algorithms, researchers have also introduced them into the work of EEG signal classification and achieved some results. Orhan et al. [20] used the coefficients of the wavelet transform as the input of MLPNN (multilayer perceptron neural network) to train and classify the two dichotomous tasks of epilepsy and non-epilepsy as well as epilepsy patients in the state of onset and non-onset. The former can achieve a recognition rate of 99.60%, while the latter can make a recognition rate of 100%. In the same way, Aspirants [21] and others have also achieved excellent results in the classification of five different emotions by using multilayer perceptron model. Yuanfang Ren et al. [22] introduced the methods of biomimetic pattern recognition (BPR) and sparse representation (SR) for EEG signal classification. After a comparative study of BPR-sr algorithm and other excellent classifiers, it is considered that the combination of SR can overcome the overlapping coverage problem of BPR.

3   Experimental Design

This paper studies the influence of the experimental paradigm on the accuracy of emotion recognition based on picture-stimulated EEG signals. Therefore, it is necessary to select pictures that can induce positive and negative emotions. The stimulus pictures are derived from the IAPS picture stimulation material library.

The nine subjects in the emotional experiment were students from the Minzu University of China, including six boys and three girls, aged between 20 and 25. The subjects were right-handed and did not have any history of mental illness, and emotional state was normal to reduce the mental state of the experiment by external factors. And this study protocol was approved by the institutional review boards (ECMUC2019008CO) at Minzu University of China. All participants provided IRB-approved written informed consent after they were explained the experimental procedure.

The specific experimental environment is shown in Fig. 2. The experiment was conducted in a quiet room. The room is dimly lit, and the temperature is controlled between 25 and 26 °C. The experiment time was chosen at 10 am, to avoid the state of fatigue in the experiment. Before the trial, the participants were told to watch different types of pictures, including positive and negative, try to keep the body in a specific posture and avoid activities, to reduce the interference of the signals such as my electricity and ocular electricity on the experimental results. During the experiment, the subjects sat in front of the computer and the pictures on the screen were presented in a set way.

Fig. 2. Specific experimental environment

The stimulus file selected 140 images, 70 of which were able to induce positive emotions and 70 to cause negative emotions. Before the experiment begins, the participants should carefully read the instructions on the screen to fully understand the flow and details of the research. Before each stimulus picture appears, a red plus comment point will appear in the middle of the screen. The background is black, and the presentation time is 500 ms, which is used to remind the subject to annotate the screen and improve the degree of gaze carefully. The stimulus material is then presented for 3 s, and a feedback interface appears to record the subject's real-time response. This experiment is mainly to study the influence of the design of the experimental paradigm on the experimental results, so three experimental paradigms were designed:

Experimental paradigm 1:140 stimulating materials are mixed and presented randomly as shown in Fig. 3.

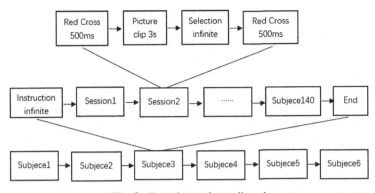

Fig. 3. Experimental paradigm 1

Experimental Paradigm 2: 140 stimulating pictures, showing 70 positive emotion pictures in order, then 70 negative pictures, the same as the experiment paradigm one, except that the pictures are presented in a different order.

Experimental Paradigm 3:140 photos of the stimulus, the positive emotion picture and the negative emotion picture are separated and experimented independently. At this time, the pictures are presented in order, because they are all the same type of pictures, so the law does not affect. As shown in Fig. 4.

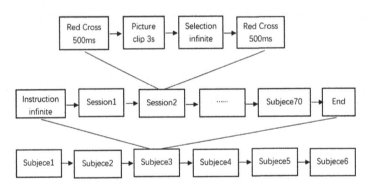

Fig. 4. Experimental paradigm 3

4   Experimental Classification Model

Experiments were carried out using the three experimental paradigms of the superior design. After collecting the data, we should select the feature extraction and feature classification methods to evaluate the experimental paradigm. We chose PCA for feature extraction and then used SVM for feature classification to identify positive and negative emotions. The principles of PCA and SVM are described below.

4.1 PCA

Principal component analysis (PCA) is a commonly used method of multivariate statistical analysis. The basic idea of this method is to transform the original multivariate variables into a new set of linearly independent multivariate variables through linear projection [23]. In calculating the principal component, it is necessary to select a projection operator that maximizes the variance of the new variable obtained after screening in all linear predictions. This projection operator is called the projection vector of the first principal component (PC). The projection operator needs to meet two primary conditions: first, it must be orthogonal to the linear projection operator that has been obtained so far; second, among all linear operators that meet the above conditions, choose the one that maximizes the variance of the new variable obtained after projection. The rectilinear projection operator of principal component analysis can be solved by using the eigenvalue decomposition method for the covariance matrix. Suppose there is a data set $X = \{x_1, x_2, \cdots, x_n\}$, the dimension is D. First zero-mean processing of the variable x_i so that the mean is zero. Then solution process of the principal component analysis projection operator of $\{x_i\}$ can be expressed as follows:
First, estimate the covariance matrix of the variable $\{x_i\}$.

$$C = XX^T \tag{1}$$

Where X is the sample data set, each column represents a sample, and C is the covariance matrix of the data set.
Secondly, Perform covariance matrix C for eigenvalue decomposition.

$$C = U\Lambda U^T \tag{2}$$

Where $U = \{u_1, u_2, \cdots, u_d\}$ is the covariance matrix C eigenvector and satisfies.
Furthermore, $U^T U = I$, $\Lambda = \text{diag}(\lambda_1, \ldots, \lambda_d)$ is a diagonal matrix composed of d eigenvalues of the covariance matrix C. Arranging the eigenvalues of the covariance matrix C in descending order. The feature vector u_i corresponding to the i-th eigenvalue is the projection operator of the i-th principal component of principal component analysis.

$$V_i = u_i^T X \tag{3}$$

Where V_i is the i-th principal component of the data set.
When using the PCA method for feature dimensionality reduction, the number K of principal components that need to be retained is usually selected based on the percentage of the variance of the first K principle components in the sum of all primary component variances. The final principal component projection matrix is the eigenvector corresponding to the first k large eigenvalues of the covariance matrix C of the original multivariate variables.

4.2 SVM

Vapnik et al. first proposed the support vector machine (SVM). It is based on the VC dimension theory of statistical learning theory [24]. This method seeks the best compromise between model complexity and learning ability based on the principle of structural risk minimization, based on sample information, to obtain the best generalization ability [25]. The key to this method is to map the feature set that is difficult to divide in low-dimensional space to high-dimensional space by kernel function. Then effectively share data points by establishing a hyperplane with maximum spacing [26]. In the case of linear separability, the sample points closest to the classification hyperplane in the training set are called support vectors. As shown in Fig. 5, which are located on hyperplanes H1 and H2 parallel to the optimal classification plane.

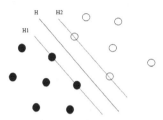

Fig. 5. Linear separable SVM classification diagram

Assumed that the data set is $\{x, y\} = \{(x_1, y_1), (x_2, y_2) \cdots (x_n, y_n)\}$ where x represents the sample point, y is the label of the corresponding category of the sample point, and the class label is 1 or -1. Because the training data set is linearly separable, you can find a hyperplane that separates the two types. Suppose the formula of the hyperplane is $x^T \omega + b = 0$, then the two types of samples satisfy the condition:

$$y_i\left(x_i^T \omega + b\right) = \gamma_i \geq \gamma, i = 1, 2, \cdots, \text{n} \tag{4}$$

Here ω represents the normal vector, which determines the direction of the hyperplane; b represents the offset, which determines the distance between the hyperplane and the origin.

By scaling up or down the values of ω and b, we can make the function interval γ equal to 1, which is done for convenience and has no effect on the optimization of the objective function. Then the above formula can be written as:

$$y_i\left(x_i^T \omega + b\right) \geq 1, i = 1, 2, \cdots, \text{n} \tag{5}$$

The optimal hyperplane can be used to maximize the geometric distance between the two hyperplanes, that is, make $2/\|\omega\|$ maximum. Therefore, the above problem translates into the problem of finding the optimal solution under constraints:

$$\max \frac{2}{\|\omega\|}$$
$$s.t, y_i\left(x_i^T \omega + b\right) \geq 1, i = 1, 2, \cdots, \text{n} \tag{6}$$

The above formula is equivalent to solving:

$$\min \frac{1}{2}\omega^T \omega$$
$$s.t, y_i\left(\omega^T x_i + b\right) \geq 1, i = 1, 2, \cdots, \text{n} \tag{7}$$

The above problem can be solved by the Lagrangian multiplier method to get the dual problem:

$$\max Q(a) = -\sum_{i=1}^{n}\sum_{j=1}^{n}\frac{1}{2}a_i a_j y_i y_j x_i^T x_i + \sum_{i=1}^{n}a_i$$

$$\text{s.t, } a_i \geq 0, \sum_{i=1}^{n}a_i y_i = 0 \tag{8}$$

Assume the dual problem's solution is a^* and the existence of j satisfy $a_j^* \geq 0$, then ω^* and b^* can be obtained:

$$\omega^* = \sum_{i=1}^{n}a_i^* y_i x_i$$

$$b^* = y_j - \sum_{i=1}^{n}a_i^* y_i x_i^T x_i \tag{9}$$

Thus, we can get the formula for classifying hyperplanes as:

$$\omega^* x + b^* = 0 \tag{10}$$

The final decision function for classification is:

$$f(x) = sign(\omega^* x + b^*) \tag{11}$$

This classification decision function is also called a linear separable support vector machine.

5   Analysis of Results

Each picture stimulates the sample. After the EEG signal is collected, the data size is a matrix of 64 * 3000, and the total sample data size is 140 * 64 * 3000. We use PCA for data dimensionality reduction and feature extraction. After testing, the first 10 principal components can account for more than 99% of the ingredients. Therefore, we uniformly reduce the data to 140 * 64 * 10 and normalize it. The raw data after feature extraction and dimensional reduction, we divide the data into a training set, and test set randomly according to 5:2. Finally, use SVM to classify the feature, using five-fold cross-validation. The results show when the experimental paradigm 1 is randomly presented, the average accuracy is 37.5%, the experimental paradigm 2 is presented in sequence, average accuracy is 85%, and the experimental paradigm 3 is presented in separate series, with an average accuracy of 55%. It can be seen from the results of the three experimental paradigms that different experimental procedures lead to significant differences in the accuracy of the final emotional classification

6   Conclusion

In this work, we induced the emotions of the subjects through image stimulation, designed three different experimental paradigms, and using PCA and SVM methods processing the collected EEG signals. The final result shows when the pictures are presented in sequence, the highest impact on the accuracy of emotional recognition. Further conclusions were verified through specific analysis.

References

1. Al, O.Z., Awad, M., Kasabov, N.K.: Anytime multipurpose emotion recognition from EEG data using a liquid state machine based framework. Artif. Intell. Med. **86**, 1–8 (2018)
2. Hsu, J.-L.: Affective content analysis of music emotion through EEG. Multimedia Syst. **24**(2), 195–210 (2017). https://doi.org/10.1007/s00530-017-0542-0
3. Perry, A., Saunders, S.N., Stiso, J., et al.: Effects of prefrontal cortex damage on emotion understanding: EEG and behavioural evidence. Brain **140**(4), 1086–1099 (2017)
4. Zhang, B.: Research status based on EEG emotion recognition (2017)
5. Li, M., Lu, B.L.: Emotion classification based on gamma-band EEG. IEEE Eng. Med. Biol. Soc. **2009**, 1323–1326 (2009)
6. Huang, N.-M.: Emotion recognition based on EEG. The South China University of Technology (2016)
7. Chen, M.-M.: Emotional information features and classification based on EEG Signals. Southeast University (2017)
8. Xu, L.: Research on emotion recognition based on EEG. Kunming University of Science and Technology (2018)
9. Hong, X., Zheng, X., Xia, J., Wei, L., Xue, W.: Cross-lingual non-ferrous metals related news recognition method based on CNN with a limited bi-lingual dictionary. Comput. Mater. Continua **58**(2), 379–389 (2019)
10. Long, M., Zeng, Y.: Detecting iris liveness with batch normalized convolutional neural network. Comput. Mater. Continua **58**(2), 493–504 (2019)
11. Niu, B., Huang, Y.: An improved method for web text affective cognition computing based on knowledge graph. Comput. Mater. Continua **59**(1), 1–14 (2019)
12. Jing, S.: Research of construction and analysis of brain network based on EEG Data (2017)
13. Frantzidis, C.A., et al.: On the classification of emotional biosignals evoked while viewing affective pictures: an integrated data-mining-based approach for healthcare applications. IEEE Trans. Inf. Technol. Biomed. **14**(2), 309–318 (2010). A Publication of the IEEE Engineering in Medicine & Biology Society
14. Hadjidimitriou, S.K., Hadjileontiadis, L.J.: Toward an EEG-based recognition of music liking using time-frequency analysis. IEEE Trans. Biomed. Eng. **59**(12), 3498–3510 (2012)
15. Lang, P.J., Bradley, M.M., Cuthbert, B.N.: International affective picture system (IAPS): affective ratings of pictures and instruction manual. NIMH, Center for the Study of Emotion & Attention (2005)
16. Pantic, M., Soleymani, M., Pun, T.: Multimodal emotion recognition in response to videos. IEEE Trans. Affect. Comput. **3**(2), 211–223 (2012)
17. Subasi, A., Ismail, G.M.: EEG signal classification using PCA, ICA, LDA and support vector machines. Expert Syst. Appl. Int. J. **37**(12), 8659–8666 (2010)
18. Wang, X.W., Nie, D., Lu, B.L.: Emotional state classification from EEG data using machine learning approach. Neurocomputing **129**, 94–106 (2013)

19. Murugappan, M., Rizon, M., Nagarajan, R., et al.: Time-frequency analysis of EEG signals for human emotion detection. In: Abu Osman, N.A., Ibrahim, F., Wan Abas, W.A.B., Abdul Rahman, H.S., Ting, H.N. (eds.) 4th Kuala Lumpur International Conference on Biomedical Engineering 2008. IFMBE Proceedings, vol. 21, pp. 262–265. Springer, Heidelberg (2008). https://doi.org/10.1007/978-3-540-69139-6_68

20. Orhan, U., Hekim, M., Ozer, M.: Discretization approach to EEG signal classification using multilayer perceptron neural network model. In: 2010 15th National Biomedical Engineering Meeting (BIYOMUT), pp. 1–4. IEEE (2010)

21. Aspiras, T.H., Asari, V.K.: Wavelet domain analysis of EEG data for emotion recognition: evaluation of recoursing energy efficiency. Proc. SPIE Int. Soc. Opt. Eng. **8058**(1), 368–371 (2011)

22. Ren, Y., Wu, Y., Ge, Y.: A co-training algorithm for EEG classification with biomimetic pattern recognition and sparse representation. Neurocomputing **137**, 212–222 (2013)

23. Abdi, H., Williams, L.J.: Wiley Interdisc. Rev. Comput. Stat. (2010)

24. Schölkopf, B.: Learning with Kernels: Support Vector Machines, Regularization, Optimization, and Beyond. MIT Press, Cambridge (2003)

25. Vapnik, V.: The Nature of Statistical Learning Theory. Springer, New York (1995)

26. Cortes, C., Vapnik, V.: Support-vector networks. Mach. Learn. **20**(3), 273–297 (1995)

Research on Rasterized Population Evaluation Method Based on Multi-class Machine Learning Method

Jin Han[1] and Jingxin Xie[2(✉)]

[1] Nanjing University of Information Science and Technology, Nanjing 210044, China
[2] Hunan Meteorological Disaster Prevention Technology Center,
Changsha 410007, Hunan, China
xie_jingxin@163.com

Abstract. The size of the city's population directly determines the economic and social structure of the construction of ideas and development policies, so the accurate assessment of the urban population is extremely important. However, this paper is different from most other population assessment studies by the national, provincial and other large-scale administrative regions as the evaluation scope, taking Hunan Province as an example to rasterize the relevant regions, and take the systematic analysis and regional comprehensive research on the grid unit scale. In this paper, 30-dimensional irrelevant data of relevant regions in Hunan Province were obtained by crawlers, and each grid population was evaluated by using neural network model, SVM model and random forest model. Compared with the past yearbook population data, the experimental findings can still obtain a lower population assessment error index by using limited data. The average error of the three models is 5.8%, 5.7%, and 3.1%, respectively. The final analysis determined that random forests performed best on population estimates at grid cell scales. Therefore, it is possible to obtain a better population assessment result for each city through the geographic grid population assessment method of random forest with only limited data, which can save a great deal of resources and manpower consumption.

Keywords: Rasterization · Crawler · SVM · Random forest · BP neural network

1 Introduction

The population problem has always been a key issue in relation to regional economic growth and social stability. Therefore, correctly predicting the population size of the urban area has important reference significance for urban construction and economic development in the urban area. It provides a certain theoretical and data foundation for the strategic planning and decision-making of population development.

From the perspective of the main subjects that each forecasting method belongs to, the methods to solve the population problem can be classified into mathematical methods, statistical methods and demographic methods [1]. Mathematical and statistical methods

© Springer Nature Singapore Pte Ltd. 2020
X. Sun et al. (Eds.): ICAIS 2020, CCIS 1252, pp. 605–615, 2020.
https://doi.org/10.1007/978-981-15-8083-3_54

mainly consider historical longitudinal data to conduct univariate population prediction, which is a relatively common population prediction method at present. Mathematical and statistical methods mainly include regression analysis and gray system analysis, BP neural network and other methods. The fatal shortcoming of the mathematical method is that it can only predict a point value in the future, and cannot predict the interval value of the result, so the introduction of statistical methods has its inevitability. Demographic methods include the single factor approach and the cohort factor approach. When considering the laws of the population itself, especially the cohort factor method, considering both the historical longitudinal data and the horizontal data of the base year, the amount of information possessed is large, so the accuracy of prediction is naturally high. However, the data acquisition channels of such methods are relatively small and the data is relatively discretized. Most of the research on population assessment is based on national, provincial, and other large-scale administrative regions, and lacks systematic analysis and regional comprehensive research on the scale of grid cells. However, this paper proposes to use the crawler to extract relevant regional information data into 30-dimensional and rasterize the region. Use raster data to predict each raster population from neural network models, SVM models, and random forest models, and compare them with past yearbook population data. The experiment found that by using limited data, a lower population prediction error index can still be obtained. The average error of the three models was 5.8%, 5.7%, and 3.1%, respectively. It was finally determined that the random forest model had the best effect on the population assessment at the county level.

2 Related Works

At present, the more accurate demographic method is a regular census, which is time-consuming and costly, and the data has a certain lag. The population prediction method is mainly based on some existing population data, using mathematical methods, statistical methods and demographic methods to predict the future population size.

The mathematical method only considers the longitudinal historical data and only makes univariate prediction, which has a low reliability. In 1968, Keyfitz [10] proposed the basic mathematical method of population prediction (Keyfitz, 1968). Later, Lee et al. also constructed a probability model for population prediction, but considering that its model is constructed based on many priori judgments, So we did not refer too much to the details of the model [9]. In the study of population assessment by establishing the corresponding mathematical model through BP neural network thought, Lu wenjun et al. [2] used BP neural network to predict and compare the total population of China from 2011 to 2014, proving the feasibility of BP neural network method. In addition, the grey model GM(1.1) was used to predict the population. However, due to the limited or incomplete data, the reliability and validity of the prediction results are not satisfactory. For example, Shan Chuanpeng et al. [3] combined the grey GM(1,1) model with markov chain and found that the population size of jiangxi province showed a declining trend in the future.

Statistical methods for population prediction are usually based on the common regression analysis curve model (logistics). For example, pan Dazhi et al. [4] discussed the Logistic biological differential model and established the Logistic model of population prediction in sichuan province, with relatively accurate experimental results. However, such models can only make predictions based on a single population factor and have certain requirements on the amount of data required by the models, which limits their use frequency. At the same time, the time series method makes use of the time attribute of the data to fully exploit the information of historical data, which can greatly improve the accuracy of population prediction. But again, such methods can only be based on a single demographic factor, without considering the impact of other factors on future population Numbers.

The demographic method mainly includes the single factor method and the multi-factor cohort factor method. Among them, the single factor method only considers a single factor of population change, and cannot include complex population change information, with low accuracy. The multi-factor cohort factor method can predict the future population according to the previous population cohort data and other parameters such as population change rate, with high accuracy. It is a relatively common standard population prediction model in the world at present. However, a variety of other demographic information required by this method, such as the rate of population change, is not readily available, which directly affects the extensive use of the model. Tian Fei et al. used the cohort factor method to predict the population of Anhui Province [5]. Keyfitz and Caswell predict the actual population through the Leslie matrix constructed by the functions of the life table [11]. Shang et al. embedded conventional population prediction corrections into random population projections when studying the quantitative assessment of fiscal sustainability impacted by population ageing [12]. In the population assessment work in recent years, the research direction also tends to combine multiple prediction methods. For example, Liu Feng et al. [6] combined Richards model and Logistic model to improve the prediction accuracy of Chinese population compared with a single model. Ren et al. [7] proved that the population random prediction method based on Leslie matrix and ARMA model is robust and has strong applicability. Cheng zhu et al. [8] took advantage of the good fitting ability of BP neural network for nonlinear trends and the simplicity of grey prediction model, and the prediction effect of the combined model was better than that of any of its sub-models.

It is easy to see that most of the research on population assessment is based on large-scale administrative regions such as the state and the province, and lacks systematic analysis and regional comprehensive research on the scale of grid cells. In view of the above situation, in order to accurately estimate the population, this paper unitizes the regional geographic grid and each grid population is obtained through BP neural network, SVM, and random forest machine learning evaluation. The results were compared with the population data of various regions in the past yearbooks, and it was found that by using limited data and less resource consumption, better results could still be obtained. The average error of the three models was 5.8%, 5.7%, and 3.1%, respectively. The final analysis concluded that the use of randomized forest rasterized population assessment can solve the difficulty of the large demand for population data in the past, and to a certain extent, greatly save human and material resources.

3 Models

3.1 Data Classification and Function

Key word

The key word data is statistical data of entities such as buildings and operations obtained through a certain keyword query in the geographical area selected by the article. In this paper, 30 key words are selected, and the key word data of 122 grid regions are collected to construct an evaluation model with data sources.

Root-Mean-Square Error

The root mean square error is the square root of the square of deviation between the predicted value and the real value and the ratio of the number of observations to n which is used to measure the deviation between the observed value and the true value. In this paper, root-mean-square error is selected to evaluate the accuracy of the population assessment results.

Error Accuracy

Error accuracy is the approximation between the observed value and the true value. In this paper, error accuracy is used to evaluate the error between the estimated population assessment and the true value.

3.2 Data Acquisition

Most population assessment methods use statistical yearbook data, questionnaire statistics or field sampling to obtain experimental data sets. However, this paper adopts a new way of obtaining data sources, that is, selecting key word data in the grid. The key word data is statistical data of entities such as buildings and operations obtained through a certain keyword query in the geographical area selected by the article. Since the key word data is closely related to various socio-economic entities in the grid area, and these entities are affected by the population of the area, the key word data is closely related to the population in the grid area. Therefore, this paper selects 30 key words that are closely related to the population, and obtains key word data of 122 grid areas through crawlers, and uses this as a data set for evaluating the population within the grid.

3.3 Data Analysis

In order to make the information contained in the key words related to population in the grid comprehensive and to accurately predict the population in the grid unit, 30 key words with low correlation were selected as the experimental data set. In statistics, the spearman correlation coefficient ρ is a nonparametric indicator that measures the dependence of two variables and can reflect the degree of association between variables. In this paper, spearman coefficient is used to analyze the values of 30 key words in 122 grid areas obtained by crawlers from 3.1, and the low-correlation is verified for the data of 30-dimensional key words. The calculation formula of Spearman correlation coefficient is as follows:

$$\rho = \frac{\sum_i (x_i - \bar{x})(y_i - \bar{y})}{\sqrt{\sum_i (x_i - \bar{x})^2 \sum_i (y_i - \bar{y})^2}} \tag{1}$$

x, y are the values of any two types of key words. By analyzing the speaman correlation coefficient of each key word on the data of other 29 key words, the absolute sum of spearman correlation coefficient of the key word data and the data of the other 29 key words was obtained. The average value of the absolute sum is used as a measure of the correlation between the key words and the other 29 key words. The mean value of spearman correlation coefficient of 30 key words is shown in Fig. 1.

As can be seen from Fig. 1, the average value of absolute correlation coefficient of all key words is less than 0.6, and the average value of correlation coefficient of 90% key words is less than 0.5. Therefore, the 30 key words selected in this paper have no strong correlation with each other. In the case of high data utilization, they can cover more comprehensive data information and achieve more accurate population assessment.

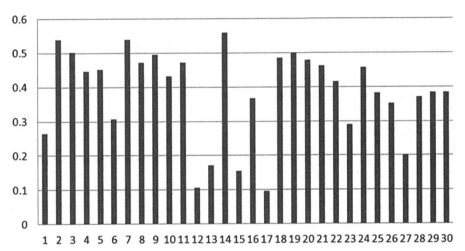

Fig. 1. Average value of the absolute value of the key words spearman correlation coefficient.

3.4 Neural Network Model

This paper uses the BP neural network to evaluate the population through the three stages of population assessment network construction, population assessment network training and population assessment network prediction. In the network construction phase, this paper constructs a BP neural network, in which the input and output sequences are (x, y), the number of network layers is three, except for one neuron in the last layer, and 128 neurons in other layers. The loss function is mse, the optimizer is adam, and the activation function is relu. The network training stage consists of the following five steps.

STEP1: Initialize the population assessment network. Initializing the connection weights t_{jk}, t_{ij} between the hidden layer, the input layer and the output layer neuron, the threshold a, b between the output layer and the hidden layer, the learning rate η and the fixed neuron excitation function;

STEP2: Calculate and output the hidden layer. The output H of the hidden layer is calculated from the input layer and the implicit inter-layer connection weight value t_{ij}, the variable x, and the hidden layer threshold a.

$$H_j = f\left(\sum_{i=1}^{n} t_{ij}x_i - a_j\right) j = 1, 2, \cdots l \tag{2}$$

STEP3: Calculate output layer. Based on the threshold b, the connection weight w_{jk}, and the output H of the hidden layer, the population estimation predicted output value O of the BP neural network is calculated.

$$O_k = \sum_{j=1}^{l} H_i t_{jk} - b_k k = 1, 2 \cdots m \tag{3}$$

STEP4: Calculate the population assessment error. The population assessment network prediction error e is calculated based on the predicted output O and the expected output Y. If the error meets the requirements, the training is ended. If it is not satisfied, continue with STEP5.

STEP5: According to the error e, after updating the thresholds a and b and the connection weights t_{ij}, t_{jk} the process proceeds to STEP2.

3.5 SVM Model

SVM is a machine learning method developed based on statistical theory and belongs to a supervised learning algorithm.

Let the 30-dimensional key word data sample set be $\{(x_i, y_i)|i = 1, 2, \ldots, n\}$, $X \in R^d$, the category label be $y \in P\{+1, -1\}$, and the classification hyperplane established in the high-level feature space be $w \cdot x + b = 0$, where w is the weight vector and b is the threshold. In the case where the optimal classification hyperplane is linearly inseparable, the original problem is converted into its dual problem.

$$\begin{cases} \max W(a) = \sum_{i=l}^{n} a^i - \frac{l}{2} y_i y_j a_i a_j K\left(x_i x_j\right) \\ s.t \, 0 \leq a_i \leq C, \sum_{i=l}^{n} a_i y_i = 0, i = 1, 2, \ldots, n \end{cases} \tag{4}$$

In the equation, C is the error penalty coefficient, a_i is the Lagrange multiplier; $K\left(x_i x_j\right)$ is the kernel function. Commonly used kernel functions include linear, polynomial, radial basis and multilayer perceptrons. In this paper, Gaussian kernel function is described as

$$K\left(x_i x_j\right) = \exp\left(-\frac{||x - x_i||^2}{2\sigma^2}\right) \tag{5}$$

According to the above analysis, the constructed population assessment model will obtain a decision function by solving a quadratic programming problem and predict the unknown population size.

3.6 Random Forest

Random forest is an algorithm that is composed of many decision trees. It belongs to an algorithm of Bagging framework, and its weak model is trained by decision tree algorithm (CART algorithm).

Randomly extract a subset from all 30-dimensional key word dataset features to train and construct each demographic decision tree model, and pass the gini value as the criterion for the segmentation node. The gini index is calculated as follows:

$$GL_m = 1 - \sum_{k=1}^{|K|} p_{mk}^2 \tag{6}$$

In the formula, k means that there are k categories, and p_{km} represents the proportion of the category k in the node m (the variation of the gini value is calculated for each node by the feature m).

4 Experiments

4.1 Access to Data Sources

Since the population of the statistical yearbook used for the evaluation of results is mostly divided by administrative districts, in order to directly compare with the statistical yearbook data, this paper selects 122 county-level regions in Hunan Province as grid units. Using Google Maps as the interface for key word data acquisition, query 30 key words in 122 grids, and use crawlers to crawl 122×30-dimensional population assessment key word data. Taking the 30-dimensional key word data obtained by Shuangfeng County as an example, the values of key word 1 to key word 30 are: 0.00272727, 0.03022727, 0.00625, 0, 0.02488636, 0.00034091, 0.02988636, 0.00397727, 0.00977273, 0.00193182, 0.00352273, 0.00181818, 0, 0.53522727, 0.07079545, 0.09920455, 0.03545455, 0.06852273, 0.03284091, 0.00386364, 0.00079545, 0.00227273, 0.00181818, 0.00147727, 0.01136364, 0.00022727, 0.005, 0.00375, 0.01136364, 0.00068182, respectively.

4.2 Evaluation Standard

Root-Mean-Square Error (RMSE)
The root mean square error is the square root of the the square of deviation between the predicted value and the real value and the ratio of the number of observations to n

which is used to measure the deviation between the observed value and the true value. The calculation formula is as follows:

$$Re = \sqrt{\frac{(D_i - d_i)^2}{n}} \tag{7}$$

In the formula, D_i is the true value, and d_i is the measured value, and n is the number of observations.

Error Precisions

Error precisions are the approximation between the observed value and the true value. The calculation formula is as follows:

$$P_i = \frac{D_i - d_i}{100\%} \tag{8}$$

In the formula, D_i is the true value, and d_i is the measured value.

4.3 Display and Analysis of Experimental Results

This article uses grid cells as the basic unit of population assessment. Through our method, the population assessment is not limited to the fixed area by administrative area. This makes the population assessment more diversified and liberalized in regional selection, providing more accurate and scientific support for social resource allocation and data statistics. The prediction results of the three types of models will be displayed and analyzed from three perspectives: the root-mean-square error, the error precision, and whether the predicted value and the true value have significant differences.

Display of Predicted Results and Comparison of Root-Mean-Square Error
The BP neural network model, SVM model and random forest model trained by 31 key word data were used to evaluate the population of 122 grid areas Because the root mean square error is mostly used to measure the deviation between the observed value and the truth value, the prediction result of the model is taken as the observed value in this paper, and the population in the yearbook is taken as the truth value. The root mean square errors of the three models are shown in Figs. 2, 3 and 4.

It can be seen from Figs. 2, 3 and 4. that the root-mean-square errors of the three population assessment models are: 268.9, 237.3, and 172.24. Obviously, the random forest model has the smallest prediction error and the highest population evaluation accuracy. The SVM model is second, and the BP neural network has the worst prediction effect. Since the data set used for training in this paper has only 122 samples, the prediction effect of BP neural network cannot be optimal in the case of small samples, which is basically consistent with the experimental results.

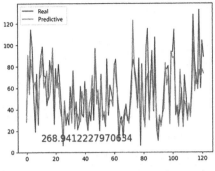

Fig. 2. BP neural network prediction results

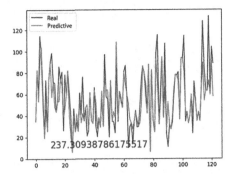

Fig. 3. SVM model prediction results

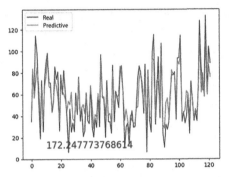

Fig. 4. Random forest model prediction results

Comparison and Analysis of Error Precisions

The most intuitive expression of the prediction effect is the error precisions between the predicted value and the true value. The population of the 122 grid cells predicted by rasterization will be summed according to the administrative district, and the population assessment of 14 cities will be compiled and counted. The error precisions are calculated by using the true value of the population on the statistical yearbook and the population after the summation. The results are shown in Table 1.

As shown in Table 1, the accuracy errors of the three models in 14 cities are: 0.06, 0.06, and 0.03. Random forest has obvious precision advantages in the research of key words and grid unit selection liberalization population evaluation area.

Combined with the above, from the analysis of different angles, it is basically summarized that the population assessment on the grid unit proposed in this paper can not only maintain its advantages in liberalization and flexibility in regional selection, but also have better accuracy in population assessment accuracy, and the random forest has the strongest prediction accuracy in the three models.

Table 1. Comparison and analysis of error accuracy.

Model	BP neural network			SVM			Random forest		
City name	Predictive value	True value	Error	Predictive value	True value	Error	Predictive value	True value	Error
Loudi	331.79	391.76	0.15	365.58	391.76	0.07	337.64	391.76	0.14
Yueyang	565.21	573.33	0.01	493.75	573.33	0.14	576.21	573.33	0.01
Changde	587.24	584.48	0.00	521.04	584.48	0.11	525.94	584.48	0.10
Zhangjiajie	134.27	153.16	0.12	106.25	153.16	0.31	204.05	153.16	0.33
Huaihua	449.87	489.33	0.08	478.26	489.33	0.02	590.93	489.33	0.21
Zhuzhou	491.19	402.15	0.22	413.34	402.15	0.03	466.32	402.15	0.16
Yongzhou	503.34	538.55	0.07	611.53	538.55	0.14	578.01	538.55	0.07
Xiangtan	292.41	285.24	0.03	309.12	285.24	0.08	318.53	285.24	0.12
Xiangxi	261.43	263.82	0.01	275.06	263.82	0.04	295.84	263.82	0.12
Yiyang	425.41	439.20	0.03	402.97	439.20	0.08	391.50	439.20	0.11
Hengyang	633.87	720.53	0.12	624.96	720.53	0.13	723.76	720.53	0.00
Shaoyang	669.82	737.54	0.09	747.16	737.54	0.01	799.31	737.54	0.08
Quzhou	454.62	473.16	0.04	488.52	473.16	0.03	534.77	473.16	0.13
Changsha	643.11	791.81	0.19	617.23	791.81	0.22	710.13	791.81	0.10
Average	460.26	488.86	0.06	461.05	488.86	0.06	503.78	488.86	0.03

5 Conclusion

At present, the mainstream population assessment method mainly uses time-varying population data to predict from a total number of fixed administrative districts using a single forecasting model. The existing problems are: predicting the required population data depends on the census, which consumes a lot of manpower and material resources; the predicted results cannot be used for detailed analysis; the method of model is single and lacks rationality of controlled reference.

Based on the idea of regional rasterization, this paper uses crawlers to extract key word data of each grid and convert it into 30-dimensional vector, which solves the data acquisition scientifically and conveniently. From the three models of SVM, neural network and random forest, the population is predicted. By comparison with actual data, the average error of the three models was 5.7%, 5.8%, and 3.1% under limited data. Through the significant difference analysis, the results predicted by the SVM and the random forest model method are not significantly different from the real values. After comprehensive consideration, the random forest model is finally selected to predict the raster data. The advantage is that the model has higher accuracy under limited data. At the same time, the predicted results are no longer confined to fixed administrative districts, and the smallest unit of population assessment is refined to the grid. It can provide detailed data for population analysis, which shows that this is a reliable method of population assessment and has certain practical value. In the following work, we will study how to optimize the selection of key words and improve the model.

References

1. Tian, F.: Research on population prediction method system. J. Anhui Univ. Philos. Soc. Sci. Ed. **35**(5), 151–156 (2011)
2. Lu, W., Liu, B.: A method for predicting the total population based on BP neural network. China Manag. Informationization **19**(20), 144–145 (2016)
3. Shan, C.: Application of Grey Markov model in population prediction of Jiangxi Province. Sci. Mosaic **26**(4), 95–100 (2015)
4. Pan, D., Liu, Z.: Application of logistic biodifferential model in population prediction. Stat. Decis. (20), 157–158 (2009)
5. Tian, F.: Population probability prediction method and application. Northwest Popul. **32**(05), 9–13 (2011)
6. Liu, F., Zhuo, H.E., Tan, X.: Comparison of richards model and logistic model in population forecasting. J. Chongqing Technol. Bus. Univ. (Natural Sci. Ed.) **34**(01), 6–9 (2017)
7. Ren, Q., Hou, D.: Stochastic method of population prediction: based on Leslie matrix and ARMA model. Popul. Res. **35**(2), 28–42 (2011)
8. Zhu, C., Ye, M., Hu, Z.: Population prediction based on optimized discrete Grey and ANN combination model. Modern Inf. Technol. **2**(5), 40 (2018)
9. Lee, R.D., Carter, L.R.: Modeling and forecasting US mortality. J. Am. Stat. Assoc. **87**(419), 659–671 (1992)
10. Keyfitz, N.: Introduction to the mathematics of population: with revisions. Addison-Wesley Series in Behavioral Science Quantitative Methods (1977)
11. Keyfitz, N., Caswell, H.: Applied Mathematical Demography. Springer, New York (2005)
12. Wu, C.W., Shie, B.E., Tseng, V.S., et al.: Mining Top-K high utility itemsets. In: Proceedings of the 18th ACM SIGKDD International Conference on Knowledge Discovery and Data Mining, pp. 78–86. ACM (2012)

Salary Satisfaction of University Teachers with Different Professional Positions

Shufeng Zhang[1](✉), Yaya Luo[2](✉), and Yu-Fan Zhou[3](✉)

[1] China Institute of Nuclear Information and Economics, Beijing, China
okzhangtt@sina.cn
[2] Department of Data Science and Intelligent Media, Communication University of China,
Beijing, China
gemini070@126.com
[3] School of Communication and Journalism, Zhengzhou University, Zhengzhou, China
3317613395@qq.com

Abstract. This study is mainly to analyze the correlation between talents with different professional positions and salary satisfaction among college teachers. A total of 1,911 valid questionnaires were collected by questionnaire survey. First of all, it is judged whether there is a significant correlation between the two through cross-contingency analysis, and then it is further determined by correspondence analysis and qualitative data modeling. Finally, the study found that there is a significant difference in salary satisfaction among different professional and technical personnel, and the higher the positions, the higher the satisfaction with their current salary level. Based on this finding, the paper puts forward targeted programs to mobilize teachers' enthusiasm, including conducting regular salary surveys for teachers, establishing a scientific and perfect performance management system, and improving teachers' income level.

Keywords: Different technical positions · Satisfaction with salary · Cross-contingency analysis · Correspondence analysis · Qualitative data modeling

1 Introduction

Nowadays, knowledge plays an increasingly important role in the economy. China also attaches more importance to the strategy of strengthening the country with talents. China's education level is getting higher and higher, and the demand for university teachers is increasing. How to attract talents has been a major concern of universities. Among university teachers, young and middle-aged teachers aged 26–45 are the main force of all university teachers, and their current situation largely represents the situation of all university teachers. Therefore, this study selects young and middle-aged groups as the research object. As an important source of income for university teachers, salary affects the enthusiasm of university teachers significantly. Based on the real data from the questionnaire survey, this paper studies whether there is a significant relationship between the professional and technical personnel and their satisfaction with salary, and further determines how the relationship exists.

© Springer Nature Singapore Pte Ltd. 2020
X. Sun et al. (Eds.): ICAIS 2020, CCIS 1252, pp. 616–625, 2020.
https://doi.org/10.1007/978-981-15-8083-3_55

2   Description of Data Sources and Indicators

In this study, young and middle-aged teachers in some colleges and universities across the country were given questionnaires and collected. Among them, 1,911 participated in the survey and 1,911 valid questionnaires were collected. Among the teachers, there are 220 junior professionals, 898 intermediate professional positions, 471 deputy senior talents and 322 senior talents respectively. The indicators related to this study covered by the questionnaire mainly include age, professional and technical post level, annual salary of the school (excluding income from scientific research performance, faculty award remuneration, etc.), total annual income (including income from scientific research performance, faculty award remuneration, etc.), salary system, salary level and economic pressure status, and satisfaction with their current salary level.

3   Salary Status of Talents with Different Technical Positions

Before researching the Salary Satisfaction of University Teachers with Different Professional Positions, it is necessary to carry out descriptive statistical analysis of their currently salary situation. The indicators selected here mainly include the salary of the school.

As can be seen from Table 1, the annual salary of the talents with different professional and technical positions is mainly below 150,000 yuan. Among them, among the interviewees with incomes of less than 50,000 yuan in different professional and technical positions, the proportion of junior professional and technical positions is relatively

Table 1. The current situation of salary and annual income of talents with different professional and technical positions

	junior	intermediate	deputy_senior	senior
below 5	47.27%	24.28%	18.68%	4.97%
5 to 10	44.09%	64.48%	61.15%	16.15%
11 to 15	6.36%	10.02%	13.59%	17.39%
16 to 20	1.82%	1.00%	3.18%	10.87%
21 to 25	0.00%	0.00%	1.27%	7.45%
26 to 30	0.00%	0.00%	0.85%	6.52%
31 to 35	0.45%	0.00%	0.42%	13.35%
36 to 40	0.00%	0.00%	0.21%	12.42%
41 to 45	0.00%	0.00%	0.00%	4.66%
46 to 50	0.00%	0.00%	0.21%	3.73%
51 to 55	0.00%	0.00%	0.00%	0.31%
56 to 60	0.00%	0.00%	0.00%	1.24%
61 to 65	0.00%	0.00%	0.00%	0.62%
66t o 70	0.00%	0.00%	0.21%	0.00%
71 to 75	0.00%	0.00%	0.00%	0.31%
76 to 80	0.00%	0.00%	0.21%	0.00%
81 to 85	0.00%	0.11%	0.00%	0.00%
91 to 95	0.00%	0.11%	0.00%	0.00%

large, accounting for 47.27%. In the income range of 50,000 yuan to 100,000 yuan, the proportion of professional and technical personnel at intermediate and deputy senior levels is relatively large, 64.48% and 61.15% respectively. Among the different professional and technical personnel with incomes of more than 160,000 yuan, the proportion of senior professional and technical personnel is relatively large, accounting for 62.49%, and its income distribution is the most scattered.

4   Research on Different Technical Positions and Attitudes Towards Salary

4.1   Cross-contingency Analysis

According to the grouping of two variables, the results are called contingency table, and the frequency analysis under cross grouping is called contingency table analysis. Firstly, the cross-contingency table of different professional and technical positions and salary satisfaction is established as shown in Table 2. Then the cross-contingency analysis is carried out to analyze whether there is a certain correlation between them, and the results are as shown in Table 3. Because Pearson Chi-square statistics and likelihood ratio Chi-square test results correspond to the concomitant probability less than 0.05, it can be explained that there is a correlation between different professional and technical positions and pay satisfaction.

Table 2. Technical positions * satisfaction with salary Cross table

		Satisfaction with salary					Total
		Very satisfied	Quite satisfied	General	Not very satisfied	Very unsatisfied	
Technical positions	junior	3	27	61	74	55	220
	intermediate	4	75	314	302	203	898
	deputy senior	1	51	154	147	118	471
	senior	17	100	115	49	41	322
Total		25	253	644	572	417	1911

Table 3. Chi-square tests

	Value	df	Asymp. Sig. (2-sided)
Pearson Chi-square	191.550[a]	12	.000
Likelihood ratio	167.036	12	.000
Linear-by-linear association	73.886	1	.000
N of valid cases	1911		

[a] 2 cells (10.0%) have expected count less than 5. The minimum expected count is 2.88.

4.2 Optimal Scale Analysis

In order to further test the correlation between the two, the optimal scale analysis in SPSS is adopted. The optimal scale analysis is also called classified regression and is mainly applied to the correlation analysis where independent variables and dependent variables are classified data. It is also possible to quantify the differences in different levels of classified variables to obtain results similar to linear regression. Because the two variables here are classified data in qualitative data, the optimal scale analysis can analyze the correlation between the two variables, with different professional and technical positions as independent variables and satisfaction with salary as dependent variables. The results are shown in Table 4.

Table 4. Coefficients

	Standardized coefficients		df	F	Sig.
	Beta	Bootstrap (1000) estimation of Std. error			
professional_and_technical_posts	−.309	0.28	2	123.736	.000

Dependent variable: satisfaction_with_salary

4.3 Correspondence Analysis

The most intuitive way to study the relationship between variables of two qualitative data is correspondence analysis. Correspondence analysis utilizes the idea of dimensionality reduction and analyses the structure of original data, aiming at revealing the correlation between attribute variables and various states of attribute variables in a concise and intuitive way. The Euclidean distance is used to measure the correspondence analysis distance. The data standardization method chooses "make the sum of columns equal, delete the average value". Table 5 gives the corresponding table. It can be seen that the total number of observations n = 1911, is equal to the original data.

Table 5. Correspondence table

professional_and_ technical_posts	satisfaction_with_salary					
	very_satisfied	quite_satisfied	general	not_very_satisfied	very_unsatisfied	Active margin
junior	3	27	61	74	55	220
intermediate	4	75	314	302	203	898
deputy_senior	1	51	154	147	118	471
senior	17	100	115	49	41	322
Active margin	25	253	644	572	417	1911

Table 6 shows the relationship between row and column scores. The inertia ratio represents the proportion of total inertia and cumulative percentage respectively explained by each dimension. It can be seen from this that the proportion of inertia in the first dimension and the second dimension accounts for 99.5% of total inertia. Therefore, two dimensions can be selected for analysis.

Table 6. Summary

Dimension	Singular value	Inertia	Proportion of inertia		Confidence singular value	
			Accounted for	Cumulative	Standard deviation	Correlation 2
1	.561	.315	.657	.657	.008	.740
2	.402	.162	.338	.995	.007	
3	.049	.002	.005	1.000		
Total		.479	1.000	1.000		

Tables 7 and Table 8 are the two sets of coordinates needed to draw the final superimposed scatter plot. The first is the point coordinate table of row variables (professional and technical positions). For example, junior (0.126, −0.829), intermediate (0.250, −0.879); Table second is the point coordinate table of listed variables (satisfaction with salary level), such as very satisfied (1.133, 0.855), relatively satisfied (0.224, 0608), etc. Specifically, they summarize the information related to the states of the rows and columns of the column-linked table. The Mass part refers to the marginal probability of the row and column of the column-linked table values, namely PI and PJ, and Score in Dimension is the score of each dimension, namely the coordinate values of the row and column in the two-dimensional graph. Inertia is the square of the weighted distance between each row (column) and its center of gravity. It can be seen that the total inertia of the row section is equal to the total inertia of the column section. The Contribution part refers to the contribution of each state of a row (column) to each dimension (common factor) feature root and the contribution of each dimension to each state feature root of a row (column). For example, in the first dimension, the value corresponding to senior is the largest, which is 0.581, indicating that senior contributes the most to the first dimension. In the contribution of dimensions to the characteristic roots of each state, we can see that the distribution of characteristic roots of other professional and technical positions except junior is mostly concentrated in the first dimension, which shows that the first dimension reflects most of the differences of different positions and states.

Table 7. Overview row points[a]

professional_and_technical posts	Mass	Score in dimension		Inertia	Contribution				
		1	2		Of point to inertia of dimension		Of dimension to inertia of point		
					1	2	1	2	Total
junior	.250	.126	−.829	.072	.007	.426	.031	.959	.990
intermediate	.250	−.879	.715	.160	.344	.317	.677	.321	.999
deputy_senior	.250	−.398	−.394	.038	.067	.096	.555	.409	.963
senior	.250	1.142	.507	.209	.581	.160	.876	.124	1.000
Active total	1.000			.479	1.000	1.000			

[a]Symmetrical normalization

Table 8. Overview column points[a]

satisfaction_with_salary	Mass	Score in dimension		Inertia	Contribution				
		1	2		Of point to inertia of dimension		Of dimension to inertia of point		
					1	2	1	2	Total
very_satisfied	.200	1.133	.855	.203	.457	.364	.709	.290	.998
quite_satisfied	.200	.224	.608	.037	.018	.184	.153	.806	.959
general	.200	−.545	.662	.069	.106	.218	.486	.514	1.000
not_very_satisfied	.200	−.802	.528	.095	.229	.139	.759	.236	.995
very_satisfied	.200	−.729	.440	.075	.190	.960	.792	.207	.999
Active total	1.000			.479	1.000	1.000			

[a]Symmetrical normalization

From Table 7 and Table 8, the following superimposed scatter plot can be obtained (Fig. 1). From the scatter plot, it can be clearly seen that with the origin of dimension 1 as the boundary, the right side is very satisfied and quite satisfied, the left side is general, not satisfied and very dissatisfied, the right side can represent satisfaction with the salary level, and the left side is dissatisfied with the salary. The satisfaction degree of the senior talents to the wage level is mainly very satisfactory and quite satisfactory, while the satisfaction degree of the middle-level talents to the wage level is mainly general, not very satisfactory and very unsatisfactory.

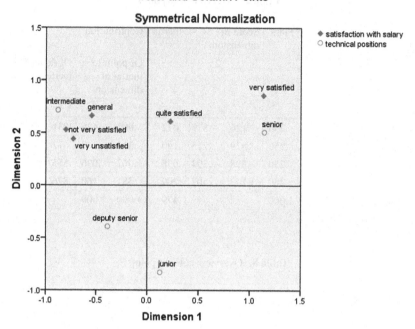

Fig. 1. Scatter plot

4.4 Logarithmic Linear Model

Logarithmic linear model analysis is a linear model in which the logarithm of grid frequency of contingency table data is expressed as each variable and its interaction effect. Then the basic idea of variance analysis and logical transformation are used to test the multivariate statistical method of the interaction size of each variable and its interaction effect. Various types of categorical variables, including their main effects and interaction effects, can be analyzed directly. The logarithmic linear model is implemented by using the loglinear model in SPSS software. Table 9 is an estimate of the parameters of the model and the test results of the parameters. It can be seen from the test results that most of the parameters passed the significance test.

α junior $= -0.529$; α deputy senior $= -0.100$; α senior $= 0.039$;
β very satisfied $= -2.425$;
β quite satisfied $= 0.116$; β general $= 0.984$
β not very satisfied $= 0.798$; β very unsatisfied $= 0.527$
γ junior quite satisfied $= -0.592$;
γ intermediate quite satisfied $= -0.314$
γ deputy senior quite satisfied $= 0.246$;
γ senior quite satisfied $= 0.392$

Table 9. Estimates of parameters

Effect	Parameter	Estimate	Std. error	Z	Sig.	95% Confidence interval	
						Lower bound	Upper bound
technical_positions*	1	.275	.378	.728	.467	−.466	1.016
satisfaction_with_salary	2	−.205	.158	−1.298	.194	−.514	.104
	3	−.267	.131	−2.038	.042	−.524	−.010
	4	.110	.129	.850	.395	−.143	.363
	5	−.592	.348	−1.700	.089	−1.275	.091
	6	−.314	.124	−2.519	.012	−.557	−.070
	7	.246	.104	2.367	.018	.042	.450
	8	.392	.106	3.710	.000	.185	.600
	9	−1.001	.514	−1.948	.051	−2.008	.006
	10	−.006	.163	−.036	.971	−.325	.314
	11	.225	.145	1.555	.120	−.059	.509
	12	.364	.146	2.488	.013	.077	.651
technical_positions	1	−.529	.105	−5.039	.000	−.734	−.323
	2	.590	.920	6.383	.000	.409	.771
	3	−.100	.133	−.751	.453	−.361	.161
satisfaction_with_salary	1	−2.425	.223	−10.867	.000	−2.863	−1.988
	2	.116	.081	1.434	.152	−.043	.275
	3	.984	.070	14.041	.000	.846	1.121
	4	.798	.072	11.019	.000	.656	.940

A positive parameter indicates a positive effect, a negative parameter indicates a negative effect, and zero is an invalid effect. Based on the above results, we may come to the following conclusion:

(i)   β very satisfied is negative and β very unsatisfied is positive, which indicates that most of the university talents surveyed are not satisfied with the current salary level.

(ii) α junior and α deputy senior are negative, indicating that junior and deputy senior talents are not satisfied with the current salary on the whole, and because α junior < α deputy senior, the satisfaction of deputy senior talents with salary is higher than that of junior talents; α senior is positive, indicating that senior talents are more satisfied with the current salary situation.

(iii) Through the study of the interaction effect between different positions and salary satisfaction, γ senior quite satisfied is positive, indicating that the senior has a positive effect on salary satisfaction; γ deputy senior quite satisfied is also positive, indicating that the deputy senior has a positive effect on salary satisfaction; γ intermediate quite satisfied is negative, shows that the intermediate has a negative effect on salary satisfaction; γ junior quite satisfied is also negative, indicating that the junior also has a negative effect on salary satisfaction. And γ junior quite satisfied < γ intermediate quite satisfied < γ deputy senior quite satisfied < γ senior quite satisfied.

5 Conclusions and Suggestions

Through the above research and analysis, it is found that, on the whole, most college teachers are not satisfied with the current salary, which needs to be paid attention to. As the main motive force and source of income for teachers to work hard, salary has a strong incentive to teachers, which affects teachers' teaching attitude and teaching effect. If most teachers are not satisfied with salary, their work enthusiasm will be difficult to mobilize, teachers' potential will be difficult to fully tap, and eventually even affect learning. The teaching quality and scientific level of the school. In addition, there are significant differences in salary satisfaction among different professional and technical personnel. Specifically, both senior and Vice-Senior talents are more satisfied with salary than middle and junior talents, and the higher the title, the higher their satisfaction with their current salary status.

Based on this study, it is found that most college teachers are not satisfied with their current salary. Therefore, the following suggestions are put forward for improvement:

(i)   Conduct teachers' salary survey regularly. Only by understanding teachers' satisfaction and expectation of salary status quo, can school administrators fully understand teachers' ideas and avoid making salary arbitrarily and causing teachers' dissatisfaction [1]. In our country, there is not much effort to carry out spot checks on teachers in the whole country, and the individual knowledge of teachers is not enough. Therefore, it is suggested that relevant departments or social organizations should carry out scientific investigations regularly to ensure that teachers' salaries are kept in mind at all times.

(ii) Establishing a scientific and perfect performance management system. The more satisfied teachers are with their salaries, the better they can fulfill their teaching and scientific research tasks in accordance with the regulations of the school. Therefore, in salary management, colleges and universities should not only tilt towards the talents at the forefront, but also ensure that the interests of all kinds of personnel are distributed in a balanced way [4]. Guaranteeing the basic vital interests of junior and intermediate professional titles and minimizing the sense of imbalance caused by Pay differences will help the smooth development of higher education and enhance the competitiveness of colleges and universities.

(iii) Increasing teachers' income level. Teachers' satisfaction with salary is low, and their turnover intention is high [5]. Compared with other professions, higher vocational college teachers are in a low state, which affects the enthusiasm and efficiency of teachers' work, and indirectly determines their willingness to pay attention. To raise the income level of university teachers is to make them reach the income level above the middle national income. Local financial institutions should improve the fund management mechanism and gradually improve the income level of teachers [5].

References

1. Xu, H.: Research on application of mathematical modeling in salary management of university teachers. Farm Staff (07), 184–185 (2019)
2. He, X.: Multivariate Statistical Analysis, 4th edn. Renmin University of China Press, Beijing (2015)
3. Cao, Y.: Research on qualitative data analysis method based on SPSS correspondence analysis. Fujian Comput. **34**(10), 4–6+20 (2018)
4. Chen, J.: University teachers' salary satisfaction on the impact of job performance and enthusiasm. China Hum. Resour. Dev. (08), 101–104 (2009)
5. Yao, M.: An empirical study on the relationship between salary satisfaction and the work enthusiasm of university staff-Putian University as an example. J. Harbin Univ. **40**(05), 133–136 (2019)
6. Sperling, J.D., Baer, R.J., Jelliffe-Pawlowski, L., Norton, M.E., Zlatnik, M.G.: 684: Gender differences in salary among university of California maternal-fetal medicine physicians. Am. J. Obstet. Gynecol. **220**(1), S452–S453 (2019)
7. Yu, Y., Li, F.: Empirical study on the impact of performance wage intensity on salary satisfaction of university staff. East China Econ. Manag. **28**(06), 172–176 (2014)
8. Quan, G., Fang, J.: Analysis on the characteristics of salary system of University of California at Berkeley and its enlightenment. Foreign Educ. Res. **44**(04), 30–39 (2017)
9. Roth, M.: To each according to their ability? Academic ranking and salary inequality across public colleges and universities. Appl. Econ. Lett. **25**(1), 34–37 (2018)

Defining Cost Function for Robust Embedding

Yanli Chen[1], Hongxia Wang[2(✉)], Hanzhou Wu[3], Yi Chen[4],
and Zhicheng Dong[5]

[1] School of Big Data and Computer Science, Guizhou Normal University,
Guiyang 550025, People's Republic of China
yanli_027@163.com
[2] College of Cybersecurity, Sichuan University, Chengdu 610065, Sichuan, China
hxwang@scu.edu.cn
[3] School of Communication and Information Engineering, Shanghai University,
Shanghai 200444, People's Republic of China
h.wu.phd@ieee.org
[4] School of Information Science and Technology, Southwest Jiaotong University,
Chengdu 611756, People's Republic of China
yichen.research@gmail.com
[5] College of Engineering, Tibet University, Lhasa 850000, People's Republic of China
dongzc666@163.com

Abstract. Embedding data into texture or high-frequency region will not arouse noticeable artifacts, meaning that, a low distortion can be achieved when suited region for data embedding is selected. It motivates us to extract texture features and spatial-correlation features to evaluate carrier characteristics for quantizing robustness. Meantime, since larger modification to cover elements provides high-level robustness, but lead to higher distortion, building a satisfactory trade-off relationship between robustness and distortion in terms of embedding modification is necessary. To this end, we take into account both the carrier characteristics and modification operation, and put forward a cost function for robust embedding. To evaluate the proposed robust cost function, we conduct simulation experiments with an embedding method based on the well-known LSB substitution, and further implement a detailed robust data hiding scheme using proposed robust function to illustrate its applicability. Experimental results have demonstrated that the proposed robust function can reflect robustness of data hiding well.

Keywords: Data hiding · Robust function · Robustness

1 Introduction

Modern data hiding (DH) refers to embedding data in cover media, such as text, image, audio, video. The embedding techniques have been developed in the past few decades [1,2]. Embedding distortion and robustness are two important

© Springer Nature Singapore Pte Ltd. 2020
X. Sun et al. (Eds.): ICAIS 2020, CCIS 1252, pp. 626–638, 2020.
https://doi.org/10.1007/978-981-15-8083-3_56

characteristics, and we always wish minimal embedding distortion and more robustness. There are a lot of works about embedding distortion [3–8], robust data hiding [9–17], and the trade-off between robustness and security [18–20], but few works about the robustness evaluation.

Usually, a DH scheme is considered more robust when more correct marked data are extracted. And also, if a DH scheme can resist some special attacks, they are also considered robust schemes. In [21], authors proposed a lossless robust DH scheme, in which a cover image was divided into a number of non-overlapping blocks and the arithmetic difference of each block was calculated, then, bits were embedded into blocks by shifting the arithmetic difference values. Owing to the separation of bit-0-zone and bit-1-zone as well as the particularity of arithmetic difference, this scheme can resist minor alteration and non-malicious attacks. In [9], it presented a robust steganography scheme which focused on embedding a secret image into a cover image in the discrete cosine transformation (DCT) domain using quantization index modulation (QIM), and mark data can also be extracted with JPEG compression and noise condition. In [11], Hadamard transform was employed as it required simple operations while it still attained robustness. Each bit of Hadamards coefficients was analyzed in terms of robustness and transparency for hiding the watermark information, and a bit-plane was found with maintaining both robustness and transparency. In [22], authors provided a solution of low capacity issue in standard least significant bit (LSB) technique by hiding multiple bits in a pixel/sample, and it also improved robustness by embedding data at the higher LSB layer. Then, it became more robust by considering multiple bit-planes randomly for embedding target data.

In most robust schemes, authors always pay more attentions on robustness by improving embedding strategies. For example, in [13], error correction code was used to improve the robustness. In sender side, before embedding, the secret message was coded using error correction code, so that in receiver side, the extracted error message can be corrected. The scheme in [11] embedded multiversions of mark data, and it was enough to extract only one version correctly. Traditional robust DH schemes often focus on embedding data in cover entities based on the statistical feature, and the image size is consistent with original image. However, there are works about DH schemes which change the image size after embedding. In [10], authors proposed a robust steganography based on texture synthesis, in which mark data was not embedded in the processing of synthesizing a texture image. Different with traditional steganography methods, this method provided an approach robustness and large payloads.

For embedding with modification, more robustness means larger embedding distortion, so the trade-off about the performance between robustness and distortion should be discussed. In [18], authors proposed an error model to analyse the fault tolerance, and used RS (Reed-Solomon) codes to improve the robustness-distortion performance. In [19], authors proposed a coefficient adjustment scheme to slightly modify original image, and made compressed version of the intermediate image same as stego-image. In [20], authors refined the robust steganographic scheme by considering asymmetric costs for different modification polarities and expanding the embedding domain for digital images, and aimed to aggregate the modifications on elements with small costs. Although these works considered both robustness and distortion, but it still is difficult to evaluate robustness directly.

Actually, there are some works relating to robustness evaluation. In [23], mark data was embedded in the frequency domain of still images, and the robustness of watermarking based on Discrete Wavelet Transform (DWT) was evaluated through evaluating the degradation of image quality caused by embedding watermark and the performance against specific attacks (scale, index color, gradation conversion, and frequency conversion). Then, they concluded that watermark in decomposition level 1 can provide better image quality, but less robust than that in level 2 domain.

Existing DH schemes usually pay their attentions on how to improve robustness of DH scheme, but few schemes concentrate on metric of robustness. In this paper, we venture to define a robust function as metric of embedding robustness, and also propose a robust DH scheme based on this function to illustrate its performance.

The remainder of this paper is organized as follows: in Sect. 2, we present the detail of robust function. In Sect. 3, the proposed robust DH scheme is described. We describe experimental results in Sect. 4, followed by our conclusions.

2 Robust Function

In this paper, we use bit plane substitution (BPS) as embedding method, in which embedding modification can be calculated by their positions, to evaluate robustness. For BPS, embedding in higher significant bit means more robustness, but more distortion. Obviously, embedding robustness and visual security contradict each other, but both of them should be considered in a DH. In this section, we mainly pay our attentions on the factors which would have impact on embedding robustness, such as image texture, spatial frequency and embedding modification, and based on these factors, construct a robust function.

2.1 The Principle of Robustness

Three different 16×16 blocks named as plain, edge and texture block are selected, and every block is divided into nonoverlapping 4×4 sub-blocks. We implement Not operation on fixed significance bit of DCT coefficients to explain the impact of every factor, and use PSNR, SSIM values to indicate embedding distortion.

2.2 Embedding Modification

Generally, embedding in higher significant bits produces more visual quality degradation, but it may make higher-level robustness. We use Fig. 1(a) to show the relation between PSNR values of marked image and corresponding positions of significant bits. The figure shows PSNR values degrade directly with higher significant bit, and we can presume that significance bit position is inversely proportional to visual quality. Figure 1(b) shows the relation between SSIM values and significant bits with different spatial frequencies. Both two figures illustrate high significant bits make serious image distortion both in pixel values and image structure. So, we consider that modification on significant bits is proportional to the image quality.

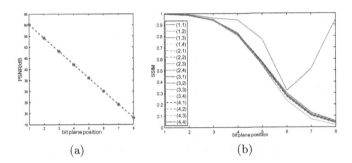

(a)   (b)

Fig. 1. Relation between quality of marked image and corresponding positions of significant bits: (a) PSNR (b) SSIM

2.3 Spatial Frequency

For embedding in a image block, the same embedding modification in different DCT coefficients would cause different visual distortion. To reveal the relation between SSIM values and spatial frequency, we embed data in all DCT coefficients. Figure 2 shows the 3-dimension curve of this relation with embedding in least 4 significant bit. Some inferences are drawn on the basis of this figure:

- The SSIM values with embedding in DC coefficients are greater than that in AC coefficients, that means the influence of modification in DC coefficients is smaller than that in AC coefficients.
- For zigzag scanned DCT coefficients, spatial frequency of neighbor coefficients is similar which result to small differences in SSIM values.
- The SSIM values in high frequency coefficients are greater than that in middle frequency coefficients for lower significant bits.

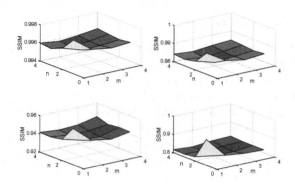

Fig. 2. 3-dimensional curve of this relation with least 4 significant bit

2.4   Texture Feature and Visual Effect

For images, abundant texture feature always produces great AC coefficient and masking effective in visual. As we illustrated in Sect. 2.3, hiding data in distinguished spatial frequencies may cause different. We use Fig. 3 to explain how texture feature influence the robustness and visual quality. The figure shows the SSIM-spatial frequency curve with different significance bit and different texture, and the SSIM values for texture blocks in the same significance bit are higher.

– Embedding in more abundant texture areas can produce less structure distortion.
– For the three frequency coefficients, visual distortion decreases with increasing texture area for embedding in the same significance bit.
– For middle frequency coefficients, distortion can attract attentions more easily than low and high frequency coefficients with high significance bit, especially in plain area.

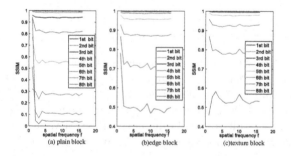

Fig. 3. SSIM-spatial frequency curve with each significance bit in different texture blocks

2.5 Expression of Robust Function

Based on illustrations above, we think that the embedding robustness is relevant to significance bit, spatial frequency, texture feature. A robust function is used to reflect their relation. To describe robust function clearly, let Sb, f and T denote the significance bit (we only consider the least 8 significance bit, $Sb = 1, 2, \cdots, 8$), spatial frequency (for 1D DCT coefficients with zigzag scanning, $f = 1, 2, \cdots, 16$) and texture feature respectively.

1. Embedding modification
   In Sect. 2.2, it was represented that robustness is proportional to significance bit, and we employ linear function to define significance bit factor as:

$$factor_{Sb} = \alpha Sb, \tag{1}$$

   where Sb denotes significance bit, α is a scaling factor.
2. Spatial frequency
   Section 2.3 indicated the effect of embedding in middle frequency, high frequency and low frequency coefficients speculatively. Embedding in lower frequency coefficients may produce higher robustness. Combining with the relation between spatial frequency and robustness, we use exponential function to express the effect of spatial frequency on robustness roughly:

$$factor_{Sf} = Sf^{-\beta} \tag{2}$$

   where Sf denotes spatial frequency in a block after zigzag scanning, and β is a real number and denote scale factor.
3. Texture feature
   In Sect. 2.4, it was illustrated that the influence of embedding in rich texture area is less than that in smoother area, and it can achieve better visual quality in higher frequency area. Naturally, we can define texture factor in spatial frequency according to the curve in Fig. 3 as follow:

$$\beta = \frac{\gamma}{T + 1} \tag{3}$$

   where γ is a real number and denote the scale factor.
4. Robust function expression
   Combining with above illustration, we present robust function as:

$$f_{robust} = factor_{Sb} \cdot factor_{Sf} = \alpha Sb \cdot f^{-\left(\frac{\gamma}{T+1}\right)} \tag{4}$$

where α, β, γ are set to be 1 in experiments.

3 Robust Data Hiding Scheme

We use a DH scheme based on proposed robust function to illustrate the validity of robust function. For an image, we use variance of AC coefficients in a block to describe the texture, and category blocks as texture, plain blocks, and edge blocks. To represent the texture of blocks efficiently, we use *texture index* (TI) to indicate the texture. The framework of this scheme is shown in Fig. 4, and we implement two phases before images transmission: preprocessing and embedding.

Definition 1: Assuming an image is divided into non-overlapping blocks, and every block is categorized based on texture feature according to variance of their AC coefficients. We use a number to distinguish the category and call it TI. Usually, image blocks are categorized into plain, edge and texture blocks, and TI values are assigned 0, 1 and 2 respectively.

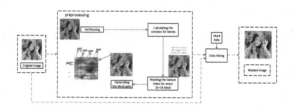

Fig. 4. The framework of proposed scheme

3.1 Preprocessing

We categorize every block with size 16×16 based on texture feature. With help of TI, we accomplish the goal of preprocessing which includes partitioning, acquiring texture index, matching blocks (shown in Fig. 4).

– Partitioning
  original image is divided into nonoverlapping 16×16 blocks, and furthermore, every block is divided into nonoverlapping 4×4 sub-blocks.
– Acquiring TI
  We calculate the variance of AC coefficients for every sub-block and assign TI values for them. At last, voting principle is used to get the category of every block.
– Matching blocks
  Every two neighbor blocks with largest TI difference is matched. Non-overlapping 3×3 blocks are gathered, and the center, around blocks are considered as the current block and neighbor blocks respectively. An neighbor block, whose texture is different from current block, is paired with current block.

3.2   Data Hiding

Assuming $b(i,j)$, $b(i',j')$ denote two paired blocks, and $b_{(m,n)}(i,j)$, $b_{(m,n)}(i',j')$ are sub-blocks in mth row, nth column of blocks $b(i,j)$, $b(i',j')$ respectively, and similar, $b_{(m,n)}^{(k,l)}(i,j)$, $b_{(m,n)}^{(k,l)}(i',j')$ indicate the DCT coefficients with spatial frequency (k,l) in sub-blocks $b_{(m,n)}(i,j)$, $b_{(m,n)}(i',j')$.

(1) Embedding location

For a sub-block, DC coefficients are selected to carry data. However, for DH scheme, larger modification means higher robustness, but more distortions. In order to demonstrate the validity of proposed robust function, we use robustness of AC coefficients in two paired sub-blocks to indicate the specific embedding location.

(2) Embedding method

The well known BPS method is used to embed data, and 1 bit is embedded in two paired sub-blocks. Assuming two paired sub-blocks are $b_{(m,n)}(i,j)$ and $b_{(m,n)}(i',j')$, the embedding is as follows.

Step1: Implementing XOR operation on the LSB of $b_{(m,n)}^{(0,0)}(i,j)$ and $b_{(m,n)}^{(0,0)}(i',j')$, and denote the result as b.

Step2: Searching the AC coefficient with maximal absolute value from two sub-blocks separately, and calculating their robustness using the proposed robust function. At last, denoting the one with more abundant as fp, and another as ft.

Step3: Comparing fp and ft, and defining the mapping between b and the compare result to embed data. let m denote to be embedded bit, the mapping relation is as follows. The embedding is accomplished by modifying the DC coefficient in smoother sub-block.

$$b = m \leftrightarrow fp \le ft, b = 1 - m \leftrightarrow fp > ft \tag{5}$$

4   Experimental Results

In this section, we will show the performance of proposed robust function. For DH schemes, high-level robustness indicates that more correct mark data can be extracted after attacks. The proposed DH scheme mainly focuses on robust embedding, and we select two kinds of noise in this experiments: Gaussian noise and Salt&Pepper noise. Without loss of generality, we use bit error rate (BER) to represent the quality of extracted data.

4.1   Experimental Setting

To reveal the validity of proposed robust function, we take into account 9 images (lena, baboon, bank, crowd, flowr, girl, hat, martha, loco) with BMP format shown in Fig. 5. In this experiments, we add multi-level noise attacks on these images, and then extract message from the polluted images.

Fig. 5. The original images used in experiments

4.2   Gaussian Noise Attack

In this part, we illustrate whether robust function can reflect actual robustness for Gaussian noise attacks. Firstly, we show the relation between actual BER, the calculated robustness with significant bits and texture in Fig. 6(a). This figure exposes that the performance of robustness on different texture feature is consistent with Sect. 2. Secondly, we show the relation between actual BER, the calculated robustness with spatial frequency, texture in Fig. 6(b). Also, the results are up to Sect. 2. At last, the relation between actual BER, the calculated robustness with spatial frequency and significance bit is exhibited in Fig. 6(c), and the curves response the Sect. 2.

In additional, BER of extracted message is shown in Table 1 in which '*' means that the embedded message size. There are some discussions about this table.

- For all images, with smaller noise, BER is moving toward 1. Table 1 shows that even if noise variance is smaller than 0.000001, data can not be extracted correctly, such as *loco, bank, girl* and *hat*. Comparing with other images, the texture in these images is less abundant than that in other images. So, the result means abundant texture can produce more robustness.
- For most images, with decreasing noise variance, BER values increase. However, for the random of Gaussian noise, it may make the texture of same blocks different and result in uncorrect extraction.
- For some images with abundant textures, such as *crowd, flowr*, abundant texture nearly exist in every block, and little modification cannot cause noticeable texture difference. That is to say, distinguishable noise attacks would produce similar results. For example, in Table 1, there are little difference for

BER of *crowd*, and for tiny Gaussian noise, the maximal AC absolute values usually change few which may lead to its robustness invariant.

Table 1. The BER of extracted data with Gaussion noise

noise variance	0.2	0.04	0.02	0.01	0.002	0.001	0.0005	0.0002	0.00002	0.000002
crowd	0.7041	*0.8120	*0.8122	*0.8232	*0.8236	*0.8236	*0.8236	*0.8236	*0.8242	*0.8248
martha	0.5653	0.6187	*0.7429	*0.8266	*0.7429	0.5895	0.8278	0.8278	0.8284	0.8286
loco	0.5491	0.6508	0.5676	*0.7733	*0.7742	*0.7749	*0.7755	*0.7828	*0.8292	0.8438
lena	*0.6234	*0.8375	*0.8380	*0.8380	*0.8380	*0.8380	*0.8380	*0.8380	*0.8391	*0.8391
bank	*0.6321	0.6658	*0.7500	0.8337	*0.8348	*0.8348	*0.8348	*0.8348	*0.8348	*0.8353
baboon	0.7333	*0.8133	*0.8240	*0.8241	*0.8241	*0.8241	*0.8243	*0.8243	*0.8243	*0.8243
flowr	0.6240	0.7270	*0.5500	0.7276	*0.7742	0.7285	0.7305	0.7342	0.8383	0.8683
girl	0.5184	0.8155	*0.7033	*0.8192	*0.8210	0.8213	0.8214	*0.8214	*0.8276	*0.8281
hat	0.6279	0.5398	0.5762	*0.7775	*0.8210	0.7711	0.7714	*0.8192	*0.8232	*0.8248

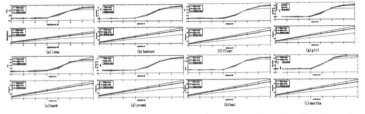

(a) Relation between significance bit and texture feature for Gaussian noise with a special spatial frequency

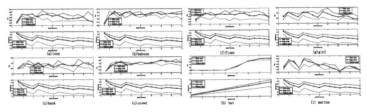

(b) Relation between spatial frequency and texture feature for Gaussian noise with a fixed significance bit

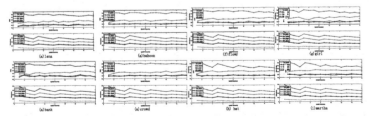

(c) Relation between spatial frequency and significance bit for Gaussian noise with the same texture feature

Fig. 6. The performance with Gaussian noise

Combining with the experimental results in Fig. 6(a), Fig. 6(b), and Fig. 6(c), the BER can keep with the robustness calculated using proposed robust function, and also Table 1 shows the experimental results are consistent with robustness regulation of DH schemes. We declare that proposed robust function is efficient for Gaussian noise.

4.3   Salt and Pepper Noise

Table 2 shows BER with Salt&Pepper attacks with different variance. Since Salt and Pepper noise can be considered as a image in which special number of pixels with values 0 and 255 are distributed randomly, it can change statistical property with great probability comparing with Gaussian noise. Table 2 shows experimental results about BER for images and the variance is less than that for Gaussian noise. The results are similar with Table 1.

Table 2. The BER of extracted data with Salt and Pepper noise

noise variance	0.005	0.003	0.002	0.001	0.0015	0.0005	0.00001	0.000001
crowd	*0.6260	0.5617	0.8155	*0.9866	*0.9794	*0.9923	1.0000	1.0000
martha	0.5795	0.5090	0.6098	0.5963	0.5788	0.6711	0.5646	*1.0000
loco	0.6699	*0.9642	*0.9762	*0.9884	0.9814	*0.9937	0.9997	0.9997
lena	0.5109	0.5880	0.5984	0.9832	0.6011	0.9440	*0.9978	1.0000
bank	0.6495	0.6870	0.7060	0.8120	*0.7929	*0.8630	0.9984	0.9984
baboon	0.6623	0.7505	0.6019	0.9300	0.5998	*0.9919	0.9997	1.0000
girl	0.6921	0.7338	0.6723	0.6804	0.6765	*0.9565	*0.9627	0.9997
hat	0.5459	0.5976	0.6137	0.5886	0.5498	0.6227	*0.9981	0.9996

5   Conclusion

This paper proposed a robust function based on image feature and embedding modification. Considering the impact from DH on images, we mainly took image texture and spatial frequency as image features, and BPS as embedding method to evaluate robustness. We discussed the relation between robustness and image texture, spatial frequency, and significance bit using experiments. And based on these relations, we defined a function as metric of robustness. And also, to illustrate the effect of robust function, we also proposed a framework of DH scheme using the proposed robust function. The results showed the proposed robust function can work well.

Acknowledgments. This work was supported by National Natural Science Foundation of China under the grant No. 61972269, No. 61902235 and No. 61561046. It was also supported by "Chen Guang" project co-funded by the Shanghai Municipal Education Commission and Shanghai Education Development Foundation.

References

1. Tew, Y., Wong, K.: An overview of information hiding in H.264/AVC compressed video. IEEE Trans. Circuits Syst. Video Technol. **24**(2), 305–319 (2014)
2. Shi, Y.-Q., Li, X., Zhang, X., Hao-Tian, W., Ma, B.: Reversible data hiding: advances in the past two decades. IEEE Access **4**, 3210–3237 (2016)
3. Nan-I, W., Hwang, M.-S.: A novel LSB data hiding scheme with the lowest distortion. Imaging Sci. J. **65**(6), 371–378 (2017)
4. Ma, X., Li, Z., Tu, H., Zhang, B.: A data hiding algorithm for H.264/AVC video streams without intra-frame distortion drift. IEEE Trans. Circuits Syst. Video Technol. **20**(10), 1320–1330 (2010)
5. Filler, T., Judas, J., Fridrich, J.: Minimizing additive distortion in steganography using syndrome-trellis codes. IEEE Trans. Inf. Forensics Secur. **6**, 920–935 (2011)
6. Zhang, W., Zhang, Z., Zhang, L., Li, H., Yu, N.: Decomposing joint distortion for adaptive steganography. IEEE Trans. Circuits Syst. Video Technol. **27**(10), 2274–2280 (2017)
7. Wang, Z., Yin, Z., Zhang, X.: Asymmetric distortion function for JPEG steganography using block artifact compensation. Signal Process. **11**(1), 107343 (2019)
8. Wang, Z., Qian, Z., Zhang, X., Yang, M., Dengpan, Y.: On improving distortion functions for jpegsteganography. IEEE Access **6**, 1 (2018)
9. Juarez-Sandoval, O., Espejel-Trujillo, A., Nakano-Miyatake, M., Perez-Meana, H.: Robust steganography based on QIM algorithm to hide secret images. Int. J. Comput. **7**(4), 145–152 (2013)
10. Qian, Z., Zhou, H., Zhang, W., Zhang, X.: Robust steganography using texture synthesis. In: Advances in Intelligent Information Hiding and Multimedia Signal Processing. SIST, vol. 63, pp. 25–33. Springer, Cham (2017). https://doi.org/10.1007/978-3-319-50209-0_4
11. Etemad, E., et al.: Robust image watermarking scheme using bit-plane of hadamard coefficients. Multimedia Tools Appl. **77**(2), 2033–2055 (2017). https://doi.org/10.1007/s11042-016-4278-1
12. Miyazaki, A., Okamoto, A.: Analysis of watermarking systems in the frequency domain and its application to design of robust watermarking systems. In: 2001 IEEE International Conference on Acoustics, Speech, and Signal Processing. Proceedings (Cat. No.01CH37221), vol. 3, pp. 1969–1972 (2001)
13. Zhao, Z., Guan, Q., Zhang, H., Zhao, X.: Improving the robustness of adaptive steganographic algorithms based on transport channel matching. IEEE Trans. Inf. Forensics Secur. **14**(7), 1843–1856 (2019)
14. Li, C., Zhang, Z., Wang, Y., Ma, B., Haung, D.: Dither modulation of significant amplitude difference for wavelet based robust watermarking. Neurocomputing **166**(20), 404–415 (2015)
15. Jayashree, N., Bhuvaneswaran, R.S.: A robust image watermarking scheme using z-transform, discrete wavelet transform and bidiagonal singular value decomposition. Comput. Mater. Continua **58**(1), 263–285 (2019)
16. Chen, Y., et al.: A robust zero-watermarking based on SIFT-DCT for medical images in the encrypted domain. Comput. Mater. Continua **61**(1), 363–378 (2019)
17. Liu, J., et al.: A novel robust watermarking algorithm for encrypted medical image based on DTCWT-DCT and chaotic map. Comput. Mater. Continua **61**(2), 889–910 (2019)
18. Zhang, Y., Qin, C., Zhang, W., Liu, F., Luo, X.: On the fault-tolerant performance for a class of robust image steganography. Signal Process. **146**, 99–111 (2018)

19. Tao, J., Li, S., Zhang, X., Wang, Z.: Towards robust image steganography. IEEE Trans. Circuits Syst. Video Technol. **29**(2), 594–600 (2019)
20. Xinzhi, Y., Chen, K., Wang, Y., Li, W., Zhang, W., Nenghai, Y.: Robust adaptive steganography based on generalized dither modulation and expanded embedding domain. Signal Process. **10**, 107343 (2019)
21. Zeng, X.T., Ping, L.D., Pan, X.Z.: A lossless robust data hiding scheme. Pattern Recogn. **43**(4), 1656–1667 (2010)
22. Samir Kumar Bandyopadhyay: A lossless robust data hiding scheme. Res. C Med. Eng. Sci. **3**(4), 1–4 (2018)
23. Okagaki, K., Takahashi, K., Ueda, H.: Robustness evaluation of digital watermarking based on discrete wavelet transform. In: 2010 Sixth International Conference on Intelligent Information Hiding and Multimedia Signal Processing, pp. 114–117, October 2010

Efficient Identity-Based Signature Authentication Scheme for Smart Home System

Dawei Song and Fengtong Wen[(✉)]

School of Mathematical Sciences, University of Jinan, Jinan 250022, China
wftwq@163.com

Abstract. The secure communication between users and devices is extremely important for Internet of Things (IoT) applications, if the communication between the two parties is not secure, user privacy and security will be threatened. So far, many solutions for secure communication between IoT devices have been proposed, but not all of them meet the security goals. Ashibani et al. proposed an identity-based signcryption scheme with message recover (IBS-MR) for smart home communications, they claimed that their solution not only provide effective authentication, but also ensure data integrity and confidentialty. But we find that it is not the case, their solution does not guarantee data integrity and is not resistant to replay attacks, in addition, it lacks formal security certification. Therefore, we propose a new identity-based signcryption scheme with message recover (IBS-MR) in smart home system to solve these problems, our scheme does not require hash-to-point operation and we prove our IBS-MR scheme secure in the random oracle model.

Keywords: Smart home · Signcryption · Authentication

1 Introduction

The Internet of Things is used in many fields, such as smart home, where people can remotely control devices and communicate with them through terminals such as mobile phones. In the smart home system, the following entities generally exist: (1) A trusted third party: it is usually a local server, while sometimes it is a cloud server, which responsible for registering new users and new smart devices, initializing the system, or pre-processing some parameters. (2) Smart home equipment: any home equipment that can be remotely controlled, the computing power of the equipment is limited. (3) End-user equipment for monitoring and controlling home devices such as mobile phones, tablets or smart watches via Wi-Fi or the Internet, and the computing power is not strong. (4) Home Gateway (HG): the gateway is the management and control center of the smart home system, which act as an intermediary between devices, and help with authentication and information exchange between devices through Wi-Fi or the Internet.

Supported by the National Science Foundation of Shandong Province (No. ZR2018LF006).

X. Sun et al. (Eds.): ICAIS 2020, CCIS 1252, pp. 639–648, 2020.
https://doi.org/10.1007/978-981-15-8083-3_57

How to communicate and transmit information securely between users and devices is an important issue. The device may contain some user privacy information, and insecure communication between devices may become the target of the attacker. Since most home devices are designed with low hardware and low power consumption, resulting in limited storage and computing power, so smart home environments require a lightweight security solution. Many lightweight security schemes based on symmetric ciphers have been proposed. Take [1] as an example, these schemes must provide each party with many shared symmetric keys for encrypting and decrypting any transmitted messages, which requires periodic replacement of keys between devices, if the key is compromised, all communication messages will be compromised. Bhattasali et al. combined with symmetric encryption and asymmetric encryption and hash function, proposed a lightweight encryption scheme [2, 3], which provides identity authentication, integrity and confidentiality. However, it mainly relies on symmetric cryptography and data encryption. In order to provide higher security, Li et al. [4] proposed a public key encryption protocol for smart home environment based on elliptic curve, which requires a trusted certificate authority to provide public and private keys, but this requires a lot of overhead. 1984, Shamir [5] first proposed the idea of identity-based cryptography, which saved the cost of certificates, but he failed to successfully build an IBE (Identity-Based Encryption) security scheme. Until 2001, Boneh-Franklin [6] established the first IBE program. Since then, the IBE scheme has emerged one after another. Salami et al. [7] proposed a lightweight solution for smart homes that uses IBE technology but still uses symmetric ciphers. Han et al. [8] proposed solution requires each device to communicate with the manufacturer, but it is obviously difficult to always access the manufacturer and send authentication information to it. Fouda et al. [9] proposed a lightweight mutual authentication scheme to reduce the amount of information exchanged during the authentication process. Although the proposed scheme implements two-step mutual authentication, it uses public key encryption and DH key exchange. The cryptographic technique suitable for solving the communication of smart home devices is based on elliptic curve IBE, which is superior to other technologies in terms of key size and encryption operation [10]. IBS (Identity Based Signcryption) is an IBE-based signcryption scheme that does not require access to trusted third parties during authentication. It only requires registration and key update. Compared to combined encryption and signature schemes, it can be more effective in meeting authentication, data integrity and confidentiality.

The remainder of this paper is organized as follow. Section 2 is preparation. Section 3 presents a brief review of Ashibani et al.'s scheme [11]. Then, we analyze their weaknesses in Sect. 4. Subsequently, we present a new scheme in Sect. 5. And we prove our scheme secure in the random oracle model in Sect. 6. Section 7 concludes the paper.

2   Preparation

2.1   Bilinear Pairing

Let G_1 and G_2 be two cyclic groups of order p which is a large prime, and $P_1 \in G_1$ be the generator of G_1.The bilinear pairing map is $e : G_1 \times G_1 \rightarrow G_2$, this map must satisfy the following properties:

Bilinear: $\forall P, Q \in G_1$ and $\forall a, b \in Z_p^*$ (Z_p^* is an multiplicative cyclic group), have $e(aP, bP) = e(P, Q)^{ab}$.

Nondegenerate: $\exists P, Q \in G_1$ make $e(P, Q) \neq I_{G_2}$ (I_{G_2} is the generator of G_2).

Computable: $\forall P, Q \in G_1$ calculate $e(P, Q)$ is valid.

2.2 Assumpution

It is known that there is no polynomial-time algorithm to solve the following problems, which form the basis of our scheme.

Computational Diffie-Hellman problem (CDH): Given $(P_1, aP_1, bP_1) \in G_1$ for unknown $a, b \in Z_p^*$ there is no polynomial time to compute $abP_1 \in Z_p^*$.

Bilinear Diffie-Hellman problem (BDH): Given $(P_1, aP_1, bP_1, cP_1) \in G_1$ for unknown $a, b, c \in Z_p^*$, it is difficult to compute $e\left(P_1, P_1^{abc}\right) \in G_1$.

Discrete Logarithm problem (DL): For an element $X \in G_1$, the DL problem is computing $x \in Z_p^*$ to make the equation $X = x \cdot P_1$ holds (Table 1).

Table 1. Used notations

Notation	Defintion
ID_{di}, ID_u, ID_{LS}	Unique identity of device di, user and LS
Q_{di}, Q_u, Q_{LS}	Public identity of device di, user and LS
S_{di}, S_u, S_{LS}	Private identity of device di, user and LS
k	Security parameter
s	Secret master key of the LS
H_1, H_2	Secure cryptographic hash functions
$e()$	Bilinear pairing
n	Plaintext length
m	Random number and timestamp encoding length
T	Effective time range
σ	Signcryption message

2.3 Identity-Based Signcryption

Identity-Based Signcryption (IBS) includes four steps:

System initialization: The local server (LS) uses k to generate system public parameters.

Registration and Extraction: The local server (LS) calculates the corresponding private key S_{di} based on the given identity ID_{di} and sends it back to the device.

Signcryption: In order to send the message M to the recipient with the identity ID_{di}, the sender encrypts the message M and then signs it consecutively using the public parameters including S_{di} of the sender and ID_{di} of the receiver, then produces σ.

Unsigncryption and Verify: When the receiver receives σ from the sender, it uses ID_{di}, S_{di} and σ to recover M after verifying the identity of the sender.

3   Overview of Ashibani et al.'s Scheme

3.1   System Initialization

1. The trusted LS generates the bilinear parameters (p, P_1, G_1, G_2, e) using k.
2. LS chooses two secure hash functions: $H_1 : \{0, 1\}^* \rightarrow G_1, H_2 : G_2 \rightarrow \{0, 1\}^n$.
3. LS chooses a random number $s \in Z_p^*$ as a master secret, and then calculates $P_{pub} = sP_1$.
4. LS published public parameters $(p, P_1, G_1, G_2, n, e, H_1, H_2, P_{pub})$ (Fig. 1).

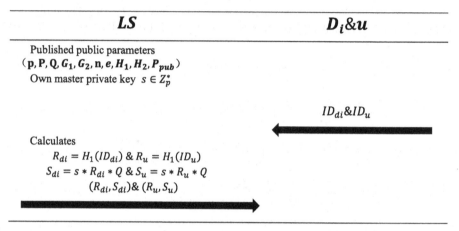

Fig. 1.   Setup and extract

3.2   Registration Phase

Each device submits its identity ID_{di} to the LS.

1. LS generates $Q_{di} = H_1(ID_{di})$.
2. LS calculates the private key $S_{di} = s \cdot Q_{di}$ using the master secret key s.
3. LS send (Q_{di}, S_{di}) with the public parameters to the registered devices over a secure channel.

3.3   Signcryption

Assume that the sender of this information exchange is d_1, the recipient is d_2. In order to signcrypt $M \in \{0, 1\}^n$ the sender works as follows:

1. d_1 generates a random integer $r_i \in Z_p^*$.

2. d_1 calculates the following: $C_1 = r_i P_1, K = H_2\big(e\big(r_i Q_{d2}, P_{pub}\big)\big)$

$$C_{enc} = M \oplus K, h = H_1(C_{enc}), C_{sign} = r_i h + S_{d1}.$$

3. d_1 sends $\sigma = \big(C_1, C_{enc}, C_{sign}\big)$ to the targeted receiver d_2.

3.4 Unsigncryption

After receiving the signcryption message.

1. d_2 verifies the received message by running the following equations:

$$e\big(P_1, C_{sign}\big) = e(h, C_1)e\big(Q_{d1}, P_{pub}\big)$$

2. If the equation holds, d_2 calculates $K' = H_2(e(S_{d2}, C_1)), M' = C_{enc} \oplus K'$.

Otherwise, it is determined to be invalid and the message will be rejected.

4 Cryptanalysis of Ashibani et al.'s Scheme

4.1 Modify Ciphertext Attack

The Ashibani's scheme have not verified whether the ciphertext was modified during the transfer. If the attacker intercepts and modifies the signature information transmitted on the channel then sends it to the device, the verifier can also pass the verification but will not find that the message has been tampered with.

4.2 Replay Attack

Ashinabi's scheme can't resist replay attacks. In the smart home environment, if the attacker intercepts the command sent by the user, he send it to the device again to complete the intrusion when the user is not at home.

4.3 Calculated Consumption and Secure Proof

Ashibani's scheme has used hash to point operations, which generates a lot of computational overhead. And they have not proved secure in the random oracle model.

5 Our Proposed Scheme

We have improved the scheme of Ashibani et al. We not only confirmed the identity of the signer but also verify the validity of the signature. We canceled the hash to point operation, simultaneously added time stamps to avoid replay attacks. At last we proved our scheme secure in the random oracle model.

As a signcryption scheme, it is also divided into four phases: Setup Phase, Extract Phase, Signcryption Phase, Verify Phase.

5.1 Setup Phase

1. LS generates the bilinear parameters (p, P, Q, G_1, G_2, e) using k, G_1, G_2 are two cyclic group of the p-order, P, Q are two generators of G_1.
2. LS chooses two secure hash functions: $H_1 : \{0, 1\}^* \rightarrow Z_p^*$, $H_2 : G_2 \rightarrow \{0, 1\}^n$.
3. LS chooses a random number $s \in Z_p^*$ as a master secret, and then calculates $P_{pub} = sP$.
4. LS published public parameters $(p, P, Q, G_1, G_2, n, e, H_1, H_2, P_{pub})$.

5.2 Extract Phase

Each device d_i and u submits its identity ID_{di} and ID_u to the LS

1. LS generates $R_{di} = H_1(ID_{di})$.
2. LS calculates the private key $S_{di} = s \cdot R_{di} \cdot Q$ using the master secret key s.
3. LS sends (R_{di}, S_{di}) with the public parameters to the registered devices over a secure channel.

5.3 Signcryption Phase

Assume that the sender of this information exchange is u, the recipient is d_3. In order to signcrypt $M \in \{0, 1\}^n$ the sender works as follows:

1. u generates random numbers $r_1, r_2 \in Z_p^*$.
2. u calculates $C_1 = r_1P$, $C_2 = r_2P$, $K = H_2\big(e\big(r_2R_{d3}Q, P_{pub}\big)\big)$

$$C_{enc} = (M \| r_1) \oplus K, \quad h = H_1(C_{enc}), \quad C_{sign} = hS_u + r_2Q.$$

3. u sent $\sigma = \big(C_1, C_2, C_{enc}, C_{sign}, T_1\big)$ to the targeted receiver d_3.

5.4 Verify Phase

Once d_3 receives σ.

1. d_3 verifies whether $T_2 - T_1 \leq T$, then if the following equation holds u is proven to be the sender and proceed to the next step, otherwise terminate the session.

$$e\big(P, C_{sign}\big) = e(C_2, Q) + e\big(hR_uP_{pub}, Q\big)$$

2. d_3 calculates $K' = H_2\big(\hat{e}(S_{d3}, C_2)\big)$, $M' \| r_1' = C_{enc} \oplus K'$ to get M', r_1'.
3. d_3 verifies whether $C_1 = r_1'P$. If the verification is passed, it means that massage has not been tampered, otherwise refuse to execute this command (Fig. 2).

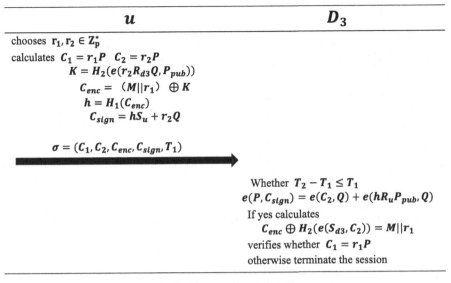

Fig. 2. Signcryption and verify

5.5 Correctness

$$e(C_2, Q) + e\big(hR_uP_{pub}, Q\big) = e(r_2P, Q) + e(hR_usP, Q)$$
$$= e(P, r_2Q) + e(P, hsR_uQ)$$
$$= e(P, r_2Q) + e(P, hS_u)$$
$$= e\big(P, C_{sign}\big)$$

$$K = H_2\big(e\big(r_2R_{d3}Q, P_{pub}\big)\big)$$
$$= H_2(e(r_2R_{d3}Q, sP))$$
$$= H_2(e(sR_{d3}Q, r_2P))$$
$$= H_2(e(S_{d3}, C_2))$$

6 Security Analysis

6.1 Security Model

We adapt the security model for signature schemes to prove the security of the proposed scheme [12]. Existential unforgeability against selective identity and chosen message attack are formally defined through a game between an adversary A and a challenger C. There are three phases in this game, as described below:

Setup Phase: In this phase, A selects a target user identity ID^*, and sends it to C. C executes **Setup** to produce the master private key s and system parameters, then returns to system parameters A.

Query Phase: In this phase, A adaptively issues *HASH* query, *Extract* query and *Sign* query. $C's$ responses to the respective queries are presented below:

1. *HASH* query: When receiving a message m, C randomly picks an element $r \in Z_p^*$, stores (ID_{di}, r) in the list L_{Hash} and returns r to A.
2. *Extract* query: When receiving $d_i's$ identity ID_i, C executes **Extract** to produce $d_i's$ private key S_{di}, stores (ID_{di}, S_{di}) in the list L_E, and returns S_{di} to A.
3. *Sign* query: When receiving $d_i's$ identity ID_i and a message m, C executes **Signcryption** to return $m's$ digital signature σ to A.

Output Phase: In this phase, A forges a digital signature σ^* of a message m^* corresponding to ID^*.
We say that A wins in the above game if all the followi σ^* ng conditions hold.

1. σ^* is valid
2. A has not made a *Extract* query with ID^*.
3. A has not made a *Sign* query with ID^*.

Theorem 1. *We say a IBS scheme for the smart home system is existential unforgeable against selective identity and chosen message attack, if and only if, no polynomial-time adversary is able to win the above game with a non-negligible advantage.*

6.2   Security Proof

In this section, we demonstrate that our proposed IBS scheme is secure under the above security model A.

Theorem 2. *Our proposed IBS scheme for the smart home system is provably secure in the random oracle model, assuming that the underlying CDH problem is hard.*

Proof. If the adversary A is able to win the game presented in Sect. 5 with a non-negligible advantage ε, then we can construct a challenger C to solve the CDH.

Given an instance (P, aP, bP) of the CDH, the task of C is to compute abP. C sets $P_{pub} \leftarrow aP, Q \leftarrow bP$ and sends the follow system parameters to A.

$$params = \left\{ p, P, Q, G_1, G_2, n, e, H_1, H_2, P_{pub} \right\}$$

C randomly picks an ID^* as challenge identities, and answers $A's$ queries as follows:

1. *HASH*(ID_{di}): C maintains a list L_{H_1} which has been initialized to empty. C checks whether a tuple (ID_{di}, R_{di}) exists in L_{H_1}. If it exists, C returns R_{di} to A; otherwise, C randomly selects a number R_{di} inserts (ID_{di}, R_{di}) to L_{H_1} and returns R_{di} to A.
2. *Extract*(ID_{di}): C maintains a list L_E which has been initialized to empty. C checks whether a tuple $(ID_{di}, r_{di}, S_{di})$ exists in L_E. If it exists, C returns S_{di} to A; otherwise, C randomly selects a number r_{di} and computes $S_{di} = r_{di} \cdot Q$. Finally C inserts $(ID_{di}, r_{di}, S_{di})$ to L_E and returns S_{di} to A.

3. $Sign(ID_{di})$: C randomly picks two elements $r_1, r_2 \in Z_p^*$ and current time T_1, calculates $C_1 = r_1P$, $C_2 = r_2P$, $K = H_2(e(r_2R_{dj}Q, P_{pub}))$, $C_{enc} = (M\|r_1) \oplus K$, $h = H_1(C_{enc})$, $C_{sign} = hS_{di} + r_2Q$. Then return $\sigma = (C_1, C_2, C_{enc}, C_{sign}, T_1)$ to A as a digital signature of m.

Finally A outputs a digital signature $\sigma^* = (C_1, C_2, C_{enc}, C_{sign}, T_1)$ of the message m corresponding to (ID_{di}, m), if $ID_{di} \neq ID^*$, C aborts the game.

Thus, we have

$$e(P, C_{sign}) = e(C_2, Q) + e(hR^*P_{pub}, Q)$$

According to [12] Lemma 8, we know that A can output another valid signature $\sigma' = (C_1, C_2, C_{enc}, C'_{sign}, T_1)$ with the probability $\eta \geq \frac{1}{9}$ by choosing another random oracle h'_1, which has the same probability distribution as h_1.

Therefore, we have:

$$e(P, C'_{sign}) = e(C_2, Q) + e(h'R^{*'}P_{pub}, Q)$$

We obtain:

$$e(P, C_{sign} - C'_{sign}) = e(C_2 + hR^*P_{pub} - C_2 - h'R^{*'}P_{pub}, Q)$$

$$= e((hR^* - h'R^{*'})aP, bP)$$

$$= e((hR^* - h'R^{*'})abP, P)$$

C outputs $(hR^* - h'R^{*'})^{-1}(C_{sign} - C'_{sign})$ as the solution to the given CDH. According to the above simulation, we know that the probability of C solving the CDH is related to the following events:

1. E_1: $ID_{di} = ID^*$
2. E_2: A is able to forge two legitimate digital signatures.

Let q_h denote the numbers of h_1 queries which A made in the above game; thus, we obtain: $\Pr[E_1] = \frac{1}{q_h}$, $\Pr[E_2|E_1] \geq \frac{1}{9}\varepsilon$.

Therefore, the probability that C solves the CDH is:

$$\Pr[E_2 \wedge E_1] = \Pr[E_2|E_1] \cdot \Pr[E_1]$$

$$\geq \frac{1}{9}\varepsilon \cdot \frac{1}{q_h}$$

$$= \frac{\varepsilon}{9 \cdot q_h}$$

Because ε is non-negligible and q_h are polynomial-bounded, we conclude that C is able to solve the CDH with a non-negligible probability $\frac{\varepsilon}{9 \cdot q_h}$. Due to the hardness of the CDH, we know that the proposed IBS scheme for the smart home system is secure in the random oracle model.

7 Analysis and Conclusion

This paper improved the scheme of Ashinabi et al. which made the information exchange more secure and reliable in the smart home environment. Compared to their scheme, we strengthened the verification process which ensured recipients can verify the accuracy of the message, thus guaranteed the integrity and confidentiality. In addition to this we canceled the hash-to-point operation, which greatly reduced the computational cost. We also added a timestamp to prevent replay attacks, although it increases the computational cost to a certain extent, it is essential to do so in a smart home environment. Finally, we provided a security prove under the random oracle model.

The development of emerging technologies such as big data and blockchain is in full swing, and security issues have also followed. Although many researchers have proposed some solutions [13], our research cannot be stopped. We must continue to work on the existing results and achieve better results.

References

1. Dobkin, D.M., Aboussouan B.: Low power wi-fi TM (ieee802.11) for ipsmart objects. GainSpan Corporation (2009)
2. Bhattasali, T.: Licrypt: Lightweight cryptography technique for securing smart objects in internet of things environment. CSI Communications (2013)
3. Ayuso, J., Marin, L., Jara, A.: Optimization of public key cryptography (RSA and ECC) for 16-bits devices based on 6lowpan. In: 1st International Workshop on the Security of the Internet of Things, Tokyo, Japan (2010)
4. Li, Y.: Design of a key establishment protocol for smart home energy management system. In: 2013 Fifth International Conference on Computational Intelligence, Communication Systems and Networks (CI-CSyN), pp. 88–93. IEEE (2013)
5. Shamir, A.: Identity-based cryptosystems and signature schemes. In: Blakley, G.R., Chaum, D. (eds.) CRYPTO 1984. LNCS, vol. 196, pp. 47–53. Springer, Heidelberg (1985). https://doi.org/10.1007/3-540-39568-7_5
6. Boneh, D., Franklin, M.: Identity-based encryption from the weil pairing. In: Kilian, J. (ed.) CRYPTO 2001. LNCS, vol. 2139, pp. 213–229. Springer, Heidelberg (2001). https://doi.org/10.1007/3-540-44647-8_13
7. Salami, S.A., Baek, J., Salah, K.: Lightweight encryption for smart home. In: 2016 11th International Conference on Availability, Reliability and Security (ARES), pp. 382–388. IEEE (2016)
8. Han, K., Kim, J., Shon, T.: A novel secure key paring protocol for rf4ce ubiquitous smart home systems. Pers. Ubiquit. Comput. **17**(5), 945–949 (2013)
9. Fouda, M.M., Fadlullah, Z.M., Kato, N.: A lightweight message authentication scheme for smart grid communications. IEEE Trans. Smart Grid **2**(4), 675–685 (2011)
10. Magons, K.: Applications and benefits of elliptic curve cryptography. In: SOFSEM (Student Research Forum Papers/Posters), pp. 32–42 (2016)
11. Ashibani, Y., Mahmoud, Q.H.: An efficient and secure scheme for smart home communication using identity-based signcryption. In: IEEE International performance computing and Communications Conference, pp. 1–7. IEEE Computer Society (2017)
12. Pointcheval, D., Stern, J.: Security arguments for digital signatures and blind signatures. J. Cryptol. **13**(3), 361–396 (2000)
13. Xin, J., Liu, M., Yang, C.: A blockchain-based authentication protocol for WLAN mesh security access. Comput. Mater. Continua **58**(1), 45–59 (2019)

A Resource Allocation Mechanism
for Edge-Blockchain

Weichao Gong[1]([✉]), Yidong Yuan[2], Dongyan Zhao[2], Wuyang Zhang[3], and Sujie Shao[1]

[1] Beijing University of Posts and Telecommunications, Beijing, China
gongweichao@bupt.edu.cn
[2] Beijing Zhixin Microelectronics Technology Co. LTD, Beijing, China
[3] Liaoning Electronic Science Institute, Jinzhou, Liaoning, China

Abstract. Blockchain technology develops rapidly, which has a broad application prospect in solving security problem of the Internet of things (IoT). However, IoT devices with limited computing resources cannot afford high computing cost of blockchain mining. To solve this problem, edge computing is introduced to improve resource allocation efficiency in trusted IoT network based on blockchain. Therefore, IoT devices can choose to offload tasks to edge servers or local collaborative mining devices. Moreover, to maximize system revenue, a two-stage auction strategy is put forward to reasonably allocate computing resources in blockchain network. In the first stage of auction strategy, computing tasks can be offloaded to edge server, and the second stage realizes resource allocation of collaborative mining devices to utilize idle computing resource adequately. Simulation results show that the proposed strategy performs better than linear search algorithm in terms of effectiveness and rationality.

Keywords: Edge computing · Resource management · Blockchain · Auction

1 Introduction

First proposed by Satoshi in 2009, blockchain has attracted attention from both academia and industry [1]. Blockchain is a distributed database replicated and shared among members of network. When transaction is created, blockchain node verify transaction safely and transparently through the mining process. Then, transactions are added into chains, where links between blocks and their contents are cryptographically protected and cannot be forged [2]. Its features include security, transparency, distribution, tamper-proof, traceability, etc.

However, the development of blockchain in IoT devices (Electricity, transportation, logistics, etc.) is hindered by a major challenge brought by proof-of-work (PoW) process [3]. The main obstacle is that mobile devices with limited energy fall short to afford high computing resources of mining process. Some researches adopts cloud computing to address this problem. A resource allocation mechanism had been proposed to offload mining tasks to cloud server in [4]. However, it is not efficient due to high latency. Therefore, edge computing is a promising technology. In [5], author proposed a method

X. Sun et al. (Eds.): ICAIS 2020, CCIS 1252, pp. 649–658, 2020.
https://doi.org/10.1007/978-981-15-8083-3_58

to offload the task to edge server to decrease delay, but resources of idle devices in network are wasted. Idle devices in network can share computing resources with miners to assist in mining, then they can obtain rewards according to their contribution [6]. To improve resource allocation efficiency and utilize idle computing resource in blockchain network, a resource allocation mechanism is proposed in this paper where mining task can be offloaded to both edge server and local collaborative mining devices.

Compared with traditional resources allocation, innovations of our work lie in offloading of devices mining tasks to both edge computing server and co-mining devices, based on our proposed two-stage auction strategy. The main contributions of this paper are summarized as follows:

- Two offloading modes are proposed in the resource allocation mechanism based on edge computing. Miners can offload their mining tasks to non-mining devices or edge server, which takes advantage of idle resources within blockchain network and reduces load on edge server.
- A two-stage auction strategy is proposed to optimize system revenue. The resource allocation for offloading computing tasks to edge server is implemented in the first stage, and the second stage realizes resource allocation of offloading tasks to collaborative mining equipment.
- Simulation is conducted to evaluate key performance parameters including number of devices, reward factors, number of transactions and so on. And simulation results show that the proposed strategy performs better than linear search algorithm.

The rest of this paper is organized as follows: Sect. 2 reviews the system model. Section 3 presents the resource allocation strategy. The evaluation function is presented in Sect. 4. Section 5 analyzes experimental results and corresponding discussions. Section 6 presents conclusions and future work.

2 System Model

2.1 Network Model

As shown in Fig. 1, we consider a scenario where edge computing server (ES) provides resources for devices with insufficient computing resource to support blockchain services. There are $N = \{1, 2, \ldots, n\}$ devices with certain computing resource under an edge computing server. Due to lack of computing resource of device, they can offload their tasks to edge server to complete consensus process. In this paper, we define the computing resource that devices need to obtain from the edge server as $d = \{d_1, \ldots, d_i, \ldots, d_n\}$, and auction price of device is $b = \{b_1, b_2, \ldots, b_n\}$. $X = \{x_1, x_2, \ldots, x_n\}$, $x_i \in \{0, 1\}$ is used to indicate whether edge server allocates computing resources to device. $P = \{p_1, p_2, \ldots, p_n\}$ denotes actual transaction price of computing resources.

In order to maintain the stability of blockchain network, a s-type utility function is used to describe benefits of blockchain network as Eq. (1) shows. With the increasing of computing resources, devices can get more rewards. Therefore, as more and more

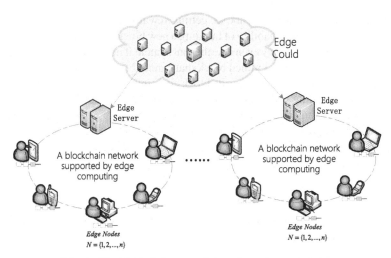

Fig. 1. The blockchain network based on edge computing

devices participate in mining process, blockchain network will also be safer and more stable.

$$\chi(d_N) = \frac{1 - e^{-\mu d_N}}{1 + v e^{-\mu d_N}} \tag{1}$$

where $d_N = \sum_{i \in N} d_i x_i$ is the sum of computing resources, and μ, v are positive parameters. It's a slowing down of the utility function, and it's going to go to 1.

2.2 Mining Mechanism Supported by Edge Server

Given x_i, d_i and g_i, device $i's$ hash capability γ_i is represented as Eq. (2).

$$\gamma_i(d_i, x_i) = \frac{d_i^{\alpha} x_i + g_i}{\sum_{j \in N} (g_j + d_j^{\alpha} x_j)} \quad i \in N \tag{2}$$

where $\sum_{i \in N} \gamma_i = 1$ and α is an exponential parameter of hash power function. g_i is defined as the computing resource of each device. $\gamma_i(d, x)$ is hash power function with parameter is set as $\alpha = 1.2$ in the rest of this section [7].

In mining competition, miners need to be the first to find correct nonce to solve POW problem and propagate the block to reach consensus. The generation of new blocks follows a Poisson process with a constant rate $1/\lambda$. Firstly, miners collect unconfirmed transactions represent by $S = \{s_1, s_2, \ldots, s_n\}$ into their blocks [8]. Secondly, miner i broadcast its block to blockchain network to reach consensus, The propagation delay is affected by the size of transactions s_i. The first miner which reach consensus can get a reward R composed of a fixed bonus T and a flexible fee affected by transactions s and the transaction fee rate r. Thus, miner $i's$ expected reward R_i is expressed by Eq. (3).

$$R_i = (T + r s_i) P_i(\gamma_i(d, x), s_i) \tag{3}$$

Through mining competition above, getting rewards involves building blocks and reaching consensus. The probability of building a new block P_i^m is equal to miner $i's$ hash power. However, the miner may even lose the tournament if its new block does not achieve consensus as first. This kind of mined block that cannot be added on to the blockchain is called orphaned block [8]. Moreover, the block containing larger size of transactions has higher chance becoming orphaned. Here, we assume that miner $i's$ block propagation time τ_i is linear to the size of transactions in its block, i.e., $\tau_i = \xi s_i.\xi$ is a constant that reflects the impact of s_i on τ_i. Since the arrival of new blocks follows a Poisson distribution, miner $i's$ orphaning probability can be approximated by $P_i^o = 1 - e^{-\frac{1}{\lambda}\tau_i}$ [9]. After substituting τ_i, P_i can be calculated as follows.

$$P_i = P_i^m(1 - P_i^o) = \gamma_i e^{-\frac{1}{\lambda}\xi\tau_i} \tag{4}$$

According to above mechanism, to maximize utility of system, an optimal function can be represented as Eq. (5)

$$Max\left\{\sum_{i\in N}(T + \eta s_i)\frac{d_i^\alpha x_i + g_i}{\sum_{j\in N}(g_j + d_j x_j)}e^{-\frac{1}{\lambda}\tau_i} - \sum_{i\in N}d_i x_i Ecs - \sum_{i\in N}g_i cs_i\right\}$$

$$s.t. \sum_{i\in N}d_i x_i \leq C, x_i \in \{0, 1\}, \forall i \in N \tag{5}$$

where Ecs refers to cost of unit computing resources of edge computing server, cs_i refers to cost of device $i's$ computing resources. Assume that computing resources of edge computing server is C. Then total computing resources that all devices can obtain from edge server should be less than C.

3 Resource Allocation Strategy

In this section, in order to solve proposed optimization problem (maximizing system benefits), a two-stage resource auction strategy is designed as Fig. 2 shows. In the first stage, VCG auction is used to realize resource allocation between edge servers and devices. In the second stage, vickrey auction is used to realize allocation between miner and sharer. In addition, we also prove the rationality and authenticity of strategy.

3.1 Allocation Between Edge Server and Devices Based on VCC Auction

In the first stage of auction, VCG auction is adopted. Device i first sent d_i and offer b_i to edge computing server. After receiving the bids from all devices, edge computing servers would select winner, allocate corresponding computing resources and determine actual transaction price according to VCG auction rules.

Thus, devices in blockchain network can be divided into two categories. As winner of the first auction, such devices can obtain computing resources from edge server, and act as miners in blockchain network. In addition, such devices also act as buyers in the second stage of Vickrey auction. Other devices are failed devices in the first phase of auction, which do not have enough computing resources to solve PoW problem, so they can only serve as computing resource sharing devices in blockchain network. We define $x_i \in \{0, 1\}$, when $x_i = 1$, device i is a miner, $x_i = 0$ means device i is a sharer.

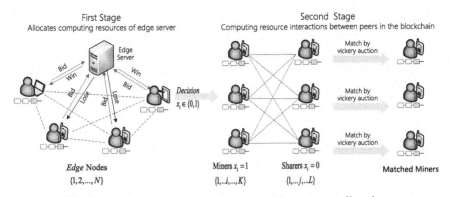

Fig. 2. Two-stage auction strategy on computing resource allocation

3.2 Allocation Between Miners and Sharers Based on Vickrey Auttion

In particular, for buyer j, we calculate and get a composition of the agreed-price matrix v_j^i. Therefore auction bidding price in the second stage can be described by means of matrix H.

$$
H = \begin{bmatrix} v_1^1 & \dots & v_1^i & \dots & v_1^K \\ v_j^1 & \dots & v_j^i & \dots & v_j^K \\ v_L^1 & \dots & v_L^i & \dots & v_L^K \end{bmatrix} \tag{6}
$$

Two problems need to be solved in the second stage of auction. The first is how to match sellers and buyers. To solve this problem, we adopt the second price matching mechanism according to the rules of Eq. (6).

$$
p_j^{2nd} = \arg \text{Second}_{j \in N/w} v_j^i, j \in N\backslash W, i \in W \tag{7}
$$

where p_j^{2nd} is final transaction price of device j.v_j^i is the agreed price where device j is in resource sharer set $N\backslash W$ and device i is in miner set W.

As for the second problem is how to determine actual transaction price between miner and sharer. $\delta \in (0, 1)$ is defined. we will determine price of device resource interaction according to the rule of Eq. (8).

$$
v_j^i = \delta v_i + (1 - \delta)v_j, j \in N\backslash W, i \in W \tag{8}
$$

where δ is the weight of pricing process, which is decided through negotiation between seller and buyer.

4 Evaluation Function in a Two-Stage Auction

In this section, in order to assess two stage auction strategy reasonably on the resource allocation strategy in blockchain network based on edge computing, we establish the profit function of edge service provider, miner and sharer, it provides a basis for simulation to verify that strategy is reasonable, flexible, and effective.

Firstly, for resource-sharing device $j \in N \backslash W$ in the blockchain network, the cost paid by device in two-stage auction process is the cost of selling its computing resources in the second-stage auction process.

$$\text{Cos}_j = g_j cs_j, j \in N \backslash W \tag{9}$$

The income obtained by resource-sharing device j in two-stage auction is obtained by assisting some mining devices in the second stage auction

$$R_j^i = g_i p_j^{2nd}, j \in N \backslash W \tag{10}$$

So device $j's$ net income is (11).

$$U_j = g_i p_j^{2nd} - g_j cs_j, j \in N \backslash W \tag{11}$$

Then for miners $i \in W$, its costs in the process of two stage auction can be divided into two parts: payment of purchasing computing resource from edge computing server in the first stage of auction, as well as costs for collaborative mining resources sharing devices in the second stage of auction.

$$M \cos_i = p_i + R_j^i, i \in W \tag{12}$$

Income of miner in two-stage auction is expected reward for participating in mining process, and miner's income is Eq. (13)

$$R_i = (T + \eta s_i) \frac{d_i^\alpha x_i + g_i + g_j}{\sum_{j \in N} (g_j + d_j^\alpha x_j)} e^{-\frac{1}{\lambda} \tau_i}, i \in W, j \in N \backslash W \tag{13}$$

Finally, for edge computing service provider, the cost obtained in two-stage auction is operating cost of edge server for selling edge computing resources:

$$E \cos = \sum_{i \in N} d_i x_i \cdot Ecs \tag{14}$$

Profit of edge computing server is paid by miners for gaining computing resource.

$$Einc = \sum_{i \in N} p_i \tag{15}$$

Therefore, edge computing service provider gains a net profit in two-stage auction process as follows:

$$U_E = \sum_{i \in N} p_i - \sum_{i \in N} d_i x_i \cdot Ecs \tag{16}$$

Above all, the overall income of whole system can be calculated as follows.

$$S_{all} = \sum_{i \in W} U_i + \sum_{j \in N \backslash W} U_j + U_E \tag{17}$$

5 Experiment Results and Performance Analysis

In this chapter, the two-stage auction strategy is simulated to verify the effectiveness and rationality of the two-stage auction strategy, and is compared with linear search algorithm mentioned above. Simulation result proves that the strategy proposed has better system benefits.

Table 1. Simulation parameter

Simulation parameters	Values
Number of devices, N	$U[10, 100]$
Edge server computes resources, C	$U[30, 300]$
Computing resource needed, d_i	$N[6, 1]$
Biding price, b_i	$N[0.4, 1]$
Transaction in block, s_i	$N[mean, 10]$
Block transaction average,mean	$N[100, 1000]$
Device's computing power, g_i	$N[1, 0.8]$
Fixed rewards for miner, T	300
Variable factor for miner, η	0.03
Fixed parameters of the poisson process, λ	800
Linear parameters of delay, ξ	1
Transaction price weight, δ	$\delta \in (0, 1)$
Edge server's cost per unit, Ecs	0.8
Device's cost for per unit, cs_i	0.2

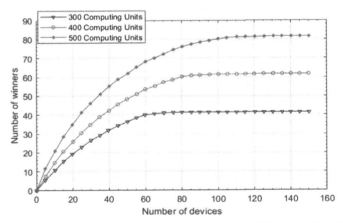

Fig. 3. The relationship between auction winners and number of devices with different edge computing resource.

We first analyze the relationship between number of auction winners (i.e., miner) and number of network devices under different amount of computing resource of edge server. In Fig. 3, as the amount of devices increases, the number of winners grows at a gradually slowing rate, and then converges to a stable value. At same time, we find that the stable value is determined by computing resource provided by edge server.

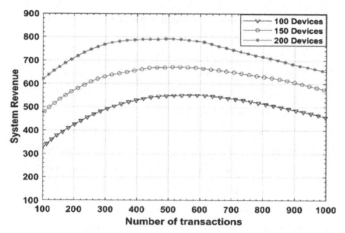

Fig. 4. The influence of transaction on system revenue under different equipment quantity.

As shown in Fig. 4, with the increasing of packaging transaction in different number of devices, the system revenue will first increase and then gradually decline after reaching maximum value. Reason is that as transaction rises, the propagation delay will also increase. Hence a larger probability of generating isolated blocks and reducing the system revenue will rise.

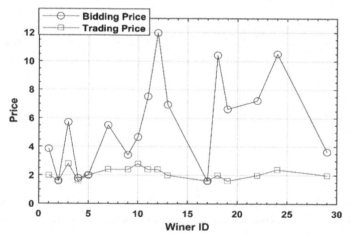

Fig. 5. The difference between bidding price and trading price.

In Fig. 5, we compared the relationship between buyer's bidding price and trading price in the first stage of auction when there are 30 edge devices. The encapsulation information of block is in optimal area value as shown in Fig. 5 and other fixed parameters are complied with Table 1. As can be seen from Fig. 5, due to the adoption of VCG auction strategy, the final price of buyers is generally lower than bidding price, thus avoiding buyers from being cheated in auction process.

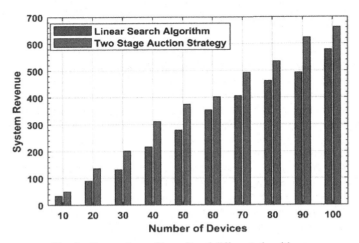

Fig. 6. Comparison of benefits of different algorithms.

In addition, we also compared our proposed two-stage auction algorithm with existing linear search algorithm. The results are shown in Fig. 6, our proposed two-stage auction strategy has better performance than existing strategy in improving the revenue of system.

6 Conclusion and Future Work

In this paper, we propose a resource allocation mechanism for blockchain network based on edge computing to solve the PoW problem, where blockchain is used to solve the security problem of IoT. In order to maximize the system revenue, a two-stage auction strategy is proposed. Offloading computing tasks to edge server is implemented in the first stage, and the second stage realizes resource allocation of collaborative mining devices. Then, in simulation, we studied the effects of various parameters such as number of devices, transaction and reward factor on policy performance. Moreover, the performance of our mechanism is compared with linear search method, the simulation results show that under our proposed mechanism, system can get better benefits. In the future, we will consider the different requirements of the devices.

Acknowledgment. This work is supported by the Science and Technology Project of State Grid Corporation of China: Security Protection Technology of Embedded Components and Control Units in Power System Terminal (Grant No. 2019GW—12).

References

1. Fakhri, D., Mutijarsa, K.: Secure IoT communication using blockchain technology. In: 2018 International Symposium on Electronics and Smart Devices (ISESD), Bandung, pp. 1–6 (2018)
2. Sun, G., et al.: Research on public opinion propagation model in social network based on blockchain. Comput. Mater. Continua **60**(3), 1015–1027 (2019)

3. Deng, Z., Ren, Y., Liu, Y., Yin, X., Shen, Z., Kim, H.-J.: Blockchain-based trusted electronic records preservation in cloud storage. Comput. Mater. Continua **58**(1), 135–151 (2019)
4. Jiang, X., Liu, M., Yang, C., Liu, Y., Wang, R.: A blockchain-based authentication protocol for WLAN mesh security access. Comput. Mater. Continua **58**(1), 45–59 (2019)
5. Samaniego, M., Deters, R.: Blockchain as a service for IoT, pp. 433–436, December 2016
6. Liu, M., Yu, F.R., Teng, Y., Leung, V.C.M., Song, M.: Computation offloading and content caching in wireless blockchain networks with mobile edge computing. IEEE Trans. Veh. Technol. **67**(11), 11008–11021 (2018)
7. Jiao, Y., Wang, P., Niyato, D., Xiong, Z.: Social welfare maximization auction in edge computing resource allocation for mobile blockchain, pp. 1–6, May 2018
8. Qin, R., Yuan, Y., Wang, F.: Research on the selection strategies of blockchain mining pools. IEEE Trans. Comput. Soc. Syst. **5**(3), 748–757 (2018)
9. Qin, R., Yuan, Y., Wang, S., Wang, F.: Economic issues in bitcoin mining and blockchain research. In: 2018 IEEE Intelligent Vehicles Symposium (IV), pp. 268–273, June 2018

Remote Sensing Image Zero-Watermarking Algorithm Based on Accurate Polar Harmonic Fourier Moment

Bin Ma[1], Lili Chang[1], Chunpeng Wang[1(✉)], Jian Li[1(✉)], and Yuli Wang[2]

[1] Shandong Provincial Key Laboratory of Computer Networks, Qilu University of Technology (Shandong Academy of Sciences), Jinan 250300, China
mpeng1122@163.com, 1jian_20@163.com
[2] Shandong Provincial Key Laboratory of Computer Networks, School of Cyber Security, Qilu University of Technology (Shandong Academy of Sciences), Jinan 250300, China

Abstract. This paper introduces a remote zero-watermarking algorithm based on polar harmonic Fourier moments (PHFM) and Logistic chaotic mapping. In this algorithm, Gaussian numerical integration is used to calculate the PHFM of the original gray image and construct a binary feature image. Finally, the binary feature image is XOR with the scrambled logo image to obtain a zero-watermarking image. When copyright protection is verified, the logo image obtained by XOR-ing the binary feature image and the image to be verified is compared with the original logo image to determine the copyright ownership of the image. The experimental results show that compared with other zero-watermarking algorithms, the proposed algorithm is robust to both conventional image attacks and geometric attacks.

Keywords: Zero-watermarking · PHFM · Gaussian numerical integration · Remote sensing image

1 Introduction

With the rapid development of Internet technology, many copyrighted digital images can easily be illegally used and spread by unauthorized persons, resulting in an increasing number of pirated images. Image security has become an important issue that cannot be ignored and needs to be solved urgently. In recent years, a large number of digital image copyright protection technologies have also been proposed, including image encryption [1], image hashing, image authentication [2], image steganography [3, 4] and image watermarking [5]. The main idea of these technologies is to find the invariant features of the image and modify them by adding a watermark. However, for some sensitive images, such as medical, military, and remote sensing images, owing to the details contained in the pixels are very important, any change can lead to mistakes made by doctors or military and remote sensing experts. So, in order to solve this problem, a new technology called zero-watermark has recently been proposed.

© Springer Nature Singapore Pte Ltd. 2020
X. Sun et al. (Eds.): ICAIS 2020, CCIS 1252, pp. 659–673, 2020.
https://doi.org/10.1007/978-981-15-8083-3_59

Wen et al. [6] first proposed the concept of zero-watermark. This scheme proposed a zero-watermarking algorithm based on Discrete Cosine Transform (DCT). The feasibility of zero-watermarking algorithm was verified by this method. Then they use the high-order cumulant to extract the features of the image and construct a zero-watermark [7]. It is proved by experiments that the zero-watermark constructed by this method has good performance. Tsai et al. [8] proposed a lossless zero-watermarking algorithm for image authentication based on the truncation mean algorithm and support vector machine (SVM). The algorithm uses the truncated mean algorithm to remove noise to enhance the accuracy of feature selection, trains SVM model to record the relationship between watermark and feature image, and uses the trained SVM to recover watermark during copyright verification. Based on the literature [8], they proposed a zero-watermarking algorithm against geometric attacks based on SVM and Particle Swarm Optimization (PSO) [9], using SVM classifier for image authentication Geometric attack. Gao et al. [10] proposed a robust visible zero-watermarking algorithm based on Bessel-Fourier moment. The Bessel-Fourier moment is used to extract feature images and construct a zero-watermark. This method can resist various attacks. Compared with other similar visible zero-watermarking algorithms and the ZM algorithm, the algorithm is also superior. Wang [11, 12] used the invariant moment theory to propose two robust image zero-watermarking algorithms against geometric attacks based on quaternion exponential moments (QEM) and polar harmonic complex exponential transformation (PCET), which can effectively resist various geometric attacks and regular image processing. Wang et al. [13] designed a new set of invariant continuous orthogonal moments, polar harmonic Fourier moments (PHFMs), which have no numerical instability. Because it does not cause numerical instability, it is theoretically and experimentally proven that under noise and various attacks, PHFM outperforms other image moments mentioned in the article in reconstructing images and identifying rotation-invariant objects.

Then based on accurate PHFM and Logistic chaotic map [14], this paper proposed a robust zero-watermarking algorithm for remote sensing images against geometric attacks. Firstly, the traditional calculation method of PHFM is improved, and an accurate calculation method is proposed, which effectively improves the calculation accuracy of PHFM. Then based on the proposed method and chaotic map, a robust zero watermarking algorithm against geometric attacks is proposed. Experimental results show that this method can effectively resist common geometric attacks such as rotation, scaling, and image flipping.

The structure of the article is as follows. The second part introduces the definition of PHFM and its traditional calculation method. Then it introduces the accurate calculation method and its reconstruction performance. The third part describes the construction and verification of zero-watermark. The fourth part is the experimental result. And the introduction of the analysis, the fifth part is the conclusion.

2 Polar Harmonic Fourier Moments

2.1 Definition of Polar Harmonic Fourier Moments

For a polar coordinate image function $f(r, \theta)$, the PHFM [15] whose expansion coefficient L_{nm} is called the (n, m) order function on the basis function $S_{nm}(r, \theta)$ is defined as follows:

$$L_{nm} = \frac{2}{\pi} \int_0^{2\pi} \int_0^1 f(r, \theta)\overline{S_{nm}(r, \theta)}rdrd\theta \tag{1}$$

Where $\overline{[\cdot]}$ the conjugate of the complex number, the basis function $S_{nm}(r, \theta)$ consists of a radial basis function $T_n(r)$ and an angular basis function $\exp(jm\theta)$:

$$S_{nm}(r, \theta) = T_n(r)\exp(jm\theta) \tag{2}$$

The radial basis function $T_n(r)$ is:

$$T_n(r) = \begin{cases} 1/\sqrt{2}, & n = 0 \\ \sin(n+1)\pi r^2, & when \ n \ is \ odd \\ \cos(n)\pi r^2, & when \ n \ is \ even \end{cases} \tag{3}$$

According to the theory of orthogonal complete function system, the original image $f(r, \theta)$ can be reconstructed approximately with a finite number of PHFM. Assuming PHFM with the highest order n_{max} and maximum repetition m_{max}, the reconstructed image function is as follows:

$$f(r, \theta) = \sum_{n=0}^{n_{max}} \sum_{m=-m_{max}}^{m_{max}} L_{nm}S_{nm}(r, \theta) \tag{4}$$

2.2 Accurate PHFM Calculation

In the traditional method of calculating PHFM [15], we first discretize the double integral of formula (1), and then perform the PHFM calculation. The discrete form of PHFM is as follows:

$$L_{nm} = \frac{2}{\pi N^2} \sum_{p=0}^{N-1} \sum_{q=0}^{N-1} f(x_q, y_p)T_n(r_{p,q})\exp(-jm\theta_{p,q}) \tag{5}$$

Aiming at the problem of numerical integration error in traditional methods [16]. This section proposes an accurate calculation method of PHFM based on Gaussian numerical integration (GNI) [17].

Assuming that there is a one-dimensional function $f(x)$, its Gaussian numerical integral over the interval $[a, b]$ can be defined as

$$\int_a^b f(x)dx \cong \frac{(b-a)}{2} \sum_{i=0}^{n-1} w_i f\left(\frac{a+b}{2} + \frac{b-a}{2}t_i\right) \tag{6}$$

Where, w_i and t_i are the weight and position of the image sample point, respectively, and n is the order of the Gaussian value integral.

Similarly, for a two-dimensional function, the expression of the double Gaussian integral in the integral region can be expressed as:

$$\int_a^b \int_c^d f(x,y)dxdy \cong \frac{(b-a)(d-c)}{4} \sum_{i=0}^{n-1}\sum_{h=0}^{n-1} w_i w_h f(\frac{a+b}{2} + \frac{b-a}{2}t_i, \frac{c+d}{2} + \frac{d-c}{2}t_h) \tag{7}$$

Now, we use the method of double Gaussian numerical integration to accurately calculate PHFM. For Eq. (6), there is

$$L_{nm} = \frac{2}{\pi N^2} \sum_{p=0}^{N-1}\sum_{q=0}^{N-1} f(x_q, y_p) \times \sum_{i=0}^{n-1}\sum_{h=0}^{n-1} w_i w_h S_{nm}(\frac{t_i + 2q + 1 - N}{N}, \frac{t_h + 2p + 1 - N}{N}) \tag{8}$$

Where,

$$(\frac{t_i + 2q + 1 - N}{N})^2 + (\frac{t_h + 2p + 1 - N}{N})^2 \le 1 \tag{9}$$

The constraint given in Eq. (9) is an improvement on the constraints in the traditional calculation method. This method of accurate calculation allows pixels whose pixel center points do not fall in the unit circle to participate in the calculation.

2.3 Comparison of Image Reconstruction Performance

This section compares the reconstructed performance between the traditional computational method and the Gaussian numerical integration method from two aspects of reconstructed image and reconstruction error. In the experiment, the order of the Gaussian numerical integration in the Gaussian numerical integration method is set to 5. The test image uses a grayscale remote sensing image airplane of size 128×128 and a grayscale remote sensing image of airplane2 size 64×64, as shown in Fig. 1:

(a) Airplane   (b) Airplane2

Fig. 1. Test image

Firstly, the effect of reconstructing the image by two methods is compared. It can be seen from Fig. 2 and Fig. 3, when the PHFM order is small, the reconstructed image effect of the traditional method and the Gaussian numerical integration method is basically the same. With the gradual increase of the order of the moment, the white area appears in the center and edge of the image reconstructed by the traditional method, and the reconstructed image quality drops sharply. The image reconstructed by the Gaussian numerical integration method becomes more and more clear, which indicates that the reconstruction effect of the Gaussian numerical integration is obviously superior to the traditional method.

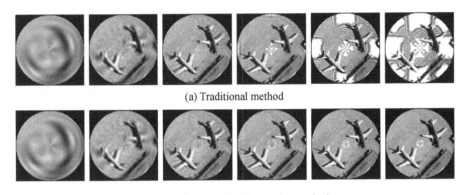

(a) Traditional method

(b) Gaussian numerical integration method

Fig. 2. Comparison of image airplane reconstruction performance (n_{max} = 5, 20, 40, 60, 80, 100)

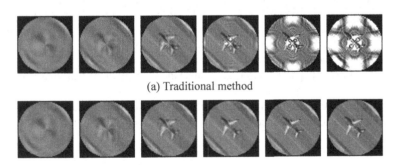

(a) Traditional method

(b) Gaussian numerical integration method

Fig. 3. Comparison of image airplane2 reconstruction performance (n_{max} = 5, 10, 20, 30, 40, 50)

Then compare the reconstruction errors of the two methods, here we use the mean square reconstruction error (MSRE) [18] to measure, the results shown in Fig. 4, we can see that when the number of moments is small, the reconstruction errors of the two methods are approximately equal, and as the order increases, the reconstruction error of the traditional method increases sharply, and the reconstruction error of the Gaussian numerical integration method continues to decrease. This shows that the Gaussian numerical integration method still maintains high accuracy when calculating high-order moments, effectively solves the numerical integration error of the traditional method and improves the calculation accuracy of PHFM.

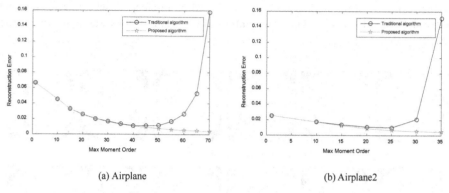

(a) Airplane   (b) Airplane2

Fig. 4. Reconstruction error comparison

3   Zero-Watermarking Algorithm Based on Accurate PHFM

3.1   Zero-Watermark Construction

Set the original image $I = \{f(x, y), 0 \le x, y < N\}$ and the original binary logo image as $Q = \{q(i, j), 0 \le i < M, 0 \le j < P\}$. The specific process of zero-watermark construction is as follows:

1)   Scrambling of logo images
Logistic chaotic map [14] is used to enhance the security of the watermark algorithm.

a)   Use the key K_1 as the initial value of the Logistic system and use the key to map out the chaotic sequence $Q_{11} = \{q_1, q_2, q_3 \cdots q_{i\times j}\}$ of length $i \times j$:

$$Q_{11} = Logistic(K_1, i \times j) \tag{10}$$

b)   Convert Q_{11} into a two-dimensional chaotic sequence Q_{11}'' of size $i \times j$ in raster scan mode:

$$Q_{11}'' = \begin{bmatrix} q_1 & \cdots & q_j \\ \vdots & \ddots & \vdots \\ q_{(i-1)\times j+1} & \cdots & q_{i\times j} \end{bmatrix} \tag{11}$$

c)   Chaotic sequence binarization. Compare the size of each coefficient and the average value in the chaotic sequence. When the coefficient is greater than or equal to the average value, record it as 1.

d) Generation of chaotic feature images. The binarized chaotic sequence $Q'_{11} = \{q(n), 1 \leq n \leq i \times j\}$ is XORed with the original watermark sequence Q_{11} to obtain a scrambled watermark sequence $Q_1 = \{q_1(i,j), 0 \leq i < M, 0 \leq j < P\}$.

2) Calculation of the original image PHFM
   The GNI method is used to calculate the exact PHFM of the original grayscale image I.

3) Select robust PHFM
   According to the key K_2, randomly select in the set S select $M \times P$ robust PHFMs, and calculate the moment amplitude to form the feature vector $\overrightarrow{A} = \{A_1, A_2, \cdots, A_{M \times P}\}$.

4) Generation of zero-watermark image
   The binary feature image Q_f and the logo image Q_1 are XORed to obtain a zero-watermark image:

$$W_Q = BITXOR(Q_f, Q_1) \tag{12}$$

3.2 Zero-Watermark Verification

The specific process of zero-watermark verification is as follows:

1) Calculation of PHFM
   The PHFM of the image I^* to be verified is calculated according to the PHFM accurate calculation method proposed in this paper.

2) Choice of robust PHFM
   Select randomly $M \times P$ robust PHFM by the key K_2, and calculate the corresponding moment amplitude to obtain a vector $\overrightarrow{A^*} = \{A_1^*, A_2^*, \cdots, A_{M \times P}^*\}$.

3) Construction of binary feature images
   Convert vector $\overrightarrow{A^*}$ to a two-dimensional feature image Q_A^* of $M \times P$, and then use threshold T to change Q_A^* to a binary feature image Q_f^*.

4) Get verification logo image
   By XORing the binary feature image Q_f^* and the zero-watermark image W to obtain the binary logo image Q_1^*:

$$Q_1^* = BITXOR(Q_f^*, W) \tag{13}$$

Finally, the obtained Q_1^* is reversed using the key K_1 to obtain a verification logo image Q^*.

4 Experiment Analysis

In order to verify the effect of the proposed algorithm, the original image we selected in the experiment is 15 256×256 grayscale remote sensing images, of which 6 original grayscale images and a 32×32 binary log image are shown in Fig. 5 shown. In the experiment, we set the maximum order of PHFM to $N_{\max} = 23$, and the experiment was carried out under the experimental environment of Matlab R2015b.

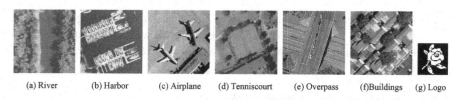

(a) River   (b) Harbor   (c) Airplane   (d) Tenniscourt   (e) Overpass   (f)Buildings   (g) Logo

Fig. 5. Experimental image

4.1 Performance Measurement Parameter

The bit error rate (BER) [18] is defined as:

$$BER = \frac{B}{P \times Q} \times 100\% \tag{14}$$

B Indicates the number of bits of the extracted watermark information error, and $P \times Q$ indicates the total number of bits of the original watermark information.

This paper uses bit correct ratio (BCR) to measure the degree of difference between the extracted watermark and the original watermark.

$$BCR = 1 - BER \tag{15}$$

4.2 Robustness Test

JPEG Compression Attack. JPEG compression will lose the pixels of the image, which will affect the accuracy of watermark extraction. Therefore, we test the robustness of JPEG compression of this algorithm, and choose 10, 30, 70 and 90 quality factors of JPEG compression. Table 1 shows the image effect after JPEG compression of the original image, and the logo image extracted with zero-watermark and its corresponding BCR value. It can be seen from Table 1 that when the quality factor is 10, the extracted watermark information is slightly worse. With the gradual increase of the quality factor, the BCR value of the extracted logo image is greater than 0.99, which is close to lossless extraction. It shows that the proposed algorithm is robust to JPEG compression attack.

Rotation Attack. Image rotation causes a change in the pixel position of the image, which in turn affects the normal extraction of the watermark. In Table 2, it can be seen from the results that the effect of the logo image extracted with the increase of the rotation angle is gradually deteriorated, but the BCR value is generally greater than 0.99, which indicates that the algorithm can resist the image rotation attack.

Noise Attack. It is common for images to be attacked by noise during the propagation process. We added Gaussian noise and salt and pepper noise to the original image to conduct experiments. From Table 3, we can see that the effect of the logo image obtained by zero-watermark XOR will gradually deteriorate with the increase of noise density. When the attack is Gaussian noise (0.01) and salt and pepper noise (0.01), the BCR values are respectively For the 0.9531 and 0.9727, the effect is worse than the BCR

Table 1. Experimental results after JPEG compression attack

Attacks	Attacked image	Verify Logo image	BCR
JPEG10%			0.9639
JPEG 30%			0.9902
JPEG 70%			0.9980
JPEG 90%			0.9961

Table 2. Experimental results after rotation attack

Attacks	Attacked image	Verify Logo image	BCR
Rotation 0.25			0.9980
Rotation 0.5			0.9971
Rotation 0.75			0.9971
Rotation 1			0.9971

Table 3. Experimental results after noise attack

Attacks	Attacked image	Verify Logo image	BCR
Gaussian noise (0.01)			0.9531
Gaussian noise (0.005)			0.9648
Salt and pepper noise (0.01)			0.9727
Salt and pepper noise (0.005)			0.9814

values of two noise densities of 0.005. However, after adding two kinds of noise, the logo image can be extracted well, which proves that the proposed algorithm can resist a certain degree of noise attack.

Scaling Attack. A large number of pixels are lost after the image is scaled, which affects the normal extraction of the watermark. Here, the original image is scaled by 0.75, 1.5, and 2 times. The scaled image and the extracted logo image are shown in Table 4. It can be seen that the quality of the watermark extracted from the scaled image is good, and the BCR values are 0.957, 0.9863 and 0.9814, respectively. Therefore, the algorithm can effectively resist certain scaling attacks.

Cropping Attack. Cropping attack can cause the extracted watermark to be distorted. In the experiment, the upper left corner of the image is selected for cutting, and the degree of clipping is 1/16, 1/8, 1/4, respectively. Table 5 is the effect picture after cutting and the effect picture of the extracted logo image. It can be seen that the logo image can be well extracted when the shear ratio is 1/16 and 1/8, but when the cut ratio is 1/4, the extracted logo image is slightly inferior. This is because when using this algorithm to accurately calculate PHFM, it is obtained by the method of inscribed circle mapping of the image, but when the cut exceeds $\frac{2-\sqrt{2}}{2}$ ratio, the content in the inscribed circle of the image will have an impact, the effect of the extracted logo image is gradually deteriorated. Therefore, the algorithm can resist a certain degree of shear attack.

Filtering Attacks. Filtering attacks are a common type of image attack. Here we perform three filtering attacks on the original image, such as median filtering, Gaussian

Table 4. Experimental results after scaling attack

Attacks	Attacked image	Verify Logo image	BCR
Scaling 0.75			0.957
Scaling 1.5			0.9863
Scaling 2			0.9814

Table 5. Experimental results after cropping attack

Attacks	Attacked image	Verify Logo image	BCR
Cropping 1/16			1
Cropping 1/8			1
Cropping 1/4			0.8398

filtering and averaging filtering. From Table 6, it can be seen that the image after the mean filtering and the median filtering attack will decrease with the increase of the filtering attack template. After the Gaussian filtering attack, the increase of the filtering attack template does not affect the image quality. The experimental results show that the proposed algorithm can resist Gaussian filtering well and can effectively resist a certain degree of median filtering and mean filtering attacks.

Table 6. Experimental results after filtering attack

Attacks	Attacked image	Verify Logo image	BCR
Average filtering 3×3			0.9912
Average filtering 5×5			0.9688
Median filtering 3×3			0.9707
Median filtering 5×5			0.9609
Gaussian filtering 3×3			0.9990
Gaussian filtering 5×5			0.9990

Flipping Attack. Image flipping, divided into vertical flip and left and right flip, it will change the pixel position of the image. In Table 7, the BCR value of the logo image extracted after the vertical flip and left and right flipped are all 1, indicating that the algorithm has good robustness against flipping attacks.

4.3 Comparison of Similar Methods

This algorithm will compare the robustness between the zero-watermark algorithm of PHFM and the existing zero-watermark algorithm. The algorithm proposed in this paper uses the PHFM in the image moment to extract the image features. In the contrast experiment, we experiment with a binary logo image and 15 original images, and take the average of 15 groups of BCR to measure the robust of the algorithm. The measurement of algorithm robustness is mainly divided into geometric attack and conventional image processing attack. The attacks added in the experiment include JPEG compression, rotation, scaling, median filtering, Gaussian filtering, Gaussian noise, salt and pepper

Table 7. Experimental results after flipping the attack

Attacks	Attacked image	Verify Logo image	BCR
Vertical flipping			1
Horizontal flipping			1

noise, and upper left corner cutting. The experimental results are shown in Table 8. It can be seen from the table that the robustness of the algorithm is better than that of the algorithm when most of the attacks are added [19] and [20], the robustness of the proposed algorithm is verified.

Table 8. Robust contrast (BCR)

Attacks	Algorithm [19]	Algorithm [20]	Proposed
JPEG 10%	0.9758	0.9639	0.9707
JPEG 30%	0.9824	0.9822	0.9907
JPEG 50%	0.9958	0.9944	0.9990
JPEG 70%	0.9980	0.9912	0.9934
JPEG 90%	1	0.9766	0.9863
Rotation 5°	0.9321	0.9805	0.9863
Rotation 45°	0.9412	0.9571	0.9902
Scaling 0.25	0.9741	0.9883	0.9885
Scaling 4	0.9980	0.9912	0.9973
Median filtering 3×3	0.9915	0.9981	0.9980
Gaussian filtering 3×3	0.9966	0.9952	0.9961
Gaussian noise (0.01)	0.9724	0.9737	0.9785
Salt and pepper noise (0.01)	0.9670	0.9336	0.9531
Cropping 1/16	1	0.9483	1
Cropping 1/8	1	0.9590	1

5 Conclusion

When the existing zero-watermark algorithm suffers from geometric attack, the robustness is poor and the security is low. Therefore, based on the accurate PHFM, this paper proposes a robust zero-watermarking algorithm for remote sensing images against geometric attacks. In this algorithm, the Logistic chaotic mapping method is used to improve the security of the algorithm; the algorithm takes the accurate PHFM of the image as the image feature, which improves the ability of resisting the conventional attack and geometric attack. Therefore, in the copyright protection of remote sensing image, this algorithm has very important significance and certain practical application value.

References

1. Fang, Z., Wang, J., Wang, B., et al.: Fuzzy search for multiple chinese keywords in cloud environment. Comput. Mater. Contin. **58**(2), 351–363 (2019)
2. Ma, B., Shi, Y.Q.: A reversible data hiding scheme based on code division multiplexing. IEEE Trans. Inf. Forensics Secur. **11**(9), 1914–1927 (2016)
3. Xiong, L., Shi, Y.: On the privacy-preserving outsourcing scheme of reversible data hiding over encrypted image data in cloud computing. Comput. Mater. Con. **55**(3), 523–539 (2018)
4. Qu, Z., Zhu, T., Wang, J., et al.: A novel quantum stegonagraphy based on brown states. Comput. Mater. Con. **56**(1), 47–59 (2018)
5. Li, J., Ma, B., Wang, C.: Extraction of PRNU noise from partly decoded video. J. Vis. Commun. Image Represent. **57**, 183–191 (2018)
6. Wen, Q., Sun, T.F., Wang, S.X.: Based zero-watermark digital watermarking technology. In: Proceedings of the 3rd National Conference in Information Hiding, pp. 102–109. Xidian University Press, Xi'an (2001)
7. Wen, Q., Sun, T.F., Wang, S.X.: Concept and application of zero-watermark. Acta Electron. Sin. **31**, 214–216 (2003)
8. Tsai, H.H., Tseng, H.C., Lai, Y.S.: Robust lossless image watermarking based on α-trimmed mean algorithm and support vector machine. J. Syst. Softw. **83**(6), 1015–1028 (2010)
9. Tsai, H.H., Lai, Y.S., Lo, S.C.: A zero-watermark scheme with geometrical invariants using SVM and PSO against geometrical attacks for image protection. J. Syst. Softw. **86**(2), 335–348 (2013)
10. Gao, G., Jiang, G.: Bessel-Fourier moment-based robust image zero-watermarking. Multimed. Tools Appl. **74**(3), 841–858 (2013). https://doi.org/10.1007/s11042-013-1701-8
11. Wang, C.P., Wang, X.Y., Xia, Z.Q., et al.: Geometrically resilient color image zero-watermarking algorithm based on quaternion exponent moments. J. Vis. Commun. Image Represent. **41**, 247–259 (2016)
12. Wang, C., Wang, X., Chen, X., Zhang, C.: Robust zero-watermarking algorithm based on polar complex exponential transform and logistic mapping. Multimed. Tools Appl. **76**(24), 26355–26376 (2016). https://doi.org/10.1007/s11042-016-4130-7
13. Wang, C., Wang, X., Xia, Z., et al.: Image description with polar harmonic Fourier moments. IEEE Trans. Circ. Syst. Video Technol. (2019). https://doi.org/10.1109/TCSVT.2019.296 0507
14. Song, W., Hou, J.J., Li, Z.H., et al.: A zero-watermarking algorithm based on Logistic chaotic system and singular value decomposition. Acta Physica Sinica **58**(07), 4449–4456 (2009)
15. Wang, C.P.: Research on several key technologies of digital image watermarking. Dalian University of Technology (2017)

16. Singh, C., Upneja, R.: A computational model for enhanced accuracy of radial harmonic Fourier moments. World Congress of Engineering, London, UK (2012)
17. Upneja, R.: Accurate and fast Jacobi-Fourier moments for invariant image recognition. Optik **127**(19), 7925–7940 (2016)
18. Wang, C.P., Wang, X.Y., Li, Y.W., Xia, Z.Q., Zhang, C.: Quaternion polar harmonic Fourier moments for color images. Inf. Sci. **450**, 141–156 (2018)
19. Wang, C.P., Wang, X.Y., Xia, Z.Q., Zhang, C.: Ternary radial harmonic Fourier moments based robust stereo image zero-watermarking algorithm. Inf. Sci. **470**, 109–120 (2019)
20. Liu, W.J., Sun, S.Y., Qu, H.C.: Fast zero-watermarking algorithm for Schur decomposition. Comput. Sci. Explor. **13**(03), 494–504 (2019)

Multi-layer Quantum Secret Sharing Based on GHZ States

Li-wei Chang[1,2(✉)], Yu-qing Zhang[1], Xiao-xiong Tian[1], Yu-hua Qian[2],
Zeng-liang Bai[1], and Shi-hui Zheng[3]

[1] School of Information, Shanxi University of Finance and Economics, Taiyuan 030006, China
changliwei002@163.com
[2] Institute of Big Data Science and Industry, Shanxi University, Taiyuan 030006, China
[3] School of Cyberspace Security, Beijing University of Posts and Telecommunications, Beijing
100876, China

Abstract. A multi-layer quantum secret sharing protocol based on GHZ states is
put forward. In this protocol, Alice wishes to share a secret, carried by the quantum state, with multiple agent nodes in the network. To be specific, the secret is
transmitted and shared layer by layer from root Alice to layered agents. Only if all
agents at the last layer cooperate together, this secret can be reconstructed accurately. Compared with existing quantum secret sharing protocols, there are two
highlights in our proposed protocol. On the one hand, the secret can be distributed
to multiple agents only with five-particle GHZ states on account of layered construction. On the other hand, we elaborately design two iterative algorithms under
the guidance of computational thinking, Algorithm 1 is helpful to quickly calculate the final collapsed state in each layer, Algorithm 2 is capable of obtaining
the specific recovery operation based on the output results of Algorithm 1. Our
proposed protocol can be applied to the wireless network in an effort to ensure the
security of information delivery.

Keywords: Quantum secret sharing · GHZ states · Multi-player sharing ·
Iterative algorithms

1 Introduction

Nowadays, with the rapid development of science and technology, human society has
stepped into the era of the integration of realistic space and cyberspace. The information
superhighway has become the basis of economic development. Thus, how to effectively
ensure the security of information is of extreme significance.

Classical cryptography is an important tool to ensure the information security. Unfortunately, quantum algorithms cause them to be broken through in polynomial time.
Thereupon, quantum cryptography, which is proven to be unconditionally secure over
an insecure channel, has attracted more and more attention from both industry and
academia. As a result, so far all kinds of quantum secure communication protocols
have been proposed by the researchers such as quantum key distribution (QKD) [1–5],

© Springer Nature Singapore Pte Ltd. 2020
X. Sun et al. (Eds.): ICAIS 2020, CCIS 1252, pp. 674–685, 2020.
https://doi.org/10.1007/978-981-15-8083-3_60

quantum secure direct communication (QSDC) [6–8], quantum teleportation (QT) [9, 10], remote state preparation (RSP) [11, 12], quantum signature (QS) [13, 14], quantum private query (QPQ) [15, 16], quantum private comparison [17] and so on.

Quantum secret sharing (QSS) is a significant branch of quantum secure communication, which is deemed to be the quantum counterpart of classical secret sharing. In fact, QSS combines quantum mechanics and the kernel idea contained in classical secret sharing to split either a classical secret (bit string) or a quantum state (unknown quantum state) into several shadows, a specific quantity of shadows can reconstruct the secret but every shadow alone cannot. The quantum secret sharing schemes were firstly proposed by Hillery et al. and Karlsson et al. at the same year [18, 19]. Since then, a great many of QSS schemes have been put forward by experts and scholars in both theory and experiment.

In 2008, Deng et al. presented an efficient high-capacity QSS protocol based on the ideas of quantum dense coding [20]. In 2010, Gu et al. proposed two robust three-party QSS protocols to be against both collective-dephasing noise and collective rotation noise with logical Bell states [21]. In 2012, Yang et al. not only summarized how to construct a verifiable quantum (k, n) threshold protocol, but also designed a specific scheme by means of Lagrange Interpolation formula and post-verification mechanisms [22]. In 2013, Hsu et al. put forward a dynamic QSS protocol with the entanglement swapping of EPR pairs to deal with the volatility of agents [23]. In 2015, Rahaman et al. elaborately devised the first QSS scheme by utilizing the local distinguishability of orthogonal multipartite entangled states [24]. In 2017, Wang et al. designed a multi-layer QSS protocol based on GHZ state and generalized Bell-basis measurement [25]. In the same year, Chen et al. came up with a QSS scheme using the Borras-Plastino-Batle (BPB) state, in which the module division and coupling of quantum communication protocols was investigated [26]. In addition, Wang et al. attempted to make use of the local distinguishability of orthogonal Dicke states and multi-qudit entangled states to construct the QSS schemes, respectively [27, 28]. In 2019, a new multi-party QSS model was built by Zhang et al. by analyzing the property of multi-qubit entangled states [29]. In the same year, a novel rational non-hierarchical quantum secret sharing protocol emerged, which is widely applicable [30].

It is easy to discover that each of aforementioned QSS schemes is deem to be a representative of one kind of QSS. Aiming at the fact that it is difficult to prepare multiparticle entangled states, based on layered structure, we put forward a multi-layer QSS protocol with five-particle GHZ states which can be created in laboratory. In our scheme, the secret, carried by one quantum state, is distributed to the multiple agent nodes in the network layer by layer from root to layered agents. Only if all agents at the last layer cooperate together, the secret can be reconstructed.

The structure of this paper is organized as follows. In Sect. 2, we come up with a multi-layer quantum secret sharing protocol by means of five-particle GHZ states. In Sect. 3, we design two iterative algorithms under the guidance of computational thinking. One is to calculate the multi-qubit entangled states carrying the secret in the last layer, while the other is to compute the recovery operations performed by the designated agent in the last layer. Finally, this paper ends up with a discussion in Sect. 4.

2 Multi-layer Quantum Secret Sharing Protocols

In this section, we design a multi-layer QSS protocol with five-particle GHZ states by using Bell-basis measurement. We take into account that the agent's number in each layer is a geometric sequence with common ratio 4. The workflow of this QSS protocol can be depicted as follows.

2.1 The Secret Sharing Process of the First Layer

Suppose that there are five participants, one sender Alice and four agents $Bob_i (i = 1, \cdots, 4)$ in the first layer. Alice holds a secret carried by the one-qubit quantum state and wants to distribute this secret to the agents $Bob_i(i = 1, \cdots, 4)$. The one-qubit state corresponding to this secret can be written as.

$$|\psi_1\rangle = \alpha|0\rangle + \beta|1\rangle, \tag{1}$$

where α and β are complex numbers, which satisfy the normalization condition $\alpha^2 + \beta^2 = 1$.

For sharing the one-qubit state with four agents, Alice first prepares a five-particle GHZ state, as shown in the Fig. 1(a), which can be expressed in

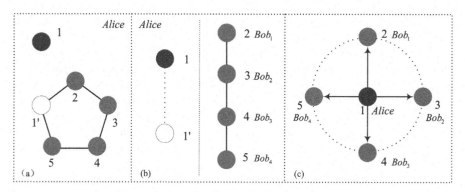

Fig. 1. The secret sharing process of the first layer

$$|\psi\rangle_{1'2345} = \frac{1}{\sqrt{2}}(|00000\rangle + |11111\rangle) \tag{2}$$

This five-particle GHZ state can be created in laboratory conditions. To set up the quantum channel, Alice sends the particle 2 to Bob_1, the particle 3 to Bob_2, the particle 4 to Bob_3 and the particle 5 to Bob_4. Therefore, the state of the whole six-particle system can be described as

$$|\psi\rangle_1 \otimes |\psi\rangle_{1'2345} = \frac{1}{\sqrt{2}}(\alpha|000000\rangle + \alpha|011111\rangle + \beta|100000\rangle + \beta|111111\rangle) \tag{3}$$

In order to transfer the secret to four agents, Alice performs a Bell-basis measurement on the particles 1 and 2 as depicted in the Fig. 1(b). This measurement basis is made up of four Bell states

$$|\varphi_1\rangle = \frac{1}{\sqrt{2}}(|00\rangle+|11\rangle)), |\varphi_2\rangle = \frac{1}{\sqrt{2}}(|00\rangle-|11\rangle)$$

$$|\varphi_3\rangle = \frac{1}{\sqrt{2}}(|01\rangle+|10\rangle)), |\varphi_4\rangle = \frac{1}{\sqrt{2}}(|01\rangle-|10\rangle) \qquad (4)$$

As a result, the state of the whole quantum system, which is composed of six particles, can be rewritten as

$$|\psi\rangle_{11'2345} = \frac{1}{\sqrt{2}}[|\varphi_1\rangle_{11'}(\alpha|0000\rangle + \beta|1111\rangle)_{2345}$$

$$+ |\varphi_2\rangle_{11'}(\alpha|0000\rangle - \beta|1111\rangle)_{2345}$$

$$+ |\varphi_3\rangle_{11'}(\alpha|1111\rangle + \beta|0000\rangle)_{2345}$$

$$+ |\varphi_4\rangle_{11'}(\alpha|1111\rangle - \beta|0000\rangle)_{2345}] \qquad (5)$$

It is obvious that the whole system will collapse to a term of Eq. (5) with the probability of 1/4, after Alice implements the Bell-basis measurement.

Table 1. Corresponding relationship between the measurement outcomes of Bob_2–Bob_4 and the unitary operations performed by Bob_1

Bob_2's SM results	Bob_3's SM results	Bob_4's SM results	Bob_1's operations
$|+\rangle$	$|+\rangle$	$|+\rangle$	I_2
$|+\rangle$	$|+\rangle$	$|-\rangle$	σ_2^z
$|+\rangle$	$|-\rangle$	$|+\rangle$	σ_2^z
$|+\rangle$	$|-\rangle$	$|-\rangle$	I_2
$|-\rangle$	$|+\rangle$	$|+\rangle$	σ_2^z
$|-\rangle$	$|+\rangle$	$|-\rangle$	I_2
$|-\rangle$	$|-\rangle$	$|+\rangle$	I_2
$|-\rangle$	$|-\rangle$	$|-\rangle$	σ_2^z

That is to say, as shown in the Fig. 1(c), the secret carried by the particle 1 is transferred to the quantum system composed of four particles 2, 3, 4 and 5. As a result, this secret is shared by four agents Bob_1, Bob_2, Bob_3 and Bob_4 through one time distribution. Only if these four agents collaborate with each other, they can recover the secret.

If Alice decides that the protocol only works in the first layer, she will announce her measurement results and designate one agent to recover the secret at random. Assume she empowers Bob_1 to recover the secret, Bob_2, Bob_3 and Bob_4 should carry out a single-qubit measurement in the basis $|X^{\pm}\rangle = \frac{1}{\sqrt{2}}(|0\rangle\pm|1\rangle)$ on their own particles respectively and publish their measurement outcomes to Bob_1 via a classical channel. According to the measurement outcomes from both Alice and Bob_2–Bob_4, Bob_1 can recover the original secret by applying a suitable unitary transformation on his particle 2. As illuminated in Table 1, when Alice's measurement result is $|\varphi_1\rangle$, Bob_1 should carry out the corresponding unitary transformations.

If Alice wishes to make more agents share this secret, she does not publish her measurement results and not designate any agent to reconstruct it. Bob_1, Bob_2, Bob_3 and Bob_4 will continue to distribute this secret to the second layer. Obviously, these four agents are not able to recover the secret accurately, because they are ignorant of Alice's measurement results.

2.2 The Secret Sharing Process of the Second Layer

After the first distribution, the entangled state, carrying the secret, shared among Bob_1, Bob_2, Bob_3 and Bob_4 can be written as Eq. (5). The target is to share this secret among sixteen agents $Charlie_i (i = 1, \cdots, 16)$ in the second layer.

As shown in the Fig. 2(a), Bob_1–Bob_4 should prepare a five-particle GHZ state respectively,

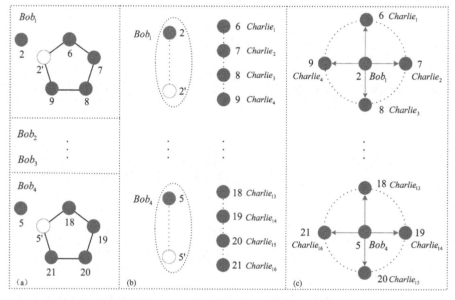

Fig. 2. The secret sharing process of the second layer

$$|\psi\rangle_{2'6789} = \frac{1}{\sqrt{2}}(|00000\rangle + |11111\rangle)_{2'6789}$$

$$|\psi\rangle_{3'10111213} = \frac{1}{\sqrt{2}}(|00000\rangle + |11111\rangle)_{3'10111213}$$

$$|\psi\rangle_{4'14151617} = \frac{1}{\sqrt{2}}(|00000\rangle + |11111\rangle)_{4'14151617}$$

$$|\psi\rangle_{5'18192021} = \frac{1}{\sqrt{2}}(|00000\rangle + |11111\rangle)_{5'18192021} \qquad (6)$$

For simplicity, the numbers 6, 7, 8, 9 are written as 6–9, the numbers 10, 11, 12, 13 are written as 10–13, the numbers 14, 15, 16, 17 are written as 14–17, and the numbers 18, 19, 20, 21 are written as 18–21.

Bob_1 respectively sends the particles 6–9 to $Charlie_1$–$Charlie_4$ with the help of decoy photons, Bob_2 respectively sends the particles 10–13 to $Charlie_5$–$Charlie_8$ with the help of decoy photons, Bob_3 respectively sends the particles 14–17 to $Charlie_9$–$Charlie_{12}$ with the help of decoy photons, and Bob_4 respectively sends the particles 18–21 to $Charlie_{13}$–$Charlie_{16}$ with the help of decoy photons.

Suppose Alice's measurement result is $|\varphi_2\rangle$, the state of the whole quantum system, which is composed of twenty-four particles, can be described as

$$|\psi\rangle = |\psi\rangle_{2345} \otimes |\psi\rangle_{2'6-9} \otimes |\psi\rangle_{3'10-13} \otimes |\psi\rangle_{4'14-17} \otimes |\psi\rangle_{5'18-21}$$

$$= \frac{1}{4}(\alpha|0000\rangle - \beta|1111\rangle)_{2345} \otimes (|00000\rangle + |11111\rangle)_{2'6-9}$$

$$\otimes (|00000\rangle + |11111\rangle)_{3'10-13} \otimes (|00000\rangle + |11111\rangle)_{4'14-17}$$

$$\otimes (|00000\rangle + |11111\rangle)_{5'18-21} \qquad (7)$$

After Bob_1 completes his measurement work, the state of the whole quantum system will collapse into

$$|\psi\rangle = \frac{1}{4\sqrt{2}}[|\varphi_1\rangle_{22'}(\alpha|0000000\rangle - \beta|1111111\rangle)_{3-9}$$

$$+ |\varphi_2\rangle_{22'}(\alpha|0000000\rangle + \beta|1111111\rangle)_{3-9}$$

$$+ |\varphi_3\rangle_{22'}(-\beta|1111000\rangle + \alpha|0000111\rangle)_{3-9}$$

$$+ |\varphi_4\rangle_{22'}(\beta|1111000\rangle + \alpha|0000111\rangle)_{3-9}]$$

$$\otimes (|00000\rangle + |11111\rangle)_{3'10-13} \otimes (|00000\rangle + |11111\rangle)_{4'14-17}$$

$$\otimes (|00000\rangle + |11111\rangle)_{5'18-21} \qquad (8)$$

Assume Bob_1's measurement result is $|\varphi_1\rangle$, after Bob_2 implements a Bell-basis measurement on particles 3 and $3'$, the state of the whole quantum system can be written as

$$|\psi\rangle = \frac{1}{8}[|\varphi_1\rangle_{33'}(\alpha|0000000000\rangle - \beta|1111111111\rangle)_{4-13}$$

$$+ |\varphi_2\rangle_{33'}(\alpha|0000000000\rangle + \beta|1111111111\rangle)_{4-13}$$

$$+ |\varphi_3\rangle_{33'}(-\beta|1111110000\rangle + \alpha|0000001111\rangle)_{4-13}$$

$$+ |\varphi_4\rangle_{33'}(\beta|1111110000\rangle + \alpha|0000001111\rangle)_{4-13}]$$

$$\otimes (|00000\rangle + |11111\rangle)_{4'14-17} \otimes (|00000\rangle + |11111\rangle)_{5'18-21} \qquad (9)$$

Assume Bob_2's measurement result is $|\varphi_1\rangle$, after Bob_3 carries out a Bell-basis measurement on particles 4 and $4'$, the state of the whole quantum system can be expressed as

$$|\psi\rangle = \frac{1}{8\sqrt{2}}[|\varphi_1\rangle_{44'}(\alpha|0000000000000\rangle - \beta|1111111111111\rangle)_{5-17}$$
$$+ |\varphi_2\rangle_{44'}(\alpha|0000000000000\rangle + \beta|1111111111111\rangle)_{5-17}$$
$$+ |\varphi_3\rangle_{44'}(-\beta|1111111110000\rangle + \alpha|0000000001111\rangle)_{5-17}$$
$$+ |\varphi_4\rangle_{44'}(\beta|1111111110000\rangle + \alpha|0000000001111\rangle)_{5-17}]$$
$$\otimes (|00000\rangle + |11111\rangle)_{5'18-21} \tag{10}$$

Assume Bob$_3$'s measurement result is $|\varphi_1\rangle$, after Bob$_4$ executes a Bell-basis measurement on particles 5 and $5'$, the state of the whole quantum system can be depicted as

$$|\psi\rangle = \frac{1}{16}[|\varphi_1\rangle_{55'}(\alpha|0000000000000000\rangle - \beta|1111111111111111\rangle)_{6-21}$$
$$+ |\varphi_2\rangle_{55'}(\alpha|0000000000000000\rangle + \beta|1111111111111111\rangle)_{6-21}$$
$$+ |\varphi_3\rangle_{55'}(-\beta|1111111111110000\rangle + \alpha|0000000000001111\rangle)_{6-21}$$
$$+ |\varphi_4\rangle_{55'}(\beta|1111111111110000\rangle + \alpha|0000000000001111\rangle)_{6-21} \tag{11}$$

If Alice empowers Charlie$_1$ to recover the secret, she will announce her measurement results. Charlie$_i$ ($i = 2, \cdots, 16$) should respectively carry out a single-qubit measurement in the basis $|X^{\pm}\rangle = \frac{1}{\sqrt{2}}(|0\rangle \pm |1\rangle)$ on their own particles and publish their measurement outcomes to Charlie$_1$ via classical channels. In the light of the measurement outcomes from Charlie$_i$ ($i = 2, \cdots, 16$), Charlie$_1$ can recover the original secret by applying a corresponding unitary transformation on his particle 6.

If Alice wishes to make more agents share this secret, she does not publish her measurement results and not designate any agent to reconstruct it. Charlie$_i$ ($i = 2, \cdots, 16$) will continue to distribute the secret to the third layer. To be apparent, Charlie$_i$ cannot recover the secret accurately, since they are unaware of Alice's measurement results.

2.3 The Secret Sharing of Higher Layer

As shown in Fig. 3, we can achieve the secret sharing of higher layer in the same way described in Subsect. 2.2. Take the third layer as an example, Charlie$_i$ needs to prepare one five-particle maximally entangled GHZ states, sends four particles to four agents in the fourth layer with the help of decoy photons, leaves one particle in her own hand, and performs a Bell-basis measurements on two particles in her own hands. Finally, the secret can be shared with 4^3 agents in the third layer. Repeat this work again and again, we are able to realize that the number of each layer of agents is a geometric sequence with common ratio 4. With the increase of layer number, the secret can be shared with more and more agents. It is worth noting that no matter how many agents the secret is shared with, our proposed protocol only needs five-particle GHZ states.

3 Iterative Algorithms

In this section, we make every endeavor to look for an appropriate manner to clearly exhibit the whole evolution process of multi-layer quantum secret sharing protocols. The

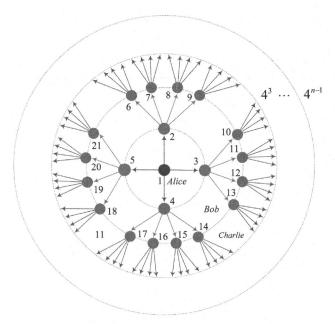

Fig. 3. The secret sharing process of higher layer

core work is how to calculate the collapsed states and recovery operations quickly and accurately. In view of the fact, we design two iterative algorithms to quickly calculate the collapsed states as well as recovery operations. Algorithm 1 is helpful to quickly calculate the final collapsed states in each layer, while Algorithm 2 is capable of obtaining the specific recovery operation performed by the designated agent in the last layer.

3.1 Algorithm 1

Algorithm 1 Calculate the final collapsed states carrying the secret in every layer

Input: The total numbers of layers m, all the measurement results $|\varphi'_{i,j}\rangle (1 \le i \le m, 1 \le j \le 4^{i-1}m)$ and the collapsed state $|\psi_{1,1}\rangle$ of the first layer

Output: Multi-qubit entangled states carrying the secret in the mth layer $|\psi\rangle$

1: Initiate $|\psi\rangle$

2: Generate a reference Table 2 in accordance with Eq.(5)

3: **for** i = 2 to m **do**

4:      $|\psi_{i,j-1}\rangle = |\psi_{i-1,4^{i-2}}\rangle$

5:      **for** j = 1 to 4^{i-1} **do**

6:          Denote α and it's symbol as α' as well as β and it's symbol as β', where α and β are the coefficients of the collapsed state $|\psi_{i,j-1}\rangle$

7:          Compare the first qubit of the collapsed state $|\psi_{i,j-1}\rangle$ with the j th one of GHZ = $|0\rangle^{\otimes 4^{i-1}} + |1\rangle^{\otimes 4^{i-1}}$ from left to right

8:          **if** They are equal **then**

9:          $|\psi_{i,j-1}\rangle = \alpha' |\underbrace{\qquad}_{4^{i-1}+3j-4}\underbrace{\qquad}_{4}\rangle + \beta' |\underbrace{\qquad}_{4^{i-1}+3j-4}\underbrace{\qquad}_{4}\rangle$

10:          Fill the last $4^{i-1} + 3j - 4$ bits of $|\psi_{i,j-1}\rangle$ into the first $4^{i-1} + 3j - 4$ ones of $|\psi_{i,j}\rangle$

11:          Query the reference Table 2 according to the current measurement result $|\varphi'_{i,j}\rangle$, find out the corresponding collapsed state and fill this collapsed state into the last four qubits of $|\psi_{i,j}\rangle$

12:      **else**

13:          $|\psi_{i,j-1}\rangle = \beta' |\underbrace{\qquad}_{4^{i-1}+3j-4}\underbrace{\qquad}_{4}\rangle + \alpha' |\underbrace{\qquad}_{4^{i-1}+3j-4}\underbrace{\qquad}_{4}\rangle$

14:          Fill the last $4^{i-1} + 3j - 4$ bits of $|\psi_{i,j-1}\rangle$ into the first $4^{i-1} + 3j - 4$ ones of $|\psi_{i,j}\rangle$

15:          Query the reference Table 2 according to the current measurement result $|\varphi_{i,j}\rangle$, find out the corresponding collapsed state and fill this collapsed state into the last two qubits of $|\psi_{i,j}\rangle$

16:      **end if**

17:      **end for**

18:      Return $|\psi_{i,j}\rangle$ to $|\psi\rangle$

19: **end for**

Before describing this algorithm, we needs to do some preparation work. To be specific, we must create a reference table called Table 2 in accordance with Eq. (5), which plays an important role during calculation. Table 2 presents the corresponding relationship between measurement results and collapsed states in the first layer, it will be called to calculate the collapsed states in next layers. Table 2 is described as follows.

3.2 Algorithm 2

In the last layer, the secret from Alice must be carried by the multi-particle entangled states. The function of Algorithm 2 is able to help the researchers to effectively acquire

Table 2. Corresponding relationship between Alice's measurement results and the collapsed states in Bob_1–Bob_4's hands in the first layer

Alice's GM results $|\varphi'_{1,1}\rangle$	The collapsed states $|\psi_{1,1}\rangle$ in Bob_1–Bob_4's hands
$|\varphi_1\rangle$	$\alpha|0000\rangle + \beta|1111\rangle$
$|\varphi_2\rangle$	$\alpha|0000\rangle - \beta|1111\rangle$
$|\varphi_3\rangle$	$\alpha|0000\rangle - \beta|1111\rangle$
$|\varphi_4\rangle$	$\alpha|0000\rangle + \beta|1111\rangle$

the recovery operations. For simplicity, in the following algorithm we assume Alice empowers the first agent in the last layer to recover the secret.

Algorithm 2 Calculate the recovery operations

Input: The multi-qubit entangled states carrying the secret $|\psi_{m,4^{m-1}}\rangle$ and the single particle measurement results $SM_i (i = 2, \cdots, 4^m)$ from the $4^m - 1$ agents in the mth layer

Output: The operations performed by the designated agent who is responsible for recovering the secret

1: Initiate the operation OP

2: Record the positions of all the 1 in the term with the coefficients α and β of $|\psi_{m,2^{m-1}}\rangle$, respectively

3: Count the number C_α and C_β of the measurement outcome $|-\rangle$ corresponding to the position of 1 in the term with the coefficients α and β

4: Generate the final collapsed state $(-1)^{C_\alpha}\alpha|\bar{0}\rangle + (-1)^{C_\beta}\beta|\bar{1}\rangle$, $\bar{0}$ and $\bar{1}$ correspond the state of the qubit in the first agent in the last layer

5: Obtain the recovery operation OP

---

4 Conclusion

This paper puts forward a multi-layer QSS protocol based on five-particle GHZ stats by adopting the layered construction. The number of each layer of agents is a geometric sequence with common ratio 4. There exist two bright spots in this paper. The first bright spot is that sharing the quantum secret in multi-party agents only needs GHZ states with less particles which can be easily prepared in the laboratory. The second bright spot is that we design two iterative algorithms for quickly calculating the collapsed states and recovery operations. The ideas of these two algorithms can make a variety of entangled states to be utilized to design multi-layer QSS protocols and wireless communication protocols.

Acknowledgements. The work was supported by the National Natural Science Foundation of China (Grant No. 61672332), Natural Science Foundation of Shanxi Province in China (Grant No. 201801D221159), Scientific and Technological Innovation Programs of Higher Education Institutions in Shanxi, China (Grant Nos. 2019L0470 and 2019L0479), the Key R&D program (international science and technology cooperation project) of Shanxi Province, China (No. 201903D421003).

References

1. Huang, W., et al.: Authenticated quantum key distribution with collective detection using single photons. Int. J. Theor. Phys. **55**(10), 4238–4256 (2016). https://doi.org/10.1007/s10 773-016-3049-0

2. Zhu, J., Zhang, C., Wang, Q.: Biased decoy-state reference-frame-independent quantum key distribution. Eur. Phys. J. D **71**(12), 1–6 (2017). https://doi.org/10.1140/epjd/e2017-80219-2

3. Zhu, K.-N., Zhou, N.-R., Wang, Y.-Q., Wen, X.-J.: Semi-quantum key distribution protocols with GHZ states. Int. J. Theor. Phys. **57**(12), 3621–3631 (2018). https://doi.org/10.1007/s10 773-018-3875-3

4. Zhou, N.R., Zhu, K.N., Zou, X.F.: Multi-party semi-quantum key distribution protocol with four-particle cluster states. Ann. Phys. **531**(8), 1800520 (2019)

5. Xiao, H., Zhang, J., Huang, W., et al.: An efficient quantum key distribution protocol with dense coding on single photons. Comput. Mater. Contin. **61**(2), 759–775 (2019)

6. Deng, F.G., Long, G.L., Liu, X.S.: Two-step quantum direct communication protocol using the Einstein-Podolsky-Rosen pair block. Phys. Rev. A **68**(4), 042317 (2003)

7. Cao, Z., Li, Y., Peng, J., Chai, G., Zhao, G.: Controlled quantum secure direct communication protocol based on Huffman compression coding. Int. J. Theor. Phys. **57**(12), 3632–3642 (2018). https://doi.org/10.1007/s10773-018-3876-2

8. Zheng, X.-y., Long, Y.-x.: Controlled quantum secure direct communication with authentication protocol based on five-particle cluster state and classical XOR operation. Quantum Inf. Process. **18**(5), 1–12 (2019). https://doi.org/10.1007/s11128-019-2239-0

9. Li, Y.H., Li, X.L., Nie, L.P., et al.: Quantum teleportation of three and four-qubit state using multi-qubit cluster states. Int. J. Theor. Phys. **55**(3), 1820–1823 (2016). https://doi.org/10. 1007/s10773-015-2821-x

10. Sisodia, M., Verma, V., Thapliyal, K., Pathak, A.: Teleportation of a qubit using entangled non-orthogonal states: a comparative study. Quantum Inf. Process. **16**(3), 1–23 (2017). https:// doi.org/10.1007/s11128-017-1526-x

11. Chang, L.W., Zheng, S.H., Gu, L.Z., et al.: Joint remote preparation of an arbitrary five-qubit Brown state via non-maximally entangled channels. Chin. Phys. B **23**(9), 090307 (2014)

12. Chang, L.-W., Zheng, S.-H., Gu, L.-Z., Jin, L., Yang, Y.-X.: Multiparty-controlled joint remote preparation of an arbitrary four-qubit cluster-type state via two different entangled quantum channels. Int. J. Theor. Phys. **54**(8), 2864–2880 (2015). https://doi.org/10.1007/s10773-015-2522-5

13. Jiang, D.-H., Xu, Y.-L., Xu, G.-B.: Arbitrary quantum signature based on local indistinguishability of orthogonal product states. Int. J. Theor. Phys. **58**(3), 1036–1045 (2019). https://doi. org/10.1007/s10773-018-03995-4

14. Chen, F.-L., Liu, W.-F., Chen, S.-G., Wang, Z.-H.: Public-key quantum digital signature scheme with one-time pad private-key. Quantum Inf. Process. **17**(1), 1–14 (2017). https://doi. org/10.1007/s11128-017-1778-5

15. Wei, C.Y., Wang, T.Y., Gao, F.: Practical quantum private query with better performance in resisting joint-measurement attack. Phys. Rev. A **93**(4), 042318 (2016)

16. Gao, F., Qin, S., Huang, W., Wen, Q.: Quantum private query: a new kind of practical quantum cryptographic protocol. Sci. China Phys. Mech. Astron. **62**(7), 1–12 (2019). https://doi.org/10.1007/s11433-018-9324-6

17. Yan, L., Chang, Y., Zhang, S., et al.: Measure-resend semi-quantum private comparison scheme using GHZ class states. Comput. Mater. Contin. **61**(2), 877–887 (2019)

18. Hillery, M., Buzek, V., Berthiaume, A.: Quantum secret sharing. Phys. Rev. A **59**(3), 1829 (1999)

19. Karlsson, A., Koashi, M., Imoto, N.: Quantum entanglement for secret sharing and secret splitting. Phys. Rev. A **59**(1), 162 (1999)

20. Deng, F.G., Li, X.H., Zhou, H.Y.: Efficient high-capacity quantum secret sharing with two-photon entanglement. Phys. Lett. A **372**(12), 1957–1962 (2008)

21. Gu, B., Mu, L., Ding, L., et al.: Fault tolerant three-party quantum secret sharing against collective noise. Opt. Commun. **283**(15), 3099–3103 (2010)

22. Yang, Y.G., Jia, X., Wang, H.Y., et al.: Verifiable quantum (k, n)-threshold secret sharing. Quantum Inf. Process. **11**(6), 1619–1625 (2012). https://doi.org/10.1007/s11128-011-0323-1

23. Hsu, J.L., Chong, S.K., Hwang, T., et al.: Dynamic quantum secret sharing. Quantum Inf. Process. **12**(1), 331–344 (2013). https://doi.org/10.1007/s11128-012-0380-0

24. Rahaman, R., Parker, M.G.: Quantum scheme for secret sharing based on local distinguishability. Phys. Rev. A **91**(2), 022330 (2015)

25. Wang, X.J., An, L.X., Yu, X.T., et al.: Multilayer quantum secret sharing based on GHZ state and generalized Bell basis measurement in multiparty agents. Phys. Lett. A **381**(38), 3282–3288 (2017)

26. Chen, X.B., Dou, Z., Xu, G., et al.: A kind of universal quantum secret sharing protocol. Sci. Rep. **7**, 39845 (2017)

27. Wang, J., Li, L., Peng, H., et al.: Quantum-secret-sharing scheme based on local distinguishability of orthogonal multiqudit entangled states. Phys. Rev. A **95**(2), 022320 (2017)

28. Wang, J.T., Xu, G., Chen, X.B., et al.: Local distinguishability of Dicke states in quantum secret sharing. Phys. Lett. A **381**(11), 998–1002 (2017)

29. Zhang, K., Zhang, X., Jia, H., et al.: A new n-party quantum secret sharing model based on multiparty entangled states. Quantum Inf. Process. **18**(3), 81 (2019). https://doi.org/10.1007/s11128-019-2201-1

30. Dou, Z., Xu, G., Chen, X.B., et al.: Rational non-hierarchical quantum state sharing protocol. Comput. Mater. Contin. **58**(2), 335–347 (2019)

Robot Scheduling System Based on Semantic Recognition

Yuan Pan[1(✉)], Zhangguo Chen[2], Bo Zhou[2], Xiangzhong Xie[1], Qian Guo[1], and Chao Hu[2]

[1] Electric Power Dispatching and Control Center of Guangdong Power Grid Co., Ltd., Guangzhou 510600, China
675679580@qq.com
[2] Nanjing NARI Information Communication Technology Co., Ltd., Nanjing 210033, China

Abstract. Dispatching the operation order is the cornerstone and foothold of the dispatching work, and is also an important guarantee and measure for power safety production. With the expansion of the construction scale of Guangdong Power Grid, the operation and management of power grid dispatching operations is becoming more and more complicated. The contradiction between the relatively decentralized service status of power grid operation and the integration characteristics of power grid operation has become increasingly prominent. As the complexity and frequency of scheduling orders increase significantly, the resulting economic losses are huge. In view of the above problems, the provincial-integrated dispatching operation robot designed in this paper realizes intelligent graphics ordering, graphic simulation preview, audit, operation order execution anti-error check, program operation and other functions by scheduling semantic recognition technology. Through the visual management of the land-saving scheduling operation cockpit, it is equipped with the functions of real-time operation risk perception of the whole network and real-time operation big data analysis of control system equipment status perception.

Keywords: Dispatching operation robot · Semantic recognition technology · Intelligent graphics ordering · Anti-error check · Cockpit

1 Introduction

With the continuous expansion of the scale of Guangdong power grid, the power grid dispatching operation is increasingly complicated, and the safety of dispatching operations is becoming more and more prominent. The contradiction between the relatively decentralized business status of power grid management and the integration characteristics of power grid operation needs to be solved, among which the operation management system [1] (OMS) and the operation control system [2] (OCS) are built independently in III and I, respectively. Regulating integration [3] refers to the grid operation management mode that combines the scheduling and monitoring services. It is to place the

© Springer Nature Singapore Pte Ltd. 2020
X. Sun et al. (Eds.): ICAIS 2020, CCIS 1252, pp. 686–698, 2020.
https://doi.org/10.1007/978-981-15-8083-3_61

dispatcher and the monitor in the same place, and the dispatching department manages it in a unified manner. This mode promotes the further integration of dispatching operation and equipment operation monitoring, realizes the integration of power grid dispatching and power grid monitoring, and further improves the scheduling and monitoring level of the power grid.

The focus of dispatching operation order has mainly focused on graphical invoicing and intelligent ordering, which has effectively improved the efficiency of grid operation management personnel, but the system deficiencies are as follows: firstly, the massive historical data of the current dispatching operation order management system is sleeping. Manual collation and archiving, the workload is complicated, and the artificial intelligence technology; secondly, the scheduling operation order generation process is separated from the grid security check, and the workload of the dispatching operation manager is increased; thirdly, traditional scheduling. The operation of the closing gate is complicated, the efficiency is low, the risk of disoperation is large, and it is difficult to adapt to the needs of the scale growth of the power grid, and the program operation is required to improve the execution efficiency of the operation order of the plant. In recent years, the development of artificial intelligence technology [4–10] in knowledge expression has provided new ideas for the construction of dispatching robot systems [11–15]. Aiming at the above problems, the scheduling robot system developed in this paper solves the problem of description, learning and reasoning of the operation order rules based on the historical data of the operation order through scheduling semantic recognition, and realizes the seamless connection with the OCS system. The pattern of I is the same as that of III, and the five defenses and the power flow check are combined to ensure the safety of the power grid operation; the on-site operation steps are simplified through the program operation, and the dispatching is characterized by intelligent, information, automation and interaction. We operate the management system and establish a centralized, unified, intelligent, efficient and safe dispatching and working flow, develop a new generation of command platform for grid intelligent dispatching, realize the coordination and unification of grid operation management and grid operation control, and realize the safety and efficiency of grid operation coordination and unity.

The remaining part of the paper is organized as follows: In Sect. 2, preliminaries about the scheduling system and semantic recognition are briefly introduced. In Sect. 3, the overall design framework of robot scheduling system based on semantic recognition is depicted in detail. Finally, Sect. 4 is dedicated for conclusion.

2 Preliminaries

2.1 Scheduling System

The scheduling system [16–18] is mainly applied in the mine emergency vehicle equipped with touch screen in the emergency command office duty room emergency center. The user can make emergency notification and command release in the fastest and most effective way, and can visually display the status of the notified object. The scheduling system generally has the following characteristics:

(1) High reliability

The system runs stably and reliably. The design adopts dual CPU, dual switching plane and dual power supply to ensure that the system can still work when there is an emergency.

(2) Strong real-time

The hardware device adopts embedded operating system and real-time communication software, which has the advantages of short startup time, fast operation response and stable system operation.

(3) Echo suppression

The system has powerful echo suppression function, which can realize 240-party conference without blocking, and the sound effect is good.

(4) Intelligent detection signaling

The device has simple outlet, convenient plugging and plugging, and the connector is firmly connected. The plug-and-play design is only possible on the interface, which reduces the cumbersome configuration. For digital relay, the device can automatically detect the signaling type and automatically configure the corresponding signaling parameters.

2.2 Semantic Recognition

The semantic web aims to provide a common semantic framework [19], realize data sharing and integration between different applications in the semantic web is to the existing model to increase the support semantics, its goal is to help a machine to a certain extent, to understand the meaning of information modeling, make the effective information sharing and machine intelligence collaborative possible semantic web [20] will provide users with dynamic active service, thus easier to machine and the dialogue between man and machine, and work together.

In response to the current exists in semantics in the field of dispatching operation is not standard phenomenon, design a semantic intelligent identification algorithm for the dispatching operation information intelligent preprocessing algorithm based on semantic dictionary management matching retrieval management four modules combined with collection and storage and retrieval algorithm preprocessing algorithm and text similarity algorithm designed an intelligent self-learning semantic intelligent processing mechanism through improved computer since the recognition rate to realize the algorithm of non-standard operation semantics, so as to enrich semantic knowledge accumulation, in order to increase the accuracy of nonstandard semantic standardization. According to the test of different types of non-standard semantic data, the obtained standard semantic data is analyzed and verified.

Dictionary management module mainly is the standard semantics and intelligent identify non-standard semantic loaded into the semantic knowledge accumulation in the library semantic vector matching is mainly the standard semantic information and enumeration of nonstandard information vector matching, semantic interpretation and returns the pre-set standard defines retrieval preprocessing module is mainly the input preprocessing, not standard semantic specification semantic information format, is advantageous to the recognition in the semantic knowledge accumulation in pretreatment mainly contains uppercase and transformation, replacement of suspicious characters in relay protection information and input ends at the end of the first relay protection information of suspicious characters such as punctuation and spaces. The retrieval management module mainly provides external retrieval entry and related resource application and release interface.

3 Robot Scheduling System Based on Semantic Recognition

The dispatching robot system has functions such as intelligent ordering, graphic simulation preview and program operation. Intelligent ordering intelligently analyzes the grid structure, wiring form, equipment status and type, and automatically forms an operation order with comprehensive anti-error verification according to the operational task requirements, using the system's rule base and terminology; graphical simulation rehearsal. The audit function is to enable the system to perform graphical simulation and preview operations on the generated operation orders, and to provide information such as the power outage range, so that the dispatcher can more intuitively review the dispatching commands, and solve the process of the dispatcher's memory operation, so that the operation order review process is more Visualization and visualization, and improve the safety and reliability of the operation; the operation order execution anti-error check has the operation order execution anti-false lock, the operation order execution sequence check, the operation order equipment status check, the operation order process permission check other functions to meet the requirements of safety and reliability during operation; program operation is "one-button operation", the dispatcher only needs to click to start operation, the system automatically performs five-proof and power-flow verification, and the verification result is satisfied. The system operates automatically and no human intervention is required.

The programmatic operation of the scheduling programmatic robot system realizes the intelligent operation of the main network scheduling operation, and has the following characteristics: (1) The scheduling operation task realizes the automatic process of the whole process; (2) The OCS and DICP are fully interconnected to realize effective information transmission, and the system Automatically determine the operating status; (3) Based on the construction of the automated main station, the whole process realizes the safety and error prevention of the state and the flow, and improves the safety of the dispatching operation; (4) Selecting the programmed operating mode according to the device status evaluation. The switch and knife gate equipment realize remote control through remote control, and do not have the order to operate on site; (5) Realizing the program operation of covering first and second equipment (including line ground knife).

3.1   Overall Architecture

The operation control system (OCS) is a provincial distributed independent construction system. Dispatching intelligent command platform (DICP) is a provincial and land integration construction mode [21]. The unified construction of main functions is centrally deployed in the central modulation. The system spans II, III area and realizes information connection which can be seen in Fig. 1).

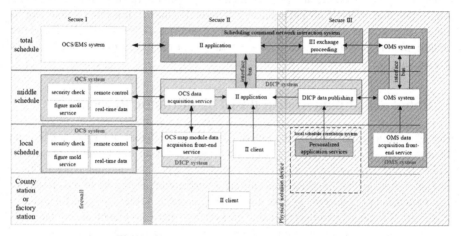

Fig. 1. Overall architecture of scheduling robot.

Through the integration of OCS security check and remote control operation, DICP network command and risk assessment and progress release and other core modules, the automatic order writing, audit link operation simulation preview, and the execution link in the operation of the value control are performed. The command (direct remote control device that can be operated remotely, and the on-site operation automatically ordered by the network without remote control conditions), real-time evaluation of operational risk and real-time release of operation progress. Under the technical protection against mistakes, the operation order is fully automated or semi-automated, maximizing safety and operational efficiency.

System function division: OCS provides graph mode output service and real-time data output service for DICP, security check (including power flow calculation), and externally output graph and real-time data in II, which are intelligent applications of II (e.g. smart order) provides data support and power flow calculation support; OCS dispatcher operates robotic actuator to implement safety check and remote control operation module which can be seen in Fig. 2).

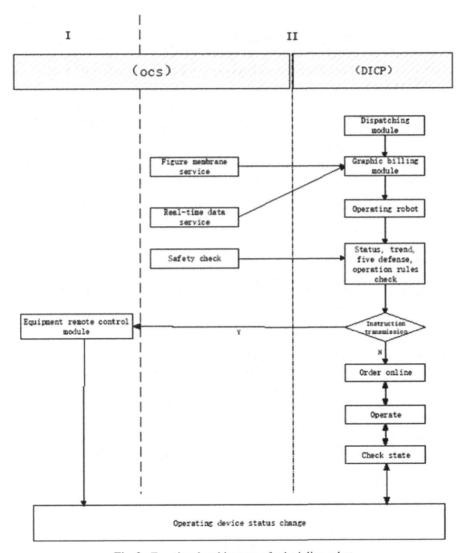

Fig. 2. Functional architecture of scheduling robot.

3.2 Functional Characteristics

Functional characteristics are mainly divided into the following four aspects:

(1) Intelligent operation order

Scheduling robot order offers a variety of ways, including all intelligent graphics make out an invoice text hand make out an invoice all intelligent graphics make out an invoice through to the power grid structure connection form operation device type equipment running state of intelligence analysis, and according to the system of rule base and the glossary, automatic equipment operation task list options listed operation tasks, the system automatically comprehensive error checking, and verify the result is given, if the check is successful, the system automatically order if validation fails, the system failure reasons were given and the analysis of the effect of a specific list of equipment calibration results.

Control personnel before the real-time remote control operation on operation order for preview, preview in the premise of success in real-time remote control in real time remote control operation, must be carried out in accordance with the preview of the operation sequence and operating equipment operation, if the operation of the equipment is not in operation practice or not according to the order of operating a rehearsal of the latching current remote control, remote control is to ensure that every step can depend on.

(2) Comprehensive anti-error check

In the whole operation process by applying state five anti blocking trend respectively, and other technical means of checking, achieve comprehensive security intelligence prevent mistake, avoid man-made wrong operation system have topology error prevention function, the network topology and the five rules combined to realize equipment operation between atresia, can accurately identify error protected atresia relationship between station, and from the entire network model error protected atresia. Tide check function, in a simulated rehearsal training in the process of the operation and real-time of make out an invoice according to the current operation flow calculation, according to the trend of the electrical island topology coloring, calculated results provide a visual display method, at the same time, according to the results of the power flow calculation of voltage the limit line or main transformer overload and the limit of check.

Before the operation order step is executed, check the equipment target completion state of the operation step correlation and the completion state of the operation order step correlation, and give the verification result. When the state is inconsistent, the system will interrupt the operation and give a prompt.

(3) Sequence control

Sensing procedure refers to the application of automatic control technology and the Internet of things technology state of automatic identification and intelligent judgment, pour tedious repetition easy wrong operation of the traditional artificial brake operating mode into operation project software prefabricated task modular structures, equipment operation status automatic discriminant interlocking intelligent checking steps into a key to start operating process automatically sequential automatic mode according to the simulated operation, the operation sequence to track every step of the change of state after operation, whether the operation properties of this step and other operation. The simulation preview and the graphical display interface work closely, and the results of each simulation preview step are displayed directly from the graph.

(4) Operating cockpit

The cockpit is for managers to provide centralized monitoring and control of power grid operation of a regional, integrated professional system information, extract the key indicators, promote business collaboration, improve operational efficiency of system in the perspective of dispatching operation, build a unified information acquisition show unified management platform, the foundation of substation panoramic views of the data obtained from the unified information platform, based on system concise, information standard, unified interface. The basic requirements of business coordination are as follows: to build three categories of business, including power grid monitoring equipment monitoring and operation and maintenance management, to provide a standardized man-machine interface for power grid monitoring to realize the functions of substation monitoring sequence control and comprehensive alarm. The device monitoring interface realizes the functions of primary device online monitoring and primary device evaluation. The operation and maintenance management interface realizes the management functions of equipment ledger defects and work orders, so as to provide one-stop service for the operation and management of the power grid and improve the work efficiency of the management personnel.

3.3 Key Technologies

Semantic Intelligent Identification. According to the design of the whole module, the modules were linked together and the algorithm was designed according to the modeling process shown in Fig. 3).

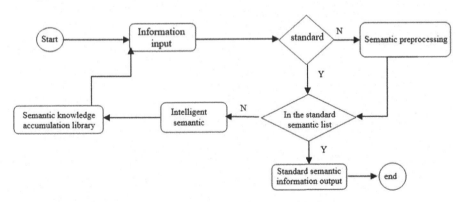

Fig. 3. Scheduling semantic library modeling.

Semantic preprocessing of semantic intelligent identification is first, then determine whether to exist in the semantic knowledge accumulation in the library if he does not exist, the standard information in the library of semantic accumulation traversal, similarity calculation in order to select high and set by the similarity threshold K to compare the less than the threshold, indicates no relevant standard semantics, don't do any processing, the input of the semantic was invalid. When the value is greater than the threshold, the preprocessed relay protection information is written into the standard semantic information list corresponding to the highest similarity value and recorded into the semantic knowledge accumulation library.

About semantic intelligent identification function, is based on the semantic and semantic knowledge accumulation in the library standard traverse semantic comparison, find out the similarity computing the similarity of the maximum compared with setting the threshold value of judging if more than the not standard semantics to the corresponding standard semantic information if set below the maximum threshold, it ignores the nonstandard semantics, not include the semantics in the accumulation of semantic repository.

By scheduling the construction of the semantic web, and 19 in the Guangdong power supply bureau of dispatching operation records have big data analysis, the normalized entire network dispatching operation, through the analysis of semantic orientation of dispatching operation scheduling robot study unceasingly thoroughly, gradually increase the dispatching operation dispatching institutions at all levels of formal writing, is advantageous to the higher and lower efficient communication scheduling mechanism.

Comprehensive Anti-Error Check Based on Interconnection. In order to ensure the security of power grid, comprehensive and multi-level verification of power grid security [22] is conducted mainly from the aspects of closed-loop management of maintenance application form, topology security check, power grid power flow security check, etc. The interactive content is shown in Fig. 4.

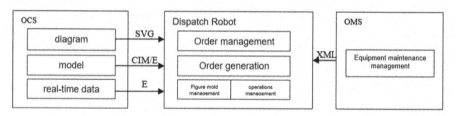

Fig. 4. The interaction architecture between scheduling robot and external system.

(1) Check on blocking and error prevention with OMS maintenance list

And OMS (Operations Management System) maintenance application form, form a closed-loop Management security prevention mechanism through docking for maintenance after the application data, then analysis maintenance application form, get construction completion date, which can automatically generate operation maintenance single associated operation order and working order, and automatically acquire construction completion date when can manually modify the repair time limit for a project, the dispatcher System automatically inform the site after the transfers (delay).

(2) Comprehensive check with OCS security check

And OCS system interface to get graphic model and real-time running data, for real-time operation system and security check to provide reliable data basis of make out an invoice, including graphic files using SVG format file, model files using standard CIM/E or CIM/XML format file, real-time data based on E format string before operation, and analysis of state grid will each electrical equipment as a node, and to establish the topology relation between equipment, the formation of grid model in the process of topology analysis, fully consider the connection mode and operation mode of power grid, pattern recognition.

In order to support system monitoring, OCS provides a service state interface, which is called by DICP on a regular basis to detect whether the service state is available. The development interface not only reduces the maintenance workload of maintenance personnel, but also realizes data sharing between various systems.

Procedural Operation. Procedural operation [23] is through the automatic program to control the operating equipment, its purpose is to improve the level of automatic control of power grid equipment, control operation error and avoid personal accident, improve operational efficiency based on the current situation. The operation order of maintenance state includes several steps in sequence, each step includes logic before operation (error-proof logic), logic after operation (confirmation of operation), etc.

In terms of the design of the main station system substation monitoring system and data transmission, the main steps of the implementation of the program operation configuration include: definition of equipment state, procedural operation order content definition, programmed operation simulation and operation order execution.

(1) Device state definition

The corresponding position combination of any switch within the corresponding interval can be defined as an equipment state, including the hot standby state of the running state, cold standby state and maintenance state through the synchronous interface with the diagram mode of OCS, and the programmed operation can initialize the equipment state, and combine the equipment state template file through the user's predefined logical relationship.

(2) Programmatic operation order definition

Take the one-time order as an example, the process definition usually includes the definition of initial device state definition, target device state definition, operation object task definition, pre-operation/post-operation check condition definition, operation delay (timeout) definition and error handling definition.

(3) Simulated rehearsal

Procedural operation definition is completed, before they will be issued to the appropriate execution, to test the correctness of the content of operation logic and application effectiveness, it is necessary to conduct a complete simulation rehearsal, simulated rehearsal operation no a real physical switch, breaker to realistic environment simulation and actual operation, testing and found that the logic and the application of defects existing in the operation and gives the corresponding revision.

(4) Operation order execution

Simulated rehearsal is completed, through the way of service calls RPC, in XML documents issued to the substation monitoring and control system execution scheduling operation device performing each step of the procedural operation, in order to ensure the safety of every step of operation, will be implemented strictly according to the operation condition definitions related to perform calibration, and in a single step execution, defined according to the operation order inspection operation success if calibration condition is met, the system will enter the next operation, otherwise the system will be according to the definition of operation order into error protected program exits or prompt pop-up action aborted or continue to dialog for the user to choose from.

The data service between DICP and OCS includes the complete order sequence data service remote control operation service, the following remote control operation service as an example, to illustrate the transmission specification between DICP and OCS, remote control operation including one-step operation request (DICP OCS) one-step operation confirmation (OCS DICP) operation confirmation information (DICP OCS) and so on. Compared with other programmed operation schemes, it increases the scheduling semantic recognition ability of programmed operation, carries on the normative check from the text description of the scheduling operation order, and introduces the comprehensive anti-error check before and after the operation, realizes the intelligent programmed operation of substation, and improves the intelligence level of programmed operation.

4   Conclusion

The scheduling robot system based on scheduling semantic recognition proposed in this paper is applicable to intelligent substations and non-intelligent substations and it can adapt to various complicated scene. From the practical application, it has achieved good results in improving the safe and stable operation level of the power grid and the working efficiency of the operating personnel. The intelligent and digital dispatching operation of the main network has been fully realized in Guangdong middle railway station and 19 power supply bureaus. It can reduce scheduling, command and communication time and risk cost. By strengthening the safety check method of dispatching operation, the efficiency of collaborative work is improved, and the coordination between the development speed of the power grid and the quality of dispatching operation is realized. Besides, the coordination between safety and efficiency of power grid operation is realized too.

References

1. Chen, C., Duan, S., Cai, T., Liu, B., Hu, G.: Smart energy management system for optimal microgrid economic operation. Renew. Power Gener. Iet 5(3), 258–267 (2011)

2. Olivares, D.E., Mehrizi-Sani, A., Etemadi, A.H., Canizares, C.A., Iravani, R.: Trends in microgrid control. IEEE Trans. Smart Grid **5**(4), 1905–1919 (2014)
3. El-Hawary, M.E.: The smart grid-state-of-the-art and future trends. Electric Power Compon. Syst. **42**(3), 239–250 (2014)
4. Lu, H.M., Li, Y.J., Chen, M., Kim, H., Serikawa, S.: Brain intelligence: go beyond artificial intelligence. Mob. Netw. Appl. **23**(2), 368–375 (2018)
5. Abbas, N.N., Ahmed, T., Shah, S.H.U., Omar, M., Park, H.W.: Investigating the applications of artificial intelligence in cyber security. Scientometrics **121**(2), 1189–1211 (2019)
6. Poniszewska-Maranda, A., Kaczmarek, D., Kryvinska, N., Xhafa, F.: Studying usability of AI in the IoT systems paradigm through embedding NN techniques into mobile smart service system. Computing **101**(11), 1661–1685 (2019)
7. Sokolov, I.A.: Theory and practice of application of artificial intelligence methods. Herald Russ. Acad. Sci. **89**(2), 115–119 (2019)
8. Bose, B.K.: Artificial intelligence techniques in smart grid and renewable energy systems-some example applications. Proc. IEEE **105**(11), 2262–2273 (2017)
9. Anitescu, C., Atroshchenko, E., Alajlan, N., Rabczuk, T.: Artificial neural network methods for the solution of second order boundary value problems. Comput. Mater. Continua **59**(1), 345–359 (2019)
10. Liu, W., Xu, Y., James, C.N., Yang, Y.W., Chi, L.: Privacy-preserving quantum two-party geometric intersection. Comput. Mater. Continua **60**(3), 1237–1250 (2019)
11. Ono, K., Miyamichi, J., Yamaguchi, T.: Intelligent robot system using "model of knowledge, emotion and intention" and "information sharing architecture". In: IEEE International Symposium on Computational Intelligence in Robotics and Automation, pp. 498–501. IEEE, Banff (2001)
12. Meng, L., Yang, D., Sun, Y., et al: Construction of energy hub model and optimal scheduling of energy internet. In: 36th Chinese Control Conference (CCC), Dalian, P. R China, pp. 10740–10744 (2017)
13. Takadama, K., Watabe, M., Shimohara, K., Nakasuka, S.: How to design good rules for multiple learning agents in scheduling problems? In: Nakashima, H., Zhang, C. (eds.) PRIMA 1999. LNCS (LNAI), vol. 1733, pp. 126–140. Springer, Heidelberg (1999). https://doi.org/10.1007/3-540-46693-2_10
14. Takadama, K., et al.: Organizational learning agents for task scheduling in space crew and robot operations. 5th International Symposium on Artificial Intelligence. Robotics and Automation in Space (ISAIRAS 99), pp. 561–568. Noordwijk, Netherlands (1999)
15. Bozejko, W., Hejducki, Z., Uchronski, M., Wodecki, M.: Solving resource constrained construction scheduling problems with overlaps by metaheuristic. J. Civil Eng. Manag. **20**(5), 649–659 (2014)
16. Calyam, P., Kumarasamy, L., Lee, C.-G., Ozguner, F.: Ontology-based semantic priority scheduling for multi-domain active measurements. J. Netw. Syst. Manag. **22**(3), 331–365 (2013)
17. Liu, W., Chen, Z., Liu, J., Su, Z., Chi, L.: Full-Blind delegating private quantum computation. Comput. Mater. Continua **56**(2), 211–223 (2018)
18. Missier, P., Wieder, P., Ziegler, W.: Semantic support for meta-scheduling in Grids. In: Talia, D., Bilas, A., Dikaiakos, M.D. (eds.) Knowledge and Data Management in Grids, pp. 169–183. Springer, Heidleberg (2007). https://doi.org/10.1007/978-0-387-37831-2_11
19. Butz, C.J., Yao, H., Hua, S.: A join tree probability propagation architecture for semantic modeling. J. Intell. Inf. Syst. **33**(2), 145–178 (2009)
20. Hewitt, C.: Open information systems semantics for distributed artificial intelligence. Artif. Intell. **47**(1C3), 79–106 (1991)
21. Zhao, J., Ji, K., Sun, D., et al.: A key technology scheme of pilot projects for provincial and local integrated power grid dispatch. Autom. Electric Power Syst. **32**, 120–125 (2012)

22. Zhang, Y., Chen, Z., Guo, M., et al.: Comprehensive anti-error study on power Grid dispatching based on regional regulation and integration. In: IOP Conference Series Earth and Environmental Science, vol. 108, no. 5, p. 052089 (2018)
23. Kim, J.H., Kim, D.H.: Design of user-oriented market operations in a smart grid ecosystem. In: The 40th International Conference on Computers and Industrial Engineering. IEEE, Awaji (2010)

Pedestrian Counting Without Tracking for the Security Application of IoT Framework

Tao Zhang[1,2(✉)], Mingming Zhang[3], Bin Yang[4], and Yan Zhao[1]

[1] School of Artificial Intelligence and Computer Science, Jiangnan University, Wuxi 214000, People's Republic of China
{taozhang,yangbin}@jiangnan.edu.cn
[2] Key Laboratory of Urban Land Resources Monitoring and Simulation, Ministry of Land and Resources, Shenzhen, China
[3] School of Digital Media, Jiangnan University, Wuxi 214000, People's Republic of China
ifismm@yeah.net
[4] School of Design, Jiangnan University, Wuxi 214000, People's Republic of China

Abstract. Currently, the security of the Internet of Things (IoT) has aroused great concern. Pedestrian counting under video surveillance has become a key problem affecting social security. In this paper we describe a novel and real-time pedestrian counting framework without using any tracking algorithms. Current research under wide overhead cameras are mainly focus on the tracking-based algorithms, however, effective tracking is difficult in most cases. Therefore, we design a line sampling process, based on this strategy, we can achieve a temporal slice image that contains useful head feature information, which can be used for pedestrian counting without the necessity for visual tracking. As is expected, our algorithm is more stable and accurate than existing approaches. In addition, we also design a two-stage detection algorithm, which is used to locate head position. Experimental results indicate that our constructed algorithm can obtain better performance.

Keywords: Pedestrian counting · IoT · Two-stage detection · Line sampling · Temporal slice image

1 Introduction

The Internet of Things (IoT) has become an important research domain, and their applications have shown their potential in recent years. In order to be successful in the commercial world, deep learning technology has been broadly used in action recognition, image recognition and computer vision fields [1,2]. Pedestrian counting is a basic component in computer vision. Counting the number of pedestrians in a region of interest (ROI) is useful for security monitoring and traffic control and management. Counting the number of pedestrians crossing a

© Springer Nature Singapore Pte Ltd. 2020
X. Sun et al. (Eds.): ICAIS 2020, CCIS 1252, pp. 699–712, 2020.
https://doi.org/10.1007/978-981-15-8083-3_62

line of interest (LOI) also helps to optimize the public services such as providing the sufficient products in a shop or services in public places. However, counting pedestrians in crowded situations is a challenging task.

Many algorithms have been proposed to count pedestrians. Applications generally involve counting pedestrians in a region of interest (ROI counting) and pedestrians passing through a line of interest in a fixed time period (LOI counting).

Existing methods for ROI counting can be generally divided into two categories: object detection and regression. Viola *et al.* detect motion patterns by utilizing the AdaBoost learning algorithm [3]. However, when occlusion occurs, the motion pattern detection method tends to suffer, and because of this some part-based pedestrian detectors are proposed. Wu *et al.* count pedestrians in crowded scenes by detecting different parts of the human body [4]. To make the part-based pedestrian detector more robust, an approach combining head-shoulder detector and moving flow is developed by Xing *et al.* [5]. Dong *et al.* match the shape of foreground segment to a database with pedestrian silhouettes [6]. This performs well when the number of pedestrians in the segment is less than 6. The above methods try to directly detect every single pedestrian in one or several frames precisely. However, detecting one people becomes intractable under some complex scenes.

The regression methods can deal with scenes with significant occlusion successfully without locating the precise position of each pedestrian. Saqib *et al.* extract texture features to count the crowds [7]. To analyze the crowd in small regions, the Local Binary Pattern (LBP) method is utilized to count pedestrians in separated areas [8]. In order to determine the number of peoples in each of the complex segments, foreground areas [9,10] and foreground edge orientations [11,12] are extracted as features. Linear function [13,14] and neural networks(NN) [15] are utilized as regression functions. A Gaussian process regression with radial basis function (RBF) kernel is proposed to capture both linear and locally non-linear features [16].

A number of papers in the literature for LOI counting relies on tracking-based approaches [17–22]. To solve the occlusion problem, current research mainly concentrate these area with wide overhead cameras. A kind of human shape model was utilized to extract the foreground region in [17]. However it is difficult for the system to achieve real-time performance when numerous pedestrians are tracked simultaneously. Therefore, a two-level tracking structure is proposed, which uses two kinds of tracking strategy to solve these problems about merges and splits of the blobs [18]. Antic *et al.* apply k-means clustering scheme to pedestrian segmentation in crowded scene [19].

However, visual tracking is computationally expensive and tracking multiple targets accurately and robustly is still a challenging problem. As a result, researchers have begun to utilize information from spatial and temporal domains [23,24]. Albiol *et al.* first store the foreground of pedestrians passing through a gate of a train in a spatial-temporal domain and segment the pedestrians with morphological tools [24]. Morphological operations are applied to deal with images that are lack of detailed features, so a Kanade-Lucas-Tomasi (KLT) feature tracker is utilized to gather feature trajectories, which are then clustered to count pedestrians in separated areas [25]. As the KLT tracker is not efficient, Cong et al. measure the flow velocity on the detection line and estimate the number of pedestrians by quadratic regression [26]. Recently, Ma et al. improve the work of Cong et al. by introducing an integer programming method to count people crossing the line based on ROI counting [27].

Followed by above research, we design a novel strategy to count the pedestrians across a line of interest (LOI) via a two-stage detection algorithm, which is more robust and efficient than existing methods. The algorithm described here has utilized many kinds of technologies comprehensively, including the adoption of Gaussian mixture model (GMM) [28] in background substraction. Here we segment the pedestrians in the second-stage detection using the affinity propagation (AP) clustering [29], while in the traditional research, mean shift clustering [30] algorithm is always used to segment each pedestrian. We compare the performances of different clustering algorithms and of two-stage and one-stage segmentation algorithms. The results reveal that our designed algorithm is unsusceptible and appropriate. The contributions of our research are summarized as follows:

1. A two-stage pedestrian detection algorithm based on support vector machine (SVM) and clustering is developed.
2. An automatic pedestrian moving direction determination method is proposed.
3. A new challenging pedestrian dataset is established.

The remainder of this research is dicpicted as follows. Details of our designed approach is presented in Sect. 2. The perfomances of our algorithm are compared with other baselines in Sect. 3. A conclusion is finally drawn in Sect. 4.

2 Proposed Algorithm

In this section, we first describe the procedures to obtain the temporal slice image, followed by feature extraction for classification. The two-stage pedestrian detection algorithm is then presented in detail. Finally, we discuss how to determine the moving direction of the pedestrians.

Whole framework of our designed strategy is depicted in Fig. 1. First, a cycle period T is set manually and Gaussian mixture model (GMM) is applied to eliminate unnecessary background information. Second, the temporal slice image ST on the LOI is obtained. Subsequently, 10 features are extracted from each foreground region in ST, and forms a feature vector $F(i)_{i=1,...,N}$, where N is the amount of foreground blocks. According to these feature vectors, the foreground regions are classified into two categories, crowd and individual. The centers of the regions labelled as individuals can be located immediately. The pedestrians in the crowd class are detected by clustering. Finally, The moving directions of each pedestrian are determined.

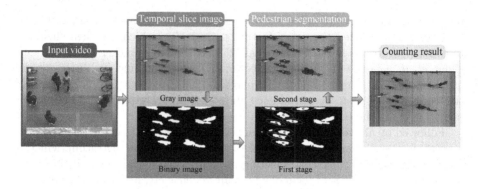

Fig. 1. Flow chart of the approach.

2.1 Background Subtraction and Line Sampling

Our designed algorithm generates a temporal slice image which indicates the location of pedestrians, and also reflecting the time information. All the frames are transferred to gray scale images before processing. Gaussian mixture model is applied for detecting moving objects. For each pixel on the LOI, $I(p)$ denotes the grayscale value of pixel p. The probability that the pixel presents this color at frame t is described as follows:

$$P(I(p),t) = \sum_{k=1}^{K} w_k(t)g(I(p),\mu_k(t),\sigma_k^2(t)), \tag{1}$$

where K depicts the quantity of mixture models (usually it is defined as Eq. 3), $w_k(t)$ represents the weight value of the kth model at frame t ($\sum_{k=1}^{K} w_k(t) = 1$), $\mu_k(t)$ is the center of the kth model at frame t, $\sigma_k^2(t)$ is the variance of the kth model at frame t, and g is a Gaussian function

$$g\left(I(p),\mu,\sigma^2\right) = \frac{1}{\sqrt{2\pi}\sigma}e^{-\frac{[I(p)-\mu]^2}{\sigma^2}}. \tag{2}$$

Typically, if

$$|I(p) - \mu_k(t)| < 2.5\sigma_k(t), \tag{3}$$

we consider that the current pixel p at frame t matches the kth model. On the other hand, if the pixel p does not match any of the models, it is labelled as foreground.

When the current pixel p matches the kth model, the kth model will be updated by

$$\begin{cases} \mu_k(t+1) = (1-\alpha)\mu_k(t) + \alpha I(p) \\ \sigma_k^2(t+1) = (1-\alpha)\sigma_k^2(t) + \alpha(\mu_k(t) - I(p))^2 \end{cases} \tag{4}$$

Here α is a preset parameter to control the updating speed. Suppose that for all the models that pixel p matches, the k_m^{th} model has the largest weight $w_{k_m}(t)$.

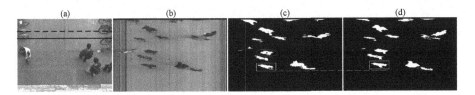

Fig. 2. a) LOIs, and temporal slice images from b) gray level, c) the initial line and d) the additional line. The red ellipse shows a special case of covering ellipse sheme in Sect. 2.2. The yellow rectangles show an example of direction determination in Sect. 2.4. (Color figure online)

Then this largest weight is updated by

$$w'_{k_m}(t+1) = (1 - \beta)w_{k_m}(t) + \beta. \tag{5}$$

Here β is also a preset parameter to control the updating speed. For other models, the weights updating scheme is defined:

$$w'_k(t+1) = (1 - \beta)w_k(t). \tag{6}$$

At last, the updated weights are normalized by

$$w_k(t+1) = \frac{w'_k(t+1)}{\sum_{i=1}^{K} w'_i(t+1)}. \tag{7}$$

When there is no model that can match the pixel p, the model that has the smallest weight will be replaced by a new model with $\mu_k(t+1) = I(p)$.

After the background subtraction on the LOI, each pixel on the LOI are labelled either white (if it is the foreground) or black (if it is the background). By applying the line sampling procedure on the LOI, the binary temporal slice image ST is obtained.

We draw two LOIs to obtain the temporal slice images (see Fig. 2a for example). The solid line represents the initial position, which can be used to collect the feature of foreground regions. The dash line, as an additional one, is used to help the solid line to verify the effectiveness of pedestrian movement direction. The gray scale temporal slice image obtained from the initial line during the current frame to the 200th frame is shown in Fig. 2b. The binary temporal slice images generated by the two lines are presented in Figs. 2c and 2d.

2.2 Feature Extraction

Features can be got from each foreground region in the binary temporal slice image. In this paper, we extract 10 low level features to form a feature vector $F(i)_{i=1,...,N}$. These pixels with respect to foreground region are fixed using appropriate coordinates $(w, t) \in ST$. $Cov = \Phi \Lambda \Phi^{-1}$ represents the covariance matrix of pixel coordinates in a foreground region, here $\Phi = [v_1, v_2]$ in which

v_1 and v_2 are the eigenvectors and $\Lambda = diag(\lambda_1, \lambda_2)$ (here $\lambda_1 < \lambda_2$) represents the eigenvalues. Finally, for these extracted foreground, we define 10 kinds of features:

1. foreground area size S;
2. long axis of the covering ellipse $a = \sqrt{S \times \lambda_2/\lambda_1}$;
3. minor axis of the covering ellipse $b = \sqrt{S \times \lambda_1/\lambda_2}$;
4. ratio between long and short axes a/b;
5. difference with respect to the time axis Δ_t;
6. difference with respect to the line axis Δ_w;
7. perimeter of the foreground area L;
8. variance with respect to the time axis σ_t^2;
9. variance with respect to the line axis σ_w^2;
10. ratio between perimeter and region size L/S.

Visual examples of our designed algorithm can be found in Fig. 2c. After feature extraction, N feature vectors $F(i)_{i=1,...,N}$ is formed according to N foreground regions in the temporal slice image ST.

2.3 Two-Stage Pedestrian Detection

Usually, it is not easy to detect each human from the temporal slice image ST under crowded scene. We propose a two-stage pedestrian detection algorithm. First the foreground regions from the temporal slice image are separated into two sperate parts using a support vector machine classifier. Then an appropriate clustering algorithm is adapted to make a correct estimate of the number of pedestrians.

In the first stage, support vector machine is applied to classify the foreground regions according to the extracted features $F(i)$. Classical C-Support Vector Classification (C-SVC) [31] is chosen in our algorithm. In detail, training vectors are denoted as $xt_i \in R^n, i = 1, ..., l$, given a label vector $y \in R^l$ so that $y_i \in \{1, -1\}$, thus, we design the following optimization strategy of C-SVC:

$$\min_{w,b,\xi} \quad \frac{1}{2}w^T w + C \sum_{i=1}^{l} \xi_i$$
$$\text{subject to} \quad y_i(w^T \phi(xt_i) + b) \geq 1 - \xi_i, \tag{8}$$
$$\xi_i \geq 0, \quad i = 1, ..., l,$$

where $\phi(xt_i)$ a mapping function and $C > 0$ is the cost. When the dimension of w is high, the optimization is usually carried in the following dual form:

$$\min_{\alpha} \quad \frac{1}{2}\alpha^T Q\alpha - e^T\alpha$$
$$\text{subject to} \quad y^T\alpha = 0, \tag{9}$$
$$0 \leq \alpha_i \leq C, \quad i = 1, ..., l,$$

where $e = [1, ..., 1]^T$ indicates ones vector, Q represents a positive semidefinite matrix, $Q_{ij} \equiv y_i y_j K(xt_i, xt_j)$, and $K(xt_i, xt_j) \equiv \phi(xt_i)^T \phi(xt_j)$ indicates the kernel function. We choose the radial basis function (RBF) as the kernel function in our algorithm, which takes the form

$$K(xt_i, xt_j) = e^{-\gamma \|xt_i - xt_j\|^2}. \tag{10}$$

The parameter γ is related to the number of features, and will be discussed (together with cost C) later in the parameter setting section. After solving problem (9), the optimal w can be expressed:

$$w = \sum_{i=1}^{l} y_i \alpha_i \phi(xt_i), \tag{11}$$

and the final decision can be made as follows:

$$\text{sgn}(w^T \phi(xt) + b) = \text{sgn}(\sum_{i=1}^{l} y_i \alpha_i K(xt_i, xt) + b), \tag{12}$$

and parameter b in Eq. (12) is

$$b = -\frac{1}{2}(\max_{i:y_i=-1} w^T xt_i + \min_{i:y_i=1} w^T xt_i). \tag{13}$$

In Fig. 3a, the foreground areas in the ellipses represent the individuals classified by the SVM classifier.

In the second stage, we apply affinity propagation (AP) clustering [29] to detect each pedestrian. The AP clustering algorithm is an iteration of responsibility and availability. First the similarity is obtained:

$$s(i, k) = \begin{cases} -\|x_i - x_k\|^2 & \text{if } i \neq k \\ \frac{\sum_{i'=1}^{N_r} \sum_{k'=1, k' \neq i'}^{N_r} s(i', k')}{N_r(N_r-1)} & \text{if } i = k \end{cases}, \tag{14}$$

where x_i and x_k ($1 \leq i, k \leq N_r$) are the coordinates of foreground region in the crowd class. Then the variables $r(i, k)$ and $a(i, k)$ can be iterated by:

$$r_{t+1}(i, k) = s(i, k) - \max_{k' \text{ s.t. } k' \neq k} \{a_t(i, k') + s(i, k')\}, \tag{15}$$

$$a_{t+1}(i, k) = \min\{0, r_{t+1}(k, k) + \sum_{i' \text{ s.t. } i' \notin (i,k)} \max\{0, r_{t+1}(i', k)\}\}. \tag{16}$$

And a damping procedure is applied to reduce oscillations:

$$r_{t+1}(i, k) = (1 - \lambda) \cdot r_{t+1}(i, k) + \lambda \cdot r_t(i, k), \tag{17}$$

$$a_{t+1}(i, k) = (1 - \lambda) \cdot a_{t+1}(i, k) + \lambda \cdot a_t(i, k). \tag{18}$$

Here λ is a preset parameter to control the damping speed. The pixel points which fulfill $r(k, k) + a(k, k) > 0$ are regarded as centers of clusters.

2.4   Direction Determination

Our algorithm designs a new approach to determine the moving directions of pedestrians through the change of movement centers of temporal slice images. However, the centers obtained for the two images by clustering may not match, as the clustering number cannot be predicted. Therefore, the number of clusters is set as the result of clustering in the first temporal slice image. The centers of pedestrians in the second temporal slice image are obtained by labelling the foreground pixel to the nearest center in the first image, and new centers in the second image can be obtained according to the labelled pixels. The centers in the two images can then be compared.

Denote $ST_c(w_m, t_m)$ as initial central position and $ST_c(w_a, t_a)$ as auxiliary position. Then we can get the direction prediction strategy:

$$\text{direction} = \begin{cases} down & \text{if } t_m - t_a > 0 \\ up & \text{if } t_m - t_a < 0 \end{cases}, \tag{19}$$

An example of direction determination is demonstrated in Figs. 2c and 2d.

3   Experiments and Results

3.1   Datasets

Most of the testing videos of LOI counting in the existing literatures are not accessible for us, so it is not easy to compare the performances of different methods. Thus, we established a new pedestrian dataset, named the SJTU dataset (available at http://www.pami.sjtu.edu.cn/people/yuzong). In this case, we did the verification on two data sets, which consist of the SJTU dataset and the UCSD dataset [32]. The SJTU dataset is created by setting up a camera in a building on the SJTU campus. 8 video clips were collected with a frame size of 320×240 and frame rate of 18 fps. The ground truth of the UCSD dataset is related to ROI counting, thus we marked the ground truth of the UCSD dataset for LOI counting (available at http://www.pami.sjtu.edu.cn/people). The line of interest (LOI) is vertically located 60 pixels from the left side.

3.2   Training and Parametric Settings

Because of the difference of pedestrian posture when crossing line locations, 24 locations are simultaneously chosen at random to get the temporal slice images in the process of training. The foreground regions in these training images are the pedestrians to be counted. There are two principles to set the cycle period T:

1. The body of a pedestrian is required to pass the line during the cycle period, so T can not be too small.
2. The counting results of a cycle should be presented in time, so T can not be set overly large.

Taking the above principles into account, we set the cycle period T to 200 frames.

In Sect. 3.1 we introduced two parameters α and β in the updating procedure of Gaussian mixture model (GMM). Large α and β lead to fast updating speed, as well as instability. In order to keep the updating procedure robust, the parameters α and β are both set to 0.02 in this paper.

LIBSVM [31] toolbox is applied to train and classify the foreground regions in the first-stage detection in Sect. 3.3. The parameter γ (in Eq. (10)) is usually set to $1/K_f$, where K_f is the number of features ($K_f = 10$ in this paper). The parameter C (appeared in Eq. (8)) is generally set to 1. Meanwhile, in order to estimate the exact value of γ and C, cross validation is applied, instead of simply taking the empirical values. What is more, the maximum value of the features can not be predicted, so normalization and cross validation are employed in each cycle.

In the damping procedure in AP clustering, we introduced the parameter λ. A quantized intermediate value named Net Similarity [29] is calculated to monitor the oscillations, which has the form

$$\text{Net Similarity} = dpsim + expref. \tag{20}$$

Similarities between the data points and its cluster centers are defined as $dpsim$, while the similarities among the cluster centers themselves (define in Eq. (14) when $i = k$) is expressed as $expref$. The Net Similarity will reach a maximum value as the clustering algorithm iterates. Figure 5 shows the Net Similarity with different values of λ, from which we can draw the conclusion that a large λ (see $\lambda \geq 0.9$ as examples) increases the number of iterations with a stable rise of Net Similarity. On the other hand, a small λ (see $\lambda = 0.6$ as an example) accelerates the iteration, but causes oscillations of Net Similarity. Taking both stability and efficiency into account, we set λ to 0.7 in the proposed algorithm.

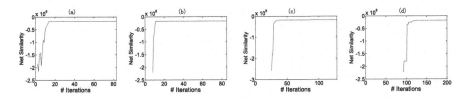

Fig. 3. Parameter setting in AP clustering. a) $\lambda = 0.6$, b) $\lambda = 0.7$, c) $\lambda = 0.9$, d) $\lambda = 0.97$.

3.3 Experimental Results

Table 1 gives the corresponding experimental results on SJTU dataset. The error rate regardless of the moving directions is 6.573%. The error rate for the number of pedestrians walking up is 7.633%, whilst that for walking down is 8.056%.

Table 1. Results on the SJTU dataset. The second and third columns indicate the actual steps up and down. The fourth and fifth columns geive the result of our proposed algorithm. Three kinds of errors are given in the remaindering columns.

Video	#of	#of	up	down	err	err	err
No	up	down			up	down	total
1	15	3	15	3	0	0	
2	12	7	13	8	+1	+1	+2
3	16	11	16	12	0	+1	+1
4	28	8	29	7	+1	−1	0
5	37	11	35	11	−2	0	−2
6	16	7	17	9	+1	+2	+3
7	13	10	13	10	0	0	0
8	8	5	11	5	+3	0	+3

In Fig. 4 we compare the tracking-based approach [18], our built strategy with and without the first-stage detection (abbreviated as 'cluster' in Fig. 4) on the UCSD dataset. By comparing the performance of our system with the ground truth and the tracking based method, we draw a conclusion that the algorithm we designed is very stable. We can also state that the two-stage detection algorithm performs better than the algorithm just applies clustering. The reasons for poor performance mainly include:

1. Clustering number increases when someone stay too long, as well as the result of counting.

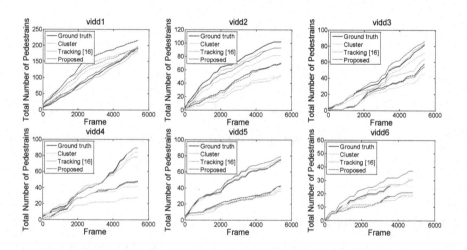

Fig. 4. Results on the UCSD dataset. The solid line indicates the left direction and the dotted line indicates the right direction.

2. Background subtraction algorithm can be heavily affected when the colors of pedestrians get mixed up.
3. There are other similar moving objects (Fig. 5).

We implement our algorithm using Matlab, and our computer configuration is Pentium dual core 3.40 GHz, 6 G memory. Running time of each step is shown in Table 2.

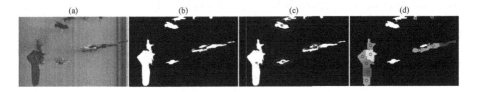

Fig. 5. Failure case. a) gray level and b) binary temporal slice images. c) results of SVM and d) clustering

Table 2. Processing time of each step.

Task	Feature extraction	SVM	AP clustering	Direction judging	Total
Cost	0.15 s	3.66 s	4.13 s	0.22 s	8.16 s

3.4   Failure Case

Although the proposed two-stage detection algorithm achieves satisfying results in most instances, it is expected to fail in some extreme situations. For instance, in Fig. 5, if one person stays on the LOI for a while, the foreground region in the temporal slice image will increase (see Figs. 5a and 5b). After the first-stage classification (see Fig. 5c) and the second-stage clustering (see Fig. 4d), the foreground region of the stationary person (labelled 1 in Fig. 5c) will be grouped into small clusters. As a result, the number of pedestrians estimated by the AP clustering algorithm will increase (see Fig. 5d). Another cause of failure is due to background subtraction error. Specifically, if the color of the moving object is similar to the background, the result of background subtraction will not be accurate. The foreground region labelled 6 in Fig. 5c is an example of this. This region should be connected to that labelled 5. It is therefore necessary to select suitable background subtraction algorithms for different situations.

4   Discussions and Conclusion

The vision-based pedestrian counting is a relatively independent part that touches wider areas, and there exist many problems that have not been solved perfectly. In our study, a novel and robust pedestrian detection algorithm is constructed to count pedestrians. Without tracking each pedestrian, our counting algorithm is both efficient and robust. Experiments demonstrate the reliability of our algorithm and suggest that our LOI counting can efficiently dealt with crowded situations. However the stationary pedestrians still causes counting errors. In future research, we will focus on how to solve above problem, as well as large moving non-human objects.

Acknowledgments. This research was partly supported by National Science Foundation, China (No. 61702226), the Natural Science Foundation of Jiangsu Province (Grant no. BK20170200), Open Fund of Key Laboratory of Urban Land Resources Monitoring and Simulation Ministry of Land and Resources (KF-2018-03-065), the Fundamental Research Funds for the Central Universities (JUSRP11854), China Postdoctoral Science Foundation (2019M661722).

References

1. Kumar, P.M., Gandhi, U., Varatharajan, R., Manogaran, G., Jidhesh, R., Vadivel, T.: Intelligent face recognition and navigation system using neural learning for smart security in Internet of Things. Cluster Comput. **22**(4), 7733–7744 (2017). https://doi.org/10.1007/s10586-017-1323-4
2. Souri, A., Hussien, A., Hoseyninezhad, M.: A systematic review of IoT communication strategies for an efficient smart environment. Trans. Emerg. Telecommun. Technol. **6**(2), 113–119 (2019)
3. Viola, P., Jones, M.J., Snow, D.: Detecting pedestrians using patterns of motion and appearance. In: 2003 Proceedings Ninth IEEE International Conference on Computer Vision, pp. 734–741 (2003)
4. Wu, B., Nevatia, R.: Detection of multiple, partially occluded humans in a single image by Bayesian combination of edgelet part detectors. In: Proceedings Tenth IEEE International Conference on Computer Vision (ICCV 2005), pp. 90–97 (2005)
5. Xing, J., Ai, H., Liu, L., Lao, S.: Robust crowd counting using detection flow. In: Proceedings 18th IEEE International Conference on Image Processing (ICIP), pp. 2061–2064 (2011)
6. Dong, L., Parameswaran, V., Ramesh, V., Zoghlami, I.: Fast crowd segmentation using shape indexing. In: Proceedings Tenth IEEE International Conference on Computer Vision (ICCV 2007), pp. 1–8 (2007)
7. Saqib, M., Khan, S.D., Blumenstein, M.: Texture-based feature mining for crowd density estimation: a study. In: Proceedings 2016 International Conference on Image and Vision Computing New Zealand (IVCNZ), pp. 11–19 (2016)
8. Wang, Z., Liu, H., Qian, Y., Xu, T.: Crowd density estimation based on local binary pattern co-occurrence matrix. In: Proceedings 2012 IEEE International Conference on Multimedia and Expo Workshops (ICMEW), pp. 372–377 (2012)
9. Zhang, T., Jia, W.J., He, X.J.: Discriminative dictionary learning with motion weber local descriptor for violence detection. IEEE Trans. Circ. Syst. Video Technol. **27**(3), 696–709 (2017)
10. Zhang, T., Li, J.J., Jia, W.J.: Fast and robust occluded face detection in ATM surveillance. Pattern Recogn. Lett. **107**(2), 33–40 (2018)

11. Zhang, T., Yang, Z., Jia, W., Wu, Q., Yang, J., He, X.: Fast and robust head detection with arbitrary pose and occlusion. Multimed. Tools Appl. **74**(21), 9365–9385 (2014). https://doi.org/10.1007/s11042-014-2110-3

12. Zhang, T., Yang, Z., Jia, W., Yang, B., Yang, J., He, X.: A new method for violence detection in surveillance scenes. Multimed. Tools Appl. **75**(12), 7327–7349 (2015). https://doi.org/10.1007/s11042-015-2648-8

13. Zhang, T., Jia, W.J., Yang, B.Q., Yang, J., He, X.J.: MoWLD: a robust motion image descriptor for violence detection. Multimed. Tools Appl. **76**(1), 1419–1438 (2017)

14. Zhang, T., Jia, W.J., Gong, C., Sun, J., Song, X.N.: Semi-supervised dictionary learning via local sparse constraints for violence detection. Pattern Recogn. Lett. **107**(1), 98–104 (2018)

15. Wu, T., Zhang, K., Tian, G.: Simultaneous face detection and pose estimation using convolutional neural network cascade. IEEE Access **14**(5), 36–48 (2019)

16. Schulz, E., Speekenbrink, M., Krause, A.: A tutorial on Gaussian process regression: modelling, exploring, and exploiting functions. J. Math. Psychol. **85**(5), 1–16 (2018)

17. Zhao, T., Nevatia, R.: Bayesian human segmentation in crowded situations. In: Proceedings IEEE Computer Society Conference on Computer Vision and Pattern Recognition (CVPR), pp. 455–459 (2003)

18. Velipasalar, S., Tian, Y., Hampapur, A.: Automatic counting of interacting people by using a single uncalibrated camera. In: Proceedings IEEE International Conference on Multimedia and Expo (ICME), pp. 1265–1268 (2006)

19. Antic, B., Letic, D., Culibrk, D., Crnojevic, V.: K-means based segmentation for real-time zenithal people counting. In: Proceedings 16th IEEE International Conference on Image Processing (ICIP), pp. 2565–2568 (2009)

20. Brostow, G.J., Cipolla, R.: Unsupervised Bayesian detection of independent motion in crowds. In: Proceedings 2006 IEEE Computer Society Conference on Computer Vision and Pattern Recognition, pp. 594–601 (2006)

21. Chen, T.H., Chen, T.Y., Chen, Z.X.: An intelligent people-flow counting method for passing through a gate. In: Proceedings 2006 IEEE Conference on Robotics, Automation and Mechatronics, pp. 1–6 (2006)

22. Leibe, B., Schindler, K., Van Gool, L.: Coupled detection and trajectory estimation for multi-object tracking. In: Proceedings IEEE 11th International Conference on Computer Vision (ICCV 2007), pp. 1–8 (2007)

23. Cutler, R., Davis, L.S.: Robust real-time periodic motion detection, analysis, and applications. IEEE Trans. Pattern Anal. Mach. Intell. **22**(8), 781–796 (2000)

24. Albiol, A., Mora, I., Naranjo, V.: Real-time high density people counter using morphological tools. IEEE Trans. Intell. Transp. Syst. **2**(4), 204–218 (2001)

25. Rabaud, V., Belongie, S.: Counting crowded moving objects. In: Proceedings IEEE Computer Society Conference on Robotics, Automation and Mechatronics, Computer Vision and Pattern Recognition (CVPR), pp. 705–711 (2006)

26. Cong, Y., Gong, H., Zhu, S.-C., Tang, Y.: Flow mosaicking: real-time pedestrian counting without scene-specific learning. In: Proceedings IEEE Computer Society Conference on Computer Vision and Pattern Recognition (CVPR), pp. 1093–1100 (2009)

27. Ma, Z., Chan, A.B.: Crossing the Line: Crowd Counting by Integer Programming with Local Features. In: Proceedings 2013 IEEE Conference on Computer Vision and Pattern Recognition (CVPR), pp. 2539–2546 (2013)

28. Stauffer, C., Grimson, W.E.L.: Adaptive background mixture models for real-time tracking. In: Proceedings IEEE Computer Society Conference on Computer Vision and Pattern Recognition, pp. 25–29 (1999)
29. Frey, B.J., Dueck, D.: Clustering by passing messages between data points. Science **315**(5814), 972–976 (2007)
30. Cheng, Y.: Mean shift, mode seeking, and clustering. IEEE Trans. Pattern Anal. Mach. Intell. **17**(8), 790–799 (1995)
31. Chang, C., Lin, C.: LIBSVM: a library for support vector machines. ACM Trans. Intell. Syst. Technol. (TIST) **2**(3), 27–38 (2011)
32. Chan, A.B., Vasconcelos, N.: Modeling, clustering, and segmenting video with mixtures of dynamic textures. IEEE Trans. Pattern Anal. Mach. Intell. **30**(5), 909–926 (2008)

Correction to: Research on Video Violence Detection Technology of UAV on Cloud Platform

Chen Zhi and Weidong Bao

Correction to:
Chapter "Research on Video Violence Detection Technology of UAV on Cloud Platform" in: X. Sun et al. (Eds.): *Artificial Intelligence and Security*, CCIS 1252, https://doi.org/10.1007/978-981-15-8083-3_33

In the originally published version of chapter 33, the name of one of the authors was incorrect. The author name has been changed to Chen Zhi.

The updated version of this chapter can be found at
https://doi.org/10.1007/978-981-15-8083-3_33

Author Index

Printed in the United States
by Baker & Taylor Publisher Services